An Introduction
to the Causes of War

An Introduction to the Causes of War

Patterns of Interstate Conflict from World War I to Iraq

Greg Cashman and Leonard C. Robinson

ROWMAN & LITTLEFIELD PUBLISHERS, INC.
Lanham • Boulder • New York • Toronto • Plymouth, UK

ROWMAN & LITTLEFIELD PUBLISHERS, INC.

Published in the United States of America
by Rowman & Littlefield Publishers, Inc.
A wholly owned subsidary of The Rowman & Littlefield Publishing Group, Inc.
4501 Forbes Boulevard, Suite 200, Lanham, Maryland 20706
www.rowmanlittlefield.com

Estover Road, Plymouth PL6 7PY, United Kingdom

British Library Cataloguing in Publication Information Available

Library of Congress Cataloging-in-Publication Data

Cashman, Greg.
  An introduction to the causes of war : patterns of interstate conflict from World War I to Iraq / Greg Cashman and Leonard C. Robinson.
      p. cm.
  Includes bibliographical references and index.
  ISBN-13: 978-0-7425-5509-9 (cloth : alk. paper)
  ISBN-10: 0-7425-5509-7 (cloth : alk. paper)
  ISBN-13: 978-0-7425-5510-5 (pbk. : alk. paper)
  ISBN-10: 0-7425-5510-0 (alk. paper)
  1. War—Causes. 2. War—Causes—Case studies. 3. Military history, Modern—20th century. 4. Military history, Modern—21st century. I. Robinson, Leonard C., 1960–
II. Title.
  U21.2.C375 2007
  355.02'7—dc22

                                                    2006101220

Printed in the United States of America

To Linda and Alicia

Contents

Illustrations

Introduction

As our televisions and newspapers and websites constantly remind us, we do not live in a golden Age of Peace. We continue to live, instead, in an Age of Conflict. For those of us who are interested in international politics, the most crucial issue has been and will continue to be war—an institution that appears to be as old as civilization. And since the seventeenth century, when the nation-state became the dominant form of governing unit, **interstate wars** have been the most destructive form of warfare. The term *interstate war* usually has been defined as sustained armed combat between two or more sovereign states that results in a minimum of one thousand battle deaths. This is the standard set by the "grandfather" of all data-gathering projects on war, the Correlates of War (COW) Project (Singer and Small 1972; Small and Singer 1982). This definition eliminates from our consideration several types of violent conflicts that might involve national militaries: minor armed clashes between states, such as "border skirmishes" that are not "deadly" enough to be classified as wars; violent conflicts between states and nonstate entities, such as imperial or colonial wars; and violent internal conflicts, such as revolutions, civil wars, and **wars of secession**.

Statistics about wars are always frightening, but the trends in war data convey both good news and bad news. First, the good news. It is generally believed that since the sixteenth century interstate wars have become less frequent, though there was a slight increase in such wars in the twentieth century. This downward trend is particularly prominent for wars among the great powers (Levy 1983, 135). And since the number of new states in the international system has increased faster than the number of wars, the average number of wars per state has declined substantially from 0.744 in the decade after 1890 to 0.171 in the 1990s (Sarkees, Wayman, and Singer 2003, 63). Not only have purely interstate wars been less frequent in the post–World War II era, but violent interstate conflicts of all kinds have steadily decreased since 1945 (Pfetsch and Rohloff 2000, 381–82). This is largely accounted for by the disappearance of "extra-systemic wars" such as imperial and colonial wars, now that most colonial states have become independent (Sarkees, Wayman, and Singer 2003, 60).

Now the bad news. There is general agreement that interstate wars are becoming more severe, at least when measured by the number of war-related battle deaths. This rise in severity, however, generally is accounted for by some very large wars. When researchers with the COW Project controlled for overall global population growth in the past two centuries, they found that the trend in battle deaths per thousand people was "generally flat"—except for the decades involving the American Civil War, World War I, and World War II (Sarkees, Wayman, and Singer 2003, 65).

The worst wars of the present age are really considerably worse than those in the past. Although the great powers do not go to war as often as in previous centuries, when they do, the resulting conflicts have been increasingly more deadly (Levy 1983, 116–36). Of all those who have died in wars of all types since the year 1000, 75 percent are believed to have died in the twentieth century and 89 percent have died since 1800. The most serious war of the seventeenth century, the Thirty Years' War (1618–1648), resulted in roughly 2 million deaths from battle, and there were about 2.5 million battle fatalities in the French Revolutionary Wars and the Napoleonic Wars (1792–1815). By contrast, the shorter wars of the twentieth century were significantly more devastating. Combat deaths among troops have been variously estimated at between 8 and 9 million in World War I and between 13 and 17 million in World War II. These figures do not include the civilian victims who succumbed to war-related causes such as disease, starvation, bombardment, or internal governmental repression. If these figures are included, then the total death toll in the Thirty Years' War and the French Revolutionary Wars reach 4 million and 4.9 million, respectively, and World Wars I and II reach 26 million and 53.5 million, respectively (Eckhardt 1991; Levy 1983, 88–91; Renner 1999, 9–19; Singer and Small 1982; Sivard 1991, 1994, 1996).

Although many interstate wars in the last one hundred years have been relatively small, the two world wars—with their global scope and magnitude, their attacks on the enemy's domestic infrastructure and civilian populations, and their massive mobilization of resources—made the twentieth century the age of "total war." Even the massive impact of World War II, which ended with the introduction of nuclear weapons, only marginally dampened the attraction of organized international violence. The Korean War, the Vietnam War, and the Iran-Iraq War each resulted in over a million battle-related deaths (Gleditsch et al. 2002, 623).

Another recent phenomenon is that interstate war has been almost absent from the more prosperous developed regions of the world, and there have been no wars between major powers since the Korean War ended in 1953. Unfortunately, war in the developing regions of the world has become endemic. The locus of war has shifted to the global periphery, and within the periphery war has become primarily an intrastate phenomenon (Marshall 1999).

In fact, the vast majority of the violent conflicts in the post–World War I era have been internal, **intrastate wars** rather than interstate wars. In the post–Cold War period (1989–2003) the Uppsala Conflict Data Project's data set of armed conflicts (which uses a threshold of twenty-five deaths per year instead of one thousand) has recorded 116 armed conflicts in seventy-eight locations, but only 7 of these have been true interstate conflicts. The vast majority—94 percent—have been intrastate wars. In twenty of these intrastate conflicts there was outside intervention that "internationalized" the conflict (Eriksson and Wallensteen

2003, 625–27). The COW Project finds a similarly distressing situation: "Civil wars are breaking out at an all-time record rate" and they have become increasingly internationalized, with intervention from outside states (Sarkees, Wayman, and Singer 2003, 62). The most depressing aspect of this is that in some of these internal wars—such as the Yugoslav wars of secession, the 1994 Rwandan conflict between Hutus and Tutsis, and the ongoing civil war in the Darfur region of Sudan—we have seen genocidal killing. *Genocide* is defined as acts committed with the intent to destroy, in whole or in part, a national, racial, ethnic, or religious group. In genocide, the atrocity of warfare reaches its lowest depths. In Rwanda, a country of about eight million people, almost one million were killed in a period of three or four months, the majority with low-tech weapons such as machetes.

It must be remembered that interstate war is (and always was) a relatively rare event. As two prominent scholars (Geller and Singer 1998, 1) point out, one way to look at the issue is to compare the number of pairs of countries that *might* go to war with the number of pairs that *actually do* go to war. Geller and Singer found that in 1993 there were about 18,000 possible "dyads," or pairs, of countries. Considering that most wars take place between contiguous countries, however, the real set of countries that were likely to go to war at that time was reduced to about 317 pairs. The relatively small number of interstate wars actually going on—at present, roughly two or three in any given year—is a mere fraction of the number of interstate wars that *might* take place. Moreover, in 45 percent of the years since 1815 there have been no wars at all. Another set of researchers calculate the odds of a randomly selected pair of states going to war with each other as roughly approximate to the odds of being killed in an automobile accident in the United States (Bennett and Stam 2004, 116).

Despite the relative rareness of full-scale interstate wars in the present age, these wars continue to be a primary concern of statesmen and international relations scholars. For it is these wars that hold the greatest potential for the devastation of human societies and, indeed, in the age of nuclear weapons, the potential for human annihilation. If we are to further reduce the chances of interstate war, we must seek to understand the causes of these wars.

CAUSES OF WAR

Since World War II social scientists have expended tremendous effort in an attempt to identify the causes of interstate war. What have we found? To some extent empirical research by political scientists has constituted a "rubble clearing" exercise. Some theories have been rejected on the basis of empirical examination and have been relegated to the status of mythology. Many other theories have survived and have been modified as a result of the research. The evidence clearly indicates that a single "master cause" of all interstate wars does not exist and no single "grand theory" prevails. Three things are becoming increasingly clear as a result of empirical research: (1) interstate wars have multiple causes, (2) these causal factors interact with one another, and (3) these causes can be found at different **levels of analysis**. Most wars occur because a number of important factors are simultaneously present, and together these factors reduce the likelihood that the states involved will resolve their differences peacefully. The more causal factors that are present, the greater the probability that war will result (see Geller and Singer 1998; Bennett and Stam 2004; also Thompson 2003).

Although scholars disagree on the appropriate number and designation of levels of analysis, we will identify five: the individual level, the substate level, the nation-state level, the level of dyadic (bilateral) interaction between states, and the international system level. These levels of analysis are essentially levels of aggregation: Each level is made up of larger units than the preceding level. At the individual level we examine the impact of single humans—primarily presidents, prime ministers, and monarchs—in determining the outbreak of war. The substate level focuses on the process by which small groups of individuals, normally elite government decision makers, make the decision for war. States are, of course, aggregate entities made up of many individuals and groups. The analytical focus at this level is on those attributes or characteristics of particular states that might make them prone to war. The dyadic level of analysis pinpoints two types of factors that increase the potential for war: characteristics jointly shared by a pair of states and the dynamics of the interaction of these two states with each other. Finally, at the level of the international system, the focus is on the combined interactions of many states and the changing dynamics of these interactions. Some of these causal factors may represent **long-term or "root" causes of war**, whereas others may be more immediate or proximate causes.

In this chapter we will set out the theoretical arguments associated with the causes of interstate war and attempt to summarize something of what we know about the causes of war in the modern age. Subsequent chapters will provide case studies of some of the most notable wars of the twentieth century in an attempt to illustrate the various patterns by which important causal phenomena interact to produce war. The cases include World War I, World War II in the Pacific, the 1967 Six-Day War, the 1971 Bangladesh War, the 1980–1988 Iran-Iraq War, and the 2003 Iraq War. (A seventh case study, the Ethiopia-Eritrea War, can be found on this book's website.) In a final chapter we will attempt to draw conclusions based on the case studies.

THE INDIVIDUAL LEVEL

Factors at the individual level of analysis are essentially short-term or **immediate causes of war**; they also are generally recognized as merely subsidiary causes of war rather than primary causes. Nevertheless, we know that individual political leaders often make a difference. Leaders are influenced in their decisions for peace and war by their **personalities**, their **psychological makeup**, their **perceptions** of the world, and their **beliefs**—both general and specific.

A leader's personality or psychological makeup may, on occasion, play an important role in determining how a leader reacts to international situations. In some circumstances, especially those involving great stress, a leader's ability to make rational decisions may be impaired by his or her subconscious needs or may be guided by ego defense mechanisms rather than by conscious, rational thought processes. Germany's Kaiser Wilhelm II's fateful decisions during the July crises of 1914 are frequently cited in this regard (Lebow 1981). Likewise, one would find it difficult to adequately explain the outbreak of World War II in Europe without an exploration of the personality of Adolf Hitler (Byman and Pollack 2001).

Beliefs are also important in guiding decisions. Social scientists have used various terms to refer to an individual's systematic set of beliefs, such as "belief systems," "images," "worldviews," "ideologies," and "operational codes." Certain belief systems possessed by national leaders (acting perhaps together with their personalities) may predispose them to support hawkish, aggressive or hardline foreign policies. Other belief systems might predispose national leaders to pursue more dovish, conciliatory, or accommodationist foreign policies. It goes without saying that the construction of leaders' belief systems will be heavily influenced by the general political and social culture of their time and place as well as by the particular institutional subcultures to which they belong.

Considerable impressionistic evidence indicates that inappropriate and seemingly illogical decisions about war and peace may be due to individual perceptions and **misperceptions**. Misperceptions occur when an individual's understanding of the world does not correspond to reality. This would appear to be an endemic problem. Misperceptions are likely when information is missing or incomplete—a normal condition in international politics, where secrecy and deception are practiced to keep rivals and opponents from knowing what they wish to know. Additionally, misperception is the result of normal human cognitive failings. Our perceptions of events and actions in the international environment are filtered through our present images of the world. These images, which are more or less kept on file in our minds, act as a screen or a filter through which we process all new information from the world around us. These current images of the world, which are of necessity somewhat simplified and biased, distort our interpretations of incoming information, seriously degrading our ability to create a realistic picture of our surroundings. Efforts to change inaccurate images must work against powerful cognitive pressures to maintain consistent images. This pressure for **cognitive consistency** means that when individuals are faced with new (and presumably accurate) information that conflicts with their current images, they are inclined to discount or reject or modify the new information in order to maintain the old (and erroneous) images.

Just as an individual's personality predisposes him to respond to certain situations in certain ways, so do his images and belief systems. The important point here is that national decision makers do not act on reality; they act on their perceptions of reality, and sometimes these are seriously distorted (Jervis 1976).

The most relevant, and most typical, misperceptions in the realm of international conflict are (1) the perception that the intentions of one's opponent are more hostile than they are in reality, and (2) the perception that the power of one's own state (or alliance) is greater than it really is and/or that the power of one's opponent (or its alliance) is less than it really is. In other words, there is a misperception about the true distribution of power, with the result that the leaders of at least one state view their chances of winning a potential war to be good. War, therefore, may be the result of "false optimism." These misperceptions about power realities are most likely to occur when the objective distribution of power is undergoing change. Unrealistic perceptions about the relative balance of capabilities frequently lead to an associated misperception: (3) that one's opponent is likely to back down in the face of demands accompanied by toughness and displays of force and fortitude (see Cashman 1993, 61–70).

Finally, a related set of optimistic perceptions about the nature of war are relevant. These perceptions may, in fact, correspond closely to reality or they may be false (and hence be misperceptions). But whether or not the perceptions correspond closely to reality, if leaders hold these perceptions, war may be more likely than if they did not hold them. These dangerous perceptions are (4) that the coming war is likely to be short and not very costly, (5) that offensive forces and strategies are superior to defensive forces and strategies, and (6) that the side that strikes first has an advantage. These perceptions have the dubious effect of simultaneously reducing inhibitions toward war, since war is presumed not to be too costly, and increasing the desirability of war, especially a preemptive war, since victory seems attainable, especially if one strikes first (Van Evera 1999, 14–34, 73–87; Cashman 1993, 61–70).

The importance of cultural and ideational factors—such as beliefs and perceptions—is the focus of what has become known as the *constructivist approach* to international relations (see Wendt 1992, 1998; Jepperson, Wendt, and Katzenstein 1996). Constructivists argue that international politics are "socially constructed." Reality is subjective rather than objective; it is what people "construct" as reality. Social and cultural processes within institutions tend to produce a shared, "intersubjective" consensus. Thus common images, expectations, beliefs, and norms may be shared by members of a state's national security team or by the society of an entire state. These shared images and expectations are created through mutual experiences and interactions, and they constantly evolve. An important result of the process is the creation of *identities*, defined as "mutually constructed and evolving images of self and other" (Jepperson, Wendt, Katzenstein 1996, 59). The shared images, expectations, assumptions, identities, norms, and beliefs possessed by national leaders give meaning to the world and thus play an important role in shaping the policies and actions of governments.

Before ending this section, we should note that theorists who deal with personalities, beliefs, and misperceptions generally put forward the argument that decisions by government leaders tend *not* to conform to models of ideal rationality because psychological or cognitive processes impair rational decision making. We therefore need to touch on **rational choice** theories of war or, more specifically, **expected utility theory**.

Rational choice theories assume that states can be seen as single (unitary) rational actors or that the decision-making process within leadership groups proceeds as if there was a single, dominant leader who controls the outcome (Bueno de Mesquita 1981, 17). Leaders are assumed to be guided by the desire to maximize the net benefits they expect from their foreign policy choices. In other words, a "policy maker will never choose an action that is expected to produce less value—or utility—than some alternative policy" (Bueno de Mesquita, 29). Very simply, an expected utility theory of war says that wars are intentional, calculated acts and that they will only occur when the initiator believes that war will yield a positive expected utility. Leaders would not start wars or continue them if they perceived the net result to be less than that of staying at peace or surrendering.

The decision for war depends on an estimation of the costs and benefits of war. Specifically, "the size of the expected gains or losses depend on (a) the relative strengths of the attacker and the defender; (b) the value the attacker places on changing the defender's policies, relative to the possible changes in policies that the attacker may be forced to accept if it loses; and (c) the relative strengths and interests of all other states that might intervene in the war" (Bueno de Mesquita 1981, 46). The expected utility of a particular war strategy is a function of the sum of the utilities of the possible outcomes times their probabilities (Bueno de Mesquita, 34, 127). We should never discount the possibility, therefore, that war is the product of a leader's rational calculation that by going to war the country will be better off than if it had not gone to war. Even if this is true, however—and in many instances it is true in some way—it is rarely the only answer to what causes war.

An "amendment" to expected utility theory is helpful to our understanding of the causes of war. Whereas traditional rational choice models of decision making emphasize war as a way to maximize utilities, prospect theory emphasizes the minimization of losses. **Prospect theory** (Kahneman and Tversky 1979) suggests that decision makers tend to think in terms of gains and losses rather than in terms of net assets; they therefore think of their choices in terms of deviations from a particular reference point—usually the status quo. In this calculus, losses loom larger than gains; the loss (or disutility) of giving up something already possessed is usually seen as greater than the gain (utility) of acquiring something new. Moreover, the perceived value of anything is proportional to the length of time it has been possessed and the effort and resources used to acquire it. In addition, losses and gains are evaluated differently in terms of risk orientation; decision makers tend to be risk averse with respect to gains and risk acceptant when trying to prevent losses. The theory suggests a bias toward the status quo: "Leaders take more risks to maintain their international positions, reputations, and domestic political support than they do to enhance these positions" (Levy 1997, 93).

Because of the role of the reference point in defining gains and losses, the identification of the reference point—the framing of a choice—is of critical importance. It matters considerably whether one frames an issue in terms of gains or losses. Newly acquired gains become part of the new status quo. Decision makers accommodate themselves to gains more quickly than they accommodate to losses. Accommodation to gains leads to risk-acceptant behavior designed to keep those gains, whereas accommodation to losses leads to a greater tendency toward avoiding risks associated with attempting to reverse the losses (Levy 1994a, 1994b).

In sum, prospect theory suggests that war is more likely when decision makers perceive that they are defending the status quo and believe that they will suffer significant losses if they do not fight to keep what they value. Decision makers are much more willing to take risks when they believe that failing to do so will result in certain losses. Fear, rather than the desire for expansion or gains, is the most significant motivating force behind war. Logically, the most dangerous situation occurs when leaders in both states in a dispute see themselves as defending the legitimate status quo (Jervis 1994, 31).

THE SUBSTATE LEVEL

Other short-term or medium-term causes of war can be found at the subnational level of analysis. Here the focus is on the making of policy decisions by small groups of leaders within government institutions—by court officials, cabinets, politburos, or juntas. Unfortunately, the shortcomings of individual government leaders may be abetted and magnified by certain dysfunctional governmental decision-making procedures that produce nonrational decisions, or at least decisions that are less than optimum. These dysfunctional procedures may (1) limit the amount and reliability of information available to the group, (2) reduce the number of alternative policy choices that are identified and analyzed, (3) inhibit rigorous and informed debate on the options, (4) inhibit the objective examination of potential risks, (5) introduce bias in favor of tough-minded solutions while denigrating cooperative solutions, (6) substitute the primacy of domestic political interests or organizational interests over national interests, (7) create inappropriate political practices such as logrolling, (8) produce decisions based on the possession of political power or on group loyalty rather than on logical assessment of the situation, (9) impose inflexible standard operating procedures on the implementation of policies, or (10) create the possibility that those who implement policy will subvert or contradict the intentions of those who make policy decisions.

Some of these dysfunctional procedures have been identified and given names. Graham Allison's **bureaucratic politics model** describes a conflictual process by which governmental decisions are made by individuals representing different organizations and agencies in competition with one another to determine national policies (Allison 1971). Institutional interests are important in determining a policymaker's preferences: "Where you stand depends on where you sit." Since most "players" tend to see foreign policy issues from the parochial perspectives of their home organizations, they tend to disagree on the proper policies to follow. Decisions, therefore, tend to be made through political processes such as bargaining, logrolling, coalition building, and compromise, as well as through outright power struggles among competing organizations and coalitions. It is also a process in which the domestic political interests of top-level players tend to intrude. Ultimately, the outcome of the decision process depends on the relative power and skill of the proponents of various alternative courses of action rather than on the individual who has the best answer.

If governments make policies according to the bureaucratic politics model, war is chosen because it is seen by a particular coalition of political factions as promoting their organizational or political interests. The decision for war may be the result of political bargaining or compromise, or it may be the result of a power struggle between two or more factions in which the balance of power within the government has come to rest with those who favor war (Cashman 1993, 102). The "steps to war" theory of John Vasquez argues that the internal domination of government positions by "hard-liners" is an important "prerequisite" for war (Vasquez 1993, 199). It is difficult for two states to go to war with each other if they are both governed by leaders who follow an accommodationist approach to foreign policy. For war to occur, **hardliners** must be in control of the government in at least one of the states. Hardliners tend to use realpolitik methods of statecraft; they use threats and ultimatums, coercive bargaining, arms buildups, the construction of alliances, and the demonstration and use of military force. This produces a particularly insidious bilateral dynamic between states. The use of such tactics by one state drastically increases the amount of tension and the perceived threat in the other state, helps to drive **accommodationists** from power in the rival state, and, therefore, helps to accelerate conflict spirals. If hardliners control power in both states, the probability of war increases substantially (Vasquez 1993, 198–224).

Jack Snyder (1991) has put forward another domestic politics theory of war, similar in many respects to the bureaucratic politics model. He attributes the expansionistic policies of nineteenth/twentieth-century Britain, Germany, Japan, and Russia/Soviet Union to the existence of **cartelized political systems**—systems in which the government was dominated by a coalition of powerful groups with narrow interests who all derived parochial benefits from foreign expansion and military activities. The coalitions were maintained by logrolling tactics in which the parochial interests of each group were supported by other members of the coalition. The classic example is the "marriage of iron and rye" found in pre–World War I Germany: Prussian Junkers received grain tariffs (antagonizing Russia), and German industrialists and the Navy got a larger fleet (antagonizing Britain).

Irving Janis (1982) describes an alternative decision-making model: **groupthink**. In groupthink, members of a cohesive, homogeneous, and insulated decision-making group strive for unanimity and cohesion, adversely affecting their ability to realistically assess the problem in front of them. The need for group cohesion is driven by situations of high stress and the inherent difficulties of making critical national-security decisions. Group cohesion serves to allay the stress felt by group members but leads to several problems: limitation of group debate, limitation of options, the closing of the process to outsiders, suppression of doubts and self-censorship, unwillingness to criticize the opinions of others, unwillingness to confront the risks of the preferred solution, selective bias in favor of the group's preferred option, and a general lack of critical thinking. The result is a policy that is ill considered, risky, and unlikely to lead to a successful outcome.

Dysfunctional decision-making processes such as bureaucratic politics or groupthink are neither necessary nor sufficient causes of war; when they are present, they are likely to be secondary or contributing factors rather than decisive factors in determining whether governments opt for war rather than peace.

THE NATION-STATE LEVEL

Political scientists have expended significant effort trying to identify certain attributes or characteristics of states that might make them prone to war. A whole host of factors have been dismissed by empirical research as possessing little explanatory or predictive value. Although these factors may be associated with some isolated instances of war, as a general rule their historical association with war over the last two centuries has been minimal. Into this category would fall factors such as lack of "war weariness" brought on by recent participation in previous wars, the nature of a country's economic system (capitalism or socialism), a particular kind of political system (democracy or autocracy), economic upturns or downturns, resource deprivation, population growth, or various forms of "lateral pressure" associated with population growth. In other words, wars have been initiated in almost equal frequencies by states with recent exposure to war and by states without such exposure, by capitalist states and socialist states, by democratic states and autocracies, by states experiencing economic downturns and economic upswings, by those with rapidly growing populations and those with declining or stable populations, and so on. (See Cashman 1993, 124–59; Geller and Singer 1998, 46–67.)

One important characteristic of states that cannot be ignored, however, is pure size and power. Numerous studies show that states with greater power capabilities are more likely than states with lesser capabilities to participate in and initiate wars (Geller and Singer 1998, 565–58). The relationship between power ranking and war involvement makes intuitive sense. In a world of rational calculators, it is more likely that large states would pick on small states than vice versa. Also, large states probably are involved in more conflicts simply because they are more involved in international politics in general: They have more interests and more international commitments, they have a greater capacity to act in the international arena, and they are more likely to see themselves as responsible for the protection of allies, as defenders of the international status quo, and as guarantors of world order. However, it should be mentioned that in the post–World War II era, although the great powers are still involved in war, they have rarely fought directly against one another.

One truly crucial short-term variable at the state level of analysis seems to be the existence of internal political conflicts and political instability. Whereas internal conflicts may provide the impetus for external war, there are several different pathways through which domestic conflict may lead to war.

If a country's domestic political and/or economic difficulties are serious enough to threaten the continued rule of the current government elites, those elites may have an incentive to initiate **scapegoat wars** or **diversionary wars** (Levy 1993). In such wars, domestic elites who see themselves as vulnerable may attempt to unify their country and shore up their own political positions by engaging in war with foreign opponents. In most cases the motive is to divert the attention of the public from those domestic troubles that threaten the regime. In some cases a particular state can be targeted as a scapegoat and blamed for the internal troubles. Note that the logic behind diversionary war theory is buttressed by insights from prospect theory: Leaders are more likely to be risk acceptant if they appear to face losses, including domestic political losses (Levy 1989, 274). The Falklands War between Argentina and the United Kingdom is usually cited as a classic modern example of this type of war. The unpopular military junta in Argentina faced a deteriorating economic situation and political demonstrations by democratic opposition forces. A successful attempt to occupy the disputed Falkland Islands (or the Malvinas, as the Argentinians called them) and detach them from British control, it was thought, would be a popular move and just might reduce the internal opposition faced by the junta. It must be kept in mind that a small percentage of all wars derive from such a situation, but the diversionary motive is an important cause of *some* wars.

Some theorists have focused on the kind of domestic political unrest that is associated with regime change. Governments undergoing fundamental transitions from one regime type to another—that is, they are in the process of **democratization** (or autocratization)—may be especially prone to war. Mansfield and Snyder argue that the initial stage of democratization is fraught with danger (Mansfield and Snyder 1995, 7, 19–20). Participation in the political system increases, but the newly formed democratic institutions may be too weak to resolve conflicts between political groups and enforce the "rules of the game" on all participants. A particular concern is that traditional elites, who are often associated with military and imperial groups, may feel that their interests are threatened by democratization. Fearing that the public and the parliament will refuse to support military ventures, they may attempt to mobilize mass support for adventuristic and aggressive foreign policies through propagandistic appeals to nationalism. Thus traditional elites may try to drag the country toward risky and aggressive foreign policies as a way to maintain their political positions in a rapidly changing domestic environment.

In extreme cases of transitional regimes, characterized by the existence of **contested institutions**, powerful domestic groups disagree about the most fundamental rules of politics, such as who should rule and what type of political and economic institutions are best for the state (Dassel 1998). In this "Wild West" scenario, all political groups—civilian and military—are forced to struggle to secure political power from their rivals. Since the basic rules of the polity are fluid and lack agreement, some groups will resort to "extraconstitutional" means to protect their interests. Because the military has certain built-in advantages in this situation (they presumably have a monopoly on the means of violence), civilian groups seek to reduce the power and influence of the military. The military will naturally resist any attempt to reduce its budget, its personnel, its resources, and its domestic political influence. Military institutions have two viable courses of action: the use of internal repression against its enemies or the use of external force (diversionary war) to increase its internal power vis-à-vis other political forces at home. According to Dassel, internal repression is the preferred option, but if its use would split the military and cause civil war, or if no civilian factions will support repression, then the military may choose external conflict as a way of protecting and promoting its interests. Early-twentieth-century Germany and Japan are classic examples of polities with contested institutions. The democratization argument and the contested institutions argument both suggest that the primary motivation for war is found in domestic politics and that wars fought by such regimes tend to have a diversionary logic behind them.

Although the diversionary war theory argues that states with internal conflict seek wars, it is also possible that such states are the *targets* of attacks by others (see Blainey 1973, 68–86). Civil conflicts may create the conditions for war by providing an opportunity for one state to settle old scores at a time when a normally stronger rival is temporarily weakened by internal troubles. The internal conflict causes a change in the dyadic distribution of power, which enables one country to do what it had previously been unable even to contemplate. We might call these **kick 'em while they're down** wars. Iraq's 1980 attack on revolutionary Iran fits this classification nicely. Saddam Hussein's government seized a short-term opportunity to reduce its long-term vulnerability to the normally more powerful Iran at a moment of internal confusion and disorder in Iran.

Revolutionary transitions or the birth of new states in revolution may be connected to wars through still another pathway (Walt 1996). **Revolutions** have a number of insidious regional and international effects. Because the policies of the new government are unclear, revolutions increase the uncertainty and anxiety in the international system. They also cause an abrupt shift in the distribution of power and, at the same time, make it difficult to measure power accurately, thus leading to considerable misperception. Additionally, revolutions increase the level of threat perceived on both sides. Other states in the region may perceive a greatly enhanced threat because revolutions typically bring to power new regimes motivated by a revolutionary ideology and dedicated to achieving national goals that challenge the international status quo and threaten the legitimacy of existing borders. The revolutionary state's neighbors may initiate an attack in order to prevent the spread of revolution to their own borders. On the other hand, leaders in the revolutionary state may perceive that the revolution is threatened by status quo powers, who they believe are about to strangle the revolution in its infancy; launching a preventive war is seen as the only solution. Both sides are likely to exaggerate their own vulnerability in such cases. This dynamic also was at work in the Iran-Iraq War. Iraqi leaders were concerned about the spread of "Islamic fundamentalism" from Iran and were frightened by the efforts of Iran to rally adherents of Shi'a Islam in Iraq to overthrow the Sunni-dominated secular government of Saddam Hussein. Thus the Iranian Revolution was seen as constituting a threat to the unity of the state of Iraq while simultaneously weakening Iran and making it a better target.

The final pathway from civil conflict to external war is through the **internationalization** of civil conflicts. Both sides in an internal conflict—the government and the rebels—are likely to have external allies who might be inclined under certain circumstances to intervene militarily on behalf of their friends. The internationalization of civil conflict may be exacerbated by ethnic and/or religious identities. If the internal conflict is based along ethnic/religious grounds, each of the various ethnic or religious communities may be supported by members of their group outside the state or by other states themselves. The same is true of conflicts based on ideological identity.

THE DYADIC LEVEL

At the dyadic level the relationships between states and their mutual dynamic interactions affect the probability of war. One of the most important elements of the relationship between a pair of states is the distribution of power between them and the changes in that distribution. **Power transition theory**, in its purest (and original) form, asserts that the potential for war is greatly increased when the power capabilities of a major power challenger who is dissatisfied with the international status quo rapidly reaches a level equal to (or almost equal to) that of a hegemonic leader who is a defender of the global status quo (Organski and Kugler 1980; Kugler and Lemke 2000). The more rapid this change in the dyadic balance, the more likely the transition will result in war. Hence, an equal balance of power is dangerous, contrary to the classical realist position, which states that equality helps to reduce the probability of war (Claude 1962, 40–93; Waltz 1979, 123–28). On the other hand, a stable preponderance of power (in the hands of a single hegemonic state) helps to prevent wars among the great powers.

The original power transition argument has now been loosened and broadened. Proponents of the theory now maintain that the logic that connects power transitions to war is applicable not just to top-level, major power contenders but also to regional power systems and, perhaps, to any **dyadic relationship** (Lemke 2002; Huth, Bennett, and Gelpi 1992; Tammen et al. 2000). The consensus of scholars is that, historically, changes in dyadic balances of power have increased the probability of war (Geller 2000, 268). (Technically, power transitions refer to a reversal of relative capabilities; the term *power shift* may be used to denote either a convergence or divergence of dyadic capabilities; see Geller 2000, 264.)

What explains the relationship between power transitions and war? First, the conjunction of power transitions and dissatisfaction means that dissatisfied states that were at one time unable to do anything about their grievances are no longer at such a disadvantage. "Rising states" have both the means and the motivation to go to war. Second, changes in the dyadic distribution of power produce an unsettling political and military environment. When states gain power relative to others, they generate fear. In other words, changes in the distribution of power are likely to bring about increased perceptions of threats to a country's national interests. Realist scholars remind us that in this situation, weak powers will tend to engage in **balancing** behavior to offset the power of strong states. Power shifts may thereby induce compensatory behaviors by "declining states" designed to enhance their security against the power of rising states, which in turn can create conflict spirals that lead to war. Alternatively, changes in power distribution may induce a rising state to engage in reckless and threatening behaviors designed to take advantage of its new-found capabilities, once again initiating conflict spirals. Moreover, when power transitions result in power equality, either side may see the possibility of victory in war, thus increasing the potential for disaster. It should also be noted that whether or not an actual change in the distribution of power is taking place, the perception of such a change may motivate political elites to take some kind of compensatory action.

Third, much of the explanation above is consistent with Stephen Van Evera's "window theory." Van Evera argues that when the actual or perceived balance of capabilities changes or is about to change, leaders may see an impending **window of opportunity**, during which they temporarily may be able to prevail against a rival in warfare. Or they may see a looming **window of vulnerability** in which they will no longer be able to prevail against a rival in warfare (Van Evera 1999, 73–87). By their very nature, windows are temporary: They never stay open or closed for long. A window of opportunity is by definition "a fading offensive opportunity," whereas a window of vulnerability is a "growing defensive vulnerability" (Van Evera 1999, 74). Windows create pressure for both preventive and preemptive wars. Declining powers may be tempted to react to such a perceived shift by choosing preventive war, thinking that it is better to strike against an opponent now (when they still have a chance of victory) rather than later (when there is little or no chance of victory). In the words of E. H. Carr, "Wars are fought in order to make one's own military stronger, or, *more often, to prevent another country from becoming militarily stronger*" (Carr 2001, 104; emphasis added). And rising powers may fear just such a preventive attack, giving them an incentive to initiate a preemptive attack "if they see a first-move advantage" (Van Evera 1999, 81).

Another important factor at the dyadic level is the existence of security dilemmas. Security dilemmas may be seen as a general aspect of the international system as a whole or as a dyadic phenomenon involving only two states. In either case, the problem is that the actions taken by leaders to increase the security of their states—building up military defenses, placing forces on alert, forming alliances, inventing new weapons—may be seen as threatening by others, who now feel less secure. Fear is the primary motivating factor in this scenario. In response to the defensive actions of another, a threatened state takes similar actions to increase its own security, which in turn make the first state feel less secure. Each side overestimates the hostility of the other. Thus national leaders motivated purely by the desire for greater security may (especially if this is consistent with their worldview or operational code) engage in competitive, realpolitik actions that create **conflict spirals** in which interaction is characterized by ever higher levels of threat, hostility, and militarization (Jervis 1976, 58–113).

Conflict spiral theory assumes that states and their leaders generally respond to others on the basis of reciprocity. They tend to react to cooperation and accommodation by others with cooperation and accommodation of their own. But they tend to respond to hostile, uncooperative and threatening actions by others with hostile, uncooperative, and threatening actions of their own. Bullying leads to bullying. Once a spiral of hostile and conflictual interactions begin, it is difficult to break. As states respond to the perceived hostile acts of others, they may be brought to the very brink of war, where one misjudgment may suffice to bring on full-scale armed conflict—even though neither side desires such an outcome. Or war may begin because leaders in one state initiate a **preemptive war** on their rival out of fear that the other is poised to do the same.

Security dilemmas and conflict spirals may not be strictly dyadic; several states may be involved simultaneously in interlocking dilemmas and spirals. The 1967 Six-Day War illustrates the potential for a "multilateral security dilemma" as well as multilateral conflict spiral patterns. Another consideration is that power transitions and security dilemmas may be related. Power transitions may trigger security dilemmas and therefore conflict spirals. The large number of dyadic power transitions taking place in the decade prior to World War I were instrumental in initiating a number of interrelated security dilemmas and conflict spirals.

Deterrence theory is in many ways the polar opposite of conflict spiral theory. It maintains that states may successfully deter attacks on themselves or their allies by making threats to retaliate. Threatening behaviors are deemed to induce caution rather than counterthreats in others. Logically, a state attempting to deter others should be successful if it (1) specifically defines its commitment to retaliate against any prohibited action, (2) effectively communicates this commitment to the potential attacker, (3) possesses sufficient military capabilities to carry out the threat and inflict unacceptable costs on the attacker, and (4) makes the deterrent threat credible by somehow demonstrating its willingness to carry out the threatened actions (Cashman 1993, 219).

If these criteria are met, war may be prevented by the threat of war. On the other hand, wars may occur because states fail to make an attempt to deter others or because others do not believe the deterrer has the physical capability or the intention to carry out the threatened retaliation. In other words, it fails because the deterrer has not effectively carried out steps 1 to 4 above. Our discussion of security dilemmas and conflict spirals should remind us, however, that the making of deterrent threats is fraught with danger. Threats may simply incite fear, hostility, and anger. Instead of preventing violence, they may provoke the opponent into risky actions and serve to escalate the conflict spiral instead of dampen it (Jervis 1976, 58–113).

At the dyadic level of analysis, a variety of other factors having to do with the nature of the two disputants are of significance. On the basis of the accumulation of statistical evidence from conflicts from the past several centuries, we can say that disputes are more likely to lead to war (1) if they take place between a pair of longstanding or "enduring" rivals, (2) if an arms race is in progress, (3) if they involve contiguous states, (4) if an actual dispute over territory is involved, or (5) if at least one of the states is nondemocratic.

Enduring rivals are pairs of states who compete with each other over a period of decades, during which time they tend to become involved in a series of crises. There is a tendency for these crises to become repeated and "militarized"—that is, to involve acts of violence or threats of violence. Indeed, these repetitive militarized disputes are a hallmark of enduring rivalries. But mutual perceptions are also an important component of rivalries. Political elites in the two states perceive each other as rivals; they mistrust each other and are deeply suspicious of the other's motives and intentions. Furthermore, the rivals not only tend to have mutual expectations of future conflicts but also expect such conflicts will probably be settled by force rather than through diplomatic means. All of these tendencies have the potential to create self-fulfilling prophecies.

Statistically, long-term enduring rivals have been responsible for roughly half of all wars, militarized disputes, and violent changes of territory in the last two centuries. More than half the interstate wars in the nineteenth and twentieth centuries occurred between enduring rivals, and disputes among enduring rivals are almost twice as likely to end in war than disputes occurring between other pairs of states (Goertz and Diehl 1992; Geller and Singer 1998, 23). As we might suspect, the relationship between enduring rivals is also sensitive to changes in the dyadic distribution of power, with war as the possible result (Geller 1998, 180–81).

Additionally, enduring rivals appear to be the victims of a particularly pernicious dynamic called **dysfunctional crisis learning**, a concept associated with the work of Russell Leng (1983). Enduring rivals experience mutual international crises that are likely to involve threats of force, demonstrations of force, and the use of force short of war. Each rival derives certain "lessons" from these periodic crises. Leaders in the state that wins the first crisis learn that victory has been achieved through "acting tough," and they therefore become committed to a similar policy in the next crisis. Leaders in the losing state in the first crisis learn that they must be "tougher" the next time there is a crisis. Domestic political pressures enhance the probability that dysfunctional learning will take place, with the result that, when the next crisis occurs, leaders on both sides are committed to "tough" policies—including the use of threats, ultimatums, mobilization of forces, demonstration of force, and so on. If the second crisis does not result in war, a third crisis will almost certainly have that effect (Leng 1983; Diehl 1998).

Arms races—competitive mutual buildups of arms at higher than normal rates—may be part of the general phenomenon of increased tension and threat that take place in the midst of conflictual dyadic interactions. Conflicts between states that are engaged in an arms race appear to be more likely to result in war than conflicts that do not involve arms races (Wallace 1979, 1982). Arms races not only increase the likelihood that disputes will escalate to war but also increase the chances that a pair of states will engage in a dispute in the first place (Sample 2000, 170–71). Arms races are associated with other dyadic phenomena as well. They are most likely to take place between states that see themselves as rivals, and they may be a crucial element within the more general phenomenon of a conflict spiral. Though the presence of an arms race is unlikely, by itself, to start a war, it does add considerable fuel to an already flammable situation by increasing the perceived level of threat, hostility, and malignant intent and by generally increasing the level of anxiety on both sides. Other dyadic factors also contribute fuel. Sample (2000, 177–78) finds that although the probability of a dispute escalating to war is 21 percent when the two disputants are both arming, the probability rises to 69 percent if other phenomena are present: a high defense burden, a territorial dispute, and equal power capabilities as a result of a rapid "catching up" that results in a power transition. She also finds that the post–World War II nuclear age has made a difference; nuclear weapons actually appear to help prevent the escalation of disputes to war (Sample 2000, 185–86).

Conflicts and crises that involve **contiguous states** are the most prone to war. That most wars involve contiguous states would seem obvious. Most of us would concede that the possibility is greater that Germany would attack France or that Israel would attack Lebanon than it is that Peru would attack Angola or China would attack Colombia. This is simply because war between contiguous states is logistically more feasible and war between noncontiguous states is militarily difficult. Additionally, neighboring countries simply have more opportunities to get into conflicts; they have more interactions (both positive and negative) with their neighbors. More important, however, geographic closeness is related to a state's willingness to go to war. Neighbors have more concerns about each other's ambitions, and disputes with neighboring states are normally viewed as more important, more threatening, and more closely related to vital national interests. Finally, and perhaps most crucially, contiguous states are most likely to develop disputes based on claims to national territories and to the people within those territories—the most dangerous of all types of disputes. Of all the possible issues that might generate conflict between states, territorial disputes have been those most likely to lead to war (Hensel 2000; Huth 2000). One scholar (Vasquez 1993, 224) even refers to territorial disputes as the most important underlying cause of war. Although such disputes might not immediately or inevitably lead to war, they are likely to produce a sequence of events that could lead to war. On the other hand, the absence of territorial disputes makes war between any pair of states extremely unlikely.

Why are territorial disputes so important? The loss of a state's territory directly affects its access to resources, its physical capabilities, its human composition and labor power, and its reputation for defending itself. All of these are seen as vital and inescapable national interests by the leaders of most states. Territorial disputes may also have ethnic, cultural, and religious dimensions. The claims of one state to the territory of a neighbor may be based on the ethnic or religious similarity of the populations within the two areas.

Conflictual relations between neighbors can be offset if the neighbors happen to have similar democratic political systems. Much has been made of the fact that even though democracies are involved in almost as many wars as other kinds of states, stable democratic states do no fight each other (see, for instance, Weart 1998; Russett and Starr 2000). This is usually referred to as the **democratic peace**. Indeed, it is now commonplace to assert that we only know two things for sure about the causes of war: Neighbors fight each other and democracies don't. If two democratic states are involved in a dispute, the presence in both states of democratic constitutions and institutions based on the principles of separation of power and checks and balances creates powerful restraints on the ability of executives to take their countries to war. Just as important, the presence of similar democratic political cultures in a pair of states creates mutual expectations that international disputes will be handled just like domestic disputes—peacefully and through the rule of law. When disputes arise between such states, they are almost always resolved peacefully. Autocratic states would appear to have no such inhibitions against war. At any rate, given the mutual inhibitions of democracies to fight each other and the lack of such inhibitions between democracies and nondemocracies, the likelihood that a dispute will end in war is increased if at least one of the disputants is nondemocratic.

THE INTERNATIONAL SYSTEM LEVEL

The most fundamental characteristic of the international system is **anarchy**, which by definition exists because the international system lacks a world government with the ability to make and enforce international law. This lack of world government (and lack of a world police force) means that at the most basic level, wars happen because there is no global authority capable of preventing them. The international system is essentially a "self help" system in which countries must ultimately provide for their own security. However, as we have already seen, unilateral efforts by states to increase their security is likely to lead to security dilemmas and the conflict spirals associated with them.

One aspect of this anarchic international system that has received an inordinate amount of attention is the global distribution of power among the states that make up the system, especially the distribution of power among its major states or great powers. The results of empirical investigations have been disappointing and mixed. There is no clear evidence that any particular type of international distribution (or balance) of power—**unipolar**, **bipolar**, or **multipolar**—is any more warlike or peaceful than any other. Whether this balance is defined simply in terms of the number of major powers in the system (one, two, three, or more) or in terms of the level of concentration of power among the major powers within the system, the results are the same. Wars occur with relative frequency in every type of system (Cashman 1993, 232–248; Geller and Singer 1998, 113–120; Geller 2000, 271–275).

Although the particular kind of balance may make no difference, changes in the global distribution of power may have a profound effect on the chances for war or peace in the system. Charles Doran's power cycle theory (Doran 1989, 1991, 2000; Doran and Parsons 1980) connects the changes in a state's relative power position to the outbreak of major power wars. Doran argues that the capabilities of states, relative to other members of the great power system, follow a cyclical path of growth, maturation, and decline which he calls a "power cycle." It is a cycle of relative power, and a state's course through it depends as much on the power of others as on the state's own internal growth or decline. Wars between the great powers are seen as most likely when a state reaches one of four **critical points** in the cycle, points at which abrupt and unpredictable changes occur. Each critical point represents a change in the previous trend. New members of the great power club usually enter the system at the lower turning point, where they begin a rapid ascent in terms of relative capabilities. At the first inflection point, a state that has been rapidly rising in power relative to others begins to decelerate. At the upper turning point, a rising state now begins to decline relative to other great powers. At the second inflection point, the once-rapid decline (relative to others) begins to decelerate. At each critical point there is a misalignment between a state's relative capabilities, on the one hand, and its interests, its aspirations, and the roles it wishes to play on the other hand. Critical points call for a drastic reevaluation of a state's foreign policies. They create anxiety and uncertainty in the international system and increase the probability that leaders will be prone to misperceptions, overreactions, and risk-taking behavior. When several great powers in the system simultaneously go through critical points, this creates massive structural uncertainty in the system and further vexes the ability of system members to make needed adjustments to manage change. Essentially, wars between great powers occur because of the inability of states to adjust to shifts in their relative capabilities and make the needed alterations to their foreign policies.

Others theorists have focused more specifically on power transitions in the dyadic balance between a systemic leader—a global "hegemon" who dominates a system that is more or less unipolar—and a rising great-power challenger who is dissatisfied with the nature of the international system. These "historical/cyclical" theories come in several varieties: the hegemonic war theory (also called hegemonic stability theory) associated with Robert Gilpin (1981), the **long cycle theory** associated with George Modelski and others (Modelski and Thompson 1989; Rasler and Thompson 2000), and the **world systems theory** of Emmanuel Wallerstein (1974). Like Doran's power cycle theory, these theories attempt to explain great-power wars rather than all interstate wars. All of these theories use the logic of power transition theory—that an equal distribution of capabilities is dangerous and that preponderance of capabilities in the hands of a single great power is conducive to relative peace and stability in the system. The hegemonic state uses its power and prestige to make and enforce rules in the system and to provide leadership. When the power capabilities of this hegemonic state begin to decline and power becomes "deconcentrated" in the international system, the chances of war between great powers begin to increase. Modelski and Thompson see hegemonic cycles as lasting roughly one hundred years. (Others see no particular duration to hegemonic rule.)

An important similarity of all of the theories that focus on changing power distributions is that the root of these changes can be found in uneven rates of economic, technological, and demographic growth within countries—a "normal" process that is not easily subjected to manipulation by states themselves. The uneven or dissimilar rates of growth among states mean that changes in the distribution of power are endemic in the system. The proponents of these theories suggest that the relative decline of the global leader is more or less inevitable, and that such a decline leads to a general deconcentration of power in the international system, which increases the chances that dissatisfied states will challenge the old-system leader, thereby increasing the probability of major power war.

What can we distill from these theories and from the empirical studies associated with them? Historically, shifts in the dyadic and/or global distribution of power have tended to increase the probability of war among great powers. There appears to be a synergistic, interactive effect between (1) the general deconcentration of power within the international system that comes about because of the declining power of the global hegemon and the rising power of a dissatisfied great-power challenger and (2) the shifting dyadic-level capabilities of other states in the system (Geller and Singer 1998, 119–120; Geller 2000, 271–76). These dyadic power shifts or transitions cumulatively alter the global distribution of power. Although there has been less investigation of the distribution of power within regional "subsystems," changes in such subsystems probably also increase the probability of war.

The connection between systemic power changes and war can be explained in a number of ways. First, power shifts generally create an environment in which anxiety, uncertainty, and the perception of threats are increased, thereby triggering security dilemmas and conflict spirals. This dynamic is particularly pernicious among states who are rivals. As at the dyadic level, changes in the global distribution of power also create perceptions of windows of opportunity and windows of vulnerability, which strengthen the perceived need for wars of either preemption or prevention. The environment created by power shifts is generally conducive to miscalculation and reckless behavior, with rising states acting prematurely and declining states acting preventively. Second, power shifts create an imbalance (or disequilibrium) between the distribution of power capabilities in the system, on the one hand, and the distribution of prestige, status, and roles on the other hand. This creates situations of **status discrepancy** in which certain states that are dissatisfied with the distribution of status, prestige, and political influence within the international system (or within their regional subsystems) have now gained the military and economic potential to redress their grievances. If these imbalances between capabilities and status are not rectified through political accommodation, violence may result. In the 1930s both Germany and Japan were states with rising military and economic power whose use of aggression was linked to dissatisfaction with the rules of the international system and their status and roles within that system. Third, the deconcentration of power at the global level may make it difficult for the hegemonic power to manage conflicts among the other great powers. The existence of an unstable hierarchy among the great powers may mean that when dyadic power shifts occur between lower-tier states within the system, these power shifts are now more likely to lead to war than in the past.

Another systemic phenomenon, **alliance formation**, is related to changes in global power distribution. Although the formation of alliances frequently precedes wars between great powers, it is generally conceded that alliances do not cause wars in and of themselves (Levy 1981). Instead, alliances confirm the already-existing tensions and hostilities among states in the system, and their formation exacerbates the degree of anxiety and the perception of threat among members of the system. (The role alliances play is probably not unlike that of arms races.) This is probably also true of polarization, an alliance pattern in which two opposing alliances become discrete and mutually exclusive, with no overlapping memberships between one alliance and the other. Although the polarization of alliances is logically problematic—they are clearly antagonistic, they reduce chances for amity, and they are likely to increase the level of perceived threat—polarized alliance systems may also reduce uncertainty. Perhaps what is most important about alliances is that they help explain why wars expand from small, bilateral conflicts to larger multilateral and global wars as countries not involved in the initial dispute join to assist their allies. Alliances may not be instrumental in causing wars, but they are crucial in determining whether wars will expand.

The massive structural change in the international system that resulted from the collapse of communist governments in Europe, the dissolution of the Soviet Union, and the end of the Cold War led many international relations scholars to think about whether and how international conflict might be different in the post–Cold War world. One controversial recent theory, Samuel Huntington's (1993) clash of civilizations theory, merits some discussion.

Huntington argues that with the demise of the Cold War bipolar system, the nature of the international system has changed significantly. States will still be the major actors, but politics will revolve around civilizations, which Huntington defines as the "highest cultural grouping of people and the broadest level of cultural identity that people have short of that which distinguishes humans from other species" (1993, 24). A civilization's central defining characteristic, at least in Huntington's eyes, is religion. Although civilizations have risen and fallen historically, Huntington claims only seven or eight exist today: Western, Confucian, Japanese, Islamic, Hindu, Slavic-Orthodox, Latin American, and, possibly, a sub-

Saharan African civilization. Huntington believes that conflict in the future will be primarily cultural, rather than ideological or economic, in nature. This is because civilizational identity is the most basic identity of all and is very difficult to change. Moreover, a variety of present-day cultural, political, technological, and economic processes are combining to intensify peoples' consciousness of their civilizational identity.

In addition to culture, Huntington is also interested in the nature of the international system (it is multipolar) and the shifting distribution of power (away from Western civilization). We might, therefore, wish to think of his theory as a kind of "cultural realism." Huntington's predictions about international conflict include the following:

1. Whereas in the past several centuries major international conflicts have primarily been intracivilizational conflicts between states within Western civilization, the principal conflicts of the post–Cold War era will be between states or groups from different civilizations.
2. Interstate wars are most likely to break out along the geographic "fault lines" between civilizations.
3. Conflicts between states within the same civilization are likely to be less frequent and less intense, and they will be less likely to spread than conflicts between states of different civilizations. (Common civilizational membership reduces the probability of violence, thus creating a kind of "civilizational peace.")
4. If interstate wars spread, this will tend to happen via common civilizational membership. (Huntington calls this "civilizational rallying.") Likewise, membership in international organizations and alliances will tend to be based on common civilizational ties.
5. The central axis of international conflict in the future will be "the West against the Rest," as other civilizations will attempt to balance off the power of the predominant cultural coalition.
6. The next world war will be between civilizations.

We should mention that Huntington's theory has significant temporal limitations; it attempts to explain only those conflicts that occur after the end of the Cold War. And since the post–Cold War era is now less than two decades old, we have a very limited universe of events or cases that may be used to test the theory. Of our cases, only the 2003 Iraq War and the Eritrea-Ethiopia War come from the post–Cold War period. Finally, the evidence we have thus far is certainly not overwhelming enough for us to concede the theory's explanatory power. The jury is still out on this one.

MULTILEVEL ANALYSIS

Finally, we should make note of one theory of war that attempts to combine causal factors at different levels of analysis: John Vasquez's "steps to war" explanation (Vasquez 1993, 2004). This theory looks at war as a process that occurs over time, with the chances of war increasing after each step. Vasquez argues that the underlying cause of wars between relative equals (which he calls **wars of rivalry**) is the presence of a dispute over territory by contiguous states—a dyadic-level variable. The other causes of war are more immediate or proximate.

If states respond to territorial disputes by using **realpolitik** methods—using coercive bargaining, making threats and ultimatums, forming alliances, demonstrating power and resolve, engaging in arms buildups and arms races—then a dyadic conflict spiral is likely to take place. Successive dyadic crises give the spiral an escalatory momentum and take the states closer to war. The spiral is likely to be intensified if the countries in question are enduring rivals. It is also likely to be accelerated by **blowback effects** on the domestic political situation in each country—a substate level phenomenon. Say the external foreign policy acts of State A have a negative effect on the internal politics in State B. They spark popular indignation and fear; they receive intense media attention, which frequently plays on nationalist themes; and they arouse rival political parties, politicians, and interest groups, who may condemn any sign of a weak response from the government in power. The combined effect of these things is to place pressure on the government of State B to pursue "tougher" external policies against State A. These actions, once taken, have in turn a negative effect on the domestic political situation in State A, forcing A to take tougher policies against B. The use of realpolitik foreign policy tactics by one state has the political effect of "proving" that a conciliatory approach will not work with the opponent. Thus, in the rival state, accommodationists are driven from power and hardliners are brought to power, thereby reducing the chances that the conflict spiral will end peacefully (Vasquez 1993, 212). The domestic political systems of the rival states are thus tightly linked in conflict spirals. Wars are most likely if hardliners are in power in both countries.

The conflict spiral is also affected by factors at the international system level. The presence of international norms against the use of force and a nonviolent conflict resolution regime help to dampen the conflict; however, their absence creates a permissive environment in which violence is more likely. Finally, whether the war escalates to involve additional belligerent countries depends primarily on other system-level factors, the most important of which are a multipolar distribution of power, a polarized alliance system, and the lack of global preponderance.

Dyadic factors—repeated territorial disputes, conflict spirals, rivalries, arms races, alliance formation, and the use of coercive diplomacy—are central to the steps to war explanation, but domestic political factors (the ascendancy of hardliners) and systemic factors (the absence of an international regime for peaceful conflict resolution) help to determine whether the conflict spiral will escalate to war.

Multilevel explanations such as the steps-to-war approach are useful in several ways. First, they move us away from both single-factor and single-level explanations of war and get us to think about the ways that causal factors interact with one another. Second, they move us in the direction of thinking about war as a process in which war is the result of a chain of interrelated factors—a chain that perhaps starts with certain root or long-term conditions that then combine and interact with more immediate factors in a way that greatly increases the probability of war.

SUMMARY

Although not all of the factors we have identified as contributing to the outbreak of war are necessary for war to occur, many of them appear frequently enough in combination with one another to cause us to be wary of their potential to bring about warfare. We will use the case studies in the following chapters to clarify how these factors (and perhaps other factors) combine to create war. These case studies have not been selected as a representative sample of wars of the last one hundred years and thus in no way constitute an attempt to empirically test our propositions about the causes of war. The cases have been selected because they appear to be some of the most important instances of war in the past one hundred years and because of their inherent interest to students of international conflict. We also tried to select cases from diverse periods of time and geographic regions, and we wanted to include wars that involved minor as well as major powers.

In examining these case studies, we use a method called **process tracing**. Essentially, we attempt to trace the causal process by which initial conditions or root causes combine with more immediate or proximate factors to develop, over time, into war. We do this by focusing on those variables or factors that the theoretical and empirical literature in international relations has identified as important causes of war. We wish to see if the causal factors identified by research using aggregate data on war apply in the particular cases selected here. More important, we wish to ascertain how the various causal factors might cluster and interact to produce war. In other words, we seek to identify and examine the causal chains that produce war and to compare the similarities and differences between the causal chains found in our cases. We consider this study to be a modest "first cut" at achieving these goals. It will certainly not end the debate on the causes of war.

We begin our investigation of the case studies by laying out a number of assumptions and expectations that are at the basis of our analysis:

1. There is no single causal factor that is responsible for interstate war.
2. Since interstate war is a relatively rare event, and since individual causal factors by themselves are likely to increase the probability of war only slightly, war is most likely to be the result of a relatively rare combination of multiple causal factors that come together simultaneously and interact dynamically to produce situations that are inherently dangerous and prone to violence (see Bennett and Stam 2004, 155–56 on this point).
3. These causal factors exist at several different levels of analysis.
4. We expect that the exact nature and number of these factors will vary somewhat from war to war and that no two cases of war are likely to result from exactly the same combination of forces.
5. Nevertheless, certain factors will appear often enough, and in combina-

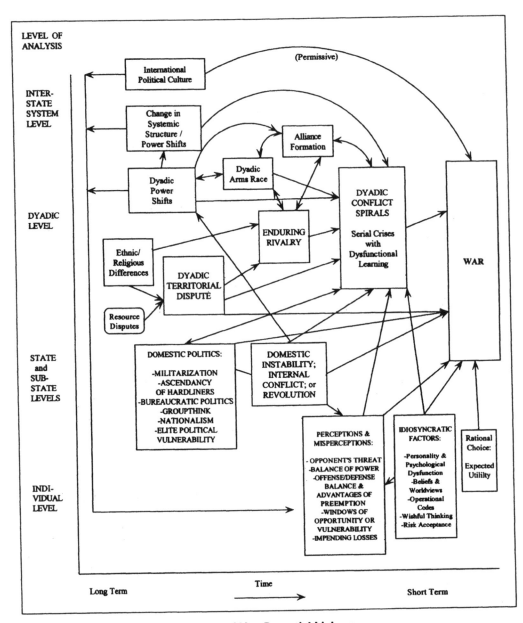

LEVEL OF
ANALYSIS

INTER-
STATE
SYSTEM
LEVEL

DYADIC
LEVEL

STATE
and
SUB-
STATE
LEVELS

INDI-
VIDUAL
LEVEL

(Permissive)

International
Political Culture

Change in
Systemic
Structure /
Power Shifts

Alliance
Formation

Dyadic
Arms Race

Dyadic
Power
Shifts

DYADIC
CONFLICT
SPIRALS

Serial Crises
with
Dysfunctional
Learning

ENDURING
RIVALRY

Ethnic/
Religious
Differences

DYADIC
TERRITORIAL
DISPUTE

WAR

Resource
Disputes

DOMESTIC POLITICS:

-MILITARIZATION
-ASCENDANCY
OF HARDLINERS
-BUREAUCRATIC POLITICS
-GROUPTHINK
-NATIONALISM
-ELITE POLITICAL
VULNERABILITY

DOMESTIC
INSTABILITY;
INTERNAL
CONFLICT; or
REVOLUTION

PERCEPTIONS &
MISPERCEPTIONS:

- OPPONENT'S THREAT
-BALANCE OF POWER
-OFFENSE/DEFENSE
BALANCE &
ADVANTAGES OF
PREEMPTION
-WINDOWS OF
OPPORTUNITY OR
VULNERABILITY
-IMPENDING LOSSES

IDIOSYNCRATIC
FACTORS:

-Personality &
Psychological
Dysfunction
-Beliefs &
Worldviews
-Operational
Codes
-Wishful Thinking
-Risk Acceptance

Rational
Choice:

Expected
Utility

Long Term

Time

Short Term

Chart 1.1. Causal Factors in Interstate War: Potential Linkages

tions and sequences that are repetitive enough, to indicate their crucial impact in turning a dispute into a full-fledged war. In other words, we expect to find clearly discernable patterns and regularities in our search for the causes of war, and these dangerous patterns—the focus of this book—may take the shape of causal chains that sequentially link causal factors together.

See chart 1.1, Causal Factors in Interstate War: Potential Linkages, for a visual sketch of the potential connections between the various causal factors outlined in this introduction.

2

World War I

On June 28, 1914, Archduke Franz Ferdinand of Austria-Hungary was assassinated and Europe was plunged into crisis. Diplomacy broke down, and in a little over a month the curtain of war had descended over the Continent. The "long nineteenth century" of international peace in Europe had ended. From the end of the Napoleonic Wars until the outbreak of World War I, the great powers of Europe had avoided the perils of a general war engulfing the Continent. Smaller, less destructive wars had been the norm: the Crimean War, the three short wars of German unification, and the wars on the periphery of Europe that forced the withdrawal of the Turks from the European Continent. World War I ended this relatively idyllic age. The war engaged most of the European states and pulled in their allies in North America, the Near East, and Asia. It was also one of the most destructive wars in history. A recent study (Ferguson 1999, 436) estimates that approximately 9.45 million died as a result of the war and concomitant disease, killing more than one out of every eight of the 65.8 million men who fought in it. In one battle alone, the Somme, there were 1.3 million dead and wounded. World War I killed roughly twice as many people as had the wars of the previous two centuries (Kagan 1995, 82). In addition to those who died in battle, another 15.4 million were wounded and almost 8 million soldiers were taken as POWs.

It was a war that no European leader clearly and consciously sought. If Europe's leaders had known in 1914 what they knew in 1918, the war almost certainly would have been avoided. But very few in 1914 were able to correctly predict the course the war would take and the momentous changes that would come in its wake.

LONG-TERM ROOTS OF WORLD WAR I

International System Level: Global Culture and Attitudes toward War

As the constructivist approach to international politics tells us, war is a social construction. It is a political institution created by men as a way of solving political problems. This socially constructed institution is buttressed by a set of attitudes,

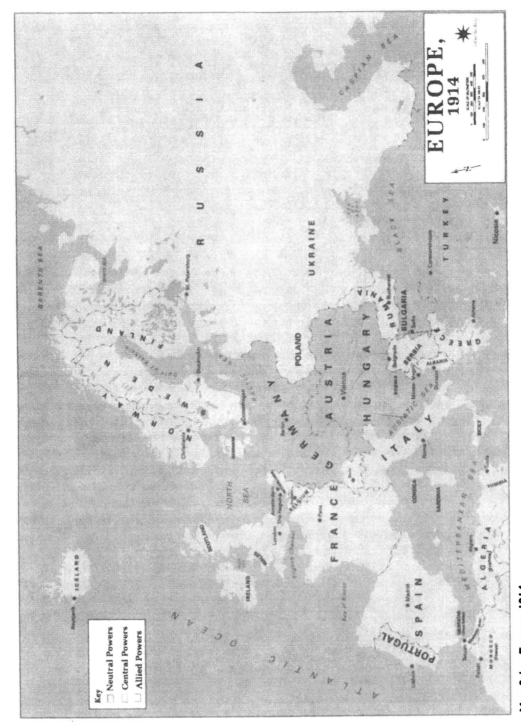

Map 2.1. Europe, 1914

beliefs, and values associated with war—all of which change over time. For want of better terminology, we may say this set of attitudes, beliefs, and norms about war is part of a **global political culture**. At any given time the global culture may be either supportive of war or inhibitive. According to Vasquez's (1993) steps to war theory, the presence of a global culture that condones or justifies interstate violence is an important factor in the explanation of war.

In 1914 a dominant feature of global political culture was the relatively benign outlook on war. In spite of the presence of many antiwar groups in 1914, the prevailing view among political elites in most countries in the "civilized" world was supportive of the institution of war. The resort to war was seen as the ultimate right of sovereign states and was legitimated by various legal and moral conceptions of "just wars."

Moreover, the prevailing norms in 1914 saw war not merely as acceptable but also as beneficial, progressive, manly, virtuous, and uplifting—something that provided spiritual regeneration. War was romanticized and seen as glamorous. Many believed wars were necessary to sweep away the decadence that infested societies during times of peace. The German general Friedrich Bernardi quoted the philosopher Hegel on this point: "Wars are terrible, but necessary, for they save the state from social petrification and stagnation." German general Helmuth von Moltke believed that war "developed the noblest virtues of man." War was also seen as deeply ingrained in human nature and therefore both natural and inevitable. The popular German historian, Treitschke, believed that war played a key role in the long-term social development of nations and that the prime duty of the state was to prepare itself for war. Support for these views was provided by the popular fascination with social Darwinist thought, which saw war as a powerful force of nature through which the stronger nations tended to prevail over the weaker in an international "struggle of the fittest." While these quotes come from Germans, they are, in fact, fairly representative of European elite opinion as a whole in the years before the war and represent the kind of language in which politicians and journalists discussed foreign affairs (Mueller 1989, 37–52; Joll 1992, 199–229). Such cultures do not appear overnight. They are the result of histories learned in school, glorified stories of the national past told to children, and the accumulated mythologies of several generations. In its attitude toward war, the Europe of 1914 appears now to be a place far, far away and long ago.

It is possible, but not necessary, to argue that in Germany in particular, the political culture was imbued with militaristic attitudes. It is certainly true that of all the countries that went to war in 1914 it was in Germany that the support for a strong army and military values most deeply affected the whole of society (Joll 1992, 71–72). It is also certainly true that in Germany the leadership surrounding the kaiser was strongly influenced by militaristic honor codes that glorified violence (and duels) as a proper way to defend one's honor (Hull 1982; Gilbert and Holmes 1996).

What is important here is not the particular political culture of Germany or any other state, but the general nature of global norms toward war. The fact is that in 1914, war was not seen as illegitimate, unethical, or illegal. It was in fact almost universally seen as a normal tool of international politics and as the ultimate legal right of all sovereign states. The international system of the nineteenth and early twentieth centuries established the legal rules and consensual norms that allowed and legitimated the unilateral use of force and established only weak procedures and institutions for the regulation and resolution of conflicts between states. In other words, the nature of global political culture and the nature of the institutions of the international system were *permissive* of war. They did not cause the outbreak of war in 1914, but they constituted an environment in which war was permitted rather than discouraged and restrained (Vasquez 1993, 263–91).

International System Level: Changing Distribution of Power

Where does one look for the roots of WWI? How far back does one go? The search for the causes of the war must go back at least as far as the creation of a unified German state under Prussian leadership in 1871, a process made possible by Prussian victories over Denmark (Schleswig-Holstein War, 1864), Austria (Austro-Prussian War, 1866), and France (Franco-Prussian War, 1870–1871). The creation of a unified, dynamic German state in the heart of central Europe significantly changed the global distribution of power. Perhaps no period in modern history has seen such rapid changes in the relative capabilities among the world's most powerful states. These changes in national power were fundamentally due to the demographic, economic, and technological dynamics occurring within countries and to uneven rates of growth among them. However, we must keep in mind here that it was not only the real changes in the distribution of power that were important but also the **perceptions** of these changes in the minds of national leaders and the effect they had on the evaluation of threats.

The unification of the German territories into the new "Second Reich" accelerated German economic and industrial growth. In the 1890s Germany's heavy industry output surpassed that of Britain, the former world leader, and its GNP growth rate was twice that of Britain's at the turn of the century. German steel production in 1914 was greater than that of Britain, France, and Russia combined, and its share of world manufacturing production was 14.8 percent, compared to 13.6 percent for Britain and 6.1 percent for France (Geller and Singer 1998, 167). Of the European powers, Germany's population was second only to Russia's, but its population was more highly educated and highly skilled. And it also was growing; between 1890 and 1913 it leaped from forty-nine million to sixty-six million (Kennedy 1984, 18; 1987, 210). Germany's economic and demographic growth was paralleled by its military growth. The country's easy victories over two of the traditional great powers of Europe demonstrated that Germany had the single most powerful army on the Continent. The growth of German power could not help but compel the other states of Europe to reevaluate their relative international positions.

The rise of German power was the single most important fact in the changing distribution of power. It also changed the evaluation of threats, as the European states increasingly saw Germany as a threat to their interests. As historian Paul Kennedy (1987, 214–15) has argued, Germany was the one great power whose growth directly undermined the European balance, it was the sole rising newcomer with the strength to challenge the existing order, and it was the one great power whose expansion to the east or west would have to come at the expense of powerful neighbors.

On the other hand, Germany began to see itself as surrounded by potential enemies and without defensible borders either to the east against Russia or (as a result of taking Alsace and Lorraine) on its southwestern frontier with France. Moreover, Germany saw itself as less self-sufficient than these two continental rivals, and unlike Britain, its coastline was easily subject to economic blockade (Calleo 1978, 69). To some German leaders, these conditions seemed to require both external and internal solutions: economic self-sufficiency assisted by protectionism and a colonial policy designed to ensure access to markets and raw materials.

What of the other great powers? On the eastern fringes of the Continent, the Ottoman Empire's European holdings were being pried from its grip by the rebellious multiethnic peoples under its rule, eagerly assisted by various European patrons. The empire was seen as a declining power whose European territories were up for grabs—with Austria and Russia hoping to be the major beneficiaries of its losses.

The Austro-Hungarian Empire was in many ways a European twin of the Ottomans. A multiethnic empire of eleven nationalities ruled by the German Habsburgs, the Dual Monarchy was itself beset by the nationalist political aspirations of its subject peoples—especially Serbs, Croats, Slovaks, and Rumanians. The empire also suffered from a relative economic and military decline. It is not that economic improvement was unknown in Austria; on the contrary, the empire experienced fairly strong industrial growth between 1900 and 1912. But in contrast to the more rapidly growing great powers, it was in relative decline. And it was living beyond its means, especially after the expense of the Balkan Wars (Williamson 1991, 29–30, 157). The empire's military also was in sad shape. Its weapons were out of date and its military starved of funding. Austria spent less per capita on the military than most other European states. In the aftermath of its defeat in the Austro-Prussian War, Austria-Hungary still held status as one of Europe's great powers, but without the resources and physical capabilities to perform in that role. Nevertheless, it hoped to be able to gain strength from the decline of its old rival in the Balkans. But the decline of the Ottoman Empire created problems as well as opportunities for Austria. The Ottoman Empire's forced exodus from Europe created newly independent or autonomous Slavic states such as Serbia and Montenegro, which encouraged other southern Slavs within Austria's empire to rebel and join together in a southern Slav confederation.

Russia, another multiethnic empire, was the champion of Slavic and Orthodox peoples in the Balkans. It also had a fundamental interest in any change in the arrangements for the straits connecting the Black Sea and the Mediterranean that might be affected by the decline of Ottoman power. Unlike Austria, Russia's fortunes seemed to be on the rise. A traditional great power in Europe because of its great size and population, Russia had always been the standard bearer for states with unfulfilled potential. A late convert to modernization and industrialization, Russia's economy was finally experiencing real growth in the last decades of the nineteenth century. Indeed, the industrial growth rate in Russia throughout the 1890s was about 8 per cent a year. It overtook both France and

Austria in steel production. By 1914 Russia had the fourth largest economy in the world, though it was a very distant fourth. However, Russia's productive economic strength was actually decreasing relative to Germany's (Kennedy 1984, 29; Kennedy 1987, 233–34). Its defeats in the Crimean War and the 1904–1905 Russo-Japanese War lowered its importance as a military ally, but they helped to further prod both military and economic modernization. Russia's economic growth was concentrated in military-related heavy industries. It had a rapidly growing population, the largest army in the world, and half a million reserves to back it up. And in the aftermath of the war with Japan, Russia was also rebuilding its fleet.

After 1910 all the European states believed that Russia's return to the top ranks of the great power club would be rapid and impressive. By 1914 Russia's allies, the British and especially the French, tended to be optimistic in their assessments of Russia's new capabilities. Russia's opponents, the Austrians and the Germans, tended to believe that Russia had not yet turned the corner, but they were both mightily concerned that in a few short years Russia's military rearmament program would inexorably spell doom for them (Wohlforth 1987). Given Russia's manifest liabilities, their fears were greatly exaggerated.

France, the major land power on the Continent for several centuries, was still a great power, but by the early days of the new century it was showing little of the vitality that was necessary to keep pace in the changing global environment. The French economy remained largely agricultural. While economic growth took place, the most important fact is that France actually experienced a relative industrial decline compared to the faster growing Britain, Germany, Russia, and United States. In 1914 France's total industrial production was only 40 percent of Germany's, and the total size of France's economy was roughly half that of Germany's (Kennedy 1984, 16; Kennedy 1987, 222–23). With a static birth rate, France's population barely grew, whereas Germany's skyrocketed. This had direct and obvious implications for the military strengths of the two continental powers. France could draw on a pool of about five million service-aged males; Germany had access to approximately twice that number (Kennedy 1987, 223).

Two non-European states had begun to emerge as true powers on the global stage. The United States had one of the most dynamic economies in the world by the turn of the century; indeed, the U.S. had surpassed Great Britain in the 1880s as the world's largest economy. And its military victory over Spain in 1898 signaled its increased military prowess. Similarly, Japan's victory over Russia in the Russo-Japanese War emphasized the creation of a new Asian powerhouse.

Finally, Britain had been for at least the last century the dominant global power; indeed, many historians and political scientists have referred to Britain as a *global hegemon*—a single country that was the dominant global state militarily and economically. Its navy ruled the seas, its leadership in the industrial revolution made it the preeminent industrial nation, and it was the world's leading merchant, financier, and insurer. In short, it was the primary state in the emerging global capitalist economy. Britain's military power rested on its industrial power. But as the century waned, Britain's economic power, while still growing, had gone into decline relative to the faster growing powers such as Germany, the United States, and even Russia (Sabrosky 1989, 68). Though Britain held a leading edge in older technologies like textiles, Germany and the United States dominated in newer industries such as steel, chemicals, machine tools, and electrical products. Between 1885 and 1913, Britain's industrial production became sluggish, rising by only 2.11 percent, whereas Germany's increased by 4.5 percent and the United States' by 5.2 percent. By 1906 Britain was surpassed by the U.S. in iron and coal production and by both the U.S. and Germany in steel production (Kagan 1995, 92). While Britain's portion of the total world manufacturing output had been 22.9 percent in 1880, by 1913 it had fallen to 13.6 percent (Kennedy 1987, 228). The former world leader was becoming decreasingly competitive in the global economy.

Not only was Britain losing its economic status, but its military had for centuries been extraordinarily one-dimensional. In the decades before WWI, British shipbuilding still accounted for more than 60 percent of the world's tonnage and 33 percent of its warships (Kennedy 1987, 229). Though Britain was a naval power of the first rank, its army was the smallest in Europe, a meager seven divisions compared to Germany's ninety-eight and a half. Furthermore, the British army had been constructed to act primarily as an imperial police force rather than to defend Britain from invasion or to fight a war on the Continent. Nothing had been done in the decades before WWI to change this, and conscription was out of the question politically and ideologically for the ruling Liberal Party.

The result of Britain's relative decline was that the international system became transformed from one in which power was concentrated in the hands of a global hegemon to a system in which power capabilities were diffused among a fairly large number of states. In other words, the system was less and less characterized as unipolar and more and more characterized as multipolar (Geller and Singer 1998, 178–79). Theories of war associated with **hegemonic stability theory**—Gilpin's theory of hegemonic war, Modelski and Thompson's long cycle theory, Wallerstein's world systems theory, and Organski's power transition theory—all argue that the presence of a global hegemonic state with a preponderance of power leads to greater international peace and stability and that the decline of the global hegemon and the consequent deconcentration of global power lead to increased probability of instability and great power wars. As hegemonic power declines, the global leader is less able to effectively constrain conflict among lesser states and conflict increases as rising states attempt to challenge the hegemon for global or regional leadership.

Another aspect of the changing power structure among the European great powers can be seen by the application of Charles Doran's theory of **power cycles** (Doran 2000, 1991, 1989; Doran and Parsons 1980). Doran has calculated power cycles for the great powers based on their relative capabilities. Each cycle contains four critical points at which the country's path changes. (These are called the lower turning point, the first inflection point, the upper turning point, and the second inflection point.) At each critical point a country's trend in its power relationship with the other great powers undergoes a change in direction or in the rate of increase or decrease. At these points there is a disjuncture between a state's capabilities and its interests, it roles and its policies. Critical points produce anxiety, apprehension, and a propensity for risk taking and miscalculation. What is remarkable about the years preceding World War I is how many great powers were going through critical points. Russia reached its lower turning point between 1894 and 1899, Germany had its upper turning point between 1902 and 1907, Britain went through its second inflection point between 1900 and 1905, the United States had its first inflection point in 1910–1915, Italy reached its lower turning point in 1907–1912, and Austria-Hungary was at its lower turning point between 1910 and 1914 (Doran 1991, 133). The fact that so many countries reached critical points compounded the tension and anxiety in the system and greatly increased the probability that miscalculation and risk taking would result in war.

The changing power realities of the late nineteenth and early twentieth centuries created conflicts over status, prestige, and role in the international system and created anxieties and perceptions of threats in most of the major capitals of Europe (Doran 1991). Great powers in relative decline, like Britain, France, Austria, and Turkey, felt impending threats to their prestige and status, to their access to the benefits of global leadership, to their economic and geopolitical interests, and to their physical security. Rising contenders like Germany and Russia were concerned that their interests be taken seriously and that they be granted the status, prestige, influence, and compensation to which their growing power entitled them. This in turn further fueled the fears of declining powers. Without doubt, the years before 1914 had produced what sociologists would refer to as a situation of **status discrepancy**. The status and prestige enjoyed by many states was inconsistent with their actual economic and military capabilities—a situation that produced multiple, interlocking grievances.

In sum, the distribution of power in Europe and in the international system as a whole was unusually fluid and unstable in the decade prior to 1914. Three interconnected structural phenomena were evident. First, dyadic power transitions or shifts took place between some of the great powers. The clearest power transition was between Britain and Germany. The German-Russian balance was also unstable, while the German-French balance was somewhat ambiguous (Geller and Singer 1998, 173–75; Thompson 2003, 465). Second, the relative capabilities of the states in the global great power system in general were in flux, as a large number of great powers went through critical points in their power cycles in the decade before the outbreak of the war. Third, the international system as a whole experienced a massive deconcentration of global power as the capabilities of the global hegemon declined relative to the other great powers. Thus dyadic balances and the global balance both moved toward greater parity of capabilities and away from preponderance (Geller and Singer 1998, 178–79). The combination of these dyadic- and system-level factors created massive structural uncertainty, anxiety, and perceptions of threat throughout the system.

The shifts in the European distribution of power and the resulting changes in the perceptions of threats cannot be discussed without also touching on changes in alliance configurations among the great powers. The changes in the power potentials of states were certainly not evaluated by European leaders in isolation, but in light of the likely alliance ties between European states. Whether or not the growing (or declining) power of a state was seen as threatening depended in large part on whom these nations might align with in a future war (Sabrosky 1989).

During the two decades between the Franco-Prussian War and 1890, Germany's chancellor, Otto von Bismarck, had constructed a complex system of diplomatic agreements that simultaneously isolated France, tied Germany into a set of cooperative relations with Russia, Austria, and Italy, and maintained good terms with Britain. Through the Three Emperors' League (created in 1873 and renewed in 1881) Germany could use its influence to restrain the more ambitious and conflictual policies of its two allies, Austria-Hungary and Russia. Through the Triple Alliance (formed by Italy joining the Dual Alliance of Germany and Austria-Hungary), Bismarck could place the same restraining hand on the potentially antagonistic relations between Italy and Austria. Bismarck even helped arrange the Second Mediterranean Agreement between Britain, Austria, and Italy to promote the status quo in the Balkans, the Near East, and North Africa. Understanding that a strong Germany might be seen as a political threat by its neighbors, Bismarck held German ambitions in check, generally refrained from overseas imperialism, and sought to dampen the conflicting ambitions of others. The newly unified Germany acted in many ways like a satisfied status quo power. But in 1888 Wilhelm II ascended the throne in Berlin, and two years later Bismarck was forced out as chancellor. German ambitions became more apparent; German leaders began to play the imperialist game, and Germany became more of a troublemaker than a conciliator. Oddly, it appeared less satisfied.

Over the next few years a revolution in diplomatic alignment took place in Europe. A fundamental rearrangement of alliance bonds was brought about by several related factors: the growing power of Germany; the insoluble problems that existed between two of Germany's allies, Russia and Austria; the simultaneous attempts by Britain and France to reduce the potential for colonial conflicts and to find allies; and significant bungling by German political leaders. When Russian-Austrian differences proved too much to continue the Three Emperors' League, Bismarck salvaged the day with a continued Triple Alliance with Italy and Austria-Hungary and a separate Reinsurance Treaty with Russia (1887). Even though the Triple Alliance was renewed for five years in 1912, increasing differences between Austria and Italy meant that the Italians would be totally unreliable. A secret anti-Russian pact negotiated in 1883 among Germany, Austria, and Rumania had the same problem: Austrian-Rumanian conflict over ethnic Rumanians in Hungary's Transylvania region made Rumania an undependable ally as well. Most important, with Bismarck gone, the new German government permitted the Reinsurance Treaty with Russia to lapse in 1890. This had two results: Germany had less reason to discourage Austrian confrontations with Russia, and Russia turned elsewhere for friends.

In 1894 the Russians and the French signed the secret Military Convention, which promised mutual defense in case of military attack by a member of the Triple Alliance. The treaty gave Russia an ally on Germany's western flank that would present Germany with its worst nightmare: the problem of fighting a two-front war. Meanwhile, given the far-flung nature of the British Empire and the multitude of potential threats to British interests, Britain concluded that it would be wise to make accommodations with at least some of its potential rivals. (The French had done similar soul-searching and had reached the same conclusion as the British.) The Anglo-Japanese Alliance of 1902 was the first fruit of this new approach. Two years later Britain abandoned its long-held role as an independent balancer of continental power and concluded the Anglo-French Entente Cordiale. The Germans had played an unwitting role in pushing the British and French together through their overly aggressive words and deeds. The German naval buildup that began in 1898 initiated a naval arms race with Britain, and German meddling in Britain's troubles in South Africa and the Boer War increased the ill will. While the Entente Cordiale was not a defensive alliance that committed either Britain or France to the other's defense—it essentially settled outstanding colonial issues between the two countries—Britain was moved progressively toward a more or less tacit commitment to do so. This development was impelled particularly by Germany's aggressive attitude in the Moroccan crisis in 1905 and 1906. The final piece of the geopolitical triangle was put into place in 1907, when France's two allies, the Russians and the British, signed an agreement settling differences on their respective spheres of influence in Persia, Afghanistan, and Tibet. While this agreement was in no way a defensive alliance, France prodded its two allies toward ever greater military cooperation, and in early 1914 Britain agreed to start negotiations on naval cooperation with Russia.

The resulting arrangements, for all practical purposes, created a Triple Entente—Russia, France, and Britain—arrayed against the Triple Alliance of Germany, Austria-Hungary, and Italy (also referred to as the Central Powers). However, between 1900 and 1909 Italy engaged in separate agreements with Russia and with France that essentially nullified Rome's commitments to the Central Powers in the event of war with either France or Russia. And conflicts between Rumania and Austria-Hungary (fanned by Russia) meant that Rumania was also likely to defect from the German-Austrian coalition as well.

In sum, alliance configuration among the European great powers had become relatively polarized by 1907, a structural arrangement that made accommodation difficult, increased and intensified antagonism, increased the level of perceived threat, and helped ensure that when war did break out, it would quickly spread to a large number of states, resulting in a war of tremendous severity and magnitude.

Dyadic Level: Arms Races, Windows, and Preventive War Doctrine

Closely related to the balance of power in Europe were arms races among its most important states. While shifts in overall power had their roots in demographic, economic, and technological phenomena, these underlying trends made shifts in military power possible as well. And to national leaders, changes in military power were perhaps the most visible and threatening of the overall changes that were taking place.

For Britain, the most concrete manifestation of the threat from Germany was the German naval program. The German kaiser, Wilhelm II, was a passionate supporter of increased naval power. A strong German navy was connected to Wilhelm's passion for the sea and for sailing, but it was more than that. A strong navy was a symbol of power: Great powers had colonial empires, and colonial empires required navies. If Germany wished to attain the status of a true world power, it needed a navy, and a Germany navy would force the British to respect Germany and its leader.

After the selection of Alfred von Tirpitz as state secretary of the Imperial Navy in 1897, the German naval building program took off. The German navy went from the world's sixth largest fleet to its second in fifteen years (Geller and Singer 1998, 167). The ultimate goal of Tirpitz's naval buildup is a matter of conjecture. Most certainly, however, his initial goal was neither superiority nor even parity; the strategy was simply to attain sufficient naval strength—approximately sixty ships—to deter British military and diplomatic actions and to prevent Britain from substantially blocking German interests. This was Tirpitz's famous "risk theory." Faced with a German fleet of sufficient size, Britain would be unwilling to risk naval war with Germany because (1) its far-flung interests would mean it would be unable to deploy its entire fleet in opposition to Germany, and (2) even if Britain were to ultimately defeat a German navy, its losses to the German fleet would leave it vulnerable to the navies of the other great powers and thus it would be unwilling to risk military confrontation with Germany. The flaws in the strategy became manifestly evident after British cooperation with the French and the Russians nullified both conditions.

The British leaders tended to see the German fleet as a luxury (Germany had a minuscule colonial empire) and their own fleet as a vital necessity. They therefore questioned German intentions and saw the German program as a real threat to British security interests. The German naval buildup had rather immediate and predictable results in Britain; it was countered with reinvigorated British building, especially under the leadership of Adm. Sir John Fisher, who became first sea lord in 1904. Under Fisher, Britain not only built more new ships but also built qualitatively better ships—dreadnaughts. The Germans responded with dreadnaughts of their own. Britain continued to build, demonstrating the determination to maintain the 60 percent superiority over German forces it felt was necessary. The British reaction to the German naval buildup was so decisive that Tirpitz's goal was quickly shown to be unattainable. While Tirpitz had originally aimed at reaching a ratio of 1.5 to 1 between British and German forces, Germany never came close to this (Ferguson 1999, 84).

In the years before 1914 the naval arms race between Britain and Germany dominated the strategic relationship between the two countries, driving a wedge between them that made efforts of accommodation on other matters more difficult. And it was a major factor in the British decision to seek accommodation with France and Russia. In both Britain and Germany there were war scares centering around naval attacks. Numerous British novels of the age were based on scenarios in which a German invasion force arrived by sea to conquer the island. In Germany there were fears of a British preventive strike against the German navy. The belief that "Fisher was coming" caused a panic in Kiel in 1907, and students were kept home from school for two days. By 1913, however, the naval race had begun to die down somewhat. While the two sides could not agree on a set ratio or on a naval moratorium, Chancellor Bethmann-Hollweg's lack of support for continued naval building and the competing demands of the German Army curbed German naval growth. By 1914 most British leaders were no longer concerned about a threat from the German navy and Lloyd George had even declared the naval race to be over (Kagan 1995, 141, 184; Ferguson 1999, 83–87). But the damage to British-German relations had already been done.

A second arms race among land powers on the European Continent was just as important. While Germany contested control of the seas with Britain, it also was engaged in an attempt to maintain its dominant position on the Continent and to counter the combined land forces of France and Russia. France began rebuilding its army immediately after its defeat in the Franco-Prussian War, and an arms race in conventional land forces between Germany and France was virtually continuous from 1871 to 1914. Germany's greatest fear was that, in the event of a continental war in Europe, it would be forced to fight opponents on both its eastern and western borders. The growing strength of the Russian army and the (not-so) secret Franco-Russian Military Convention of 1894 made this scenario infinitely more likely. Germany's army had been somewhat neglected during the early phases of the naval buildup. Stimulated by the Agadir crisis of 1911, the First Balkan War in 1912 and the expulsion of Turkey from much of Europe, Germany attempted to redress this situation with a rapid increase in the size of its forces in 1912 and 1913. Between 1910 and 1914 Germany's army budget went from $204 million to $442 million (Kennedy 1987, 212).

France responded by extending the term of military service from two years to three. By 1914 France was conscripting 89 percent of eligible youths, compared to 53 percent in Germany (Kennedy 1987, 212). Between 1911 to 1914, the French army increased from 638,500 men to 846,000, and the German army from 626,732 to 806,026 men (Huntington 1958, 62; figures from other sources differ somewhat). Germany also had a sizable and growing population advantage over its neighbor. The population of France was about thirty-nine million; Germany's was sixty-five million. Saddled with a relatively flat population rate, French leaders saw the state at a disadvantage vis-à-vis a militarily dominant Germany with a rapidly growing population (Huntington 1958, 51–54, 62–63). Nevertheless, political and financial constraints in Germany made it difficult for it to turn this population advantage into a military advantage.

Meanwhile, in the aftermath of the disastrous defeat by Japan in 1905, the Russians had undertaken an extensive military reorganization program, though it was only in 1910 or 1911 that this program really got underway. The Russian military program included increasing the size of the army by about half a million men; the production of more and better weapons, including the modernization of field artillery; the restocking of Russia's European arms depots; and a significant improvement in the strategic railway network, including railway lines built to the German frontier in western Russia. If war broke out with Germany, France required an immediate Russian offensive to the east. For this purpose, the French invested heavily in railway construction in Russia. The much-heralded rail program cut Russia's mobilization time, thus allowing it to position a larger percentage of its forces at the front in the first weeks of a war. Russia's 1913–1914 "Great Program" of armament and its mobilization plan (Plan 20) would give her the ability to put seventy-five divisions into the field in just eighteen days, compared to the previous thirty days (Ferguson 1999, 96). The new Russian mobilization plan emphasized offensive scenarios rather than defensive ones—a move very much encouraged by Paris. Not surprisingly, the German General Staff became increasingly concerned about these developments. It was generally recognized that if Russia's tremendous natural resources could ever be matched with technological modernization and efficient leadership, the future would belong to Russia. More specifically, German leaders feared that improvements in the Russian army and a shortening of its mobilization time line would make their own mobilization plan, the Schlieffen Plan, virtually inoperative.

It should not go unnoticed that Germany's actions probably worsened its own situation. In a classic example of the **security dilemma**, Germany's military buildup had provoked an even greater Russian and French buildup, thereby deepening German leaders' perception of a coming window of vulnerability. The French and Russian buildups actually resulted in Germany and Austria losing ground in terms of men at arms. Not counting colonial manpower, on the eve of war in 1914 Germany and Austria-Hungary had a combined troop strength of 1,239,000 while France and Russia could count on 2,272,000. Serbia had 52,000 troops, and Britain possessed 248,000 forces for the European theater (Ferguson 1999, 91–93).

While the arms races had the general effect of increasing tension, anxiety, and perceived hostility throughout Europe, the most profound effect of the arms races was not on the winners of those races but on the losers, the two Central Powers. The arms races (along with the changes in the dyadic and systemic distribution of power) created the perception among leaders in Germany and Austria that the window of opportunity for a military victory was closing quickly and would in the near future be replaced by a window of vulnerability—a point at which German and Austrian forces would be unable to prevail against their opponents in the Entente. This perception affected the willingness of German leaders to run military risks in the present rather than wait for a less advantageous future. When perceptions of power transitions and power imbalances are combined with perceptions of impending windows of vulnerability, perceptions of threats from others tend to become exaggerated (Lebow 1984, 184).

The response of the Central Powers to their perceived impending vulnerability was to seriously contemplate **preventive war** against the Entente. (A preventive war is one fought now in order to avoid the risks of having to fight a war later under worsening circumstances. It is a strategic response to perceived long-term threats. A preemptive war, on the other hand, is undertaken because an adversary's attack is perceived as imminent. See Levy 1987, 90.) For Austria, Russian military modernization meant that Russian forces available for war on the Dual Monarchy's border would almost double (Williamson 1991, 117–18). War Minister Alexander Krobatin, Chief of Staff Conrad, and other Austrian military leaders generally backed preventive war as a solution. And after the assassination of the archduke, Foreign Minister Berchtold joined them. Until 1914, however, this strategy had always been rejected by civilian authorities in Austria.

Several generations of German chiefs of staff—from Moltke the Elder, to Waldersee, to Schlieffen, to Moltke the Younger—also had pushed the idea of preventive war as a way to address the closing window of opportunity. German mobilization plans incorporated first strike notions. This had been the strategy of the elder Moltke in the 1870s and it once again had become the dominant German strategy in the 1890s under Schlieffen. And since it was believed that the Entente powers would certainly win a protracted war because of their greater resources, it was also understood that Germany must devise a strategy capable of winning decisively and quickly. Once again, preventive war seemed the best course.

In 1905, in 1909, and at the famous "War Council" in 1912, the military supported a German preventive war against Russia and France while victory could still be assured—that is, while a window of opportunity still existed. But as in Austria, the military's advice was rejected by civilian leadership. It is interesting to note, however, that one week before the assassination in Sarajevo, Kaiser Wilhelm II stated his agreement with the idea. In a conversation with banker Max Warburg, the kaiser said he believed Russian railway construction was probably a prelude to a Russian attack in 1916, and he wondered whether it might be better for Germany to strike now rather than to wait (Ferguson 1999, 100–101). Confronted with Russia's military buildup and railway expansion and given the deepening of Entente cooperation, the situation in 1914 looked worse than ever. German and Austrian leaders were no longer looking at a situation of a declining window of opportunity so much as they were faced with forestalling a fast-approaching window of vulnerability (Lebow 1984, 152).

The various causal factors we have been discussing did not work in isolation from each other; rather, the dynamic was much more synergistic in nature. The combined impact of the changing European distribution of power, the changing alliance configurations, and the momentum of the arms races all added up in the same direction. They produced increased perceptions of threat, increased anxieties and tensions, increased influence of windows of opportunity and vulnerability, and an increased perception that war was imminent. And especially in Germany, there was an increased belief that preventive war might be the best alternative if Germany was forced to fight on two fronts. Unless German diplomats could devise some ploy to break up the Entente coalition, Germany might have to contemplate preventive war.

Let us summarize the arguments advanced thus far. A partial explanation for the outbreak of World War I is that by the eve of war there existed a causal chain of events that begins with (1) uneven rates of industrial and demographic growth among the European states, which create (2) unstable power relationships at dyadic and systemic levels, as indicated by dyadic power transitions, the arrival of numerous states at critical points in their power cycles, hegemonic decline and deconcentration of systemic power, all of which lead to (3) an increased perception of threats. These changes are all associated with (4) ongoing arms races and (5) changes in alliance configurations leading to alliance polarization. These dynamic long-term trends, in turn, created within the Central Powers (6) perceptions of rapidly closing windows of opportunity and rapidly impending windows of vulnerability. The perception of windows gave rise to (7) a preventive motivation for war.

Prevention is not the only reason for war; nor does war occur in every case where a state has a preventive motivation, but the preventive motivation makes war more likely, especially in association with other conditions. The strength of German and Austrian preventive motivation in 1914 was buttressed by several interrelated factors to be discussed in the following sections: (8) the dual perceptions that offensive forces and strategies had an advantage over defensive forces and strategies and that there was an advantage in striking first, (9) the perception that the probability of victory for the Central Powers in 1914 was still high, and (10) the twin perceptions that war was inevitable and that there was a high probability that the Entente powers would initiate war during the coming period of vulnerability, both of which are related to (11) the existence of enduring rivals with histories of conflict.

Box 2.1. Cast of Characters: Europe 1914.

The Triple Entente
  Britain
      Herbert Asquith, prime minister
      Sir Edward Grey, foreign minister
      Sir Eyre Crowe, permanent secretary, Foreign Office
      Sir Arthur Nicolson, undersecretary, Foreign Office
      Lord Richard Haldane, minister of war
  France
      Raymond Poincaré, president, 1913–1920 (premier, 1912–1913)
      René Viviani, premier
  Russia
      Nicholas (II) Romanov, tsar
      Alexander Izvolsky, ambassador to France
      Sergei Sazonov, foreign minister

The Triple Alliance
  Germany
      Wilhelm II, German emperor
      Prince Bernhard von Bulow, chancellor, 1900–1909
      Theodore von Bethmann Hollweg, chancellor
      Gottlieb von Jagow, foreign minister
      Alfred von Kiderlen-Wachter, foreign minister, 1910–1912
      Count Helmut von Moltke, chief of General Staff
      Prince Karl von Lichnowsky, ambassador to Britain
      Count Friedrich von Pourtales, ambassador to Russia
      Count Heinrich von Tschirschky, ambassador to Austria-Hungary

  Austria-Hungary
      Count Leopold Berchtold, foreign minister
      Gen. Franz Conrad von Hotzendorff, chief of General Staff
      Franz Ferdinand, archduke to Habsburg throne
      Franz Joseph, emperor
      Gen. Alexander Krobatin, war minister
      Istvan Tisza, prime minister of Hungary

We should add at this point that the preventive motivation for war is also buttressed by the logic of prospect theory. Prospect theory argues that national leaders tend to be willing to accept risks with respect to preventing losses, while they tend to avoid risks associated with pursuing gains. In other words, states are more likely to fight to maintain the status quo than to change the status quo in their favor. Preventive war is essentially a strategy designed to minimize expected losses from a future decline rather than to maximize gains by fighting now (Levy 1987, 87–88).

MEDIUM-TERM FACTORS IN THE PATH TO WAR, 1905–1913

Dyadic Level: Enduring Rivals, Great Power Interaction, and Dysfunctional Crisis Learning

The outbreak of World War I did not occur out of the blue. A series of crises initiated the long, downward slide toward war. Each of these crises invigorated the European security dilemma and propelled the great powers closer to war by creating threatening perceptions of the opponent and by creating "lessons" that should be applied in the next crisis. In the decade leading up to WWI, two interlocking factors combined at the dyadic level to produce a situation highly conducive to war: the presence of enduring rivals and the presence of dysfunctional crisis learning.

There is a tendency for crises between enduring rivals to become "militarized"—that is, to involve acts of violence or threats of violence. These crises also tend to become repeated. The two states not only tend to have mutual expectations of future conflicts but also expect that such conflicts will probably be settled by force rather than diplomatic reconciliation. Enduring rivals account for a large proportion of the world's conflict and war (Goertz and Diehl 1992; Geller and Singer 1998, 23). It is also notable that the relationship between enduring rivals is sensitive to changes in the dyadic balance of power. Unstable power balances are highly associated with the outbreak of war (Geller 1998, 180–81).

Enduring rivalries are usually operationally defined as pairs of states who engage in at least six militarized disputes over a period of at least twenty years. A list of such states (Goertz and Diehl 1998, 107) shows the existence of at least seven relevant pairs for the period of 1905–1914 (omitting enduring rivals who end up on the same side in WWI): UK-Germany, France-Germany, and Austria/Hungary–Italy, as well as UK-Turkey, France-Turkey, Italy-Turkey, and Russia-Turkey. The list omits three other pairs that, intuitively, should also be termed enduring rivals but do not meet the specific criteria in 1914: Germany-Russia, Austria/Hungary–Russia, and Austria/Hungary–Serbia. If we relax the formal criteria for the existence of enduring rivals and use an alternative approach that identifies rivalries based on mutual perception of rivalries, these three dyads may be added to the list. Thompson's list of rivalries cites all ten rivalries for major states in pre–WWI Europe (Thompson 2001, 570–73). Of the ten, only the British-German relationship was moving in a more cooperative direction in 1914 (Thompson 2003, 464).

Many of these rivalries were intertwined with territorial disputes, a factor that tended to intensify conflicts between them. The most important of these territorial conflicts were between France and Germany (over Alsace and Lorraine) and Austria-Hungary and Serbia (over Bosnia-Herzegovina). The German-French rivalry, arguable the most central of all, was especially active. The two were engaged in six militarized international disputes (MIDs) between 1870 and 1919, with the final one ending in World War I (Geller and Singer 1998, 185–86).

The presence of **multiple rivalries** is arguably a much more dangerous situation than the existence of an isolated rivalry dyad. In prewar Europe these ten dyadic rivalries existed simultaneously in a geographically confined space and were tightly coupled. They interacted with each other, reinforcing the potential for escalation to war. In Thompson's words, "The basic point is that dense and proximate rivalry fields are highly susceptible to producing complex and unanticipated interactions. What takes place in one rivalry can have implications for the course of several other rivalries. If they are also tightly coupled, 'failures' in one or more rivalries to manage their levels of conflict can spread throughout the system" (Thompson 2003, 461).

Not only were there a large number of rival dyads, but many of them were "ripe" for hostilities. Instead of smoldering or cooling off, many of them were extremely active and intense. The ripeness of these rivalries for violent interaction was very much a function of alliance polarization, the existence of power shifts, and the serial progression of crises involving great powers in the heart of Europe (Thompson 2003, 471).

Serial crises have an important (and perverse) impact on the interaction of enduring rivals. Leaders in both states tend to learn dysfunctional lessons from their perpetual crisis encounters with each other. Leaders invariably come to believe that their failure in a previous crisis with a rival was due to insufficient demonstration of toughness and they should therefore adopt a more coercive strategy in the next confrontation with the rival. On the other hand, the state that was victorious in the last crisis "learns" that bullying has worked and becomes even more committed to a reliance on coercive strategies. Thus both sides become locked into tough-minded, coercive strategies and the two rivals mutually escalate the level of coercion in each successive encounter. Since neither side is willing to back down and make concessions, by the time the rivals engage in their second or third crisis, a full-scale war is the almost inevitable result (Leng 1983). We now examine the progressive crises that shook the great powers in the decade before the war.

Round One: The First Moroccan Crisis, 1905–1906

The first Moroccan crisis constituted "round one" in this process, primarily engaging Germany against France and Britain. Trying to drive a wedge between the members of the new Anglo-French Entente and isolate France diplomatically, the Germans sought to undermine French power in semi-independent Morocco. The kaiser made a stop in March 1905 at Tangier, where he asserted German support for Moroccan independence (as well as Germany's equal rights there). The Germans demanded an international conference on Morocco and talked of war, though this was not Germany's goal. Germany supported its demands with some fairly moderate military activities such as speeding up the provisioning of its army. France, Britain, and Belgium responded with some low-level military measures of their own, and the German leadership, careful not to create a conflict spiral, refrained from escalating. In May 1905 Schlieffen actually proposed a preventive attack on France, but this was quickly vetoed by Wilhelm II (Stevenson 1991, 129–32).

On the other hand, France's position was weak. Its main ally, Russia, had just been defeated by Japan, and the Anglo-French Entente was still in its infancy. Nevertheless, when the conference finally took place (January–April 1906) at the Spanish town of Algeciras, the participants, except for Germany and Austria-Hungary, supported French dominance in Morocco. German leaders had hoped to convince France that its British ally was unable or unwilling to help it. But German bullying had backfired, and Berlin dropped its demands. However, German actions frightened and alienated the French and the British as well as the Italians. The crisis strengthened the Entente rather than splitting it. More important, during the crisis, the British General Staff was forced to consider how Britain would respond to the possibility of a German attack on France, probably through Belgium. The result was that although the new foreign minister, Sir Edward Grey, made no formal promise of military support in case of war, he secretly approved talks between the British and French general staffs (Remak 1995, 43–45; Kagan 1995, 149–50). These talks eventually led to important decisions about the size and potential deployment of a British expeditionary force on the Continent and to a decision to divide naval patrol areas. The Entente was growing teeth. And within a year the British and the Russians, prodded by the French, had settled some longstanding colonial issues. The Triple Entente—Britain, France, and Russia—had now been fashioned as a counter to contain and deter the aims of the Triple Alliance.

Round Two: The Bosnian Annexation Crisis, 1908

Round two, the Bosnian annexation crisis, followed hard on the heels of round one; this time the attention of the great powers turned to the Balkans, engaging the Austrians and Germans against the Russians and Serbs. The Russo-Turkish War of 1877 had liberated Bosnia and Herzegovina from Ottoman rule, and the Treaty of Berlin in 1878 granted Austria the right to occupy those areas, with the unspoken understanding that it might annex them at a later date. (It was at this point that Serbia was also given full independence.) Thirty years later, in October 1908, at the urging of Austrian chief of staff Conrad, the Dual Empire decided to cash in its chips and unilaterally announced its formal annexation of Bosnia and Herzegovina. Austrian leaders hoped that Serbia, Turkey, and Russia would all be compelled by their various weaknesses to accept this **fait accompli**. They also hoped that Serbia would drop its desire for these same territories and its goal of creating a "Greater Serbia" made up of southern Slavic peoples currently under the rule of the Ottomans and the Austrians (Kagan 1995, 158).

Predictably, the Serbs were furious at Austria's land grab. They denounced the annexation and demanded its reversal. Public support for war against Austria was high in Serbia, and the Serbian army was mobilized: Enough reserves were called up to triple the size of the army. Montenegro mobilized as well. The Dual Monarchy responded with a phased escalation of its own and then, in November, moved troops into Bosnia-Herzegovina and reinforced them in the spring of the next year (Stevenson 1991, 133). The Austrian and Serbian armies remained in a state of partial mobilization for several months. Russia, in support of Serbia, denounced the annexation, demanding an international conference to determine compensation for Serbia and, for good measure, a revision of the straits convention.

German chief of staff Helmut von Moltke and Kaiser Wilhelm II had both given assurances to Austria-Hungary that if war broke out with Russia, Austria could count on German assistance. The potential for a European-wide conflagration clearly existed. A Russian mobilization against Austria would trigger a German mobilization and, given the strategy contained in the Schlieffen Plan (and the assumption that France would aid Russia), Germany would respond by attacking France through Belgium, triggering in turn a British intervention. In other words, it was made clear that a Balkan war would set off a continental war. The kaiser understood this (Kagan 1995, 163). The German General Staff in fact supported using the crisis to launch a preventive war against Russia and France while military success was still feasible. German chancellor Bulow sent an ultimatum to Russia on March 21 making it clear that Germany would support Austria and demanding that Russia compel Serbia to accept the annexation.

The real possibility of war was remote, however, as Bulow knew. German evaluations of the Russian predicament concluded that it would be irrational for Russia to risk war in light of its military deficiencies and its internal unrest (Wohlforth 1987, 361). The analysis was correct. During the 1908–1909 Bosnian crisis, Russia's military leadership informed political officials that Russia's forces "were completely unfit for battle" owing to the recent debacle of the Russo-Japanese War, budget cuts, and the fact that fully one-third of the troops were being used for internal security. Russian military leaders rejected a proposal for partial mobilization of forces in the west (Wohlforth 1987, 365; Stevenson 1991, 135). Russia required peace in order to pursue domestic rebuilding. War was not an option; conciliatory policies would have to be pursued. It was also clear to the Russians in 1908 that they were diplomatically isolated; neither Britain nor France would back the use of military force and instead counseled restraint.

In the end (March 1909) Russia and Serbia capitulated to Bulow's ultimatum. Russia forced Serbia to accept Austria's annexation without compensation; Germany declined the opportunity for a preventive attack and war was avoided. Though it ended peacefully, the crisis set off cascading animosities. Having to back down was galling for both the Serbs and the Russians. It was the "point of no return" in Austro-Serb relations (Lebow 2000–2001, 597–98). Anti-Austrian feeling intensified, and the crisis led the Serb government to create and support various pro-Slav nationalistic organizations, such as the Black Hand, which carried out terrorist activities across the border—a policy that culminated in the assassination of Austria's crown prince in 1914. The crisis also pushed Serbia closer to Russia. In Russia the crisis ended a decade of Austro-Russian attempts at cooperation, and it produced a patriotic reaction and a determination that Russia not be humiliated again by its inability to help Serbia in a showdown with the Austrians. To this end it redoubled its effort to strengthen its military. Russia also sought to promote the creation of a Balkan League of Slavic states that was inherently anti-Turkish but also anti-Austrian. Finally, in Austria and Germany the crisis produced the impression that in any future confrontation, the Russians and the Serbs would back down if only the Germans and Austrians acted together and acted strongly—a belief that was crucial in 1914. The strategy followed by

German chancellor Bethmann in 1914 was clearly modeled on Bulow's line of action in 1909, in spite of the fact that Bulow had warned his successor *not* to repeat this strategy in the future, as Russia could not allow itself to be humiliated again (Lieven 1983, 37; Lebow 1981, 123).

Round Three: The Second Moroccan Crisis, 1911

Round three, the Agadir Crisis (or second Moroccan crisis), engaged Germany once again against France and Britain in North Africa. A local revolt in Morocco led in 1911 to French military intervention. (The French probably intended to use their presence there to make Morocco a protectorate.) The Germans responded by reminding the French that under the terms of previous agreements, Morocco was still nominally independent and French actions there were subject to limitations. The Germans declared that they would not oppose French intervention in Morocco as long as they got compensation somewhere else, say, the entire French Congo. In July, the German naval gunboat *Panther* was sent to the Moroccan port of Agadir to drive home the point. In these endeavors the Germans were probably motivated by the desire to reverse their previous diplomatic defeat in Morocco and by the need to produce a visible foreign policy victory for a government in domestic troubles at home, where unpopular taxes brought about by the naval program had led to the rapid growth of the Social Democratic Party.

France's allies were disconcerted with the prospect of another confrontation with Germany. The Russian General Staff informed its allies in France that it would be militarily unready for war with Germany for at least two years. In Britain, Prime Minister Herbert Asquith's cabinet was split. "Radicals" in the Liberal Party pushed the French for concessions in order to avoid a war, and "hawks" in the Foreign Office, who saw the crisis as a trial of strength, vigorously supported the French. The deadlock was broken by David Lloyd George, the radical chancellor of the exchequer, who gave a speech declaring that acceptance of German terms would be detrimental to British prestige; indeed, peace at the price of knuckling under to German demands would be "a humiliation intolerable for a great country like ours to endure" (Remak 1995, 49–50). Britain decided to stand firmly behind France. Its navy moved to "high readiness," and its army undertook defensive measures, canceling scheduled maneuvers (Stevenson 1991, 137).

Alfred von Kiderlen-Wachter, the German foreign minister who had orchestrated the confrontation with France, feared the internal repercussions of war in Germany. And neither the kaiser, nor Chancellor Bethmann Hollweg, nor War Minister Heeringen, nor Admiral Tirpitz favored war at this point. Despite considerable talk among military and colonial officials in Germany in favor of war, the Germans backed off, declined to enter the military mobilization game, and agreed to settle for less—a meaningless slice of territory in the French Congo.

The domestic blowback in Germany surrounding the humiliating foreign policy setback was severe; German newspapers savaged the kaiser and his chancellor for their lack of nerve. German leaders came out of the crisis convinced that they could not back down in a future confrontation; another humiliating defeat would be disastrous. For the Triple Entente, the message was also clear: The

Entente must hold together in the face of an increasingly assertive and threatening Germany. British-French military discussions were intensified and tentative plans were made to send a British expeditionary force to the Continent in the event of a German attack on France—though there was still no specific binding commitment by Britain to defend France. Finally, the lack of Russian support during the Agadir Crisis led some French leaders to take the position that to ensure the full participation of Russia against Germany in the future, France would have to provoke a showdown over an issue or region that held a real, primary concern for Russia (Snyder 1985, 173–74). The Balkans constituted just such a place.

Round Four: The Balkan Wars, 1912–1913

Round four, the Balkan Wars of 1912 and 1913, once again focused the attention of the great powers on southeastern Europe. In 1911 the Italians, emboldened by the success of the French in Morocco, decided to detach Tripoli from Ottoman rule. The victorious Italian effort compelled the Turks to cede Tripoli, which the Italians renamed Libya. Turkey's evident weakness and the fact that its forces were tied down by the Italians on another continent lured an odd collection of Balkan states to try their own hand at severing Turkey from its European realms. In the spring of 1912 Russia had used its influence to engineer an anti-Turk alliance—the Balkan League—between Serbia and newly independent Bulgaria. Greece and Montenegro were then added, once again with Russian sponsorship. The creation of the alliance led to mobilization of Turkish forces and then mobilization by league members. In early October Montenegro declared war on Turkey in an attempt to grab the Ottoman Empire's last European possessions, Macedonia and Albania. One by one, the rest of the Balkan League piled on. The smaller powers of Europe, acting independently of their great power supporters who wanted no part in a Balkan conflict, had started a war in Europe.

The Turks were defeated, losing almost all of their Balkan territories, and Macedonia was divided. The Serbs demanded to be allowed to annex the conquered Turkish province of Albania with its ports on the Adriatic. The Austrians, however, objected to this last conquest and maintained that Albania must be independent. Russia predictably supported Serbia's occupation of Albania's coast. Sensing a potential major power conflict, states began to increase military forces along their borders. In September, Russia went ahead with a preplanned "trial mobilization" in its four western districts. Moreover, it kept its third-year cohort of draftees—scheduled to be released from duty—on active duty, thereby increasing its forces by over two hundred thousand men. Presumably, this would be useful in deterring an Austrian move against Serbia. As the Russians mobilized, and as the Serbs advanced toward Albania, Austria-Hungary undertook its own mobilization, calling up two hundred thousand reservists in mid-November and sending military units to the Russian border in Galicia as well as the Serb border with Bosnia-Herzegovina. In December, Austria-Hungary activated more troops and two "hawks" were returned to power: Conrad as chief of the General Staff and Krobatin as war minister. The war seemed doomed to spread. But Austrian foreign minister Berchtold resisted pressure by the military and Franz Ferdinand for a direct clash with Serbia, believing that the Germans would not support such a move. The Austrian emperor, Franz Joseph, sided with his foreign minister in the crucial December meetings (Williamson 1991, 130–32; Stevenson 1991, 142–44).

Once again, Austrian and German leaders doubted that Russia would fight in support of Serb rights to a port on the Adriatic. Once again they were correct. The Russians told the French that they would be unable to fight in the event of an Austrian attack on Serbia; the military had not yet attained a state of sufficient readiness, and the internal political conditions in the country were still dicey in the aftermath of the 1905 revolution. Foreign Minister Sazonov and other civilian leaders refrained from partial mobilization, thus preventing an escalation of the conflict spiral (Williamson 1991, 132–33). In addition, while it was clear that Germany would ultimately support Austria-Hungary, Germany did not encourage Austrian ambitions and pushed for a diplomatic solution. None of the major civilian players in Germany—Foreign Minister Kiderlen, Chancellor Bethmann, and Wilhelm II—supported a military confrontation. Germany refused to mobilize, thinking it unnecessary (Stevenson 1991, 145). Russia and Britain agreed that Albania should have independence and that Serbia must go without an Albanian port. Once more the Russians pressed the Serbs to withdraw their demands for an opening on the sea. Serb and Montenegrin troops withdrew from the disputed areas, a reversal compelled in part by Austria's call-up of its remaining reserves. The First Balkan War was over, though Austria and Russia did not demobilize until March 1913.

During the Balkan crisis the British secretary of state for war, Lord Haldane, had told the German ambassador in London, Prince Lichnowsky, that if Germany were to attack France, Britain would unconditionally assist France in order to maintain the balance of power in Europe; Germany could not be allowed to become the leading power on the Continent. This piece of information infuriated the kaiser, who called a meeting of his military advisers on December 8, 1912, sometimes referred to as the "War Council." The kaiser openly opposed his own chancellor's attempts to seek accommodation with the British and threw his support behind an immediate preventive war against France and Russia. Chief of Staff Moltke concurred in the need for a preventive war. He believed war was inevitable and, given Russia's military modernization plans, Germany's chances of winning such a war were better now than in the future: By 1917 the combined power of Russia and France would put Germany and Austria in a position of military inferiority. The logic of "windows" was very much on display. Admiral Tirpitz, however, opposed a war because the German fleet was not ready at that time. Moreover, the crisis appeared over, leaving Germany with no real pretext for war. Anger was vented against the Entente powers, but the meeting ended without serious decisions being taken. Chancellor Bethmann, who had not attended the War Council, was much opposed to the idea of preventive war. He agreed with Bismarck's famous quip that preventive war was "like committing suicide for fear of death" (Kagan 1995, 187). In December 1912 the German and Austrian governments had both gone to the brink and decided not to jump.

A Balkan peace treaty was signed in London at the end of May 1913, but within weeks the erstwhile Balkan allies fell out over the spoils. The Serbs felt aggrieved; Serbia was the only Balkan state with no border on the sea. Forced to forgo territorial gains in Albania, it occupied all of Macedonia, denying Bulgaria its fair share. In June, Bulgaria attacked Greece and Serbia. Montenegro, Rumania, and Turkey then joined against Bulgaria. The Balkan League had collapsed. By August, the Second Balkan War was over, with the Treaty of Bucharest giving Bulgaria's gains in Macedonia to Greece and Serbia instead. Albania was established as a nominally independent state. As October dawned and Serb forces had still failed to leave Albania, Austria (supported by its Triple Alliance partners, Germany and Italy) was forced to issue an ultimatum. With that, Serbia (pressured by Russia) backed down.

Though the full extent of Serb ambitions was unfulfilled, Serbia emerged from the Balkan Wars with substantial territorial gains: Its land area and population virtually doubled. Serbia also emerged from the war with a seasoned military, increased confidence, and an appetite for even greater territorial acquisitions. The Dual Monarchy's Bosnia-Herzegovina was especially coveted. Austria, a major loser of the Balkan Wars even though it was not a participant, was concerned with the future goals of both Serbia and Russia. As long as Serbia remained a strong and independent Slavic state in the Balkans, it served as a revolutionary beacon to Slavic peoples within the Austro-Hungarian Empire and as a threat to slice off Slavic pieces of the Austrian Empire—Bosnia, Herzegovina, Croatia, and Slovenia—in order to create a Greater Serbia of some sort. **Nationalism** in the Balkans was becoming an increasing problem for Austria. Feelings of South Slav unity, fanned by Russia, had been revived by the Balkan Wars, and there was open talk of political union among southern Slav territories. (One of these was a proposed merger of Serbia and Montenegro that would give Serbs access to the sea—a situation totally unacceptable to Austria.) Serbia had emerged as the principal threat to Habsburg interests. Meanwhile, Turkey and Bulgaria, two states that Austria and Germany relied on to balance Serbian power, had been defeated. To make matters worse, Russia had shown its willingness to foment trouble in the area by sponsoring the Balkan League: It abetted pan-Slav activities and supported the creation of a Greater Serbia.

What did Austria learn from the Balkan Wars? A new consensus was emerging in Vienna. While Conrad and others had consistently backed military force in the Balkans, Berchtold and Franz Joseph had been reluctant. But the continual Balkan crises had militarized attitudes of the principal actors. The existence of a Russian-supported Balkan League and a stronger Serbia constituted not only an external threat to the Dual Empire, but also an internal threat to its tenuous unity (Lebow 2000–2001, 599). With the Balkan Wars over, former "doves" like Foreign Minister Berchtold had concluded that diplomacy would not work to constrain Serbia and to deal with the South Slav problem. Only by threats of force had Austria managed to get Serbia and Montenegro to abandon Albania. Moreover, Conrad, for one, consistently maintained that Russia would accept an Austrian attack against Serbia. He believed that Austria's countermeasures to Russia's "trial mobilization" had effectively forced Russia to back down. If Austria were to use force, however, obtaining the support of Germany was essential, and this could only be achieved by acting strongly (Williamson 1991, 108, 135, 141, 155; Kagan 1995, 181). But the Balkan Wars had somewhat shaken Vienna's confidence in German support; while the kaiser occasionally talked tough, in the end Berlin counseled caution and kept its guns holstered.

What had the Russians learned? The consensus in Russia was that even though there was no defensive treaty or formal alliance that bound Russia to assist Serbia in case of war, Russia could not afford to back down again. After being unable to support Serbia in the Annexation Crisis or in the Balkan Wars, a third consecutive failure would be a disaster. Russia would gain a reputation as a state that would not support its allies in the pinch. Its power and prestige would be irretrievably diminished (Stevenson 1991, 159). Moreover, the public reaction was strong; there was a wave of anti-German nationalism in Russia between 1913 and 1914. Tsar Nicholas II remarked that if he were to make further concessions, "Russia will never forgive the Sovereign" (Joll 1992, 125). There would be no backing down. In the meantime, Russian officials encouraged Serbia to prepare for a war against Austria at a more propitious moment (Van Evera 1999, 206).

Prior to 1914 the alliance systems had to some degree allowed Germany to restrain Austria, France to restrain Russia, and Russia to restrain Serbia. But with each succeeding crisis, restraint became more difficult. As Charles Maier (1989, 254) puts it, "Russian, French and German statesmen might all fear that their partners would see little purpose to the respective pacts were they only to serve as instruments for restraint." Too much restraint could encourage defection from the alliances. Similarly, each demonstration of resolve meant that a higher level of "toughness" would be required to attain the same effect in the future (Maier 1989, 262).

By 1914 important players on all sides, winners and losers alike, had all come to the same conclusion as the result of their experiences in the crises of 1905–1912. The next time, there would be no backing down. They all had to support their allies; they all had to pursue "strong" policies; they all had to go to the brink. The European crises associated with the Balkan Wars were highly militarized. In addition to the armed forces of the actual combatants in those wars, approximately 750,000 forces had been called up—mostly in Austria and Russia (Stevenson 1991, 140). Mobilizations were now commonplace. Restraint during crises was successively weakened by the series of European crises (Stevenson 1991, 128–29). In the future, leaders might have to take greater risks. The next step would be for countries to actually use these forces in combat.

MEDIUM-TERM FACTORS AT THE STATE AND SUBSTATE LEVEL

Political leaders may take their countries to war as a response to the presence of economic or political conditions at home that threaten the current rulers or the nature of the regime itself. These wars are called either scapegoat wars or diversionary wars because they constitute conscious efforts by ruling authorities to maintain or improve their domestic political power. The primary motivation behind them is to divert the public's attention from disastrous internal conditions and to use foreign wars to rally the public behind the regime. Most political leaders have a "gut-level" understanding of the concept that sociologists call the **in-group/out-group hypothesis**—that under certain circumstances conflicts with external enemies (out-groups) can increase cohesion among internal groups (Levy 1993). Fortunately, most political leaders also understand that under certain conditions, conflicts with other countries can actually *increase* internal conflict, thereby decreasing popular support for a regime. As a result, true scapegoat wars are relatively rare. Did leaders in 1914 attempt to go to war to ameliorate domestic conflict and solidify internal support for their shaky regimes?

The effects of domestic conflict on the decisions of the European powers' decisions for war in 1914 are a matter of controversy. However, one fact is indisputable: Each of the European great powers experienced some degree of sociopolitical crisis in the years prior to 1914.

In France, major political issues—electoral reform, income taxes, compulsory military service—bedeviled the governments of the day. Ideological struggles between Left and Right were relatively intense. The constitutional rules of the Third Republic made it somewhat unstable under normal conditions, but when the government faced controversial and intractable issues, that instability increased. Between January 1912 and July 1914 the Third Republic had seven different governments and six different prime ministers.

Across the Channel, Britain suffered from a variety of disorders: a constitutional crisis centered on the power of the upper house, upheavals and violence associated with women's suffragettes and the trade unions movements, growing class conflict, and the prospect of **civil war** over the question of Irish home rule. The government of Prime Minister Asquith was a minority government with limited ability to pass controversial legislation. In both Britain and France domestic political considerations generally led to cautious foreign policies. As we will see, the inability of the British government to effectively deter Central Power aggression was due largely to domestic political considerations, though not to large-scale internal conflict per se within Britain.

Russia's defeat by Japan precipitated a revolution in 1905 that weakened the Romanov dynasty and Russia's position as a Great Power. Rapid industrialization in Russia also meant that it would suffer all the problems that bubble up when semifeudal aristocracies attempt to hold on to political power while they undergo economic and social modernization. Russian political leaders certainly had a rudimentary understanding of the need for external peace in order to maintain internal order, but they also believed that Russia's survival as a Great Power required that it reassert itself in the international sphere, especially by expanding its influence in the Balkans. On the one hand they hoped that a vigorous and assertive foreign policy would rally support for the tsar; on the other hand they understood that if a vigorous foreign policy led to war, that war might rekindle the fires of revolution in Russia. As in Britain and France, domestic and foreign considerations were inextricably mixed, whether consciously or subconsciously, in deliberations during the July crisis, and they pushed both ways—for war and against it.

For the Austro-Hungarian Empire, the most significant internal problem was the growing tide of nationalism and the dissatisfaction of southern Slavs—Serbs, Croats, and Slovenes—in the Magyar-dominated realms of Hungary. Rumanians in Hungary were also aggrieved politically. Any attempt by these minorities to create for themselves greater power or autonomy within the empire was perceived as a threat by the German and Magyar rulers. But lack of accommodation pushed the southern Slavs toward demands for independence. Such demands were backed, and indeed instigated, by the Serb government and Russia. (A Serbian group, Narodna Odbrana, carried out propaganda efforts in Bosnia-Herzegovina, and Serb military officers founded the secret Black Hand organization which was dedicated to the use of force to create a Greater Serbia at the expense of Austria-Hungary.) In a true multinational empire, any concessions to ethnic minorities might start the empire down the slippery slope toward a complete breakup. By 1914 Austro-Hungarian leaders believed that the only solution to the problem was strong action to reduce the influence of Serbia. The decisions of Austrian leaders in the July crisis were a direct product of the internal political situation (Joll 1992, 110–11; Williamson 1991, 11, 15).

In Serbia, a political crisis of major proportions existed. In 1903 an army group assassinated the king and replaced him with a rival from a different dynastic house. The new king thus owed his throne to the military. In the spring of 1914 rumors abounded of a military coup by the Black Hand against Prime Minister Pasic. Disagreements between the army and the government led to a crisis in early June 1914. A move by the chief of staff to persuade King Peter to dismiss Prime Minister Pasic was thwarted by Russian support for Pasic. At this point the king withdrew from politics and Crown Prince Alexander became the prince regent. Pasic took the opportunity to dissolve the parliament and call for elections to be held on August 1. The assassination of Franz Ferdinand also created political repercussions in Serbia. The fateful decision of the Serb government to reject the clauses in the Austrian ultimatum that would permit an Austrian investigation in Serbia was of course based on the knowledge that such an inquiry would discover that the head of Serbian military intelligence, Colonel Dimitrevic, was the man behind the assassination in Sarajevo. And the investigation would also have revealed the extent of Dimitrevic's influence (and that of the Black Hand) on the political and administrative institutions within Serbia.

It is in Germany that the effects of domestic conflict and domestic politics are most controversial. One historian describes Wilhelmine Germany as an inherently unstable state faced with an insoluble dilemma (Gordon 1974, 218). Though Germany pursued rapid modernization and economic development, these processes had generally unsettling effects. Industrialization inevitably increased the size of those social classes who were bound to join trade unions and socialist parties and to oppose the regime. The Second Reich, officially a limited constitutional government, was an authoritarian state dedicated to the preservation of the power and privileges of a semifeudal ruling class and its allies—the conservative landed Prussian aristocracy (Junkers), the military and bureaucratic elites, and industrial barons in the west. The regime attempted to escape the political consequences of industrialization by limiting the political power of not only the working class but also the bourgeoisie. Instead of accommodating the demands of the new classes and sharing power with them, German leaders used repression and extraconstitutional methods to counter their power. And it manipulated foreign policy for domestic political purposes.

To some extent this arrangement had its roots in the twenty-year global depression that began in 1873. As a result of the depression, German heavy industry, normally in favor of protectionism anyway, increased the pressure on Bismarck's government for restrictive tariffs. Similarly, German agricultural interests who were also being hurt by cheap foreign imports demanded government protection. The result was that in 1878 Bismarck abandoned his liberal, free-trade approach and pursued a more competitive, protectionist policy. With protectionism came a strong impulse toward creating German self-sufficiency and an imperialist urge to exert German control over foreign markets and raw materials (Calleo 1978, 12–17, 68). Domestically, Bismarck fashioned a new political alliance to support this new direction. Thus was born the conservative political coalition of "iron and rye"— German heavy industry and the landed aristocracy of the Prussian Junkers.

By 1900 the regime, now under Chancellor Bulow, began the conscious manipulation of foreign affairs as a response to the perceived domestic threats of socialism and democracy. The policy of Weltpolitik (world policy) was born. The essential elements of Weltpolitik were the building of a large naval fleet, the construction of a (modest) colonial empire, the creation of tariffs to support home industries and to make Germany self-sufficient in food production, and a generally active and vigorous foreign policy aimed at increasing German prestige and influence in world affairs (which included aggressive and often bullying behavior). All these policies were accompanied by nationalistic and chauvinistic rhetoric and mass agitation. Of lasting consequence was the change in trade policy. Bulow allowed the prewar free trade treaties to expire and imposed protectionist treaties on Russia and Austria-Hungary that kept the markets of those countries open to German industrial exports while German agriculture was protected against foreign competition.

Weltpolitik performed two political functions. First, it was useful in rallying public support for the regime and for the kaiser. Second, it revitalized the core ruling coalition in the German system. The alliance cemented relations between German government leaders (the emperor, the chancellor, and the government ministers) and various entrenched interest groups and institutions, including political elites in the Reichstag. This marked the resurgence of the iron-and-rye coalition first engineered under Bismarck and now joined by pro-navy and pan-German pressure groups.

Jack Snyder (1991) has made the argument that the nature of the German system and its path toward economic development created special problems. As a "late industrializing" state, Wilhelmine Germany developed as a nondemocratic cartelized political system—one in which power was "concentrated in the hands of parochial groups, each with very narrow interests focused around a particular economic sector or bureaucratic sphere" (Snyder 1991, 31). Such political systems tend to rely on **logrolling** tactics "in which each group gets what it wants most in return for tolerating the adverse effects of the policies its coalition partners desire" (Snyder 1991, 44). The logrolling bargains centered around Weltpolitik ensured that German industrialists would benefit from industrial protectionism and the massive naval construction program, the Junkers would benefit from the high tariff walls that protected German agricultural products and inflated the price of grain, the military would be able to retain its high degree of autonomy and pursue buildups and offensive strategies, and the various nationalistic and militaristic movements would be pleased by the active foreign policy measures (Snyder 1991, 98–99).

The policy of Weltpolitik had serious international repercussions. First, the Junkers got high grain tariffs, which angered Russia and forced it into an alliance with France and Britain. German Junkers wanted to eliminate competition from cheaper Russian grain while German industrialists wanted access to Russia's market. Both attained their goals through Bulow's trade agreements. Those agreements were due to run out after 1914. Obviously, Russia resented the one-sided agreement and was opposed to their continuance. Russia would in the future insist on coupling low Russian industrial tariffs with low German grain tariffs. In this way, domestic political conditions in Germany led to protectionist policies that set Germany on a collision course with Russia (Gordon 1974, 206; Calleo 1978, 39, 76). Second, the navy and heavy industry got a fleet that threatened Britain and eliminated the option of an Anglo-German settlement. And third, the army got an offensive war plan that ensured that if war broke out, virtually all of Europe would side against Germany and Austria (Snyder 1991, 99). In sum, Germany's pursuit of Weltpolitik set in motion a chain of events leading to the July crisis and war. The assertion of German power, the economic conflict with Russia, the bullying of France and Britain in the two Moroccan crises, and the arms race with Britain led subsequently to fears of German power, to the creation and tightening of the Triple Entente, and to relative German isolation, precipitating German fears of encirclement and the willingness to risk preventive war.

It is important to note that the architects of Weltpolitik—Bulow, Tirpitz, and others—did not contemplate war as part of the policy (Snyder 1991, 84–91; Kaiser 1983, 445, 452). The idea was to use foreign policy measures short of war in order to shore up support for the regime. It was to a great extent political posturing to divert middle-class and lower-class attention that might otherwise be focused on political and constitutional reform (Calleo 1978, 21). The goals of Weltpolitik were unusually moderate: to demonstrate to the public through relatively cheap successes that Germany was "keeping up" with its rivals in the global struggle for influence and territory and to do this without the risk of war. It was heavy on the pursuit of prestige and light on concrete results. It was a policy of limited goals and limited risks (Kaiser 1983, 450–51). No one in the German government pushed for war during the Moroccan crisis in 1905. And Tirpitz, refusing to risk the fleet, consistently opposed war in every crisis from 1897 through 1914. The fleet itself was probably designed less to challenge the British Empire directly and more to make sure that when the decrepit Chinese, Ottoman, and Portuguese empires crumbled, Germany would be in a position to secure its fair share of the booty (Kaiser 1983, 450).

The powerful nationalist sentiment inherent in Weltpolitik took on a political life of its own, outside the control of its creators. When Bulow, the architect of Weltpolitik, was forced to resign as chancellor in 1909, his policy was criticized as being *too moderate*. The often jingoistic and bellicose rhetoric of German leaders had created higher expectations than the government's own leaders were willing to pursue. Weltpolitik and imperialism had grown into a kind of national obsession. Indeed, most Germans had by this time come to accept the idea that Germany needed to expand, and educated Germans agreed that Germany's population and industrial growth required a larger colonial empire and a fleet to protect it (Kaiser 1983, 449, 457–58). In the second Moroccan crisis in 1911, when

Germany settled for a slice of the French Congo, outrage was expressed in the Reichstag and in the press. Once again the government lagged behind right-wing opinion on foreign policy, which maintained that Germany's failure to expand would trigger stagnation and then decline. A victim of their own rhetorical excesses, German elites were not always able to limit the mass passions they unleashed on behalf of Weltpolitik.

Regardless of the caution exerted by Bulow and his successor, Bethmann Hollweg, the activist policies pursued by Germany and the perception of these advances by Germany's rivals created reciprocal reactions by other European states that evolved into a conflict spiral that ended in war.

Clearly some in Germany believed that war, and only war, would solve Germany's internal problems and preserve the regime. This sentiment was especially strong after the 1912 elections in which the Social Democrats emerged as the largest party in the Reichstag. It was at this point also that right-wing forces in Germany increasingly supported the idea of a coup d'état from above to eliminate the socialist threat. However, Chancellor Bethmann did not share this belief. Like Bulow before him, he believed that even a German victory in war would do little to rally the public around a conservative and nationalist government; instead, the forces of liberalism and social democracy would gain strength (Joll 1992, 139; Kaiser 1983, 445, 455–56, 470). But Bethmann was not especially concerned about the Social Democratic threat. He attempted to gain the support of the Social Democrats in the parliament and was successful on many occasions; indeed, the socialists had supported taxes to finance the army increases in 1913. (And they were to unanimously support emergency war credits in August 1914.)

Domestic crises and politics in Germany led to war not because German leaders sought war in 1914 as a solution for domestic problems (the scapegoat thesis), but because Weltpolitik—a set of active, assertive, and moderately aggressive policies initiated for domestic political purposes—led to a conflict spiral between the Central Powers and the Entente that in 1914 escalated into war.

It is at this point that we may contemplate the synergism of two important factors. While we know that under some conditions leaders faced with domestic political troubles may initiate scapegoat wars, we also know that under other circumstances leaders facing these internal troubles do not initiate war. "Decision makers faced with decline in military strength as well as internal divisiveness," Levy suggests, "may be particularly willing to gamble on a war that might solve their external and internal problems simultaneously, and thus be driven to war by the interaction of scapegoat and preventive motivations" (Levy 1988, 96). Nevertheless, domestic political considerations probably played a relatively minor role in the German decision for war in 1914.

SHORT-TERM FACTORS AT THE DYADIC LEVEL: THE JULY CRISIS

The Security Dilemma and Conflict Spirals

A fundamental problem in international relations is the security dilemma. The security dilemma exists because actions taken by national leaders to bolster the security of their states—increasing armaments and the size of the military, annexing buffer zones, forming alliances, inventing new weapons—may be seen as threatening by others, who consequently feel less secure. In response, these other states take similar actions to increase their own security, which in turn make the first state less secure. National leaders motivated by the desire for greater security tend to engage in competitive realpolitik actions that create dyadic conflict spirals—dynamic interaction patterns in which the actions of states become progressively more threatening, more hostile, more intense, and more militarized until war eventually breaks out. Once the spiral of hostile actions begins, it is difficult to break the cycle and reverse or "de-escalate" the hostilities. The primary motivating factor in this cycle is fear: All states take actions that they see as legitimate defensive responses to the perceived hostile actions of others. But these "legitimate defensive responses" are seen as illegitimate offensive provocations and therefore trigger equally legitimate defensive responses by others. The result is a dangerous cycle of competitive and threatening actions resulting in war. From this perspective, wars are not consciously sought; rather, they occur when one state sees no other way of defending itself than by striking first. The actions of the European states in the July 1914 crisis constituted a classic conflict spiral.

Round Five: The July Crisis

June 28–July 23

On June 28, 1914, Archduke Franz Ferdinand of Austria, the heir to the Dual Monarchy's throne—held at the time by the eighty-four-year-old Emperor Franz Joseph—was assassinated along with his wife in the Bosnian capital of Sarajevo. The assassination kindled demonstrations in Bosnia against Austrian rule. The leading roles in the assassination were played by Gavrilo Princip and Nadjelko Cabrinovic, Bosnian Serbs who were members of a student terrorist group, the Mlada Bosna (Young Bosnia). The assassins had been trained in the Serbian capital of Belgrade by members of the Black Hand, a secretive underground organization whose goal was the creation of a Greater Serbia. The Black Hand, led by members of the Serbian government and military—including Col. Dragutin Dimitrevic (known as Apis), the head of Serbian military intelligence—used nationalistic and pan-Slavic propaganda, terrorism, and subversion to undermine Austro-Hungarian control over the Slavic portions of its empire. While the Serb government per se had not organized the plot, certain of its officials had been involved. The Serb prime minister, Nikola Pasic, had actually discovered the plot and had then made only the most ineffectual attempt to warn the Austrian government of the plot's existence.

Austrian officials immediately rounded up six of the seven conspirators—all ethnic Serbs. While it was strongly believed that Serbian officials were behind the assassination, at the time of the investigation no "smoking gun" could be found that definitively proved that the Serb government was directly involved in the plot. (The links to "Apis" came out after the war had begun.) Nevertheless, the investigation showed that the assassins had clear links to low-level Serb government officials. That was enough.

Government officials in Vienna determined that Serbia must be punished and its ability to cause mischief in Austria's Slavic domains ended. They viewed the assassination as an opportunity to create a showdown with Serbia. They also perceived a need to demonstrate strength to Serbia and Russia and to "act like a great power" (Stevenson 1991, 147; Williamson 1991, 179). Any Austrian action against Serbia would require, at a minimum, the acquiescence of Germany. If a war between Austria and Serbia triggered Russian intervention, Austria would need German help. On July 5 and 6, one week after the assassination, Kaiser Wilhelm II and Chancellor Bethmann met in Potsdam with Austrian ambassador Szogyeny and Vienna's special envoy, Count Hoyos. In response to the official letters from Emperor Franz Joseph and Foreign Minister Berchtold, Wilhelm and Bethmann both promised unequivocal support for Austria in its actions toward Serbia. Even though the official Austrian request did not mention the possibility of war, the kaiser specifically promised that if Austrian retaliation against Serbia led to war with Russia, Germany would stand with its ally.

German leaders clearly understood that an Austro-Serbian war could ignite Russian intervention and a European-wide war but appeared willing to risk it. The kaiser's notes, written into the margins of Berchtold's letter, indicate his temperament: "Now or never. . . . The Serbs must be disposed of and that right soon!" (Kagan 1995, 189). The guarantee of German support has frequently been referred to as a "blank check" given to Austria, permitting the latter to choose whatever course of action (presumably a local war with Serbia) it felt appropriate. In fact, German leaders were worried that the Austrian response would not be sufficiently "tough" and prodded Austria to take the strongest actions against Serbia as quickly as possible, while Austria still had the benefit of a European sympathy for slain members of its royal family.

What was the kaiser's motivation? As we shall see, Wilhelm II was an impulsive and impetuous man who frequently acted out of personal motivation, but he was certainly profoundly shocked by the assassination of a close friend and his wife. More important, however, he was also mindful of his reputation as a weak and ineffectual leader who had been castigated for his timidity in previous confrontations with the Entente powers. On July 6 he seemed eager to impress industrialist Alfred Krupp: "This time . . . I shall not chicken out" (Kagan 1995, 190).

Chancellor Bethmann focused on the political. He opposed a German initiation of a European war, as he had previously opposed a preventive war. He also knew that an Austrian war against Serbia risked a rapid escalation that might engulf all the great powers. But he was willing to risk it in 1914, especially if Germany could not be blamed for its initiation, because he believed that a war was inevitable, that time was not on Germany's side, and that its chances for victory declined with every passing year (Lebow 2000–2001, 596).

On the basis of previous experience, the kaiser and other German leaders felt sure that a strong German reaction to the assassination would deter any potential Russian intervention on behalf of the Serbs. Kaiser Wilhelm, Chancellor Bethmann, and Ambassador Pourtales all expected that Russia would back down (Lebow 2000–2001, 604; Lebow 1981, 122–29). It had done so during the Bosnian Annexation Crisis and again during the Balkan Wars. Moreover, Tsar Nicholas II, the kaiser's first cousin, would surely be reluctant to take action in support of Serbian regicides. The Russian royal family, so often a victim of assassination attempts in its own country, would certainly understand the need to punish the Serbs. Finally, Germans leaders were worried that a mild response would weaken the perception of Austrian power, thereby reducing the value of Germany's only true ally. They were similarly concerned that if they did not back Austria, it would either be forced to gravitate towards the Western powers or would collapse, leaving Germany without an ally. The problem was that in supporting Austria, Germany risked being dragged into a war with Russia.

Nevertheless, if war did break out, the Balkans crisis created the conditions under which Germany might maximize its chances of winning: The Serbian scenario guaranteed that Austria would join Germany in a war against Russia and France, and the assassination in Sarajevo gave the Central Powers a plausible excuse for military action, creating the possibility that Britain would remain neutral. Under these conditions, German leaders were quite ready to contemplate a preventive war (Van Evera 1984, 82–83).

Austro-Hungarian plans for a potential war in the Balkans had been developed over the years. The war plans contained two main options, both offensive: one with Serbia as the primary target of attack, the other with Russia as the target. The two plans shared a common core: Twenty-eight and a half divisions would be mobilized near the Russian frontier to the northeast (in Galicia), and eight divisions would be mobilized on the Serb frontier to the south (in Bosnia-Herzegovina). A remaining twelve divisions would be placed either to the north (to execute Plan R against Russia) or the south (to execute Plan B against Serbia), depending on which front was to engage in offensive operations. Conrad was confident Austria could defeat Serbia if Russia stood on the sidelines; twenty Austrian divisions would face only ten or eleven Serb divisions, while twenty-eight Austrian divisions guarded the northern frontiers. Austrian chief of staff Conrad was also confident that Austria could force Russia to back down (as it had in 1909). A war with Russia would, however, be a horse of a different color. Though Conrad thought little of the quality of Russia's forces, the empire's forty divisions would face one hundred Russian divisions. Austria might be aided by perhaps twelve German divisions, but clearly more German divisions would have to be transferred to the east. Moltke had assured Conrad that a quick German victory against France would permit this (Williamson 1991, 118, 181–82).

The paramount problem with the war plan, and the scenario most likely to occur, was the situation that would occur if Austria mobilized its forces in Plan B against Serbia *and then Russia intervened.* Austrian forces would be in the wrong place. Moreover, Austrian execution of Plan B would also interfere with Germany's Schlieffen Plan, whose success depended on Austria attacking and holding down Russian forces in the east while Germany dispensed with France. Austro-German military discussions never addressed this scenario (Williamson 1991, 181).

On July 7 the Austro-Hungarian Common Ministerial Council met with the country's military leadership. The option of an immediate attack on Serbia—supported by Krobatin and Conrad—was scotched; the political leadership, except for Hungarian prime minister Tisza, favored issuing an ultimatum before the initiation of war (Williamson 1991, 198–99). Though the Austrians were worried that a weak, delayed response would lose them the support of their only ally, Germany, the ultimatum would not be issued for two more weeks.

The assassination of Franz Ferdinand had changed the internal balance of power in the Dual Empire. The heir to the throne had gradually become a "moderate": He was sure that an Austrian war with Serbia would bring Russian intervention, and he did not believe that Austria was ready for war (Williamson 1991, 51). His assassination left moderates without a strong voice and in fact pushed some of them to take tougher positions. The hardliners were now in ascendance. The most extreme hawks were led by the chief of the General Staff, Gen. Franz Conrad von Hotzendorff. Conrad had consistently argued for a strategy of preventive attack by Austria against its enemies: Italy, Albania, and, especially, Serbia. His martial urgings were just as consistently resisted by Berchtold, Franz Joseph, and Franz Ferdinand (Williamson 1991, 35–37). In the aftermath of the assassination, Conrad was supported by War Minister Krobatin and General Potiorek, the governor of Bosnia-Herzegovina, as well as Austrian prime minister Sturgkh and Common Finance Minister Bilinski.

The hardliners' desire for immediate war had been rejected at the July 7 Ministerial Council meeting as too provocative. The key figure here was Prime Minister Tisza, who supported a diplomatic approach and whose consent for war was constitutionally required (Williamson 1991, 191–93). His support for stronger measures was obtained with the promise that war would not result in Austrian annexation of Serb territory—a provision designed to minimize the probability of Russian intervention as well as the number of troublesome Slavs contained within the Empire. He was eventually convinced that a weak response to Serbia would encourage Romanian nationalism in the Empire's province of Transylvania (Williamson 1991, 200).

At the urging of German leaders, Austrian foreign minister Berchtold, who also supported war against Serbia, devised a plan that would provide some diplomatic cover. Austria would confront Serbia with an ultimatum blaming Serbia for the assassination and laying out a set of demands. The terms of these demands would be made so unacceptable that Serbia would be forced to refuse the conditions, thereby providing Austria with the diplomatic excuse that it needed to take military measures. The tradeoff was that in deciding not to wage immediate war, Austria lost the advantage of favorable public opinion. Preparations for the ultimatum, which consumed another two weeks, continued despite warnings from the Russian foreign minister, Sergei Sazanov, that Russia would not permit Austria to use military measures against Serbia and despite a reminder from French president Raymond Poincaré that France was allied with Russia.

Two other factors fostered delay. First, a sizable portion of the Austro-Hungarian armies had been given "harvest leave" to work in the fields. Canceling these leaves would not only have disrupted the harvest and confused the mobilization process, but it would also have tipped off the Entente powers of an impending military action. Second, it was determined that the ultimatum should not be issued while President Poincaré and French prime minister Viviani were on a state visit in Russia, scheduled for July 20–23.

The ultimatum was approved by the emperor on July 21, and finally, at 6:00 pm on Thursday, July 23, almost four weeks after the assassination, the ultimatum was presented to Serbia. It demanded a reply in forty-eight hours.

July 24

The Russian reaction was immediate. On the morning of July 24 the Austrian ambassador to Russia, Friedrich von Szapary, read the terms of the ultimatum to Foreign Minister Sazonov. Sazonov replied that Austria's demands were unacceptable and that Austria appeared to be seeking a war. Sazonov's perception of the situation was that Austria and Germany clearly intended to attack Serbia. He believed that Germany had interpreted Russia's past concessions as proof of Russian weakness; therefore, Russia needed to stand firm. Despite his belief that Russia was not yet ready for war, Sazonov believed that this time Russia must support Serbia. Russia's security interests, its reputation, and its international prestige were on the line. Accepting the ultimatum would essentially turn Serbia into a protectorate of the Dual Alliance, ending Russian influence and prestige in the Balkans and detaching Serbia from the Russian side of the power equation. Russian leaders also perceived that if Serbia fell to Austria, there would be a domino effect in which Bulgaria and Romania would also fall under the domination of the Central Powers. Germany would eventually assert its control over the Turkish Straits and the Black Sea—areas where Russia had important strategic and commercial interests (Kagan 1995, 195–96; Van Evera 1984, 219). The Russians, however, incorrectly believed the Serbian government to be innocent of the assassination in Sarajevo, and they also incorrectly assumed that Austria was bent on taking large chunks of Serbian territory—two misperceptions that stiffened their resolve to react forcefully to Austria's provocation (Van Evera 1999, 51–52).

When the Russian Council of Ministers met later the same day, there was uniform agreement for Sazonov's position that Russia's bargaining reputation and its international prestige were at stake and that another diplomatic setback at the hands of the Central Powers was not acceptable, even if it meant war (Lieven 1983, 141–44; Huth 1988, 189). Therefore, on July 24, even before Serbia's reply to the ultimatum, the Council of Ministers approved Sazonov's proposal that the Russian military be partially mobilized for action against Austria. "Premobilization" measures for a "period preparatory to war" were to go into effect on July 26. These measures applied to military districts opposite Austria-Hungary and Germany (a fact that did not escape the attention of Berlin) and to the Baltic and Black Sea fleets. Supplies were to be purchased, mobilization arrangements were to be checked, and munitions were to be distributed (Stevenson 1991, 152). Austria was warned that it would not be allowed to crush Serbia; Russia would not be "indifferent" to its fate. If all went well, this demonstration of Russian firmness might deter aggression by the Central Powers. But if Serbia was attacked, the Council of Ministers decided that Russia would initiate partial mobilization against Austria-Hungary but not Germany.

On the other hand, seeking to defuse the crisis, Russia also cautioned Serbia not to give offense to Austria and requested Austria to extend the ultimatum. Between July 24 and 29 Sazonov would present numerous proposals to Germany and Austria concerning the negotiation of a settlement. He would receive nothing more than evasive replies.

The British government, in the person of Foreign Minister Sir Edward Grey, proposed a diplomatic conference: Ambassadors from France, Germany, and Italy were invited to meet with him to mediate the Austro-Serb conflict. The German ambassador in London, Lichnowsky, urged Germany to accept the British mediation offer. The Germans passed this mediation proposal on to Vienna without recommending it. The Austrians were uninterested. Meanwhile, British, French, and Russian pleas to extend the ultimatum deadline were also rejected by Germany and Austria.

July 25 and 26

The Serbian answer to the ultimatum came at 5:58 pm on Saturday, July 25, two minutes before the deadline. The response was conciliatory: It accepted almost all of the demands save those that directly impinged on its sovereignty. It specifically rejected the demand for a joint Austria-Serbian committee to investigate the assassination. Throughout Europe, diplomatic support for the Serb response was positive and widespread. Nevertheless, the Austro-Hungarian ambassador in Belgrade immediately informed the Serbs that the response was unsatisfactory and that diplomatic relations would be broken. The Austrians were intent on using the lack of total Serb cooperation as an excuse for military action. Three and a half hours later Emperor Franz Joseph gave the order to mobilize two-fifths of the empire's forces beginning on July 28. Franz Joseph ordered that no measures should be taken on the Russian border; Russia was to be given no pretext for war. Conrad now had five days to determine whether circumstances would permit an attack on Serbia (Plan B) or whether Austria would have to implement Plan R against Russia instead (Williamson 1991, 205; Stevenson 1991, 148). Before the night was out, initial preparations for war were being made all over Europe.

Earlier in the day, even before Serbia's response to the ultimatum, Russia's Tsar Nicholas II had tentatively approved orders for a partial mobilization against Austria in case of need and then authorized premobilization measures, giving secret orders for a "period preparatory to war"—canceling military leaves, calling up reservists, promoting military cadets early, taking protective measures along borders, and preparing troops stationed in the east to move west. This was seen in St. Petersburg as a deterrent warning to Austria (and Germany), though Russian diplomats denied the mobilization was taking place. For its part, France assured Russia of its support and initiated secret precautionary military measures. The following day, the British fleet was ordered to remain at its stations.

German and Austrian leaders had believed, perhaps in a fit of wishful thinking, that a military confrontation between Serbia and Austria could be kept localized, that Russia would not intervene on behalf of Serbia, and that even if Russia did intervene, France and certainly Britain would not get involved. Germany, in fact, refrained from military preparations at this point so as not to provoke Russia (Stevenson 1991, 148). Diplomatic cables, however, warned that a localized war might well be mythical. On the day of the Serbian reply, and again on the twenty-sixth, the German ambassador in London, Prince Lichnowsky, advised his superiors in Berlin that Britain would probably not remain indifferent to a war between Germany and France, and he urged Berlin to accept Grey's proposal for mediation. While the Italians and the French accepted Grey's proposal, the Austrians rejected them on the twenty-sixth and the Germans on the twenty-seventh.

July 27

On Monday the twenty-seventh the anxiety and the threatening behavior intensified. Late in the afternoon German intelligence had concluded that Russia's military premobilization efforts had in fact begun. Bethmann told the German ambassador to Russia, Pourtales, that preparatory military measures by Russia aimed at Germany would compel Germany to mobilize and that mobilization by Germany would mean a European-wide war. For its part, Russia warned Austria that it would mobilize if Austria crossed the Serb frontier. In light of the accumulating events, the kaiser, who curiously enough had been cruising in the Baltic on his yacht during the period of the Austrian deadline and had now returned, began to have second thoughts. The kaiser's chancellor and foreign minister, afraid that Wilhelm's resolve would weaken, had withheld from him the content of Serbia's reply to the ultimatum "until they thought it was too late for him to intervene" (Lebow 1981, 140). Having finally read the Serb reply himself, the kaiser declared it to be a great Austrian success and "all reason for war is now gone." On the evening of the twenty-seventh he asked the Austrians to accept the Serb reply as a basis for negotiation.

July 28

Tuesday the twenty-eighth was another day of frantic activity and deepening anxiety. In the morning the kaiser, attempting to reverse the conflict spiral, advanced his own solution to prevent war—the Halt in Belgrade proposal. Austria's armies should stop after reaching Belgrade, creating a breathing spell that could be used for further talks. Lord Grey in Britain supported a very similar plan of his own, but Chancellor Bethmann was unenthusiastic and delayed sending his revised version of the kaiser's proposal to the Austrians, all the while encouraging Austrian boldness, ensuring that Vienna received mixed signals about German desires. By the time the amended proposal arrived in Vienna, the Austrians had officially declared war against Serbia—one month to the day after the assassination in Sarajevo. *A crucial point had been reached: Austria-Hungry had initiated war.* Limited bombardment of Belgrade signaled the start of the Third Balkan War. By the next morning eight Austrian divisions were mobilized against Serbia and the bombing of Belgrade intensified, though no preparatory measures were yet taken against Russia and there was little real fighting for the next two weeks.

What had led Austria to war? The fear of domestic disintegration brought on primarily by the perceived threat to the empire from pan-Slavic nationalism aided and abetted by Serbia, the perceived approach of a window of vulnerability vis-à-vis Russia, the increased level of German support for Austrian military action, the absence of Franz Ferdinand as a key supporter of moderation in internal struggles over foreign policy and the consequent strengthening of Conrad's hawk-ish faction, and the general conclusion, even among moderates, that after the seemingly endless Balkan crises, war was the only solution to "the Serbian prob-lem" (Williamson 1991, 211–15).

Having been informed that Austria had declared war on Serbia, Sazonov now decided that premobilization measures were not sufficient. It was time to make good on the tsar's earlier tentative approval for a partial mobilization against Aus-tria, in spite of the fact that Austria-Hungary had mobilized only against Serbia and had taken only defensive preparations on the Russian front. Partial mobilization would be ordered for Russia's four southern districts on the Austrian frontier as well as for the Baltic and Black Sea Fleets. It is possible that Sazonov believed that such an act, openly announced by Russia, would serve to shock the Austrians to their senses, deterring further actions against Serbia and preventing war. On the other hand, if war broke out, Russia would need to be prepared. For the Russians, mobilization did not automatically mean war; mobilization plans permitted the Russian army to stay within Russian borders for an extensive period before an at-tack began. At any rate, Sazonov announced to the other great powers that Rus-sian mobilization was set for the following day, Wednesday the twenty-ninth.

To some extent, Sazonov and the other Russian decision makers were being pushed forward by the French ambassador in St. Petersburg, Maurice Paleologue. With President Poincaré and Prime Minister Viviani out of communication, re-turning to Paris by sea after their visit to Russia, Paleologue, a champion of a strong Franco-Russian alliance, gave verbal support to the Russian government that far exceeded his formal instructions (Remak 1995, 117). Specifically, he in-formed Sazonov of France's willingness to fight with Russia if war broke out. Thus unlike the Bosnia annexation crisis in 1909, when France refused to back Russia in support of Serbia, this time Russia would not be alone. While France's strategic and reputational interests were not directly at stake in the Balkans, the alliance with Russia was the anchor to its geopolitical strategy and the basis of its protection from Germany.

July 29

On Wednesday, July 29, as Austrian ships in the Danube bombarded Belgrade, diplomatic activity reached a crescendo. Beginning to fear that the crisis had very much gotten out of control, Kaiser Wilhelm II sent a telegram to his cousin, Nicholas II, emphasizing his attempts to induce the Austrians to arrive at an agreement which might satisfy the Russians. A daylong series of communica-tions ensued. Nicholas replied to the effect that he hoped his cousin would exert his influence on Austria to prevent it from "going too far and to avoid a calamity such as a European war." Wilhelm's counter was to bring up the one issue that worried Germany most, rumors of Russian mobilization. (The German consulate in Moscow had wired on the twenty-eighth that Russian mobilization was al-leged to be in progress. And indeed, on the twenty-eighth, Russia announced that it was beginning partial mobilization against Austria on the twenty-ninth.)

In St. Petersburg, Sazonov had been informed by the Austrian ambassador that Austria refused to negotiate any of the demands in its ultimatum to Serbia.

Moreover, on the twenty-ninth Chancellor Bethmann (through his ambassador, Pourtales) had warned Sazonov that regardless of whether Russia announced a mobilization, further implementation of the "Period Preparatory to War" would force Germany to mobilize and this would mean a European-wide war. Sazonov concluded at this point that it was hopeless to pursue the diplomatic track; Russia must now turn its energies toward the preparation for war. Perceiving (incorrectly) that Germany wanted a wider war, and convinced (rightly) that Germany would mobilize even upon Russian partial mobilization against Austria, Sazonov now decided that Russian partial mobilization (originally planned against Austria-Hungary) would be inadequate. Russia must, as the military had urged, pursue general mobilization against both Germany and Austria (Stevenson 1991, 152–54).

Russian preparations for a partial mobilization had, at any rate, run into a bureaucratic *snafu*. The Russian chief of the General Staff, Janushkevich, was a recent appointee and had not realized that the Russian military had no contingency plans at all for a partial mobilization. A Russian partial mobilization would therefore be "pure improvisation." Military strategists had believed that if war broke out in the west, it would inevitably be against both Austria and Germany, and therefore Russia's mobilization plans were all designed against *both* western opponents rather than just one. On the twenty-ninth Russian military officials informed the tsar that they were unable to perform a partial mobilization; attempting it would render useless any plan to perform a full mobilization at a later date. A partial mobilization followed by a general mobilization was technically infeasible. The only real choices were to initiate a complete general mobilization or none at all (Van Evera 1984, 49, 63, 86–89; Levy 1989, 155–58). Russian leaders also understood the need to begin offensive operations as early as possible in order to insure the French ability to survive a German offensive. A delay in Russian mobilization against Germany might place the survival of France at risk. The tsar initially agreed therefore to a general mobilization against Germany as well as Austria and then, incredibly, after reading the previously mentioned letter from the kaiser, reversed himself, opting once again for the (technically infeasible) partial mobilization option.

In Germany on the twenty-ninth, as the kaiser was involved with his telegraphic conversations with Nicholas II, the impending gloom darkened. The General Staff had already picked up evidence that Russia was reinforcing its frontier posts during the premobilization period. By 3:25 pm the German Foreign Office received a telegram from the German military attaché in St. Petersburg confiding that Russia considered a general war to be almost inevitable now that Austria had declared war on Serbia. Within minutes, the German General Staff also learned of Belgian military preparations, and by 5:00 pm Foreign Minister Jagow had learned of Russia's partial mobilization. Shortly after 9:00 pm, more bad news arrived. The German Foreign Office received Ambassador Lichnowsky's report from London saying that British foreign secretary Grey had indicated that while Britain would remain neutral in a local war between Austria and Russia, it could not stand aside in a continental war involving Germany and France, a statement that shattered the last remaining German hopes (and misperceptions) of British neutrality. Unless Austria could now be persuaded to stop its actions immediately, Germany and Austria would find themselves at war with Serbia, Russia, France, and Britain. Moreover, Germany could find itself left behind in the mobilization race: Up to this point, German measures had been minimal and defensive in nature (Stevenson 1991, 148–49).

July 30

In the middle of the night (3:00 am on Thursday, July 30) Chancellor Bethmann, pushed by the increasing reality that war was drawing near, tried frantically to reverse the tide of events. Throughout the crisis, guided by the assumption that Britain could be kept neutral and that Germany could defeat France and Russia, Bethmann had essentially forced Russia and France to choose between a humiliating diplomatic defeat or war. The illusions now shattered, he tried another tack. Continuing to fend off the requests from his own generals to begin preparations for mobilizations, he now sent several telegrams to Vienna urging Austria to accept the Halt in Belgrade proposal or to enter into direct negotiations with Russia to devise a negotiated settlement. He received no reply.

The Austrian leadership, having been strongly pressured over the last weeks by the German emperor, foreign minister, chancellor, and chief of the General Staff, had spent enormous reserves of emotional and psychological capital and had taken the plunge: They had rejected the rather conciliatory Serb reply and had declared war. It would have taken a truly gargantuan effort by the Germans to bring about a reversal at this late date and an equally monumental summoning up of courage by the Austrians to reconsider their decisions. Neither happened. Political leaders in Vienna perceived that a retreat at this point would weaken Austria's prestige. (And the Austrian war plan had not called for an attack on the Danube front, so its troops were not in a position to occupy Belgrade anyway.) The wheels of war continued apace.

Around the same time, early on the thirtieth, the kaiser received the final telegram from Nicholas II. In response to the kaiser's inquiries about Russian mobilization, the tsar admitted that the "military measures which have now come into force . . . had been decided on five days ago for reasons of defense on account of Austria's preparations." The kaiser, angry at what he believed to be Russian deviousness, misinterpreted this remark to mean that Russia had mobilized *against Germany* five days earlier, a situation that might give Russian forces an advantage unless Germany countered with its own mobilization in short order. As if this were not enough, the kaiser also received a rather alarmist report from the German naval attaché in London saying that the British navy would immediately attack Germany at sea if war broke out.

Finally, at 1:00 pm on Thursday the thirtieth, Wilhelm II read Ambassador Lichnowsky's report of his conversations with Grey in London to the effect that Britain would indeed support France if war broke out on the Continent. The coincidence of these three indications of bad news for the Germans had a tremendous psychological effect on the kaiser. He concluded, amazingly, that the three Entente powers had conspired among themselves to use the Serbian crisis to wage war against Germany (Lebow 1981, 141–45).

Pursuant to Chancellor Bethmann-Hollweg's last-ditch attempt to rein in Austria's behavior, Chief of Staff Moltke urged Austria not to declare war on Russia. But later in the day, going behind Bethmann's back, both he and the new German war minister, Erich von Falkenhayn, encouraged Conrad to stand firm and to begin a general mobilization against Russia—an action the Austrians had already decided to take on the next day. (From the Austrian perspective, the Russian mobilization on the Austrian border had to be countered; furthermore, continued mobilization against Serbia would be detrimental to the Schlieffen Plan, which depended on Austrian action against Russia.)

Bethmann tried to dampen down Austrian actions once more at 9:00 pm on the thirtieth, cabling the German ambassador Tschirsky to urge Vienna to accept mediation. By 11:20 pm this advice had been countermanded and Bethmann's diplomatic offensive was over. In the interim, Moltke and the General Staff had convinced the chancellor that German mobilization was imperative as a response to Russia's partial mobilization against Austria. (Plus, by 11:00 pm the General Staff had its first—erroneous—indications that Russian general mobilization had begun.) The stiffening of Moltke's position on July 30 can be traced in part to his discovery that Belgium had virtually doubled its army by calling up reserves and had begun defensive military preparations around Liege, the key target in the Schlieffen Plan (Trumpener 1976, 80; Stevenson 1991, 152). On the thirtieth as well, the British announced their rejection of Bethmann's last-ditch effort of the previous day—a deal in which Germany promised not to annex continental French territory, to respect Dutch neutrality, and to restore Belgian territorial integrity at the war's end in return for British neutrality. German officials had come to the conclusion that diplomacy had failed.

Meanwhile, in Russia, in the afternoon of July 30, the tsar had finally given in to his advisers and ordered a general mobilization to begin, in secret, on the next day. Once the tsar gave the order for the Russian general mobilization, Sazonov telephoned the Russian chief of staff with the news that there would be no further changes of policy: "Now you can smash your telephones. Give your orders, General, and then—disappear for the rest of the day" (Stoessinger 2005, 15). Russian haste in this decision was propelled to some extent by promises made to the French that Russian forces would advance on East Prussia by the fourteenth day of mobilization—a move which would presumably draw off at least five German corps, helping to relieve the German attack on France in the west. Full mobilization by Russia might gain a day or two on Germany. And if the Russians were really lucky, their mobilization might deter a German attack altogether (Snyder 1985, 177–78).

Haste was the order of the day in Paris as well. The French chief of staff, Joffre, had become convinced (erroneously) that Germany had already begun its mobilization; he therefore called up thousands of French reservists and threatened to resign unless the government agreed to mobilize. It did.

July 30 was also a fateful day in Vienna. In a comedy of errors, Conrad initiated the military's Plan B against Serbia in spite of strong evidence of a Russian intervention. When on the next day Vienna learned of Russia's order for general mobilization, Austria was caught; it had to permit the trains carrying its troops to finish their southern journey and then turn the trains around and proceed north to Galicia and the Russian front. Conrad was only able to begin full mobilization on August 4, setting Plan R in motion (Williamson 1991, 208).

July 31

Now that it was clear that the conflict could not be kept localized, that the current diplomatic gambits had failed and that continuing the aggressive strategy regarding Serbia meant continental war against the three Entente powers, German generals were nevertheless still determined to plunge ahead, pressing for mobilization. Moltke urged the kaiser and the political leadership in Germany and Austria that the current situation was favorable. Chancellor Bethmann was at last won over. His primary concern was, as ever, to keep Britain out of the war; he had counseled his peers that if war were to break out, Russia should appear as the aggressor rather than Germany. Once Berlin learned of the Russian partial mobilization against Austria, the chancellor accepted the advice of the military and agreed to a German mobilization by noon on the thirty-first. The deadline was achieved by a scant five minutes: At 11:55 on Friday the thirty-first Berlin received reliable information confirming that Russia had switched from partial mobilization to general mobilization. Germany could now make a plausible case that it had responded to Russian aggression. The kaiser proclaimed a "state of imminent war" at 1:00 pm, initiating preliminary measures just short of mobilization. A twelve-hour ultimatum was sent to Russia demanding a cessation of the Russian military measures on the German frontier. If not, German mobilization (and by implication, war) would be the result. An eighteen-hour ultimatum was sent to France demanding French neutrality in a Russo-German war (plus temporary German occupation of a French fortress on the German border as a sign of good faith). There were no replies.

France set its mobilization to begin on the following day, though French troops were ordered to simultaneously carry out a ten-kilometer withdrawal in order not to appear provocative. (The French, worried about British willingness to support them, were also concerned that they not be seen as the aggressors.) Lord Grey asked Germany and France to pledge to respect Belgian neutrality. The French immediately agreed; the Germans, predictably, gave no reply.

August 1 and After

Doom approached with increasing rapidity. On Saturday, August 1, French mobilization began about 3:55 pm, though the troops were kept ten kilometers behind the border. German mobilization followed five minutes later. However, a report from Lichnowsky in London that British neutrality, and even French neutrality, might still be possible if France were not invaded led the kaiser at the last moment to contemplate scrapping the Schlieffen mobilization plan in favor of a mobilization against the east only. At that point Moltke disingenuously advised the kaiser that this would be impossible; he told Wilhelm that no such alternative plan existed. In fact, the German General Staff had annually updated an alternative plan for a priority attack on Russia (Levy 1989, 162). Germany began an all-out offensive.

Germany declared war on Russia at 7:00 pm on August 1, and on Sunday, August 2, Luxembourg was invaded, though not without second thoughts. The kaiser's cautious nature led him to attempt to delay the attack by stopping trains from crossing into Luxembourg. Moltke again intervened by refusing to sign the delay order. Finally, a telegram arrived from London saying that an earlier suggestion of British neutrality had been the product of a "misunderstanding." The attack began. With its troops now in Luxembourg, Germany demanded free passage into Belgium in return for a pledge to return all Belgian territory after the war. Belgium rejected the German ultimatum on Monday, August 3, and appealed to Britain and other signatories of the 1839 Belgian neutrality treaty for aid. Germany declared war on France. Britain issued an ultimatum to Germany to respect Belgian neutrality, and the government finally gave the order for mobilization of British forces. Belgium was invaded by the Germans on the night of August 3–4 and Britain declared war on Germany on the fourth at midnight. On the sixth Austria declared war on Russia. Continent-wide war had broken out in Europe. The Third Balkan War had become World War I.

WHY WAS THE JULY CRISIS DIFFERENT?

As Choucri and North (1975, 234–36) have shown, there was no "snowballing" of violence between 1905 and 1914. Previous levels of violence between the members of the Triple Alliance and the Triple Entente were fairly modest and had always died down without culminating in war. Why did the July crisis escalate to war when previous crises had not? Several reasons are important. On all sides, leaders of the European states were applying lessons from past crises— lessons that were in a very real sense dysfunctional. (Only the British still believed that diplomacy could work better than threats and toughness.) Remembering the two Moroccan crises, German leaders believed that they must not back down again. The Austrians, remembering the previous Balkans crises, believed that they could repeat their earlier victories by acting strongly and obtaining German help. As the southern Slav problem worsened, they came to believe that only force would be effective against Serbia. The Russians, remembering their betrayals of Serbia in earlier Balkan crises and buoyed by their military rebuilding program, took the pledge "never again"—the next time, they would have to be tough. And this time, unlike the previous Balkans crises, Serbia's independence was vitally threatened. And perhaps, most important, by 1914 the Russian military had been sufficiently rebuilt and modernized that its leaders could actually contemplate its use. Decisions in Paris, St. Petersburg, and Berlin were motivated primarily by fear.

The war was not exactly "accidental," but it was "inadvertent." In most cases the crucial decisions for war were made reluctantly. Civilian leadership generally held back, in awareness of the potential for inadvertent crisis escalation (Stevenson 1991, 155). The great powers and Serbia all preferred a negotiated settlement to a world war (Levy 1991, 71). But there were points beyond which they were unwilling to sacrifice the security of their state or its reputation. All were willing to risk a war in Europe under certain circumstances. And in 1914, after a series of militarized crises in Europe, all were willing to run greater risks (Stevenson 1991, 154–56). Austria went to war against Serbia deliberately and cautiously, but was willing to risk Russian intervention. The Germans preferred a war in 1914 as opposed to later, and they were committed to war at the first sign of Russian mobilization. The Russians, knowing that they would not be alone, preferred to fight rather than let Austria dominate Serbia. The French were not happy about fighting for Serbia, but felt threatened by Germany. The British were especially reluctant, but feared German domination of the Continent if they stayed at home.

SHORT-TERM FACTORS

Dyadic Level: Deterrence Failure

In July of 1914 there were two major issues of deterrence: Could Germany and Austria deter Russia from intervening on behalf of Serbia and could Britain deter a German attack on France? We will focus on the second issue. Before we address the issue of British deterrence, we should state that the attempt by Germany and Austria to deter Russia intervention failed simply because the bullying tactics used by the Central Powers and their unwillingness to seriously consider alternatives to Serbia's humiliation were perceived by Russian leaders as threatening to Russia's national security interests. And given the history of Russian concessions to German power in the past, Russian prestige was engaged. With the Russian military in a better position than in previous crises, Russian leaders feared the costs of inaction more than the costs of a possible military confrontation. Its reputation as a European power was at stake (Huth 1988, 191, 194–95).

The case of potential British deterrence against German aggression is more problematic. One argument (Levy 1990–1991) is that because German support for Austria was a necessary condition for an Austrian war against Serbia, and because the German expectation of British neutrality was a necessary condition for German support for Austria, the perception of British neutrality held by German political leaders was a key component in the calculus of war. In the July crisis German leaders had concluded reluctantly that war between Austria and Russia might be ignited by an Austrian invasion of Serbia. They concluded as well that Austria must be supported. They hoped that France might be kept out of the war, but they were much more certain that Britain would fail to intervene on behalf of the other members of the Entente. Under those circumstances, German military leaders were relatively confident of victory.

The Germans had some reason to believe that alliance bonds among the Entente countries were weak; after all, alliance pledges were not always kept. The Germans themselves understood full well that Italy, the third member of the Triple Alliance, would probably not support Germany or Austria if war broke out. But German leaders also knew that the treaties among the Entente powers had sufficient loopholes to permit defection as well. The Anglo-Russian agreement of 1907 was entirely related to colonial issues and contained no provisions for mutual defense, though at the urging of Paris, British and Russian leaders had begun in 1914 to discuss cooperation on naval issues.

The terms of the Anglo-French Entente (the Entente Cordiale) were not particularly robust either. It was originally developed to settle colonial issues and contained no provisions for assistance in case of an attack on either power. Informal military conversations had led to agreements about the dispersal of naval forces, but not to a specific pledge of mutual defense, though the French continually pushed for just such an understanding. Bethmann's strategy in the July crisis was to avoid provoking Britain and to ensure that German actions were not the ones that started the confrontation. If the war's initiation could be blamed on Russia or France, Britain could be kept out of the war.

Could Germany have been deterred from war by a strong warning by Britain that it fully intended to fight alongside France and Russia in a war with Germany and Austria? Did Britain fail to use its ability to deter aggression? The argument is, of course, that if German leaders had known that Britain was committed to the defense of its allies, they would not have risked war.

According to deterrence theory, successful deterrence requires a credible deterrent threat. The conditions for such a threat occur if a defender specifically defines its commitment to intervene, communicates this commitment to the potential attacker, possesses sufficient military capabilities to carry out the commitment, and demonstrates its willingness to carry out the commitment. If any of these conditions is absent, credibility is lost and one can reasonably expect deterrence to fail (Cashman 1993, 219).

Certainly there was, until the last moment, no unambiguous British warning to Germany. Why not? There are four reasons. Two are strategic in nature. First, German secrecy about the Schlieffen Plan meant that Britain did not know that for Germany, mobilization meant war and that, therefore, British efforts should be aimed at preventing a German mobilization (Van Evera 1984, 99–101). Second, British policy had been to resist giving either France or Russia any guarantee that might encourage them to be more aggressive as the crisis unfolded.

A third reason deals with Anglo-German relations in the immediate prewar period. Foreign Minister Grey was the dominant voice in the British cabinet for a strong British Entente with France and Russia and a strongly anti-German policy. He believed that of all the great powers, Germany represented the greatest threat to Britain's interests. Britain had strategic interests in maintaining the territorial integrity of France, in preventing a single power (Germany) from dominating the Continent and in making sure that a hostile power did not control the Continent's Channel ports, thereby threatening British naval operations. Grey's anti-German position was clearly a minority position within the cabinet, but it was largely supported by the opposition Conservative Party, which tended to see Grey as one of their own, at least when it came to foreign policy. Grey had a limited amount of freedom in foreign policy, a freedom preserved to some degree by his being "economical with the truth." He did not always inform the cabinet, let alone the Parliament, about his discussions with the French. Grey's "Germanophobia" and pro-Entente zeal were supported by other high-level officials in the Foreign Office, such as Undersecretary Sir Arthur Nicolson and Sir Eyre Crowe, the permanent secretary. The military's General Staff was also supportive. By 1911 the Committee on Imperial Defense (CID) had taken the position that in case of war on the Continent, it was imperative that Britain send six army divisions to support the French.

In November 1911, however, Grey's position was decisively defeated when the cabinet voted fifteen to five to the effect that no communications between the British General Staff and the staffs of other countries could commit Britain to intervention; no commitments could be given without the consent of the cabinet. Grey had also been savagely attacked by members of his own Liberal Party for bringing Britain to the brink of war with Germany in the Agadir Crisis. As a result, London moved in the direction of a "mini-detente" with Germany. Anglo-German cooperation at the London Conference of 1912–1913 helped to end the Balkan Crisis. In 1913 the two sides negotiated an agreement on the potential division of Portuguese colonies in Africa. And in June of 1914 an agreement between Britain and Germany settled a long-standing dispute concerning the Baghdad Railway project. The naval arms race had even wound down. While no formal agreement existed, Germany seemed resigned to a 16:10 ratio in capital ships, acquiescing to British naval superiority. On the eve of the July crisis therefore, leaders in both countries believed that Anglo-German relations had warmed (Lynn-Jones 1986, 135). To be clear, the German belief that Britain would remain neutral was not a result of any previous British lack of resolve in confrontations with Germany; Britain had strongly supported France against Germany in the two Moroccan crises. The German belief was based on the mini-detente of 1912–1914 (Huth 1988, 196).

It should be noted, however, that by 1914 Bethmann's attempts to deepen Anglo-German cooperation and to detach Britain from the Entente had pretty much reached an impasse. The secret Anglo-Russian naval talks of June 1914 had been discovered by German espionage, thereby undermining Bethmann's hopes for the long-desired neutrality agreement with Britain (Kaiser 1983, 466–67; Calleo 1978, 41).

Some scholars (Lynn-Jones 1986; Huth 1988) have argued that this detente produced counterproductive consequences in both countries. It led the British to believe that Anglo-German cooperation could resolve the 1914 crisis peacefully. And it permitted the Germans to retain the belief that Britain would remain neutral in a war on the Continent, especially if Russia and Serbia could be portrayed as the aggressors, thus encouraging its risky course. According to this argument, leaders in both Germany and Britain were seduced into misperceptions; they each underestimated the hostility of the other. Grey appeared to believe that the most effective way to deal with Germany was to emphasize cooperation and diplomacy over threats and bluster. In fact, despite his relative hawkishness, Grey may have erroneously concluded that there was a politically significant group of "accommodationists" in Berlin whose political power had been strengthened by the success of the detente with Britain (Huth 1988, 198; Lynn-Jones 1986, 147). In this view, it was not until the initiation of hostilities between Austria and Serbia that Grey abandoned his illusion that Germany wanted to avoid war (Kagan 1995, 200).

A fourth reason for the absence of a strong British deterrent threat has to do with the nature of British politics in the prewar years. Prime Minister Asquith's Liberal government was electorally weak, and Foreign Minister Grey was in no position politically to make a definitive deterrent threat. The 1910 election had created a Parliament with Liberals and Conservatives both winning 272 seats;

the Liberal government relied for its majority therefore on 42 Labour Party members of Parliament (MPs). Conservatives subsequently won sixteen of twenty by-election contests, giving the Liberals and their allies a slim 12-seat majority in Commons (Ferguson 1999, 120). On top of this, by the summer of 1914 Britain was consumed by a severe domestic crisis created by Irish demands for home rule.

A relative hardliner (and an imperialist) within a Liberal Party that had a strongly pacifist wing, Grey had limited room for maneuver. Though Foreign Office officials like Crowe and Nicolson urged Grey to issue a blunt deterrent warning to Germany, the foreign minister could not commit Britain to the defense of France without the cabinet's support. It was well known that the cabinet was deeply divided on the question of intervention; many within Asquith's government opposed a commitment to France, and about three-fourths opposed any intervention. Only two members of the cabinet, Grey and Churchill (a former Conservative who was first lord of the Admiralty), favored intervention; several favored complete neutrality; and the majority, including the prime minister and his chancellor of the exchequer, Lloyd George, had not made up their minds. The official British policy was that if war came and France was attacked, the cabinet would decide what to do depending upon the circumstances.

Britain's first official response to the crisis gave no signs of British willingness to fight. On July 24, the day after the Austrian ultimatum was announced, Grey met with Ambassador Lichnowsky and urged Germany to restrain Austria and to support a mediation effort. Grey also predicted that the crisis could lead to war among Germany, Austria, France, and Russia. That Grey did not mention British participation was certainly noticed by Chancellor Bethmann Hollweg (Huth 1988, 190). Britain's initial position therefore did not challenge the long-held perceptions of German leaders about British neutrality. Of all the countries, Britain seemed most desirous of heading off the crisis, and its foreign minister was at the forefront of those who attempted to find diplomatic ways of settling the crisis. This probably had the unintended effect of encouraging the Germans in the view that Britain would not fight if war broke out.

On July 27 several of the cabinet neutralists threatened to resign if the government decided to enter the conflict. Grey was unable even to give the Belgian ambassador a guarantee that if Germany violated Belgian neutrality, Britain would aid Belgium. On August 1 the cabinet rejected a proposal to dispatch the British Expeditionary Force to the Continent and it forbade Churchill from ordering a full mobilization of the navy. That same day, Grey was still discussing with Lichnowsky how Britain might remain neutral. Even as late as August 2, a cabinet majority could not be attained in favor of a British pledge of support to France. The British were able to support the sending of an expeditionary force only after the German ultimatum to Belgium on the second, followed by King Albert's appeal for assistance on the third and Germany's subsequent invasion of that country on the fourth. Importantly, these events were accompanied on the second by a note to Asquith from the Conservative opposition leader, Bonar Law, stating the Tory position that any hesitation in supporting France would be fatal to Britain's honor and security and offering "united support" for British intervention. The implied threat was that if the Liberal government should fall because it was unable to decide the question, a new Conservative government would quickly make the decision for intervention (Ferguson 1999, 165).

The cabinet deadlock did not prevent Grey from issuing his famous warning to Lichnowsky on July 29 that Britain could not stand aside in case of war. But Grey's warning had to be a *private* communication rather than an official one, and it had to be couched in wording which was fairly obtuse. At the time that the statement was made, it certainly did not represent government policy.

Was the German leadership's belief that Britain would remain neutral a rational expectation based on their evaluation of the 1911–1914 detente? British officials appear to have given their counterparts in Germany the impression that Britain would remain neutral. This was the distinct impression given to German ship owner Albert Ballin in his meetings in late July with War Minister Haldane, Churchill, and Grey; it was also an impression given to the kaiser's brother, Prince Heinrich of Prussia, in his conversations with King George V on July 26 and reported on July 28, one day before Grey's warning (Lynn-Jones 1986, 141, n. 100). And on August 1 Lichnowsky reported that Grey suggested that Britain would remain neutral and even guarantee French neutrality if Germany did not attack France. In other words, the German government received information that was sufficiently contradictory that those who believed that Britain would remain neutral did not have to re-examine their assumptions.

The British cabinet believed that if the other European states (on both sides) did not know what Britain would do, this would induce caution rather than risk taking (Huth 1988, 191). As one historian (Ferguson 1999, 156) puts it, the result of the British policy of "studied ambiguity" was "so garbled that it could be interpreted more or less according to taste. By Sunday 26 July the French thought they could count on Britain, while the Germans felt 'sure' of English neutrality." German leaders were certainly faced with ambiguous information and mixed signals coming from Britain. One reason for Grey's ambiguity was, of course, that he had to try to deter Austria and Germany while at the same time not encouraging Russia and France to act recklessly.

If Grey had been able to make an early and definitive deterrent threat, would Germany have acted differently? British neutrality was a key consideration for Chancellor Bethmann, whose willingness to risk a war in Europe depended on British abstention. When he learned of the British warning, on July 29, he immediately attempted to restrain Austria, belatedly pushing the Halt in Belgrade proposal. The kaiser's reaction was equally strong; he felt betrayed by the British threat. If Britain had made the threat earlier, Bethmann would probably have attempted to restrain Austria earlier, and the crisis might have turned out differently (Lynn-Jones 1986, 143–44). The Anglo-German detente and German perceptions of British neutrality created the conditions under which German decision makers could confidently pursue risky policies regarding Serbia.

On the other hand, the German military was less concerned about British intervention. The General Staff doubted that the British Expeditionary Forces would have any effect on the outcome of the war on the western front (Ferguson 1999, 154). Britain had done virtually nothing in the last decade to create land forces that could make a serious contribution to the French effort against Germany on the Continent. However, the German military played a marginal role in the initial decisions of the July crisis (Lynn-Jones 1986, 144; Kaiser 1983, 469; Levy 1991, 73). The chancellor and the kaiser were the key decision makers in the crucial initial phases of the July crisis. (Moltke was absent from Berlin until August 2, and Tirpitz was ensconced at a spa when the kaiser decided to back Austria.) It wasn't until July 29 that the military began to exert heavy pressure on the civilian leadership for mobilization.

To conclude, it cannot be argued that WWI was the result of a deterrence failure on the part of Britain. Germany and Austria did not discount the British threat; *there was no real threat to discount*. No clear-cut, binding defense treaty existed, no unequivocal statement of British commitment had been made, no serious British expeditionary force existed, and no clear British political will to intervene was present. Discounting what was left was easy. For reasons having to do primarily with internal politics, Britain did not make a serious effort to deter a German attack on France through Belgium and Luxembourg. The existence of the Belgium Neutrality Treaty, the Anglo-French Entente and the Anglo-Russian Agreement were by themselves insufficiently credible to prevent German aggression. Ad hoc statements by British officials of commitment to France, such as the one by Haldane in 1912, were likewise insufficient statements of British intent. In the July crisis of 1914 the British went to great lengths to deny that they were automatically bound to assist France; they conveyed this to the French as well as to the Germans. As one scholar notes (Kagan 1995, 211), "Not only could Britain's friends and enemies not be sure what the British would do until the last minute, the British themselves did not know." Only clear and credible statements of British commitment to defend its allies would have made a difference. This was not forthcoming. When Grey's warning did come on the twenty-ninth, it was too late—overtaken by the logic of interlocking military mobilizations.

SHORT-TERM FACTORS AT THE INDIVIDUAL LEVEL: MISPERCEPTIONS, PERSONALITY AND PSYCHOLOGICAL FACTORS

In all the European countries, errors of fact and misperception of events played a role, though perhaps not a decisive one. Decision makers in Russia, Germany and France all believed premature and exaggerated reports of the mobilization measures taken by their opponents (Van Evera 1984, 103). One of the most important findings of the Stanford studies of perceptions in the 1914 crisis was that leaders in the two Dual Alliance countries—Germany and Austria—overperceived the threat posed by the actions of the Triple Entente countries (Holsti, North, and Brody, 1968). While the German military strategist Clausewitz is famous for writing about the "fog of war," which makes it impossible for battlefield commanders to know exactly what is happening as the battle itself takes place, it should be noted that there is a similar *prewar fog*, which prevents decision makers from knowing exactly what is happening in the days preceding the outbreak of war. As one author has said, "Decisions were made with no time for proper reflection, messages crossed each other, and some of the most fateful errors were committed from motives no more profound or sinister than lack of information or sleep" (Remak 1995, 114). On the other hand, Stevenson has argued that the errors were fairly minor and that most reports of opponents' mobilizations were fairly accurate (Stevenson 1991, 129, 150).

While leaders in all of the European capitals had *misperceptions* about the nature of events and of their adversaries in 1914, it is proper to focus on the misperceptions and miscalculations by German leaders, since the decisions in Berlin were arguably those that were most crucial. These misperceptions were of two kinds: misperceptions about real world events and actors, and misperceptions about future contingencies, about what would happen in the future. The latter are perhaps more correctly categorized as *miscalculations* rather than misperceptions. Nevertheless, they were important to the reasoning of leaders at the time.

German appraisal of the July Crisis rested on several misperceptions and miscalculations. The blank check given to Austria was based on the assumption that a war between Serbia and Austria could be kept localized. Russia would back down in the face of joint Austro-German threats just as it had done earlier. Based on past experiences, German leaders were predisposed to see Russian threats to support Serbia as mere bluffs (Huth 1988, 186). Even if Russia did intervene on behalf of Serbia, it was believed that France would not aid Russia. And Britain would not support its allies, even if France was involved. Russia and France were believed to be unprepared for war, and Britain was seen as unwilling to fight over Serbia. Decision makers in Germany and Austria assumed that the July 1914 crisis would be a repeat of the 1909 Bosnian annexation crisis and failed to understand the differences between the two situations. (This time Serbia's sovereignty was at stake; this time Russia was more prepared militarily; this time Russia's allies were more supportive; this time the endangered status of everyone's reputation prevented concessions.) They assumed that bullying and other realpolitik tactics would force their opponents to back down. If bullying failed, they were willing to accept the risk of continental war (at least without Britain's participation) because they believed that Germany and Austria could win a war against France and Russia. These assumptions persisted in the minds of German leaders well into the crisis and long after sufficient evidence to the contrary had accumulated (Lebow 1981, 121–22). Had these misperceptions not existed, or had their wrongheaded notions been discovered and accepted early enough so that corrective measures could be taken, war might not have broken out. What, then, accounts for the persistence of these misperceptions?

We have already mentioned the ambiguous nature of the British commitment to France. This is an important reason, but it is not the only piece of the puzzle. Important contributory factors can be found at the substate level, within the governmental bureaucracy. The German diplomatic corps had become infested with toadyism and were habitually unable to give political leaders in Berlin objective and unbiased analysis; instead, they tended to give their superiors advice that they knew was desired. The belief that Russia would not support Serbia persisted in Berlin in part because the German ambassador in St. Petersburg, Pourtales—who had listened to Russian foreign minister Sazonov's impassioned warnings of Russia's commitment to Serbia and who therefore knew his superiors were mistaken—nevertheless refused to tell them they were wrong (Lebow 1981, 125–27).

Part of the answer to this question also derives from the normal cognitive processes of human thought. The human mind has a natural tendency toward cognitive consistency. We resist incompatible ideas and facts (which create "cognitive dissonance") and therefore tend to fit new information into our thinking in a way that is consistent with old ideas and previously accumulated facts. Once the dominant belief had been established in the minds of the kaiser and his advisers that Russia would back down, most information would henceforth be interpreted in a way which was consistent with that belief. Russian protests and threats would merely be interpreted as bluffs. And once the top leadership had taken the position that Britain would remain neutral, contradictory information was liable to be selected out. The problem was, in part, one of "premature cognitive closure" and "selective attention" within German leadership circles (Lebow 1981, 119–47). Once German decision makers had concluded that the war could be kept localized, it became difficult for evidence to the contrary to be taken seriously. Contradictory information was ignored or treated as the product of untrustworthy observers or as simply disinformation attempts by Germany's enemies. The entreaties of the lone German diplomat who consistently warned Berlin of the folly of counting on localization, Ambassador Lichnowsky in London, were ignored until late in the crisis.

Refusal to reexamine these ideas might also be attributed to the **motivational biases** of individual leaders. Because notions of British neutrality and localized war were so critical to the thinking of civilian leaders in Germany, a certain emotional commitment to these beliefs naturally developed. If these beliefs were challenged, subconscious ego-defense mechanisms such as "wishful thinking," "denial," and "defensive avoidance" would be engaged to thwart the challenge (Lebow 1981, 111–19). And the more crucial the belief and the greater the consequences if it was wrong, the greater the tendency of the individual to deny its falseness.

Finally, a complete picture requires an examination of the role played by the personality of Kaiser Wilhelm II. Many of the critical decisions in 1914 were made by the kaiser: the blank check to Austria, the initial push for a strong Austrian reaction to the assassination, the risky and assertive behavior toward the Entente powers, the inept attempts to find a peaceful solution to the July crisis, the fateful overreaction to the news of July 29–30, the miscalculations about British neutrality and the ability to keep a war in the Balkans localized, and the final decisions to mobilize the German army and invade Luxembourg and Belgium. What do we know of the kaiser that could help us understand the actions he took in 1914?

Wilhelm II came to the throne at age twenty-nine in 1888. His mother was the oldest child of Queen Victoria of England. Young Wilhelm entered the world cruelly. He was born with a physical deformity, a useless left arm which would be permanently shorter than the right, the result of a breech birth which tore the nerves connecting the hand and arm muscles to the spinal column in the neck. He also suffered from painful growths and inflammations of the inner ear. It is possible that he also suffered brain damage during birth.

Contemporaries spoke of the kaiser's problematic behavior. Many who knew him wondered about his sanity. In 1900 and again in 1908 serious consideration was given in top political circles to Wilhelm's fitness to rule (Rohl 1987, 23; Waite 1990, 153). It was not only Germans who were concerned. Foreign Minister Grey declared his belief that the kaiser was "not quite sane," that he appeared somewhat like "a battleship with steam up and screws going, but with no rudder," and that some day he just might "cause a catastrophe" (Rohl 1987, 21).

It seemed to many that he never matured psychologically and that he frequently behaved like a child. (The following section is based on Rohl 1987, 11–27.) His behavior was often described as impulsive, mercurial, and unstable; he seemed uncertain of his aims and incapable of sustained efforts. Frequently seen to be a "ditherer," he tended to run away from problems and choices, but when he did make decisions, they were often the result of vanity and personal feelings rather than rational calculation. The kaiser also had a tremendous capacity for seeing the world the way he wanted to see it; he literally had a propensity for swearing that black was white. Vulnerable to flattery, he greatly overestimated his own abilities and was virtually unable to take constructive criticism or feel guilt. He tended to dismiss his cabinet ministers as ignoramuses and rarely listened to their counsel. Like a child, he was seemingly incapable of learning from advice or experience. He also had grandiose visions of himself that bordered on a kind of "Caesar-mania": He believed that he was a special agent of the Almighty with a mission to rule the entire world.

The kaiser appeared to possess contradictory traits in abundance. He was intelligent and quick, but his behavior was frequently bizarre. Half English, the kaiser had decidedly ambivalent views of his maternal motherland. Like many Germans of his day, Wilhelm II both despised and admired England. Before ascending the throne he remarked, "One cannot have enough hatred for England." He was simultaneously aggressive and insecure; he was impulsive and yet cautious. The kaiser's verbal saber rattling and aggressive public outbursts were mostly for public consumption, however, a facade used to compensate for feelings of inadequacy. He was generally cautious in his approach to foreign affairs (Lebow 1984, 163).

Though this is highly speculative, some would add one more complication to this impressive list of rather debilitating traits: sexual confusion (Rohl 1987, 19–20; Waite 1990, 153). As a young bachelor, Wilhelm had romantic relationships with several women, but he was also drawn to a coterie of homosexual males in the "Liebenberg Circle." The leader of the circle was one of Wilhelm's most intimate friends, Prince Phillip Eulenburg. In 1908 Eulenburg became the defendant in a very public trial in which his homosexuality—a crime in Germany—was directly at issue.

It would be unusual if the kaiser's personality were not affected by his social and psychological environment. Saddled with conspicuous birth deformities, without a nurturing family life, and confronted with the burden of living up to the accomplishments of his predecessors on the throne, the kaiser would depend heavily on subconscious ego-defense mechanisms. Psychic defenses protected an anxious, conflicted, and childlike person who needed reassurance but trusted no one. Grandiose self-concepts, assertions of power, and "compensatory belligerence" constituted psychological defenses against feelings of inadequacy and perhaps also fears of homosexuality (Waite 1990, 157). Clearly, Wilhelm II was emotionally unstable. Many of the leading psychiatrists of the day diagnosed the kaiser as a manic-depressive. Sigmund Freud defined his problem as "neurasthenia," a neurosis that was a manifestation of his inability to cope with emotional conflicts and feelings of inferiority (Rohl 1987, 25; Lebow 1981, 143). Medical authorities had, in fact, warned the German royal family that while young Wilhelm was not clinically insane, neither would he ever be entirely normal; he would always be subject to sudden bursts of anger, and he would not always be capable of making wholly rational decisions. As a result, some warned that his accession to the throne would be dangerous (Rohl 1987, 21).

To the extent that sexual confusion was part of the psychological baggage carried by the kaiser, the July crises probably touched off critical internal dynamics for the kaiser, both conscious and unconscious. The 1908 Eulenberg Trial had been an emotional personal trial for Wilhelm. Three years later, the kaiser's masculinity was called into question by the German press during the Agadir Crisis. He had been labeled as "Wilhelm the timid" and "the brave coward." After these events, there is no doubt that the kaiser was well aware of his need to appear more outwardly masculine (Waite 1990, 153). Masculine behavior required decisiveness, toughness, belligerence, and assertiveness in the foreign arena; it meant shunning diplomacy, compromise, and concessions. "Compensatory belligerency" would become standard operating procedure (Hull 1982, 262–65). The July crisis would in some ways become a public test of his manhood, and as he told the German industrialist Krupp, "This time I won't cave in."

We have already seen that in response to Lichnowsky's warnings of July 25 the kaiser had gradually begun to move toward a more moderate position; his cautious side was in the ascendant. Jagow and Bethmann, perhaps sensing a weakening of the kaiser's resolve, withheld from him the conciliatory Serbian reply to Austria's ultimatum until the twenty-eighth. His reading of this document prompted the kaiser's Halt in Belgrade proposal, the transmission of which to Vienna Bethmann subsequently helped to undermine through delay and alteration. The kaiser's advisers had also withheld from him Grey's warning of July 29, but on the thirtieth the kaiser finally received the information that would completely shatter his illusions about a localized war. First came Nicholas II's final cable admitting Russian partial mobilization, next came an overly alarmist note from the German naval attaché in London warning of an immediate British naval attack, and finally, at 1:00 pm, came Lichnowsky's cable detailing Grey's warning that Britain would support France.

We cannot discount the notion that the kaiser's angry overreaction to the news of July 29–30 had its source in the inner compulsions of his mind. One analyst (Lebow 1981, 142) suggests that the kaiser suffered an acute "anxiety reaction" on July 30. In the context of the other two messages, the kaiser misinterpreted the telegram from Nicholas II stating what was already known, that Russian had begun military mobilization *against Austria* five days previously, as having meant that Russia had begun mobilizing *against Germany* five days ago. His normal cognitive functions impaired, he appeared to have been overcome with a mood of despair and aggression and fatalism. His response to Nicholas's note verged on the paranoid: Drawing on his long-held perception of a Germany encircled by hostile powers and his ambivalent love-hate relationship with Britain, he concluded that there was a British, Russian, and French conspiracy to keep Germany negotiating while the Entente powers mobilized for an attack on Germany. He treated the news from Britain as a personal affront. In the margin of the dispatch from Nicholas, the kaiser scribbled anti-British diatribes filled with intense invective. His reaction to Grey's warning: "This means they will attack us. Aha! The common cheat" (Stoessinger 2005, 13). Placing the blame for the coming war squarely on Britain, the kaiser's reaction appears very much as an ego-defensive mechanism to cope with anxiety and stress. Confronted with information that the war could not be localized, he was overcome with anxiety and his self-confidence destroyed. According to Lebow (1981, 142–43):

> Wilhelm's paranoid response was perhaps indicative of his need to resort to more extreme defense mechanisms to cope with the free-floating anxiety triggered by the breakdown of his former defenses. No longer able to deny the probability of Russian, French and British intervention, yet unable to admit just how grievously he had miscalculated, Wilhelm chose instead to escape from his own aggressiveness and its consequences by portraying Germany and himself as helpless victims of the aggressiveness of other powers. Paranoid delusions of persecution are typically triggered by environmental or inter-personal stress, although they tend to occur only in persons who have formerly maintained an unstable psychological balance by resorting to denial or other defense mechanisms. The kaiser was such a person.

The belief in the Entente's scheming was far removed from reality. Russia was still recovering from the dual trauma of defeat in war and social upheaval. Britain was beset by labor violence and the threat of civil war in Ireland, and its government was headed by a Liberal cabinet with a strong non-interventionist wing. France was politically torn between Left and Right, each competing to be less belligerent than the other. No Entente power sought a war.

Making a decision for war is a tremendous responsibility for a national leader—the kind of decision Wilhelm tended to respond to with procrastination or "defensive avoidance." Clearly, a leader's decision to go to war can be made easier if he is able to evade or repudiate his responsibility for the decision by attributing the decision to external pressures or by convincing himself that he is a victim of the actions of others. When confronted with the reports of Russian mobilizations, the kaiser convinced himself that his choices had now been outpaced by events, that there were no other options. German mobilization was now impelled by the actions of others. He bore no responsibility for what would happen next (Lebow 1984, 159, 164–66).

While it is difficult to determine their exact weight, individual level factors such as belief systems, misperceptions, inner psychological dynamics and emotional reactions to international events clearly played a role in the events of the July Crisis. A final set of beliefs and perceptions, however, must still be examined—those dealing with military strategy.

SHORT-TERM FACTORS AT THE INDIVIDUAL LEVEL: MISPERCEPTIONS OF THE OFFENSE-DEFENSE BALANCE

An important misperception held by leaders in almost all the major capitals of Europe had to do with the nature of warfare. While military technology in the late nineteenth century had produced inventions which gave a decided advantage to defensive forces (particularly railroads, barbed wire, the repeating rifle and the machine gun), in 1914 European military forces and the strategies designed to guide them were offensive in nature. All four of the great land powers in Europe—France, Germany, Austria, and Russia—pursued offensive strategies in 1914. Why they did so is the subject of much debate, though most agree that it was not because of the desire to make territorial gains.

Sagan (1986) argues that even though European leaders realized that offensive doctrines were problematic, nevertheless, they were compelled to rely on them by political and strategic objectives—mainly the need to protect and support their exposed allies. If war occurred, Russia needed to attack Austria in order to prevent Serbia from being destroyed, and it needed to attack Germany in order to prevent France from being overcome by a concentrated German attack in the west. Defending Russian territory would not address these needs. France needed to attack Germany in order to protect Russia. Germany needed to attack France because slow Russian mobilization meant that Germany *could* successfully fight both France and Russia, but only serially, by attacking France first. Austria needed to attack Russia to give Germany time to defeat France, even though leaders in Vienna really preferred to attack Serbia instead and keep Russia out of a war. In other words, offensive doctrines seemed to be a rational response to the dynamics of a potential war involving multiple alliance partners.

Others suggest that the continuance of offensive doctrines in the age of defense was the result of a misperception of recent military experiences. Somehow, despite a rather vigorous and open debate in the military community, European militaries missed the warning signs provided by recent military experience. The American Civil War, the Russo-Japanese War, and the Boer War pointed to the new potency of defensive technologies and the decreased utility of such offensive maneuvers as the direct frontal assault. Despite these portents, European military leaders clung to the belief that the next wars in Europe would be just like previous wars—the Franco-Prussian War and the Austro-Prussian War—short and sweet, due to offensive power. This misperception of the actual balance between offensive and defensive forces is what Jack Snyder (1985) calls a "perceptual security dilemma" rather than a real or "structural" security dilemma.

Other scholars have argued that a powerful "cult of the offensive" developed within the military high commands of the European powers (Van Evera 1999, 1984; Snyder 1984; Levy 1989). According to this argument, the roots of this cult were bureaucratic and sociopolitical rather than rational. European militaries adopted offensive doctrines primarily because, unlike defensive doctrines, they enhanced the power and size of military organizations, they promoted the autonomy of the military, they enhanced the prestige and morale of military professionals, and they minimized uncertainty. For a variety of bureaucratic and psychological reasons, most organizations and the individuals within them tend to be reluctant to reconsider core values and beliefs. Once adopted as policy, offensive doctrines and the beliefs upon which they were based were naturally resistant to change. (We can consider offensive military doctrines to be part of the **operational code** of military leaders.)

The Defensive Realist school of thought argues that the likelihood of war can be linked to the balance between offensive and defensive weaponry and strategies

(Jervis 1978; Snyder 1982; Van Evera 1999; Lynn-Jones 1995). In an offense-dominant system, conquest is easy; in a defense-dominant system, it is difficult (Van Evera 1999, 118). Defensive Realists argue that war is more likely to occur in offense-dominated international systems—or in systems perceived to be offense-dominated—rather than ones in which defensive forces and strategies are dominant. In such systems, leaders perceive a greater incentive to use force. Since true offense-dominated systems are believed to be rare, perceptions of offensive domination must explain much interstate war (Van Evera 1999, 122).

The widespread belief in offensive superiority in 1914, erroneous as it was, had a number of significant results (Van Evera 1984, 1999):

1. Wars were assumed to be short and inexpensive and therefore expansion became more tempting because the cost of aggression was perceived to be small. After all, if offenses were superior to defenses, then logically, someone's offensive forces would overwhelm someone else's defensive forces rather quickly, and the war would be over.
2. Leaders believed that the side which mobilized or attacked first had a military advantage, thereby creating a "hair trigger" situation in which preemptive wars became more likely. Restraint, on the other hand, was likely to be dangerous.
3. The perception of relatively small shifts in the distribution of power caused greater alarm (or hope), creating bigger perceived windows of opportunity or vulnerability. As a result, the perception of offensive dominance helped to promote arms races and to increase the incentive for preventive wars to close windows of vulnerability. Attacking now was seen as preferable to defending later.
4. States tended to adopt a more competitive style of diplomacy, using brinkmanship tactics and faits accomplis.
5. States enforced tighter political and military secrecy since leaks of important information were perceived to have greater potential for harm. Thus security dilemma problems in 1914 were heightened by potential power shifts, by the overestimation of the hostility of others, and by the tendency to overrate the advantages of the offense.

None of the great powers entered the war set to carry out a defensive operation to protect its own territories. All believed that the best defense was a good offense. Influenced by the **cult of the offensive**, Germany, Russia, Austria-Hungary, and France (though not the small states like Belgium and Serbia) had devised war plans that were essentially offensive in nature: Germany's Schlieffen Plan, Russia's Plan 20, and the Austro-Hungarian plans B and R. And offensive mobilization plans were interactive. Once the outline of the Schlieffen Plan was understood, the French pushed Russia into an offensive doctrine. They insisted that further loans to Russia be tied to improvements in Russia's offensive capabilities. French survival was deemed to depend on a Russian attack on Germany's eastern front.

And since military and civilian elites all believed that the state that mobilized (and/or attacked) first had a decisive advantage, they all believed that they needed either to mobilize before their opponents, or at the very least *immediately* after their opponents. Everyone believed that a few days or hours difference could mean the difference between winning and losing the war. As a result, political leaders in all countries on the Continent were under strong pressure from their militaries to order mobilization at the soonest possible moment. Mobilization decisions in the European capitals were tightly coupled. This created the potential that war might begin by preemption. Consequently, Nicholas II ordered preliminary mobilization of the Russian army at a time when Russia was not directly threatened by the crisis in the Balkans—before the Serb reply to the Austrian ultimatum and before the Austrian mobilization against Serbia. And Russia initiated its full mobilization in response to premature and exaggerated accounts of a German mobilization. In other words, Russian mobilization decisions revealed haste brought on by the beliefs that time was of the essence, that offenses were dominant, and that huge military gains would accrue to the state which mobilized first. The inaccurate perception of first move advantages placed a hair trigger on crisis decision making.

Similarly, leaders believed that it was important that their own mobilizations be kept secret from their opponents. It was especially important for the German military that the Schlieffen Plan's opening attack on the rail junction at Liege in Belgium be kept a secret, as success depended upon capturing Liege with its bridges and tunnels intact, and therefore victory depended in large part on surprise. One result of the extreme secrecy was that Bethmann Hollweg, Jagow, Tirpitz, and perhaps even the kaiser were unaware of the planned attack on Liege—it had only been added to the plan in 1913—leading civilian leaders to treat mobilizations as mere diplomatic tools in an extended bargaining process (Van Evera 1984, 93; Van Evera 1999, 63; Waite 1990, 161).

Leaders also feared the ability of their opponents to keep their mobilizations secret. The decision by Russian leaders for a partial mobilization against Austria on July 29 was influenced by the perceived need to prevent Russia from being taken unawares by an Austrian mobilization. (This had actually happened in the Balkan Crisis of 1912, when Austria had mobilized forces in Galicia without Russian detection.) And Russia's later full mobilization was influenced by its lack of confidence in being able to detect German mobilization. Likewise, French generals were concerned about being caught napping by an undetected German mobilization (van Evera 1999, 209–11).

The beliefs that offensive forces were superior and that the initiator had the advantage, and that mobilizations could be kept secret, along with the presence of offensive forces following offensive mobilization plans, combined to create conditions for a preemptive war in 1914. These conditions were major factors in the decisions by Russian and French leaders to mobilize their forces, which in turn triggered the German mobilization (van Evera 1984, 79).

Germany adopted the Schlieffen Plan for continental war in Europe in 1905, without the consent of its ally Austria-Hungary, thus turning the Dual Alliance from a defensive pact against Russia into an offensive pact whose first target would be France. The German mobilization plan differed from the plans of the other European states in one important respect: It called for an attack on Luxembourg within the first day of mobilization and an attack on Liege on the third day of mobilization. From there, the German army would march on France and seek to capture Paris within weeks of the opening shots.

The Schlieffen Plan made sense if the military environment was indeed of-fense-dominated and if Germany's neighbors were hostile. The German military assumed France would attack Germany if Germany and Austria fought Russia. Germany thus would be faced with the danger of a two-front war. Because the French army was superior to the Russian army, because its mobilization time was shorter, and because French armies were much closer to Germany's essen-tial Rhine valley, a French offensive against Germany would constitute a greater threat than a Russian offensive. France, therefore, had to be dealt with quickly, while slow Russian mobilization would give Germany a tactical window of op-portunity in the west. German planners were committed to striking first, against France, if war appeared on the horizon. And they were committed to doing it through neutral Belgium as a way of flanking French forces and because the cen-tral rail yards in Liege were normally undefended. Germany's mobilization would be almost entirely a mobilization toward the west. Once France had been defeated, Germany would have time to turn its armies to the east. In the mean-time, it was essential that Austria slow the progress of the Russian thrust on the eastern front. Conrad had, in fact, promised a Galician offensive against Russian forces in Poland. In return, Moltke pledged enough German forces in the east to give Conrad enough time to shift his forces northward if Austrian troops were in-volved in a war with Serbia to the south—a pledge the Germans failed to keep in 1914 (Williamson 1991, 88).

Mobilization meant war for Germany. For the others, the resort to war was probable but not automatic. Austria-Hungary and Serbia had mobilized parts of their forces in 1890 without going to war; likewise, the Balkan Wars saw alerts or mobilization by Britain, France, Austria, and Russia (in addition to the actual participants), without leading to a wider war. However, in 1914 the mobilization decisions of the European powers were essentially interdependent and interlock-ing. A mobilization against Serbia by Austria-Hungary would trigger a Russian mobilization; Russian (or French) mobilization, no matter how cautious or re-strained, would trigger a German mobilization; and a German mobilization would mean war.

The motivation was fear rather than desire for conquest. German leaders overestimated the Entente's hostility; they therefore saw war as inevitable, and they concluded that a current window of opportunity would quickly turn into a window of vulnerability vis-à-vis the Entente powers, especially Russia. Thus Germany's best strategy was for a preventive war rather than a defensive or de-terrent strategy (Snyder 1985, 170–71). The beliefs associated with the cult of the offensive played a role in generating the perception of these windows. In sum, the threat to Germany and Austria from France and Russia depended on the as-sumption that offenses were dominant. If the strategic environment was one in which defenses were dominant, then Germany and Austria had much less to worry about from the growing power of their neighbors. For Russia (or France) to be a real threat in a defensive strategic environment would require extremely large shifts in the size of its armies relative to the Central Powers (van Evera 1984, 79–84).

Russian leaders were aware of German thinking about windows of opportunity and windows of vulnerability. They knew of German discussions of preventive war, and they expected Germany to use the Serb crisis in 1914 to mount such a preventive war. If deterrence failed, Russian mobilization could be used to preempt a presumed German preventive strike against Russia (van Evera 1984, 87–88). In 1914 both preventive and preemptive motives existed.

Finally, note must be made of the rigidity of mobilization plans and its effects on the course of the crisis in 1914. In part, what made the war plans so disastrous was that in practice, mobilizations were carried out somewhat inflexibly, making it difficult for statesmen to pursue less coercive and threatening paths. This is an argument consistent with the organizational process model of government behavior that is closely related to Graham Allison's (1971) bureaucratic politics model. The German military and its leaders refused to consider alternatives to the Schlieffen Plan and they refused to delay the crossing into Luxembourg, the Austrian war plans could not accommodate the Halt in Belgrade proposal, and the Russian military's attempt to counter Austria without provoking Germany through a partial mobilization interfered with the ability to execute a later full mobilization.

Moreover, especially in Germany, war plans were made without input from civilian political officials, resulting in a plan which—in the context of the 1914 crisis—made no real political sense and ensured the worst possible outcome for Germany: The attack on France guaranteed a two-front war over a conflict in the Balkans, and the attack through Belgium guaranteed British intervention. Additionally, military secrecy surrounding the Schlieffen Plan was so tight that political leaders were unaware of some of its more sensitive aspects. Thus German civilian leaders were disposed to look at the use of mobilizations as one more instrument in the toolbox of coercive diplomacy rather than a step which meant war.

SUMMARY

If ever a war was overdetermined, it was World War I. A large variety of causal factors combined together in 1914 to produce the war; many of these are related to a comprehensive and multifaceted security dilemma. Unequal rates of growth among the European great powers had, by the turn of the century, created significant dyadic power transitions, changes to the global balance of power, and a deconcentration of systemic power associated with the decline of Britain as the hegemonic power. These in turn produced perceptions of threat as well as perceptions of windows of opportunity and vulnerability. Combined with an unrealistic assessment of the offense-defense balance, German leaders became convinced of the necessity of preventive war as a method of ensuring security. The drive for security that accompanied these upheavals in the military balance led to arms races and changes in alliance configurations that increased the polarization of the system; both of these factors increased the general level of perceived hostility, threat, and anxiety that already existed in the European system.

The general result was that the European great powers, many of whom were already enduring rivals, became engaged in a series of crisis interactions in the decade before 1914. The fact that there were tightly coupled multiple rivalries among geographically contiguous states, several of whom had unresolved territorial issues, meant that any conflict in Europe had the potential to become intensified. Throughout the successive crises, the willingness by almost all parties to use military coercion and to take risks increased. These interactions resulted in dysfunctional crisis learning: In Berlin, Vienna, Paris, and St. Petersburg political leaders came to believe that toughness was the key to winning crisis confrontations. The catalyst for the 1914 conflict was the assassination of the Austrian crown prince in Sarajevo, an event that precipitated a classic conflict spiral among the participants. The upward spiral was exacerbated somewhat by interaction of individual misperceptions, personality and psychological needs.

The long passage toward these fateful events was aggravated by the domestic political factors in several states. In Germany, a cartelized system led to policy making through logrolling, which resulted in the pursuit of an aggressive Weltpolitik. This policy helped to trigger arms races, changes in alliance configurations, and perceptions of threat—ultimately producing in Germany feelings of being surrounded by threatening neighbors, producing the crisis interactions. German domestic politics also produced an environment in which diversionary motives lay just under the surface of foreign policy calculations. In Britain the domestic political situation made it impossible for Britain to issue deterrent threats to the Central Powers. And in Austria the domestic situation compelled decision makers in Vienna to desperately search for a "final solution" to the Serbian problem.

When the crisis came in 1914 it was in the context of a global political culture that saw war as a natural, inevitable, and even beneficial tool used by sovereign states in pursuit of their interests. And it was in the context of the final stages of a decade-long series of crises at the end of which no country saw compromise or backing down as a viable foreign policy strategy. Germany, Austria-Hungary, Russia, and France were committed to making forceful responses to any perceived threat or provocation.

The year 1914 represents in effect "a perfect storm"—the near simultaneous combination of an extremely large number of factors associated historically with the outbreak of war. The presence of these factors interacting synergistically with one another did not make war inevitable, but it did increase the probability of war to an extremely high level. Almost all of the underlying conditions identified by political scientists as producing war were present. Richard Ned Lebow (2000–2001) has argued that the onset of war requires a conjunction of these underlying causes with an appropriate catalyst. He sees WWI as highly contingent: Despite the large number of underlying causes, war would not have happened without the assassination of the Austrian archduke. The assassination, he argues, was the one event capable of producing the necessary changes in thinking and policy in Germany, Russia and Austria-Hungary. William Thompson (2003) takes the opposite approach. Catalysts, he argues, are like "streetcars": If one doesn't come along now, there will be another one in a few minutes. Any streetcar will do. The authors tend to support Thompson's view. Whether wars actually occur is always probabilistic. It is possible that war would not have broken out in 1914 without the assassination in Sarajevo, but—given the large number

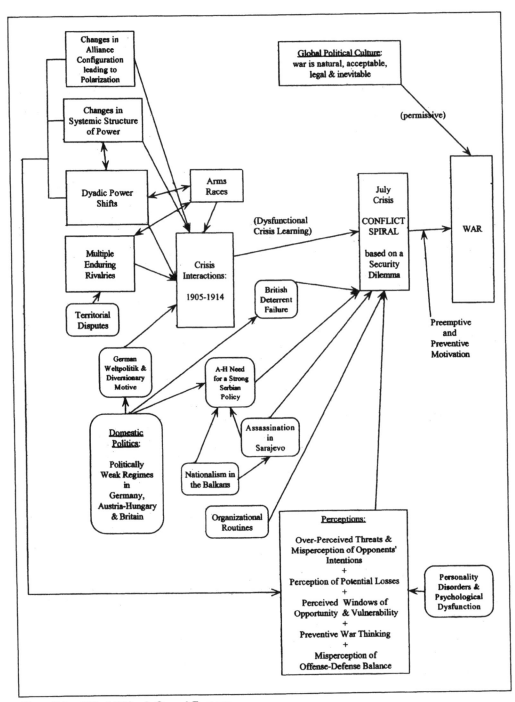

Chart 2.1. World War I: Causal Factors

of causal factors at work—the exact requirements for an "appropriate" catalyst were extremely broad in the second decade of the 20th century.

AFTERMATH

World War I changed the world dramatically. It permanently destroyed two empires (the Ottoman and the Austro-Hungarian) and temporarily dissolved two others (the German and the Russian). In the process, the Romanov, Habsburg, and Hohenzollern dynasties were toppled and monarchies were replaced by republics. The war briefly enlarged the colonial empires of Britain and France, primarily in the form of League of Nations mandates, and eventually created a wave of new states, thereby validating the power of nationalism and the principle of national self-determination. Among the new creations: a separate Hungary and Austria; new states called Czechoslovakia, Yugoslavia, Saudi Arabia, Syria, Iraq, Lebanon, and Jordan; and an especially difficult entity called Palestine. As the Second Reich was dismantled, a significant German diaspora was created in Central and Eastern Europe, creating the seeds of future conflicts. The war also ignited the Russian revolution, creating the first communist government anywhere in the world. It propelled the rise of American power (though the U.S. continued its isolationist policies for another quarter century) and made world politics somewhat less Euro-centered. And it gave birth to the first global international political institution of the modern age, the League of Nations. The war also led to a diplomatic conclusion—the Treaty of Versailles—which saddled Germany with reparations and the war guilt clause and returned Alsace and Lorraine to France, laying the basis for German dissatisfaction with the postwar world order, the rise of Hitler and the National Socialist Party in Germany, and the outbreak of World War II. Finally, among the developed countries of the west, World War I produced a change in political culture regarding attitudes toward war. As a result of the devastation of the war years, many in Europe and North America began to see war as being too costly, even for the victors. War was now seen as immoral, unethical, irrational, economically impractical, uncivilized, and futile—in short, a historical anachronism.

3

World War II in the Pacific

The Japanese attack on Pearl Harbor on December 7, 1941, initiated a bitter war in the Pacific between Japan and the United States. The war was not inevitable, but its onset had a certain feel of predestination to it. Indeed, one is reminded of Gabriel Garcia Marquez's famous novella *Chronicle of a Death Foretold*, in which the death of the protagonist is a foregone conclusion about which everyone knows before it happens. From the 1931 Manchurian Incident—Japan's armed invasion and occupation of China's three northeastern provinces—to Japan's push into Southeast Asia in 1940 and 1941, Japan and the United States proceeded on a collision course with each other as their interests in the Asian-Pacific region became increasingly incompatible over the decade.

Like most wars, the Pacific phase of World War II was the result of the interaction of many factors. The most important causal forces include the presence of transitional democratic institutions in Japan, which threatened the interests of the military and created internal conflicts and diversionary motivations for war, a rapidly changing international system that created perceptions of temporary windows of opportunity, the framing of choices in a way that promoted risk-taking, security-driven territorial issues, and an entrenched conflict spiral between rivals fueled by coercive diplomacy on both sides.

Perhaps the best way to begin is to examine a state-level phenomenon that was crucial to bringing about the war: the nature of the Japanese political system in the period between WWI and WWII.

LONG-TERM FACTORS: STATE AND SUBSTATE LEVELS OF ANALYSIS

Democratization, Contested Institutions, and Diversionary War

The domestic roots of the war in the Pacific can be found within the nature of the Japanese state. Japan officially entered the modern age in 1868 with the overthrow of the shogunate and the restoration of imperial rule under the emperor Mutsuhito, named Meiji. The Meiji restoration committed Japan to economic and political modernization. By the end of the 1880s Japan had a new constitution, a prime minister and a cabinet, and an elected lower house. In truth, Japan was merely in the

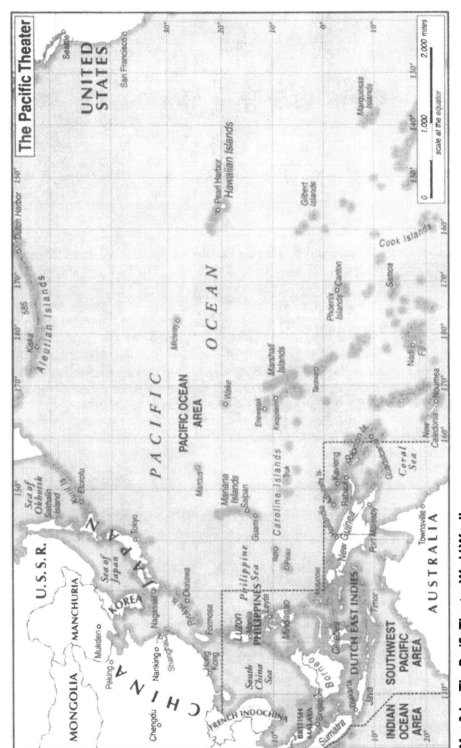

Map 3.1.   The Pacific Theater, World War II

initial stages of a democratic transition, and its system was only "semidemocratic." Whether it would become a fully democratic state was open to question.

According to the constitution, ultimate political sovereignty was possessed by the emperor, who was considered to be "sacred and inviolable." Undergirding the institution of the emperor was the Shinto state religion, according to which the emperor was a direct descendant of the sun goddess Amaterasu. The emperor had the power to issue imperial decrees with the force of law and to veto all legislative acts. And he was given supreme command of the army and the navy. Beyond that, however, the position of the emperor was, by design, somewhat vague. Since the emperor had to be protected from real participation in the making of government decisions so that his infallibility could not be challenged, he was "to reign but not rule." The government would to some extent act in the name of the emperor.

The prime minister was not chosen by the lower house (as he would be in a true parliamentary system) but was nominated by the *genro*—a group of elder statesmen. Individual cabinet ministers were appointed by, and were directly responsible to, the emperor rather than to the prime minister. The principle that cabinets should be based on party composition in the lower house was never strongly established, though "party cabinets" did become part of the political landscape from 1918 to 1932. Only the House of Representatives, the lower house of the Imperial Diet, was popularly elected. The appointed upper house, the House of Peers, could reject acts passed by the lower house. Moreover, the cabinet could promulgate imperial ordinances, in effect going over the heads of the elected legislature.

In the final analysis, the military, the cabinet, and the elected members of the Diet could all claim to be rightful interpreters of the "imperial will," acting in the name of the emperor. The result was "a curious sort of pluralism in which many participated and no one was ultimately responsible" (Jansen 2000, 496).

A significant aspect of this system was the relative power and autonomy of the military. The chiefs of the military staffs were independent of the civilian government with respect to military matters, and the army and navy ministers reported directly to the emperor. To further ensure the autonomy of the military, in 1882 an imperial rescript was issued that declared that the emperor's supreme command of the army and navy was never to be delegated to others. The military was able to claim that it acted on behalf of the emperor, and—lacking an indication to the contrary by the emperor—political leaders were unable to challenge military actions (Kato 1974, 235). The rescript also said that troops were to refrain from politics and not to question imperial policies; they must be absolutely loyal to the emperor. The logical flaw in this set of rules—which became readily apparent in the 1920s and 1930s—was that if a soldier's only duty was to the emperor, it became legitimate to rebel against civilian leaders who appeared to be in opposition to the emperor's will (Buruma 2003, 55).

Over time, the military also won acceptance of the rule that only active duty military officers could serve as ministers of the army or navy. (This rule was abolished between 1913 and 1936, allowing retired generals and admirals to fill these slots, but the influence of the military remained strong.) Hence, *all* cabinets included several representatives of the military, guaranteeing the services the right to participate directly in the political process. In addition to its control over the two military cabinet positions, military personnel often held "civilian" posts in the cabinet as well. Between 1885 and 1945 the military occupied approximately 28 percent of the civilian posts (LaFeber 1997, 163). Furthermore, military ministers could bring down the prime minister and his government by resigning their cabinet posts and then refusing to agree to a successor to fill the vacant slots unless they got their way in choosing a new prime minister.

Moreover, powerful interest groups, such as the Imperial Military Reserve Association, lobbied on behalf of military interests, and the *zaibatsu*, Japan's giant business conglomerates, were closely linked to the military. Military influence on the economy was strong and pervasive: From 1890 to 1919 military expenditures accounted for as much as 20 percent of the national income, and from the Manchurian Incident of 1931 until the end of WWII, military expenditures accounted for between 30 and 50 percent of the government budget (McDermott 1995, 183). Finally, to the extent that an effective public opinion existed in Japan, it tended to be fairly nationalistic. Japan's military aggression, at least in the 1930s, was extremely popular in Japan—a popularity that was fueled by the mass media and the entertainment industry and by government propaganda (LaFeber 1997, 163; Buruma 2003, 92). In sum, the military possessed both political allies and an extensive set of tools in its political arsenal. As one observer has noted, the military did not need to "overthrow the system" to gain power; it merely had to assert the power that it already possessed (Kato 1974, 225–26).

The Japanese war effort in China produced several new decision-making structures. In November 1937 the emperor ordered the creation of an Imperial Headquarters to coordinate military policy. Its members were to include the emperor, the army and navy chiefs of staff, the army and navy ministers, the chiefs of operations, and the emperor's own military aide. The prime minister, foreign minister, and other civilian officials were purposely omitted from this grouping. Next, an Imperial Headquarters–Government Liaison Conference was created to facilitate military-government cooperation. Between 1940 and 1941 the Liaison Conference became the single most important forum for military-security decisions, usurping the decision-making functions of the cabinet (Bix 2000, 387). Joint decisions worked out at a Liaison Conference would then be formally presented to the emperor for his approval at imperial conferences, attended by the top military and government leaders. According to Bix (2000, 329), "The imperial conference was *the* device for legally transforming the 'will of the emperor' into the 'will of the state.' And because everyone who participated in its deliberations could claim to have acted by, with, and under the unique authority of the emperor, while he could claim to have acted in accordance with the advice of his ministers of state, the imperial conference diffused lines of responsibility. In that sense, it was the perfect crown to the Japanese practice of irresponsibility."

With the death of Emperor Meiji in 1912, Japan entered the period of the Taisho emperor (1912–1926). This is usually portrayed as a liberal period in which democracy was strengthened at home and Japan joined in cooperative arrangements with Western countries in international affairs. It was also, especially after 1922, a time in which elite political consensus began to break down, generating a period of tremendous political instability. Japan's "Taisho Democracy" ultimately deteriorated into military-led authoritarianism after 1931. The power of the elected legislature declined, and after 1932 cabinets were no longer party cabinets based on the results of parliamentary elections. Between the Manchurian Incident in 1931 and the end of World War II, Japan had fourteen governments, with eleven different prime ministers; eight of these governments were led by generals or admirals in the position of prime minister.

How is one to explain the increasing authoritarianism and militarization of the political system? In part, it was because the process of democratization is by its very nature a messy process and hardly ever proceeds in an upwardly ascending straight line from authoritarianism to full democracy (Mansfield and Snyder 1995, 24). More specifically, in Japan the problem was related to the vagaries of dynastic succession. The Taisho emperor, Yoshihito, suffered from both physical and mental disabilities that made the performance of his duties virtually impossible. In short, he was mentally incompetent. The weakness of his central authority naturally abetted the rise of a more pluralistic democracy, but it also stimulated political competition among political elites—a battle in which the military had significant advantages.

The succession in 1926 of the Showa emperor, Hirohito, reversed this trend toward greater democracy. Hirohito and his court officials were intent on reviving the power of the monarch. The political system became more authoritarian, but it also became more militarized. The military, however, was not monolithic. Numerous political splits existed—between officers from different geographic regions, between junior and senior officers, between the army and navy, and along ideological/strategic lines.

The two most important military factions were formed primarily from graduates of the Army Staff College. Both factions desired a "purer" and more powerful Japan with a military dictatorship under the emperor dedicated to imperial expansion. The Imperial Way (or Spirit) faction was avowedly "Asian" and strongly anticommunist and anti-Russian in orientation. It supported expansion in Manchuria and Northeast Asia as a strategy of self-defense against the perceived threat from the Soviet Union. It emphasized "national spirit" rather than technological modernization as the key to Japanese military superiority. The faction was led by the older generation in the army centered around three generals from Choshu Province—Yamagata Aritomo, Terauchi Masatake, and Tanaka Gi'ichi. In the 1930s leadership passed to a younger generation of officers led by Araki Sadao (the war minister from 1933 to 1935) and Gen. Mazaki Jingaburo. The power of this group was drastically reduced as a result of its failed attempt in the 1936 Tokyo Rebellion.

The Total War (or Total Mobilization or Control Group) faction was centered around Nagata Tetsuzan (head of the military affairs bureau of the War Ministry), Minami Jiro, Ishiwara Kanji, Suzuki Teichi, and Tojo Hideki. This faction came to dominance after the 1936 rebellion. Its members emphasized the need to mobilize the entire population and the economy—with government control over capital, labor, and raw materials—in order to establish a "national defense state." The faction supported military reform and modernization. Its members believed that Japan needed to engage in a wider war beyond Manchuria. Consequently, it wanted to develop China's resources as a prelude to creating a planned economy geared to fighting a total war later with the Soviet Union and the United States.

The views of Ishiwara Kanji, who engineered the Manchurian Incident, are representative of this group:

> Japan, acting through the army, was destined to save the world from Marxism and other corrupting ideologies. This would require a series of wars, first against Russia, then against Britain, finally against the United States, in which Japan would stand as the champion of Asia and the embodiment of Confucian righteousness. The culminating struggle would be a holocaust in which warfare would take on a wholly new dimension . . . bringing into action entire populations and the totality of their resources. (Beasley 1987, 182)

The fundamental problem for all military factions in the Taisho era was that political forces advocating parliamentary democracy were in the ascendant. The powers of the Diet and of the prime minister were growing. The active duty rule for the positions of army and navy ministers had been abolished, and Japan had established party cabinets based on the results of legislative elections, giving civilian officials more legitimacy and more power. By the mid-1920s the position of the Taisho emperor had declined to the status of a mere figurehead (Bix 2000, 93).

Moreover, during the Taisho era, Japanese governments pursued foreign and domestic policies inimical to military interests. The government of Kato Tomosaburo approved the various Washington treaties of 1922. The Nine Power Treaty compelled Japan to partially divest herself of her territorial gains from World War I. It had to give up the Shantung Peninsula in Manchuria and pledge to respect the territorial integrity of China. The Naval Disarmament Treaty limited Japan to a 6:10:10 ratio in capital ships compared to the United States and Britain. In the same year Japan withdrew intervention forces from the Soviet Far East without extracting territorial gains. With the Siberian intervention over, the civilian government approved three rounds of personnel cuts in the army to take place from 1922 to 1924. And in spite of the opposition of the General Staff, in 1925 the government further reduced the army by four divisions. The navy began scrapping older ships. Total military spending by the two services decreased steadily. It was hard to justify continued high military expenses in the absence of a serious foreign threat to Japan, especially when it was clear that previous arms spending had taken the government to the brink of bankruptcy (Bix 2000, 148, 152, and 705 n. 58).

The trend continued in the early years of the Showa emperor, Hirohito. In 1928 the government frustrated the army's desire to intervene in north China in the Chang Tso-lin affair. And in 1930 the Hamaguchi government ratified the new London Naval Convention, which further restricted naval competition among the great powers, even though its terms were unanimously opposed by the Naval General Staff. This last policy split the navy between the protreaty faction and the "fleet faction" and led to a brutal naval propaganda campaign against the prime minister, the purging of protreaty officers, and eventually to the assassination of Prime Minister Hamaguchi by an ultranationalist—setting off a period of political violence by army and navy extremists as well as civilians (see Bix 2000, 225).

Thus prior to the Manchurian Incident, military personnel, regardless of factional ties, had grievances against the political authorities in Tokyo with respect to the reduction of military resources and the general direction of Japanese foreign policy. Just as important, the military was concerned about the increasing power of political parties and the strengthening of parliamentary democracy. These latter developments were seen by officers in both the Imperial Way and the Total War factions as a threat to the survival of military values in Japanese society (Snyder 1991, 138–39). The primary goal of democratizers was the complete subordination of the military to civilian control, a change that would reverse hundreds of years of Japanese political history (Dassel 1998, 133). A primary goal of almost all military factions, therefore, was to prevent further civilian encroachment on military power (Snyder 1991, 142).

Despite their internal divisiveness, all military elites could agree that developments during the Taisho era presented serious threats to the military's institutional interests. These interests included enhanced funding of military programs, maintaining military values in Japanese society, maintaining autonomy over military decisions, and establishing a paramount power position among the competing domestic elites that made up the political system. War was the one pathway guaranteed to achieve these goals. Indeed, wars against China (1894–1895) and Russia (1904–1905) had already institutionalized a strong military with substantial claims on budgetary resources.

In response to these developments, the officer corps became intensely politicized in the late 1920s and early 1930s. Military officers publicly railed against the Washington treaty system as a Western plot to prevent Japan from expanding, and they lambasted the political parties for undermining Japan's ability to defend itself. Many officers saw the government's moderate foreign policies and its support for a liberal, capitalist international system as making Japan dependent on the West. Foreign policy became a partisan issue. Military officers essentially went into open conflict with the Wakatsuki government in 1931, and "the army as an institutional entity showed signs of spiraling out of control" (Bix 2000, 155, 211, 226–27). Various elements within the military successfully used threats of coups and the assassination of political rivals at home to influence political results. In 1931 Prime Minister Hamaguchi was assassinated by a right-wing patriot. The following year Prime Minister Inukai was assassinated by naval officers. Both prime ministers had pursued foreign policies opposed by military factions.

Japan seemed ripe for a military coup; indeed, the Seiyukai Party (the more promilitary of the two main parties) at times even encouraged such a venture. There were two attempted coups in March and October 1931 undertaken by the secret Cherry Blossom society of right-wing officers. While both attempts failed, their perpetrators went largely unpunished by the emperor, thereby weakening the government's ability to exert control over the military. A third attempt, the infamous Tokyo Rebellion of February 26, 1936, dramatically illustrated the danger that a military coup might trigger an all-out civil war involving military factions.

The rebellion was led by young officers of the army's Imperial Way faction. It was touched off by the announcement that the 1st Division would be transferred from Tokyo to Manchuria—a move seen as an attempt by the rival Total War faction to reduce the power of the Imperial Way by sending one of its major units as far from the center of political power as possible (Butow 1961, 63). The coup was aimed at reversing Japan's pro-Western, liberal-capitalist-internationalist orientation by creating a military dictatorship based on traditional Japanese culture (Iriye 1987, 7). Specifically, its goal was to force the emperor to announce a "Showa restoration" that would reduce the power of the court advisers, install Gen. Mazaki as prime minister, distribute government and military positions to members of the Imperial Way faction, strengthen the push for military rearmament, undertake an all-out mobilization of national resources, and then use the newly mobilized military resources to resolve the conflict in China. In February 1936 roughly fifteen hundred rebel soldiers occupied Tokyo police headquarters and other government buildings and cut off Tokyo's communication links. The rebels assassinated four high government officials, but Prime Minister Okada escaped assassination by hiding in a closet for two days. The coup attempt was put down quickly, and the anticipated spontaneous uprising of troops failed to occur. Most important, the Tokyo Rebellion put on display the extremely sobering sight of loyal naval marines and the Imperial Guard fighting against rebel forces of the Imperial Army. Such an intermilitary civil war was to be avoided at all costs.

The immediate result of the rebellion was to increase the political power of the military at the expense of "terrorized" and intimidated civilians (Kato 1974, 233). The civilian elites threw their support behind the Total War faction, giving them a free hand to suppress the Imperial Way. But the price for order at home was that the government had to make concessions to the military (and the now ascendant Total War faction) on foreign policy and give it a free hand overseas (Butow 1961, 70). The civilian government lost the ability to control military actions abroad.

The path from domestic politics in Japan to her war in Asia can be explained by a complex of three interrelated theories that focus on the connection between interstate wars and internal conflicts, especially within countries making the transition to democracy. These theories are Snyder's (1991) theory of cartelized political systems, Mansfield and Snyder's (1995, 2005) theory of democratization and war, and Dassel's (1998) theory of contested institutions. All three may be seen as variations of the theory of diversionary war (Levy 1989).

Snyder notes that Japan, like Wilhelmine Germany, was late in undergoing industrialization. Economically, this situation led to a rapid, state-led modernization effort under the Meiji government, but politically it created a cartelized political system—a system dominated by a number of powerful, concentrated interest groups with narrow, parochial interests. As Snyder explains, the political system of such states requires the construction of political alliances between these elite groups. In the case of Japan, the political system was dominated by an alliance among the army, navy, local landowners, government bureaucrats, nationalist politicians, and certain state-supported business interests (Snyder 1991, 133, 146). While the system was pluralistic, its pluralism produced effects that were not entirely benign.

Rather than merely insisting on its own program and attempting to veto the interests of others, each such group found that the only way to formulate policy was to cooperate through logrolling tactics, in which groups supported each other's preferred policies in the pursuit of mutual benefits (Snyder 1991, 58). In early- and mid-twentieth-century Japan, the one policy that benefited the vast majority of relevant groups turned out to be imperial expansion in Asia. Each group supported the preferences of the others, even though the result of such a process—war with China and the Western powers—might be detrimental to the greater "national" interest.

This ruinous political dynamic was exacerbated in Japan by its incomplete process of democratization in the Taisho period and afterward. As Mansfield and Snyder (1995, 7, 19–20) note, the problem with the initial stage of democratization is that while participation in the political system is increased, the newly formed democratic institutions may be too weak to resolve conflicts between political groups and enforce the "rules of the game" on all participants. Moreover, older, traditional elites—typically associated with military and imperial groups— feel that their interests are threatened by further democratization. Primarily, they fear that the public (and the parliament) will refuse to bear the costs necessary to subsidize the military and its interests. Typically, such traditional elites attempt to mobilize mass support for their views through the use of propagandistic nationalist appeals and the use of prestige strategies (i.e., aggressive policies against foreign enemies). They may logroll with other like-minded groups in this strategy. The result is the use of reckless, adventuristic, aggressive, nationalistic policies to maintain and build domestic political support. All of these insights apply to the situation in Japan.

In Japan the process of democratization was even more dysfunctional than might normally have been the case. As we have seen, by the mid-1920s with the incompetent Taisho emperor on the throne, political arrangements in Japan had begun to break down, creating a very fluid Wild West situation in which all political groups, civilian and military, were forced to fight as best they could to secure political power from their rivals. This extreme phase of democratization is best captured by Kurt Dassel's term "contested institutions"—a situation in which the most important political groups fundamentally disagree about the basic rules of the political game (Dassel 1998, 108). While the conflict in Japan was complex and multifaceted, certainly a major aspect of it was a conflict between civilian leaders who supported Western-style democratic institutions, diminished roles for the emperor and the military, and an accommodationist approach to foreign policy and a coalition made up of certain military factions, nationalists, and business groups whose foreign policy orientation was more hard line and who supported an authoritarian, militarized state that would pursue the creation of a self-sufficient Japanese empire (Vasquez 1998, 198).

Many groups were simply unwilling to play by the rules of the present Taisho system of semidemocracy and resorted to "extraconstitutional" methods. Under these conditions civilians naturally sought to challenge the autonomy of the military and exercise control over it because it represented a threat to them. In return, the military was forced to protect its organizational interests in one of two ways: use force internally to repress opponents or use force externally to increase its internal power over other political actors.

In Japan, as Dassel (1998, 133–36) explains, the normal tendency to use force against internal opponents through repression or military coup was ruled out by two things. First, the military was itself broadly representative of Japanese society as a whole and was therefore fragmented. Consequently, a coup by any particular faction would have resulted in a civil war in Japan with the various military factions arrayed against each other. Second, the emperor was adamantly opposed to a military coup, even one nominally on his behalf. In the absence of a coup that created a military government, what the military factions could all agree on was that it was in their interest to promote external conflicts as a way of increasing their budgets, their personnel, their resources and their domestic political influence vis-à-vis various civilian opponents. And since some civilian political actors supported foreign intervention for their own reasons, the result was that the Japanese military came to rely on the external use of force and expansion abroad as a way to buttress its internal political position. For military elites, diversionary motives were always a powerful incentive for war.

Consistent with Snyder's focus on cartelized political systems, factionalism within the military also encouraged interservice *logrolling*. For instance, in the 1930s the navy sought to convince other groups that Japan needed to break out of the limits imposed by the 1930 London Treaty, even though this would provoke Britain and the United States. The Imperial Army's war in China and its contemplated war against Russia were largely land operations that were "infantry intensive" and left little for the Imperial Navy to do. Moreover, the army understood that a naval buildup would increase the international opposition— from the USSR and the U.S.—to the army's encroachments in China, thereby increasing both the expense and the risk of the operation. Nevertheless, even though army-navy preferences were mutually counterproductive, they both got their way. Military policy was based on a simple logrolling tradeoff: The army supported the navy's breakout from the treaty limits and her preparation for a naval war against the United States, and the navy supported a simultaneous effort by the army to prepare for a war with the Soviet Union in Asia.

Especially after the middle of 1936, the various national security elites—the prime ministers, foreign ministers, the two service ministers and the two chiefs of staff—no longer attempted to deal with their disagreements by attempting to compromise or seek consensus. They simply stated their views in various policy statements that coexisted "side-by-side" (Bix 2000, 308–10). This represented a simple but uneasy solution. It suggested that the interests of all parties could be satisfied equally without making any difficult choices and without recognizing the consequences. Thus according to the August 1936 Criteria of National Policy, the Imperial Army could advance on the Chinese mainland while the Imperial Navy could advance into the vaguely defined "Southern Oceans."

The army and navy tended to take different approaches to the issue of Japanese expansion. While both favored expansion, the navy, dependent on foreign oil supplies, naturally tended to emphasize Southeast Asia, where supplies of oil might be secured. The army, more militant and ideological than the navy, focused on China as part of a more general strategy to systematically control the economies of Asia. By 1941, however, it was the army that was pressing for war against Britain and the United States. While the army generally had more political clout than the navy and was usually able to get its way, the Imperial Navy was not without power. Generally, the navy was the most reluctant of the military factions to pursue aggression abroad, because it was well aware of its disadvantages compared to the British and the American navies. Presumably, it could have prevented war in December 1941 by simply refusing to accept the army's proposals. However, the likely consequence of such a refusal was an army coup or a direct interservice clash. The Imperial Navy's leaders, Chief of Staff Nagano and Navy Minister Shimada, believed it preferable to back the army's plans for war than to face the unthinkable: internal war between the army and navy (Marder 1981, 254; Dassel 1998, 135–36). In the final analysis, even Emperor Hirohito believed that expansion of the war to the south of China, including the possibility of war with the United States, was preferable to paralysis and continued conflict over the proper strategic course. The emperor "expressed fears that not taking some kind of warlike action . . . would jeopardize the imperial system of government and eventually damage the imperial institution itself. For Hirohito domestic conflicts were more dangerous than the escalation of war, for they carried the risk of eroding the monarchy" (Bix 2000, 429).

Bureaucratic Politics

The notion that a government's policy (war) may be highly influenced by the political decision-making process is well understood. Much of the above discussion is consistent with insights from the bureaucratic politics model of decision making associated with Graham Allison (1971). The bureaucratic politics model argues that government decisions are not necessarily the result of a rational process; instead, decisions are made through a conflictual political process by individuals who represent institutions with different interests, outlooks and preferences (like the Imperial Navy and Imperial Army). Any decision, therefore, reflects the prevailing balance of power among the various competing individuals and groups involved in the process.

Though a general consensus existed in Japan about the desirability of imperial expansion, there was significant conflict over how, where, when, and against whom this policy should be carried out. In other words, there were conflicts over the tactics and strategy of imperial expansion and war. As we shall see, the decisions for war were truly collective decisions made among representatives of competing political institutions who saw issues from different perspectives and had different institutional interests. The Imperial Army, Imperial Navy, and Foreign Ministry constantly blocked one another's desires (Bix 2000, 429). Decisions were the result of a political process involving lengthy internal conflict, extended debate, compromise, logrolling, coalition building, power plays, independent action by policy implementers, and back-stage resorts to imperial authority. At many points in the process, especially as the crucial decision on attacking the United States neared, the debates among government leaders were so contentious that "cooling off" breaks were required. The process was clearly incremental in nature with a significant amount of agonized second-guessing over past policies. In addition, domestic political considerations were important for many of the participants.

To arrive at a decision for war required the formation, at minimum, of a majority coalition. In the end such a coalition was formed among leaders of the army and navy and the civilian cabinet politicians. Perhaps the crucial component in the coalition was the Imperial Navy, whose conversion to the prowar stance was the key factor in a long, drawn-out process. In short, the process is entirely consistent with what political scientists have called the bureaucratic politics model of decision making.

The bureaucratic politics model also predicts that since policymakers and policy implementers are not necessarily the same people, "official" policy may be frequently undermined and overridden by those in charge of implementation. This was certainly the case in Japan. Given its organizational autonomy and its privileged relationship with the emperor, the military had considerable control over its own activities abroad and it also proved adept at using its force abroad to create military and political faits accompli. Examples of such faits accompli are well known. Japan's Kwantung Army arranged the murder of Manchurian warlord Chang Tso-lin in 1928 in order to ignite a full-scale Japanese invasion of Manchuria. This gambit was unsuccessful, but three years later autonomous actions by the Kwantung Army precipitated the Manchurian Incident, and local Japanese army leaders frequently initiated incursions beyond Manchuria in defiance of Tokyo. Subsequent independent actions by the army in the 1937 "China Incident" were instrumental in pushing the government toward full-scale war in the Far East.

LONG-TERM FACTORS AT THE NATION-STATE LEVEL OF ANALYSIS

Nationalism and Militarism

While Japan's victories over China and Russia at the turn of the century strengthened its sense of cultural nationalism, a major step toward a more militant nationalism took place in the 1920s. The enthronement of Hirohito marked a new "emperor cult" and concerted efforts by the state at "national spiritual mobilization" (Bix 2000, 195, 201). The Education Ministry and other government agencies propagated an elaborate mythic history of the Japanese state, which was said to have been founded in 660 BC by Emperor Jimmu, a direct descendent of the sun goddess, Amaterasu. This history not only gave the emperor a divine origin, but it attributed racial, cultural, and moral purity to the Japanese people (Dower 1986, 205, 217). Prior to this, the Japanese had never actually worshiped the emperor as a supreme, living deity.

The new nationalism, referred to as kodo, the "imperial way," was a homegrown concoction that blended ideas from Shintoism, Buddhism, neo-Confucianism, and Western monarchism. Of fundamental importance was the fact that kodo preached Japanese superiority to Western political values such as liberalism, democracy, capitalism, materialism, and individualism. Kodo spread widely in both popular and elite circles.

Japanese nationalism incorporated desires for outward expansion, not unlike the idea of manifest destiny in the United States. Japan was believed to have a historic mission to expand into East Asia to secure peace and prosperity for its peoples and to protect (and indeed to purify) them from Western imperial oppression and Western culture (Mueller 1989, 72). Moreover, there was also a millenarian facet of kodo, emanating particularly from the Nichiren sect of Japanese

Buddhism. Specifically, there was the belief that the Japanese state was uniquely positioned not only to lead an Asian renaissance but also to overthrow the current unjust world order and unify the world.

Kodo was also "linked to a willingness to use force against those who rejected [the emperor's] fatherly benevolence" (Bix 2000, 11). In the words of a 1934 Imperial Army pamphlet, war was declared to be "the father of creation and the mother of culture"; and there was a mystical belief in an apocalyptic final victory. War was seen as a creative and constructive force having the ability to "purify" the nation and the world (Bix 2000, 326–27; Dower 1986, 215–17; Mueller 1989, 72). Moreover, since the emperor was a living god and the state was the incarnation of morality and justice, by definition Japan engaged only in "just wars." Wars became "sacred struggles" in pursuit of a national mission to unify the world under the benevolent rule of the emperor. The goal of war was frequently seen as the creation of a "new world order" that would "enable all nations and races to assume their proper place in the world" (Dower 1986, 205). The more concrete meaning of the "proper place" of other nations and races was that they would be subservient to Japanese leadership.

The Nichirens strongly opposed Taisho democracy and were especially hostile to a Western-style parliamentary democracy. They maintained that the foundation of the *kokutai* (the national polity) was the direct personal rule and absolute authority of the emperor. Not incidentally, many top-level military officers and right-wing civilian politicians were Nichirens, including Ishiwara Kanji and Honjo Shigeru, the "rogue officers" behind the Manchurian Incident. The Nichiren movement was a driving force behind Japanese ultranationalism and it was instrumental in fostering the idea of a Japanese national mission to unify the world (Bix 2000, 163–69).

A second, more ancient, cultural strand meshed with the new emperor-centered nationalism. Even though the samurai, Japan's traditional military class, had been abolished and universal conscription had been adopted in 1873, strong military values persisted. An important legacy of the samurai period in Japan was the continued existence, though in altered form, of the *bushido*, the "way of the warrior" code of the samurai warriors. In early-twentieth-century Japan *bushido* had become more or less institutionalized as a general "legitimating ideology" of the ruling military elites (Snyder 1991, 131–32). The samurai code, like many honor codes, glorified loyalty, obedience to superiors, military discipline, and honorable death as the highest personal values, and it provided cultural support for a belligerent, macho, zero-sum approach to interpersonal, intergroup, and interstate relations. After Japan's victory over Russia in 1905, Japanese army manuals were rewritten to emphasize the *bushido* code (Bix 2000, 34, 51). And the early-seventeenth-century primer of samurai morality, the *Haga Kure*, was revived as a popular classic during the early Showa era. There was a decidedly romantic component to the samurai spirit: a willingness to take up any challenge, despite monumental odds. General Tojo's justification for the dangerous attack on Pearl Harbor, that sometimes it was necessary "to make a great leap into a ravine with one's eyes closed," is often cited as an example of this (Butow 1961, 267).

Starting in 1873, all able-bodied Japanese males were required to serve three years in the army and four years in the reserve. Many learned to read and write during their period of military service. As one would expect, conscripts got a good dose of nationalist propaganda and military values in their education (Buruma 2003, 54–55). In 1925 Japan established a mandatory system of military training in the middle, upper and normal schools. Active-duty officers provided instruction to school children, inculcating military values and "right thinking" in the youth of Japan. And in general, the education system "systematically and uncritically taught the virtues of patriotism and allegiance to the Emperor" and glorified Japanese military victories such as its defeat of Russia in 1905 (LaFeber 1997, 42, 91). To put it more bluntly, "national education was military education," and the spread of the samurai ethic was a deliberate national policy. Emperor Hirohito himself was educated by military instructors steeped in the *bushido* tradition and had a military style education, though combined with instruction in the liberal arts and sciences.

As in Germany, Japanese militarism and nationalism were linked to ideas of racial superiority. Japanese nationalists used social Darwinistic principles to demonstrate Japanese superiority, citing Japan's self-propelled rise to great power status since 1868. Emperor Hirohito's tutor in international affairs, Sugirua Shigetake, passed on to his pupil a neo-Darwinian view of international politics in which the white and yellow races were "locked in conflict and competition" (Bix 2000, 66, 148). An essential part of Japanese nationalism was contempt for the backwardness of other Asian peoples. In this view, some Japanese tended to see themselves as akin to (white) Europeans, while the Chinese were backward (colored) Asians. Japanese colonial conquests over such people were a sign of Japan's relative greatness and modernity (Buruma 2003, 50–51; Dower 1986, 208–9). For example, Prime Minister Konoe saw the world in terms of racial conflict between East and West and "cast the problems besetting Sino-Japanese relations in terms of conflict between the white and yellow races and asserted the spiritual superiority of the Japanese over their pale opponents" (Bix 2000, 266; Butow 1961, 101). At the same time, many Japanese elites tended to think that the Asian heritage shared with China made the Japanese brand of imperialism more acceptable to the Chinese than Western imperialism (Butow 1961, 28).

Though the parallel should not be overstated, the nationalism of the early Showa period had much in common with European fascism: deification of the national racial community and its embodiment in a mystical cult figure, militarism and the glorification of war, political dictatorship, the idea of national mission, emphasis on moral regeneration and national spirit, and inflammatory nationalist rhetoric (Bix 2000, 203; Buruma 2003, 53). Ultimately, the presence of nationalism, militarism, and racism were part of the worldview of the Japanese leadership and could not but color their views of the world and Japan's role in it. They were part and parcel of the perceptual lens through which the Japanese political and military elite viewed the world.

LONG-TERM FACTORS AT THE INTERNATIONAL SYSTEM LEVEL: CHANGES IN SYSTEMIC DISTRIBUTION OF POWER

Important changes in the structure of the international system occurred throughout the first half of the twentieth century. These massive structural changes created conditions that directly led to World War I. In the aftermath of that war, global power distribution continued to change, increasing the likelihood of a second wave of warfare in Europe and in Asia.

The United States and Japan joined the club of great powers at the top of the international system at almost the same time and in much the same way. Both countries were prototypical ascendant states in the late nineteenth century. Both experienced rapid economic growth and modernization. Both became great powers with convincing victories over traditional European powers—the United States in the Spanish-American War in 1898 and Japan in the Russo-Japanese War of 1904–1905. And both were on the winning side in the first global war of the twentieth century.

Restructuring of global power relationships continued in the wake of World War I. Of the major states one might have predicted to dominate global politics in the third decade of the twentieth century, Germany had been soundly defeated and reduced to penury and Russia lay devastated by revolution and civil war. The biggest beneficiary of the war was the United States. As Paul Kennedy points out, the vibrant nature of the U.S. economy put the United States on a course to overtake the economies of Europe in total output by 1925; WWI merely reduced the time table (Kennedy 1987, 280–81). But the United States, while becoming an economic giant, shunned the role of global leadership and retreated to isolationism. Japanese power also emerged much enhanced from World War I. During the war Japan became a net creditor, its imports and exports tripled, and its manufacturing boomed, including its vital chemical, electrical, and shipbuilding industries. By 1938 it had overtaken France in its manufacturing and industrial production (Kennedy 1987, 298–99).

The structure of the international system in the period between WWI and WWII can be characterized in a number of ways. First, the system was power multipolar, with a large number of great powers of somewhat (but not entirely) equal strength. Second, by the late 1930s the international system was also becoming polarized (or bipolar) in terms of its alliance configurations as the numerous great powers were dividing themselves into two rival alliance blocs. Third, the period was also characterized by a continued deconcentration of power. The previous systemic hegemon (Britain) had lost her economic and military edge over the other great powers, creating an unstable hierarchy—a dangerous systemic condition in which the disparity of power among major actors was greatly diminished (Geller and Singer 1998, 139). Moreover, no clear replacement had emerged to take her place—portending the possibility of a dangerous conflict over global leadership. All of these conditions—power multipolarity, alliance creation, alliance polarization, and deconcentration of global power—have similar effects. They create uncertainty about power and status, they increase anxiety about security, they bring about perceptions of threat, and they increase the potential for risk taking—all at the same time that the system's dominant state is unable to enforce security. They are all reputed to be associated with a greater probability of major power warfare (Cashman 1993, 224–78).

But it was the general nature of constantly shifting power relations that is perhaps most useful in explaining the war in the Pacific. Charles Doran's power cycle theory helps us understand the situation. According to Doran (1991, 133, 154–57), the interwar period was characterized by rapid structural change, as indicated by the fact that a great number of major powers were going through critical points in the years immediately preceding the war. Between 1916 and 1945 five great powers passed through critical points in their power cycles—France, Germany, Italy, Japan, and China. For each of these states, the change in their relative positions meant a wrenching change in foreign policy. The fact that so many states were undergoing these changes created a ripple effect throughout the entire system. Most important for the events that were to follow, Germany reached its second inflection point between 1933 and 1938, and Japan reached its first inflection point between 1939 and 1944, just as WWII started in Europe.

Japan's passage through the first inflection point created anxiety about the slow-down in her industrial advance, an anxiety illustrated by her search for raw materials such as oil and iron ore. More generally, it created anxiety and doubt about its ability to maintain its place in the competition for power with the Western great powers. With future prospects appearing to dim, Japan might never be in a better position. Its economic, and therefore military, vulnerability appeared increasingly problematic. In this respect, the strategy adopted by the United States to deal with Japan exacerbated the problem: "By cutting off sales of raw materials and recycled metals, the United States threatened Japan with future constraints on economic growth. At precisely the time that Japan discovered its own economic decline in growth rate . . . it was confronted with external resource shortages that seemed to confirm its worst fears about decline" (Doran 1991, 156).

All of this led, eventually, to an increased willingness by Japan's leaders to risk the use of force to acquire access to the resources of Southeast Asia and Indonesia, thus creating conflict between Japan and the Western allies.

Status Discrepancy

Despite Japan's economic and military achievements in the first three decades of the twentieth century, Japanese elites still perceived their country to be a second-class citizen among the great powers. In this respect Japan was the typical "dissatisfied overachiever" described in Johann Galtung's status discrepancy theory (Galtung 1964). Victories over China (1894–1895) and Russia (1904–1905) proved that Japan had achieved great power rank on the military dimension, and it was gaining rapidly in the economic sphere. But Japanese elites perceived other states were unwilling to grant her the political status (and thus the increase in her international roles) commensurate with her new power (Iriye 1987, 56). One historian (Beasley 1987, 251) observes that in the period after the Russo-Japanese War, Japan behaved like "an abrasive latecomer, seeking equality of esteem, not only through an insistence on treaty rights, but also through the acquisition of spheres of influence." Japanese elites regarded their country as a "have-not" power in a struggle against the Western "haves," such as Britain and the United States (Iriye 1987, 56). Japan constantly pushed for rights in China equal to those of the Western imperial powers. In the 1890s, as the Western powers finally relinquished the rights granted to them in Japan by the old unequal treaties, the Japanese were anxious to act like the Europeans and inflict their own unequal treaties on the Chinese (Buruma 2003, 51). However, the "spoils" of its victories over China and Russia were reduced by the other great powers.

In the 1920s it seemed to many that Japan had indeed achieved its goal of membership in the club of great powers. It became a full-fledged member of the Washington conference system. It signed the Washington Naval Treaty, the Nine Power Treaty, and the Four Power Treaty. It was a member of the League of Nations and had signed the 1928 Kellogg-Briand Pact that renounced war as an instrument of national policy. It had adopted the capitalist economic system and accepted the gold standard that underlay that system. In other words, it was an important participant in the basic institutions and rules that were part of an evolving international global structure (Iriye 1987, 3).

But Japan continued to hold grievances against the "haves." First, Japanese elites perceived that within the Asian regional system created by the Washington treaties, Japan was treated as a "junior partner" rather than a full member of the team (Vasquez 1998, 196–97). While the system granted Japan equal footing with the other great powers in China, this was an area in which Japan believed that it should be granted status as the *primary* regional power. Second, the West refused to adopt a Japanese-sponsored racial equality clause into the League of Nations Covenant. Third, the Washington Naval Treaty locked Japan into numerical inferiority with Britain and the U.S., and the Western powers refused to accept equality as the basis for future arms control agreements. The fourth grievance was the discriminatory immigration policy followed by the United States: the 1924 U.S. Immigration Act, which excluded Japanese from eligibility for immigration into the United States.

As a result of these grievances, commitment to a liberal international order coexisted uneasily in Japan with realpolitik "old thinking." Forces on the political Right saw war as a vital, natural, and progressive force that gave effect to the most heroic aspects of mankind. They believed that national security "could only be measured in the hard cash of border adjustments, colonial acquisitions, and reparations" (Kennedy 1987, 284). Shouldn't Japanese economic and military power be translated into a "special" position in Asia—particularly in China? Wasn't Japan entitled to its own sphere of influence, just as the United States? Wouldn't adherence to a liberal world order that sought to promote peace by maintaining the status quo permanently condemn Japan to the position of a second-rate power? Many Japanese in the 1930s and 1940s believed that her future economic development depended on her dominance in Asia, particularly in China, while participation in an integrated global system would condemn Japan to economic dependence on the West. The Open Door would simply open China to exploitation by others.

Essentially, Japan—like Germany—had become a **revisionist state** dedicated to changing the nature of the international system and Japan's role in it. And her newly acquired military and economic might gave her the wherewithal to pursue this goal. Japan's adventure in Manchuria in 1931 signaled that the dominant political coalition in Japan had rejected the Wilsonian world order and Western dominance of the system and had decided to replace it—at least in Asia—with a system based on older, realpolitik principles. Essentially, Japan hoped the West would recognize the new regional status quo created by Japanese imperialism. In return for Western recognition of Japanese primacy in China, Japan would guarantee peace and order in East Asia (Iriye 1987, 22). The

United States and its partners, however, were unwilling to permit "flexibility" in the rules of the game to grant Japan a special status in Asia (Vasquez 1998, 197, 218). Japan's resort to imperialistic, unilateral, autarkic, regionalist policies were unacceptable to the Western "haves," who believed in an integrated, global system based on liberal principles.

WEAKNESS OF SYSTEMIC NORMS PROHIBITING THE USE OF FORCE

Another background condition in the international system has to do with the presence or absence of rules against the use of force. Vasquez (1993, 263–91) argues that wars are more likely when the international system lacks strong rules for the peaceful management of international conflict, lacks established and legitimate norms that limit the use of force, and lacks robust international organizations capable of resolving international disputes through peaceful means. The absence (or weakness) of such rules and such organizations can be seen as a "permissive cause" of war, especially in the presence of an alternative "realist" international culture that emphasizes forceful actions to resolve problems.

In the aftermath of WWI, the old balance of power politics was repudiated, and the victorious allies attempted (though somewhat halfheartedly) to construct a new global order centered in the West and motivated by the ideals of Wilsonian liberalism. Rules and organizations to promote peaceful dispute resolution were constructed—embodied in the Kellogg-Briand Pact and the League of Nations Covenant. The majority of elite and popular sentiment in the interwar period, at least in the West, believed that war had become morally repugnant and economically counterproductive and that institutions like the League of Nations should henceforth render war impossible. With regard to Asia in particular, treaties associated with the Washington conference system attempted to construct a regime for peaceful conflict resolution. These rules and institutions were fragile and weak, and competing values and practices (especially the realpolitik approach) continued.

Unable to win Western acceptance of Japanese dominance in Asia, Japan eventually repudiated the Washington conference system and withdrew from the League of Nations.

The regional system in Asia returned to the pre-Wilsonian world. The breakdown of the (already weak) league between 1931 and 1933 and the Washington conference system removed international institutional constraints on Japanese actions.

THE DYADIC LEVEL OF ANALYSIS: CONFLICT SPIRALS, TERRITORIAL DISPUTES, AND ENDURING RIVALRIES

The central dynamic leading to the Pacific War in 1941 was a conflict spiral involving the United States and Japan. It is possible to think of U.S.-Japanese relations from the 1890s onward as a single, long (and discontinuous) conflict spiral, and certainly the perception of the United States and Japan as rivals goes back to this period. But the rivals became trapped in a more intense phase of the conflict spiral from the Manchurian Incident onward. It is a spiral that picks up considerable steam in the last year before the attack on Pearl Harbor. While expansionist pressures propelled each country toward the Asia-Pacific area, putting the two rising great powers on a collision course, conflictual interactions between Japan and the United States were largely a product of Japanese expansion in East Asia and American reaction to that expansion.

Moreover, the U.S.-Japanese conflict dynamic grew out of, and merged with, an older Japanese-Chinese rivalry that dated to the 1870s (Goertz and Diehl 1998, 107). This conflict expanded as supporters of China (mainly the United States) developed their own rivalries with Japan. Territorial disputes, which were at the root of the Sino-Japanese conflict, "shaped Japan's relations and rivalries with all the other major states" and were "the central factor escalating hostilities in the various rivalries and eventually pushed them all to war" (Vasquez 1998, 196–97). Repeated crisis interactions negatively affected both the internal political environments in the rival states and subsequent interstate interactions. Political elites in each country increasingly took hard-line positions with regard to their international rivals. Over time, these interactions took on more threatening dimensions, leading eventually to war. We will now look at the development of this conflict spiral.

The Rise of Japan, Rivalry, and the Roots of the Conflict Spiral

The new power of Japan was first demonstrated in its victory in the Sino-Japanese War of 1894–1895, a war fought primarily over the control of Korea and against a China overwhelmed by foreign penetration. In the Treaty of Shimonoseki, which followed the war, Korea was granted independence from China (leading to de facto Japanese control there), and Japan acquired Taiwan, the Pescadores, the Liaotung Peninsula in Manchuria, and an indemnity. However, diplomatic pressure from Russia, Germany and France forced Japan to give up Liaotung. (The Russians secured a lease on the territory from China.) Japanese elites, always sensitive to any slight to Japan's international status, were deeply offended. Nevertheless, Japan emerged as an imperial power in Asia and with a growing military. It also found great power backing in the form of the Anglo-Japanese Alliance of 1902.

At roughly the same time, the United States, by virtue of its victory over Spain and its acquisition of the Philippines in 1898, had become a Pacific power. With outlandish expectations of benefits from an enormous "China trade," the primary American consideration in Asia was the perpetuation of the Open Door Policy. The Open Door, dating to diplomatic correspondence by Secretary of State John Hay in 1899, proclaimed the principle that any economic concessions or rights guaranteed to one foreign power in China should be guaranteed to all, thereby granting all foreign powers an equal access to China's markets and resources.

Japan's expansion into Manchuria conflicted with the imperial ambitions of neighboring Russia. Conflicts in that region (which was officially part of the Chinese empire) led to the Russo-Japanese War. While Japan lost more than one hundred thousand lives in this war, her victory over Russia—initiated by a pre-emptive attack on Russian positions in Port Arthur—solidified her position as a great power. Through the Treaty of Portsmouth, mediated by President Theodore Roosevelt, Japan received the Russian lease on the Liaotung Peninsula, rights to the Southern Manchurian Railway, the southern half of Sakhalin Island, recognition of her paramount interests in Korea, and the restoration of (fictitious) Chinese sovereignty over Manchuria, but no indemnity. The Japanese public had expected more and felt betrayed by Roosevelt. The ensuing anti-American riots were so violent that martial law had to be declared to end them.

Japan's two wars in Asia changed the international environment. They made Japan a great power, they gave her possessions on the Asian mainland and an appetite for more, they diminished Russian and Chinese power, and they created continuing tensions with the other great powers who considered themselves players in the region. They created anti-Japanese colonial movements in Korea (which Japan formally annexed in 1910) and elsewhere, and they generally helped to stimulate Chinese nationalism against foreign intrusion. They also helped to perpetuate Japanese beliefs of national and racial superiority and a sense that Japan was destined to become the leading power in Asia. Finally, they helped to institutionalize the power of the military within the Japanese political system. None of these would bode well for the future of peace in Asia.

In response to Japanese victories over China and Russia and to her growing imperial acquisitions, American and Japanese elites began for the first time to see each other as rivals—economically and militarily. Thompson (2001, 572) dates the rivalry to 1900. After Japan's victory over China, leading supporters of naval power in the United States like Theodore Roosevelt and Alfred Thayer Mahan pushed the government to build more battleships so that the U.S. Pacific Fleet would not fall behind the Japanese (LaFeber 1997, 56). In 1905–1908 there was much discussion of a potential U.S.-Japanese war, and fanciful stories of future war between the two new Pacific powers were prevalent in the media of both countries (Small 1980, 235). In 1906 the Roosevelt administration actually initiated the first American war plans against Japan, and the president sent secret orders to the commander of the Philippines to prepare his forces for a possible Japanese attack (Butow 1961, 11).

Japan's rivalry with the west temporarily abated when it joined with Britain, France, Russia, and the United States in World War I. In the course of the war, its forces moved southeast from the Liaotung Peninsula to occupy the Shantung Peninsula in China and took the port of Tsingtao from the Germans. In 1915 Tokyo issued its infamous Twenty-One Demands to Yuan Shih-kai's Chinese government. These demands—for control over territory, resources, and economic enterprises in Shantung, southern Manchuria, Inner Mongolia, and Fukien Province—alienated Western states, which were appalled at the enormity of Japan's new ambitions. Japan also aligned itself with the Russian White forces in the civil war against the Bolshevik's Soviet government. Its Siberian Expedition (1918 to 1922) was largely motivated by hopes of territorial gains at the expense of Russia.

Talk of a Japanese-American war surfaced again in Japan between 1919 and 1922, promoted by the media. The hysteria was due to the accumulation of a number of grievances: lingering resentment over the Treaty of Portsmouth; discrimination against Japanese in the United States; U.S. opposition to the Twenty One Demands, to Japan's continued presence in Shantung, and to its overlong occupation of Siberia and northern Sakhalin; the refusal to include in the League of Nations Covenant a racial equality clause introduced by the Japanese; and the refusal of the United States and Britain to accept Japanese parity in naval forces. At the end of WWI, military planners in Tokyo and Washington alike saw the other country as the most likely adversary in a future war (LaFeber 1997, 89–90, 122). Naval rivalry had something to do with this. Both countries had been propelled to great power status on the basis of naval victories over traditional powers. Since 1900 the U.S. Navy had advanced from seventh place to second or third, behind Britain and Germany; Japan had risen to fifth (LaFeber 1997, 89).

Late-nineteenth-century Japan adopted not only Western technology but also traditional Western attitudes toward foreign relations. From the Meiji restoration through its emergence as a great power, Japan had followed a foreign policy typical for nineteenth-century European great powers—a policy based on a realpolitik worldview and centered around military power, colonial conquest, spheres of influence, bilateral treaties, balance of power politics, and the use of war as the ultimate right of a sovereign state (Vasquez 1998, 196). As a victor over Russia in 1905 and as an ally in the war against the Central Powers, Japanese leaders had expected that joining the great power club would also mean that Japan would become a full-fledged partner in the imperialist club. They believed Japan should have rights in China similar to American rights in, say, Cuba or Panama. Secret war aims formulated during WWI proposed that "all of China was to become a Japanese protectorate, the Russian sphere of interest in northern Manchuria was to be pushed back, the resource-rich Dutch East Indies (present day Indonesia) were to be wrested from Dutch control, and the West was to be put on notice that Asia should be controlled by Asians (that is, Japanese)" (Bix 2000, 146).

As we have seen, just as Japan was getting good at the game of realpolitik, her Western counterparts changed the rules. In the wake of World War I, liberal idealism replaced realpolitik in the capitals of Europe. Japan's dependence on the United States for imports of steel, oil, and other raw materials, and for much-needed investment capital meant that its expansive goals had to be abandoned; it was necessary to cooperate with Western powers. The leader of the pro-cooperation forces in Japan was Shidehara Kijuro, the Japanese ambassador to the United States and, later, Japan's foreign minister. Cooperation with the West, however, came with a price: Japanese respect for Western rights and interests in China. The November 1917 Lansing-Isshi Agreement attempted to reconcile some of these conflicting positions. The agreement, initially kept secret, stated that the two sides accepted that "territorial propinquity creates special relations," and the United States thereby specifically recognized that Japan had "special interests" in those areas of China contiguous to Japanese possessions, such as Manchuria and perhaps the Shantung Peninsula. On the other hand, Japan was forced to agree that neither Chinese sovereignty nor the principle of the Open Door should be impaired by the activity of foreign powers in China. Japan would refrain from seeking special rights in China at the expense of others.

In the 1920s, therefore, Japan joined the liberal new world order, though this stance was less than universally popular at home. Japan became a member of the

League of Nations and signed the Kellogg-Briand Pact. It also ratified three treaties associated with the Wilsonian liberal ideas of capitalism, free trade, arms control, and international cooperation that had been negotiated at the Washington Conference of 1921–1922. The Four Power Treaty between Britain, France, Japan, and the United States, which replaced the Anglo-Japanese Alliance, guaranteed the Pacific possessions of the signatories. The Four Powers also pledged to consult with one another when crises threatened international stability. In the Nine Power Treaty, Japan—led by its chief delegate, Shidehara—joined with the other great powers in pledging to respect the status quo in the Pacific and to uphold the sovereignty and territorial integrity of China (though, importantly, Japan's activities in Manchuria were generally exempt from this) and to generally cooperate on Chinese affairs. Treaty language also committed the signatories to the Open Door Policy's equal opportunity economic policies in China. As part of the agreement, Japan gave up the Shantung Peninsula, though it kept control of the key railways there.

And finally, Japan ratified the Five Power Naval Arms Limitation Treaty, which committed Japan to a ratio of 6:10:10 in capital ships compared to the United States and Britain. (France and Italy were each limited to a ratio of 3:4:10.) The three Washington treaties officially recognized Japan's status as one of the world's great powers and they assured the hegemony of the treaty powers in Asia. Japan was granted de facto superiority in the Pacific, and its special position in Manchuria appeared to have been recognized. Japanese policymakers hoped that these treaty commitments would be compatible with Japan's colonial interests (primarily in Manchuria) and they assumed that the Western powers would accept Japanese domination in Asia (Bix 2000, 150). In this assumption they were to be gravely disappointed.

The death of the Taisho emperor in 1926 and the succession of Hirohito mark a transition. Japan began to abandon the cooperative policies of the immediate postwar period and moved toward a more imperial and confrontational policy. Prime Minister Wakatsuki and his accommodationist foreign minister, Shidehara, fell from power in 1927 and were replaced by General Tanaka Gi'ichi, an anti-Soviet, "Manchuria-first" nationalist.

In 1927 and 1928, amid the uncertainties of the civil war in China, Japan's military renewed its interest in the Shantung Peninsula in China. Chiang Kai-shek had established his nationalist (Kuomintang) government in Nanking in April 1927 and resumed his "Northern Expedition" to unify China in the spring of 1928. Japanese dominance in Manchuria was clearly threatened by the extension of Nationalist control and the reassertion of Chinese sovereignty over Manchuria. As the civil war engulfed China, Japanese leaders perceived a greater need to protect the lives and property of Japanese citizens living in China. In March 1927 Nationalist forces had pillaged the Japanese, British, and American consulates in Nanking. The two Western powers retaliated militarily, but Japan refrained from doing so. The acts were sensationalized by the Japanese press, and eventually the new emperor agreed to dispatch troops to Shantung Province. When an additional contingent of troops was sent to the port of Tsingtao in April 1928, the local Japanese commander, General Fukuda, exceeded his orders and pushed his forces inland, resulting in clashes with Chinese troops. Reinforcements were sent to Tsinan, where the seventeen thousand Japanese troops "unleashed a reign of terror" on the Chinese residents (Bix 2000, 214–15). However, in spite of the army's desire for a direct intervention in northern China to stop the advance of Chiang Kai-shek's forces, the Tanaka government withdrew Japanese forces from Shantung in March 1929.

Meanwhile, Japanese attention was also engaged in Manchuria. While legally Chinese territory, Manchuria's southern part was controlled by Japan and it was quickly becoming an integral part of the Japanese economy. By 1931 Japanese investments in Manchuria totaled over $500 million, and her coal and other mineral deposits had become crucial to Japanese industrialization (LaFeber 1997, 161).

In early June 1928 the Japanese army made its first of many attempts to take direct control of Japanese foreign policy. Senior officers of the Japanese Kwantung Army, led by Col. Komoto Daisaku, assassinated the local Manchurian warlord Chang Tso-lin, whose attempt to consolidate control of Manchuria and northern China threatened the interests of both Japan and Chiang Kai-shek. Kwantung army spokesmen alleged that the assassins were rogue elements of China's Southern Army. Colonel Komoto and the Kwantung Army assumed that the Tanaka government secretly wanted the army to take action to separate Manchuria from the rest of China, and they hoped that the "assassination" would help spur a decision by the government to seize control of Manchuria (Beasley 1987, 187). Politicians in Tokyo were not taken in by this subterfuge, and neither the government nor the army took steps to exploit the situation. But when Prime Minister Tanaka's attempt to punish those officers responsible for the assassination received no support, the Tanaka cabinet fell. (Chang Tso-lin was succeeded by his son, Chang Hsueh-liang, who immediately recognized Chiang Kai-shek's Nationalist regime, granting official Kuomintang control over Manchuria.)

The new prime minster, Hamaguchi Oschi, was a politician from the more moderate Minseito Party. In the aftermath of the Chang Tso-lin incident, Hamaguchi's foreign minister, Shidehara Kijuro, recognized Chiang's Kuomintang government in China and attempted to negotiate a diplomatic settlement with it. Prime Minister Hamaguchi also forced the navy to accept the new 1930 London Naval Treaty's expanded limits on naval vessels (light cruisers and submarines) at the ratio of 6.975 to 10 for the U.S. and Britain. The domestic fallout of the treaty in Japan was direct and violent: Hamaguchi was assassinated by a right-wing "patriot." The successor government of Prime Minister Wakatsuki Reijiro kept Shidehara as foreign minister.

The Manchurian Incident: The Conflict Spiral Enters Its Intense Phase

Manchuria was the name given to the three northeastern provinces of China, Heilungkiang, Kirin, and Liaoning. Bordered on the north and northeast by Russia, on the west by Mongolia, on the southwest by China, on the southeast by Korea, and with its Liaotung Peninsula jutting into the Yellow Sea, Manchuria was strategically located. In the period after the Russo-Japanese War, Manchuria was legally Chinese territory; however, its northern part was controlled by Russia and its southern part by Japan. Both major powers operated important economic leaseholds (such as railways) granted to them in unequal treaties by China.

The September 1931 Manchurian Incident was the first major crisis among the great powers in Asia. Japan at the time controlled the areas along the South Manchurian Railway, including most of the cities of Harbin and Mukden. The port cities of Port Arthur and Darien were under direct Japanese administration. The army, which tended to see Manchuria not as a legitimate part of China but as a lawless "no-man's-land" to which Japan would bring order, wanted more (Buruma 2003, 88). Perhaps the foremost motive for the land grab was the desire to develop Manchuria in order to produce Japanese economic **autarky**. At any rate, field officers in the Kwantung Army—aided by elements of the army general staff and the war ministry—resumed their defiance of official government policy and conspired through unilateral action to bring the three Manchurian provinces under Japanese control.

While rumors of the Kwantung Army's imminent action abounded, efforts of the government to prevent it were decidedly halfhearted, and the plot was carried to fruition. The planning of the operation was led by Komoto's replacement in Port Arthur, Lt. Col. Ishiwara Kanji, one of the Imperial Army's top strategists and a leader of the Total War faction, and by the senior staff officer at Mukden, Col. Itagaki Seishiro. The plot included the newly appointed Kwantung Army commander, Gen. Honjo Shigeru, as well as senior officials within the Army General Staff; even the army minister, Gen. Minami Jiro, was aware of the plan (Bix 2000, 230).

On September 18, 1931, the plotters planted and detonated a bomb—without any serious damage—on the tracks of the Japanese railway north of Mukden. The "attack" on the South Manchuria Railway was blamed on the army of Chinese warlord Chang Hsueh-liang, and bodies of several dead Chinese were planted at the site to increase the believability of the claim. Within hours, Japanese troops attacked the barracks of the Chinese Manchurian Army in Mukden. Then the Kwantung Army commander, on his own, ordered a military "response" against Chinese troops and garrisons, not just in Mukden, but elsewhere in Manchuria (Iriye 1987, 8). The emperor learned of the incident through newspaper reports the next day.

The Kwantung Army quickly advanced beyond the area of the Japanese leasehold. When Japanese forces ran into heavy resistance, reinforcements were sent from Korea without authorization from the government or the emperor. The cabinet approved the action after the fact. All local attempts to settle the affair peacefully were overruled as interference with the command prerogatives of the military. Although the cabinet's initial reaction was to prevent the expansion of the fighting, this policy was willfully ignored by the military in Manchuria whose insubordination was backed by the war minister. When it became known that the emperor had approved the cabinet's nonexpansion policy, army spokesmen brazenly suggested that the emperor was being advised by traitors (Butow 1961, 37).

The government covered up the conspiracy, and all official press releases accused the Chinese of blowing up the railway. The actions taken by the military in the Manchurian Incident, sensationalized in the Japanese press, were very popular in Japan and served to increase support for militarists and to weaken support for accommodationists such as Wakatsuki and Shidehara (Vasquez 1998, 198).

The Wakatsuki government, receiving no support from the military and little from the emperor, resigned in December 1931, to be replaced by the government of Prime Minister Inukai Tsuyoshi of the more hawkish Seiyukai Party. Inukai's new minister of war was the militant leader of the Imperial Way faction, Gen. Araki Sadao.

Eventually, the local Chinese forces were defeated, and the three provinces of Manchuria were detached from China and renamed Manchukuo. By March 1932 a puppet government of "Manchukuo," headed by the last Manchu emperor of China, Henry Pu Yi, was established under the control of the Kwantung Army. Japanese leaders assumed that the great powers and China would accept this new geopolitical arrangement, one of several miscalculations they were to make (Iriye 1987, 10).

As we have stated, one of the primary motivations for Japanese expansionism in Manchuria was autarky, or economic self-sufficiency. Autarky was an important part of the worldview of Japanese elites. It was consistent with Japanese nationalism, it was a fundamental tenet of the Total War faction, it resonated with those who rejected a new liberal international order based on free trade, and, as Japan's imperial adventures in Asia continued, it would become self-perpetuating. Autarky satisfied diverse political and economic groups in Japan. The military supported it out of the perceived need for critical resources and the desire to counter its resource dependence on others; businesses desired secure markets and protection for their own products; and it fit the desire of Japanese nationalists for "Asian solidarity." But in the final analysis, the drive for autarky was counterproductive. Japan's economic problems in the late 1930s were actually caused by her decision to pursue autarky through imperialism. As Snyder (1991, 118–19) notes, virtually any other policy designed to address Japan's economic condition would have produced better results.

To some extent Japan's drive for self-sufficiency through imperialism was fostered by how Japanese elites read the "lessons" of World War I and the depression. First, many in the Japanese military believed that World War I had been won by the United States and Britain because these two states had most effectively created self-sufficient industrial economies. Thus total mobilization was necessary if Japan was to prevail in competition with the West. Second, as Japanese exports fell drastically during the depression, many noticed that her exports increased to those areas Japan directly controlled, Korea and Formosa. Imperialism worked; Japan could gain secure access to markets and raw materials through conquest (LaFeber 1997, 161–62).

While the Japanese economy grew in the late nineteenth and early twentieth centuries, her vulnerability to global economic currents also grew. Japan was especially vulnerable to events in the United States—Japan's most important Western trading partner and the emerging leader of the global economy. The 1929 Wall Street crash and the subsequent protectionist trade policy of the U.S. were major spurs to Tokyo's policy of autarky (Beasley 1987, 255; LaFeber 1997, 154–55).

Japan's industrialization was driven primarily by capital accumulated through textile exports. China was the key. It consumed three-quarters of Japanese cotton goods, and Japanese trade with China was five times her trade with Korea and Taiwan combined. For Japan, the promise of the China market was real. Just as important, Japan had a trade surplus with China that helped offset her chronic deficit with her other trading partners (McDermott 1995, 193–94). Moreover, China supplied many of the raw materials that fed Japan's heavy industry and absorbed much of Japan's foreign investment (LaFeber 1997, 99–100).

Japan's Achilles' heel was her heavy dependence on foreign sources of petroleum, minerals, and other raw materials—a dependence that increased as Japan's industrialization proceeded. Japan's steel industry depended on pig iron and ore from China and Malaya. It had insufficient supplies of coal and copper, and, most important, it relied almost totally on foreign sources of petroleum fuels. Approximately 90 percent of Japan's petroleum supply was from imports and about 85 percent of her imports were from the United States. Japan similarly relied on the U.S. for a high percentage of other strategic imports (Kennedy 1987, 300; Maechling 2000, 41–42; Paul 1994, 65). Japanese leaders were constantly tempted to use foreign conquest as a method of countering her vulnerability to economic warfare.

In part, therefore, Japan's military forays into Manchuria and North China were aimed at establishing control over the resources found in those areas. Military actions, however, created their own economic dynamics. The war effort increased the need for resources, and soon Japanese leaders were talking about the need to create a larger continental economic system, the Greater East Asia Co-Prosperity Sphere (GEACPS), which would include not only Korea, Manchukuo, and China but also Indochina, Malaya, and the Dutch East Indies. (Indochina had rice, tin and rubber; Malaya had tin, nickel, iron ore and rubber; and the Indies had oil.) GEACPS was not fueled by any Japanese need to find an outlet for surplus investment capital to invest; capital was never plentiful. And it was only secondarily about creating markets for Japanese products; business leaders were not the major voices in policymaking councils in Tokyo (Beasley 1987, 251; LaFeber 1997, 161). It was primarily about securing access to resources.

As we have seen, internal political conflict in Japan and the tendency of the military to protect its institutional interests led to the external use of force for diversionary reasons. The presence of "soft" targets in a weak neighborhood made the probability of war even more likely. An important background condition responsible for the conflict in East Asia was the ongoing revolution in China. Historically, the presence of revolutions has been linked to subsequent international conflict in several ways (Walt 1996). One such dynamic is that the presence of a revolutionary struggle temporarily weakens a regime so that its neighbors have an opportunity to make economic or territorial gains at its expense. The Japanese response to the long revolution in China, beginning in 1911 with the collapse of the Manchu Dynasty, fits nicely with this dynamic.

Chinese factional conflict between Nationalists and Communists and the tendency toward local warlordism kept China divided and helped to make possible the Japanese creation of Manchukuo as well as the later invasion of north China and the coastal areas. Essentially, the revolution in China provided Japanese leaders with the *opportunity* for conquest, and it was this conquest that put Japan on a collision course with the United States. Of course, it might be argued that with or without the revolution, China was such a weak state that opportunities for Japanese expansion would have existed anyway. It is clear, however, that many Japanese leaders considered a successful revolution by Chiang Kai-shek's Kuomintang (or by any Nationalist leader) that would unify China as a threat to the ability of Japan to dominate Manchuria and East Asia in general. Thus Japanese leaders had added incentive to make sure that the revolution was not successful.

The Manchurian Incident was a crucial point on the path toward conflict between Japan and the U.S.—unleashing events with important consequences, both internationally and within Japan. It was seen as a violation of the League of Nations Covenant and the Nine Power Treaty and as a threat to all the great powers that had interests in Asia. It intensified those rivalries that already existed between Japan and China, Japan and Russia, and Japan and the United States, and it turned Britain, a previous ally of Japan, into a rival as well (Vasquez 1998, 198). In many ways the Manchurian gambit was the point of no return; Japan had isolated itself from those who counted in the Far East—the Soviet Union, Britain, and the United States.

China had, of course, immediately appealed to the League of Nations, and in October 1931 the League of Nations Council issued a resolution condemning Japanese action as contrary to the Kellogg-Briand Pact and the League of Nations Covenant and called on the Japanese military to withdraw to its original position. The tepid response was indicative of the weakness of the league. The U.S. reaction came in January 1932. President Hoover's secretary of state, Henry Stimson, announced that the nonrecognition principle (also known as the Stimson Doctrine) would apply to Manchuria; the U.S. would not recognize the legality of any political change in the status of Manchuria brought about through Japanese military force. Nor would Washington recognize any Japanese-Chinese agreement that violated the open door rights of others. There was, however, no direct threat of American retaliation.

In Japan, as always, there was a significant *blowback* from the international realm onto the domestic political realm. The application of the Stimson Doctrine and strong international opinion against Japan stimulated Japanese nationalism and increased the suspicion of the United States. Public opinion at home, rallied by the press, increasingly came to support the Kwantung Army's actions in Manchuria. Naturally, this domestic rallying effect undercut the political influence of accommodationists within the government (Bix 2000, 242; Vasquez 1998, 198).

The Shanghai Incident, the Jehol Invasion, and the Anti-Comintern Pact

In late January 1932, as the Manchurian crisis was unfolding, a second international crisis in Asia occurred—the Shanghai Incident. Shanghai was an important coastal trading city that was home to a large contingent of foreigners. Its residents had boycotted Japanese goods over the Manchurian Incident, and tensions between Japanese and local Chinese were running high. When a Japanese army major instigated a Chinese attack on Japanese Nicherin priests, local Japanese navy officers, motivated primarily by interservice rivalry with the army, decided to use the incident as a pretext to demonstrate their military capabilities. Unfortunately, they picked a fight with the Chinese Nineteenth Route Army, which proceeded to trounce them. The navy called in reinforcements, and when that proved ineffective, they were forced to call on the army for help. The army then also ran into trouble and had to be reinforced. Eventually twenty thousand Japanese troops were sent to Shanghai. Since the Japanese military preferred to focus its attention on Manchuria, it eventually accepted an armistice in May (Bix 2000, 250–51).

The Inukai government attempted unsuccessfully to restrain the Japanese Army in Manchuria and in the Shanghai area. For his attempts at moderation, Inukai and several other members of his government were assassinated on May 15, 1932, by disaffected junior officers of the army and navy and their civilian ultranationalist allies. This ended Japan's experiment with civilian party government, and the emperor chose the aging Adm. Saito Makoto as his new prime minister.

The following year Japanese forces advanced south from Manchuria into the province of Jehol just across the Great Wall from Peking. (The Kwantung Army had always considered Jehol to be part of Manchuria.) Though Adm. Saito's government and the emperor opposed the action, they refused to step in. Instead, they approved the operation with the condition that the army not cross the Great Wall that separated Jehol Province from Hopei Province and Peking. The invasion began on February 23, 1933, and was completed within a week; Jehol was annexed to Manchukuo. Two Kwantung Army incursions also crossed south of the Great Wall to the outskirts of Peking, both without prior authorization of the government or the emperor. Finally, at the end of May 1933 Japan signed the Tangku Truce whereby Chiang Kai-shek's Nationalist government recognized Manchukuo with its newly expanded borders. The truce produced very little cessation of warfare; fighting between Japanese and Chinese forces continued.

The Jehol action was the third crisis in as many years involving Japanese territorial expansion in Asia. In October 1932 the Lytton commission had issued its report on the Manchurian Incident to the League of Nations Assembly. The day following the Jehol invasion, the league assembly adopted the Lytton report. In the spring of 1933 the League of Nations, by a vote of forty-two to one, denied recognition to Manchukuo and criticized Japanese aggression. Tokyo's response was a symbolic watershed: It withdrew from the league. While the decision was due in part to the international situation and to increasing anti-Western sentiment, in the main it represented a decision by civilian elites to stabilize the domestic political situation in Japan—rocked by a series of military-supported assassinations and failed coups—by placating the military on the issue of Manchuria (Bix 2000, 269). Increasingly, the volatile nature of domestic politics in Japan compelled government leaders to grant the military what they wanted: expansion in Asia and a buildup of military forces.

By the spring of 1934 Tokyo had begun to openly justify its military policies by referring to a "Japanese Monroe Doctrine" for Asia, claiming the same kind of sphere of influence, the same latitude to act unilaterally, and the same mission to maintain peace and stability in Asia that the United States possessed in Latin America. Washington failed to see the parallel, and the State Department fended off a proposal by Foreign Minister Hirota for a Japanese-American spheres of influence agreement.

While the War Department preferred to write off East Asia as a Japanese sphere of influence, neither the U.S. Navy nor the president was so inclined. President Roosevelt's initial response to the situation in China was to endorse the nonrecognition principle and to increase assistance to Chiang's Kuomintang government. And while FDR was initially willing to accept the new status quo in Manchuria and to make no direct challenge to Japan, he did back a vigorous naval program, the Vinson-Trammell Act of 1934. At the same time, British and American negotiators resisted Japanese appeals for naval parity (Iriye 1987, 27–28). Late in 1934, after the failure of Japanese diplomats to achieve equal naval ratios, Japan abrogated the Washington Naval Treaty.

Japan drifted increasingly into an anti-Western direction toward the world's other revisionist great power. By November 1936, in the aftermath of the Tokyo Rebellion, with Japanese armies bogged down in northern China, and having failed to negotiate an agreement with Chiang, Japan signed the Anti-Comintern Pact with Hitler's Germany. While the pact was not an iron-clad defensive agreement, a secret provision obligated the two countries to consult with each other if either was attacked by the Soviet Union.

The China Incident and the Sino-Japanese War

Prime Minister Hayashi resigned in June 1937 and was replaced by Prince Konoe Fuminaro, a proponent of imperialism who had vigorously supported military action to control the resources of Manchuria. Konoe's new government came to power amid rumors of impending unilateral action by Japan's North China Army against Chiang Kai-shek's forces. Konoe's attempt to block this move was, predictably, unsuccessful. On the night of July 7, 1937, the China Incident took place on the Marco Polo Bridge in Peking. A Japanese private wandered off for a walk in the demilitarized zone long enough to be presumed missing. When the Japanese commander demanded a search, his Chinese counterpart proposed a joint search, which the Japanese took as an insult. Small-scale violence broke out when a Japanese company was fired on near the bridge, though no lives were lost. A local Japanese regimental commander, acting on his own, ordered an assault on Chinese garrison forces in order to redress the perceived insult to the Japanese army. The military disingenuously suggested to political authorities that the incident was connected to a larger Chinese offensive that was quite possibly supported by the Soviets; a strong Japanese response was deemed imperative.

Ill prepared for a new war with China, neither the hawkish prime minister nor the army supreme command initially desired an expansion of the conflict. However, the Konoe government was pummeled in the press for its weak response to a "national humiliation" (Iriye 1987, 42). The military was initially split. One group within the army wished to use the incident as an opportunity to expand operations in North China. This view was supported by the Kwantung Army staff officers and officials of the South Manchurian Railway Company. On the other hand, some members of the army's General Staff, led by (now) Maj. General Ishiwara, feared that a major war in China would suck Japan into "an endless bog" and jeopardize its ability to prepare for the inevitable conflict with the Soviet Union (LaFeber 1997, 183). The government, prodded by public and elite opinion, sided with the first group and dispatched three divisions to the area, just as the Tientsin Army had worked out a cease-fire with local Chinese officials. The cease-fire was rejected by Chiang, who sent reinforcements and then appealed to the United States and the other members of the Nine Power Treaty for aid.

While officials in Tokyo ordered that military activities be limited to the Peking-Tientsin area, the conflict spread rapidly in China. It also became apparent that Japanese forces would be needed in much larger numbers. Japan's Chinese Garrison Forces would no longer be required to simply protect Japanese citizens living in China, they would become an occupying force, and this would inevitably lead to Chinese attacks against Japanese occupiers. (This, in turn, would produce angry responses by an outraged Japanese public thereby stimulating tougher Japanese occupation policies.) A Japanese offensive in late July led to the rapid occupation of Peking and Tientsin. When Chiang's forces shifted south to Shanghai, attacking Japanese naval airplanes and the Third Fleet flagship, *Izumo*, the Navy Ministry reversed its position and became a vigorous supporter of an expanded war in China (Bix 2000, 323). In mid-August 1937 several days after the fighting began in Shanghai, the Konoe government officially abandoned its attempt to limit military expansion and sanctioned a war to "chastise" China's military. The brief exchange of rifle fire on the bridge in Peking had ignited a full-scale war—referred to by most countries as the Sino-Japanese War, though Japan persisted in referring to it as the China Incident.

By mid-December 1937, in search of a decisive battle to end Chinese resistance, Japan had captured Nanking. Japanese soldiers began to execute military prisoners and deserters and engaged in a general rampage that involved the massacre and rape of Chinese civilians and the pillage and destruction of Chinese property. This "Rape of Nanking" coincided with a Japanese attack on British gunboats and the deliberate sinking of the U.S. ship *Panay* in the Yangtze River as it was helping to evacuate foreigners from Nanking. These developments outraged foreign opinion and led to protests by the U.S. and other governments. The events also helped create in the United States an image of Japan as an inhumane, bloodthirsty, and militaristic nation bent on aggression.

The capture of Nanking served to increase the demands previously put forward by the Japanese for a settlement, and by mid-January 1938 the Konoe government had decided it would *not* negotiate with Chiang's government. Diplomatic relations were severed and mediation attempts (by the Germans) were ended. Over the objection of the army's General Staff, the navy's tougher position won out; the decision was made to "annihilate" the Nationalist government by launching an all-out offensive.

By October 1938, the Japanese army had reached its high point; the coastal cities of Hsuchow, Hankow, and Canton had been taken, as well as Wuhan, forcing the Nationalists to move their capital to Chungking. From this point on, China was essentially a quagmire for Japan, with little prospect of victory. Japan's military and civilian leaders had underestimated China's ability to resist. The Sino-Japanese War had not been planned by any of the various Japanese military factions, but Japan's initial success meant that it could not return to the pre-1937 status quo; significant concessions were no longer tenable. But the continued fighting would be costly. By the end of 1937 the war cost Japan $5 million a day (Kennedy 1987, 302). More important, it also increased Japan's need to import oil and munitions and other goods, increasing her balance of payments deficit and deepening her trade dependence on the United States and Britain—thus re-creating the very situation Japan had tried to eradicate by establishing her Asian empire.

The Shifting International Environment and the Intensification of the Conflict Spiral

Across the Pacific, Roosevelt's early attempts to counter Japanese moves in China were hampered by the continued economic depression at home, by internal executive branch divisions about Asian policy, and by an isolationist Congress that had passed a series of Neutrality Acts. Washington's refusal to officially recognize the existence of war in China meant that the U.S. continued to sell arms to China, but it also continued to sell oil and raw materials to Japan. In October 1937 the United States joined in the league's condemnation of Japan and the president made his famous "Quarantine Speech," though this produced no real economic quarantine of Japan. The president understood that at this point American public opinion would not support coercive countermeasures against the Japanese. Interaction between the U.S. and Japan was largely asymmetric; Japanese aggression in Asia did not yet trigger similar levels of hostility from the United States.

At the turn of the new year, however, in response to the rape of Nanking and the *Panay* incident, the United States began to take concrete steps to counter Japanese expansion in China. In late December 1937 Roosevelt approved military staff talks with the British; in January he ordered portions of the U.S. fleet moved from the Atlantic to the Pacific; and in May the new Vinson-Trammel Act (the Naval Act of 1938) authorized $1.1 billion over ten years for the construction of sixty-nine new American ships—with the goal of building a "Navy second to none." U.S. bases in Wake Island, Guam, and Midway were fortified. Congress also appropriated money for three thousand more U.S. warplanes. And in July the United States retaliated for the indiscriminate Japanese aerial bombardment of Chungking by increasing military aid to China and embargoing the export of airplane parts to Japan—the first set of U.S. economic sanctions on Japan. Unlike the Western response to Hitler's actions, appeasement of Japan was virtually out of the question. The vast majority of Americans sympathized with China, were increasingly outraged that American exports helped the Japanese plunder of China, and were in favor of a tougher stand against Japanese aggression (Dower 1986, 8–9, 33–73; Iriye 1987, 66).

In November 1938 Prime Minister Konoe announced a new rationalization for the China Incident—the establishment of a "New Order in East Asia," a regional bloc based on Asian cultural and political norms. The new formula explicitly called for abandoning the Washington treaty structure and asserted a Japanese right to hegemony in Manchuria, North China, and Korea. To drive home the point, Tokyo declared in a later diplomatic note that it considered previous treaties and principles no longer valid (LaFeber 1997, 186; Iriye 1987, 68). It goes without saying that the assertion of a special Japanese position in East

Asia and the attempt to establish regional autarky exacerbated longstanding American concerns about the Japanese threat to Open Door principles in Asia.

The New Order declaration was denounced by the Roosevelt administration, and in December Washington announced a $25 million loan to Chiang's Nationalist government to be used to purchase trucks and arms from the U.S.—a clear signal to the Japanese. The Soviet Union also extended aid to China. Meanwhile, Germany, originally a supporter of Chiang's Nationalists in the civil war against the Communists, recognized the Japanese puppet state in Manchukuo and reoriented its foreign policy in the Far East toward Japan, ending its aid of Chiang. The international battle lines were being drawn.

Japan's territorial conflicts with China also led to further territorial conflicts with the Soviet Union. The newly created borders of Manchukuo created friction with the Soviets at several different points: in the Amur River area, in Changkufeng (on Manchukuo's border with the Soviet Maritime Provinces), where a brief border skirmish broke out in early August 1938, and, most important, near Nomohan in the Gobi desert at the intersection of Manchuria and Mongolia (a Soviet ally). In the summer of 1939 the Japanese Kwantung Army ignored the General Staff's policy of avoiding confrontations and authorized the crossing of the Mongolian border for a "punitive expedition." The action ignited four months of fighting between Japanese and Soviet (and Mongolian) forces, including large-scale tank battles.

The Japanese army had tended to see the Soviet Union as the largest threat to Japanese interests in Asia and had focused much attention on the possibility of a future war with the USSR. Accordingly, the diplomacy of Konoe and Foreign Minister Arita had attempted to prod Germany into a specific alliance against the Soviets. The Germans resisted; they had wanted the treaty to apply to the U.S. in addition to the Soviet Union, while Arita wanted to keep the commitment more limited. The Japanese were taken more than a little off guard by the surprise announcement on August 23, 1939, of the German-Soviet Non-Aggression Treaty. The pact meant that Russia would have a free hand against Japan while Germany turned its attention to Europe—a stunning affront to the spirit of the 1936 Anti-Comintern Pact. Within weeks Japan signed a peace treaty in the Nomohan War, which had been going badly.

The German change of strategy also led to the fall of the Japanese government. The new prime minister, Gen. Abe Nobuyuki, and his foreign minister, retired admiral Nomura Kichisaburo, attempted to reorient Japanese foreign policy toward accommodation with the U.S. and Britain without abandoning the idea of a New Order in East Asia. This was a difficult task. At home Abe and Nomura faced opposition from those whose preferred strategy was to **bandwagon** with the apparent winners in Europe—Germany and the Soviet Union—by creating a grand coalition in opposition to Anglo-American status quo powers. A Japanese-Soviet pact was attractive because it might help to solve the China problem. (Russia was still the major supplier of aid to Chiang.) The Abe government, however, did not favor an alliance with Germany and Russia, fearing that it would merely antagonize further the U.S. But rapprochement with the U.S. had its own problems. Since Nomura could not give up Japan's special rights in Manchuria and China, he had few bargaining chips to entice Washington.

In the meantime, the U.S. had become increasingly committed to using **coercive diplomacy**—the use of threats, sanctions, and demonstrations of commitment—to defend China against Japanese expansion and to deter the extension of Japanese power in the Far East. The United States would reciprocate aggressive Japanese actions with increasingly tough policies and actions, propelling dyadic interactions into an upwardly ascending conflict spiral. American hardliners—Treasury Secretary Morgenthau, Interior Secretary Ickes, and most of the State Department's Asian specialists—believed that bullying might work: Japan was now seen as being on the defensive and could be pushed into further retreat by the U.S. tightening the screws (Iriye 1987, 74–75, 87). An important signal of this was the U.S. government's announcement (July 26, 1939) of its intent not to renew the U.S.-Japanese Treaty of Commerce and Navigation when it expired on January 26, 1940. There were other signs as well: the president's order in October to reposition part of the American fleet from California to Pearl Harbor and his request for an extra $500 million for defense.

Talks aimed at preventing American abrogation of the commercial treaty began between the Foreign Minister Nomura and the U.S. ambassador to Japan, Joseph Grew, but by December 1939 these talks had failed to produce agreement. And in January 1940 the U.S. formally ended its Treaty of Commerce with Japan, just as Japanese imports from Europe had dried up due to the war, making Japan even more dependent on the United States (Iriye 1987, 93). The Abe cabinet collapsed as a consequence of the international situation on January 14, 1940. The new prime minister, Adm. Yonai Mitsumasa, and his foreign minister, Arita Hachiro, agreed on the need for accommodation with the U.S., but the United States' abrogation of the treaty within days of the formation of the new cabinet gave them little real chance to succeed.

With Japanese-American relations deteriorating, the Imperial Navy's General Staff began to reassess its situation. By the spring of 1940, it had begun to see the Vinson-Trammel naval buildup in the U.S. as directed not at Germany but as a crash program designed to create American superiority in the Pacific and to restrain Japanese expansion (Crowley 1974, 285). The logical strategic consequence was that Japan would need to gain control of the resources of the Dutch East Indies in order to keep pace. And Japan would have to take a more bellicose stand against the U.S. A Japanese treaty with the Axis powers—long seen by the Imperial Navy as too provocative—might scare the Americans off and reduce the chance of war, but Japan would have to prepare for the worst (Crowley 1974, 284–85). Japanese strategy was inexorably shifting its focus from north to south, and since Japan therefore needed to stabilize relations with the Soviet Union while the southern strategy was implemented, attention turned to the desirability of a neutrality treaty with the Soviets.

The German attack on Poland and the war in Europe meant the global distribution of power was shifting in favor of the Axis. This was good news for Japan. Its attempt to construct an economic empire in Southeast Asia might now have somewhat easier going, as the chief colonial powers—Britain, France, and Holland—would be weakened by German attacks and tied down on the continent. Indeed, by mid-1940, with the fall of France and the Low Countries and with the Dutch government in exile, a window of opportunity was perceived to have opened. On June 25 Army Minister Hata Shunroku urged his staff to "seize this golden opportunity" (Sagan 1988, 326). While struggling with the continued war in China, the Japanese were now more firmly fixed on a southern expansion. In the spring of 1940 Japan issued several demands: that it be guaranteed access to a supply of raw materials from the Dutch East Indies, that the French end the movement of arms to China through French Indochina, and that Britain withdraw troops from Shanghai and close the Hong Kong frontier and the Burma Road, through which supplies were also reaching Chiang's forces in Chungking. To drive the point home, Japan moved troops to the border with Hong Kong. The French conceded, the British closed the Burma Road and the Hong Kong frontier for three months, but the Dutch negotiators hung tough.

The British and the French had appealed to Washington for a direct commitment, but FDR's government was in no position to make one at this point. What the U.S. *could* do was to respond to these developments with diplomatic, economic and military actions that signaled resolve without making a direct threat to take action. As part of its deterrent strategy, in April 1940 the U.S. had already warned Japan that any change in the Dutch East Indies except by peaceful means would be seen as prejudicial to the peace and security of the region—a warning perceived by the Imperial Navy's General Staff as meaning war (Crowley 1974, 286). This was followed by a decision to beef up the Pacific Fleet: Ships on exercises in that area were to remain in Hawaii indefinitely rather than returning to their home bases. By the summer of 1940, FDR's cabinet took on an even more hawkish complexion. Roosevelt appointed two pro-British Republicans who buttressed the ranks of the hardliners within his cabinet: Henry Stimson as his secretary of war and Frank Knox as his secretary of the navy.

In July 1940, after France had fallen to the Nazis, Congress passed the National Defense Act permitting the president to keep at home all products that might be needed for defense. The White House would now be able to exercise export control over all war-related products. The president immediately embargoed forty key materials, placing arms and war material, critical raw materials, airplane parts, machine tools, and other items under license. Scrap iron and oil were omitted from the initial list of products as a carrot to induce good Japanese behavior and to retain further sticks for future use. Predictably, the prospect of an American embargo merely served to convince the leadership in Tokyo of the necessity for self-sufficiency through conquest (Vasquez 1998, 204).

As always, policymaking was unsettled in Japan. Both the Abe government (August 1939 to January 1940) and the Yonai government (January to July 1940) were committed to the attempt to prevent a crisis with the United States and opposed to an alliance with Germany. Both governments were brought down by military opposition. On July 22, 1940, the second Konoe government was formed explicitly to settle the problems of China, the southern area, and Japanese-German relations. It was considerably more hawkish than its predecessors. Konoe himself had presided over the initiation of the war in China in 1937, and the army minister was Gen. Tojo Hideki, a leader of the army's expansionist Total War faction. While the emperor was still committed to friendly relations with the U.S. and Britain, the army would only accept a foreign minister who supported a Japanese-German alliance (Iriye 1987, 107). The foreign minister, therefore, was Matsuoka Yosuke. Matsuoka was strongly anti-American, a supporter of a Japanese-German alliance, and in favor of a southern strategy coupled with a de-escalation of the war in China. The Konoe government was determined to take advantage of the new international situation caused by German victories in Europe.

Within ten days of the formation of the Konoe cabinet, Roosevelt had signed a bill for a two-ocean navy (July 20) and had announced (on July 25) that the export of scrap metals and all grades of oil would now be subject to U.S. government licenses—though the initial restrictions were somewhat limited.

The new Konoe government wasted no time in adopting a strategy. A July 27, 1940, Liaison Conference officially sent Japan down two parallel paths. First, Japan would conclude a military alliance with Germany and Italy. The pact had been debated within government and military circles for several years, but it had been opposed by the emperor and by the navy, who correctly feared that it would provoke the Western powers and drive Washington closer to the British (Crowley 1974, 280; LaFeber 1997, 194). The fall of France in June 1940 changed the strategic climate to the extent that the navy, hoping to end its internal conflict with the army over this issue, dropped its opposition to the pact. An alliance with Germany would have an added advantage for the navy: Because Germany had a nonaggression pact with Russia, the diplomatic dynamics would make it more difficult for the Japanese army to fan the flames of a war with Russia (Bix 2000, 368–69). The second decision was that Japan would focus its attention to the south—the Imperial Navy's preferred sphere of activity—in an attempt to control the strategic assets of French Indochina, the Dutch East Indies, and British Malaya. Initial plans and preparations were made for an attack on British and Dutch territories and for a possible war with the United States.

Japanese elites supported this compromise southern strategy for different reasons. Some believed that it would cut off essential supplies to Chiang's government, helping Japan to walk out of the China quagmire and end the war on favorable terms. Others believed that regardless of the China situation, Japan must move to the south as rapidly as possible in order to create the necessary military infrastructure (advanced positioning of soldiers and supplies and the creation of bases, ports and airfields) for Japan to impose its will over the area and gain access to the essential raw materials necessary for economic autarky. And this had to be done in spite of the inherent risks of war with Britain and the United States. Indeed, most Japanese elites had reluctantly come to accept the possibility of war with the United States, and although all agreed there was little chance of success in a drawn-out war, an alliance with Germany might make the difference (Iriye 1987, 115–16). While a southern strategy was approved in principle, the Imperial Navy refused at this early point to agree to an attack on British and Dutch territories unless it could be clearly ascertained that there would be no American intervention (Sagan 1988, 327–28). Caution was still required.

On August 1 Foreign Minister Matsuoka announced Japan's intent to create a Greater East Asia Co-Prosperity Sphere to exploit the area's markets and raw materials. While the previous New Order in East Asia had explicitly asserted Japanese economic hegemony in Manchuria and North China, the new formulation, with the term "Greater" prominently displayed, alluded to much larger ambitions.

While foreign observers assumed that Japan intended to include the Dutch East Indies, French Indochina, British Malaya, and other parts of Southeast Asia and the Pacific, a secret Japanese document extended the sphere even further—to Thailand, Burma, India, Australia, and New Zealand.

Japan began its long-awaited southern advance in September 1940. Vichy France was in no position to oppose Japanese expansion. After two days of skirmishing, the French surrendered, and Japanese soldiers quickly occupied Tonkin Province (the northern portion of what is now Vietnam). Early in 1941 Japan negotiated for guaranteed supplies of rice, rubber, zinc, tungsten, manganese, tin, chromium and coal from French Indochina and procured for Japanese manufacturers unrestricted access to the Indochina market. In keeping with Japanese policy, no war was declared, but the southern advance represented a significant expansion of the Sino-Japanese War, and it more directly engaged American interests. (Like Britain, the United States obtained its rubber from Indochina.) The southern advance represented, for all practical purposes, the opening shots of Japan's participation in World War II, firmly setting Japan on a collision course with the United States. Indeed, a September 1940 policy paper from U.S. military chiefs predicted that Japan would eventually attack U.S. possessions in the Pacific, most likely within a year or two (Small 1980, 228).

American retaliation for Japanese expansion in Indochina (and response to the report of the upcoming Tripartite Pact between Germany, Italy, and Japan) was fast and furious. In late September the U.S. announced another loan to China and imposed export control over scrap iron and scrap steel. The latter act elicited a formal protest: Japan deemed the U.S. control of iron and scrap steel an "unfriendly act." At about the same time, Congress enacted a military draft. The U.S.-British "destroyer for bases" deal in early September was an additional sign of allied unity in spite of formal American neutrality.

The Spiral Continues: Alliance Building, Sanctions, and Threats

As the conflict spiral gathered momentum, the search for geopolitical allies became an important part of the interaction between the great powers. The Tripartite (or Axis) Pact was signed by Germany, Italy, and Japan on September 27, 1940. As usual, different factions supported it for different reasons. While the Imperial Army hoped that the treaty would frighten the Soviets, Konoe and his foreign minister desired the pact because they believed it might effectively deter the United States from overt conflict with Japan—or failing that, provide assistance to Japan if it had to fight the United States (Iriye 1987, 116). Indeed, Konoe perceived significant benefits from a policy of bullying: "A humble attitude will only prompt the United States to become more domineering. Therefore, a demonstration of Japanese strength is necessary" (Crowley 1974, 287).

The treaty pledged the three powers to provide military, economic and political assistance to each other in the case of an "attack by a power at present not involved in the European war or in the Sino-Japanese conflict"—wording clearly aimed at the United States and the Soviet Union. However, as the Imperial Navy feared that a German-American war would drag Japan into an unwanted conflict, a secret protocol, inserted at its insistence, mandated that the determination of whether an ally had been attacked would be made independently by each party. Additionally, Germany and Italy recognized Japanese dominance in "Greater East Asia." With the signing of the Axis Pact, Japan had crossed the proverbial Rubicon and helped to seal its fate in the war that was to come.

The effect of the pact in the United States was that hardliners, such as Stimson, Morgenthau, Knox, and Ickes, were energized to push for tougher economic sanctions—a policy opposed by Secretary of State Hull, Chief of Staff Marshall, and the chief of naval operations, Admiral Stark (Sagan 1988, 331). For the moment, though, the president resisted the oil embargo supported by administration hardliners. However, the new Axis Pact did make the U.S. more receptive to appeals from its own allies for assistance against Japan, and Churchill successfully pressed FDR to hold formal British-American military talks. Japanese activities, rather than cowing the Americans, the British, the Chinese, and the Dutch (the ABCD powers) into submission, hardened their resolve to respond forcefully (Vasquez 1998, 211; Iriye 1987, 117).

At the end of November 1940, having failed at a last-ditch attempt to get Chiang to accept Japanese terms, Japan formally recognized the Chinese government of Wang Ching-wei, a puppet government set up by the Japanese and located in Nanking, as an alternative to the Nationalist government of Chiang Kai-shek. In return, Wang recognized the independence of Manchukuo and formally permitted Japan to station troops on Chinese soil.

Within days, Roosevelt responded. He announced on November 30 a new $100 million aid package to Chiang, coupled with the promise of fifty U.S. military aircraft with American civilians to fly them. He sent ships and planes to the Philippines to beef up the U.S. presence there, and he widened the ban on exports to Japan. From this point on, Washington added other items to the list almost weekly. In December iron ore, pig iron, steel, and many types of tools were added, and in January 1941 copper, brass, bronze, zinc, nickel, and potash were added. At about the same time the U.S. entered staff talks with the British and Dutch to coordinate military contingencies. Though the talks were officially secret, Washington very much desired that Tokyo know of their existence (Sagan 1988, 333). Their "discovery" would send a signal to the Japanese of allied solidarity. On February 14, 1941, the United States delivered two deterrent threats to Japanese officials. President Roosevelt warned Ambassador Nomura that the U.S. was determined to support Britain, even at the risk of war, and that if Japan were to occupy Dutch or British areas in the Pacific, it would create havoc for the British war situation. On the same day, the U.S. counselor in Tokyo made a similar warning to the vice minister of foreign affairs regarding a possible Japanese attack on Singapore.

FDR and the hardliners believed that the use of diplomatic warnings, material support for China, diplomatic assistance to British and Dutch colonial authorities in Asia, and the presence of the American fleet in Hawaii would illustrate a strong American stand in Asia, thereby deterring Japan from further aggression. At the same time, however, the United States had to avoid provoking a war for which it was not yet ready (Iriye 1987, 122).

Increasingly committed to a southern strategy, Japan shelved its plans for war in the north (the Army's preference) and moved to stabilize its relations with Moscow. In late October 1940 Japan proposed a nonaggression pact to Soviet foreign minister Molotov that included an Asian spheres of influence division. The Soviets declined. Foreign Minister Matsuoka also attempted to interest Germany in a Four Power Pact that would array Germany, Italy, and Japan with Russia in a grand alliance against the British and the Americans. The plan did not entice the Germans, who, unknown to Matsuoka, had their own designs against Russia. His diplomatic strategy in tatters, the best that Matsuoka was able to do was a Japanese-Soviet five-year Neutrality Pact, signed in April 1941. Russian commitment to neutrality with Japan strengthened further the hands of those in Japan who supported a southern strategy.

Given the gravity of the clash of American and Japanese interests, U.S. Secretary of State Hull agreed to begin negotiations with Nomura (now ambassador to the U.S.). The two met frequently at Hull's hotel suite in Washington between February and December 1941. While Roosevelt was preoccupied with the war in Europe, Hull had managed Asian policy. A Wilsonian idealist, he was determined that a settlement be based on universal liberal principles rather than on some amoral, realpolitik compromise. Hull's proposal, delivered on April 16, was that the two states should agree to "Four Principles" as the basis of an agreement: territorial integrity, noninterference in the internal affairs of other states, equal commercial opportunities, and peaceful change of the status quo. Consistent with those principles, Hull insisted that Japan accept the Open Door and remove its forces from China, if not from Manchuria. Essentially, Japan must rejoin the status quo powers in a liberal international order. For his part, Nomura pressed the U.S. to accept the new status quo in Asia, to prevail on Chiang to make peace with Japan, and to cut off aid to the Nationalists if he refused. Nomura also declined to give assurances that Japan would refrain from using force in the Pacific. From the perspective of many American officials, the talks had little chance of success; their primary purpose was, therefore, as a tactical maneuver enabling the U.S. to gain time to prepare for war (Iriye 1987, 135).

As Hull and Nomura talked in Washington, the U.S. was busy constructing the basis for an anti-Japanese alliance. The American military held staff talks with their British counterparts, producing a report called ABC-1 that adopted a joint strategy for the Asian-Pacific region. And in April, with ABC-1 as the cornerstone, military officers of the two states conferred with their Dutch counterparts and agreed on a common military plan for the Chinese front (Iriye 1987, 134). FDR also signed off on a scheme to use "retired" American airmen to create a volunteer air force in China—the famous Flying Tigers. And in June the United States sent bombers to China with ranges capable of attacking targets in Japan.

Washington also gradually and inexorably increased the economic pressure on Japan. In May 1941 Congress extended the National Defense Act to all U.S. territories and possessions, permitting the White House to control exports from the Philippines to Japan. And on June 20 it was decided that no more oil would be exported from America's eastern seaports to Japan.

The American strategy of coercive diplomacy toward Japan was now well established. It involved activity on several fronts: support for Nationalist China in its war with Japan, incremental economic sanctions on Japan coupled with tentative negotiations, diplomatic support for British and Dutch attempts to resist Japanese encroachment in Southeast Asia, military coordination with the British in the Asia-Pacific region, and U.S. rearmament programs coupled with a minimal forward deployment of the U.S. Navy in the Pacific to deter Japanese aggression. Many American leaders assumed that Japan would not dare further military actions due to the tremendous U.S. superiority in overall capabilities that would be arrayed against them in war (Paul 1994, 66). Japanese perception of the strategy was that it was directed at closing down Japan's access to strategic materials, at gaining naval superiority, and at forcing Japan out of Manchuria and China—all of which were unacceptable to Tokyo (Crowley 1974, 291).

On June 22, 1941, Germany launched Operation Barbarossa and invaded the Soviet Union, throwing Japanese strategic planning into chaos once more. The attack stimulated renewed conflict among Japanese elites over the rapidly changing international situation and forced yet another reassessment of strategy. Konoe himself favored dumping the Axis pact and seeking rapprochement with the United States by making needed concessions. This was unacceptable to the military and to Foreign Minister Matsuoka. In spite of the neutrality treaty that he himself had recently negotiated, Matsuoka wanted an immediate attack on Russia, while the army and navy commands favored a "wait and see" approach. The army's General Staff demanded a clear decision: Would there be a war with the Anglo-American powers or would Japan undertake a northern campaign? (Iriye 1987, 141–42).

Within days, several high-level meetings had been held, culminating in an Imperial Conference on July 2 that outlined Japanese strategy. Japan was now deep into its fourth year of war in China, and the Japanese army's progress had slowed to a halt. The war was not lost, but neither had it been decisively won. Chiang's Nationalist government and Mao Tse-tung's Communist forces continued to hold out, supported by American, British, and Russian assistance. The Japanese puppet government of Wang, meanwhile, generated no real popular support and received no international recognition. The Imperial Conference determined that a settlement of the China problem would require an advance to the south in order to create the GEACPS. The effort, it was determined, should begin with Thailand and southern French Indochina; Camranh Bay and Saigon were specifically marked as essential. For the army and its chief of the General Staff, Sugiyama Gen, the move was seen as necessary to cut the supply line between Chiang's government in China and the United States and Britain. For the navy, and its chief of operations, Adm. Nagano Osami, the move was necessary to prepare for a possible war with the American-British-Dutch (ABD) countries. U.S. naval construction was a crucial factor in pushing the military and the government toward war in the Pacific (Crowley 1974, 292). The Imperial Navy, traditionally the most cautious service, was beginning to abandon its aversion to risk.

Foreign Minister Matusuoka predicted that a Japanese invasion of southern Indochina would lead to a war with the United States and Britain. Most in the army and navy, however, believed that the immediate moves to the south were relatively safe steps that would not precipitate war—an assessment that illustrates a startling capacity for **wishful thinking** on the part of strategic planners. There was, however, a conscious understanding that a Japanese move into Indochina was likely to precipitate an oil embargo (Iriye 1987, 143–45). To be safe, the southern strategy had to be combined with preparation for a possible war with the United States, Britain, and Russia. The state was to be placed on a war footing.

Japan should maintain the alliance with Germany. And even though many in the army were sorely tempted by the prospect, Japan would not join with Germany in the attack on Russia, though this option was not entirely ruled out. Sixteen divisions were to be stationed in Manchuria for this contingency. Japan would prepare for *either* a northern *or* a southern advance. Much would depend on future contingencies (see Bix 2000, 397–99).

There was one contingency that the Japanese had *not* counted on: In August 1940 the United States had broken Japan's vital top-priority diplomatic code (Code Purple) through its MAGIC deciphering equipment. Within a week, Japan's plan for a southern advance was intercepted and decoded by the U.S.

The Southern Push and Oil Embargo: Conflict Spiral at High Intensity, July and August 1941

Japan's implementation of its southern strategy gathered force in July 1941. On the fourteenth it demanded the Vichy government permit Japanese forces to enter the southern part of Indochina and to occupy French air and naval bases. The French relented on the twenty-third and within days Japanese forces began to occupy southern Indochina. This was a critical turning point for U.S. policy. It pushed FDR and Secretary of State Cordell Hull closer to the administration hardliners who had been pushing for a tight oil embargo. The president told Stimson that the time for "appeasement" of Japan was over and that a "firm policy" was necessary (LaFeber 1997, 201). American retaliation against the Japanese expansion was immediate. On the twenty-fourth Roosevelt personally warned Ambassador Nomura, "If Japan attempted to seize oil supplies by force in the Netherlands East Indies, the Dutch would, without the shadow of a doubt, resist, the British would immediately come to their assistance, and, in view of our policy of assisting Great Britain, an exceedingly serious situation would immediately result" (Russett 1972, 49).

Roosevelt was willing to probe Japanese intentions and offer some "carrots" to induce cooperation—he proposed that if Japan refrained from occupying Indochina, the U.S. would persuade its allies to categorize Indochina as "neutralized"—but "sticks" predominated over "carrots." At the end of the month FDR sent substantial lend-lease shipments to China, ordered more aircraft for the Flying Tigers, ordered a strengthening of the defense of the Philippines and a mobilization of the Philippine army, and appointed Gen. Douglas MacArthur commander in chief of U.S. military forces in the Far East. He even authorized a covert plan to permit American civilian pilots to participate in the bombing of mainland Japan while flying American planes with Nationalist Chinese markings (Small 1980, 245).

Most important, on July 25, in a clear American retaliation for Japanese moves, Roosevelt issued an executive order freezing Japanese assets in the U.S., effectively bringing all of Japan's financial and trading transactions in the U.S. under the control of the federal government—including the export of oil on a case-by-case basis. (After progressive embargos on more and more export items, oil was for all practical purposes the only commodity that remained to be withheld.) The decision was clearly a victory for the administration hardliners. In principle, export of oil from American companies to Japan was still possible, and the president did not desire the freeze to become a total ban. American policymakers understood that it might be desirable to export a certain amount of petroleum products, like low-octane gas, so as not to provide Japan with an excuse to take the Dutch East Indies. Nevertheless, State Department officials responsible for implementation of the policy interpreted the freeze order in the most restrictive way possible. Japan received no oil from the United States after July 25.

Within hours of the U.S. announcement, Britain (which had already imposed economic sanctions on Japan) froze Japanese assets. Two days later London abrogated Japan's commercial treaties with India and Burma. New Zealand, the Netherlands, and the Philippines followed suit by freezing Japanese assets. On August 23 the Dutch East Indies refused to allow the export of oil to Japan unless Japanese troops were withdrawn from Indochina and Japan promised not to attack the Indies. And a week later it imposed a total ban on the export of oil and bauxite to Japan. The economic noose tightened considerably around Japan. These actions effectively illustrated to Tokyo the potential of a trade embargo by the combined ABD countries and their overseas possessions. It also strengthened the perception by Japanese leaders of Japanese "encirclement" by the ABCD powers.

There is an old saying that nothing concentrates the mind like the realization of impending death. This was certainly the effect FDR's freeze order had on the Japanese. The U.S. and allied economic sanctions threw the Konoe government into a "near panic" (Bix 2000, 401). For the Japanese, the oil embargo was tantamount to an act of war. Japan now had approximately a year's supply of oil in its reserves for its army and eighteen months for its navy (Maechling 2000, 46). At the very most oil reserves might last two years. Since Japan produced only 10 percent of its own fuel supplies and attempts at developing alternative fuels had failed, its ability to attain imports was crucial. Unfortunately, it imported 80 percent of its fuel from the United States. The embargo meant that Japan was immediately forced to begin drawing down its reserves of oil at the rate of twelve thousand tons a day (Sagan 1988, 334, 337, 341). Army planners concluded that they could wage war for no longer than two years without capturing the resources of Southeast Asia and the Pacific (LaFeber 1997, 200). Oil wasn't the only problem: Japan was also running short of other critical materials—tin, bauxite, nickel, rubber, and rice—all normally imported from the Dutch East Indies or British Malaya (Russett 1972, 46).

Japan was forced to make some hard choices that it had thus far been able to avoid—and make them quickly. With its eyes on the resource problem, the army began to switch to a view that the military priority should be to win a war against the United States quickly (Bix 2000, 403). The Japanese army had at any rate concluded by August 9 that it was impossible to go to war against Russia; military planning from this point on focused squarely on the potential conflict with the ABCD powers (Iriye 1987, 149; Kennedy 1987, 343). The Imperial Navy, always cautious when it came to a war with the American Navy, now began to support what appeared to be the inevitable.

The Conflict Spiral's End Game Begins, August to November 1941

In the first week of August 1941, Nomura rejected FDR's proposal of a "neutralized" Indochina. Japan's position was that it would agree not to station troops *beyond* Indochina, that Japanese troops there would be withdrawn after a settlement had been reached on China but that Japan would retain special status in Indochina even after its military withdrawal, that the U.S. must suspend all military measures in the southwestern Pacific, and that the U.S. must use its "good offices" to settle the China conflict. The talks were now deadlocked. As a last resort, Prime Minister Konoe sought a summit meeting between himself and President Roosevelt.

The timing was poor. Roosevelt and Churchill were engaged in their own summit the second week in August off Newfoundland. The resulting Atlantic Charter set forward eight common allied principles, including self-determination, nonaggression, collective security, and the Open Door. It was a reassertion of the Wilsonian liberal principles that the Japanese associated with the old Anglo-American world order, and in their minds it signified the intent of the two powers to attain "global domination" and therefore constituted a "de facto declaration of war" (Iriye 1987, 15–56). At the Atlantic Conference, Churchill pleaded with Roosevelt to join with Britain and the Dutch East Indies in a clear warning to Japan to prevent her southern expansion. FDR agreed with the general principle but did not believe that the time was right for a confrontation with Japan. (The War and Navy Departments constantly pressured the president for more time to prepare.) U.S. strategy was still to maintain a firm deterrent stance against Japan but to avoid provoking a crisis that might actually lead to war—a fine line indeed. While no official statement of warning was ever issued, Roosevelt did deliver a message to Japan (though not the version agreed upon with Churchill) that permitted the Japanese to read between the lines. Thus on his return to Washington, FDR warned Nomura, "If the Japanese Government takes any further steps in pursuance of a policy or program of military domination by force or threat of force of neighboring countries, the Government of the United States will be compelled to take immediately any and all steps which it may deem necessary toward safeguarding the legitimate rights and interests of the United States and American nationals and toward insuring the safety and security of the United States" (Feis 1950, 257).

Though most U.S. tin and rubber came from the Southwest Pacific, it was, of course, an open question whether Japanese conquest of the British or Dutch possessions in Asia would constitute a clear threat to essential U.S. national interests. It was also an open question whether the American public would see such Japanese aggression as a proper casus belli. However, by November, when the president polled his cabinet, the unanimous opinion was that the country would support war against Japan if it attacked Malaya or the Dutch East Indies (Russett 1972, 50–52).

Throughout August 1941, a sense of strategic urgency descended on Tokyo, and the Imperial Navy began to push the argument that the oil embargo and the other economic sanctions had created a critical time constraint on Japanese strategy. If not quickly countered by a full-scale invasion of western colonies in Southeast Asia and the control of their vital resources, the embargo would rapidly and severely diminish Japanese capacity to wage war and defend itself. The window *of opportunity* was closing rapidly. Naval leaders argued that if war with the United States were to occur, it would be best if it happened now rather than later. Moreover, seizing the Dutch East Indies would almost certainly mean war with the U.S. and Britain, in which case Japan might as well consider *preventive war* in order to start hostilities under the best conditions possible.

On August 22 the Japanese navy presented to the army a plan for an attack on Pearl Harbor. It had not been constructed out of the blue: A question about planning such an attack had been on the final exam for graduates of the Japanese Naval Academy since 1931 (Paul 1994, 82). The plan's principal proponent was Adm. Yamamoto Isoroku, the commander in chief of the Combined Fleet. Yamamoto appears to have been originally opposed to war with the United States, but once it was clear that the government was committed to this course, he accepted the decision only on the condition that Pearl Harbor be included in the attack plan; otherwise, he felt the entire plan for the conquest of Southeast Asia would be jeopardized. He seems to have persuaded Navy Chief of Staff Nagano, who initially believed the plan too risky; indeed, the navy itself predicted that its losses in the attack would be one-third of their forces (see Wohlstetter 1962, 69, 368, 373). The army immediately accepted the plan, and on September 2 the navy began war games, including a surprise attack on Pearl Harbor, against U.S and British fleets.

At the September 6 Imperial Conference the first tentative decision for war was made. Accepting the strategic urgency argument, Hirohito and his advisers concluded that the military should prepare to initiate war against the ABCD powers, with the preparation to be completed by late October. In the meantime, diplomacy would continue and the government would be given until October 15 to obtain American agreement to Japanese terms. At that point a decision for war would be made. Japan's terms were as follows:

1. The U.S. and Britain must not aid Chiang.
2. They were not to establish military facilities in Thailand, Dutch East Indies, China, or the Far Eastern provinces of the USSR, nor increase existing force sizes in the area.
3. They must reestablish trade in essential resources with Japan.
4. For its part, Japan would promise no further military expansion in Asia and would withdraw its troops from Indochina after a settlement in China, would guarantee Philippine neutrality, and would refrain from hostilities against Russia if it observed the neutrality pact (Iriye 1987, 160). In short, Japan was willing to abandon the southern advance but not to surrender the benefits of the China Incident.

A week later, on September 13, another Liaison Conference prepared for the ongoing Hull-Nomura negotiations. It set forth Japan's minimal terms regarding China: an independent Manchuria, Japanese troops in parts of Inner Mongolia and North China, a continuation of Japan's special position in China, and the merging of Chiang's Nationalist China with Wang's Chinese government (Iriye 1987, 163). None of these conditions would be acceptable to the United States.

On October 2, at a meeting with Nomura, Secretary Hull responded to the Japanese terms. Instead of trying to negotiate the Japanese down from their positions, he simply reiterated the Four Principles of April. There appeared nothing that the two sides could agree on. As a result, American officials—led by Hull, who believed that Konoe was a "captive of the military" and would be unable to offer anything acceptable to the U.S.—rejected the proposed Roosevelt-Konoe summit (Small 1980, 247). The continual hardening of the administration's position to some extent represented the triumph of the State Department's China specialists over its Japan specialists. As LaFeber (1997, 203–6) points out, "By October 1941, the differences among U.S. officials were not over whether, but how, to stop Japan. Hornbeck [the State Department's China expert] persuaded many, including Hull and FDR, that the slipknot [U.S. sanctions] would continually tighten as the Japanese struggled against it. Japan would not try to cut the knot (that is, declare war), because it knew it could not defeat the United States." U.S. officials generally failed to see how desperate the Japanese had become and what this desperation might cause them to do.

October 1941 had arrived. The Japanese government's grace period to salvage a diplomatic settlement appeared to have lapsed without success. More bitter disputes among military and civilian elites took place in Tokyo. Army Minister Tojo and Army Chief of Staff Sugiyama believed that talks had now conclusively failed and a decision for war must be made by October 15. The navy was divided. Though many of its leaders believed it would be madness to fight the U.S., they would not say this openly and navy representatives did not speak strongly against the need for an immediate decision for war (Iriye 1987, 164). Prime Minister Konoe attempted to persuade the army to accept a political accommodation on the China issue. At a meeting on October 12 in Konoe's residence, Foreign Minister Toyoda urged a compromise on a China troop withdrawal. Tojo, the army's most vocal advocate for war, opposed this. He argued that concessions to the Western powers could not solve the China problem and would only increase American demands for further concessions; negotiation had failed and Japan now needed to act decisively. Navy Minister Oikawa, though supportive in principle of making concessions to the U.S. to prevent war, refused to state flatly that the Imperial Navy would be unable to win a war against the U.S. Navy. Fearing an army coup if negotiations continued, he insisted that the prime minister must make the decision for war or peace. Tojo, however, argued that even if the prime minister made the decision for peace, the army might not follow: They were bound by the decision of the September 6 Imperial Conference to prepare for war (Iriye 1987, 165).

Two days later, at the last Konoe cabinet meeting, Tojo renewed his argument against concessions, declaring, "If we yield to America's demands, it will destroy the fruits of the China Incident. Manchukuo will be endangered, and our control of Korea undermined." It would mean a reversion to the "Little Japan before the Manchurian Incident" (Bix 2000, 417). The army could not make concessions on the issue of China. In the meantime, mobilizations were in progress; they could be halted only by American acceptance of Japanese conditions.

Prime Minister Konoe himself was increasingly pessimistic, both of the chances of a German victory in Europe and of a Japanese victory over Britain and the United States, and there appeared to be no point in going to war if Japan was going to lose (Bix 2000, 417; Sagan 1988, 340; Iriye 1987, 166). The lack of consensus and the prime minister's unwillingness to choose war, led to the resignation of the Konoe government on October 16. At this point, only a military cabinet was workable. The emperor, having by now moved close to Tojo's position, approved General Tojo as prime minister. Though Tojo selected as his foreign minister Togo Shigenori, a supporter of accommodation with the U.S., the Total War faction of the military had consolidated its power and hardliners were now clearly in control in Tokyo. Their ascendance was seen by many in Washington as a commitment to war by Tokyo (Bix 2000, 419). Indeed, Admiral Stark, the U.S. chief of naval operations, warned the fleet on October 16 that the new government in Tokyo would be more nationalistic and more anti-American and that Japan might now launch attacks on Russia, Britain, or the United States (Wohlstetter 1962, 132–33).

The mandate of the new Tojo government was to reconsider the September 6 decision. It had to choose between making genuinely unpalatable concessions to the United States or opting for a war that held a rather significant chance of disaster. Between October 23 and November 2 there were almost daily liaison conferences between cabinet ministers and Japan's supreme military command. The strategic urgency created by the factors of time and oil continued to loom large for all participants. The navy alone expended four hundred tons of oil per hour (Butow 1961, 314, 319).

At a sixteen-hour Liaison Conference on November 1–2 an immediate decision for war backed by the army was scuttled. The emperor and the prime minister opposed that path. The option to persevere without war, backed by Foreign Minister Togo and Finance Minster Kaya Okinori, was also blocked. Prime Minister Tojo interceded to persuade greater flexibility on the part of the military, enabling a majority to cobble together a compromise decision. They agreed to put forward a revised set of final proposals—the so-called preferred Plan A and a set of minimally acceptable terms called Plan B. If the U.S. did not accept these terms by midnight November 30, war would begin soon after December 1. Officers of the supreme command warned that if the cabinet let the December 1 deadline pass without a decision for war, it could not be held responsible for the defense of the state (Butow 1961, 320). In many ways the compromise looked much like the earlier September 6 decision; the deadline had simply been moved forward.

The terms of Plan A, preferred by the Imperial Army, called for the withdrawal of Japanese forces from most of China within two years of a truce, maintenance of troops in North China, Inner Mongolia, and Hainan Island for up to twenty-five years, withdrawal of troops from Indochina after settlement of the war with China, and Japanese acceptance of the principle of nondiscrimination in trade.

The "fallback" Plan B, whose main architect was Foreign Minister Togo, contained Japan's absolute minimum conditions (Iriye 1987, 175). Two goals were deemed essential to Japan—access to the resources of the Dutch East Indies and maintenance of Japanese power in China. Specifically, therefore, Plan B stated:

1. Japan would pledge not to advance in Southeast Asia and the Pacific beyond Indochina.
2. The U.S. and Japan would cooperate with the Dutch East Indies to procure resources.

3. The U.S. must lift its freeze of Japanese assets, restore trade with Japan, and supply Japan with required quantities of oil.
4. The U.S. must refrain from obstructing attempts at peace between Japan and China.
5. If the U.S. agreed to these terms, Japan would withdraw from Indochina and ultimately from the whole peninsula when peace was restored with China or there was an equitable peace in the Pacific. In the meantime, Japan would transfer its troops from the southern part of Indochina to the northern part—if necessary. (Feis 1950, 309; Butow 1961, 323; Iriye 1987, 175–76)

Plan B was the object of intense negotiation, but in the end it was accepted, in part because many leaders feared that Foreign Minister Togo might resign if the military refused to agree to its inclusion. Ultimately, Prime Minister Tojo and Gen. Muto Akira (chief of the Military Affairs Bureau) persuaded the army's General Staff to go along, and the package was accepted unanimously by the government (Butow 1961, 323). War was now seen as inevitable unless the United States accepted Japan's conditions. Unknown to decision makers in Tokyo, U.S. officials had, of course, learned of the decisions almost immediately, thanks to the MAGIC code breakers.

On November 5 the Imperial Conference approved the decision. Hirohito had, barring a diplomatic breakthrough, made the decision for war. The two military services had papered over their differences, making possible a majority coalition in favor of war. The navy had, essentially, gone along in order to preserve military harmony and prevent overt conflict between the services. "Preparation for operations" was now to be completed, and Navy Chief of Staff Nagano ordered Admiral Yamamoto to prepare the combined fleet for war against the ABCD powers by early December. It should be noted that some officers of the Naval General Staff had opposed Yamamoto's plan to attack Pearl Harbor, believing the attack could be confined to British and Dutch territories and the Philippines. Under threat of resignation by Yamamoto, however, the navy agreed to the plan (Sagan 1988, 343). On November 10 Admiral Nagano ordered all ships to complete their preparations by the twentieth and to assemble in the Kuriles.

Meanwhile, on November 7, Nomura had presented Plan A to the Americans. It was dead on arrival, though Hull did not formally reject it until the fifteenth. On November 17 Japan's special envoy, Kurusu Saburo, arrived in Washington to assist with the negotiations. Three days later Nomura gave Secretary Hull Proposal B, Japan's final terms.

Good news arrived in Tokyo on the twenty-first: The Germans had pledged to declare war on the U.S. if war broke out in the Pacific. The next day the Liaison Conference affirmed that an American rejection of Plan B would lead to a Japanese decision for war. However, if the Americans softened their stand on the crucial issue of oil, Nomura and Kurusu were to put forward a concrete demand for five or six million tons of oil per year (Butow 1961, 334). Tokyo informed Nomura on November 22 that it had agreed to extend the deadline four days, until November 29: "This time we mean it, that the deadline absolutely cannot be changed. After that, things are automatically going to happen" (Wohlstetter 1962, 189–90). The note was translated by MAGIC on the same day.

Policymakers in Washington knew that time was limited. MAGIC intercepts confirmed preparations for an upcoming Japanese move. The consensus of Roosevelt's advisers was that the attack would target British and Dutch possessions in Southeast Asia; if American territory was to be hit, the Philippines were seen as the most likely target. Army G-2 and Navy Intelligence predicted the campaign would start on November 30 (Wohlstetter 1962, 241, 386). For the United States, breaking the diplomatic impasse centered on a counterproposal to Japanese Plan B, in which the U.S. would lift the oil embargo for three months in return for a Japanese withdrawal from southern Indonesia. This so-called modus vivendi had been pushed by administration accommodationists as a way of delaying war, and the president had given his tentative approval to it. However, after consulting with British, Dutch, and Chinese diplomats, Secretary Hull, with Roosevelt's approval, decided against putting forward this counteroffer (Small 1980, 250; Wohlstetter 1962, 242).

Hull instead presented Japan on November 26 with his "comprehensive basic proposal" or outline for a "Proposed Basis for Agreement" offered as "Strictly Confidential, Tentative, and Without Commitment." The note was intended, according to Hull, to provide an example of a possible solution. An explanatory oral statement was also presented to the Japanese negotiators. It is probably fair to say that the Hull note represented the United States' maximum terms, though it did keep the door open just barely for further negotiation. Essentially, Hull stated that Japan must abide by the Four Principles, agree to nonaggression for the Far East, and withdraw all military forces from China and Indochina. (The wording left China undefined, permitting the possibility that Japanese forces could stay in Manchuria. Indeed, no mention at all was made of Manchuria in the proposal.) From the American perspective, any agreement with the Japanese conditions would be tantamount to appeasement and, therefore, unacceptable. The American public would take it badly and U.S. allies were certainly opposed to compromise.

The Conflict Spiral Ends in War: The Final Decision

Word of the Hull note first arrived on November 27 in Tokyo, as a Liaison Conference was in session, from the Japanese military and naval attachés in Washington rather than from Nomura, whose less pessimistic report arrived later. The analysis of the military attachés was that further negotiation was now "completely hopeless." The reaction in Tokyo was similar; conferees were "dumbfounded" at the "provocative" American response (Butow 1961, 343). The prevailing opinion was that Washington knew its proposal could never be accepted by the Japanese government. Tojo deliberately misrepresented the note as an ultimatum, which it was certainly not (Bix 2000, 428). Nevertheless, the American proposal was immediately dismissed by Liaison Conference as just that—a humiliating ultimatum that left Japan no alternative except complete submission. (It should be noted that when the Hull note was presented, the Pearl Harbor task force had been underway for twenty-four hours—though it could be called back, pending a diplomatic breakthrough, up until twenty-four hours before "D day.")

Japanese elites were burdened by the heavy weight of previous decisions to carry out a southern strategy, by the momentum of military preparations, and by

the stiff American rejection of their diplomatic efforts. It had now become difficult to retreat. Foreign Minister Togo tersely summed up official Japanese opinion: "Japan was asked not only to abandon all the gains of her years of sacrifice,
but to surrender her international position as a power in the Far East." For him,
accession to American demands would be the "equivalent of national suicide"
(Feis 1950, 327). For the army, withdrawal from China was out of the question.
Its prestige and its claim on resources were based on its fighting the war to a successful conclusion. Tojo and Togo, however, appeared to have erred in their belief that the Hull note demanded a reversal of the status quo in Manchuria. This
is perhaps due to their assumption that references in the note to "China" applied
to Manchuria (Butow 1961, 343–44 n. 56). In addition, Tojo feared that any concession on this vital issue would risk open revolt by the more extremist elements
of the army. And while the navy might have been willing to abandon China, it
could not forgo the access to the raw materials of Southeast Asia (Russett 1972,
47–48). Territorial issues were important—Japanese hardliners would not permit
the government to abandon the territorial gains made in China—but so were considerations of prestige and internal politics.

Meanwhile, the public mood in Japan appeared to be extremely bullish. According to the *New York Times* Tokyo correspondent, militaristic speeches by
members of the Imperial Diet were "so belligerent that the government appears
moderate by comparison" (Butow 1961, 332–33). The Japanese media pounded
out ultranationalistic statements by the truck load and many nationalist organizations openly petitioned Tojo to go to war with the United States (Butow 1961,
333, 354). Moreover, on the twenty-eighth Japanese leaders received assurances
from Berlin that if Japan went to war with the United States and Britain, Germany would enter the war at once.

In Washington, a "War Council" meeting agreed that the president should issue a warning to the emperor of American willingness to fight in response to a
Japanese advance to the south. The president delayed sending the message until
9:00 pm on Saturday, December 6. He planned to wait until Monday night for a
reply. If there was no answer, he would formally warn Japan on Tuesday afternoon or evening (Wohlstetter 1962, 269).

On November 29 Hirohito consulted the *jushin*, the country's "senior statesmen" (primarily former prime ministers) concerning the decision for war. The
jushin constituted a rare top-level council that might, by offering their own independent judgments, serve as an effective counterweight to the military and civilian politicians who had decided on war. After a briefing by cabinet ministers,
which did not include any reference to the secret attack on Pearl Harbor, the *jushin*
presented their opinions. While they advised caution, none of the senior statesmen
opposed the war; nor did anyone offer an alternative to war (Butow 1961, 344–48).

On November 30, as the Japanese reached their negotiating deadline, the emperor summoned naval leaders to determine if the navy agreed on war; he had
heard disconcerting news of naval opposition from his brother, Prince Taka-
matsu. The navy minister and navy chief of staff discounted these rumors and assured him of success. A Liaison Conference followed, and the next day, December 1, an Imperial Conference, with Prime Minister Tojo presiding, took place.
First Tojo and then Togo presented the case for war: The Americans had refused

to make any concessions whatsoever and had demanded that Japan unconditionally withdraw troops from China, rescind the recognition of Wang's government, and disavow the Tripartite Pact. In their view, the United States was intent on preventing the realization of Japan's quest to create GEACPS. Acceptance of U.S. conditions would mean forsaking the goal of domination over East Asia and unfettered access to its resources; it would mean the destruction of Japanese power; and it would endanger the existence of the state (Butow 1961, 359–61). When Privy Council president Hara misrepresented Hull's note by claiming that Hull had demanded Japanese withdrawal from *all* of China, Foreign Minister Togo was asked to clarify if indeed Hull had meant to include Manchuria. Togo's answer was evasive but tended to back the misperception that Manchuria was included. In fact, as Togo fully understood, Hull had agreed early on to recognize the Manchukuo government and had never even brought up the issue of troop withdrawal from Manchuria (see Bix 2000, 431–32). In response to Hara's question about the probabilities of Japanese victory, Admiral Nagano was similarly evasive: He argued that the war in Europe would mean that neither the Americans nor the British would be able to transfer the bulk of their naval strength from the Atlantic to the Pacific (Butow 1961, 362).

In the end, the decision for war was made without comment from the emperor, as was the custom. The order was given to Japanese forces to carry out a planned series of surprise attacks on multiple targets. The list included not just Pearl Harbor but also British Malaya and Borneo, the Philippines, Guam, Wake Island, Hong Kong, the Dutch East Indies, Thailand, and, later, Java and Burma. The die had been cast. From this point on, the war plan was on "automatic pilot." Pearl Harbor would be attacked at dawn on December 7 (December 8 Tokyo time).

The goals of the attack on Pearl Harbor were both tactical and strategic: to destroy the immediate offensive capability of the U.S. Navy in the Pacific, to enable Japan to successfully occupy Southeast Asia and the islands of the Southwest Pacific, which would in turn enable Japan to extract desperately needed raw materials from those areas in order to pursue the war in China and to prepare for a war with the United States, and to create a better defensive position from which to fight this war with the United States. Essentially, the Japanese hoped to buy some time which would be used to supply themselves with the raw materials from Southeast Asia and the Pacific, hoping to win enough victories and inflict enough damage on the United States early in the war to convince it to negotiate a modest settlement instead of pursuing the war to its conclusion—which the Japanese understood would mean the military defeat of Japan. The Japanese analysis was permeated with a strong dose of wishful thinking.

The full range of potential options was, of course, never examined (Bix 2000, 408). Significant concessions were out of the question. Japan *had* to remain in China, it *had* to exercise control over the resources of the Asia and Pacific region, and it *had* to achieve economic self-sufficiency. Hirohito and his advisers did not examine the possibility of using troops from the Manchurian-Soviet border to defeat the Chinese, nor did they consider simply sitting out the war in Europe in order to benefit economically from it.

Nor did planners delve deeply into the full range of consequences. They did not gather much information on how the United States would react to an attack on its navy (Jervis 1989, 200). And little serious effort was put into examining in detail the real costs of a military defeat for Japan.

DYADIC LEVEL OF ANALYSIS: ELEMENTS OF THE CONFLICT SPIRAL

Arms Races

An integral part of the conflict spiral was an arms race—a dual military buildup on the part of the two major antagonists. In fact, the Pacific conflict saw the interaction of arms races involving three sets of rivals: U.S.-Japan, Britain-Japan, and the Soviet Union–Japan (Vasquez 1998). In the U.S.-Japan case, the race centered primarily on naval construction. As we have seen, Japan's naval capabilities and its expansionism in Asia caught the attention of the American military early on. By 1917 the U.S. Navy was pushing for a fleet twice the size of Japan's, and after Versailles, American and Japanese political elites began to see themselves as rivals who might someday find themselves at war with each other (Vasquez 1998, 206). At least as early as 1930, the Japanese navy had determined that its goal was to achieve a "qualitative edge" over the U.S. and British navies in the Pacific arena (Paul 1994, 71). As a result, both countries enlarged their fleets, though an arms race was temporarily avoided by the Washington Naval Treaty of 1922. In reality, the Imperial Navy secretly exceeded the treaty limits while its Western rivals were economizing. Its *Yamamoto*-class battleships, built in the late 1930s, were the largest in the world (Kennedy 1987, 300–301). Japanese diplomats failed to persuade the United States and Britain to accept equal limits in a subsequent treaty. Thus in December 1934 Japan gave two years' notice that it would repudiate the 1922 treaty, thereby eliminating all restraints on naval building as of 1937. Japan put its shipbuilding program in high gear, with the understanding that time was not on its side (Paul 1994, 72).

Given its isolationist foreign policy and economic woes, military spending in the U.S. was sorely depressed in the period after World War I. Nevertheless, the election in 1932 of Franklin Roosevelt, a naval enthusiast, led to the first serious U.S. naval buildup since World War I. Japanese naval power was clearly a consideration, even at this early stage (Vasquez 1998, 207). Hardliners within the Roosevelt administration saw Japan's abrogation of the naval treaty as an opportunity to increase the American navy. The 1934 Vinson-Trammel Act authorized a vigorous naval buildup, and between 1934 and 1937 U.S. naval expenditures doubled, though the United States still kept within the treaty's limits. After 1937, with the treaty limits gone, both the U.S. and Britain responded to Japanese buildups (Vasquez 1998, 207–8). The 1938 Vinson-Trammel Naval Act authorized $1.1 billion to construct sixty-nine new ships over a ten-year period, but the real expansion in U.S. military spending did not begin until the defeat of France in 1940. In that year Congress authorized the doubling of the U.S. Navy's combat fleet, a major expansion of the Army Air Corps, and the establishment of an army of just fewer than one million men (Kennedy 1987, 331).

Almost all military buildups create security dilemmas, and the Japanese-American arms race was no exception. The United States had entered the arms race for defensive and deterrent purposes. Given the military gap between itself and the Axis powers, the U.S. buildup served as a hedge against the U.S. being drawn into the war. It could also boost the credibility of the American deterrent threat and buttress its strategy of coercive diplomacy. However, the American military buildup (especially in the Pacific) produced dramatically higher levels of insecurity in Japan. The Japanese response was to take preventive military action before American actions became decisive.

The arms race was an important part of the conflict spiral and its effects were both mutual and negative. It served to ratchet upward the level of anxiety, tension, and mutual hostility that existed between the United States and Japan. It increased the perception of threat and insecurity on both sides, promoted the use of preventive war logic, increased the power of hardliners on both sides, and led to further buildups and to a search for allies and, therefore, a heightening of the conflict spiral and an intensification of rivalries. What the arms buildups did *not* do was deter war (Vasquez 1998, 206–9).

What effect did the rapid Japanese naval buildup have on dyadic distributions of power? Given the tremendous American advantage in potential military capabilities, Japan was never in a position to draw equal with the United States—or with Britain for that matter. The best that Japan could attain was about 60 percent of U.S. naval strength and a similar percentage of British capability. In the end, the Imperial Navy would actually achieve 40 percent of the combined U.S. and British fleet strength (Paul 1994, 64). What was most important, of course, was not the ratio of total forces but the ratio of forces in the Pacific.

In December 1941 Japan entered the war with ten aircraft carriers, eleven battleships, and about three thousand aircraft. In contrast, the U.S. fleet in the Pacific numbered only three carriers and nine battleships, but it had over fifty-two hundred aircraft. In other words, Japan had achieved a quantitative naval advantage *in the Pacific* (Paul 1994, 70–71, 195 n. 5). A month before the attack on Pearl Harbor Admiral Nagano informed the Imperial Conference that "the ratio of our fleet to that of the U.S. is 7.5 to 10, but 40 percent of the American fleet is in the Atlantic Ocean, and 60 percent in the Pacific" (Ike 1967, 233). A shift in the dyadic balance had taken place—at least in the category of military forces that mattered. (Any war between Japan and the U.S. would, of necessity, have to be primarily a naval conflict.) It was also clear to Japanese leaders that this was only a temporary advantage; the U.S. would undoubtedly be able to outbuild the Japanese in the long run.

One theorist who has studied why weaker states attack stronger ones, suggests that Japan's short-term advantage, particularly in aircraft carriers, was "a determining factor" in the decision to attack Pearl Harbor, and that the offensive capability based on Japan's carrier advantage was seen as a "necessary condition" for war (Paul 1994, 71, 84).

Recent empirical analysis of the determinants of war strongly suggest that dyadic shifts in power interact synergistically with global changes in power distribution, particularly during periods of a deconcentration of global power (Geller and Singer 1998, 119–20; Geller 2000, 273–75). Shifts at both levels are related to the absence of stability in the international system. As we noted earlier, the global distribution of power was incredibly unsettled in the 1930s and 1940s. As the relative power distribution fluctuated madly, the system experienced a deconcentration of power and increased multipolarity, with many states passing through critical points in their power cycles. This rearrangement of global power intensified the impact of the dyadic U.S.-Japanese power shift in the Pacific region. The unsettled international condition, which appeared to give advantage to the revisionist bloc of powers, coupled with a temporary Japanese naval advantage in the Pacific, increased the potential for miscalculation and war.

Deterrent Failure

We now turn our attention to an aspect of the conflict spiral that deserves separate consideration, the failure of American and Japanese policies designed to prevent the outbreak of war. Scott Sagan (1988) has analyzed the Pacific war as a mutual failure of deterrence. The Japanese attempted to pursue a policy of expansion in Southeast Asia while deterring American intervention. U.S. policy was aimed at deterring Japanese expansion while avoiding action so provocative that Japan might be compelled to choose war. Neither policy was successful.

The theory of deterrence assumes that deterrent threats will prevent attacks if the deterrer: specifically defines its commitment, communicates its commitment to the potential attacker, possesses sufficient military capabilities to carry out the commitment and inflict unacceptable costs on the attacker, and makes the deterrent threat credible by somehow demonstrating its willingness to carry out the threatened actions. The Pacific war illustrates that, in fact, deterrence may fail even when the conditions are fully met, with threats credibly made and with robust capabilities to back them up.

The United States approached the impending conflict with Japan with caution. In the spring of 1940 officials in Washington had decided the U.S. should try to prevent Japanese expansion, but without any direct action that would be too provocative. It should do this through the threat of an oil embargo and by the more subtle threat of military intervention. However, threats of an oil embargo were always seen as risky because they might just provoke Japan into an attack on the oil fields of the Dutch East Indies—the exact event the U.S. hoped to deter. Thus in July 1940, as the U.S. began imposing economic sanctions, the decision was made *not* to impose an oil embargo. At the same time, Washington wished to convey to Japan the impression that the U.S. Navy was ready and able to intervene in the Pacific if necessary (Sagan 1988, 328–29).

In addition to risking provocation, American policymakers faced other constraints on their ability to make credible threats to prevent Japanese expansion. It was fairly clear that the majority of Americans did not support the risk of war with Japan, especially if it was on behalf of British, French, and Dutch colonial territories in Southeast Asia. After the 1940 presidential elections, however, Roosevelt was in a better position to accede to allied pressure to make deterrent threats against Japan. Though he continued to be skeptical that U.S. public opinion would support American intervention against a Japanese attack on British and Dutch possessions, he began to make a more strenuous effort to persuade Japan that we would do just that (Sagan 1988, 331–32). In February 1941, in the aftermath of the Atlantic Conference, FDR warned Nomura against a Japanese attempt to change the status quo regarding Dutch and British colonies in the Pacific (and by implication, warned of U.S. backing for Britain), though a more explicit U.S. threat to intervene militarily was prevented by isolationist sentiment in Congress and in the public. A second warning followed in July. Overt activities were designed to indicate the credibility of U.S. threats: joint military staff discussions with the British and the Dutch, the general American military buildup, support for Nationalist China's war against Japan, strengthening the defenses of the Philippines, the gradual escalation of economic sanctions on Japan, and the increasing size of the American fleet based at Pearl Harbor (though in reality the U.S. Pacific Fleet was actually reduced in 1941 as ships were being sent to the Atlantic).

The July 1941 decision to freeze Japanese assets in the United States, taken in response to Japan's southern advance, was a major step in the American attempt to deter Japanese aggression. The U.S. military (especially the navy) feared an embargo would precipitate a Japanese attack on Malaya and the Dutch East Indies, pulling the U.S. into a war on behalf of the British (Wohlstetter 1962, 113–25). President Roosevelt's position was that the freeze should not be used to create a total oil embargo on Japan; some purchases were to be permitted. The Japanese had made explicit warnings that an embargo would force them to get oil elsewhere (Sagan 1988, 334). Nevertheless, when the president left the country in the following weeks for the Newfoundland conference with Churchill, those in charge of approving disbursements from Japanese accounts used the occasion to institute a total oil embargo. Assistant Secretary of State Dean Acheson, in charge of the Foreign Funds Committee, believed that an oil embargo was a good deterrent tool and should not be feared. He reasoned that it would not provoke hostilities because the Japanese would be crazy to embark on war with the United States. By the time Roosevelt had returned, the embargo had become so well entrenched politically that to reverse it would appear to be a conscious act of appeasement. Roosevelt permitted the embargo to stand (Sagan 1988, 334–36).

The Japanese, on the other hand, had decided on their southern advance—at least initially—because it had seemed a safe step to take. The Imperial Navy, the institution most cautious about entanglement with the U.S., believed that a limited drive into Indochina would not precipitate an American oil embargo, because they believed that officials in Washington knew that an oil embargo would force Japan to attack the Dutch East Indies (Sagan 1988, 334).

With the decision to embargo oil, American policy had crossed the line that both countries knew existed. Deterrent threats at some point risk becoming *provocations*, thereby initiating the very wars one seeks to prevent. Both countries knew that an oil embargo sat on the center of that line. As we have seen, the embargo hit strategic planners in Tokyo hard; it *was* treated as an act of war. Additionally, as Sagan (1988, 347–48) notes, U.S. policy moved from trying to *deter* Japan's southern advance to trying to *compel* a Japanese withdrawal from China. Japanese leaders saw this as both humiliating and politically impossible. The oil embargo *was* a provocation, and the Japanese reacted just as many officials in Washington predicted they might.

In the final analysis, as early as the spring of 1941, many Japanese leaders concluded that despite the lack of a specific American warning statement, the

United States would in fact intervene in Southeast Asia if Japan took over British and Dutch possessions in the region. Indeed, they came to see war with the United States as inevitable. In other words, *Japanese leaders believed the American willingness to intervene was credible, even in the absence of an explicit threat or a treaty commitment by the United States.*

Knowing what they knew, Japanese leaders should have been deterred. They understood that a surprise first strike would not defeat the United States. While no Japanese organization made a major study of U.S. productive capacity prior to the decisions for war, some Japanese strategists calculated that if the United States chose to fight a long war, American war potential would be seven or eight times that of Japan. Admiral Yamamoto pointedly indicated to Konoye, "If you tell me it is necessary that we fight, then in the first six months to a year of war against the U.S. and England I will run wild, and I will show you an uninterrupted succession of victories; I must also tell you that, should the war be prolonged for two or three years, I have no confidence in our ultimate victory" (Wohlstetter 1962, 350). At the November 1 Liaison Conference, Navy Minister Shimada gave essentially the same prediction, adding that even though Japan could have no confidence in winning a long war, negotiations would simply prolong the initiation of war to a later date when the U.S. would be better prepared (Wohlstetter 1962, 351).

Japanese leaders chose to initiate war because they thought a successful attack on Pearl Harbor might give them a year's head start in controlling Southeast Asia and its resources. Japanese leaders were aware that if a war began, the American strategy was to fight a long-term war of attrition against Japan. T. V. Paul (1994, 67) argues that the Japanese military did not see the American deterrent threat as effective, because they believed the American strategy would allow them to achieve their short-term goals of conquest. They might be able to finesse the long-term problems. The conquest of Southeast Asia would give Japan the resources needed to fight a protracted war with the United States—a war that could not be won, but might be settled if the enemy could be convinced that fighting a long and costly war might not be worth the effort. In other words, it was possible that the U.S. would accommodate to the loss of the fleet at Pearl Harbor, agree to fight a limited war, and negotiate a political compromise in Asia rather than fight an all-out war. While it was essential that the war be short, Japan had no plan to ensure that this would happen.

This crucial rationale appears so far from reality, at least as far as the Americans would evaluate it, as to be the product of wishful thinking. While we can only speculate on the deliberative processes of Japanese leaders, in this case wishful thinking appears to be based on motivated bias—"deviations from what is usually considered rationality that stem not from purely cognitive limitations, but from psychological pressures and needs" (Jervis 1989, 196–97). As Robert Jervis points out, when leaders become committed to a particular policy (attacking ABD possessions in the Pacific), "they will feel strong psychological pressures to perceive that the threats they face can be overcome" as a way of coping with desperate situations (Jervis, Lebow, and Stein 1985, 26–30). When policymakers face certain losses and all alternatives are seen as problematic, decision makers will have a tendency to exaggerate the chances of the preferred policy's success and misperceive the world in ways that are "comforting" (Jervis 1989, 197).

The rational flaw in the Japanese plan, as Scott Sagan (1988, 346–47) points out, was that the attack on Pearl Harbor was such a closely held piece of tactical information that the full Liaison Conference was never informed of it. An attempt to negotiate a midwar settlement with the U.S. might have been feasible if the war had started with a strike against British and Dutch possessions, but the attack on Pearl Harbor made any future negotiation impossible. This contradiction was addressed neither in Cabinet meetings nor in Liaison Conferences nor in Imperial Conferences, most likely because many participants were left uninformed of the location of the attacks. The plan was so secret that not even Naval Intelligence was aware of it. Planning was done by the Operations section alone (Dower 1986, 260). The only discussion of the issue appeared to be among navy officials, and all objections were overruled by Yamamoto (Wohlstetter 1962, 373). The admiral, having spent several years in the United States as a naval attaché, should have known that the U.S. was not likely to seek a negotiated settlement under these circumstances. Nevertheless, he hoped that a devastating blow at Pearl Harbor would leave the American people and their military "so dispirited they will not be able to recover" (Dower 1986, 36). There was no serious attempt by any Japanese department to assess the psychological effect of a surprise attack on a U.S. base (Dower 1986, 260).

As John Dower (1986, 36) has argued, the self-deception of Japanese elites was based in part on cultural stereotypes buttressed by government propaganda that "portrayed Western culture as effete and the average American and Englishmen as too selfish to support a long war in a distant place." They assumed that the American war effort would be undermined by cultural forces such as labor strife, racial conflict, war profiteering, and by "softness" and other flaws in the national culture (Dower 1986, 260).

Ultimately, however, deterrence failed and Japanese leaders opted for war because the costs of not going to war were perceived as even higher than war itself (Sagan 1988, 350). Some of these costs were external, but some were based on internal politics. Refraining from war would mean continued domestic political conflict, with the high possibility of an army coup and the destruction of the imperial system. It would mean the end of political careers. It would mean relinquishing the gains won since the 1930s in China and Indochina and perhaps even Manchuria. It would mean that Japan would abdicate its status as a great power. It would mean subordination and dependence. It would mean the superiority of the Caucasian powers of the West over Asia. If Japan did not go to war, it could lose everything—reverting back to the position it held in the world in the 1920s. For many Japanese leaders, there was no conceivable way out. No alternative could promise a positive outcome, but the costs of the alternatives to war, even a losing war, appeared to be extremely high. In that case, opting for war, even though the chance for success was low, might in some sense be rational.

For their part, of course, American policymakers failed to calculate Japanese willingness to accept extreme risks. By our own standards, the risks for Japan of starting a war with America and Britain in the Pacific simply appeared too high, and too irrational.

Our discussion has now clearly taken us into the realm of immediate or short-term factors responsible for the decision for war. At this point, insights from prospect theory and bargaining theory will help us explain the decision for war.

SHORT-TERM FACTORS

The Individual Level of Analysis: Prospect Theory

While prospect theory is essentially an individual level theory of decision making, its insights are also useful in adding to our understanding of how national leaders make decisions in groups (Levi and White 1997). Let us briefly review the propositions put forward by prospect theory (Kahneman and Tversky 1979; Levy 1994a, 1994b; Jervis 1994). First, decision makers tend to think in terms of gains and losses rather than in terms of net assets; they therefore think of their choices in terms of deviations from a particular reference point—usually the status quo but sometimes an expectation level. Second, losses loom larger than gains in this calculus. Third, the perceived value of anything is proportional to the length of time it has been possessed and the effort and resources used to acquire it. Fourth, losses and gains are evaluated differently in terms of risk orientation: Decision makers tend to be averse to risks taken in order to make gains, but they tend to be acceptant of the risks taken in order to prevent losses. Fifth, because of the role of the reference point in defining gains and losses, the identification of the reference point—the framing of a choice—is of critical importance. Sixth, people tend to accommodate to (or come to accept) gains more quickly than losses. Newly acquired gains become part of the new status quo. Finally, if elites accommodate quickly to gains, this leads to risk-acceptant behavior designed to keep those gains. But accommodation to losses inhibits the tendency to take risks to reverse those losses (Levy 1994 a and 1994b).

In sum, prospect theory suggests that war is more likely when decision makers believe that they are defending the status quo and believe that they will suffer significant losses if they do not fight to defend the status quo. Decision makers will be much more willing to take risks when they believe that failing to do so will result in certain losses. Fear of loss, rather than the desire for expansion or gain, is the most significant motivating force behind war. The most dangerous situation occurs when *both* states in a dispute see themselves as defending the status quo (Jervis 1994, 31).

For the Japanese leadership, particularly hardline army officers, making territorial concessions to the United States—that is, abandoning the GEACPS and withdrawing forces from China and Manchuria—clearly constituted losses. Accommodating quickly to the gains that they had made throughout the 1930s and early 1940s, they considered Manchuria and the occupied portions of China to already be theirs. According to one analysis (Taliaferro 2004), Japanese leaders set their reference point not at the real or existing status quo but at an expectation level—the achievement of a Japanese New Order in East Asia—that included Manchuria and much of China. By mid-1940 Japanese elites perceived themselves to be facing losses in regard to this expectation level and they "found it extremely difficult, if not impossible, to abandon an expectation level that by all objective measures was no longer achievable." In response to their predicament, "senior officials not only escalated their commitment to the failing war in China, but undertook additional high-risk strategies vis-à-vis other great powers in the region" to solidify their position (Taliaferro 2004, 95–96).

As we have seen, at the October 16 cabinet meeting Tojo declared that giving in to American demands would "destroy the *fruits* of the China Incident" (Bix 2000, 417; emphasis added). Japanese decision makers saw themselves as defending the legitimate status quo in Asia, though it was a recently created status quo (or more realistically, a status quo in progress). And they were willing to take risks to maintain these possessions, especially given the significant costs that had been incurred in producing them. Togo, in a statement filled with references to loss, made this argument at the November 27 Liaison Conference: "Japan was asked not only to *abandon* the gains of her years of *sacrifice*, but to *surrender* her international position as a power in the Far East" (Feis 1950, 327; emphasis added). And Tojo emphasized the logic of "sunken costs" at the crucial November 5 Imperial Conference: "We sent a large force of one million men [to China], and it has cost us well over 100,000 dead and wounded, [the grief of] their bereaved families, hardship for four years, and a national expenditure of several billions of yen. We must by all means get satisfactory results from this" (Levi and White 1997, 805). (This logic applied less to Southeast Asia, which was acquired more recently and at much less cost. Japanese leaders were more flexible with regard to this issue.)

Japanese decision makers therefore believed that all the options they faced were unpleasant. They could make concessions to the U.S. and see their territorial sphere reduced to the pre-1931 levels; they could keep negotiating while the embargo progressively eroded Japan's relative economic and military strength; or they could strike American forces in the Pacific and initiate a war that could probably not be won (Levi and White 1997, 805).

On the other hand, American leaders perceived Japanese "gains" to be both illegitimate and temporary. They saw themselves as the rightful defenders of an Asian status quo, but the status quo they perceived predated the 1931 Japanese conquest of Manchuria. Thus both sides framed the situation in a manner that created the most dangerous situation possible: They both perceived themselves in the role of protecting the legitimate status quo against losses to the opponent (see Levi and White 1997 for a slightly different analysis).

In the end, Japanese leaders opted for the risky choice, despite the low probability of success, because it was the only option that might offer some chance, however slim, of preventing the loss of Japan's Asian sphere of influence and its relative power and international status. All other choices promised an absolutely certain loss.

Dyadic Level: Bargaining Theory

Bargaining theory can also help us understand the decision for war. As James Fearon (1995) argues, in a general sense all wars can be seen as bargaining failures—failures of states to resolve their differences short of war. Several insights from bargaining theory can help us understand how Japan and the United States arrived at a diplomatic impasse in December 1941.

First, the Japanese-American conflict process starkly illustrates the structure of a **two-level game** of diplomatic bargaining as described by Robert Putnam (1988). In Putnam's view, states are rarely unitary actors and therefore bargaining occurs simultaneously at two levels. Level I bargaining takes place *between* the two states (the U.S. and Japan), and Level II bargaining takes place *within* each government among the various political groups that have a say in the decision. Success at one level is dependent on success at the other level, since any agreement reached at Level I will be undone unless it is ratified by all the relevant parties in the Level II negotiations. Each side has a "win set" of possible outcomes (terms or conditions) that it will accept. If the win sets of the two states overlap—that is, if they both contain some identical conditions—then an agreement is possible. The larger each side's win set (that is, the range of conditions it is willing to accept), the more likely the two win sets will overlap and the more likely an agreement can be reached.

Several things are immediately apparent with regard to the ability of the U.S. and Japanese governments to negotiate a peaceful solution to their differences. First, any solution on the Japanese side had to have the agreement of the army, the navy, and the emperor. The main impediment to a diplomatic solution here was the army's insistence that the gains of the China Incident not be sacrificed. As Putnam suggests, the domestic constituents whose interests are most affected can be expected to exert special influence and to hold the most extreme position. This was certainly true with regard to the Imperial Army. Second, while the Level II bargaining within the United States pitted hardliners against accommodationists within the Roosevelt administration, other parties were also involved in the American political coalition. The United States' allies—the British, Dutch, and Chinese—weighed in and helped to turn the tide against the accommodationists who wanted to offer a modus vivendi as a diplomatic counter to Japan's Plan B.

Third, the conflict in the Pacific appears to be a classic example of diplomatic failure due to lack of mutual win sets. Of the issues that divided the two sides—Japan's participation in the Axis Pact, its advance into Southeast Asia, and the occupation of China—Japan was willing to dispense with the first and modify the second, but was unwilling to compromise on the third. The U.S., on the other hand, made Japanese withdrawal from China the *sine qua non* for any agreement (see Small 1980, 242). Hardline factions in the United States would adamantly oppose any agreement that did not include Japanese withdrawal from China, and any such concession would open the administration to charges of appeasement. As a result, no agreement would satisfy the relevant parties in both countries.

Finally, even though the costs of nonagreement were extremely high—a destructive and costly war for both sides—this did not significantly increase the size of the win set for either country. The threat of war did not produce significant concessions. Important players on both sides came to believe that despite the cost of war, giving in to the demands of the other side involved too much lost prestige and would exact too high a cost politically among the groups whose support the regime needed.

Further insight into the Japanese-American impasse can be gleaned from Fearon's (1995) analysis of war based on bargaining theory. Fearon starts with the proposition that since wars are costly for both sides, both should logically prefer other options. There should be some set of conditions acceptable to both that are preferable to war. The existence of war indicates a bargaining failure. War can be therefore be explained by explaining why negotiations fail to arrive at a peaceful alternative.

To greatly simplify Fearon's analysis, wars occur for one of three reasons—two of which are relevant here. First, one of the parties may hold private information (information not known by other parties). Examples of such private information would be knowledge about relative military capabilities, the willingness to use force over specific issues, war plans and strategies, or the reliability of allies (Fearon 1995, 381, 393, 398; Lake 2003, 82). Moreover, parties have an incentive to withhold or misrepresent this information. This is because although both wish to avoid the costs of war, they also wish to do well in bargaining and obtain a result favorable to their own interests (Fearon 1995, 395). Thus private information is often withheld and decisions are not made in the presence of full and complete information, and states may therefore hold quite different perceptions of the true balance of power between themselves.

Private information clearly played a role, but not perhaps in the way that Fearon's theory might have predicted. One example was Japan's ability to effectively use air-launched torpedoes in shallow waters. The best example of private information in 1941, however, involved Japanese war plans, specifically, the decision to initiate the war by attacking Pearl Harbor. This information was withheld from the U.S. for obvious reasons. But the real effect of private information was inside Japan itself. The Pearl Harbor portion of the plan was a closely held secret within the Japanese government. Only top-level planners within the Imperial Navy knew of the plan until the final days. Within the Imperial Army, few knew of the secret except the chief of staff and his deputy. Even the army and navy cabinet officials were probably in the dark until December 1. Civilian cabinet ministers, including the foreign minister, were not told of the plan until the task force had left its rendezvous point (Wohlstetter 1962, 380, 393). (Emperor Hirohito was fully briefed on the complete plan on November 15; see Bix 2000, 421–22.) Had the circle of leaders knowledgeable about the Pearl Harbor plan been widened, there may have been less support for the decision to end negotiations and initiate war. In other words, the existence of private information had an effect on the Level II bargaining *within* Japan among members of the Liaison Conferences and Imperial Conferences. It made it more likely that the relevant political elites in Japan would approve the plan. Not only did Japanese military officials have an incentive to withhold information about war plans from the U.S., but they also had an incentive to withhold the same information from their domestic rivals within the decision-making unit.

The second issue identified by Fearon is that *commitment problems* may exist in which one party's willingness to carry out the bargain is not perceived as credible. If Party A believes that B has an incentive to renege on the agreement, then A may lack faith in B's promise to carry out the deal. A typical problem is created by the perception that the opponent's power is expected to increase in the future, thereby decreasing any incentive in the future to abide by an agreement negotiated at a time of previous weakness. This problem, in which one state's power grows at a faster rate than the other, may lead to preventive wars. Declining states attack their rivals because they are fearful of the terms of the settlement they would have to accept in the future after their rival has increased its power (Fearon 1995, 381, 406; Lake 2003, 83).

Japanese leaders were well aware of the rapidly increasing power of the United States relative to that of Japan. One effect of this was that they tended to believe that any settlement reached with the U.S. in late 1941 would be worth little, since rising American power would put it in a position to demand further revisions or to simply renege on the agreement at a point when its military supremacy made such actions possible (Van Evera 1999, 78–84). In other words, Japanese leaders perceived that the U.S. could not be trusted to abide by a settlement. Their response was to try to negotiate the strongest agreement possible, thus reducing the potential for a mutual win set.

We turn now more specifically to the perceptions of Japanese leaders with regard to the decision to initiate a preventive war on the United States with an attack on Pearl Harbor.

Individual Level: Perceptions of Windows and Perceptions of Offensive Advantage

Many types of individual perceptions have been linked to decisions for war. Two perceptions that form a crucial part of Stephen Van Evera's **offense-defense balance theory** are particularly relevant in the Pacific war. The first is a perception of the existence of windows of opportunity and vulnerability that are brought on by shifts in global and/or dyadic distributions of power. The second is the perception that the offense-defense balance is in favor of offensive forces and strategies (Van Evera 1999, 73–104, 117–92).

The U.S.-Japanese dyadic balance is difficult to disentangle from the overall global balance. Both must be considered. After WWI, Japan made a rapid ascent through the ranks of global great powers. Japanese power was at an all-time high by the late 1930s. Moreover, as we have seen, in its dyadic relationship with the United States, Japan had achieved a tenuous military advantage in the Pacific. The U.S. counterbuildup did not move into high gear until the defeat of France in May 1940. Events in Europe dictated that the United States redeploy a quarter of its fleet to the Atlantic in the spring of 1941. In addition, the war in Europe tied down British and French forces in the west, and the defeat of France and Holland left the Asian/Pacific colonies of these states unprotected from Japanese advances. Thus as early as June 1940, Army Minister Hata was urging his staff to "seize the opportunity" (Sagan 1988, 326). The German attack on Russia in June 1941 improved Japan's position even more by reducing the threat of Soviet intervention against Japan in the Asian theater. Thus the shift in the global balance of power and the immediate consequences of the war in Europe created for Japan a sizable window of opportunity—by definition, an offensive opportunity that would eventually dwindle and disappear. (All windows of opportunity are by nature present-oriented and short term; they will eventually close.) Indeed, Japanese leaders perceived a "never to be repeated" opportunity to create for themselves an Asian empire (Van Evera 1999, 89–90; Ike 1967, xix; Butow 1961, 180). They also calculated that if the U.S. fleet in the Pacific was destroyed, the U.S. would be incapable of offensive actions for at least one year (Paul 1994, 67).

However, the window of opportunity perceived by Japanese elites in 1940 and 1941 was coupled with strong perceptions of an impending window of vulnerability—by definition a growing defensive vulnerability. (The nature of windows of vulnerability is that they are future-oriented and therefore long term.) Part of this impending vulnerability had to do with the huge size of the U.S. economy which might be harnessed for military purposes. As we have seen, some Japanese military strategists calculated total American war *potential* to be seven to eight times that of Japan (Russett 1972, 54). Even this astounding figure was probably understated. According to historian Paul Kennedy (1987, 303), in those fundamental attributes of national power that are especially important in long wars, the United States "had nearly twice the population of Japan, and seventeen times the national income, produced five times as much steel, and seven times as much coal, and made eighty times as many motor vehicles each year. Its industrial potential, even in a poor year like 1938, was seven times larger than Japan's; it might in other years be nine or ten times as large."

The increased U.S. naval buildup, coupled with the U.S. oil embargo in July 1941, triggered the perception by Japanese leaders that there was limited time to make use of its window of opportunity. Japanese oil stocks would last two years at the very most. Furthermore, Japanese naval advantages would soon be lost. Japanese naval planners thought Japan had a chance to win a war with the United States if its overall naval balance with the latter was 5:10 (because the U.S. had to split its fleet across two oceans). They also calculated that while the ratio was expected to climb to 7:10 in late 1941, at current rates of construction, it would decline to 5:10 in 1943 and to 3:10 in 1944 (Van Evera 1999, 89, citing Pelz 1974, 224). In 1941 pessimism about the coming war with the U.S. abounded.

In a Liaison Conference several days before Washington announced its freeze of Japanese assets, Naval Chief of Staff Nagano declared that if Japan went to war with the United States immediately, it would "have a chance of achieving victory" though this chance would decrease as time passed (Bix 2000, 401). When questioned by Emperor Hirohito about this several days later, on July 30, Nagano declared that "if we are going to fight, then the sooner we do so the better because our supplies are gradually dwindling anyway" (Bix 2000, 402). In early August, Adm. Takagi Sokichi, a naval leader with close ties to the Imperial Palace, summed up the situation, noting that "if Japan lets the time pass while under pressure from lack of materials [the oil embargo], we will be giving up without a fight. If we make our attack now, the war is militarily calculable and not hopeless. But if we vacillate, the situation will become increasingly disadvantageous for us" (Bix 2000, 406–7).

The perceptions of short-term opportunity and long-term vulnerability combine to increase the likelihood of war. In 1941, the nature of the international and dyadic environments created a "now or never" atmosphere among Japanese leaders, especially within the military. The general belief was that the chances of victory against the major Western powers would be minimally acceptable in the short term but would diminish rapidly with time. It is this perception that lay behind the Japanese decision to embark on a more risky strategy of imperial conquest to the south at the expense of the Western colonial powers.

Added to the perception of a window of opportunity was a perception that a significant military advantage could be gained from a first strike against U.S.

military targets (Van Evera 1999, 35, 39; Paul 1994, 68). (The same perception in-fluenced Japanese leaders in their decision to initiate the Russo-Japanese War in 1904. Indeed, the success of that strategy against Russia greatly influenced strate-gic thinking in Japan.) A war initiated by a surprise attack would create smaller risks and greater rewards for going to war, thus changing the perceived calculus and tempting Japanese leaders to adopt a policy of war. A preventive logic permeated Japanese thinking: The military especially was tempted to launch an "early" war against the United States, not because it feared the U.S. would strike Japan first and therefore Japan needed to preempt, but because if Japan waited until the power shift in America's favor was complete, not only would all chance of future gains be lost, but past gains would have to be surrendered.

SUMMARY

During the 1920s and 1930s, multiple conditions at several levels of analysis combined to create the potential for conflict between the United States and Japan in Asia.

In the first two decades of the twentieth century significant changes in the distribution of power had taken place within the international system. Rapid structural change—brought about by World War I and by disparity in economic growth rates—took several forms. There was a general deconcentration of power at the global level as British hegemony ceased to exist and as the system moved toward a multipolar system made up of several great powers with relatively equal power, thereby setting up a conflict over global leadership. In the late 1930s this system was also becoming more polarized, as the great powers of Europe and Asia were involved in the formation of mutually exclusive alliances. Rapid structural change also meant that several states, including Japan, passed through critical points in their power cycles. Dyadic power shifts between ma-jor power rivals had a cascading effect throughout the international system, in-tersecting with more general, systemic shifts in power distribution. All of these changes created increased uncertainty, increased anxiety, increased perceptions of threat, and increased propensity for risk taking. For Japanese leaders, these changes triggered perceptions of windows of opportunity and windows of vul-nerability that also increased the likelihood of risk taking.

Rapid systemic changes also created an imbalance between power and role and status in the system, creating a situation of status discrepancy. Japanese elites tended to see Japan as an unwanted and unappreciated member of the club of great powers. They believed that Western powers had not accorded them the respect and prestige they were rightfully due on the basis of their bona fide eco-nomic and military might. They identified themselves with other dissatisfied re-visionist states that had much to gain by radically revising the postwar interna-tional system. The existence of a dissatisfied "challenger" of the current global order that is also a "rising" military power was a dangerous combination.

Moreover, the lack of strong systemic norms against the use of force made a challenge by revisionist states more likely and more dangerous. In the aftermath of World War I, global norms against the use of force and international institu-tions created to maintain these norms had been constructed, but they were not well institutionalized. On the contrary; they were nascent, fragile, and weak. In Japan, some elites supported these new liberal international norms and institutions, but those who rejected these norms proved the stronger domestically. The nineteenth-century realpolitik approach to foreign policy continued to dominate the political scene in Tokyo.

At the nation-state level of analysis, the most important factor was that Japan was in the midst of a democratic transition. The process of democratization was chaotic, fragile, and often violent. The Japanese system in the 1920s and 1930s is probably best characterized as a political system with contested institutions, in which powerful groups, including the military, were locked in mortal combat with one another to protect and promote their interests and their political power. The Japanese military was both highly politicized and relatively autonomous in its ability to act; and it used its autonomy and political clout to circumvent the more conciliatory policies of the government by taking independent military action to create "facts on the ground." Moreover, in its struggle with civilian political leaders, the military tended to see foreign adventure as crucial to its institutional survival and well-being; thus Japanese military expansion always had a diversionary logic behind it. In the absence of the ability of the military to protect its interests by coup d'état, the existence of foreign wars was the preferred strategy of the military. The domestic political struggle in Japan resulted in the ascendancy of hardliners over accommodationists. Especially after the end of party governments in 1932, a coalition of the army, navy, state-supported businesses, and right-wing politicians controlled Japan's foreign policy and appealed to the nationalist impulses of the population through "prestige strategies" abroad. The decision to attack Pearl Harbor was due in part to considerations of domestic politics: War would be preferable to continued paralysis, which would surely bring open internal warfare and a coup that might undermine the monarchy.

At the dyadic level, multiple rivalries were involved, but the U.S.-Japan rivalry was of central importance. The two countries had become rivals at the dawn of the twentieth century, and the rivalry intensified in the 1930s and 1940s due to intractable territorial issues (Japan's conquest of Manchuria and China). Intransigence on territorial issues led to the use of coercive bargaining tactics that were reciprocated by the other side, leading to the increased power of hardliners on each side and therefore to the use of more coercive bargaining behavior and greater risk taking. Territorial conflicts between China and Japan, associated with the latter's policies of autarky and imperialism, led to the Japanese foray into Manchuria and then into northern China. These regional wars in Asia precipitated a long conflict spiral between Japan and the United States centered over the issue of China. As the conflict continued over the decade between 1931 and 1941, repeated crisis interactions taught all sides that "force was the only way to deal with the situation" (Vasquez 1998, 197–98).

The attack on Pearl Harbor was the last of a long series of mutually antagonistic and hostile acts undertaken by the Japanese and American governments in response to the actions of the other. Japanese policies of aggression against China, fueled in part by autonomous actions by the military, followed by further aggression in Southeast Asia largely designed to "save" the situation in China, compelled the United States, Britain, and Holland to impose progressively punitive economic sanctions that dramatically challenged Japan's security. Unable for political reasons to give up territorial gains on the mainland and unwilling to accept the loss of international status that territorial concessions would entail, Japan pushed doggedly forward, seeking to establish secure sources of raw materials that it would need to fight a war against the United States, Britain, and Russia—a war that would almost certainly occur if Japan refused to make territorial concessions. Japan's efforts to solidify its gains in Asia only increased Western perceptions of its aggressive intent, and Western reactions to Japanese expansion increased Japanese perceptions of Western hostility.

The conflict spiral involved most of the normal, realpolitik tactics of foreign policy that one would expect: coercive techniques of international bargaining such as the buildup of military forces, the use of economic sanctions, construction of alliances, the threat of force, the use of force, and so on. Adding to the conflict spiral and increasing the tensions and fears was an arms race between Japan and the United States in the Pacific. At the dyadic level, although overall American military and economic power was vastly superior to that of Japan, in the theater that counted, the Asian-Pacific region, the dyadic balance was, at least temporarily, in favor of Japan. While the Japanese leaders understood that U.S. overall superiority could be rather quickly applied to the Pacific, they also perceived a window of opportunity that would end if Japan declined to take immediate action. Moreover, they perceived a first-strike advantage.

American deterrent threats failed to work because Japanese leaders perceived that the costs of *not* going to war were higher than war itself, even if Japan were to suffer defeat. The presumed costs of inaction were both internal (domestic conflict, the possibility of a coup, and the destruction of the imperial system of rule) and external (loss of territorial gains, loss of great power status, economic dependence, and political subordination). Consistent with prospect theory, policymakers in both the United States and Japan saw themselves as defending a legitimate status quo. Japanese leaders in particular were willing to take significant risks to maintain gains already achieved, especially given the tremendous costs that had been incurred in producing these gains.

AFTERMATH

On August 6, 1945, a single American bomber unleashed "Little Boy," a uranium fission bomb produced by the Manhattan Project, over the Japanese city of Hiroshima. And on August 9 a plutonium bomb nicknamed "Fat Man," was dropped on Nagasaki. Seventy thousand Japanese died that first day in Hiroshima, and perhaps forty thousand in Nagasaki. (By the end of the year, deaths from the two bombs had reached 210,000, and by 1950 perhaps 340,000 had died from the two explosions.) On August 10 Japanese authorities told the Allies of their intent to surrender, and by the fifteenth Japan had accepted Allied terms. A long American occupation followed, with the end result being the reconstruction of Japan as a democratic, capitalist state.

Most of Europe and Asia lay in ruins. Total military and civilian deaths associated with the war probably surpassed fifty million. Even the victors emerged with grievous losses. The sole state to emerge in a strong position was the United

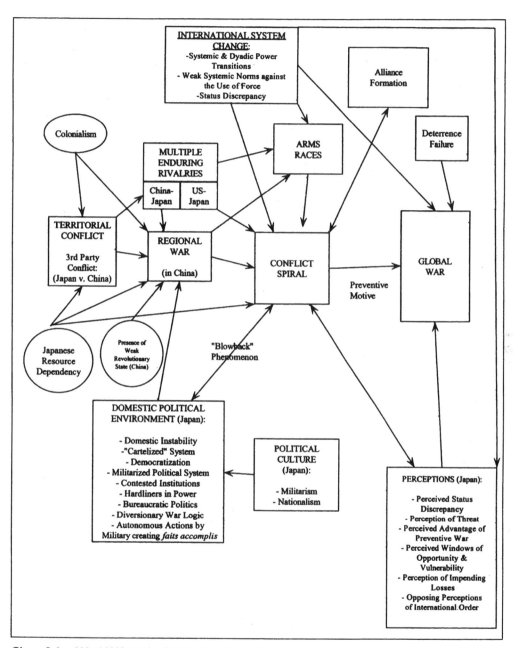

Chart 3.1.   World War II in the Pacific: Causal Factors

States, whose continental territories had escaped attack. Though it appeared that two "superpowers" had emerged from the ashes, the power of the Soviet Union in the immediate aftermath of war was largely built on smoke and mirrors; its Western realm had been utterly devastated by the war. Keeping its relative weakness a secret would become a primary objective.

Most global wars end with a reorganization of the international system. World War II was no exception. By 1945 a new global political and economic order was under construction. The foundations of this new system were the United Nations and its sister institutions such as the International Court of Justice, the International Monetary Fund, the World Bank, and the Global Agreement on Tariff and Trade (GATT). Though these new global institutions were jointly constructed by the victorious Allies, the power behind this new order was in the hands of the new global hegemon, the United States—the only state with the economic and military strength and the global reach to ensure the functioning of the system and to enforce the rules of the game.

While it had been hoped that the Allied powers would cooperate to provide international harmony in the postwar world, within three or fours years of the war's end, Allied cohesion had proved unsustainable. The Cold War had become an international fact of life. The world was divided into two camps, both of which created exclusive military alliances and trading groups. The bipolar conflict between East and West became the central dynamic of international politics until the collapse of the Communist bloc and of the Soviet Union in the years between 1989 and 1991.

As usual, the defeated states lost their empires. Korea was liberated from Japanese control and quickly became divided between a northern Soviet-occupied zone and the southern zone occupied by U.S. forces, thus laying the seeds for the first armed combat associated with the new Cold War. As Japanese forces left China and Manchuria, Chiang Kai-shek's Nationalist KMT resumed its long death struggle with Mao's Chinese Communist Party, a struggle that would end with Communist victory in 1949.

Not only did the defeated powers lose their colonial possessions, but the war simultaneously invigorated the principle of national self-determination and weakened the ability of European states to maintain their empires. In 1947 Britain permitted India and Pakistan to become independent states. The age of decolonization had begun. In some cases colonial powers voluntarily withdrew; in other cases bloody national liberation struggles began. Within the next fifty years, more than one hundred new sovereign states would be created, creating a more complex and diverse international system. The new states quickly became the subject of bipolar competition between the superpowers.

Finally, the nuclear age that had begun in August 1945 initiated a nuclear arms race, with the USSR joining the nuclear club in August 1949. Nuclear proliferation was the order of the day. Britain and France attained the new weaponry first, but the nuclear genie would not be confined to the former great powers. China, Israel, South Africa, India, Pakistan, and eventually North Korea would all make the nuclear leap. Others would try: notably Iraq and Iran. The world had become in many ways a more dangerous place.

4

The Six-Day War

Just before 8:00 am on June 5, 1967, the armed forces of the state of Israel struck Egypt. The Jewish state's offensive caught the bulk of Egypt's Soviet-supplied air force still on the ground, where the planes were sitting ducks for Israeli pilots. Lacking air support, Egyptian ground forces were no match for Israeli troops and armored units. Egypt's army was badly mauled in the fighting, permitting Israeli forces to gain control of the Sinai Peninsula and the Gaza Strip. Meanwhile, to the east Jordan's King Hussein, acting on erroneous reports sent to him by Gamal Abdel Nasser about Egypt's "success" on the battlefield, and ignoring a warning from Israeli prime minister Levi Eshkol to stay out of the fighting, ordered his army to begin an artillery barrage of Israeli positions. The Israelis responded by launching an effective counterstrike, seizing control of the West Bank and Arab East Jerusalem after heavy fighting. Finally, Israel turned its attention to the Syrian frontier, where after several days, Israeli forces occupied the strategically vital Golan Heights. In six short days, the strategic, political, territorial, and psychological landscape of the Middle East had been fundamentally altered.

To many observers, the Six-Day War may appear to be another inevitable chapter in the long-running Arab-Israeli conflict. And yet, it is important to note that all available evidence points to the fact that as late as one month before the war, none of the actors to the conflict expected that a major outbreak of interstate violence was on the horizon. "The Six-Day War between Israel and its Arab neighbors in June 1967 burst upon an unsuspecting world as suddenly as a summer storm" (Brown and Parker 1996, 1). This chapter identifies the forces, events, and decisions that provided the spark which precipitated this sudden "storm" over the Middle East. We will begin with an overview of the historical roots of the Arab-Israeli conflict, and then proceed with an analysis of the immediate-term causes of the Six-Day War.

Map 4.1. Israel and the Surrounding Arab States

ROOTS OF WAR: LONG-TERM CAUSES

Religion

Chronicling and explaining the complete history of the conflict between Jews and Arabs in the Middle East is indeed a daunting task. In fact, such an effort is beyond the analytical scope of this chapter. However, a brief summary of the religious roots of tensions in the region is in order, if for no other reason than to highlight some commonly held misconceptions about both the duration and nature of the conflict.

It is tempting to assume that the conflict between Jews and Muslims is grounded solely in religion. Ironically, both peoples claim to trace their lineages back to Abraham: Jews believe they are descendants of Isaac, son of Abraham and his wife Sarah; Muslims trace their roots to Ishmael, son of Abraham and Hagar, Sarah's handmaiden (Bickerton and Klausner 1998, 3). Religious identities and territorial claims intertwine inside the walls of the old city of Jerusalem, which is the holiest city in the Jewish faith, and the third holiest city (behind Mecca and Medina) for Muslims. Is this simply a case then of two nations of people with conflicting religious claims to the same plot of land?

To depict and explain the conflict solely in religious terms is a gross oversimplification. For one thing, during the vast expanse of time between the dispersal of Jews from Palestine by the Romans around AD 70 and the founding of the modern Zionist movement at the end of the nineteenth century, there were relatively few Jews living in the Middle East, particularly in the area near the Holy Land. At the beginning of the nineteenth century, only about twenty-five thousand Jews lived in Greater Syria, a region that encompassed the modern territorial units of Syria, Lebanon, Jordan, and Israel/Palestine. These Jews lived under the Ottoman system of *millets*, in which minority groups such as Jews and Christians were considered along with Muslims to be "People of the Book." As a result of this status, Christians and Jews, although not treated as political equals to Muslims, were permitted a significant degree of autonomy, particularly in religious, social, and judicial matters (Farsoun and Zacharia 1997, 27). By the 1850s, the position of Jews within the Ottoman Empire improved even further as a result of the Tanzimat reforms, under which enhanced religious and political freedoms were promised for all the empire's subjects. It was only after these reforms, the timing of which happened to coincide with a surge of anti-Semitism in Eastern Europe, that Jewish immigration to Palestine began to increase (Bickerton and Klausner 1998, 19–20). Put simply, interaction between Arabs and Jews in the region was fairly limited, and not very conflictual, prior to the turn of the twentieth century.

Furthermore, to view the conflict purely through the spectrum of religion clouds the differences that exist *within* the Jewish and Arab communities respectively. The Jewish population in Israel has always been divided sharply between religious and secular Jews. An additional split between Jews who hail from Europe (the Ashkenazim) and those whose roots are in Africa or the Middle East (the Sephardim) had (and continues to have) a major impact on Israeli politics.

In the Arab world, divisions exist both between Muslims and non-Muslims, and within the Muslim community itself. According to the seventh edition of the Congressional Quarterly publication *The Middle East*, as of 1990 Christians comprised nearly 50 percent of the population in Lebanon, about 10 percent of the population in Syria, and about 5 percent in both Egypt and Jordan. In fact, two of the founding figures of the modern Arab secular nationalist movement were the Syrian political thinkers Antun Sa'ada and Michel Aflaq, both of whom were Christians. It is not surprising that Christian philosophers would espouse a secular notion of national identity in the Arab Middle East, since the alternative basis of identity—religion—would place the Christian minority at a potential disadvantage vis-à-vis the Muslim majority.

Among Arab Muslims, a controversy developed in the late seventh century AD over the question of the appropriate line of the succession from the Prophet Mohammad. From this conflict over the right to rule the main schism within Islam emerged and persists. Although the large majority of Muslims today adhere to the Sunni faith, approximately 10 percent are members of the Shi'a sect, including the majority of the citizens of the wealthy Persian Gulf state of Bahrain, and a full 30 percent of the populations of Lebanon and Kuwait. Iran, a Persian country, is virtually 100 percent Shi'a. In Syria, Alawites, who belong to a secretive offshoot of the Shi'a branch, are just 10 percent of the population, but leading figures of the Alawite community—in particular the Asad family—have dominated the Syrian political system through their control of the ruling Ba'ath Party for over three decades. Finally, Druze Muslims, another Islamic sect, are found in Syria, Lebanon, and the former Palestine.

Recognizing the divisions that characterize both Islam and Judaism does not mean that one should completely ignore the religious aspects of the conflict in the region. As the failed Camp David negotiations in 2000 illustrate, the competing Palestinian and Israeli claims to sovereignty over Jerusalem severely complicate the objective of achieving a full settlement to the Middle East conflict. However, the problem of how to resolve the Jerusalem issue is the exception, rather than the rule, in the Middle East. In fact, the violence that is triggered by religion in the Middle East is quite often inwardly directed. That is to say, it is commonly aimed by radical fundamentalists at their own regimes. For example, both Egyptian president Anwar Sadat and Israeli prime minister Yitzhak Rabin died at the hands of extremists from within their own populations.

On the other hand, as is evidenced by the completion of peace treaties between Israel and Egypt (1979) and Israel and Jordan (1994), religious animosity between Jews and Muslims does not automatically preclude the achievement of formal agreements between political elites at the level of state-to-state relations. In fact, given the avowedly secular nature of the governments that represent the most powerful state players in the regional conflict drama—Israel, Egypt, and Syria—religious divisions offer at best only a partial underlying explanation for the long-running Arab-Israeli dispute.

Ethnicity and Nationalism

Just as focusing solely on religion as the catalyst for violence in the region is incorrect, it is also inaccurate to portray the Arab-Israeli conflict as a simple case of two monolithic, ethno-national blocs engaged in an inevitable struggle for dominance over each other within a limited, contested territorial space. In particular, such a view ignores the role played by external powers in stoking the flames of mistrust and dispute in pursuit of their own narrow self-interests, as well as the impact of domestic divisions upon the behavior of the parties to the conflict in the Middle East. That having been said, the emergence in the late nineteenth and early twentieth centuries of ethno-national movements within the Jewish and Arab communities alike, and their competing claims to the territory known then as Palestine, created obvious intercommunal tensions in the region.

The very concept of a Jewish nation is a slippery one at best. As scholars Ian Bickerton and Carla Klausner put it, "Jews are not simply a nationality, are not a race, and are more than a religion" (Bickerton and Klausner 1998, 4). Nor can one rely on language, the typical wellspring of nationalism, as the primary criterion for Jewish national identity, since Hebrew is not the native language for most Jews.

Historically, the roots of modern Jewish nationalism can be traced to conditions in late-nineteenth-century Europe. At that time and place, Jewish national aspirations came to be expressed by the Zionist movement. Led by Theodor Herzl, the Zionists first appeared in Eastern Europe in response to the rising wave of anti-Semitism and *pogroms* (persecutions) to which the Jews in this region (in particular those under the rule of tsarist Russia) found themselves subjected. Seeking to escape a life of poverty and persecution, many Jews fled Eastern Europe for the United States, while others began to contemplate migration to Palestine. Eventually, six *aliyas* (waves) of Jewish immigration into Palestine occurred between 1882 and 1948. From a total of 24,000 in 1882, the Jewish population in Palestine grew to over 650,000 on the eve of Israel's independence in 1948. As a percentage of the total population in Palestine, the Jewish community grew from 4 percent in 1882 to 33 percent in 1948 (Massoulie 1999, 68).

Support among European Jews for the idea of a secular Jewish state picked up further momentum in Western Europe in 1894, when a Jewish officer in the French army, Alfred Dreyfus, was convicted of treason and sentenced to death. Although the sentence was eventually overturned (after another officer confessed to the crime) and Dreyfus set free, the level of anti-Semitism in France and the rest of Europe stunned many Jews. The so-called Dreyfus Affair energized the fledgling Zionist movement. In 1897, the World Zionist Congress met in Basel, Switzerland. Led by Herzl, the delegates to the conference issued a statement defining Zionism's goal as being "to create for the Jewish people a homeland in Palestine using public law" (Bickerton and Klausner 1998, 22–24).

It is important to recognize the fact that Herzl and the other Zionist leaders at that time did not frame their movement as an attempt to achieve a specifically religious outcome. Nor, despite the 1897 proclamation, were all early Zionists absolutely wedded to the idea that Palestine must be the site of the Jewish homeland. In 1899, Cyprus was proposed as a possible location. In 1902, Herzl seriously considered a British offer to establish a Jewish homeland in the Sinai. In 1903, the "Uganda Plan" designated a part of Kenya as a potential site (Bickerton and Klausner 1998, 24). Although ultimately the Zionists rejected each of these proposals and set their sights on the biblical land of Israel as the preferred location for their state, their willingness in the early stages of the movement to consider areas other than Palestine underscored the fact that many of them defined the challenge of creating a Jewish homeland as a practical political problem which might require a compromise solution, rather than treating it as a religious crusade (Mansfield 1991, 160).

Having learned the art and practice of politics in post-Enlightenment Europe, the early Zionists saw the objective of their movement largely in secular terms. They aimed for the creation of a Western-style nation-state whose population would be comprised of citizens who shared the Zionist dream of a homeland for Jews, preferably in Palestine. Zionism was clearly a nationalist movement; it was not, however, exclusively, or even primarily, an ideological religious movement.

In the case of the Arabs, the attempt to construct a single sense of national identity was complicated by the territorial, religious, and ideological divisions in the Middle East, as well as by the historical legacy of external domination. Arab nationalism—the vision of a single Arab nation spanning (and essentially obliterating) state boundaries in the Middle East—has had to compete first with familial, local, and religious identities, and later with state identities, for the hearts and minds of Arabs. Ideologically, as will be discussed in greater detail later in this chapter, the so-called Arab world was plagued by divisions throughout the latter part of the twentieth century.

It is critical to note that the Jewish national movement got a significant head start on its Arab counterpart. The successful Arab revolt against Ottoman rule during World War I both influenced and was influenced by the initial stirrings of Arab nationalism. However, this nascent spark of nationalism was quickly dampened by the boundaries that were forced on the region by Great Britain and France after the war, about which more will be said below. In the words of scholar Fred J. Khouri, "Just at the time when most Jews in various countries were uniting to support the Zionist cause in Palestine, the Arab World found itself split into many territorial units—mandates, protectorates, and 'independent states'" (Khouri 1985, 19). Weakened by shallow roots and poisoned by conflicting interests and identities, nationalism was never as strong a mobilizing force for Arabs as it was for Jews, at least prior to the appearance of Nasser on the scene in the early 1950s.

The most significant impact of ethnicity has been within the context of the status of Palestine. The Zionists' dream of founding a secular state for Jews in Palestine, and the Arabs' resistance to that plan, created the conditions by which an intercommunal conflict could emerge, fester, and eventually boil over. The fact that since 1948 large numbers of Palestinians have found themselves living either in Israel proper or in Israeli-occupied territories has underscored the ethnic dimension to the conflict. In that sense, ethnicity has played a role in providing a motivation, or some might more cynically say a rationale, for the Arab states to proclaim their solidarity with the Arabs of Palestine, and to resort on occasion to force against Israel. It is the presence of what they view to be an alien nation in their midst that informs the Arabs' opposition to the existence of Israel.

On the other side, for the early Zionists who created a Jewish island in a sea of Arabs, the question of ethnicity had, and continues to have, critical international, domestic, and psychological implications. Externally, the early Jewish settlers relied on Zionists around the world to supply monetary support for their cause. In fact, Israel today continues to seek international support during times of crisis, as evidenced by advertisements that appeared in late 1999 in popular Western periodicals calling for foreign donors to contribute money to the Jewish National Fund in order to combat the problems caused by a severe drought in Israel. Internally, the sticky issue of preserving Israel's "Jewishness" while at the same time absorbing hundreds of thousands of non-Jews (i.e., Palestinian Arabs) through successive territorial conquests in 1948 and 1967 has created a policy challenge for Israeli decision makers. Psychologically, the link between Jewish identity and the ancient land of Israel forges a "relationship to the land [that] supersedes and becomes superior to all other relationships" for Zionists (Peri 1988, 47). Thus at its core the Arab-Israeli conflict is a dispute over territory.

Territory

In its early stages, the dispute in Palestine primarily involved the struggle between the indigenous Arab population and the rising tide of Jewish immigrants for control over the same parcel of land. By the 1940s, the cast of players in the drama was widened to include the Arab states, which, being vulnerable in their infancy, saw the Palestine question as a way to strengthen their fragile internal security environments. In fact, the intercommunal aspect of the dispute was largely eclipsed between 1948 and 1967 by its interstate component, as Palestinians looked to the Arab states to secure for them their national rights and as Arab state leaders looked to bolster their own shaky political regimes by taking a hard line in defense of the Palestinian people (Aruri 1988, 73). And yet, if one peels away the layers of domestic politics and inter-Arab intrigue, the struggle to control the territory of Israel/Palestine has remained at the center of the Arab-Israeli conflict.

In order to grasp the roots of the twentieth-century territorial dispute in the region, it is necessary to start with World War I and its aftermath. Between July 14, 1915, and January 16, 1916, British official Sir Arthur Henry McMahon sent a series of letters to a key Arab leader, Sharif Hussein, asking that Hussein lead a revolt against the Ottomans. The so-called Hussein-McMahon correspondence resulted in an agreement under which the Arabs would seek to undermine Ottoman rule in exchange for the promise of an independent Arab state after the war.

At about the same time the British reached their agreement with Hussein, they were also engaged in secret negotiations with the French over the postwar division of territory in the Middle East. These talks led to the Sykes-Picot Agreement, named after the chief British and French representatives responsible for negotiating the accord. Under the terms of the agreement, the British would control modern Iraq and Jordan, while the French would govern Syria and Lebanon. Palestine was designated to become an international zone. Although the secret deal was leaked in 1917 after the Communists came to power in Russia, the Sykes-Picot Agreement eventually served as the blueprint for colonial control of the region after the war.

Further complicating the situation, on November 2, 1917, British official Lord Balfour issued the Balfour Declaration, in which the British government announced that it looked "with favor (upon) the establishment in Palestine of a National Home for the Jewish people." However, in a nod to the interests of the

Arab majority in Palestine, the Balfour Declaration promised that "nothing shall be done to prejudice the civil and religious rights of existing non-Jewish communities in Palestine" (Andersen, Seibert, and Wagner 1998, 70). In effect, the colonial powers had made conflicting promises to the Zionists and Arabs regarding the future status of Palestine.

The disintegration of the Ottoman Empire after the war left a power vacuum in the region that the victorious European powers, Britain and France, scrambled to fill. The colonial division of territory, in which London and Paris would draw new territorial boundaries in the Middle East, was given the stamp of international approval in 1922 when the League of Nations officially recognized British and French mandates in the region. The British mandate included Iraq and Palestine, the latter of which was placed under direct British control rather than being internationalized, as was suggested in the Sykes-Picot Agreement. The British chose to cleave the east bank of the Jordan River away from the Palestine mandate, in the process creating a new territorial entity known as Trans-jordan (later shortened to Jordan) east of the river. In an effort to placate the Hashemite family, which had spearheaded the Arab revolt against Ottoman rule and now agitated for Arab independence, the British named one Hashemite brother, Feisal, king of Iraq, while the other brother, Abdullah, was named king of the newly created territory of Trans-jordan. Meanwhile, the French controlled Syria and Lebanon. Under the mandate system, the colonial powers were charged with working toward preparing the territories under their control for eventual independence.

Over the next two decades, the decision to accept the mandate over Palestine would come back to haunt the British as the tension between Jews and Arabs mounted. As early Zionist leader Ze'ev Jabotinsky correctly predicted, violence between Jews and Arabs was an inevitable consequence of the attempt to secure a Jewish homeland in Palestine. "Colonization (of Palestine by Zionists) is self-explanatory," wrote Jabotinsky, "and what it implies is fully understood by every sensible Jew and Arab. There can be only one purpose in colonization. For the country's Arabs, that purpose is essentially unacceptable. This is a natural reaction and nothing will change it" (quoted in Lustick 1996, 4).

The issues of immigration and land purchases put the Zionists on a collision course with the Palestinian Arab population. The first major instance of intercommunal bloodshed under the mandate broke out around the Wailing Wall in Jerusalem in August 1929. In the wake of the violence, which saw scores of Jews killed by rioting Arabs, the British government launched an investigation into the causes of the crisis. The report that was submitted by the commission headed by Sir Walter Shaw blamed Arabs for being the immediate catalyst for the conflict, but then went on to observe that the Arab population in Palestine perceived itself, with some justification, as being under increasing political and economic pressure from the rising tide of Jewish immigration.

In the aftermath of the report, Sir John Hope-Simpson was dispatched to the region in order to examine in greater detail the tension over immigration and land issues. He passed his analysis on to the British government, which incorporated his recommendations into the first of a series of official government statements on Britain's Palestine policy that would be issued throughout the length of the British mandate period. The Passfield White Paper of 1930 enforced tight restrictions on Jewish immigration to Palestine and stated that land should only be sold to landless Arabs. The new policy caused a firestorm of protest from Zionists in London against British prime minister Ramsay MacDonald. The domestic political pressure being too intense to bear, MacDonald quickly relented, essentially repudiating the findings and recommendations of the Passfield White Paper (Bickerton and Klausner 1998, 52).

The question of immigration would become even more complicated in the mid-1930s, as the rise to power of Adolf Hitler in Germany fueled a wave of Jewish immigration into Palestine. In 1930, just four thousand Jews entered Palestine. By 1935, that number had jumped to sixty-two thousand. Once more, Arabs demanded that the British curtail Jewish immigration, as well as the sale of land to Jews. When the British failed to do so, the various Arab factions came together to form the Arab High Committee, under the leadership of the grand mufti of Jerusalem, Hajj Amin al-Husseini. The Arab High Committee called for and maintained a general strike for six months and organized the unsuccessful Arab Revolt against British rule from 1936 to 1939.

In 1937 the Peel Commission concluded that the rift between the Jews and Arabs in Palestine was so deep that the only solution was the creation of two states. However, the Zionists had severe reservations about the plan, which kept Jerusalem and Haifa under British rule. For their part, Palestinian Arabs firmly rejected the partition plan and increased their efforts against Jewish land purchases and immigration, as well as against British rule (Mansfield 1991, 205–6). In fact, the Palestinians became so fierce in their opposition that the British moved to smash the Arab High Committee, an action that caused the grand mufti to flee the mandate territory (Khouri 1985, 25).

Ultimately the Arab Revolt failed, and it had the short-term effect of enhancing ties between Britain and the Zionists in Palestine by forcing the British to cooperate with Jewish guerrilla forces in opposition to Arab military activities. However, it also caused growing consternation among those in the British government who were increasingly obsessed with events on the European continent. With Europe teetering on the precipice of another major war, and with the Jews, for obvious reasons, ready to support any alliance opposed to Hitler's Germany, the British calculated that a missing piece to their global strategic puzzle was broad Arab support for British war aims.

With this in mind, another government report, the White Paper of 1939, attempted to address some of the Arab populations' concerns in Palestine, with the goal being to draw the Arabs closer to Britain. The report declared that Palestine would be granted full independence within ten years and that Jewish immigration would be limited to seventy-five thousand over the next five years. After that, any further Jewish immigration was subject to Arab consent. The combination of the five-year numerical restriction on immigration and the requirement for Arab approval thereafter guaranteed that, upon independence, the Arabs would still form the majority of the population in Palestine. The report stated that the British government, in putting tight limits on Jewish immigration, in fact rejected the argument by some "that all further Jewish immigration into Palestine should be stopped forthwith." In what is in retrospect a chilling understatement, the paper goes on to explain the government's refusal to completely end Jewish immigration by noting "the present *unhappy plight* of large numbers of Jews who seek a refuge from certain European countries" (*The White Paper of 1939*, as published in Bickerton and Klausner 1998, 65–66; emphasis added). Put simply, London chose to downplay the Holocaust because its security interests dictated that Britain improve its relations with the Arabs at the end of the 1930s.

In the aftermath of World War II, the pressure to create a Jewish homeland in Palestine increased. In May 1946 the joint Anglo-American Committee of Inquiry issued a report calling for, among other things, the issuance of one hundred thousand permits to Jewish refugees in Europe allowing them to immigrate to Palestine; the creation of a multireligious, democratic government under the umbrella of a UN trust; and an end to certain land and employment practices by the Jewish National Fund that were judged to be prejudicial to the Palestinians. The U.S. administration of Harry Truman, keenly aware that critical congressional elections were coming up in the fall of 1946, embraced the parts of the plan that seemed more favorable to the Zionists, while taking a wait-and-see attitude toward the rest of the proposal. For their part, British government officials complained loudly that there was no way they could absorb one hundred thousand refugees into the mandate over a short period of time. Meanwhile, the Palestinians were angry over the Americans' selective approval of the parts of the plan that seemed to threaten their (i.e., the Palestinians') interests, while Zionist leaders argued for the immediate need to create an independent Jewish state in Palestine. Needless to say, the plan withered and met a quick death (Khouri 1985, 34–35).

By 1947 it was clear to the government in London that Britain's position in Palestine was rapidly becoming untenable. Domestically, British public opinion was sharply divided between those who sympathized with the plight of the Jews after the genocide of World War II and those who were angered by the increasingly violent attacks carried out by Jewish militants in Palestine against British targets there. In the realm of foreign policy, British leaders believed that their interests in the Middle East lay largely with maintaining good relations with the Arab states. Yet at the same time, Britain was reliant on U.S. economic assistance, and American policy clearly favored increased Jewish immigration and the immediate partition of Palestine into Jewish and Arab territories.

Faced with these swirling cross-currents of interests and demands, the British announced that they were prepared to relinquish their mandate in Palestine and turned the problem over to the United Nations (UN). The UN Special Committee on Palestine (UNSCOP) subsequently issued a report in August 1947 calling for the political partition of the territory. Under the plan, the two territories would stay unified economically and Jerusalem would be placed under international control. With the strong backing of both the United States and the Soviet Union, the partition plan was adopted by the UN General Assembly on November 29, 1947 (Mansfield 1991, 234).

Although the majority of Zionists embraced the UN plan, it was bitterly opposed by most Arabs. Arab criticism of the plan focused on the fact that the Jewish state would incorporate 55 percent of the territory, despite the fact that Jews comprised only 33 percent of the population of Palestine in 1947. Moreover, under the plan a large number of Palestinians would live within the boundaries of the Jewish state (about 45 percent of the total population of the Jewish state would be Palestinian).

However, there was not blanket Arab opposition to the proposed partition. The primary exception to Arab outrage was King Abdullah of Trans-jordan, a nation that had been granted its formal independence by Britain in 1946. Calculating that he and the Jewish Agency (the vanguard institution of the Zionist movement in Palestine) shared an interest in thwarting the emergence of an independent Palestinian state, Abdullah held secret meetings with Zionist representatives, including future Israeli prime minister Golda Meir. From these meetings there emerged the outlines of an understanding between the parties under which Abdullah agreed not to oppose the creation and existence of the future Jewish state in exchange for the Zionists' acceptance of Jordanian rule over the West Bank territory that was supposed to be set aside for a Palestinian state. Eventually, however, the agreement foundered when the Jordanian monarch relented to intense pressure to close ranks with other Arab leaders in opposing the partition of Palestine (Bickerton and Klausner 1998, 93–94).

The tension caused by the proposed partition of Palestine boiled over into full-scale civil war between Palestinians and Jews in late 1947 and early 1948. By this point—after the UN voted for partition on November 29, 1947, but before the April 15, 1948, deadline Britain had set for its withdrawal from Palestine—the British were eager to minimize their own casualties and thus chose largely to stand aside as the fighting intensified. The UN had provided no detailed plan for how the partition of Palestine was to be carried out or paid for, and the British had no intention of trying to implement a policy that was based on a peaceful process of division while violence and bloodshed was rampant in the territory.

The Zionists finally realized their dream of establishing a Jewish state in Palestine on May 14, 1948. On that date the British completed their pullout a month behind schedule, and the Zionists proclaimed the founding of the state of Israel. Almost immediately, both the U.S. and the USSR recognized the fledgling state, while the surrounding Arab states of Egypt, Syria, Jordan, and Iraq launched an offensive against Israeli positions, the stated intention of their attack being to protect the 45 percent of the territory that had been set aside for the Palestinian state (Mansfield 1991, 237). Not for the last time in the Arab-Israeli conflict the actual military balance of power between the two sides stood in stark contrast to the demographic balance of power, which should have given the Arabs an overwhelming advantage, given the fact that they outnumbered the Zionists forty million to six hundred thousand. However, the Arab forces were poorly commanded and even more poorly coordinated. The Arab leaders harbored conflicting objectives in fighting the war, with each seeking to use the conflict to bolster his domestic legitimacy as well as his claim to regional leadership (Bickerton and Klausner 1998, 98). As a result, not only did the various Arab states fail to create an effective, integrated command structure, but they also managed to bring a paltry 21,500-strong army to the field to face a well-trained, highly motivated Israeli force that numbered about 60,000.

The fighting between Jews and Arabs continued throughout 1948. After initial success, the Arab forces quickly found themselves on the defensive. By January 1949, the Arabs had been reduced to controlling a thin strip of land around the city of Gaza along the Mediterranean coast and the area along the West Bank of the Jordan River that had been allocated to the Palestinians under the UN partition plan. Meanwhile, Israel not only managed to retain all of the land originally allocated to the Jews under the plan but also had gained control over a area of coastline between Jaffa and Gaza, that part of the eastern Negev desert that had not been awarded to the Jews by the UN, and a chunk of territory in the middle of the country, including the western part of Jerusalem. A series of armistice agreements were reached between Israel and its foes (with the exception of Iraq, which nevertheless agreed to withdraw its forces).

The armistice agreements froze in place the distribution of territory as it existed in January 1949. Israel had achieved substantial territorial gains as a result of the war. Whereas the original UN partition plan granted 55 percent of the land to the Jews, by the end of the war Israel controlled over 76 percent of prewar Palestine. Israel's territorial gains included all of the northern part of the country (a substantial portion of which had been allocated to the Palestinians under the UN scheme) as well as areas surrounding the Old City of Jerusalem that were to have been treated as an international territory under UN control (Farsoun and Zacharia 1997, 112, 123–24).

At the same time, the Palestinians found themselves stateless. Egypt assumed control over the Gaza Strip, while Jordan's King Abdullah took advantage of the war to achieve that which he could not secure through secret negotiations with Zionist leaders prior to the creation of Israel: Jordanian occupation of the West Bank and Arab Jerusalem. Quickly thereafter, Abdullah annexed the West Bank and East Jerusalem and announced the formation of a new Hashemite Kingdom of Jordan that would unify the Arab territories along the eastern and western banks of the Jordan River. More than any other action taken by Arab leaders during this period of time, King Abdullah's occupation and annexation of the West Bank and East Jerusalem created bitter resentment among Palestinians, who believed the land rightfully belonged to them. Two years later, Abdullah would pay for this perceived betrayal to the Arab cause with his life when he was assassinated in East Jerusalem by a Palestinian assailant while his young grandson, the future King Hussein, looked on in horror.

The 1948 War created two realities on the ground that would sow the seeds of future conflict for generations to come. First, the establishment of the state of Israel caused great resentment in much of the Arab Middle East and would form the focal point for attempts at rallying the Arab states to set aside their growing ideological and political differences in the name of defeating the common enemy. In this environment, the concept of Arab nationalism took strong root in the region. By the mid-1950s, there emerged in Egypt a single charismatic leader—Gamal Abdel Nasser—who came to symbolize for Arabs across the Middle East their hopes and aspirations, including the restoration of Palestine, the end of colonialism and imperialism in the region, and the creation of a great Arab state that would unite the Arab people as a single nation living in a single territory, in the process eliminating the Western-drawn boundaries in the region.

Second, the plight of Palestinian refugees would haunt the region for decades to come. Estimates of the number of refugees created by the conditions surrounding the war ranged from 520,000 by the Israeli government to 770,000 by

Palestinian sources and up to 810,000 by British officials (table 4.1 in Farsoun and Zacharia 1997, 125). The refugee crisis created a huge social, economic, and political challenge for the neighboring Arab states that had to absorb the flow of Palestinians into their territories while also providing the context and pretext for Arab animosity toward the fledgling Jewish state.

Enduring Rivals: At the Nexus of Domestic, Regional, and International Politics

The conflict between Israel and the Arab states evolved into one of the most heated and enduring interstate rivalries in the Cold War international system. Israel's fiercest regional rivals during the 1950s and 1960s were Egypt and Syria. In addition, conflict dyads involving Israel and Jordan, Israel and Lebanon, and Israel and Iraq all contributed to Arab-Israeli tensions in the region.

Several issues were at the core of the rising tensions between Israel and the Arab states. These issues included differing interpretations over provisions within the armistice agreements, tension over access to and use of critical waterways such as the Jordan River, the Suez Canal, and the Gulf of Aqaba, and the problem of cross-border infiltrations and retaliatory raids. Disagreements in these areas fueled the conflict environment in the region, enhancing the sense for the parties on the ground that the militarization of disputes was the rule rather than the exception.

On the issue of the armistice agreements, the Arab states espoused the traditional diplomatic argument that the armistice agreements dealt purely with military matters. Under this interpretation, the final status of political issues such as the final demarcation of borders and the fate of Palestinian refugees were still unresolved. The Israelis, on the other hand, increasingly pushed the notion that the armistice demarcation lines marked the official, final borders of the states in the region and argued they had the right to carry out any activities they deemed necessary within the the demilitarized zones (DMZs) (Khouri 1985, 182–83).

In 1951, Israel began to lay territorial claim to large portions of the three DMZs that separated the armed forces of Syria and Israel. On April 4, 1951, seven members of an Israeli military unit that had moved deep into Syrian-controlled territory in order to "show the Israeli flag" were killed by Syrian army forces. The Israeli air force responded with an attack on the village of al-Hamma. A subsequent attack by Israeli ground forces in May triggered an angry rebuke from the UN Security Council, which demanded that the Israelis allow Arab inhabitants of the region to return (Shlaim 2001, 72). Stung by this early criticism, most Israeli officials, including Prime Minister David Ben-Gurion, quickly came to the conclusion that they could not count on the UN to protect Israel's interests (Khouri 1985, 187). Given this mindset, it is not surprising that both the Mixed Armistice Commissions (MACs) and the United Nations Truce Supervision Organization (UNTSO) were increasingly ignored by the Israelis in the early 1950s.

The water issue was closely linked to the armistice agreements, particularly in the case of Israel and Syria. Many key waterways lay within the three DMZs that had been established along the Israeli-Syrian lines. In 1951, Israel's plan to drain Lake Hulah, part of which lay within one of the DMZs, sparked a firestorm of protest from the Syrians. Meanwhile, tensions were also high at Lake Tiberias (the Sea of Galilee), where Syrian artillery routinely fired at Israeli fishing boats, and Israeli armed patrol boats sought to keep Syrian fishermen from using the lake (Bickerton and Klausner 1998, 123). A series of American-sponsored meetings designed to reach a final settlement on the territorial divisions within the DMZs foundered in 1953 on the rocks of Israel's insistence that it enjoy exclusive rights over the Sea of Galilee and the upper parts of the Jordan River. Finally, in 1955 the Arabs and Israel accepted a quota proposal developed by American emissary Eric Johnston for allocating the waters of the Jordan River. Under the terms of the plan, Israel would control 45 percent of the water, the rest going to the Arab states (Shlaim 2001, 71–76, 109).

Meanwhile, to the south Israel's relations with Egypt were severely complicated by Cairo's official closure of the Suez Canal to Israeli ships and to those foreign ships carrying "contraband of war" destined for Israel. The Egyptians further antagonized Israel by extending its search and seizure policy to the Gulf of Aqaba. On September 1, 1951, the UN Security Council passed a resolution demanding that Egypt open the canal to all ships. The Egyptians ignored the resolution and, in fact, upped the ante in 1953 by adding "foodstuffs and all other commodities" to its list of contraband that could be seized.

By far the most frequent source of tension between Israel and its Arab neighbors in the 1950s was the issue of cross-border movement. Although it is true that many of the Arab incursions into Israel were conducted by criminals, smugglers, and guerrillas, it is also the case that a large number of the early incidents of cross-border incidents actually represented attempts by civilian refugees to return to their former homes (Khouri 1985, 186). However, even these innocent attempts at infiltration had serious political implications, given the fact that Israel steadfastly opposed the return of Arab refugees to the former Palestine. Moreover, with violent infiltrators engaging in such acts as the mining of roads, the blowing up of pipelines and bridges, and the murder of civilians, the Israeli government was under pressure at home to take a tough stand on the issue (Bickerton and Klausner 1998, 123). Thus from the outset Israeli officials, led by David Ben-Gurion, advocated an aggressive policy toward thwarting infiltrators. The "free-fire" policy of shoot first and ask questions later led to the deaths of several thousand infiltrators between 1949 and 1956 and to a significant increase in tensions between Israel and its Arab neighbors (Shlaim 2001, 82–83).

Over time, the Israeli government adopted Ben-Gurion's maxim that Israel could best deter Arab hostility by enacting a formula of "two Israeli blows for one Arab blow." A cycle of strike and counterstrike emerged, leading to an environment in which reciprocal violence became the norm. The policy was designed to punish severely the Arab states that aided and abetted infiltration activities. The overall goal was to force those states to do a more effective job of policing their borders while also sending a larger message that Israel would make peace only on its own terms (Khouri 1985, 187).

In 1954 a foreign policy debacle sparked a domestic crisis in Israel. The Israelis had long been worried about the economic and strategic threat posed by Egyptian control over the Suez Canal. In July 1954, this concern motivated the Israeli government to carry out an ill-conceived and poorly implemented campaign of sabotage against Western targets in Egypt. The purpose of the bombing attacks, which were designed to appear to have been the work of Egyptian radicals, was to reinforce the image of Egypt, now led by army officer Gamal Abdel Nasser, as being hostile toward Western interests. The Lavon Affair, so named after the defense minister who was in office in Israel at the time, was a spectacular failure. The plot was quickly uncovered by Egyptian intelligence, which arrested the espionage ring inside of Egypt. The spies were subsequently tried, found guilty, and executed (Shlaim 2001, 110–12).

In the aftermath of the Lavon Affair, Ben-Gurion came out of retirement, taking the role of minister of defense, and by the end of 1955, Ben-Gurion had replaced Moshe Sharett as prime minister. Just a week after Ben-Gurion returned as minister of defense, Israel launched its biggest military strike against Egypt since the signing of the armistice in 1949. Code-named Operation Black Arrow, the Gaza raid resulted in over thirty civilian deaths and led to the adoption of a UN Security Council resolution condemning Israel for the operation (Khouri 1985, 200).

From the perspective of an American journalist who was close to Nasser, Operation Black Arrow "transformed a stable level of minor incidents between the two countries into a dialogue of mounting fear and violence in which the distinction between measures of defense and acts of aggression faded and became invisible to the world at large" (Love 1969, 1). In addition, the rising cycle of violence was one of the factors that drove Nasser toward a more militant position at home and abroad. Initially, Nasser followed a pragmatic course in his internal and external policies. Domestically, although some of the policies enacted by Nasser, including land reform, wage reform, and shorter working hours, seemed to place him firmly on the left of the political spectrum, he was far from being a dyed-in-the-wool socialist.

In the realm of regional politics, upon entering office Nasser left the door open to the possibility of reaching a negotiated settlement with Israel. In fact, during Moshe Sharett's term as prime minister, Nasser and his representatives engaged in discussions with Israeli government officials on a wide array of topics, ranging from the fate of the Lavon Affair spies to the possibility of economic cooperation. However, domestic opposition from hawks in both governments doomed the talks. By the middle of 1955, any hope at achieving a diplomatic breakthrough in the Egyptian-Israeli dyad had disappeared. Nasser claimed that his trust in the Israelis as a good faith partner in negotiations was destroyed by the Gaza raid. In fact, there is evidence that Egypt did not actively begin to sponsor *fedayeen* (guerrilla) forays from Egyptian and Jordanian territory into Israel until after the Gaza raid of 1955, and even then the Jordanian government stepped up its efforts to thwart attempts at infiltrations from Jordan. Thus Ben-Gurion's policy failed in the sense that it led to more, rather than fewer, cross-border attacks by Arab guerrillas. For their part, the Israelis countered that Nasser had never really been serious about securing a peace settlement, and that the launching of cross-border guerrilla attacks was simply the latest example of Arab hostility toward Israel (Shlaim 2001, 121–29).

Internationally, Nasser initially pursued a neutral line in the Cold War, balancing his relationship with the United States and Soviet Union. Relations between Egypt and the Soviet Union began to warm in 1955, as Nasser strove to insulate Egypt from Western imperialism and Soviet leader Nikita Khrushchev tilted Moscow's policy in the region away from support for tiny Communist parties in the Arab states and toward Arab leaders such as Nasser, who were seeking to distance themselves from Western influence (Mansfield 1991, 253). Moreover, Egypt and the Soviet Union were thrown together in 1955 by a common threat: the creation of the U.S.-conceived, British-sponsored Baghdad Pact, consisting of the pro-Western states of Turkey, Iran, Iraq, and Pakistan.

On the other hand, Nasser did not close the door on constructing a better relationship with the U.S. than Egypt had enjoyed under the monarchy. However, American-Egyptian relations, which initially warmed in 1954 (as evidenced by an increase in the amount of technical aid and economic assistance flowing from Washington to Cairo), began to falter badly in 1955 and 1956. In the aftermath of Operation Black Arrow, the Egyptians sought to improve their military preparedness by signing an arms agreement to receive Soviet weapons via Czechoslovakia (Massoulie 1999, 77). Nasser further angered American officials by recognizing Communist China in 1956. In response, on July 20, 1956, the Eisenhower administration decided to withdraw an offer of U.S. aid in helping to construct the High Aswan Dam. Less than a week later, Nasser reacted by nationalizing the British- and French-owned Suez Canal. This set the stage for the next major war in the region.

In the aftermath of Nasser's nationalization of the Suez Canal, the British and French sought to reestablish their control over the waterway in such a way that they would not expose themselves to charges of neocolonialism. At the same time, hardline elements within the Israeli government, led by David Ben-Gurion and Moshe Dayan, chief of staff for the Israeli Defense Forces (IDF), had come to the conclusion that it was in Israel's interest to induce a new war with Egypt at the earliest possible date. Having defined Nasser as posing the biggest threat to Israel's security, the fundamental objective of the war would be to cause domestic unrest in Egypt, and ultimately the collapse of Nasser's regime (Shlaim 2001, 141–42).

In this environment, a scheme was developed under which Israel would launch an attack against Egyptian forces, and Britain and France would intervene as "objective" third parties in order to separate the warring sides as well as protect the canal for international shipping. The operation was set to be launched in late October 1956, a period of time during which the Soviet Union was bogged down with the anti-Soviet revolt in Hungary, and the United States was distracted by the looming presidential election. For the French and British, successful completion of the operation would permit them to reassert their hold over the Suez in the supposed name of peace and free passage. For Israel, it meant loosening the noose of economic isolation brought about by an Arab economic boycott of Israel and the Egyptian blockade of Israeli shipping through the Straits of Tiran and the Suez Canal, along with the possible overthrow of Nasser.

The Anglo-French-Israeli military plan was implemented on October 29, 1956. However, it quickly ran into difficulties, as the British and French offer of peaceful intervention came so rapidly that hostilities between Egypt and Israel had barely begun. In fact, Israeli troops were still far from the Suez Canal when their European allies issued the demand that the two sides withdraw their forces from the canal area and accept the Anglo-French offer of peacekeepers along the canal in order to assure the safe passage of foreign shipping. Sensing that something was afoot, Nasser refused the demand and ordered his troops to withdraw from the Sinai Peninsula in order to concentrate on defending the Suez Canal. The British and French responded with massive air strikes, and by November 5, 1956, Israeli forces were in full control of the entire Sinai.

The Anglo-French-Israeli alliance, however, met with stiff resistance in the international arena. On November 1, 1956, the U.S. sponsored a UN resolution demanding that Israel withdraw to the 1949 armistice line and that *all* UN members (read: Britain and France) refrain from sending military supplies to the region, while also demanding that Egypt reopen the Suez Canal to all shipping. Egypt immediately accepted the resolution, but the other parties refused, as they tried to push their military advantage on the ground. Finally, on November 6–7, with the Suez still not firmly occupied by British and French ground forces, the colonial allies and the Israelis reluctantly agreed to abide by the UN resolution. In exchange for the complete withdrawal of Israeli, British, and French forces from Egyptian soil, Egypt agreed to the placement of the United Nations Emergency Force (UNEF) on the Egyptian side of the border with Israel. (The Israelis refused to accept UN forces on their side of the frontier.) As a historical footnote, the UNEF was the first peacekeeping operation ever undertaken by the United Nations.

The Suez crisis reordered the internationalization of the Arab-Israeli conflict with the introduction of UN forces, and the end of Anglo-French attempts to dominate the region. However, as the era of European colonialism drew to a close, the Middle East found itself increasingly ensnared in the global conflict between the United States and the Soviet Union. As one chapter in the history of international penetration of the region came to a close, a new chapter was just beginning.

A sense of uneasy calm characterized the Arab-Israeli dispute in the years following the Suez Crisis of 1956. Over the next decade or so, Israel sought to strengthen its ties with the West in order to bolster its armed forces and to secure international support for the Jewish state. Meanwhile, although leaders such as Nasser paid lip service to the ideal of Arab nationalism, the Arab world in fact was split by what has been called "the Arab Cold War" (See Kerr 1971). Unable to put aside their political differences in a common effort to restore Palestine, the Arabs found themselves divided between radical and conservative camps. Radical Arab states such as Egypt, Syria, and, by 1958, Iraq drew support from the USSR, while conservative regimes in Jordan, Lebanon, and the Persian Gulf region aligned themselves with the U.S. Such events as the pro-Nasserist coup in Iraq in 1958, the threat of Nasserist-inspired political unrest in the pro-Western states of Jordan and Lebanon in the late 1950s, and Egypt's intervention during the 1960s in the Yemeni civil war highlighted the degree of inter-Arab tension that existed during this period of time.

Nasser did achieve a major victory in 1958, when the Syrian Ba'athist regime approached the Egyptian president about forming a political union between the two countries, despite the fact that the two states did not share a contiguous border. While it is true that Ba'athist ideology paralleled that of Nasserism in its support for a limited brand of socialism and advocacy of pan-Arabism, it is also true that the primary motivation behind the Ba'ath Party's offer was to gain Nasser's support in crushing Syrian Communists, who were threatening the Ba'athists' domestic position of power. In Egypt, Nasser had moved quickly to crush potential Communist rivals to his rule, and the Ba'athists hoped that he would help them to do the same in Syria. The temporary nature of the Ba'athist-Nasserist alliance was underscored by the short history of the "United Arab Republic." Founded in February 1958, the union collapsed just three years later when Syrian military officers intervened and withdrew Syria from the pact. In the words of Arab scholar Bassam Tibi, "Nasserism and the pan-Arab Ba'ath Party . . . never enjoyed harmonious relations—at best only tenuous passing alliances" (Tibi 1993, 67).

Meanwhile, Israel and Syria still found themselves involved in an unending spiral of low-grade warfare in the DMZ, most often revolving around the struggle to control the access to the tributaries and headwaters of the Jordan River. The various schemes that were undertaken to alter the flow of the river inevitably reinforced the established pattern of strike and counterstrike between the two parties. The flash point of tension over the issue became the area near the nexus of the Israeli-Syrian-Lebanese border, where a significant armed exchange between Israeli and Syrian forces took place in November 1964. In the face of mounting pressure from the U.S. and the UN for both parties to desist from their diversionary activities and to cease firing on each other, a series of border clashes occurred throughout 1965 and 1966, centered around the fear on both sides that the other would succeed in diverting the river. On August 15, 1966, a major exchange involving planes, artillery, and patrol boats took place in the area of Lake Tiberias. The Lake Tiberias battle occurred just a month after Israel had responded to Palestinian infiltrations from Syria with a large-scale aerial assault on targets eight miles inside of Syrian territory (Khouri 1985, 231–32).

Syria's ongoing support for Palestinian *fedayeen* infuriated the Israelis, who beginning in January 1965 had to deal with attacks from the Fatah (Conquest) guerrilla organization. All of this sparked what was branded "the Syrian syndrome" by Israeli brigadier general Israel Lior. "Service on this front, opposite the Syrian enemy, fuels feelings of exceptional hatred for the Syrian army and people," Lior later recalled. "We loved to hate them" (quoted in Shlaim 2001, 229).

While the military conflict between Syria and Israel persisted at a fairly sustained rate and moderate level during the 1960s, both the Egyptian and Jordanian fronts became comparatively tranquil, at least in terms of the frequency of military exchanges along those frontiers. In retrospect, this represented the calm before the storm, as all the parties continued to build their arsenals in preparation for a possible future war in the region.

Regional Arms Race

In response to such factors as the Arab-Israeli dispute, the inter-Arab conflicts, and the global Cold War, the Middle Eastern states sought to upgrade their military capabilities throughout the 1950s and 1960s. Originally, the United States, in an effort to retain good relations with conservative Arab states, avoided selling weapons to Israel. In fact, in 1955 the Eisenhower administration turned down an Israeli request for arms, with Dulles telling Israel that it should look to the UN and collective security to protect itself from Arab attacks. The U.S. did, however, quietly support European arms transfers to Israel, including deals involving the delivery of weapons from West Germany and France. However, both of those sources began to dry up in the 1960s, as the West Germans bowed to Egyptian pressure to halt military transfers to Israel, and the French reevaluated their Middle Eastern policy in the wake of Algeria gaining its independence from France in 1962. No longer concerned with the possibility that Nasser would support Algerian nationalists in their war for liberation from French colonial rule, Paris turned its attention toward warming relations with the Arab states (*The Middle East* 1991, 70). It was during this time that Israel began to look increasingly to the U.S. as a source of military aid.

By the early 1960s, a regional arms buildup, with ample external assistance, was in full swing, with Egypt and Israel at its center. The arsenals of the two major regional actors were bulging with an ever-growing supply of tanks, planes, and missiles. Between 1960 and 1965, the percentage of gross national product (GNP) devoted to defense outlays increased from 7.0 percent to 12.2 percent in Egypt, and from 8.6 percent to 11.5 percent in Israel (Safran 1969, 148, 158). Each state accused the other of accelerating the arms race, and each warned that it was prepared to initiate a preemptive war in the event that the other appeared poised to attain a substantial military advantage (Khouri 1985, 305).

Meanwhile, policymakers and analysts struggled with the issue of precisely how to calculate the military balance of power in the region. In Israel, a widely shared strategic outlook informed the debate regarding the distribution of military capabilities and the preparation for a possible future war with the Arabs. Most Israeli leaders, including Ben-Gurion, believed strongly in the doctrine of self-reliance (Shlaim 2001, 97). According to this perspective, given the Jews' experience with the Holocaust, it would be unrealistic—and perhaps fatal—to the survival of the Jewish state to rely on external forces to ensure the security of Israel.

In theory, the doctrine of self-reliance meant that Israel had to plan for a multitude of military exigencies involving a potential war with various possible combinations of Arab foes. One way to simplify this complicated set of strategic calculations was to work to ensure Israel's military superiority over any and all of the Arab armies. Dating back to the writings of revisionist Zionist visionary Ze'ev Jabotinsky prior to the creation of Israel, this approach to addressing the security threat posed by the Arabs is embedded within the "iron wall" theory (Shlaim 2001, 14). According to the iron wall theory, it was rational for the Arabs to reject Israel's existence, since the Zionists essentially occupied Palestine as a colonizing force. The strategic implication of this theory is clear: Peace could only come about by convincing the Arabs that Israel had the military capability to inflict costly defeats on any combination of its adversaries (Lustick 1996, 5).

At the same time, there was a desire to create the image of a "beleaguered Jewish state" in order to enhance international support. For propaganda purposes, Israeli leaders tended to frame the balance of capabilities according to a formula by which Israeli military power was measured against the combined advantage in raw manpower and material enjoyed by the Arab states. This subjective and selective comparison of military power between Israel and a hypothetical pan-Arab army was presented for foreign public consumption despite the widely held, though not universal, belief within Israel's decision-making hierarchy that the Israeli army was "at the zenith of its strength in manpower, skill, fighting spirit, and military equipment" and was in a position to "defeat the [Arab] aggressors" (Brecher 1980, 96).

It is true that Israel's budget outlays on defense of $2.2 billion between 1960 and 1966 were far outpaced by Arab military expenditures during the same period. Taking the combined budgets of the front-line states (i.e., those which share a common border with Israel—Egypt, Syria, Jordan, and Lebanon) and other influential actors in the region (i.e., Iraq and Saudi Arabia), the Arabs spent over $5.3 billion during this same period of time (figures calculated from Safran 1969, 158–89). Of course, the Arab states also enjoyed an overwhelming theoretical advantage in manpower, although as Safran points out, the Arabs were unable to place as many troops in the field as rapidly as the Israelis (Safran 1969, 258).

In January 1964, Arab leaders agreed to create the United Arab Military Command, with an Egyptian general at the top of the command structure. Arab elites also vowed to work toward a plan by which the supply of water to Israel could be curtailed by diverting the tributaries that ran through Arab territory to the Jordan River (Mansfield 1991, 270). At the same Cairo summit meeting, the Arab state leaders created a new Palestinian nationalist organization, dubbed the Palestine Liberation Organization (PLO). According to the official report published at the end of the conference, the PLO's raison d'être was "the organizing of the Palestinian people and enabling them to play their role in the liberation of their country and their self-determination" (Cobban 1984, 28–29). Palestinian lawyer Ahmed Shukairy was named as head of the PLO, a choice that put Shukairy on a collision course with Yassir Arafat, head of the existing Palestinian Fatah guerrilla movement. By the end of the decade, both Arafat as an individual and Fatah as a group would emerge as the leading forces within the PLO's superstructure.

The facade of Arab unity that was displayed at the Cairo summit barely hid Nasser's real objectives in calling the meeting: to rob other Arab states of their freedom of action toward Israel so that Egypt would not be dragged into a premature war in defense of a potentially adventurist Arab state such as Syria, facilitate burden-sharing between the Arab states in terms of defending Arab interests in the conflict with Israel, and create a pliant Palestinian nationalist organization that was answerable to Nasser, thus hopefully minimizing the chance that Egypt might be the target of Israeli military retribution in response to uncontrolled Palestinian guerrilla activity. Having said that, taken at face value, the budget statistics and pretense of Arab unity seemed to support the perception that Israel was surrounded by increasingly more powerful and belligerent neighbors bent on the Jewish state's destruction.

In reality, it was clear in the early to mid-1960s that the ideological divisions between so-called radical (i.e., Soviet supplied) and conservative (i.e., Western supplied) states in the Arab world was so pronounced as to render the concept of "Arab unity" a fiction. Even if Arab leaders in the region had wanted to set aside their political differences in the name of genuine Arab unity—and there is little evidence that they wished to do so—any attempt at integration of the armed forces of the Arab states into a cohesive fighting unit was severely complicated by the fact that some states relied on Soviet-bloc aid, while others received Western military assistance.

Furthermore, security concerns for the Arab states were much more varied, and thus harder to manage, than were those of Israel. While Israel focused exclusively on building up its arsenal in order to balance the combined power of the front-line Arab states, the Arab states were driven to bolster their arsenals in response to a series of theoretical threat scenarios. Among the scenarios that were included in the Arab states' strategic balance calculations were each state's individual military capability vis-à-vis Israel, the combined might of the most probable Arab participants in a possible war with Israel (i.e., Egypt and Syria, and possibly Jordan, Lebanon, and Iraq as well), the threat posed by Arab states who stood on the other side of the "Arab Cold War," the threat in certain countries (e.g., Jordan, and Syria) that internal foes presented to the stability of the state, and, in the case of Egypt, the costly and inconclusive intervention in the Yemeni civil war.

It is simply incorrect, therefore, to define the arms buildup in the Middle East as being a classic case of a bilateral arms race, since one side to the conflict (the Arab side) in fact was comprised of multiple actors, each of whom gave different weights to the various regional and domestic threats they faced in determining the balance of power. Israel "tended to add the forces of other Arab countries to Egypt's in its reckonings, [whereas] Egypt . . . could not count much if at all on the accretion of power to other Arab countries in connection with its contest with Israel and . . . therefore sought to achieve a favorable balance with Israel all by itself" (Safran 1969, 145). Essentially, the arms race in the Middle East during the 1960s involved "a primary race between Egypt and Israel, in which Egypt endeavored to obtain by itself a position of military superiority over Israel, while Israel strove to provide against the military effort of Egypt *plus* any number of other Arab countries likely to join it in a hostile coalition" (Safran 1969, 191).

In the other Arab states, however, patterns in defense spending had little or no consistent correlation with developments in the conflict with Israel. Instead, the focus in these states seemed to be primarily on using the military to guarantee internal cohesion, as was the case in Jordan, Lebanon, Iraq, and, to a lesser extent, Saudi Arabia, and/or on using increased military capability in order to deter other external Arab forces from threatening the sovereignty of the state, as was the case in Saudi calculations. In addition, for states such as Egypt, Syria, and Iraq, military spending was useful as a way to project an image of prestige in the region, the purpose of which was to bolster each state's claim to pan-Arab leadership as well as to legitimize the state's regime in the eyes of its domestic population. The complex combination of internal and external threats fueled "the need of these countries for more armed forces and . . . fed into Israel's motivations and calculations" to increase its own military capabilities (Safran 1969, 145).

Thus by the mid-1960s the combination of external support for regional actors, a regionwide weapons buildup (although, to reiterate, not a typical dyadic arms race), a constant concern with the relative balance of power between Arab and Israeli forces (particularly on the part of Israeli leaders), inter-Arab disputes, domestic crises within several Arab states, and the persistence of the unresolved Palestinian question combined to create an extremely volatile situation in the Middle East. The Cold War provided the rationale by which the Western and Eastern blocs in the international system could justify providing arms to their client states in the region. The flow of arms into the Middle East exacerbated the extremely complicated, multilateral security dilemma for actors in the region, particularly for the Arab states, because arms that one state might purchase in order to balance against a perceived threat from Israel could quite possibly, due to the inter-Arab conflict, be understood as posing a security threat to another Arab state, which would then feel compelled to respond in kind. Meanwhile, the Israelis would likely view the increase in Arab military capability purely through the lens of the Arab-Israeli conflict, and therefore seek to bolster their military even further, thereby initiating a subsequent dilemma cycle.

Furthermore, the nagging concern in a number of Arab states with domestic threats to the survival of the ruling regimes drove leaders in those countries to seek both to increase their capacity for internal military coercion *and* to use the Arab-Israeli conflict as a legitimizing tool. Under these circumstances, it was in the short-term domestic interest of state leaders to fan the flames of the anti-Israeli sentiment among their citizens. However, once their populations were mobilized to "rally around the flag" in order to "destroy the Zionist enemy" and "restore the legitimate national rights of the Palestinian people," these state leaders found themselves compelled to continue to push the envelope of the Arab-Israeli conflict ever closer to war, regardless of whether their armed forces were really prepared for such a development. In fact, as will be seen in the forthcoming discussion of immediate causes of the Six-Day War, we cannot understand why that war occurred without taking into account the domestic concerns that plagued each of the major participants, and in particular the Arab states.

IMMEDIATE/SHORT-TERM FACTORS

Few if any actors in the Arab-Israeli drama saw the storm clouds of war looming just over the horizon in the first half of 1967. Reporting from Cairo on June 4 and 5, *New York Times* journalist James Reston observed that Egypt "did not want war . . . [and] (was) certainly not ready for war" (cited in Khouri 1985, 247). As for Israel, although some Israeli analysts have claimed in recent years that there were radical elements within the Israeli armed forces who were seeking an excuse to "finish what they had started" in 1948, thereby realizing the vision of the creation of Greater Israel (a charge which is currently the subject of a heated debate within Israeli academic circles—see Oren 1999), at that time it was assumed by many in the West that Israel would not start a war, short of extreme Arab provocation.

All of which raises a basic question: If no one anticipated, or for that matter even wanted, a major war in the Middle East, why did one occur? Several short-term factors seem to have played a crucial role in contributing to the outbreak of war. These factors include the emergence of the Palestinian Fatah guerrilla movement, the actions of which increased tensions between not just the Arab states and Israel but also radical and conservative Arab states; the growing sense of domestic crisis that characterized the political systems of Jordan, Syria, Egypt, and Israel; the construction of mutual-defense pacts involving Egypt and Syria and Egypt and Jordan; and a series of statements, claims, and decisions that created and fueled a conflict spiral in the region, beginning in May 1967.

Regional Politics: The Palestinian Resistance Movement

The Palestine Liberation Organization was created in 1964 (see above). From the organization's founding, both the PLO and the original leader of the group, Ahmed Shukairy, were viewed with a great deal of suspicion by many Palestinians. Wary of the control that Nasser and the other Arab state leaders clearly hoped to exercise over the PLO, it was denounced early on as "an organization with no relations to the (Palestinian) masses." Others charged that the PLO was a "colonialist, Zionist conspiracy aiming at the liquidation of the Palestinian cause." Nor did the organization or its leader fare any better with some of its Arab state creators. Shukairy's public claim in July 1964 that the territory of Palestine included all traditional Palestinian lands west *and* east of the Jordan River played poorly at the royal palace in Amman, Jordan, since the Kingdom of Jordan consisted entirely of "traditional" Palestinian land (Cobban 1984, 30–31).

The heavy-handed way in which Nasser and the other Arab leaders put together the PLO and tried to present it as the sole voice of Palestinian nationalism ignored the fact that other, indigenous nationalist movements already existed. The most important of these alternative groups was Fatah, which consisted of a small but extremely committed group of Palestinian nationalists. The core of the group first began to coalesce in 1959 around a few Palestinian activists living in Kuwait. By building connections with similarly minded Palestinian nationalists in other parts of the Middle East as well as in Europe, these activists created Fatah in 1962, with Khalil al-Wazir seen as the head of the movement. The group espoused five central tenets: the drive to "liberate" Palestine from what they viewed as an illegal and immoral Zionist occupation, the need to use armed struggle in pursuit of this goal, the building of Palestinian self-organization, the desire to cooperate with friendly Arab parties, and the necessity to seek cooperation with international supporters (Cobban 1984, 23–24).

Perhaps the most groundbreaking claim in the Fatah program was that while Arab unity was a long-term objective, for Palestinians the achievement of the liberation of Palestine must take precedence. This argument was later included in the Palestinian Charter of 1968, which stated that Palestinians must "safeguard their Palestinian identity and develop their consciousness of that identity" (Cobban 1984, 268). In making this statement, the group's ideology contradicted the pan-Arabist ideology which then dominated the region. According to Nasser and his many followers, the key to restoring Palestine was Arab nationalism, which required that all Arabs unify behind his leadership. In fact, as one of the early Fatah activists noted, Nasser's pull on Arabs, including Palestinians, was extremely strong in the mid-1960s, and the movement only began to pick up significant support when they initiated their campaign of military action in 1965 (Cobban 1984, 24–25).

Interestingly, the most important early state benefactor of *Fatah* was Syria. Beginning in the early 1960s, Syrian air force commander Hafiz al-Assad and chief of military intelligence Ahmed al-Sweidani established contacts with the guerrilla group and signaled Syria's willingness to allow the Palestinians to establish two military training camps on Syrian territory. By permitting the Fatah guerrillas to set up camps in Syria, the Syrian regime clearly was attempting to nurture and support an alternative to the Egyptian-backed mainstream PLO. Thus it is fair to interpret Syria's policy on this issue as being one more example of inter-Arab rivalry (Cobban 1984, 32).

Operating under the organizational nom de guerre "al-Asiyfa" (the Storm), commandos from the Fatah movement launched their first military operation in early 1965, carrying out a total of thirty-nine strikes by the end of the year, most of which were designed to disrupt Israel's water diversion project. In another interesting twist to the Fatah story, the first attempted attack came from the Egyptian-controlled Gaza Strip. Subsequently, the large majority of guerrilla operations were initiated from Jordanian territory, the frontiers of which the raiders found to be rather lightly guarded and thus fairly easy to traverse. Undoubtedly, the guerrillas were also encouraged by Syria to use Jordan as their base of attack, because in doing so the Syrians could strike at Israel while avoiding the inevitable round of Israeli retaliatory strikes.

Furthermore, the radical regime in Damascus may very well have hoped that the cycle of strike and counterstrike between Jordanian-based Palestinian guerrillas and Israeli forces might spark domestic unrest in Jordan, and thus result in the downfall of the conservative Hashemite regime there. In fact, King Hussein found himself in the extremely awkward position of having to cooperate, albeit quietly, with Israel by trying to stop infiltrations across the Jordanian-Israeli border. Jordan's efforts in this area were illustrated by an incident in 1965 in which a Palestinian was killed by Jordanian troops as he returned from a raid in Israel (Cobban 1984, 33; Khouri 1985, 229). Despite Jordan's attempts to curtail guerrilla activity along its frontier, a steady cycle of violence continued throughout 1965 and into 1966, with Jordanian villagers feeling the brunt of Israeli retaliation.

Also in 1966, the Israelis, recognizing that Syria was the genuine source of support for Fatah, began to hit Syrian targets as well. For their part, the Syrians argued that they should not be expected to act as policemen by defending Israel's border from attacks. Thus guerrilla infiltration joined the water dispute as a source of violent confrontation between Syria and Israel. Finally, tension along Syria's border with Israel began to cool in November 1966 as a result of Nasser's ability to rein in Syria through the mutual-defense pact the two countries signed in November 1966 (Khouri 1985, 233–34).

The short respite from violence was shattered on November 13, 1966, when two Israeli armored columns launched an assault on Jordan, centered on the town of as-Samu. The well-planned attack, which was in response to a string of guerrilla operations over the previous six months, was a major embarrassment to King Hussein. Large-scale riots broke out among Palestinian civilians in Jordan, many of whom blamed the king for not doing a better job of standing up to the Israeli assault. Both Nasser in Egypt and the Ba'athist regime in Syria, which by 1966 was ruled by Gen. Salah Jadid, branded King Hussein a traitor, with the Syrians even going so far as to offer support for those inside Jordan who wished to overthrow the monarchy (Khouri 1985, 234–35). Although the king weathered the immediate domestic crisis, the events of late 1966 put concern over the survival of his regime squarely at the top of his policy agenda and further exacerbated the split between moderate and radical Arab states a mere six months before the onset of war in June 1967.

Domestic Politics

As Janice Gross Stein correctly points out, most wars in the Middle East have been wars of vulnerability. In other words, state leaders choose to go to war not because they calculate that they will gain by doing so but because they perceive that they will lose by failing to do so. This focus on loss minimization is the core assumption of prospect theory, which has emerged in recent years as an alternative to traditional rational choice theory. According to Stein, the "interactive impact of strategic and domestic vulnerability explains wars that occur inadvertently, unplanned, and unintended, or wars in which leaders see no alternative but to resort to the use of force if they are to avoid significant loss" (Stein 1993, 56). Because we will focus shortly on the role played by strategic vulnerability in affecting the outbreak of war in June 1967, for now let us examine the impact of domestic vulnerability.

Typically, accounts of the events leading up to the outbreak of the war in 1967 emphasize the role that domestic politics played in influencing the behavior of Arab state leaders (see Stein 1991, 1993). However, it also is important to take into account domestic factors within the context of Israeli decision making. In particular, disagreement within the Israeli government over the likelihood of war and the probable outcome of a conflict with the Arabs, combined with the increasing economic, social, and psychological burden of maintaining mass mobilization and a heightened state of alert to create "an intolerable situation" within the country by late May (Churchill and Churchill 1967, 53–54). In the words of Bernard Reich, there existed in Israel "domestic pressures deriving from economic problems and the general sense that the government must 'do something' about the deteriorating situation, which put the future of the state at stake" (Reich 1996, 121).

Moreover, in recent years there has emerged in Israel a school of thought which argues that Israel's decision to go to war was heavily influenced by a prolonged economic slump during the mid-1960s, and a desire on the part of the government to create a foreign policy crisis in order to divert attention from its failed policies at home. "It is conspicuously anomalous," writes political economist Michael Shalev, "to encounter in the mid-1960s a period of recession and unemployment in the midst of nearly two decades of rapid economic growth. Beginning in the autumn of 1966, unemployment reached double-digit levels" (Shalev 1992, 200). Under this scenario, by instigating increased tensions with the Arabs, Israeli leader Levi Eshkol hoped to foment a foreign policy crisis in order to convince the domestic population to put aside its grievances against the government and to unite in the face of a foreign threat. It has been argued that as early as 1964 the Israeli government began purposely to pursue policies that were designed to antagonize the Arab states in order to induce a diversionary war. Although this hypothesis has been severely criticized by some Israeli analysts (see, for example, Oren 1999), the very fact that it seems plausible to others (for example Shalev 1992) underscores the logic behind the linkage between domestic politics and foreign policy.

Putting aside the debate regarding the causal relationship between socioeconomic crisis and Israel's war policy in 1967, it is beyond dispute that Syrian politics and society were torn with divisions on the eve of the war. The radical neo-Ba'athist faction that seized power over the political system in February 1966 was led by members of the secretive (and according to mainstream Sunni Muslims, heretical) Alawite sect. The fact that the rural-based, minority Alawites controlled the levers of state power was a source of a great deal of resentment among Syria's Sunni majority, many of whom lived in and around the cities. The neo-Ba'athist regime relied for internal support on a narrow populist alliance of radical urban intellectuals, traditionally powerless rural peasants, and minority religious communities. At the same time, the regime's economic program of land redistribution and nationalization of industry was bitterly opposed by a broad cross-section of Syrian society, where the logic of the market had always been a powerful economic force (certainly much more so than in Egypt).

In a desperate attempt to construct some basis of internal legitimacy, the neo-Ba'athists took to the forefront in "pushing the envelope" on the Arab-Israeli conflict. The unfettered radicalism of Syrian foreign policy was of such concern to the Soviet Union that they prodded Egypt into securing a defense pact with Syria in late 1966. The collective defense pact was designed to bolster the security of the vulnerable Syrian regime, while also in theory facilitating Nasser's ability to constrain the Syrian regime in its foreign policy adventurism toward Israel.

Meanwhile, in Egypt Nasser struggled for the first time with the possibility of significant internal opposition to his rule. Egypt faced a severe balance of payments crisis by the mid-1960s, and a general sense of economic malaise prevailed (Stein 1993, 62–64). Unemployment among Egypt's youth was very high, despite the fact that state law guaranteed employment to school graduates, thereby forcing the state to create thousands of redundant jobs that contributed nothing to the country's economy. In comparative terms, prior to the aforementioned economic slump in Israel in the mid-1960s, the Jewish state's annual real GNP growth rate of 11 percent between 1953 and 1963 far outpaced that of Egypt (Safran 1969, 201–2, 259). In addition, Nasser's reputation in the Arab world was suffering as a result of Egypt's inconclusive and controversial intervention in the Yemeni domestic conflict, a war which was also draining Egypt's coffers.

One more critical domestic pressure deserves to be mentioned (see, for example, Baghdadi 1977, Fawzi 1980, and Riad 1986). Throughout the 1960s, Nasser became increasingly concerned with the growing independent influence that his Army commander, Marshall Abd al-Hakim Amr, exercised over the officer corps. Several times throughout the decade, Nasser tried to force Amr out of his post due to his (Nasser's) belief that Amr was incompetent, only to have a large number of officers verbally rally to Amr's defense. By 1967 Amr had consolidated his control over the Egyptian armed forces, a fact that Nasser, fearful of the possibility of a military coup, grudgingly accepted. Interestingly, more than any other advisor it was Amr who pressed Nasser the hardest to accept the notion in May 1967 that Egypt was ready for war with Israel. Apparently, Nasser's fear of the potential negative internal consequences of disputing Amr's assessment motivated the Egyptian president to adopt his general's sanguine—and completely unrealistic—views about Egypt's preparedness. "The picture which increasingly emerges," observes Robert Parker, "is of a leader who in effect was a prisoner of an incompetent general" (Parker 1993, 83–89).

This combination of factors created a domestic environment by 1967 in which, as Stein phrases it, "important elements (in Egyptian government and society) . . . were in opposition to the regime" (Stein 1993, 64). In Stein's view, only by taking into account Nasser's desire to divert attention away from his internal vulnerability in May 1967 can we fully understand the political framework within which Nasser made his policy decisions prior to the outbreak of war on June 5. His confrontational stance toward Israel bolstered his domestic and regional standing, and therefore Nasser was willing to accept the risk that they might trigger a war with the Israelis. In fact, in April 1967, after meeting with Nasser, U.S. official Lucius Battle reported back to Washington that he believed that the Egyptian leader was anxious to create a foreign policy crisis in order to deflect mounting internal pressure against his regime (Quandt 1992, 200). Faced with growing domestic and regional opposition, Nasser took strategic risks in order to try to minimize his political losses.

Of all the major actors in the events of 1967, it was Jordan's King Hussein who was most hemmed in by his domestic constraints. The majority Palestinian population in Jordan agitated both for action to destroy Israel and for the overthrow of the conservative regime in Amman, particularly in the aftermath of the devastating Israeli assault on the Jordanian village of as-Samu on November 13, 1966. In the wake of that attack, Jordan was besieged by a wave of antigovernment disturbances, led by Palestinians who challenged the legitimacy of the Hashemite regime. The fact that the Israeli action at as-Samu was in direct response to a *Fatah* raid that in fact was launched from Syria further heightened King Hussein's sense of severe vulnerability. In the words of Jordanian scholar Samir Mutawi, senior Jordanian government officials, including Prime Minister Wasfi Tel, believed in 1966 and 1967 that Israel's strike on Jordan was designed "to entice Jordanian public opinion to rebel against the government" (quoted in Zartman 1996, 102).

At face value, this seems to be an absurd contention, considering the fact that having a moderate, pro-Western regime in power along Israel's eastern border should have been in the Jewish state's interests. However, as L. Carl Brown notes regarding the Jordanians' frame of mind at the time, "Perceptions are important" (quoted in Zartman 1996, 102). What is critical to understand is not the objective reality of Israeli foreign policy at the time, which in fact included the belief by most Israeli elites that maintaining Hashemite control in Jordan was good for Israel's security, but the subjective fear in Amman that Jordan was an attractive target for Israeli aggression, both because of Jordan's relative military weakness when compared to Egypt and Syria, and because some in Israel believed that the creation of a Palestinian state in Jordan would settle the issue of Palestinian refugees once and for all. Beset with this combination of domestic and regional threats, King Hussein turned to alliance politics as the last best hope for preserving his teetering regime.

Security Pacts and Security Dilemmas

One of the foreign policy tools available to states in the anarchic international system is to forge alliances. By pledging to provide military support to each other in the event of a war, the parties to an alliance hope to increase their individual and collective defense capabilities, and to deter aggression. However, as expressed by the theory of the security dilemma in international relations, steps taken by one party to increase security automatically increase the insecurity of potential foes. Such was the case in the Middle East in 1966 and 1967.

Although technically a so-called Unified Arab Command had existed among the front-line Arab states for several years, in practice this did little to deter Israel's willingness to strike against the Arab states along its borders. By 1966, the Unified Arab Command was more a source of conflict between the Arabs than it was a pillar of cooperation. In particular, King Hussein felt betrayed by Nasser's refusal to come to Jordan's defense in response to Israeli attacks on Jordanian territory. Specifically, King Hussein taunted Nasser for failing to meet his obligations, as the king saw it, to respond with force to Israel's November 13, 1966, assault on the village of as-Samu and accused Nasser of hiding behind UN peacekeepers instead of fulfilling his self-proclaimed role of leader of the Arab world (Parker 1993, 40). These charges increased the domestic and regional pressure on Nasser to be more aggressive in the future in supporting his Arab "allies" against Israeli provocations.

In early November 1966, just prior to the attack on as-Samu, Egypt and Syria signed a mutual-defense pact under which each pledged to come to the defense of the other in the event of a war with Israel. The pact meant different things to each of the major front-line Arab states. In Egypt, it was perceived as a way to rein in the radical regime in Damascus, and therefore to avoid a war with Israel in the near future, at a time when Egyptian economic and military resources were being diverted to support Cairo's intervention in the Yemeni civil war. In Damascus, it was hoped that the pact would deter Israel from striking with force against the Syrians in response to cross-border incidents, although that hope was dashed on April 7, 1967, when Egyptian forces remained quiet as Israeli planes shot down six Syrian MiGs in a dogfight over Syrian air space. (In response to complaints from Syrian officials on Egypt's inaction, Nasser replied that such actions were considered "local" in nature, and thus did not fit the criteria for assistance). Although Israeli chief of staff Yitzhak Rabin publicly stated in the aftermath of the air battle that the Israeli "air force had proven its strength so persuasively that one could not suppose that the Arab states would seriously contemplate challenging Israel," the Syrians in fact became even more bellicose and defiant after April 7 (Stein 1991, 128). In the tough Syrian response we see evidence of the blowback effect, as the perception of Israeli hostility toward Syria engendered broad popular support among the Syrian population to take a tough stand toward Israel.

In Jordan, the pact was seen as exposing the already vulnerable regime to possible future Israeli aggression. In the words of Jordanian air force chief of staff

Amer Khammash, in the event of general hostilities in the region, "the West Bank was a primary target and would not be spared." (Mutawi 1987, 58). The Jordanians perceived that they were caught in a vice: They believed that in its military planning Israel made no attempt to differentiate the moderate Hashemite regime from the more confrontational governments in Cairo and Damascus; at the same time, the Egyptian-Syrian defense pact seemed to signal that neither of Jordan's Arab partners would come to its assistance in the event of an Israeli attack.

Meanwhile, in Cairo the stark possibility that Egypt might actually be forced to come to the aid of their Syrian partners, per the conditions of the pact, hit home in mid-May. In fact, as early as February 1967 Israeli officials publicly raised the possibility of launching a strike into Syria (McInerney 1994, 108). Furthermore, in the second week of May, Israeli chief of staff Yitzhak Rabin reportedly told the press that Israel was considering strong military action against the Syrians if cross-border guerrilla activity did not cease. The circumstances surrounding the report are still subject to much debate. On the one hand, United Press International reported in regards to a May 11, 1967, briefing that a "high Israeli source said today that Israel would take limited action to topple the Damascus army regime" if the cross-border attacks continued. On the other hand, Israeli officials insisted that they had been misquoted. In their version, an IDF spokesman issued a sharp warning to the Syrian regime on the serious consequences of failing to stop the attacks. However, that same spokesman went on to note that there were military alternatives between limited counterstrikes and an "all-out invasion of Syria and conquest of Damascus" (Parker 1993, 15–16).

Putting aside the issue of what Israeli officials really did or did not say, there is no dispute that the Syrians believed, or at least claimed to believe, that the statements from Israel should be interpreted as a direct threat to the survival of the regime in Damascus. The Syrian Foreign Ministry proclaimed as much in press statements issued within a day or two after the story broke, and the Syrian version of what the Israelis had said was accepted at face value by the rest of the Arab world. The apparent explicit verbal threat to Syria's security, which was reinforced by Soviet intelligence reports forwarded to Nasser in Cairo that the Israelis had mobilized ten to twelve brigades along the Syrian border (this report will be discussed in more detail below) left Egypt no wiggle room within the context of its defense pact with Syria. Clearly, this was the type of threat the pact was designed to address. With Nasser's domestic, regional, and international prestige on the line, the Egyptian president took a series of fateful decisions, including the mobilization of troops, the movement of Egyptian forces into the Sinai, demanding the withdrawal of UN peacekeepers from along the Egyptian-Israeli border, and closing the Straits of Tiran to Israeli shipping.

The clouds of war that suddenly loomed on the horizon looked particularly ominous from the vantage point of the dusty, rolling hills of the Jordanian capital of Amman. Feeling ever more isolated as the tension in the region rose, King Hussein faced a difficult set of options. The king saw a war against Israel as being a folly that would almost certainly result in defeat for the Arabs. And yet, at the same time, the Hashemite regime recognized that the blowback from failing to participate in a possible Arab-Israeli war meant domestic suicide, since it was expected that such a policy would trigger a large-scale revolt among Jordan's Palestinian majority. A cousin of the king, Zaid Ben Shaker, who also held a top post in the Jordanian army, lamented in late May, "If Jordan does not join the (possible) war, a civil war will follow in Jordan." In the words of King Hussein, the Hashemite regime "had the following choice: either to act at the right time with no illusion of what the results might be ... or not to act and to have an eruption occur within, which would cause us to collapse" (quoted in Stein 1993, 66). Faced with these two dark scenarios, the king chose the policy path he hoped would minimize his, and Jordan's, losses. He traveled to Cairo on May 30, 1967, and signed a mutual-defense pact with his longtime Arab nemesis, Nasser. By agreeing to place Jordan's military under Egyptian command, Hussein and Nasser created an image of military coordination between the Arab allies that in reality was virtually nonexistent.

In retrospect, it is clear that the military pacts that were forged by the front line Arab states in 1966–67 increased, rather than decreased, the possibility that war might erupt in the region. In particular, Jordan's late decision to sign a defense pact with Egypt exacerbated the threat environment within which Israeli leaders operated. In the words of Gideon Rafael, who in 1967 was the Israeli ambassador to the UN, "For Israel, strategically, it meant that the ring was closed: Syria to the north, Egypt to the South, Jordan to the east. That was a clear indication of us moving into a military confrontation" (quoted in Parker 1996, 106).

Furthermore, even from the perspective of the Arab states it would appear that alliance politics made war a more likely prospect. For one thing, the pact between Egypt and Syria emboldened the Syrians to continue their policy of confrontation with Israel, if for no other reason than for domestic consumption. In addition, the pacts enhanced the fog of prewar in the sense that they increased confusion over the context within which each party might or might not meet its obligations under the treaties. The potential gap between what the parties seemed to promise in writing and what in fact they would be willing to do if and when a large-scale armed conflict erupted created an atmosphere of uncertainty and mistrust among the Arab states in the weeks leading up to the outbreak of war, and made it very difficult to engage in rational planning once the crisis began to pick up steam in May 1967.

Regional Conflict Spiral and the International System

A spiral of events in the region, beginning in the second week of May 1967, helped to spark the war in the Middle East. Any analysis of regional factors and the outbreak of war in 1967 must begin with Yitzhak Rabin's widely reported threats that Israel was prepared to invade Syria. Within a day of Rabin's warning of Israeli military action against Syria, the Soviets informed their Syrian allies of intelligence reports regarding supposed Israeli troop mobilizations and movements toward the Syrian border. The Syrians quickly passed this information on to the Egyptian government, which initially treated the claims with an ample dose of skepticism. It was not until the Soviets informed the Egyptians directly of the purported troop buildup that Cairo began to take the reports seriously.

There is much disagreement as to the manner in which the Soviets delivered their report. It is claimed by some who were involved that the report was delivered by the Soviet ambassador to Egypt, Dimitri Pojidayev, to Egypt's undersecretary for foreign affairs, Ahmad Hassan al-Fiqi, while others state that the report was passed on by a Soviet intelligence officer to Salah Nasr, Egypt's director of intelligence (Parker 1993, 5–6).

However, while there may be no common account of how the Soviets notified their Egyptian allies of their concerns regarding the position and intent of Israeli troops along the Syrian border, there is widespread agreement on two other points. First, the reports were delivered by Moscow on or about May 13, approximately three weeks before the outbreak of the war. Second, there was at the time no independent confirmation, nor has any evidence been uncovered since then, to support the Soviets' claim regarding the purported massing of Israeli forces near the Syrian frontier. The Israelis themselves issued a vigorous denial at the time, even going so far as to invite the Soviets to tour northern Israel to analyze the situation firsthand, an offer which the Soviets declined. In addition, Egyptian military officials traveled to the border region on May 14 and found no evidence of the Soviet claim of an Israeli troop buildup, an interpretation of the situation that was supported at the time by the Syrians themselves, at least in private discussions with the Egyptians. The evidence was so overwhelming against the claim of an Israeli escalation that a scant two weeks later Egyptian minister of war Shams Badran pressed the Soviets in late May to offer an explanation for why they had provided misleading information to the Egyptians, pointedly telling Soviet premier Aleksei Kosygin that the false report "is what moved us to send troops into the Sinai." Finally, further supporting the argument that the Soviet claim was not true is the fact that the Jordanian radar station at Ajloun reported no Israeli troop movements along the northern border at that time (Parker 1993, 8–9).

There has been much speculation as to what may have motivated the Soviets to plant this false story in the minds of the Egyptians. One school of thought argues that the Soviets in fact truly believed that, in the absence of American intervention on the side of Israel, the Kremlin's Arab allies would triumph in a war. Under this scenario, the Soviet Union supposedly pushed the Egyptians and Syrians to pursue a policy of escalation that they thought would result in an Arab military victory over Israel. This interpretation of events seems highly unlikely, however, given the overwhelming evidence, as discussed shortly, that by the latter stages of May the Soviets sought to put the brakes on Nasser's provocative statements and actions. There was a recognition in Moscow that an actual shooting war could result in strategic and political disaster for Soviet allies in the region.

A more plausible scenario focuses on the claim that, while the misinformation was not part of "a well-planned Soviet exercise in brinksmanship . . . Moscow may have been interested in a limited, controlled increase in tension" (Brecher 1980, 45). This interpretation of the Soviets' motivation is supported by the fact that the Soviets pleaded with their Egyptian allies to act in a restrained way during a high-level visit of Egyptian officials to Moscow in late May and by the fact that the Soviet ambassadors to Cairo and Tel Aviv were instructed to wake Nasser and Eshkol respectively in the early morning of May 27 in order to urge caution and thus avoid a war (Parker 1993, 12).

If one accepts this second scenario as the more likely of the two, then one is driven to ask, what motivated the Soviet Union to risk the possibility of a disastrous war in the region by initiating an increase in tensions on the ground? Again, the most persuasive explanation for Moscow's risky behavior during this period of time is provided by prospect theory, with its focus on loss aversion (McInerney 1994). Contrary to the assumptions that form the basis of the standard rational choice/expected utility theory of decision making, prospect theory posits that actors are most motivated to take risks when they calculate that doing so will minimize their losses in those things which they already possess and value. In other words, actors are more likely to take risks in order to protect the status quo than they are to attempt to achieve gains beyond what they already possess.

In this case, the Soviets were concerned with trying to preserve the fragile, radical regime in Damascus. The neo-Ba'athists who had seized control of the government on February 23, 1966, seemed an excellent fit for Soviet ideological and strategic purposes in the Middle East. Domestically, the new, pro-Soviet Provisional Command espoused the path of scientific socialism (McInerney 1994, 104). In the realm of foreign policy, a strong call went out from Damascus in 1966–1967 for Arab unity in order to meet the strategic threat posed by Israel, and to oppose American imperialism in the region. In the eyes of the Kremlin, these external positions, combined with the ideological purity of Syrian socialism (as compared to Nasser's version of Arab socialism) and the fact that the Syrian regime's vulnerability might make Damascus more pliant to Soviet demands, significantly bolstered Syria's utility within the context of the Soviet Union's regional designs. In addition, given the divisions which existed within the Syrian regime on the issue of the Sino-Soviet split, the Soviet Union was driven to try to increase its role as a military and political patron to Syria in order to coax the neo-Ba'athists into the USSR's sphere within the international communist camp (McInerney 1994, 113).

However, much of Syria's domestic population did not share the Soviet Union's warm embrace of the secular, socialist, minority-dominated neo-Ba'athist contingent that was now in control in Damascus. In fact, internal antiregime activity rose sharply during the first several months of 1967, at least partially in response to an article in the Syrian army newspaper which appeared to attack Islam as a threat to the secular ideology that supposedly formed the core of the "New Arab Man" (McInerney 1994, 109). Religious-based opposition to the regime intermingled with the economic grievances which the Damascene merchant class held toward the radical socialist policies of the state to form a powerful brew of antiregime sentiment within Syria. The one action which the embattled neo-Ba'athists could pursue in order to burnish their domestic position was to turn up the heat in the conflict with Israel. Unfortunately for the regime, such a policy greatly increased the risk that eventually the Israelis would feel compelled to strike at the heart of, and even overthrow, the radical Syrian government.

In the minds of the Soviet leadership, the combined domestic external and internal challenges to Moscow's allies in Damascus put into play what is referred to in prospect theory as the "certainty effect" (McInerney 1994, 112). In this case, Soviet elites came to the conclusion that doing nothing would result in the *cer-*

tain collapse of the neo-Ba'athist regime, whether or not a general war erupted in the region. On the other hand, they calculated that concocting a controlled crisis in the region, while increasing the risk of all-out war (and thus the possibility of a devastating set of strategic and diplomatic losses to Soviet interests in the region), was not certain to result in such an overwhelmingly negative outcome. They were willing to take a gamble on the *possibility* of a more extensive array of severe losses in the region in order to avoid the *certain* loss of their allies in Damascus.

Under the best case scenario, by creating and then managing the crisis in such a way that the Arab states could be perceived as having faced down the Israelis without going to war with them, Moscow could have the best of both worlds: increasing the domestic legitimacy of the pro-Soviet Syrian regime, without risking its destruction in an actual war. Such an outcome would have met the long-term objectives of the Soviet Union in the Middle East, which according to Dr. Vitaly Naumkin, who was a student in Cairo at the time of the war and went on to become the director of the Russian Center for Strategic Research and International Relations, centered on Moscow's desire to strengthen leftist Arab regimes and to protect its own strategic and political position in the Middle East. Naumkin further states that there was a division within the Soviet government at the time between military experts who believed that Israel enjoyed a decisive military advantage over the Arabs and ideologues within the Politburo who were passionate in their hatred of Israel and Zionism (Brown 1996, 36–40). This depiction of the difference of opinion between Soviet military and civilian elites is contradicted by other accounts, which claim that military elites pushed for the Arabs to take a tougher stance toward Israel while the civilian leadership advocated a more cautious approach (see McInerney 1994, 109). Regardless of the precise nature and placement of the policy disagreement within the elite class, such divisions within Soviet policymaking circles may have triggered a situation whereby the radicals (be they civilian government leaders or military commanders) pushed to pursue a more confrontational stance toward Israel while the realists (again, be they civilian government leaders or military commanders) lectured patience and restraint. The compromise between these two positions would be to turn up the pressure on Israel while at the same time trying to avoid a war.

As for the rationale on the part of the Arab states, and in particular Egypt, to accept the Soviet report, part of the explanation lay in the simple fact that the Arab governments trusted their Soviet patrons. Thus when American diplomat and scholar Richard Parker asked former Egyptian official Ahmad Hassan al-Fiqi why Cairo chose to ignore evidence offered by the CIA station chief in Cairo debunking the claim of Israeli troop concentrations, Fiqi responded, "Because we trusted the Soviets more than we trusted you." In fact, on May 23, 1967, Nasser himself explicitly referred to a past instance of bad information from Washington—a promise prior to the Suez invasion in 1956 that Israel was not preparing to attack Egypt—as evidence that the Americans could not be trusted on such issues (Parker 1993, 14).

As might be expected in a case of enduring rivalry, the Arabs were also willing to accept the Soviets' claim of an Israeli buildup because such a claim fit a preconceived notion of inevitable Israeli hostility. The longstanding belief in

Arab capitals that Israel was preparing to strike was validated by the reports of Rabin's threat to launch an assault against Damascus. Thus a situation existed in which the faulty information supplied by Moscow simply reinforced a preexisting assumption that an Israeli military offensive was inevitable.

Sensitive to the domestic and regional heat he had taken in the past for failing to rally to the defense of Egypt's Arab allies, on May 14 Nasser ordered Egyptian troops into the Sinai. At that point in time, Israeli leaders believed that Nasser was prepared to launch a retaliatory strike against any Israeli attack on Syria. They calculated that such an attack would be designed primarily to protect the Egyptian president's image and prestige at home and in the region, while falling short of provoking a full Israeli response (Brecher 1980, 46). For their part, the Israelis responded to the growing imbalance in terms of the numbers of Egyptian troops (thirty thousand and growing) and Israeli forces (one battalion and several dozen tanks) along the border by sending armored units toward the region and placing regular army units on alert. Although concerned about the rapid buildup of Egyptian forces near the border, Israeli intelligence reports on May 15 noted that the newly arrived Egyptian troops appeared to be taking defense positions. Meanwhile, in an effort to calm the situation the Israelis informed the Egyptians through UN contacts that they had no aggressive designs on Syria (Brecher 1980, 47–48).

On May 16, Egypt demanded the partial withdrawal of UN observers from along the Egyptian-Israeli border. UN Secretary General U Thant responded that a partial withdrawal was unacceptable, primarily because it would so weaken the UN's presence along the border area as to render it incapable of serving its peace-keeping role. Therefore, either all UNEF forces must be allowed to remain in the region or all would be withdrawn. Faced with the UN leader's "all or nothing" answer to Egypt's request for a partial pullout, on May 18 Egypt demanded the complete withdrawal of all UNEF forces from the area, and the UN commanders on the ground began to comply in short order. U Thant's attempt to play hardball with Nasser backfired, and in the aftermath the rapid move by Egyptian forces to fill the territorial vacuum left by UNEF troops significantly increased the threat environment within which Israeli leaders perceived they were operating, particularly once the Egyptians occupied the strategically vital town of Sharm al-Shaykh (Brecher 1980, 50). By gaining control of Sharm al-Shaykh, the Egyptians placed themselves in a position to cut off the flow of Israeli ships and other vessels carrying cargo and supplies to Israel via the Straits of Tiran and up through the Gulf of Aqaba.

Moreover, the rhetoric that was employed by the parties deepened the sense of hostility. The increasingly bellicose cry for war that emanated from the state-owned media in the Arab states highlighted the sense that war was inevitable. The statement on Radio Cairo that Egypt and its Arab allies were "determined to wipe Israel off the face of the earth" and a further statement by PLO leader Ahmed Shukairy that he expected that "none of them (i.e., Israeli Jews) will survive (a possible war)" greatly increased the perception in Israel that the Arab states were preparing to launch a war (Brecher 1980, 133–34). Conversely, factors such as Rabin's threat to attack Syria and the mobilization of Israeli forces increased the belief for the Arabs that Israel intended to strike first, as had been the case in 1956. As Egyptian journalist Muhammad Heikal noted at the time, given the circumstances in the region, it was his opinion that "Israel must attack" (Stoessinger 2001, 160).

Meanwhile, in Washington the Johnson administration struggled to find the correct policy response to the building crisis. The fundamental goal of American policymakers, particularly in the early stages, appears to have been to avoid a war in the region, although it is important to note that according to estimates by the U.S. Central Intelligence Agency (CIA) at the time the Israelis would score a decisive victory in any war fought in the region. In the words of Richard Helms, who in 1967 was director of the CIA, "If the Israelis attacked first, it was going to be a short war; if the Egyptians attacked first, it was going to be a somewhat longer war, but there was never any concern about who was going to win" (Bergus 1996, 217).

President Johnson and his advisors urged restraint on the actors in the region. In a May 17 letter to Levi Eshkol, Johnson warned the Israeli prime minister that he would not "accept responsibility for situations which arise as the result of actions on which we are not consulted" (Quandt 1992, 201). In a speech to the American people on May 22, Johnson stated that U.S. policy "strongly opposes aggression by anyone in the area, in any form, covert or clandestine." On the same day, the newly appointed U.S. ambassador to Egypt, Richard Nolte, met with an Egyptian official and delivered a message from Johnson in which the American president proposed that Vice President Hubert Humphrey serve as a mediator between the disputants in the region (Parker 1993, 48).

Johnson's speech and Nolte's meeting occurred just hours after the Egyptian government took the decision to close the Straits of Tiran on May 21. "Under no circumstances," said Nasser the next day in explaining the decision, "can we permit the Jewish flag to pass through the Gulf of Aqaba. We say they are welcome to war, we are ready for war. . . . These our are waters" (Brecher 1980, 116). The Egyptian president may have been emboldened to take his tough stand by the strong display of public support he received from the Soviet Union, which on May 22 issued a statement that any attack on an Arab state would be met by a unified Arab response with vigorous backing from Moscow. The strongly worded communiqué out of Moscow appears to have strengthened Nasser's perception that the Soviets were prepared to take an extremely active role in support of their Arab allies (Parker 1993, 49).

Nasser's closure of the Straits of Tiran took the tensions in the region close to the boiling point. As far back as 1957, the U.S. government under Eisenhower had recognized that under UN Charter Article 51, Israel would have the right to resort to force if the straits were closed by force. Furthermore, Eshkol had stated in a letter written to French leader Charles de Gaulle in the early stages of the crisis that Israel would not initiate war with Egypt "until or unless they close the Straits of Tiran to free navigation by Israel." As Michael Brecher concludes in his exhaustive account of Israeli decision making during the 1967 crisis, "The announcement of the decision to close the Straits was, for Israel, a major escalation: in fact, it was a point of no return on the path to war" (Brecher 1980, 111, 117).

Recognizing the closure as the spark that might very well light the tinderbox of war, Lyndon Johnson's approach to managing the crisis from May 23 forward focused on continuing to work to restrain the Israelis, Egyptians, and Syrians from being the first to strike, while also attempting to build domestic and foreign support for an international effort to reopen the waterway. The policy options under consideration for achieving this objective ranged from international diplomacy to the creation and utilization of a multinational naval flotilla to force open the strait. The one option that was clearly off the table was unilateral military action by the U.S. Neither Johnson, Congress, nor the American people had the stomach for such an operation in the midst of the ongoing Vietnam War.

In response to the escalation of tension in the region, Washington at once sought to reassure Israel of American support (on May 23, Johnson approved a $70 million military aid package to Israel) while also requesting that the Israelis exercise a forty-eight-hour delay prior to the initiation of any military action. At the same time, the Americans worked with British naval officials on a proposal to call for freedom of navigation through the Straits of Tiran and to try to create a so-called Red Sea Regatta of ships that would pass through the straits. While progress was being made in building international support for the flotilla idea, the plan caused divisions within the U.S. government, with the Department of Defense expressing grave concerns over its logistical practicality, and the Department of State generally expressing enthusiastic support for the plan as a politically viable way to open the straits while also avoiding either unilateral American action or a general war in the region. Given their differing views on the attractiveness of the plan, it is not surprising that the problem of bureaucratic politics arose between the State Department and Defense Department. "Unfortunately," William Quandt notes, "there was little coordination between the two" (Quandt 1992, 204–7).

For their part, Israeli leaders privately placed little faith in the international flotilla scheme. By May 23 the war option was clearly at the top of the menu of options being considered by Israel. Although Prime Minister Eshkol fretted that "it seems there is no way out" of resorting to the use of force, his military commanders decided to recommend that all diplomatic options be exhausted before the choice for war was made. Such a path would allow the Israelis to probe the Soviets for their intentions regarding the crisis, while also shoring up Western support for Israel in the event that war later broke out (Brecher 1980, 118–20).

On May 25, Israeli foreign minister Abba Eban began a series of meetings with U.S. officials. In an apparent attempt to guarantee the maximum possible level of American support while also laying the groundwork for rationalizing the necessity of launching a preemptive strike, Eban surprised his American counterparts by arguing that an Egyptian assault on Israel was imminent. In response to this threat, the Israeli government, through Eban, asked that the U.S. government issue a declaration that any attack on Israel would be considered an attack on the United States. Such a statement would commit the U.S. to go to war in defense of Israel in the event of aggression. The Americans responded on both May 25 and 26 that U.S. intelligence could uncover no evidence of a pending Egyptian attack, that should an attack occur the balance of military capability in the region heavily favored Israel, and that the type of iron-clad commitment the Israelis were requesting was reserved solely for America's NATO allies. In a meeting between Johnson and Eban on May 26, the president reiterated his view that "the appraisal in Jerusalem about an imminent Egyptian attack was not shared by the United States" and repeated the warning that should Israel choose to start a war, "the United States would have no obligations for any consequence that might ensue." In more blunt terms, Johnson told Eban, "Israel will not be alone unless it decides to go alone" (Brecher 1980, 131–37; Quandt 1992, 207–13).

While Eban was in Washington, Egypt's minister of war, Shams Badran, was in Moscow attempting to sound out Soviet officials on just how far they would be willing to go in aiding Egypt should war occur. Badran received decidedly mixed signals during his four-day visit. On one hand, Soviet premier Kosygin and a chorus of other Soviet officials constantly hammered home the need for Egypt to proceed with great caution in order to avoid provoking an Israeli attack. On the other hand, Soviet defense minister Andrei Gretchko told Badran as he prepared to board his plane to depart on May 28, "Rest easy about all your requests. We will give them to you. . . . I want to make it clear that if America enters the war we will enter it on your side. . . . I want to confirm to you that if something happens and you need us, just send a signal" (quoted in Parker 1993, 32).

Bolstered by Badran's report of Gretchko's apparently unambiguous promise of support for Egypt, as well as by the pending Egyptian-Jordanian Defense Pact, which King Hussein had signaled he was ready to sign, and the perceived unwillingness on the part of Israel to pull the trigger on choosing to go to war, Nasser and some other Egyptian officials publicly began to exude a sense of confidence that bordered on cockiness. At a May 28 news conference, the Egyptian president confidently predicted an Arab victory in any conflict and repeated a theme that he had first publicly sounded two days earlier during a speech—that Egypt's objective should fighting break out would be the destruction of Israel (Brecher 1980, 151). Meanwhile, General Amr laughingly told Nasser that he had ordered reconnaissance flights by two MiGs over Israel, and that the planes had purportedly conducted the operations with nary a response from the Israelis. In general, there was a growing perception in Cairo that the Israelis were afraid to go to war (Parker 1993, 52). Given this perspective regarding Israel, Nasser appears to have calculated that he could have the best of both worlds: garnering the political capital from publicly taunting the Israelis while managing to avoid a potentially devastating war with Israel.

Here it is important to return briefly to Israel's iron wall theory. The theory assumed that the Arabs, as rational actors, would be deterred from behaving in an aggression manner when they recognized that the balance of military capabilities so clearly favored Israel that diplomatic compromise was the only reasonable option for resolving the regional conflict. In 1967, the iron wall strategy failed to deter the Arabs, and in particular Egypt, for two reasons.

First, the Egyptian president and his aides appear to have badly miscalculated the relative balance of power between Egypt and Israel. As an Egyptian intelligence report summarized the situation during the crisis, given Egypt's superiority in firepower, "Israel was not about to commit suicide" by launching an offensive. Surely, many Arabs reasoned, with the Arab states now better organized and mobilized (as compared to the situation in 1948–1949), and with the possibility of great powers fighting alongside Israeli forces (as had been the case in 1956) virtually nonexistent, the balance of power favored their side (Lustick

1996, 9). In addition, Nasser was motivated to believe blindly in the best case scenario (i.e., to engage in wishful thinking) because it allowed him to engage in a policy that would burnish his domestic and regional image, apparently without actually going to war with Israel (Stein 1991, 136–37).

Second, although Syria (and to a lesser extent Jordan) had experienced frequent, and occasionally intense, military exchanges with Israel since the 1950s, the Egyptian-Israeli front had been virtually silent since the failed Suez Canal operation of 1956. The iron wall theory, as put into practice by Israeli political and military elites, assumed that deterrence would only be effective when exercised at the point of an Israeli bayonet (Lustick 1996, 5). However, the Egyptians had not experienced the "Israeli bayonet" in any meaningful way since 1956. In particular, the failure of the Israelis to immediately respond with force to such Egyptian provocations as the removal of UN peacekeepers and the closure of the Straits of Tiran served to reinforce the image in Cairo that the Israelis were ill prepared and weak willed.

Nasser's increasingly bellicose language, along with a series of Arab actions that were perceived by Israel to signal growing aggressiveness, changed the mindset among Israeli leaders regarding the attractiveness of the war option. On May 27, Eshkol's cabinet was split on whether to go to war. On the thirtieth, Abba Eban publicly warned that the buildup of Egyptian troops and the closing of the Straits of Tiran must "be rescinded . . . within the shortest possible time." Eban added that, in the event that international diplomacy failed to achieve these changes, "normal rationality" suggested that Israel would use force in order to do so. He would later note that the signing of the Egyptian-Jordanian Defense Pact, which was announced on the same day as his statement warning of the possibility of war, "made it certain that war would break out" (Eban, quoted in Brecher 1980, 153–54). The sense among Israeli policy elites that war was inevitable was enhanced by the rallying of other Arab states to Nasser's siren song of confrontation with Israel. Among other things, Morocco promised to supply troops in the event of war and King Hussein invited Iraq to station some forces in Jordanian territory.

In Israel, political and military preparations for war intensified. Drawn-out negotiations over the formation of an emergency unity government were finally concluded on June 1. Among the key decisions reached was to appoint the popular war hero Moshe Dayan to the post of defense minister, a position that had been held by Prime Minister Eshkol. Dayan's addition to the cabinet tilted the balance of power toward hawkish elements within the government as the final preparations for war continued. On June 2 Israeli military commanders began to finalize their strategy for the upcoming war, focusing on an initial aerial strike on Egyptian planes, airfields, and installations, followed quickly by a ground assault on Egyptian forces in the Sinai (Brecher 1980, 160). Prime Minister Eshkol envisioned a limited war whose objectives would be to eliminate the threat to Israel's security that was being posed by the massive buildup of Egyptian forces along the border. Beyond that, the Israelis seem to have had no firm military plans for the Jordanian and Syrian fronts, and in fact appear to have genuinely wanted to avoid a war with Jordan. In an ironic twist of historical fate, the territory that would most come to symbolize the post-1967 Arab-Israeli dispute—the

West Bank, Jerusalem, and the Golan Heights—was seized not as a result of any rational, well-thought-out military plan but as the outcome of decisions that were made "on the fly" as the Israelis scored massive early advances in the war (Shlaim 2001, 242–43).

Lack of strategic foresight aside, it is clear that June 1 marked the point in time in Israeli government circles when the tide turned decisively in favor of war as the best policy for resolving the crisis. As the idea of using an international flotilla to force open the Straits of Tiran began to lose support, the U.S. quietly backed away from its demand that the Israelis desist from, or at least delay, military action. Moreover, the Egyptian-Jordanian defense pact increased the sense that the Arab noose was tightening around Israel's neck. Within the Israeli government, there was a strong push from Moshe Dayan that it would be to Israel's advantage to launch a *preemptive war*. Dayan strongly favored launching a preemptive strike, and fretted over the risks of waiting to absorb the first shot. "Put bluntly, I (Dayan) said [in a cabinet meeting held on June 4] our best chance of victory was to strike the first blow. . . . (I)t would be fatal for us to allow them to launch their attack" (quoted in Brecher 1980, 167). This last statement by Dayan reflected a long-held belief that lay at the cornerstone of Israeli strategic planning: In any war with the Arabs, it was crucial to strike and defeat them as quickly as possible, before they could effectively unify their forces and overwhelm Israel by sheer dint of manpower (Khouri 1985, 258).

Dayan not only favored a preemptive strike, he also worked toward achieving the fullest possible element of surprise in launching the war. Toward that end, he held a press conference on the afternoon of June 3 in which he assured the assembled reporters that war was not imminent, and allowed thousands of soldiers to be released from service for a weekend holiday. The trap was set.

Meanwhile, in Washington Johnson was under mounting pressure from important pro-Israeli forces in the U.S. domestic arena to take a firm public stand in support of Israel, including from U.S. Supreme Court Justice Abe Fortas. The justice served as an informal advisor to Johnson during the crisis, while also conversing on a regular basis (apparently with Johnson's approval) with Israel's ambassador to the United States, Avraham Harman. Fortas supported the idea of the U.S. publicly committing itself to using any means necessary to force open the Straits of Tiran. Furthermore, he advocated to the president that, if the United States was not ready to resort to force itself, it should at least support the concept that Israel had the right and responsibility to act on its own to defend its self-defined strategic interests (Bergus 1996, 212; Quandt 1992, 215).

In addition, Johnson had come to believe by the end of his meeting with Eban on May 26 that the Israelis were determined to launch a strike against Egypt, either with or without overt and unqualified support from the United States. In fact, during that meeting Johnson was careful not to warn Eban in absolute terms against attacking first. Rather, his argument focused on the fact that *should* Israel choose to launch a preemptive war, the Jewish state would be on its own. Such a decision, Johnson told Eban, "was Israel's affair" (Brecher 1980, 137).

This "yellow light" to Israel from Washington—refusing to publicly support a first strike but also choosing not to explicitly denounce it as being illegitimate—flashed again when Meir Amit, the head of the Israeli intelligence service

Mossad, visited Washington at the end of May and beginning of June. At that time, Amit received a report that U.S. Secretary of State Dean Rusk had responded to a journalist's question regarding the Johnson administration's position on the prospect of war in the Middle East by saying, "I don't think it is our business to restrain anyone." This perception of a subtle (but important) shift in American policy was reinforced at a meeting with Secretary of Defense Robert McNamara during which McNamara failed to voice a strong objection to the use of force by Israel. Finally, in their interaction with several U.S. officials and associates of President Johnson in early June, a common message seemed to emerge: The U.S. president appreciated the restraint the Israelis had shown since the crisis began and the ball was now in Israel's court. Whether or not such statements reflected official U.S. policy or simply the personal sentiments of the figures to whom they are attributed (Supreme Court Justice Abe Fortas, U.S. Ambassador to the UN Arthur Goldberg, and Democratic Party financial contributor Arthur Krim), the Israeli government interpreted them as winks and nods from Washington signaling that Johnson would not stand in the way of a preemptive strike.

Any lingering doubts that Johnson may have had about Israel's intentions were apparently resolved on the evening of June 3, when he was reportedly informed by Democratic Party fund-raiser Abe Feinberg that war "can't be held any longer. It's going to be within the next twenty-four hours" (Quandt 1992, 218–23). Thus although Washington did not completely close the door to a possible peaceful resolution to the crisis (in fact, an Egyptian delegation headed by Vice President Zakariya Muhieddin was scheduled to visit Washington on June 7 for talks with U.S. officials, and the State Department was floating the idea of submitting the straits issue to the International Court of Justice), by June 3 Johnson and his advisors appear to have reluctantly accepted the fact that war was virtually inevitable.

Individual Psychological Factors and Perceptions

Numerous studies have demonstrated that the belief systems, as well as the psychological and cognitive make-up of decision makers, along with variables such as time constraints and stress, may all have a tremendous impact on individuals as they cope with crisis decision making (for a review of this literature, see Rosati 2000). To explain the types of complex decisions that political leaders must make when navigating the uncharted waters of a crisis setting, it is important to take into account the mental shortcuts they use to try to simplify and make meaning of their very uncertain world.

Certain psychological and cognitive factors influenced Israeli decision making during the crisis. As a **historical analogy**, what has been referred to as the "Holocaust syndrome" was a key component of the attitudinal prism shared by Israeli policymakers. In particular, there was a sense that the survival of the Jewish state and people was at stake in the current crisis. In reference to the closing of the Straits of Tiran, Yitzhak Rabin remarked that "the problem is not freedom of navigation, the challenge is the existence of the state of Israel, and this is a war for that very existence." In a June 1 letter to Premier Kosygin, Eshkol noted that

THE SIX-DAY WAR   195

just twenty-five years had passed since "a third of the Jewish people were cruelly annihilated by the murderous forces of the . . . Nazi enemy. . . . Only 19 years have passed since (the) survivors won their independence and began reconstructing the ruins of their national existence." He went on to characterize threats against Jews as attempts at "collective assassination." Yigal Allon, who was minister of labor in June 1967, declared after the war that, if the Arabs had prevailed, "they would have committed genocide" (Brecher 1980, 38–39). The Holocaust syndrome prevented Prime Minister Levi Eshkol and his advisors from taking under consideration the possibility that the bellicose language emanating from Cairo and Damascus was in large part bluster, designed primarily to strengthen the domestic legitimacy of the Arab regimes while also hopefully, at least from Nasser's perspective, convincing the Israelis to back down from a war about which the Egyptian leader felt ambivalent at best.

The fact that many Israelis, including David Ben-Gurion, harbored an image of Arabs as inherently primitive, violent, and bent on the destruction of the Jewish state undoubtedly reinforced the "siege mentality" that gripped Israel during the crisis (Shlaim 2001, 96). Eshkol appears to have shared Ben-Gurion's image of the Arabs, emphasizing in his own writings and speeches that the only way to deal effectively with Arabs was through the threat or use of force (Brecher 1980, 40). This demonization and dehumanization of Israel's adversaries made a peaceful resolution seem unimaginable to Israeli officials who held such an image.

In addition to cognitive prisms, images, and biases, the stress that individuals feel in addressing a crisis can have an impact on their decisions. Research shows that low and moderate amounts of stress may actually increase the quality of decision making, as individuals apply more energy and attention to the problem at hand. Under high stress scenarios such as that which existed in this case by late May 1967, decision making regarding simple tasks over a short period of time may improve. However, as stress levels rise in response to the complexity, ambiguity, and pressure of a prolonged international crisis, decision making often suffers (Rosati 2000, 69).

At least two key Israeli decision makers exhibited clear symptoms of the strain they felt as a result of the crisis. First, on May 23 Army chief of staff Yitzhak Rabin, suffering from what has variously been branded as exhaustion or even a brief nervous breakdown, was taken home and ordered to undergo complete bed rest. Reportedly, Rabin felt acute anxiety over the fact that his verbal threats directed at Syria earlier in the month were primarily responsible for placing the Jewish state on the course of war (Brecher 1980, 123). In addition, Rabin was rebuked by the old warhorse and hero of Israel, David Ben-Gurion. "I very much doubt whether Nasser wanted to go to war," said Ben-Gurion, "and now we are in serious trouble." Moreover, Ben-Gurion blasted Rabin for ordering the full mobilization of the Israeli army before it was necessary, telling him, "You have led the state into a grave situation" (Shlaim 2001, 239). The verbal dressing down from one of his mentors was too much for Rabin to bear, and he suffered a mental collapse shortly thereafter.

Second, on May 28, Prime Minister Eshkol suffered an apparent panic attack while delivering a nationally broadcast radio address that was supposed to be designed to calm the nation. Stuttering and stumbling his way through the speech,

Eshkol's performance had the opposite effect. In order to reassure average Israelis that the government was ready to tackle the awesome task at hand, Eshkol was forced to relinquish his seat as minister of defense (a position he held jointly with the premiership) and to name popular Israeli military figure Moshe Dayan as minister of defense.

In general, there was a feeling in Israel that time was running against the Jewish state—that the Jewish state faced a widening window of vulnerability. On May 30, Egypt and Jordan signed their joint defense pact. On June 2 the French government, which had long been a crucial supplier of military assistance to Israel but also ardently opposed the launching of a new war in the Middle East, announced that it would initiate an arms embargo, effective as of June 5. On June 3 it was discovered that an Iraqi armored division had crossed into Jordan and appeared to be heading in the direction of the Israeli border. These events increased the sense on the part of decision makers that they were under severe time constraints, an environment which makes rational decision making more difficult to achieve. In the words of Israeli politician Menachem Begin, "The (military) commanders . . . revealed their concerns that every additional day without a decision would increase our losses when the hour of implementation arrived" (quoted in Brecher 1980, 160).

Meanwhile, in Cairo the buildup of tensions in May 1967 gave Nasser the opportunity to nurture his flagging image as champion and hero of the Arab world. As Stein notes, the decisions in May to request the withdrawal of UN peacekeepers and to close the Straits of Tiran emanated from a desire on the part of Nasser to respond to the "humiliation he had suffered in April when he failed to come to Syria's aid" (Stein 1993, 64). The severe depression that seems to have hit Nasser once the depths of the Arabs' battlefield losses in June became known, and caused Nasser to tender his resignation as Egypt's president on June 9, 1967 (an offer that was refused and drew tens of thousands of Egyptians into the streets to express their continued support for Nasser), highlights the mental strain the embattled Egyptian felt himself under during this period of time.

Furthermore, Nasser's style of ad hoc decision making during this time is indicative of classic crisis behavior, and in particular of a failure to engage in a thorough and thoughtful rational choice analysis of the menu of options available, and the costs and benefits attached to each option. On this point it is interesting to note that former Mossad chief Meir Amit believes that Nasser's decisions during the run-up to the war were made without much forethought. In Amit's words, Nasser "was making one move without predicting the next move" (Reich 1996, 137).

Although Nasser himself gave conflicting accounts of the amount of preparation that went into Egypt's war plans in 1967, the bulk of his comments appear to support the contention that the Egyptian president was trying to manage the crisis "on the fly." For example, at one point in late May he stated that Egypt "had no plans prior to May 13, because we did not believe that Israel would make such an impertinent statement (threaten an invasion of Syria), or take action against any Arab country" (Parker 1993, 93). Moreover, many members of the army complained in May that they were sent to the front with no clear orders, lacking many basic supplies, and with no coherent plan for how to place Egyptian troops across the Suez Canal (Parker 1993, 94). Interestingly, it has been argued by many that blame for the logistical failures of the Egyptian military in preparing for the war should be placed primarily in the lap of Deputy Commander in Chief Abd al-Hakim Amr, who apparently misled Nasser about the readiness (or the lack thereof) of Egypt's armed forces for war. As Parker acidly notes on Nasser's handling of the crisis, "In a society which relie[d] for its survival on a degree of discipline and cooperation unique in the Arab world, there seems to (have been) no organization or functioning command structure which [could] come up with an objective assessment" (Parker 1993, 98).

As was noted in the previous section, Nasser seems to have utilized *wishful thinking* in dealing with the growing crisis. He simply refused to believe that war was imminent until just two or three days before the Israelis launched their assault. Furthermore, he had come to believe that, should war break out, the Arabs would prevail. The same man who for so long had cautioned the Arabs against becoming involved in a premature war with Israel told UN Secretary General U Thant in May 1967, "My generals all say they are ready to go to war now" (Parker 1996, 309–12). One general in particular—the controversial deputy commander in chief Marshall Abd al-Hakim Amr—consistently assured Nasser of the military's readiness (Parker 1993, 54). Thus when Nasser warned his senior officers on June 2 that an Israeli attack was likely within the next three days, the Egyptian president's attempt to convince his own generals that Israel would attack fell on deaf ears. Given this mindset, it is not surprising that Egyptian decision makers professed to be shocked in the aftermath of the war, both by the fact that the war had occurred at all, and by the poor performance of Egypt's army.

SUMMARY

A complex and interrelated set of factors caused the Six-Day War. At the international level, the behavior of the great powers contributed greatly to instability in the Middle East. Under the League of Nations mandate system, Britain and France failed to prepare the Middle East territories under their control adequately for independent statehood. In the case of Palestine, Britain's pattern of waffling between meeting the demands of Jewish settlers and meeting the demands of the native Arab population satisfied neither the Zionists nor the Palestinians, and provided the territorial basis for an enduring rivalry between Israel and its Arab neighbors within a geographic space that included a city—Jerusalem—that was (and still is) of tremendous religious significance to Jews and Arabs alike.

Later, during the Cold War era, the efforts by the United States and the Soviet Union to protect their allies and to extend their influence in the region contributed to an arms race in the Middle East. This created a multidirectional security dilemma, thus complicating the strategic calculations for Arab and Israeli state leaders. Moreover, the importance of certain regional clients to the superpowers—and in particular the ascension of the Syrian star among the Soviet Union's constellation of client states—caused Moscow to identify the survival of the neo-Ba'athist regime as a core objective in the Middle East. It was the Soviet Union's concern over the possible collapse of the Syrian regime from internal pressure that provided the rationale for the Soviets to plant the false story of a pending Israeli invasion of Syria. In turn, this inaccurate report regarding an imminent Israeli strike was the proximate spark that triggered the crisis that eventually erupted into full-scale war.

At the state and substate levels, in the postmandate period Arab leaders found themselves in charge of unstable states whose legitimacy was questioned by large segments of their own populations. In some cases, specific colonial decisions, such as the creation out of thin air of the new state of Trans-jordan and the French policy of privileging the minority Alawite community in Syria during the preindependence period, clearly contributed to the domestic instability within these fragile new states. Overall, the weakness of these states exposed them to external threats and internal challenges. Under these conditions, the Arab regimes became addicted to foreign assistance to meet their strategic needs and to ensure their political survival. Egypt and Syria were apt to believe the Soviet Union's claims regarding Israel's aggressive intentions because they trusted their international patron to tell them the truth, and because it permitted the Egyptian and Syrian leaderships to manipulate an external crisis with Israel in order to bolster their internal standings.

At the dyadic level, enduring rivals engaged in a complicated conflict spiral. Domestic politics played a key role in fueling this spiral. No Israeli leader could be perceived as being "soft" on Arab guerrilla activity and expect to survive politically. Thus the policy of "two Israeli blows for every one Arab blow" came to be an accepted maxim of Israel security policy for political as much as for strategic reasons. At the same time, the political blowback in the Arab domestic systems forced leaders in Cairo, Damascus, and Amman to respond with toughness to acts of perceived Israeli aggression.

At the individual level, the Soviet reports of an Israeli move toward the Syrian border fit the image that the Arabs had of Israel as being an inherently aggressive state. In addition, the domestic payoff that Nasser received from his bellicose stance toward Israel in May and early June 1967 motivated the Egyptian president to push the envelope in acting and talking tough toward Israel. In dealing with the possibility that his provocative behavior might trigger a war with Israel, Nasser engaged in wishful thinking by accepting without much question his military commanders' claims that Egypt would emerge victorious should war with Israel break out.

For Israeli leaders, events such as the removal of UN peacekeepers and monitors from along the Israeli-Egyptian frontier and the closure of the Straits of Tiran to Israeli shipping, as well as the barrage of verbal threats cascading from Cairo and Damascus, reinforced the perception that the crisis in the region might threaten not just the strategic interests of Israel, but the very survival of the Jewish state. There was a sense that the iron wall Israel had constructed against its Arab rivals was being encircled and a growing demand by hawks such as Moshe Dayan that Israel strike first. The perception in Israel that war was imminent was heightened at the end of May 1967, when King Hussein signed a mutual-defense pact with Nasser. Ironically, the Jordanian monarch signed the pact precisely because he feared that he and his regime would collapse under the weight of domestic and pan-Arab outrage if he failed to participate in a possible war in the region. Thus a complicated security dilemma, informed by the unique strategic and political requirements of each actor, triggered a conflict spiral that culminated in the Six-Day War of June 1967.

THE WAR AND ITS AFTERMATH

At 7:45 on the morning of June 5, 1967, Israeli planes swooped down on the unsuspecting Egyptians. In all, nineteen air fields were eventually struck, and most of Egypt's air force was destroyed while the planes still sat on the runways. By the early afternoon of the first day of fighting, the Israelis had successfully knocked out all of Egypt's twenty-three radar stations. Lacking air support, the Egyptian army was no match for Israel's well-trained and motivated armed forces, which quickly overwhelmed the Egyptians in the Sinai. In fact, the Israeli aerial assault was so effective that the Egyptians publicly (and falsely) claimed that Israel had received direct support from the Americans and British in planning and carrying out the operation.

Around noon on June 5, the Israelis turned their attention to Syria and Jordan, launching strikes on the Syrian air base in Damascus, as well as on the Jordanian air fields in Amman and Mafraq, and the Jordanian radar site at Mafraq. In response to an Iraqi air force raid on the Israeli town of Natanya, the Israelis bombed an Iraqi air base along the Jordanian-Iraqi border. On the ground, eager to gain a total victory and fearful that pressure from the international community might dash those hopes (as had happened in the Suez Canal Crisis of 1956), the Israelis moved three divisions of troops into the Sinai to attack seven Egyptian divisions. As with so many other things during this brief war, the Israeli ground offensive in Egypt worked almost to perfection.

On the Jordanian front, King Hussein received a message from Prime Minister Eshkol via a UN emissary: "We will not initiate any action whatsoever against Jordan. However, should Jordan open hostilities, we shall react with all our might and he (King Hussein) will have to bear full responsibility for all the consequences" (Churchill and Churchill 1967, 127–28). The king, who early on received false reports from Nasser indicating that the fighting was going well along the Egyptian front, ignored Eshkol and ordered his forces to begin to bombard the Jewish sector of Jerusalem. By June 7, the Israelis had driven Jordanian forces out of all of Jerusalem and entered inside the walls of the Old City. They then turned their attention to the West Bank, eventually routing the Jordanians from that area as well, but only after the fiercest fighting of the war.

Along the Syrian front, apparently taken in by Nasser's false claims of Egyptian advances, on June 6 Syrian forces began shelling across the border on a line running from the Sea of Galilee to the south and north to Banias, near Mount Hermon. Having secured victory versus the Egyptians and Jordanians, the Israeli forces turned their (almost) full attention toward the Syrians between June 8 and 11. Also on the eighth, the Israelis became involved in an incident that today is still clouded in mystery and controversy. On that day, Israeli war planes attacked and heavily damaged the USS *Liberty*, an American intelligence-gathering vessel sailing near the Egyptian coast. Thirty-four U.S. sailors were killed in the assault, and 164 were wounded. Although the Israelis insisted that the attack was an accident, they eventually apologized to the victims and their families and paid $3 million in reparations.

At the United Nations, the United States and the Soviet Union, eager to put the brakes on a war that brought forth the specter of direct superpower intervention and conflict, supported Security Council Resolution 234, which called for an immediate and unconditional cease-fire. The Jordanians accepted the cease-fire on June 7, and the Egyptians followed suit a day later. The Syrians formally accepted the UN's call for a cease-fire early on the morning of June 9. However, Israeli decision makers reasoned that to stop the fighting at that point would deny them their objective of capturing the Golan Heights, from which the Syrians had shelled Israeli settlements in the past. Thus Levi Eshkol and his military commanders chose to act as if they were unaware of Syria's acceptance of the cease-fire, and the Israeli onslaught resumed. When the Israeli offensive continued unabated on June 10, the Soviets broke diplomatic relations with Israel.

By June 11, Israel controlled the strategic Golan Heights, and organized Syrian resistance had virtually melted away. For the Israeli army, the road to Damascus was wide open. However, taking Damascus was not part of Israel's strategic plan, and the Israeli army did not pursue the chance to seize Syria's capital city, an act that would have increased the likelihood of direct superpower involvement in the war exponentially.

As was noted at the beginning of this chapter, the Six-Day War fundamentally altered the territorial, strategic, political, and psychological landscape of the Middle East. Territorially, Israel emerged from the war having significantly increased the amount of land under its control, having occupied the West Bank, all of Jerusalem, the Golan Heights, the Gaza Strip, and the Sinai. This in turn changed strategic calculations in the region by providing the Israelis with a degree of territorial depth that it had lacked since its founding.

The Israeli occupation of Arab lands also left a bitter taste in the mouths of many in the region, and in particular in the mouth of King Hussein, who in the span of six days lost his stewardship over Muslim holy sites in Jerusalem as well as control over the West Bank land that his grandfather, King Abdullah, had seized and incorporated into Jordan. Speaking on the condition of anonymity, one Jordanian cabinet minister and advisor to King Hussein told the author in a 1997 interview in Amman that the late king never forgot his humiliating defeat in the Six-Day War and dreamed of regaining the lands he had lost in June 1967. That hope was finally dashed in 1993, when Israel relinquished parts of the West Bank to Palestinian control as part of the Oslo Accords.

Ironically, on the political front the war provided the basis for a new diplomatic formula for bringing peace to the region. In the aftermath of the war, UN Security Council Resolutions 242 and 336 called for the exchange of land for peace via the process of direct negotiations. Put simply, the UN proposed that Israel give back the land it had seized from the Arabs in 1967, in return for which the Arab states would recognize Israel's right to exist in peace and security.

Three other major political realities emerged from the war. First, the decision by the Soviet Union to sever diplomatic ties with Egypt left Moscow on the outside looking in during the 1970s and 1980s, as the Americans worked toward peace in the region. This was the case given the fact that the U.S. was the sole superpower to enjoy diplomatic relations with both the Arab states and Israel. Obviously, the Soviet Union could not help to broker talks involving a party (Israel) with which it had no diplomatic ties.

Second, the Six-Day War signaled the beginning of the end of Nasser's dominance of the Arab world, as well as the decline of the pan-Arab vision that he promoted. By late 1970, Nasser would be dead, replaced by Anwar al-Sadat, whose policies clearly privileged Egyptian state interests over the interests of the broader Arab nation. In Syria, Hafiz al-Assad, who had commanded the Syrian air force in 1967, came to power in late 1970 as well. Like Sadat, Assad was committed to placing the interests of his own state above the pan-Arabism that lay at the core of Ba'athist ideology. Later in the decade, the general ideological framework of secular pan-Arabism came under increasingly effective assault in the region from political Islam. More than one Arab Muslim came to believe that Allah had punished the Arab people in 1967 for embracing a secular, socialist-leaning political ideology.

Third, the utter failure of the Arab states to protect the interests and meet the demands of the Palestinian nation caused a growing majority of Palestinians to look toward their own nationalist movement for salvation. In the aftermath of the Six-Day War, the PLO, and in particular the Fatah faction of that organization led by Yassir Arafat, moved to the fore of the fight for Palestinian rights. Gradually, the centrality of the Arab state–Israeli conflict in the region was eclipsed by the Palestinian-Israeli conflict.

Before the Palestinian issue seized center stage, however, one more major interstate war occurred. In October 1973 the Egyptian and Syrian armies launched a surprise attack on Israel. After scoring significant advances early in the war, the Arabs were forced to retreat. However, for Sadat, the war was a political victory. The primary purpose (at least in Sadat's mind, if not Assad's) of this well-planned and coordinated assault was to change the psychological environment of the Arab-Israeli conflict. Sadat, ready to abandon Egypt's patron-client relationship with the USSR and eager to create better relations with the U.S., recognized that the most obvious way to curry America's favor (and to gain U.S. economic assistance) was to enter negotiations with Israel. However, he also knew that the Israelis, given the supreme confidence they felt about their own military superiority after their stunningly easy victory in the Six-Day War, felt no compulsion whatsoever to enter into negotiations, or even to consider a land-for-peace deal. Ultimately, Sadat's plan bore fruit in 1979, when he signed the historic Camp David Peace Treaty with Israel. As a result of that agreement, Egypt regained the Sinai from Israel and put itself in position to become the recipient of billions of dollars per year in assistance from the United States. In fact, since 1979 Egypt has trailed only Israel in the amount of aid flowing from Washington.

The Camp David Accords also led to a significant reduction in the likelihood that a major Arab-Israeli interstate war would take place in the foreseeable future. With Egypt removed from the military equation in the region, the possibility that the Arab states might be able to field an army that would be capable of defeating Israel on the battlefield became extremely remote. The weakening of the Arab strategic position, which was further eroded in the late 1980s and early

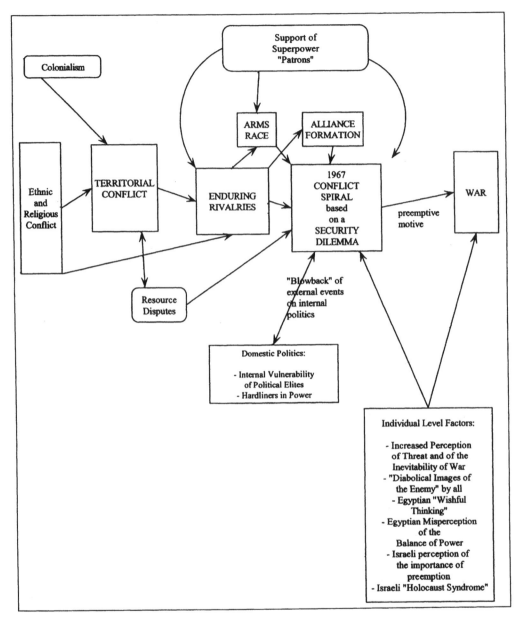

Chart 4.1. The 1967 War in the Middle East: Causal Factors

1990s by the collapse of the Soviet Union and the defeat of Iraq in the U.S.-led Desert Storm operation, eventually led the major parties to the conflict (i.e., Syria, Jordan, the Palestinians, Lebanon, and Israel) to search for a peaceful resolution through the Madrid peace process. These negotiations resulted in the 1993 Oslo Accords between Israel and the PLO, in the 1994 peace treaty between Jordan and Israel, and in a near-breakthrough on the Israeli-Syrian track of the peace process prior to Israeli prime minister Yitzhak Rabin's assassination at the hands of a Jewish extremist in November 1995. The difficulties that have emerged on the Palestinian-Israeli and Syrian-Israeli tracks of negotiations since 1996 cannot erase the fact that the formula for peace in the region is still the one that first emerged in the aftermath of the Six-Day War: land for peace.

5

The Indo-Pakistani War of 1971

With the possible exception of the Arab-Israeli conflict, no modern international dispute has proven as resistant to resolution as that which has existed between India and Pakistan since 1947. India and Pakistan fought major wars in 1947–1948, 1965, and 1971. In addition, since 1998 the two South Asian nuclear powers have engaged in bloody, low-grade warfare in the disputed territory of Kashmir.

This chapter focuses on the 1971 Indo-Pakistani War. The selection of that war for analysis from among the "menu" of Indo-Pakistani conflicts is justified due to a number of reasons. First, the outcome of the fighting of December 1971 fundamentally altered the distribution of power in South Asia, and subsequently set the stage for the nuclearization of the region. As a result of the 1971 war, the entire eastern wing of the Pakistani state gained its independence, thereafter forming the independent country of Bangladesh. In the process, Pakistan was robbed of 55 percent of its population and of fifty-five thousand square miles of land. The structural balance of power, which had always favored India due to its larger population base (estimated to be nearly five times that of Pakistan in 1961) and its more robust, industrialized economy, shifted even further against Pakistan in 1971 (Brown 1972, 3).

Desperate to balance against the widening power advantage India enjoyed following the conflict (in particular after India exploded an atomic weapon in 1974), Pakistan sought to achieve nuclear parity. In 1998 both states conducted well-publicized nuclear tests, and the world was put on notice that the two strongest powers in South Asia had indeed joined the nuclear club. Thus today the stakes in the conflict between India and Pakistan have never been higher. It is indeed sobering to consider that nuclear weapons now reside in the hands of rival states which historically have shown an inability to resolve their disputes through peaceful means. In fact, prior to leaving the presidency Bill Clinton branded South Asia "the most dangerous place on earth" (Ganguly 2001, 1).

The 1971 Indo-Pakistani War also provides a rich case study of the important role that external great powers play in shaping the conflict environment in lesser-developed regions of the international system. In this case, China, which was allied with Pakistan and had fought a war with India in 1962, was a key player whose presence in the region altered the strategic calculations for both India and

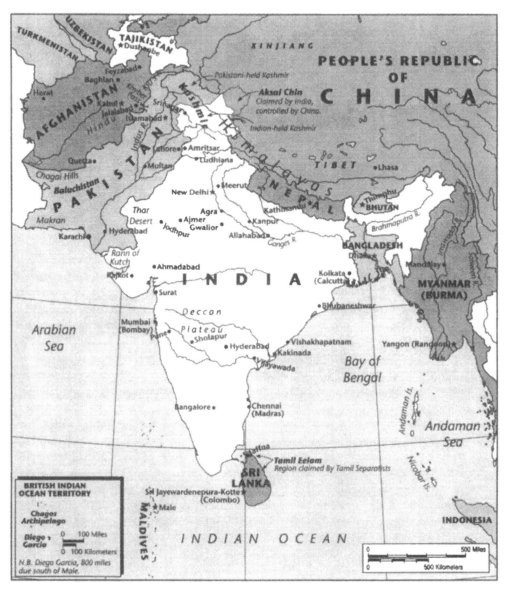

Map 5.1. India, Pakistan, and Bangladesh

Pakistan and created a complex security dilemma in South Asia. As the weaker power in South Asia, Pakistan needed Chinese support to balance against India's strength, especially given the lukewarm support Pakistan received from its traditional ally, the United States, throughout much of the 1960s and 1970s. India, on the other hand, felt threatened by the Sino-Pakistani alliance and sought to address the two-front threat from China and Pakistan both through a policy of internal balancing (i.e., undertaking a massive military buildup) and through external balancing by forging a tighter relationship with the Soviet Union (Mitra 2001, 373–74). Ultimately, the military and diplomatic support the great powers provided to India and Pakistan increased tensions in the region; at the same time, "the limited obligations accepted by the major external powers in South Asia deprived them of the capacity—or will—to impose 'peaceful' methods for the resolution of disputes on their supposed 'client' states" (Sisson and Rose 1990, 53).

In addition, the 1971 conflict underscores the importance of misperception and mistrust as a source of war in the international system, particularly within the context of an enduring rivalry. Sisson and Rose (1990) describe "a legacy of misperception" between India and Pakistan. Pakistani elites continued to assume, based on statements that had been made immediately after the partition of India by the British in 1947, that the Indian state still denied the legitimacy of Pakistan's existence. For their part, Indian decision makers tended to take a condescending view toward their Pakistani counterparts; they explained away Pakistani concerns over India's intentions toward Pakistan as being indicative of the incapacity of Pakistanis to grasp the moral basis of India's foreign policy orientation (Sisson and Rose 1990, 44–45). As a result of these mutual misperceptions, both India and Pakistan displayed an "unwillingness to even make an effort to understand each other's positions on a broad series of issues and events (a tendency which) no doubt contributed to the outbreak of war" (Sisson and Rose 1990, 46).

Finally, more so than the wars of 1947–1948 and 1965, the war of 1971 highlights the interesting (and crucial) linkage between domestic crisis and foreign conflict. Specifically, both parties faced tremendous domestic challenges in 1971. In the case of Pakistan, the unexpected outcome of the December 1970 elections, in which Sheikh Mujibur Rehman's Bangladeshi Awami League won the majority of seats, meant that the power was scheduled to be turned over to a party from East Pakistan that had demanded at the very least autonomy for Bangladesh (i.e., East Pakistan), if not outright independence. Ultimately, the brutal response of the Pakistani military to the perceived challenge posed by the Awami League electoral victory to Pakistan's territorial unity triggered a massive flight of refugees from eastern Pakistan to India. This relocation of up to ten million people from Pakistan to India seemed to threaten the domestic economic and political stability of India and drove the Indian government to intervene directly in the internal conflict within Pakistan. India armed, trained, and gave safe haven to the Bangladeshi rebels, eventually fighting alongside the rebels against Pakistan. As the fighting intensified in East Pakistan, the Pakistani government took the risky, and strategically faulty, decision to launch a second front along the western Indo-Pakistani border. Having widened the war, Pakistan then paid the price as superior Indian forces made quick work of their weaker, disorganized foe.

Pakistan was divided, Bangladesh became independent, and India gained unquestioned regional dominance. What had started out purely as a domestic crisis in Pakistan resulted in a war between the two most powerful states in South Asia that had long-lasting implications for the region.

ROOTS OF WAR: LONG-TERM CAUSES

Religion

The conflict between India and Pakistan is often presented as a conflict between Hindus and Muslims, one that links religious rivalry with territorial identity. As Mitra notes, the "standard view tracks the hostile relations down to the unresolved issue of Kashmir, the unfinished agenda of the Partition of British India on religious lines and the growth of Hindu and Islamic fundamentalism in South Asia" (Mitra 2001, 361). Renowned scholar Samuel Huntington sees the ongoing conflict between India and Pakistan as providing empirical evidence for his hypothesis that the international system will be characterized increasingly by a so-called clash of civilizations between seven or eight great cultural blocs within the system. Conflict between these civilizations is particularly likely, says Huntington, in areas where they come into contact and overlap with each other, as is the case with Muslim Pakistan and Hindu India in South Asia. Moreover, a kin-country syndrome purportedly exists in which states are particularly likely to provide material support, and perhaps even to undertake direct military intervention, in defense of their cultural brethren elsewhere. In an interview published in 1998 after India and Pakistan had both successfully tested nuclear weapons, Huntington bluntly states, "The nuclear status certainly confirms the thesis that the clash between civilizations—in this case Islam and Hinduism—has replaced the ideological confrontation of the Cold War as the main characteristic of conflict in today's world. Obviously India and Pakistan represent different civilizations. They have had 3 wars in the last 50 years" (Huntington 1998).

Stoessinger argues that the core trigger for the twentieth-century wars between India and Pakistan was the history of religious friction between the faiths in South Asia. "The fact that the two hostile religions were represented by sovereign states made the conflict even more ferocious," he observes. "Nationalism and religion were now fatefully fused with the modern nation-state serving as a handmaiden to religious warfare" (Stoessinger 2001, 112). "Had it not been for long-standing and bitter enmity between Hindus and Muslims," concludes Stoessinger, "a single state, rather than two hostile ones, would have emerged out of the British colony" (Stoessinger 2001, 134).

In order to analyze the utility of religious friction as an explanatory variable, it is important to understand the long history of the interaction between Islam and Hinduism prior to the partition of India in 1947 and to consider the actual degree to which religion served as a source of identity and conflict within and between the Muslim and Hindu communities of preindependence India. What first brought these two "incompatible" religions into contact was the spread of Islam into South Asia. Although Turkish armies began their raids into the Indian subcontinent as early as 1001, it was not until 1206 that the Qutb-ud-din Aibak government organized the Delhi sultanate.

Muslim rule in India continued for over five centuries. During the sixteenth century, the Muslim sultanate of Bengal was integrated into the Mughal empire, which had been established in the northern section of India. The conversion of Bengalis to Islam, followed by the absorption of Bengal into the Mughal dynasty, created the conditions in which tensions would eventually emerge within the Bengal territory. Although the Muslim elite class in Bengal embraced the Urdu language and began to identify more strongly with the larger Muslim world, average Bengali Muslims never let go of their unique cultural heritage, including the Bengali language. Later, interest in Bengali culture enjoyed a renaissance once the British began to move into the region (Jackson 1974, 9–10). Increasingly, ethnicity, rather than religion, became the crucial source of identity for Bengalis during this period of time.

As will be discussed in more detail below, the long arm of British colonialism began to make inroads into India in the 1600s and 1700s. In 1757 forces of the British East India Company scored a military victory at Plassey in Bengal. The British followed this up with a defeat of the Mughal army at the Battle of Buxar in 1764, after which the British East Indian Company took over revenue collection and administration in Bengal, with the consent of the Mughal dynasty (Brown 1972, 42). Using Bengal as their base of power, the British extended their rule across the length and breadth of the region, so that by the mid-nineteenth century they were in control of virtually all of India, territory that when divided in 1947 would comprise the modern independent states of India and Pakistan.

During the ninety or so years of direct colonial rule in India, the British were certainly not above playing the divide-and-rule game so typical of colonial policy at the time. Specifically, the British administration in India encouraged both Muslims and Hindus to emphasize their respective, unique religious backgrounds at the expense of any shared sense of territorial identity. After the Hindu-dominated (albeit avowedly secular) Indian National Congress (INC) was created in 1885 as the first organized nationalist movement, the British Raj permitted—even facilitated—the creation of the Muslim League in 1906. By welcoming the construction of a religious-based, Islamic alternative to the INC, the British reinforced not just communal divisions in India, but also the legitimacy of religious political organizations in the era of the secular state. Three years after the founding of the Muslim League, the British further institutionalized the connection between religion and politics by creating a system of communal electorates in India (Nayar 1972, 7).

In 1916 the INC and the Muslim League signed a nationalist alliance agreement, the Lucknow Pact, one element of which was that the INC agreed to support the concept of separate communal electorates for Muslims, Sikhs, and Hindus, as well as a quota system for guaranteeing Muslim representation in the legislature. Moreover, the INC, anxious to create a united front against British colonialism in India, agreed to the right of the Muslim League to review any law affecting Muslims in India. In retrospect, the Lucknow Pact was a spectacular failure. Not only did intercommunal cooperation fail to take root (by 1922 riots between the religious communities wracked India), but the terms of the pact simply reinforced the unique identities of each of the communities rather than building a bridge between them (Heitzman and Worden 1989, 14).

In the 1930s Muslim League theorists began to tout the "two-nation" theory, arguing that the differences in cultural and social values were so deep between Muslims and Hindus in India that it was impossible for the two peoples to live in peace within a single political system (Sisson and Rose 1990, 35). In fact, in the case of Pakistan religion served as the raison d'être of the state. Led by Muhammad Ali Jinnah and his Muslim League party, Muslims in India framed their argument for an independent state on the basis of the supposedly irreconcilable differences between the peoples of the two faiths. "Our sense of values and objectives in life and politics differ so greatly," said Jinnah in comparing Islam and Hinduism (Nayar 1972, 18).

It is important to note that most Muslims in India prior to partition believed that this formula should result in the creation of two independent "Muslim" states that would be carved from India, one in the northwest region, where Muslims comprised the majority of the population, and the other in the northeast, where they also formed the majority (Sisson and Rose 1990, 35–36). Communal ties aside, the Muslim League leadership was realistic about the inherent difficulties involved in any attempt to hold together a hypothetical Muslim state that might politically unite the northwest and northeast regions, which were geographically separated by more than one thousand miles of Indian territory. However, Britain's rushed plan for Indian independence after World War II created a new status quo—a Pakistan that united the northwest and northeast Indian territories into a single independent Muslim state—that the Pakistani leadership felt bound to defend. As is predicted by prospect theory, once the two Muslim corners of India were united, independence for the eastern wing of the Pakistani state represented an unacceptable loss that the central government was driven to attempt to avoid via the risky path of fighting simultaneous domestic and international armed conflicts in 1971.

Religion undoubtedly has played some role in stoking the flames of war on the Indian subcontinent. However, its impact as a determining explanatory factor in the Indo-Pakistani conflict is generally overstated in much of the literature. As Mitra points out, it is a mistake to define India and Pakistan as being "natural" adversaries due to their religious differences. From the Indus War Treaty of the 1950s through the meetings in recent years between the political leaderships of the two countries, the states of India and Pakistan have been able to pursue cooperation with each other when their respective leaders calculate that it is in their interests to do so (Mitra 2001, 365).

Furthermore, it is historically inaccurate to depict each of the two communities as monolithic blocs. The Muslim "nation" in Pakistan is undermined by the traditional split between Sunni Muslims, who comprise approximately 77 percent of the population, and Shi'a Muslims, who make up about 23 of Pakistan's population (Kak 1998, 2). In addition, the Muslim community is characterized by significant ethnic diversity, with the major ethnic groups being Punjabis, Sindhis, Pakhtuns, muhajirs (refugees from India), and Baloch. Numerous dialects are spoken, and each ethnic group tends to concentrate in its own geographic base (Blood 1995, 105).

Meanwhile, the Hindu religion in India is characterized by "local, regional, and historical peculiarities," and Hindu society is marked by the well-known caste-based class divisions, all of which renders the concept of a single Hindu polity a fiction (Ganguy 2001, 2). As contemporary Indian diplomat and scholar K. Shankar Bajpai correctly observes, "There is no parallel in history to the modern Indian state. Never have so many diverse groups—linguistic, racial, regional, and religious—in such huge numbers, been encompassed within a democratic framework" (Bajpai 2003, 119).

In addition, if most Hindus in India in fact harbored lingering rage against Muslims over the treatment of the Hindu community during the Mughal dynasty, how can one explain widespread (though admittedly not universal) Hindu support for the secular, multinational platform of the INC, both during and after colonial rule? Rather than reaching out in an effort to incorporate the minority Muslim community into an anticolonial coalition, Hindus should have sought to exclude Muslims and to degrade their standing in Indian society if in fact they were driven by a shared cultural memory of religious discrimination while under Muslim rule. The fact that they failed to do so calls into serious question the level of communal animosity felt by Hindus toward Muslims as the British colonial period drew to a close. Put simply, in isolation from other factors, primordial religious hatred between the Muslim and Hindu communities in India should not be treated as the primary independent variable in explaining the conflict between India and Pakistan.

The Colonial Legacy

As was noted above, the relationship between the Hindu and Muslim communities was manipulated by India's colonial master in an attempt to maintain their control over India. Thus in order to fully understand communal tensions in this case, we must begin with a detailed analysis of the impact of British colonial policy in India. In turn, this will lead us to explore the manner in which that policy contributed to the emergence of competing ideological visions between Hindus and Muslims, visions that drove both parties to make aggressive, mutually exclusive claims to certain territories.

"I told Jinnah that his moth-eaten Pakistan will not last more than 25 years." These were the words of warning that Mountbatten, the final British governor general in India, claimed to have uttered to the founder of Muslim Pakistan in 1947 (Nayar 1972, 1). Given the eventual territorial evisceration of Pakistan with the founding of Bangladesh, Mountbatten, who recalled his premonition during an interview in 1971, appears to have been a prophet. However, what he failed to recognize in lauding his own powers of prediction was that British colonial policy was largely responsible for the emergence of separate Hindu and Muslim states in India, for the creation of the culturally and territorially untenable union of the western Muslim territories and eastern Muslim territories into a single Pakistani state, and for the failure to resolve the status of Kashmir prior to the partition of India on August 15, 1947.

London's policies in India were driven primarily by Great Britain's economic interests. The timing of the seizure of India by Britain was economically propitious; it permitted the British Crown access to cheap raw materials and gave the

British carte blanche to force open the Indian market to the dumping of British manufactured goods. In the process, the domestic Indian craft and textiles sectors were decimated as British machine-made goods undersold the handmade items produced by Indians. Among other injurious policies enacted by the British, an excise tax was placed on all India textile products that pegged the value of those goods to similar items that were produced in Britain (Brown 1972, 52–53; Kulkarni 1973, 119).

In organizing their control over Indian territory, the British distinguished between two types of states. The first category consisted of those states that came under direct British rule; the second category was comprised of the "princely" states. States falling within this latter category—562 in total—were granted autonomy in most affairs (except in the areas of foreign policy, defense, and communications) in exchange for recognizing the ultimate authority of the crown (Ganguly 1995, 169).

In an attempt to forestall the development of a unified anticolonial front in India, by the late nineteenth century the British had firmly in place a system of communal preferences, designed both to create loyalty to the crown and to cause divisions within and between the various communities in India. Although a merit-based civil service emerged, in other areas of government opportunities were based on loyalty and subservience rather than on competency and intelligence. For example, in the military the British came increasingly to favor soldiers drawn from the Sikhs, Rajputs, and Dogras, all communities defined as being "warrior" in nature and all groups that predictably, given their minority status, tended to be largely pliant to British rule.

In economic life, traditional elites, particularly in Muslim regions, found themselves forced down the socioeconomic ladder. The Muslim aristocracy were increasingly isolated and alienated, even as a new rising Hindu middle class and upper class began to slice out a larger role within the Indian economy. As Muslims found themselves lagging ever further behind Hindus, their frustrations mounted. In the words of one Muslim commentator at the time, "The landlord is Hindu, the peasant Muslim. The money lender is Hindu, the client is Muslim. The jailor is Hindu, the prisoner is Muslim. The magistrate is Hindu, the accused is Muslim" (Heitzman and Worden 1989, 12).

At the dawn of the twentieth century, however, the British and Muslims found themselves drawn increasingly toward each other as they sought to counter the shared threat posed by mounting Hindu nationalism. In response to the threat from Hindu nationalists, in 1905 the British governor general, Lord George Curzon, acceded to the Muslim demand for the partition of Bengal. Although the move was made ostensibly for administrative purposes, it is also clear that Curzon sought to bolster the conservative, Urdu-speaking Muslim elites' ability to provide a counterweight against Hindu nationalism. Although the government eventually bowed to Hindu pressure and reintegrated the territory in 1911, the boundaries of Bengal were redrawn at that time to provide for a Muslim majority in the province (Jackson 1974, 10–11).

In 1906 the All-India Muslim League was formed as the Muslim organizational response to the Indian National Congress. The league proclaimed that its mission was "to protect and advance the political rights and interests of the

(Muslims) of India" (Heitzman and Worden 1989, 14). Meanwhile, an INC-led boycott of British-made goods in favor of *swadeshi* (Indian-made products) picked up steam. In order to stem the growing tide of anticolonial agitation, the British enacted constitutional reforms in 1909. The reforms, which were reinforced in 1935, institutionalized the system of separate communal electorates in India.

World War I posed a potentially perilous challenge to British hegemony in India. Would Indians rally behind the crown in its war efforts, or would they seize the opportunity to revolt against British rule? Although Britain's fear that India might slip from its grasp during this period of time proved to be unfounded, the British still sought to reinforce their tight control over the region. In March 1919 the British enacted the Rowland Acts, which legalized draconian measures in order to address the threat from "seditious conspiracy" in India. Almost immediately a round of strikes was called by Mohandas Gandhi, the rising figure within the INC. Tensions finally exploded on April 13, 1919, when British troops fired upon ten thousand Hindus who had gathered to celebrate a religious festival. When the shooting subsided, nearly four hundred Hindus were dead and more than eleven hundred were wounded. The massacre at Jallianwala Bagh fundamentally altered the course of the INC, which under the guiding hand of Gandhi began to pursue the course of *swaraj* (independence) through *satyagraha* (nonviolent civil disobedience).

Throughout the 1920s and into the 1930s, pressure for independence continued to build, spearheaded by the INC. Also during this period, the Muslim League and the INC continued to wrangle over the issue of separate electorates: the league defended the idea, the INC opposed it. The Congress issued the Nehru Report in 1928, rejecting the concept of separate electorates. The league responded with the 14-Point Program, built on the consociational model of government in which a specific percentage of legislative seats and service posts would be reserved for Muslims and legislation could be defeated if three-fourths of any community's legislative representatives opposed it (Nayar 1972, 8–9). Muslim leaders such as Muhammad Iqbal argued that Muslims formed a distinct nation "based on unity of language, race, history, religion, and identity of economic interests" (Blood 1995, 28). Framing the argument in this manner was effective not just for internal consumption among the Muslims of India but also for external consumption since it seemed grounded in the Wilsonian notion of self-determination based on national identity.

Finally, the British announced the Government of India Act of 1935, establishing federalism, provincial autonomy, and the protection of minority communal interests as the core principles of the new constitution. In 1937 provincial elections seemed to bolster the INC while discrediting the Muslim League. The Congress gained majorities in the majority of provinces and even did well in those provinces that consisted of a Muslim majority. In fact, the Muslim League managed to capture only 57 out of 482 Muslim seats. Although the outcome of the elections might have dealt a death blow to the Muslim League, World War II intervened. When the British government declared war on behalf of India against the Axis powers without consulting with Indian representatives first, the Congress angrily withdrew its elected leaders from their provincial leadership posts.

In the political vacuum that followed the Congress's decision, Muhammad Ali Jinnah, who had taken the leadership post in the Muslim League in 1934, seized the opportunity to push his idea of separate states for Muslims and Hindus in India. Jinnah had been a liberal Muslim supporter of the INC but apparently became disillusioned with the concept of intercommunal cooperation after the failure of the Lucknow Pact. His unhappiness with the INC turned into outright opposition once Gandhi ascended to the leader role within the Congress. Leading INC figure Jawaharlal Nehru argued that Jinnah split from the Congress "because he could not adapt himself to the new and more advanced ideology" (e.g., nonviolent resistance), and "even more so because he disliked the crowds of ill-dressed people, talking in Hindustani, who filled the Congress" (Nayar 1972, 10).

In 1940 the Muslim League held their annual convention at Lahore. The delegates to the convention adopted the so-called Lahore or Pakistan resolution. The language of the resolution, which specifically called for the creation of multiple independent states in the predominantly Muslim areas of Pakistan, underscores the point made in the previous section of this chapter that the Muslim League did not at this time envision the creation of a single, unified Muslim state in India.

During World War II, the Muslim League sought to curry favor with British authorities by supporting the war effort. By comparison, the Congress launched two ill-fated rounds of anti-British agitation between 1940 and 1942, including Gandhi's Quit India movement, which resulted in the arrest of over sixty thousand individuals and the banning of the INC (Heitzman and Worden 1996, 45). An attempt by British official Sir Stafford Cripps to broker an agreement with the INC in which Britain would grant dominion status *after* the war to India in exchange for strong defense links failed, with Gandhi branding the offer "a postdated check on a crashed bank" (Blood 1995, 30). The tension between the Congress and the British bolstered the Muslim League's status, which Britain saw as a counterweight to the more radical nationalists in the INC. "The British," one observer later noted, "trimmed their sails to follow the direction of the Muslim League's wind" (Nayar 1972, 7).

The outcome of two elections—the first in Britain in July 1945, the second in India in March 1946—set the stage for Indian independence and for the partition of Indian territory. In Great Britain, war-weary voters brought the Labour Party to power. The new government moved quickly to resolve the Indian issue, particularly after a naval mutiny erupted in Bombay in 1945. Seeking to negotiate a peaceful transition to independence, British officials held failed talks with Indian representatives in Simla in 1945. Afterward, the decision was made to call for elections in 1946. The outcome of those elections, which were widely viewed as a referendum on the level of support for the Muslim League's call for the partition of India, illustrated the spectacular inroads that the Muslim League and its message had made in the Muslim community since 1937. Whereas the Muslim League had won a paltry 4.5 percent of the Muslim seats in 1937, nine years later it captured 90 percent. The league controlled every Muslim seat in the Central Assembly and 442 out of 509 Muslim seats at the provincial level (Blood 1995, 30–31; Nayar 1972, 28).

Several days after the election, the British government dispatched a mission to India in a last-ditch effort to achieve an agreement by which Britain could transfer power to an independent, unified India. Abdul Kalam Azad, one of the few Muslim leaders within the INC, proposed a plan based on a federal system of government in which the provinces would have full autonomy, except in the areas of defense, foreign affairs, and communications. Britain, which in 1935 had espoused the utility of federalism in organizing the Indian system, offered what became known as the Cabinet Mission Plan. It proposed a three-tiered structure: At the top layer would be the entire country, including the princely states, at the middle level territories would be grouped together into several geopolitical units, and at the bottom would be the territories and princely states themselves. Under the proposed constitution, the midlevel groups would have autonomy over all issues except defense, foreign policy, and communications, which would be delegated to the central government at the top of the structure. Residual powers would reside with the individual provinces.

On July 6, 1946, the Muslim League accepted the plan, which grouped the six Muslim provinces together. The INC also accepted the plan, but with reservations that undermined the proposal. Specifically, Nehru chose to interpret a clause stating that provinces could opt out of their preassigned territorial groups as meaning that the INC was essentially free to modify the plan as it saw fit, without first consulting with the other parties to the proposal and without waiting for elections, an interpretation that put Nehru at odds with both Gandhi and with Jinnah. Nehru's viewpoint won out over Gandhi's within the INC, as the Congress rejected a British proposal to submit the issue to the Federal Court in India. For Jinnah and the Muslim League, the INC's backtracking on the Mission Plan, combined with the results of just-concluded Constituent Assembly elections in which the league won just 76 seats against 292 for the Congress, signaled the death knell for the federalism concept in India. The election results seemed to underscore Jinnah's argument that Muslims would be consigned to permanent second-class status in a unified, federal India in which Hindus would form the large majority of the population (Nayar 1972, 31–33).

Jinnah's anger boiled over when the British colonial administration moved forward and formed an interim government without the Muslim League. He called for a day of "direct action" on August 16, 1946. Massive communal riots erupted, leading to the deaths of thousands of Hindus and Muslims. Eventually, Jinnah decided to join the interim government in order to work with British and Hindu officials to quell the bloodshed.

By early 1947, the British government had decided that the situation in India was becoming so untenable that the best policy was to quit the territory as soon as possible. In February 1947, the British government of Prime Minister Clement Attlee appointed Lord Mountbatten to the post of viceroy and charged him with the responsibility to extricate Britain from India by June 1948. Once on the ground, Mountbatten quickly concluded that communal tensions were running too high to take another sixteen months to resolve the situation. He proposed a plan by which India would be given its independence on August 15, 1947, with the Muslim majority provinces that had been under direct British rule being separated from the rest of India to form the independent country of Pakistan. In other words, the Muslim majorities in northwest and northeast India would be combined into a single Muslim state.

Although in theory the nominally independent princely states could choose to strike out on their own, in reality the British pressured the leaders of those states to choose to join either India or Pakistan. As expected, the princely states based their decisions largely on geographic proximity and religious identity. Of the over 560 princely states, only three—Hyderabad, Junagadh, and Jammu and Kashmir, proved to be a problem. The status of Hyderabad and Junagadh, both of which were populated largely by Hindus but which had Muslim rulers, was resolved quickly as they were absorbed into India, with whom they shared borders. The problem of Jammu and Kashmir, which shared boundaries with both states but had a Hindu ruler and a Muslim majority, proved to be more difficult, as the unique ideological rationales for the Indian and Pakistani states motivated the leaders of both states to link control of territory with the legitimacy of their founding ideologies.

Ideology, Territory, and the Creation of an Enduring Rivalry

India and Pakistan have competing, irreconcilable definitions of the ideological bases of the state (Sisson and Rose 1990, 36). On the one hand, the secular ideology of the INC carried over into the construction of the Indian state, with the political system placed firmly on a constitutional framework of secularism. On the other hand, the state of Pakistan, although certainly not designed to be a theocracy, owed its very existence to the concept that religion can (and should) serve as the basis for political sovereignty and political identity. As Ganguly argues, the competing ideological visions of the Indian and Pakistani states "upped the ante" for the two states when it came to territorial disputes.

For Pakistan, both its dogged (albeit doomed) attempt to hold on to Bangladesh and its persistent claim to Kashmir are rooted in the need to prove that religion can be a legitimate source of state identity. As one Pakistani official argued nearly forty years ago in regard to Kashmir, "If a Muslim majority can remain part of India, then the *raison d'etre* of Pakistan collapses. . . . Pakistan is incomplete both territorially and ideologically without Jammu and Kashmir" (quoted in Ganguly 2001, 32).

For India, Bangladesh's successful drive for independence from Pakistan seemed to prove the poverty of religious-based state legitimacy, and by comparison the inherent superiority of the secular model. By the same token, successful integration of Muslim-dominated Kashmir into India would reinforce the triumph of secularism over religious particularism (Ganguly 2001, 5). On the other hand, permitting Pakistan to absorb Kashmir would have signaled "the triumph of one ideology and the defeat of the other. By acquiescing in Kashmir's conquest, India would have for all practical purposes conceded Pakistan's claim to the loyalty of all Muslims in the sub-continent" (Jain, in Nanda 1976, 50).

At the time of independence, although the British plan met the basic demands of Jinnah and the Muslim League, in recognizing the importance of religion as a source of territorial and political identity Britain created a whole new set of practical challenges. As the INC's Abdul Kalam Azad warned the Muslim League, Muslims who lived in territory awarded to India would "discover overnight that they have become aliens and foreigners" in the newly independent, Hindu-dominated Indian state. Muhammad Ali Jinnah's response was that the Muslims left behind "can take care of themselves" (Nayar 1972, 18–19). Of course, millions of Hindus also faced the challenge to "take care of themselves" in Muslim-dominated Pakistan, all of which triggered a migration disaster of epic proportions, as over ten million terrified Hindus and Muslims chose to relocate to their newly christened religious "homelands" rather than face the uncertainty of being a minority in their birth lands. In addition to population transfers, both sides were responsible for the wholesale massacre of fleeing civilians, particularly in the newly divided state of Punjab (Nayar 1972, 47–50).

In concocting their partition plan, the British chose to redraw the boundaries of several territories. Most significantly, the desire to group Muslims with Muslims and Hindus with Hindus drove Britain to divide both Punjab and Bengal (Jackson 1974, 13). The British lawyer who was in charge of the Boundary Commission, Cyril Radcliffe, later admitted that he was too rushed to make a reasoned and informed decision on the final delineation of boundaries. "Even accurate district maps were not there and what material there was, was also inadequate," he later recalled. "What could I do in one and a half months?" Radcliffe went on to observe that if he had it do all over again, he would have given Hindus more territory in Punjab and Muslims more territory in Bengal (Nayar 1972, 45).

While it is difficult to call Britain's withdrawal from India "hasty" (after all, Britain had been in India for well over two hundred years by 1947), it is undoubtedly true that the desire to pull out as quickly as possible from the colonies in order to focus on rebuilding Britain after World War II caused the British to speed up the process of Indian independence, particularly once the conclusion was reached that independence was inevitable. Britain had played the divide-and-rule game as the colonial power in India, reinforcing exclusive identities within the Muslim and Hindu communities. This strategy, although useful in the short run as a tool of colonial control, also helped to nurture the emergence and growth of the Muslim independence movement in India. Against the backdrop of Britain's desire to expedite its withdrawal from India, the British cobbled together a new map of the region that fully satisfied neither Muslim Pakistan nor Hindu India, and which laid the groundwork for future conflict.

As is true in much of the rest of the decolonized world, postcolonial South Asia has been bedeviled by the problem of **irredentism**. Where irredentism exists, there is a common ethnic bond between the population in one state and a segment of the population in another, often adjoining, state. This bond leads to the demand by members of the multistate ethnic population for the redesign of current territorial boundaries, with the goal being the incorporation of the entire ethnic group within a single state's boundaries. Of course, such a demand threatens the territorial integrity, and therefore the stability, of the state whose ethnic minority is connected with the population in the neighboring state.

Irredentism can be linked in certain instances with **diasporas**. Stephen Van Evera (1994) identifies the existence of diasporas as a possible source of nationalist conflict. Nationalist movements, according to Van Evera, can react to diasporas in one of three ways: They may be "diaspora accepting" and thus content with a partial union which leaves some of their nation outside of the boundaries of their nation-state; they may be "immigrationists," attempting to unify the nation by encouraging immigration to the nation's territorial homeland; or they may be "diaspora annexing," which involves a drive to incorporate the members of their diasporas through territorial conquest (Van Evera 1994, 12). In the case of India and Pakistan, the competing ideological visions of the two countries have driven both states to follow a policy of diaspora annexation in regards to Kashmir, thus contributing to their underlying conflict environment.

Saideman and Ayers (2000) argue that members of a dissatisfied ethnic group have two paths available for opting out of the current political system within which they perceive themselves to be disadvantaged: The group may seek a union with ethnic kin in adjoining territories or they may seek to create their own state through a secessionist movement. The quantitative analysis conducted by Saideman and Ayers of irredentist and separatist groups shows that "a group whose kin dominate a neighboring state has a significantly higher probability of irredentism" (Saideman and Ayers 2000, 1136). Under this set of circumstances, the aggrieved ethnic group will probably seek union with their kin across the border rather than full independence. In summary, irredentism is most likely to occur when an ethno-national group is distributed across two or more states, when that ethno-national group dominates at least one of the states and is sensitive to and protective of its aggrieved kin across the border(s), and when that group feels disadvantaged by government policy in one of the states they do not dominate.

In India and Pakistan, at the time of independence the potential territorial "wildcards" under the British partition plan were the princely states. Jammu and Kashmir (the name of the state has come over time to be reduced in common parlance simply to "Kashmir") became the most obvious sore point. The rugged territory, which shares borders with the former Soviet Union, China, and Afghanistan, was of great strategic significance to both India and Pakistan. Of course, in 1947 the future status of Kashmir was far from determined. Although technically the leaders of the princely states could choose independence, in practice all were expected to accede to either India or Pakistan, based on the criteria of geographic location and demographic composition. However, the Hindu leader of Kashmir, Maharaj Hari Singh, put off making a final decision on the status of Kashmir until after Independence Day, August 15, 1947.

Geographically, Kashmir shares borders with both India and Pakistan. Demographically, however, Kashmir was at the time and continues to be today a heavily Muslim state. Census figures from 1941 showed that over 77 percent of the population of four million was Muslim, while Hindus comprised 20.12 percent of the population. The rest of the population was made up of a scattering of Sikhs, Buddhists, and Christians (Brown 1972, 179).

In theory, because Kashmir's shared borders with both Pakistan and India rendered the geographic criteria inconclusive, the fact that the majority of the population is Muslim seemingly should have meant that the state's future lay with Pakistan. However, Hari Singh was a Hindu whose order of preference placed incorporation into Pakistan as third on his list of ideal outcomes, after independence for Kashmir and integrating into India. Finally, a full seventy-two days after August 15, Hari Singh agreed that Kashmir would accede to India (Wirsing 1994, 14).

Hari Singh's reluctant decision to join with India was triggered by the fighting that had erupted in Kashmir during the first week of October 1947. At that time, rebellious tribesmen, agitated by the pattern of Dogra atrocities in Kashmir as well as by the tales of the massacre of Muslims, who had tried to flee Punjab for Pakistan, launched attacks against the Kashmiri government in the Poonch region (Ganguly 1994, 40–42). Quickly thereafter, regular Pakistani forces disguised as tribesmen joined the rebellion. On October 22 the combined Pakistani-tribal forces captured the town of Muzaffarbad, where they were joined by the Muslim troops stationed there in the massacre of Hindu forces.

The Free Kashmir rebel legion then turned its sights on Srinagar, the capital of Kashmir. With the rebel columns moving ever closer to the city, and the issue of his own physical safety open to serious question in the event that the Pakistani-affiliated rebels should capture the capital, Hari Singh formally requested that India supply military assistance. Nehru agreed, but only on the condition that Kashmir be ceded to India. Believing that his choices were to accept Nehru's offer of a deal or else face total annihilation of his government at the hands of the rampaging rebel forces, Hari Singh reluctantly signed the Treaty of Accession on October 27, 1945.

India kept its part of the bargain, immediately airlifting an infantry brigade into the capital city. After enjoying initial success in pushing back the rebel forces, the Indians themselves were forced to retreat in December, owing to supply shortages and the difficulties that many Indian troops had in trying to cope with the bitter cold weather in Kashmir. Free Kashmir forces launched a mostly ineffective offensive, to which the Indians responded with a counteroffensive in the spring of 1948. As the war dragged on in 1948 and the Indians began to seize the upper hand, Pakistani forces became increasingly involved in the fighting. Much as India's intervention had staved-off the rebels in the fall of 1947, so Pakistan's intervention helped to staunch Indian advances. In fact, the effective placement of Pakistani forces west of the city of Jammu threatened the communication and supply lines for Indian forces on the ground in Kashmir.

By early 1948 the Indian government had come to the reluctant conclusion that achieving a complete victory over Pakistan would require expanding the war into Pakistan itself, an endeavor the Indians had neither the resources nor the stomach to undertake. Seeking a diplomatic solution to the crisis, the Indians asked the United Nations on January 1, 1948, to take up the issue of Kashmir (Ganguly 2001, 17–18). Finally, the UN managed to broker a cease-fire between India and Pakistan, which went into effect on January 1, 1949. As part of the agreement, Pakistani forces were to be withdrawn, followed by Indian troops. In addition, the UN Security Council called for a popular plebiscite in Kashmir to determine whether Kashmir should accede to India or to Pakistan. Neither of these demands was ever met. In the case of the proposed plebiscite, the Indians would later argue that a 1952 vote in the Jammu and Kashmir Constituent Assembly in which the majority of legislators voted to confirm the accession to India was sufficient (Heitzman and Worden 1996, 520). A third UN proposal, one involving the insertion of a UN observer unit on the ground to supervise the cease-fire, was enacted beginning in 1949.

Although the cease-fire did manage to cool the fires of war, albeit temporarily, the crisis in Kashmir was never far from the minds of Pakistani and Indian leaders. Particularly in Pakistan, the tough stand on Kashmir became a glue to bind the young country together during a time of political uncertainty. The death of Muhammad Ali Jinnah in 1948 was followed by the assassination of his successor, Liaquat Ali Khan, in 1951. In turn, Khwaja Nazimuddi, who had succeeded Liaquat Ali Khan, was driven out of office in 1953 by a constitutional coup led by the governor general, Ghulam Mohammad, who then placed Muhammad Ali Bogra, who had been Pakistan's ambassador to the U.S., in the prime ministership. Of course, India had experienced the trauma of Gandhi's assassination in 1948, but India's secular, democratic institutions were much better designed to absorb such a shock than were the underdeveloped political institutions of the increasingly authoritarian and militarized Pakistani state. In fact, the coup of 1953 effectively ended any pretense of parliamentary rule in Pakistan, as a coalition of military officers, civil servants and landed elites from Punjab joined forces to exercise increasing control over the country's domestic and foreign policies (Blood 1995, 41).

Meanwhile, the UN's efforts at brokering a permanent settlement in Kashmir had proven fruitless. After a coup in Pakistan in 1953 a period of limited detente emerged, characterized by bilateral talks between the two prime ministers, Nehru of India and Bogra of Pakistan. In August 1953, India and Pakistan agreed that they would not resort to force to resolve the conflict in Kashmir. Furthermore, the two sides agreed that a plebiscite would be held in Kashmir to determine the final status of the disputed territory, and that a plebiscite coordinator from a small Asian country would be appointed to administer the vote (Ganguly 2001, 24). The warming of relations between the two countries, however, was short-lived. As will be discussed below, a series of security alliances to which Pakistan became a party, including a bilateral pact with the U.S., along with the decision to join the Southeast Asia Treaty Organization (both in 1954), followed by Pakistan's participation in the U.S.-sponsored Baghdad Pact beginning in 1955, internationalized the Indo-Pakistani conflict. Once the dispute over Kashmir became intertwined with Cold War international politics, the hopes for a peaceful solution were severely complicated. A halfhearted attempt by Iskander Mirza, who had become the new governor general of Pakistan in 1955, to restart bilateral talks failed. The bilateral diplomatic door was further slammed shut in 1958 after a military coup brought Gen. Ayub Khan to power in Pakistan. Nehru, arguing that "the normal checks which occur in a government or society are absent" under military dictatorships, refused to negotiate with the new Pakistani regime (Ganguly 2001, 24–27).

Meanwhile, in the early 1960s the Indian government focused its attention on its border dispute with China. In many ways, the origins of the 1965 Indo-Pakistani War can be traced to the 1962 Sino-Indian border conflict and the events that followed. In October 1962, China used military force to seize territory in the Himalayan heights from India. India's swift defeat at the hands of China's People's Liberation Army (PLA) destroyed Indian leader Nehru's dream of building an Asian alliance between his country and China and humiliated the Indian military. When Nehru died in 1964 and was replaced by Lal Bahadur Shastri, whom the Pakistanis perceived to be less prone to use force than his predecessor but just as likely as Nehru to refuse to give in on the Kashmir issue, the leadership in Pakistan sought to seize upon this short-term window of opportunity to address the Kashmir issue (Mitra 2001, 373).

In early 1965, Pakistan began to test the mettle of the new Indian leader by initiating a small-scale incursion in the Rann of Kutch, a fairly flat, barren wasteland of no strategic value. When the Indian army responded in a timid fashion to the incursion, the Pakistanis mistakenly assumed that domestic uncertainty within Indian policymaking circles would preclude India from responding effectively to a larger military operation. In fact, the limited nature of India's response to the Rann of Kutch incursion reflected rational decision making on the part of its military elites. With the Pakistani army exposed on the ground in this terrain, the Indians easily could have used air power effectively to meet the incursion. However, this would have undoubtedly triggered the use of air power by the Pakistanis to protect their ground forces, which in turn may have triggered an escalation into an all-out war (Ganguly 1995, 172). Far from proving indecision and weakness, India's relatively weak response to the incursion reflected a rational calculation by the Indians that the costs of an all-out war with Pakistan at that time and over that territory outweighed any benefits.

Misreading India's readiness to fight a war if backed into a corner, and not recognizing the intense domestic pressure on Shastri to redress the Kutch "defeat," Pakistan embarked on a campaign to destabilize and then invade Jammu and Kashmir (Stoessinger 2001, 121). Disguised as Kashmiri fighters, Pakistani forces secretly entered the territory during the summer of 1965. The plan was simple: The disguised troops would quietly cross the cease-fire line (CFL) and foment a revolt, which would then create conditions in which Pakistan could justify intervening with its forces on the ground to protect its co-religionists. After seizing the territory in a quick war, the Pakistanis would then appeal to the international community for a cease-fire.

The plan, however, ran into significant difficulties from the beginning. First of all, the Pakistani troops did not receive the universally warm welcome predicted by their political leaders and military commanders. Instead, many residents contacted the nearest Indian outpost to report the infiltrators. Second, the response from Indian forces was much more vigorous—and effective—than the Pakistanis had predicted. Instead of a walk-over victory, the Pakistanis found themselves locked in a bloody stalemate with Indian forces throughout August and September. Furthermore, the joint Anglo-American arms embargo against both parties seriously damaged Pakistan's war effort, given the fact that the Pakistanis relied on the U.S. for nearly 100 percent of its military aid, while India, unlike Pakistan, had some indigenous military industrial capability, support from the Kremlin, and received only minor military aid from Washington (Choudhury 1975, 122).

Finally, on September 20 the UN Security Council unanimously passed a cease-fire resolution. Shocked by the poor performance of its own military and by the stiff resistance put up by India, Pakistan accepted the resolution. For their part, the Indians, fearful of undermining India's improved relations with Washington that had emerged during the Sino-Indian War (the U.S. had supported India during that contest), also accepted the cease-fire. After the fighting, with the U.S. increasingly embroiled in the war in Vietnam, the USSR took an active role in brokering the Tashkent Agreement in January 1966, in which India and Pakistan agreed to withdraw their forces to the previous CFL, as it had existed on August 5, 1965 (Ganguly 1995, 172–74).

The treaty, however, turned out to be simply a truce in the Indo-Pakistani conflict. Both countries continued to lay claim to Kashmir. By now, India and Pakistan had become enduring rivals; relations between the two states, though occasionally civil, were characterized by deep suspicion. "Both Pakistanis and Indians," note Sisson and Rose, "had standard negative interpretations of each other's motives and objectives." Although the perceptions regarding each other's objectives were often inadequate or simply incorrect, "they were never modified in the course of events prior to 1971. Developments that reinforced old stereotypes were given great prominence; those that did not were ignored." Both sides were stuck in a cycle of self-fulfilling prophecies, "assuming the worst about each other, and acting and reacting accordingly, and thus usually triggering further animosity" (Sisson and Rose 1990, 45). "Each side viewed the intentions and declarations of the other as fundamentally hostile" (Sisson and Rose 1990, 275). In this atmosphere poisoned by mistrust, a genuine political solution to the Kashmir problem seemed impossible.

Specifically, each side harbored stereotypical assumptions that greatly hindered any attempt to find a peaceful resolution to the conflict. Pakistani leaders tended to assume that India had never accepted the partition of colonial India into two states and thus was behind every instance of political instability in Pakistan. The Indian leadership believed that the Pakistanis were intellectually inferior and Pakistan was a second-rate power. Thus the Indians discounted the Pakistanis as a potential peace partner. The **mirror-imaging** that the leaders of both parties projected on each other—the tendency to define themselves as rational and peace loving, while seeing the other as being irrational and warmongering—drove both parties to take a dark view of the intentions of the other throughout the second half of the 1960s.

After the 1965 war, India, fueled by its rivalry with Pakistan and with an eye as well toward its defeat at the hands of the Chinese in 1962, undertook a spectacular spending spree on military equipment throughout the rest of the 1960s. In a classic example of the security dilemma in international relations, India's military buildup triggered "great concern," as stated by Pakistan's air force chief at the time. Put simply, the Pakistanis doubted that India's buildup was designed for any purpose other than to prepare for the destruction of Pakistan (Ganguly 2001, 37–38).

Meanwhile, following the 1965 war the political leadership in Pakistan was forced to revisit once more the sticky issue of the viability of the Pakistani nation-state. As Wieland argues in reference to states such as Pakistan, the "ethnic concept does not live long once the goal of an ethnonational state is reached. It is more of a dynamic than a consolidating concept, as can be seen in Pakistan. . . . Once the ethnonational camps are fenced in by state borders, new cleavages occur within the supposed ethnic group" (Wieland 2001, 208). In short, far from being grounded in fixed, objective characteristics, ethnic identity is a contested, largely subjective concept whose appeal is formed and shaped to a significant degree by the specific historical context within which it emerges and evolves.

In certain settings individuals may have a rich menu of "ethnic characteristics"—religion, language, tribe, race, and so on—from which to choose. As was noted above, in what would later become East Pakistan, the assertion that Islam was and is the primary source of identity for the majority of the population has long been open to debate. Clearly, beginning in the 1950s, and certainly by the 1960s, the majority Bengali-speaking population of East Pakistan chafed against its domination by less-populated, non-Bengali West Pakistanis. East Pakistanis by and large subscribed to the principle of majority rule. After all, had not the foundational basis for Pakistan been the notion that those areas of India in which Muslims formed the majority should be administered by Muslims? Should not the same principle of majority rule apply to independent Pakistan, where Bengalis comprised the bulk of the population? And since political and economic elites in West Pakistan refused to allow the Bengalis to assume their "natural" position of authority within the state, did not East Pakistan have the right to split from the West (Cohen 2002, 112)?

Of course, the drive for Bengali independence threatened the very legitimacy of the Pakistani state. Originally, Muslim leaders in preindependence India made no claim to Muslim regions of Bengal based on irredentism or diaspora annexation. However, once Britain attached that territory to the new Pakistani state, its leaders had no choice but to define the continued territorial unity of the eastern and western wings of the country as being a core state interest worth fighting to protect. Just as state leaders were so obsessed with Jammu and Kashmir because incorporation of those territories into Pakistan would "prove" their claim that Islam could indeed bind various ethnic groups into a single nation, so the loss of Bangladesh would deal a serious blow to that claim. As will be discussed in greater detail later in this chapter, by 1971 it was clear that the central government of Pakistan would go to any lengths, including the large-scale use of force, to try to preserve the dream of a unified Pakistan.

THE COLD WAR, THE SECURITY DILEMMA, AND THE ROOTS OF THE INDO-PAKISTANI CONFLICT

The Cold War system played a major role in defining the opportunities and constraints available to Indian and Pakistani leaders in conducting their relations with each other. Upon gaining their independence, both India and Pakistan claimed to adhere to a policy of nonalignment. In fact, people across the third world, including many in India and Pakistan, shared a gnawing fear in the late 1940s and early 1950s that becoming allied with one or the other of the Cold War superpowers would inevitably result in a new form of colonialism.

The leaders of India and Pakistan quickly discovered, however, that a fundamental contradiction existed between their philosophical commitment to the nonalignment movement that was then gaining momentum in the developing world and the practical need to defend themselves within the anarchic system. First Pakistan and then India came to the conclusion that the instability of the South Asian regional system meant that all lofty claims to neutrality and nonalignment aside, building secure and predictable relationships with a great power patron (or patrons) would be essential, unavoidable components of their security strategies. Thus eventually "the Cold War rivalry between the two Great Powers percolated down to South Asia" (Thapliyal 1998, 1). In that sense, India and Pakistan were no different from other third world states that eventually sought aid from an external power in order to increase their security within their own regional subsystem.

However, two factors made the Indo-Pakistani case fairly unique. First, the size and geostrategic location of India and Pakistan made them particularly valuable prizes in the superpower competition for third world allies. As Ayoob points out, under such circumstances the Cold War "client state" enjoyed a degree of leverage that most third world countries lacked in their dealings with the superpowers (Ayoob 1995, 94). Second, the Indo-Pakistani conflict was unique because of the two states' proximity to the third great power in the Cold War international system, China. As Wirsing notes in his book on the conflict in Kashmir, "None of the greater powers has been more intrusive . . . than China" (Wirsing 1994, 91). In fact, by 1960 the international system was in transition from a tight bipolar system to a loose bipolar system, as ideological differences and territorial disputes drove a wedge between Moscow and Beijing. With Sino-Indian relations already on shaky ground, and both the Soviets and Americans providing aid to India, strengthening ties with Pakistan was the only real choice left to Beijing for thwarting Soviet designs in the region.

As has already been seen, since the early 1950s Pakistan has actively sought external assistance. Pakistan's early enthusiasm for foreign aid—compared to the consistent resistance that India exhibited early on to being drawn into any sort of binding relationship with an external patron—is understandable given the balance of power in the region. Since the founding of the independent states of India and Pakistan, India has enjoyed a clear power advantage. Pakistani political and military elites have long viewed "India as a powerful state with hegemonic ambitions" (Chawla 2001, 4).

Pakistan has had two choices for addressing the maldistribution of power in South Asia: It can choose to bandwagon with India or it can choose to balance against India. Interestingly, until 1962, the Pakistani government approached the Indian government multiple times on the subject of building a defense alliance, a move which would have allowed Pakistan to bandwagon with India. However, the Indians consistently refused these overtures, arguing instead in favor of a "non-war" pact between the two states (Burke 1973, 48, 53–56).

Unable to arrive at a mutually satisfactory bilateral security arrangement, Pakistan has been forced to focus its efforts on balancing. This has been a particularly daunting task, given the fact that India has an overwhelming advantage in terms of structural, internal measures of power. Writing in 1999, Rajesh Rajagopalan noted that India's population is nearly ten times larger than that of Pakistan; in fact, the Muslim minority population in India is larger than the entire population of Pakistan. The Indian economy is six times as large as that of Pakistan, a situation that allows India to meet its defense needs much more easily than Pakistan, which, in terms of percentage of GNP, must spend twice as much as India. And yet the size of the Indian economy and society means that India's military budget is several times larger than that of Pakistan and its army is twice the size of the Pakistani army. In other words, although Pakistan devotes twice as much of its GNP to defense, its military budget is still several times smaller than in India, and its army is only half the size. As Rajagopalan bluntly states, "The balance of power between India and Pakistan is overwhelmingly in India's favor"(Rajagopalan 1999, 1–3).

Unable to rely on its domestic capabilities to balance against India, Pakistan has been forced to look upon its external relations as a key source of power. As one Indian scholar argues, "In the fifties, Pakistan did what it could to exploit the Cold War so as to steal a march over India" (Nanda 1976, 9). In fact, as early as 1949, Pakistan clearly cast its lot with the West, and in particular with the United States, as it proclaimed itself an ally in the war against communism (Burke 1973, 148). Although the Soviets and Pakistanis briefly flirted with each other in 1950–1951, the Pakistanis essentially were biding their time, waiting for an opportunity to build stronger ties with Washington.

This early tilt westward within the context of the Cold War can be explained by several factors: the western orientation of the elite class, many of whom had educational, social, and cultural ties to Great Britain and the United States; the suspicion with which many Pakistanis viewed atheistic, Marxist ideology; the vocal criticism the Kremlin heaped upon Pakistan, whose very raison d'être (i.e., Islamic national identity) was scorned by Soviet ideologues; and the simple geographic fact that, given their proximity to Pakistan, the USSR and China might feel tempted to expand southward into Pakistan, whereas the U.S., in far away North America, was more likely to pursue the defensive policy of trying to contain communist expansion in South Asia (Choudhury 1975, 9–10; Burke 1973, 267).

Although technically it is true that Pakistan was the first of the South Asian powers to abandon nonalignment for an alliance with a superpower, it is also true that, for India, "nonalignment was interpreted in an arbitrary manner so as to suit India's national interests" (Vali 1976, 89–90). In the early stages of the Cold War, Pakistan sought to address its insecurity by bandwagoning with its stronger neighbor India via a proposed mutual-defense pact, an overture that was rejected by Indian leaders. Meanwhile, India sought to bandwagon with its stronger neighbor China. Indian prime minister Nehru originally focused his energies on building a viable third bloc of Asian and African states in the international system, with India and China at the vanguard of this proposed third bloc. He hoped to build "a thousand million strong cooperative of the Chinese and Asian peoples, the base of a larger Asian-African cooperative, and ultimately a new cooperative world order" (quoted in Nanda 1976, 16). One of the most popular slogans in India at this time was *Hindi-Chini bhai bhai*, meaning "the Indians and Chinese are brothers" (Choudhury 1975, 157). However, the dreams of a "brotherly" third bloc alliance led by India and China were dashed during the 1950s, although India would continue for a number of years to reach out to its powerful neighbor.

Inside the U.S. the fall of China to Mao's forces fueled even further the growing obsession with the communist threat. Nehru visited America in 1949; however, his public commitment to nonalignment and his push for bridge building between nations did not play well in Washington, which by now had drawn the geopolitical map of the international system into pro-American and pro-Soviet camps. In this era of rabid anticommunism, American policymakers had little patience for a third world leader who professed the desire to stay out of the Cold War dispute. At the same time, the very fact that Nehru met with U.S. officials drew the ire of the Kremlin, which derided Nehru's third bloc of nonaligned countries as "an imperialist device."

In addition, a series of policy stances taken by Nehru in the early 1950s increasingly put him at odds with Washington. First, in a July 1950 speech ostensibly made to condemn North Korea's invasion of South Korea, Nehru also called for Communist China's admission as a member of the UN Security Council and emphasized the importance of the USSR's return to that body. The U.S. responded coldly that the issues of North Korean aggression and the composition of China's delegation at the Security Council should not be linked. Many suspect that Nehru's public support for China in 1950 was meant to smooth relations with Mao's government at a time when the Chinese were beginning to press their claim over Tibet. If in fact this was Nehru's objective, the plan failed miserably; in October 1950, China seized Tibet, in the process ignoring loud complaints from India.

As the decade unfolded, Nehru emerged as a leader of the nonaligned movement in Asia and the broader third world, in the process becoming increasingly critical of what he saw as the continued economic and military dependence of many decolonized states on the West. Overall, Nehru's willingness to oppose American policies on key issues endeared him to the Soviet government, which began to take a much more positive view of India, particularly after Stalin's death in 1953 (Choudhury 1975, 15–19).

In Pakistan, a change in leadership triggered a tilt toward the United States. Prime Minister Liaquat was assassinated in 1951 and was replaced by Mohammad Ali Bogra, who took a staunchly pro-American stance. The public shift in Pakistan's attitude toward the Cold War made the country a potential target for U.S. aid, particularly once Dwight Eisenhower was elected to the presidency in 1952. Under Eisenhower the U.S. aggressively explored ways to contain the perceived Soviet threat to American interests around the world. Toward this end Eisenhower sent U.S. Secretary of State John Foster Dulles to the Middle East. Dulles was charged with seeking to cobble together a regional security pact in the region, patterned after the North American Treaty Organization (NATO). However, although Pakistan under Muhammad Ali Bogra was eager to strengthen ties with the U.S., the Americans, fearful of driving the Indians permanently into the arms of the Soviets, moved cautiously.

Finally, in February 1954 the first arms deal between the U.S. and Pakistan was sealed, involving the transfer of a number of jet aircraft, as well as hundreds of surplus U.S. army tanks. In April 1954 Pakistan signed a mutual-defense pact with Turkey and the United States and later that year joined the U.S.-sponsored South East Asia Treaty Organization, or SEATO. In 1955, Pakistan agreed to join the Baghdad Pact, or CENTO, an anticommunist defense organization consisting of Great Britain, Pakistan, Turkey, Iraq, and Iran, with U.S. support behind the scenes.

It should be noted that, although few within the Pakistani government put much faith in the utility of either SEATO or CENTO as effective defense pacts, in the final analysis the choice was made to sign on to both organizations, the hope being that by doing so, Pakistan would cement its position as America's most treasured ally in South Asia (Choudhury 1975, 85; Thapliyal 1998, 2). As Pakistani prime minister Muhammad Ali Bogra argued in 1954, "At present, we can't get a settlement, mainly because India has greater military strength. . . . When there is more equality of military strength, then I am sure that there will be a greater chance of a settlement" (quoted in Rajagopalan 1999, 3).

For its part, India responded to Pakistan's foreign defense pacts by signing an agreement with China that was designed to regulate economic relations between India and Tibet. In addition, the preamble of the agreement promoted the policy of *panschsheel*, which included five principles: respect for each other's territorial integrity, nonaggression, non-interference in each other's domestic affairs, equality and mutual benefit, and peaceful coexistence (Burke 1973, 223–24). However, by the beginning of the 1960s tensions between India and China overwhelmed this temporary era of Sino-Indian rapprochement.

In addition to trying to construct better relations with China, India gradually strengthened its ties with the Soviet Union. In 1955, the Soviets signed an agreement to assist in building a steel mill in India. Also during the mid-1950s, in response to the increase in U.S. military aid to Pakistan, the Indians strengthened their military relationship with Moscow. As the Soviets sought to balance against the U.S. presence in South Asia, they reached out to India, offering to sell MiG fighter jets to India and publicly siding with India in the Kashmir dispute. However, fearful of being drawn too closely into the Kremlin's orbit, Nehru was careful not to rely exclusively on the Soviet Union for aid, going so far as to wait four years before finally accepting the proposed MiG deal (Choudhury 1975, 23–25). Still, as one Russian writer proclaimed, at least for a brief period of time in the mid-1950s, "shoulder to shoulder, Moscow, Peking, and Delhi (were) fighting the great battle for world peace" (quoted in Burke 1973, 225).

Interestingly, Nehru's unwillingness to be drawn exclusively into the Soviet camp can be explained at least partially by the declining state of India's economy, and by a change in U.S. policy in response to developments inside India. By 1957 an economic crisis seemed to threaten the stability of the Indian democracy. Declining food production, a sharp increase in defense spending (which, the Indians argued, was necessitated by the U.S. aid package to Pakistan) and a rapid rise in the costs of raw materials and capital goods combined to create a foreign currency crisis. In Washington, support for providing more aid to India grew after the Indian national elections in March 1957, in which the Communist Party won control of the Indian state of Karala. Fear grew in Washington that the electoral victory in Karala would provide the Communists with a "significant beachhead" from which to spread their influence throughout India (McMahon 1994, chap. 7, 1–2).

Facing the perceived "rising threat" from communism in India, the U.S. administration moved quickly to provide emergency aid to the country. The United States cobbled together the international Aid to India Consortium in order to facilitate the transfer of large amounts of assistance quickly to India. Whereas in 1956 India received just under $93 million in economic assistance from Washington, in 1957 U.S. aid to India skyrocketed to nearly $365 million. Thereafter, American assistance to India continued to grow, reaching three-quarters of a billion dollars in 1962. By way of comparison, U.S. aid to Pakistan increased as well, although not nearly as dramatically as did American assistance to India. In 1956, Pakistan received about $162 million in aid from Washington; by 1962, aid flows from the U.S. to Pakistan stood at just over $400 billion (Burke 1973, 255).

Pakistan's disadvantage in terms of access to external assistance was exacerbated by the fact that India continued to receive huge amounts of aid from the Soviet Union, even as its assistance flows from America soared. Meanwhile, although some small breakthroughs occurred in Soviet-Pakistani economic relations in the early 1960s (e.g., an oil agreement in 1960–1961 and a barter trade agreement in 1963), Pakistan continued to rely almost exclusively on Western aid (Choudhury 1975, 34, 38). Thus between 1957 and 1961, India received approximately $3 billion in aid from the U.S. and the Soviet Union, whereas Pakistan received barely over $1 billion during the same period (Burke 1973, 255).

Not surprisingly, America's attempt to take a more balanced approach toward its South Asian policy angered many Pakistanis. According to a U.S. government report that was issued in March 1957, a growing number of Pakistanis were becoming "increasingly disillusioned with their country's Western ties and increasingly vocal in their advocacy of a more independent foreign policy." The growing public frustration with perceived "lack of returns" from Pakistan's alliance with America was further fueled by the fact that the country's close ties with Washington left Pakistan alienated from much of the rest of the Muslim world, including Nasser's Egypt. Meanwhile, a U.S. government report issued in June 1958 complained that despite sending over $700 million in aid to Pakistan during the previous decade, the U.S. had not yet achieved its objective of helping to construct a "viable nation" in Pakistan (McMahon 1994, 9).

In the words of John Foster Dulles, America's allies in countries such as Pakistan, Iran, and Turkey were in a "state of considerable gloom" by the late 1950s. Soviet influence seemed to be on the march, with the overthrow of the pro-Western Hashemite monarchy in Iraq, the attempted overthrow of Jordan's King Hussein, and instability fomented by pro-Soviet Nasserist forces in Lebanon. These events triggered a reassessment of U.S. foreign policy. Although the administration did not wish to abandon its ties with India, the events described above forced U.S. policymakers to seek to strengthen relations with Pakistan. "The strategic importance of Pakistan," admitted the Joint Chiefs of Staff, "has increased tremendously" as a result of the events in the Asia/Middle East region (McMahon 1994, 10).

In Pakistan, after a series of power struggles, Gen. Ayub Khan emerged as the undisputed leader of the country in the fall of 1958. With martial law declared and the levers of constitutional, democratic government suspended, Ayub moved to bring stability to the country. In Washington, U.S. officials, clearly concerned that instability within Pakistan might invite Soviet intrigue, quietly applauded Ayub's seizure of power. Ayub Khan bolstered his anticommunist credentials when he published a book in 1959 in which he stated one of his main objectives was to devise a strategy to combat "the offensive of Hinduism and Communism against the ideology of Islam." Later he dismissed communism as a false cure for "an acutely diseased society" (quoted in Burke 1973, 93). Ayub's anticommunist rhetoric paid dividends in 1959 when the U.S. said it would continue military and economic aid to Pakistan and promised to defend Pakistan in the event that it was the target of military aggression (Burke 1973, 194–95).

Ironically, America's commitment to defend Pakistan served to muddy even further the security situation in the region. Among the interested parties (i.e., Pakistan, India, the U.S., USSR, and China), only the Pakistanis chose to interpret the statement as providing an iron-clad assurance that the United States would defend Pakistan in the event of war with any potential foe, including India. In doing so, the Pakistanis overlooked the key phrase "as is envisioned in the Joint Resolution." The congressional resolution to which this statement refers specifically authorized U.S. assistance to any country that was the target of "armed aggression from any country controlled by international Communism" (Burke 1973, 195). Thus, contrary to Pakistan's interpretation of the American statement—an interpretation that seems to be a classic case of wishful thinking on the part of the Pakistanis—the U.S. was formally committed to coming to Pakistan's defense in the event of an attack by Soviet or Chinese forces, but *not* in the event of an attack by India.

In regards to the Soviets, Ayub initially seemed emboldened to take a tough stand vis-à-vis the Soviet Union in 1960. On May 1, 1960, an American U-2 spy plane that had taken off from Peshawar, Pakistan, was shot down over Soviet territory. Although the Pakistanis argued—and the evidence largely supports their contention—that they did not know that the plane was being used for espionage purposes, Soviet leader Nikita Khrushchev still threatened to launch attacks against Pakistan if another spy plane flew from Pakistan into Soviet air space. Refusing to be intimidated, Ayub blasted the Soviet Union and warned that any Soviet attack on Pakistan would result inevitably in world war, as the Americans would surely come to Pakistan's defense (Burke 1973, 197).

As Pakistan grappled with a potential threat from the Soviet Union, by the end of the 1950s India dealt with a threat from China that was all too real. In March 1959, the Chinese army brutally suppressed a revolt in Tibet, forcing the Dalai Lama and thousands of his followers to flee to India (McMahon 1994, 13). Whereas during the 1950s the Chinese aggression was focused almost exclusively in Tibet and the broader Himalayan region, in 1960 Mao upped the ante when Chinese forces launched an assault against Indian troops in Kashmir, in the process seizing and retaining a large tract of territory. In general, China became more aggressive in its policy toward border disputes with India; increasingly, the Chinese began to take the land it wanted by force, leaving the Indian leadership "surprised, shocked, enraged, and completely astounded" (Brown 1972, 375).

As the tension between India and China grew, in the U.S. the newly elected Kennedy administration became increasingly concerned about the security and survival of India. Although a 1961 meeting between Kennedy and Nehru did not go as well as expected (apparently the two leaders did not hit it off very well on a personal level), the American president identified China's threat to India as being a threat to U.S. security interests as well (Nanda 1976, 12–13). In response to the "communist threat" to India, the U.S. committed itself to a huge aid package for India, totaling as much as $5 billion (Choudhury 1975, 103).

Of course, the blossoming relationship between India and the United States set off alarm bells in Pakistan, where Ayub was coming under withering domestic criticism for linking Pakistan's security too closely to American support. As the U.S. administration prepared to host separate visits from both Nehru and

Ayub in 1961, the Pakistani president demanded to come to America six months earlier than originally scheduled in order to ensure that his meeting with Kennedy would occur before Nehru was scheduled to arrive. In an impassioned speech before Congress, Ayub pleaded Pakistan's case. Pakistan, he argued, was the United States' only truly reliable ally in all of Asia. In response, Kennedy, although refusing to use the power of the purse to try to force India to make concessions on Kashmir, reaffirmed the United States' commitment to the territorial integrity and independence of Pakistan and promised Ayub that the U.S. would provide military aid to India only if the security of the region was under serious threat, and even under those circumstances, the U.S. president guaranteed that Pakistan would be consulted in advance before any American military assistance was sent to India (Choudhury 1975, 105). The fact that Kennedy blatantly broke that promise in 1962, when the U.S. provided military aid to India during the war with China, sparked a great deal of anger in Pakistan at the time.

Although the aforementioned meeting between Kennedy and Nehru did not go nearly as well as did Kennedy's meeting with Ayub, U.S. ties with India became much stronger in 1962 in response to the Sino-Indian War of October–November 1962. Both the United States and Britain answered India's call for help immediately. After the war, in a rare and remarkable example of American and Soviet strategic interests intersecting, India found itself the recipient of huge caches of arms from sources both West and East. The United States, Great Britain, and the Soviet Union all increased their assistance to India in order to bolster India's defenses and to deter further Chinese aggression.

Although the U.S. felt that the military aid to India was a short-term necessity, Kennedy admitted during a press conference a year later, "Everything we give India adversely affects the balance of power with Pakistan, which is a much smaller country" (Choudhury 1975, 109–10). President Kennedy's comment highlighted the complexity of the security dilemma in South Asia. Whereas Pakistan calculated the balance of power in the region almost solely according to its power capabilities vis-à-vis India (with the exception of a few isolated incidents, such as the U-2 crisis of 1960, the concern that the USSR posed a major threat to Pakistan's survival as an independent state had largely dissipated), India felt compelled to balance not just against smaller, weaker Pakistan but also against larger, stronger China. However, as India's threat environment seemed to be transformed for a few years in the early 1960s in response to the rising threat from China, for Pakistan India remained the primary threat. Thus India's military buildup during the first half of the 1960s, which was designed to a significant degree to deal with China, increased the perception in Pakistan that the balance of power within the Indo-Pakistani dyad was tilting even more so than before in favor of India.

Given the growing perception within Pakistan's government that the threat from India was greater than ever, it is not surprising that the Pakistani leadership was acutely sensitive to any window of opportunity for addressing Pakistan's long-term strategic vulnerability. Such an opportunity seemed to present itself after the 1962 Sino-Indian War. Nehru quickly discovered that the Kennedy administration was willing to use its newfound leverage—India was increasingly dependent on military aid from the U.S. and Britain—to bring the Indians into bilateral talks with Pakistan over Kashmir. Reluctant to anger his new external patrons, Nehru unenthusiastically agreed to participate in the talks, which were to be brokered by a joint Anglo-American delegation.

From the outset, the negotiations, which were launched on December 26, 1962, in Pakistan, seemed doomed to fail. Neither the Pakistanis nor the Indians were willing to compromise over Kashmir. Pakistan continued to demand a plebiscite in the disputed region, while India stood firm on its argument that a political arrangement based on religious identity had no place in a secular state.

Meanwhile, Ayub wrote a letter to Nehru in late October 1962 assuring him that he was committed to achieving peaceful relations with India, and he followed up that letter with one to Kennedy in early January 1963 in which he told the president that "a just and speedy Kashmir settlement" was the only way to bolster Pakistan's security. Behind the scenes, however, the Pakistanis were conducting talks with China over two thousand square miles of territory in Kashmir which Pakistan controlled and which China treasured. As early as 1959, the Pakistani government became aware that China had territorial ambitions in the area in question (Burke 1973, 290). By agreeing to cede the territory, Pakistan achieved three key objectives: recognition by China that the rest of Kashmir was indeed, as Pakistan contended, a "disputed" area; defusing the possibility that Pakistan would be the next target for Chinese aggression in Kashmir; and, more generally, addressing Pakistan's constant obsession with balancing against Indian power. With this single agreement, the "fairly straightforward bilateral contest over Kashmir between India and Pakistan that had existed at the start of the 1950s, [was replaced] in the early 1960s with a three-cornered, trans-Himalayan 'security' complex that was infinitely more complicated than the preceding arrangement" (Wirsing 1994, 91, 93).

The Indians, of course, were confused and outraged by the content and timing of the agreement. Nonetheless, the second round of talks, which were held from January 16 to 19, 1963, in New Delhi, seemed to show greater promise. At the end of the second round, India and Pakistan issued a joint communiqué in which each side pledged to seek a peaceful settlement to the dispute, to delimit an international boundary in Kashmir, to pursue military disengagement in the disputed region, and to promote bilateral cooperation. Throughout the winter and spring of 1963, rounds three through six of negotiations were held. However, despite direct diplomatic intervention by the United States, which hoped that resolving the conflict would result in an Indo-Pakistani counterweight to Chinese power in the region, no headway was made (Ganguly 2001, 32–35).

Even before the negotiations drew to a close, Pakistan formalized its agreement with China to hand over territory in Kashmir, with the two parties signing the deal on March 2, 1963. Sino-Pakistani cooperation intensified rapidly thereafter. On July 17, 1963, Pakistani foreign minister Zulfiqar Ali Bhutto told Parliament that in the event of an attack by India on Pakistan, the military aggression would be viewed in China as a threat to "the territorial integrity and security of the largest state in Asia." In August the two countries signed an air transport agreement, and in September a barter agreement was reached (Burke 1973, 293). By the end of 1963, Ayub was engaged in a difficult political high-wire act—attempting to use Pakistan's improving relations with China to address the imbalance of power with India, while not going so far in reaching out to China that he would risk doing permanent damage to Pakistan's relationship with the United States.

The bond between Pakistan and China was strengthened further by several developments that took place in 1964 and early 1965. First, at the end of a state visit to Pakistan in February 1964 by Chinese premier Chou En-Lai, a joint communiqué was issued, calling for the resolution of the Kashmiri conflict "in accordance with the wishes of the people of Kashmir, as pledged to them by India and Pakistan." With this simple statement, China for the first time in public seemed to signal its support for Pakistan's contention that the status of Kashmir could only be settled by holding a plebiscite. In return, the Chinese received Pakistani support for their argument that the United Nations would not be a truly representative international organization until such time that the People's Republic of China was given a seat in the body. Later in 1964, China offered to extend to Pakistan a $60 million interest-free loan, repayable over an extended period of time in primary commodities and manufactured goods (Burke 1973, 295).

In March 1965 Ayub marked the second anniversary of the border agreement between China and Pakistan by visiting China. During the visit, it became clear that Pakistan and China still had fundamental policy differences, in particular on the issue of the U.S. military action in Vietnam. On this issue, the two sides essentially agreed to disagree. The Chinese government made sure that no anti-American demonstrations took place during Ayub's visit, and when the Pakistani leader declared during a speech that both the U.S. and China must accept that each state had its own legitimate security interests in Asia, the crowd quietly ignored the statement (while wildly cheering other parts of Ayub's speech). The communiqué that was issued at the close of the trip reaffirmed in unambiguous language that the question of Kashmir could only be resolved by meeting the wishes of the majority of the population there and reiterated Pakistan's support for China's claim to a UN seat. In addition, for the first time Pakistan publicly condemned the United States' two Chinas policy and criticized the U.S. for introducing nuclear weapons into the Indian Ocean (Burke 1973, 296). It should be noted that Ayub's shift away from a strategy of a tight alliance with the United States and toward a more balanced foreign policy was highly popular in Pakistan, where many Pakistanis resented the U.S. for its growing support of India in recent years.

Within the international system, Pakistan's overtures to China paid additional dividends, as relations between Pakistan and the USSR warmed considerably during this period. The Soviet Union feared that its traditional South Asian ally, India, might be in the process of "switching sides" in the Cold War and moreover sought to check growing Chinese influence in the region. In August 1963 the USSR provided a loan of eleven million pounds sterling to Pakistan and signed a barter agreement with the Pakistanis, followed by an air agreement in October 1963. Although further economic agreements followed, the Soviets still refused to provide military aid to Pakistan. This policy irked the Pakistanis, particularly given the USSR's ongoing military relationship with India; in September 1964 Moscow pledged to provide India with another $140 million in military supplies (Burke 1973, 300–301).

U.S. policy in South Asia during this period seemed to take an increasingly pro-Indian tilt. In large part, this shift in America's attitude reflected the evolving strategic situation in the region, including China's support for North Vietnam. In addition, many Americans, including key administration officials and U.S. politicians, were attracted to India due to the democratic, secular nature of the Indian state. In March 1964, Secretary of Defense Robert McNamara publicly restated the U.S. policy of providing military aid to India. In late 1964, the U.S. ambassador to India, Chester Bowles, promised in the aftermath of China's first successful test of an atomic bomb that the U.S. was prepared to use its entire arsenal, including atomic and hydrogen bombs, to protect India. In February 1965, McNamara observed that the improvement in Sino-Pakistani relations increased the threat which communism posed to India's security. Meanwhile, as economic aid flowed unencumbered from the U.S. to India, assistance to Pakistan was delayed by several months (Choudhury 1975, 116–17).

Improved relations with China and the Soviet Union notwithstanding, in pure balance of power terms, in 1964–1965 Pakistan's power potential versus India had not improved in any appreciable sense. The Indians, relying on their larger economic base and the influx of external assistance, and smarting from the embarrassment of the loss to China in 1962, embarked on an intensive program of military buildup. By 1965, India's army boasted sixteen divisions; Pakistan had just half that many divisions in the field. India had two armored divisions, while Pakistan had one. India had more than seven hundred aircraft, compared to Pakistan's total of fewer than three hundred. By every conceivable measure of military capability, the gap between India and Pakistan was growing rapidly (Ganguly 2001, 37).

And yet, as was noted in the previous section, Pakistani leaders calculated in 1965 that a brief window of opportunity existed for striking at India. Of the various factors that explain the mindset of Pakistani decision makers at the time—Nehru's death, India's poor performance in the war with China, the lethargic response by India to Pakistan's initial military thrusts in 1965, and so on—for the purposes of this part of our discussion the most important factor was the perception in Pakistan that China was ready to come to Pakistan's defense. In fact, the precise nature of the Chinese commitment to Pakistan was at the time, and remains nearly forty years later, open to debate (Rajagopalan 1999, 4).

What is most important, however, is not the objective reality of China's level of commitment to Pakistan's security but the perception in Pakistan as to the extent of that commitment. One can assume that the greater the belief in Pakistan that China was ready to take an active role in defending Pakistan, the more emboldened the Pakistanis would be to take provocative actions toward India. On this point, it is interesting to note that G. W. Choudhury, a former Pakistani government official, insists that China was ready to use force to protect Pakistan in 1965. During Ayub's state visit to China in early March 1965, Chinese leaders assured the Pakistani president that in the event of an attack by India upon Pakistan, "China would definitely support Pakistan" (Choudhury 1975, 184). Interestingly, although the statement which Choudhury attributes to Chinese leaders does not specifically promise that China would use military force to protect Pakistan, apparently the Pakistani leadership chose to interpret that, in fact, the Chinese were committing themselves to military intervention, if required.

In reality, the Chinese military did not become directly involved once the war began in earnest in the fall of 1965. It is true that the Chinese government issued loud criticisms of what it viewed as "an act of naked aggression" by India against Pakistan and demanded that India dismantle its border posts. In addition, Chinese forces along the border with India were put on alert, as Indian officials frantically consulted with their American, British, and Soviet counterparts on what to do in the event of China's entry into the war. In fact, Choudhury claims that the Chinese conveyed to Pakistan a readiness to enter the conflict against India as the war went badly for Pakistan, but that, in the end, Pakistan buckled under to pressure from the U.S., USSR, and UN to accept a cease-fire before a two-front war could be launched. Nonetheless, Choudhury takes the view that China was quite willing to intervene in the war on behalf of Pakistan, if Pakistan had formally asked China to do so (Choudhury 1975, 189–91).

The objective level of China's wartime commitment to Pakistan notwithstanding, Pakistan's poor performance in fighting the 1965 war combined with the Anglo-American arms embargo and the growing domestic unrest in East Pakistan to put Pakistan at a further power disadvantage in South Asia after the war. In addition, Pakistan's erstwhile great power ally, the United States, turned its attention almost exclusively toward Southeast Asia and the Vietnam War. In particular, under the Nixon Doctrine, South Asia was given low priority. In the words of one American diplomat, "No critical U.S. security interests are at stake in South Asia" (Choudhury 1974, 203, 207).

The American disengagement from South Asia left a power void in the region. With Sino-Soviet friction increasing across Asia, the Soviets jostled with the Chinese in an attempt to fill that void. As we shall discuss in greater detail below, this emerging contest between China and the Soviet Union for influence in South Asia, along with the forging of a new era in Sino-American relations under President Richard Nixon, played a key role in fueling the Indo-Pakistani conflict environment in 1971.

IMMEDIATE/SHORT-TERM CAUSES OF THE WAR

Although it is true that tensions remained high between India and Pakistan following the 1965 war, a unique set of circumstances suddenly converged to act as a catalyst for the third major round of warfare between the two countries in 1971. In fact, as late as the beginning of 1971, U.S. officials assumed that the likelihood for another Indo-Pakistani war to break out soon in South Asia was remote. "At the beginning of 1971," Henry Kissinger later recalled, "none of our senior policymakers expected the subcontinent to jump to the top of our agenda. It seemed to require no immediate decisions except annual aid programs and relief efforts in response to tragic natural disasters in late 1970" (Kissinger 1979, 849). By the end of the year, the U.S. and the rest of the world would find that South Asia once more seized their attention and the headlines as a third Indo-Pakistani war erupted.

The Great Powers and the 1971 Indo-Pakistani War

We have previously noted that the second half of the 1960s was a time of great change in terms of the evolving nature of Soviet, Chinese, and American involvement in South Asian affairs. In particular, Sino-Soviet tensions increased significantly during this period, as characterized most graphically by the armed clashes along the Chinese-Soviet frontier in 1969. These developments were viewed with great satisfaction in Washington, as indicated by U.S. Secretary of State William Rogers's comment in May 1969 that the USSR had ascended into "the first rank of China's enemies" (quoted in Choudhury 1975, 203).

As both Moscow and Beijing sought to increase their own influence at the expense of the other, India and Pakistan garnered greater attention from the USSR and China. The Soviet Union sought to pull the Indians even closer into its orbit in order to put further pressure on the common threat which the USSR and India shared—China. However, despite their history of close ties with India, the Soviets, taking advantage of American disinterest in South Asia following the 1965 war, still sought to maintain decent relations with Pakistan. Given the cooling of U.S.-Pakistani relations during the 1960s, the Pakistanis were cautiously open to Soviet offers of aid. Against this geo-strategic backdrop, Moscow provided limited assistance to the Pakistanis right up to, and even for a short time following, the outbreak of violence in East Pakistan in late March 1971.

On the other hand, China's belief that India played a vital role in the Soviet Union's plan to roll back Chinese power and influence in South Asia precluded Beijing from reaching out to the Indians, as did the ongoing border disputes which China had with India. In fact, Sino-Indian relations at this point were marked by mutual suspicion and animosity, if not outright hatred. Thus much as the Soviets saw a strong India as bolstering Moscow's ability to counter the threat from China, so the Chinese sought to strengthen Pakistan in order to balance against the threat to China from India and the Soviet Union. Economic and military aid flowed freely from China to Pakistan during the late 1960s and early 1970s. However—and this is a critical point which the Pakistanis consistently ignored at their own peril—after 1965 the Chinese never went so far as to guarantee that China would intervene with military forces to defend Pakistan in the event of another round of Indo-Pakistani fighting.

What explains this shift in China's policy between 1965 and 1971? Several factors were critical in motivating China to proceed with greater caution. First, the domestic situation in China was still unstable, given the bloody and chaotic Cultural Revolution in which Mao purged his internal "enemies" and built a cult of personality around his leadership. In September 1971, behind a wall of secrecy, several top Chinese elites were ousted, including Lin Piao, the minister of defense who had been designated by the Communist Party to be Mao's eventual successor (Kissinger 1979, 769). Given this uncertain domestic situation, which now included the fact that an aging and ailing Mao had no successor in waiting, the Chinese were in no mood to take on another major foreign crisis.

Second, China was at a power and threat disadvantage vis-à-vis the Soviets in South Asia at this time. Whereas the Soviets were concerned almost solely with China's designs for the region (after all, Pakistan posed an extremely limited threat to the Soviet Union's security), the Chinese felt directly threatened by both the Soviet Union and India simultaneously. China had fought a war with India in 1962 and exchanged fire with the Soviet Union in 1969. In Beijing there was real concern that if China intervened on behalf of its Pakistani allies it faced the prospect of a two-front war with the USSR and India.

In the midst of this heightened threat environment, China looked to the United States as a "counterweight to Soviet pressure" (Kissinger 1979, 685). For the United States, China's major importance in terms of U.S. Cold War foreign policy was as the third axis of power in the global system. Forging a better relationship with China would pay real dividends for the U.S. because it would tilt the balance of power within the international system away from the Soviet Union, and might provide America with some degree of influence over China's policy toward the fighting in Southeast Asia, where China supported the Communist government in North Vietnam and Communist insurgents in Cambodia.

Richard Nixon's decision in 1971 to "play the China card" reverberated across the international system, including South Asia. Within the context of the Cold War, the Soviet Union responded by seeking to improve its own relations with the United States. In fact, the establishment of diplomatic relations between the U.S. and China helped facilitate the launching of detente between the U.S. and the USSR shortly thereafter.

Nixon's historic breakthrough with China had the side effect of reinforcing the United States' interest in events in South Asia. Most important, the U.S. did not want renewed tensions between India and Pakistan to threaten the U.S.'s new relationship with China. The best way to do this was to tilt toward China's and the United States' erstwhile ally Pakistan while also pushing hard for a peaceful settlement of the dispute. The real fear in Washington was that an Indian victory (which the U.S. believed would be the inevitable outcome of any Indo-Pakistani war given the imbalance of power against Pakistan) would also be a victory for Soviet influence in South Asia (Kissinger 1979, 875).

For the Soviets, the startling news of the Sino-American rapprochement forced the Kremlin to reassess its South Asian policy. Although threatened by the strategic inroads now afforded to the United States in the region, the Soviets also saw "an opportunity to gain influence in New Delhi" (Donaldson, quoted in Choudhury 1974, 215). Certainly, India felt severely threatened by these developments. In the words of one American scholar, the thawing in Sino-American relations was perceived to be so dangerous because "the visit of the American President to the capital of India's adversary number two had been facilitated through the cooperation of India's enemy number one. . . . [I]t seemed as though the apparent convergence of interest of the two super-powers in supporting India as a bulwark against Chinese ambitions was being outdistanced by the events of the 1970s" (Donaldson, quoted in Choudhury 1974, 215).

Just after Nixon announced his scheduled trip to China, a proposed Indo-Soviet Treaty of Friendship and Cooperation, which by some accounts had been drawn up as early as 1969, was once more brought forth by the Soviets for Indian consideration (Jackson 1974, 71). Previously, in a decision that was anchored in its formal claim of nonalignment in the Cold War, India had refused to sign such an agreement. Now, India rushed to reach an agreement with the Soviet Union. The rapidity with which these events unfolded seems to hint at their cause-and-effect relationship: On July 15, 1971, Nixon announced his intention to visit China; on August 9, 1971, India signed the Treaty of Friendship and Cooperation with the Soviet Union.

Thus in a scant three weeks the strategic landscape of South Asia was fundamentally altered. The relationship between Moscow and New Delhi was now cemented. Arms flows from the Soviet Union to India increased during the second half of 1971, the Soviet Union doggedly protected India from international pressure in the UN, and, although Moscow did not favor another war in South Asia, increasingly the Soviets placed the blame for Indo-Pakistani tensions squarely and solely on the shoulders of Pakistan.

During this period Pakistan's strategic situation in terms of international support was in decline, although the Pakistani regime seemed to fail to recognize this fact. In particular, deep divisions with the U.S. government over U.S.-Pakistani relations would severely hinder the Nixon administration's ability to assist the Pakistani government in the aftermath of the Pakistani army's crackdown in East Pakistan in late March (see below). Within the U.S. government, the battle lines were drawn quite sharply on the Indo-Pakistani issue. Richard Nixon and his national security advisor, Henry Kissinger, were on one side, wanting to prevent what they viewed as India's grand design to use the crisis in East Pakistan as an excuse to destroy the entire state of Pakistan once and for all. In their view, such an outcome would bolster Soviet influence in the region, put the Chinese in the untenable position of having to choose between two very unappetizing policy options (either stay on the sidelines and be accused of abandoning the Pakistanis or enter the war and face the prospects of Soviet military retribution), and undermine America's new relationship with China. On April 28, 1971, Nixon made his policy clear in a handwritten note he added to a memorandum for the president regarding the United States' policy options: "To all hands: Don't squeeze Yahya at this time" (Gandhi 2002). On May 10 Henry Kissinger sought to ease Pakistan's concerns over the Nixon administration's support for the embattled Pakistani regime by assuring Pakistani officials that Nixon felt "high regard" and "personal affection" for Yahya (Gandhi 2002). Later on the same day, President Nixon told the Pakistani delegation that he "could understand the anguish of the decisions which [Yahya] had to make" and promised the Pakistanis that the United States "would not do anything to complicate the situation for President Yahya or to embarrass him" (Gandhi 2002).

Meanwhile, the Department of State and Congress, each in the dark about the China breakthrough until the summer of 1971, condemned Pakistan as the villain in the crisis and pressed hard to isolate and punish the Pakistani government for its behavior in East Pakistan. On March 28, the U.S. consul general in Dacca, Archer Blood, described a "reign of terror by the Pak [sic] Military" in East Pakistan (Subject Numeric File 1970–73, Pol and Def, Box 2530, RG 59, NA, accessed online). Over the next several days, Blood continued to press his argument that systematic atrocities were being carried out by Pakistani forces in East Pakistan, concluding with a scathing cable on April 6 in which Blood accused the Nixon administration of "bending over backwards to place the West Pak (sic) dominated government" at a time when "the overworked term genocide is applicable" (SNF 1970–73, Pol and Def from: Pol Pak—U.S. to: Pol 17–1 Pak-U.S. Box 2535, RG 59, NA, accessed online).

The extent to which certain members of the State Department were willing to go in ignoring the "official" policy of the Nixon administration was dramatically illustrated in April 1971. In 1970, Nixon had approved a one-time exception to the arms embargo against Pakistan, agreeing to a $35 million package in which twenty aircraft and three hundred armored personnel carriers would be sold to

Pakistan (by way of comparison, India, which had a thriving domestic arms industry, also received an estimated $350 million in foreign military aid in 1970). In April 1971 the State Department moved without prior White House knowledge or approval to cut off the delivery of that military equipment to Pakistan, effectively reducing the package to just $5 million. In addition, the State Department began to put roadblocks in the way of the delivery of economic aid to Pakistan, telling the White House that the situation on the ground made it impossible from a logistical standpoint to deliver the aid (Kissinger 1979, 854).

A review of Henry Kissinger's experience in dealing with the issue, as chronicled in his book *White House Years*, underscores the extent to which bureaucratic politics plagued the U.S. government throughout the South Asian crisis of 1971 (Kissinger 1979). "It was nearly impossible to implement (the administration's) strategy," Kissinger lamented, "because our departments operated on different premises." Part of the problem had to do with the organizational structure of the State Department: South Asia fell under the jurisdiction of the Near East Bureau, rather than to the East Asian Bureau. This meant that those in the State Department who were charged with dealing with the Indo-Pakistani crisis both downplayed and at times even maligned the importance of Nixon's overtures to China and largely ignored China in their analyses of the situation in South Asia in 1971. When China was included in the State Department's reports on the crisis, the recommendations put forth were absurd given Nixon's China's policy. For example, a July 23, 1971, report recommended that in the event that China intervened in defense of Pakistan, the U.S. respond by cooperating with the USSR and Great Britain to provide military assistance to India. If enacted, this policy surely would have killed off the budding relationship between Washington and Beijing.

Time and again, Nixon's policy of "tilting towards" Pakistan was simply ignored by those in the government who disagreed with him. The Department of State consistently advocated—and actively pursued—a policy designed to undermine Pakistan's ability to meet the rising threat from India, even after U.S. intelligence sources detected an early Indian plan for an Israeli-style lightning strike on West Pakistan in May 1971. While the State Department worked hard to cut off all U.S. assistance to Pakistan, it pushed equally hard to retain the United States' aid package to India. In the case of Pakistan, State Department officials argued that squeezing aid to Pakistan could be used as a stick to force Pakistan to seek a peaceful solution to the crisis. However, in the case of India, the same officials argued that India was not susceptible to such a power play from Washington, and that therefore aid from the U.S. to India should continue unabated. The State Department's claim on this issue baffled Henry Kissinger, who countered with the argument, "If anything will tempt the Indians to attack, it will be the complete helplessness of Pakistan." Even after the U.S. government received reports on November 22 indicating that Indian troops had begun to move in substantial numbers into East Pakistan, the State Department claimed that the evidence of an Indian incursion into Pakistan was inconclusive, and continued to argue that the U.S. should press Pakistan to make further concessions in order to avoid all-out war with India. When Nixon, deciding that the evidence on an Indian move into Pakistan was in fact conclusive, ordered that U.S. aid to

India be cut off, the State Department explained that it would be impossible to trace and stop assistance from Washington to New Delhi. Keep in mind, this is the same State Department that had no trouble identifying, tracing, and stopping aid to Pakistan earlier in the year (Kissinger 1979, 842–89).

Given these divisions in U.S. policymaking circles, more and more Pakistan had to rely on China as an external guarantor of Pakistan's security. However, Yahya's attempt to draw an iron-clad promise from China to protect Pakistan in the event of a war with India failed. In November 1971, he sent a delegation to China in an effort to elicit a stung guarantee of Chinese assistance for Pakistan in the event of general war. Instead, the mission received only a generic, tepid "declaration of support." Moreover, the Chinese pressed Pakistan to seek a political settlement, calling for a "rational solution" to the crisis in East Pakistan (Choudhury 1975, 213).

Interestingly, even after failing to elicit a security guarantee from the Chinese less than a month before the outbreak of war, the Pakistani delegation declared upon returning home that China would provide Pakistan with complete support in the event of war. In reality, as the crisis unfolded in 1971, China chose the path of nonintervention. As retired Pakistani major Agha Humayun Amin (2000) later observed, the vaunted "Chinese card on which so much hope was based had limited and seasonal validity." By the time full-scale war erupted in early December, with the Himalayan passes blocked by early winter snows, the Chinese government was prepared to offer formal support to Pakistan but little else in the way of tangible assistance that could make a genuine difference on the battlefield (Amin 2000; Choudhury 1975, 212–13).

It is likely that, even if the war had erupted in midsummer rather than early winter, China would have opted to stay on the sidelines. Fresh off of their diplomatic breakthrough with the Americans, sensing the instability of Yahya's regime and the hopelessness of Pakistan's war prospects, and fearful of becoming entangled in a direct military conflict with the Soviets, China had no stomach for becoming embroiled in any fighting on the subcontinent in 1971. The United States, at least at the presidential level, offered humanitarian aid and diplomatic support to Pakistan but, like China, refused to intervene with force to protect Pakistan. Meanwhile, the Soviets, calculating that India would not require direct intervention in order to win another war with Pakistan, confidently supported India's increasingly provocative policies in the region. Those provocative policies by India were undertaken in the aftermath of the bloody military operation that was launched by the Pakistani army in East Pakistan in late March, and the subsequent mass exodus of refugees from East Pakistan into West Bengal, India.

Domestic Upheaval and the Spillover Effect

By far, the most important single cause of renewed tensions between India and Pakistan in 1971, and ultimately the primary cause of the war which erupted in December of that year, was the domestic crisis in Pakistan that had boiled over into full-scale violence when forty thousand Pakistani troops moved in to try to impose the central government's will on seventy-five million East Pakistanis. In the words of retired Pakistani army major Agha Humayun Amin, President

Yahya Khan "believed in the power of the bayonet and thought that the East Wing could be kept in the federation through military action. The (internal and external) consequences of the surgical and brief military action were not fully grasped by Yahya and most of the West Wing's politicians" (Amin 2001).

The origins of the internal problems that plagued Pakistan in the late 1960s and early 1970s can be traced back to deteriorating conditions inside the country in the aftermath of the 1965 Indo-Pakistani conflict. The cost of that war put the brakes on an impressive period of structural economic development, as increased military spending combined with the simmering conflict between West and East Pakistan to slow an economy that had been among the fastest growing in the third world. Defense spending more than doubled between 1964–1965 and 1965–1966, and during the same period defense spending as a percentage of GDP rose from 4.82 percent to 9.86 percent (Chawla 2001, 3). Although eventually the share of the state's budget devoted to defense fell due to increased external aid from China and several Arab states, by the late 1960s, Pakistan still spent nearly 6 percent of its GNP on defense. And, in 1970–1971, as the central government fought desperately to hold the two wings of Pakistan together while also dealing with the threat from India, defense expenditure comprised a whopping 55.66 percent of total government expenditures (Chawla 2001, 2). In fact, since the founding of the state in 1947, levels of defense spending in Pakistan have been so consistently high as to lead some analysts "to describe Pakistan's political economy as defense oriented, rather than development oriented" (see for example Rajagopalan 1999, 2).

Meanwhile, during the same period defense expenditures in India consumed only about 3 percent of GNP. And yet in raw dollars, India's defense budget was over six times larger than was that of Pakistan. Again, it bears repeating that India's huge domestic industrial base—the largest in the developing world—provided the country with a built-in, seemingly insurmountable advantage in terms of its ability to convert internal elements of power into an enhanced military capacity (Rajagopalan 1999, 1–3).

In the political realm, criticism of President Ayub Khan was on the rise; his foreign minister, Zulfiqar Ali Bhutto, resigned his post after the war, warning that, in the aftermath of Tashkent, India was involved in a concerted campaign to woo Pakistan into its (i.e., India's) sphere of influence by offering inducements. Bhutto went on to form his own party, the Pakistan People's Party, whose platform emphasized an end to military rule, and eventually seized power in 1971 (Burki 1986, 58–59).

Political conditions deteriorated further in 1968, when Ayub Khan suffered a heart attack. The 1962 Constitution stipulated that the speaker of the National Assembly run the government until the president recovered. However, rather than permit the speaker, a Bengali named Jabbar Khan, to take his constitutionally mandated position as temporary leader, Ayub Khan turned the reins of power over to a small group of loyal civil servants. In circumventing the constitution, Ayub simultaneously undermined the legitimacy of constitutional government and further alienated the Bengali population in East Pakistan (Burki 1986, 59).

Much of the internal tension within Pakistan during this period centered on relations between the dominant western wing of Pakistan and the eastern, rump region. As has been noted, the unity of the state of Pakistan hinged solely on religion. The very rationale for the political linkage of the eastern and western wings was linked to the shared religious identities of the peoples in the two territories. However, in linking these noncontiguous regions, the British created a country that was characterized by geographic separation, political and social inequality, cultural diversity, and economic disparity. These factors combined to create a volatile political situation.

Geographically, the western wing of Pakistan was separated from the eastern wing of Pakistan, which included Bengal, by twelve hundred miles of Indian territory, and there was no direct land communication between West and East Pakistan. Moreover, the two wings were more than twenty-four hundred miles apart by sea. In terms of territory, West Pakistan was nearly six times the size of East Pakistan. However, 1961 census figures showed that East Pakistan's population was approximately fifty-one million, while the population of West Pakistan stood at about forty-three million (Brown 1972, 208).

Despite their numerical superiority, East Pakistanis were woefully underrepresented in the halls of power. All top political offices were filled by elites from West Pakistan. Furthermore, just 16 percent of the civil service slots were occupied by East Pakistani. In the military, Bengalis comprised only 5 percent of the army's officer corps, 15 percent of the air force's officer corps, and 20 percent of the officer corps in the navy. Moreover, of the sixteen major generals, just one was from East Pakistan. This pattern of discrimination was caused by two factors: self-interest on the part of West Pakistani elites who wished to preserve their traditional place of power in Pakistan, and the widely held belief in West Pakistan that members of the Bengali nation lacked the physical and psychological attributes necessary for leadership, particularly in the military realm (Ganguly 2001, 53).

Not only were the ranks of the military dominated by West Pakistani, but the strategic policies of the Pakistani state seemed to ignore the East as well. During the 1965 war, East Pakistan had essentially been left unprotected by the Pakistani army. In fact, fighting in the East was very limited in 1965, but that was more because of "Indian sufferance" than because of any proactive policy on the part of the central Pakistani government to defend East Pakistan from Indian aggression (Ganguly 2001, 45). The disruption that was caused when East Pakistan's economic relations with India were severed as a result of the war further reinforced the growing perception among many in the East that their interests were more closely linked to India than to the western wing of their own state (Jackson 1974, 21). In the words of Amin, "The 1965 War further convinced the Bengalis that the army was not a national army, but one designed to defend the West Wing. Thus from 1965 the rift between the internal and the external fronts became much wider and the army was increasingly viewed as a foreign entity in the East Wing. . . . By 1971 Pakistan's 'Internal Front' was seriously eroded and this in turn greatly weakened its external front" (Amin 2001).

Culturally, while virtually all of the population of East Pakistan spoke Bengali, West Pakistan was comprised of four main ethnic groups—Punjabis, Pakhtuns, Sindhis, and Baluchis—each of which spoke their own language. Urdu, which was the chosen language of the Western-dominated political elite in Pakistan, was the mother tongue of a very small percentage of the total population of Pakistan. The experience of a shared language gave Bengalis a tremendous sense of a common history and cultural pride, and the fact that the central government refused to recognize Bengali as an official national language further stoked the fires of nationalism in East Pakistan. As early as 1952 riots centered on the language issue had erupted in East Pakistan (Burke 1973, 398; Ganguly 2001, 52).

Economically, East Pakistan was hampered from the outset by the fact that the majority of Muslim capitalists who migrated from India to Pakistan around the time of the partition settled in Karachi, West Pakistan (Burke 1973, 397). Thus the two regions incorporated markedly different economies, with West Pakistan being characterized more by capital-intensive industrial activities and East Pakistan relying primarily on raw materials to generate wealth. Although Bengali exports represented between 50–70 percent of the state's revenues, East Pakistan received just 25–30 percent of the country's income (Stoessinger 2001, 124). Much of East Pakistan's export revenues ended up being transferred to the western wing of the country to pay for the west's economic development (Burki 1986, 125). Furthermore, East Pakistanis argued that they were compelled as part of a state-mandated Import-Industrialization Substitution program to purchase goods and services from West Pakistan which could be purchased more cheaply on international markets (Jackson 1974, 20). In addition, nearly two-thirds of the foreign assistance provided by the U.S. to Pakistan was distributed in West Pakistan (Ganguly 2001, 52–53). State investments in development were heavily tilted toward West Pakistan, where rates of return were anticipated to be higher given that region's more advanced stage of development (Horowitz 1981, 177).

Although Ayub Khan tried to address the economic concerns of the East by increasing state investment in the eastern economy, capital flows continued to be skewed heavily toward West Pakistan (Blood 1995, 46). As a result, the economy of West Pakistan registered a much more robust pattern of economic growth during the 1960s than was the case in East Pakistan. In 1959–1960 per capita income was nearly one-third higher in West Pakistan than in East Pakistan; by 1969–1970, the West's per capita income was nearly two-thirds larger than that of the East (Jackson 1974, 20). Overall, the central government's economic policies heightened the perception in East Pakistan that the national leadership favored the West.

All of this was simply too much for many in East Pakistan to swallow. As public support grew for the East Pakistani nationalist Awami League, that organization's leader, Sheikh Mujibur Rahman, announced his six-point plan for eastern autonomy in 1966. The six points included a federal, parliamentary system, with representation based on population; limiting the power of the central government to defense and foreign affairs; two separate currencies and regional federal reserve banks with the power to halt capital flight and transfer from one region to another; overall responsibility for fiscal policy would lie with the regional units; regional governments would have the right to negotiate foreign aid packages and trade deals, as long as they did not contradict the foreign policy of the national government; and the creation of regional militias (Jackson 1974, 166–67). The six-point manifesto was so popular in East Pakistan that it served as the guiding framework for East Pakistanis in their negotiations with the central government over the next five years.

Meanwhile, Ayub Khan also faced growing dissent in the West. Zulfiqar Ali Bhutto's Pakistan People's Party espoused a populist platform, combining a message of support for the downtrodden of Pakistani society with unremitting hatred toward India (Jackson 1974, 21). At about the same time, support for Ayub within the military establishment began to erode. Bhutto was joined in his opposition to Ayub by Major General Peerzada and other military officers, who were angered by Ayub's decision to pass over Peerzada for commander in chief in favor of Gen. Yayha Khan (Choudhury 1974, 21–22).

The year 1968 signaled the beginning of the end of Ayub Khan's rule. Both West and East Pakistan were wracked by riots, all while Ayub Khan struggled to recover from a heart attack. Finally, on March 26 1969, Ayub Khan turned the reins of power over to the army chief, General Muhammad Yahya Khan. Under Yahya, power was centralized in the hands of the president, and the army was granted even greater access to the halls of power (Jackson 1974, 26). Given the strong nationalist sentiment of the military men around Yahya, it is not surprising that in the long run he would find his options for dealing with the Bangladeshi crisis substantially limited. The military establishment simply refused to consider any policy option that was not designed to maintain the full territorial unity of the existing Pakistani state.

The new president believed that the best way to save Pakistan was to address at least some of the grievances held by those in the eastern wing. In November 1969 he announced that for the first time in over a decade, nationwide elections for a civilian prime minister would be held near the end of 1970. Given East Pakistan's population advantage, it seemed quite likely that the outcome of that election would be the domination of the new national government by East Pakistan. Many in the military, as well as other Pakistani nationalist leaders such as former foreign minister Bhutto, voiced alarm that, once elected, the Bengalis would use their power in the parliament essentially to seize control of the country. They demanded that Yahya try to control the potential for Bengali hegemony over the political system by writing the Legal Framework Order (LFO) that was to govern the election process in such a way as to limit provincial autonomy after the elections (Choudhury 1974, 90–91).

At the same time that he was being pressured by the army and others to reduce the possibility that East Pakistan would emerge from the elections as the undisputed winner, Sheikh Mujib and his supporters from the Awami League continued to press hard on the president to accept their six-point proposal as the guideline for holding the elections. Yahya and his advisors worked hard to arrive at a compromise that would be acceptable to both of the extreme wings of the Pakistani political spectrum. In its final form, the LFO consisted of five principles: that Pakistan was based on Islamic ideology, that the country should have a democratic constitution based on free and fair elections, that Pakistan's territorial unity must be constitutionally protected, that the economic and social disparities between the country's two wings should be corrected through legal means, and that the provinces be granted maximum autonomy within the context of a federal system in which the national government would be in charge of maintaining the territorial unity of the country (Choudhury 1974, 93–94).

At the time the LFO seemed to some to represent a brilliant compromise, especially given the fact that Mujib had never publicly called for East Pakistan to secede from the West. However, as the election unfolded, it became clear that

Mujib was saying one thing for public consumption while saying something quite different in private. During a meeting of Awami League elites, Sheikh Mujib scoffed at the notion that he would feel compelled to abide by the LFO once elected, telling his colleagues that he would "tear the LFO to pieces as soon as the elections are over." Meanwhile, in the face of a martial law regulation prohibiting the promotion of territorial disunion, *Joy Bangla!* (Victory to Bangladesh!) became the rallying cry of Mujib's campaign and its supporters. On August 14, Pakistan's Independence Day, the Bengali flag flew across the region and students at Dacca University put a map of the proposed independent country of Bangladesh on display (Choudhury 1974, 98–99).

The elections were scheduled for October 1970. As has already been noted, based on demographics, the East Pakistani–based Awami League seemed to have the upper hand. Two horrendous natural disasters dealt the final death blow to whatever faint hope the traditional West Pakistani elites had for retaining power. First, in August East Pakistan was hit by significant flooding, forcing the government to postpone voting until December. Then, in November 1970, a massive cyclone plowed into East Pakistan, causing enormous damage. The central government did a poor job of responding to both catastrophes, as its disaster relief programs proved to be woefully inadequate. As the election loomed on December 7, 1970, one American official in East Pakistan characterized the government's failure to deal effectively with the humanitarian crisis that was triggered by these natural disasters as "a mandate from heaven" for the Awami League and its leader, Sheikh Mujib (Ganguly 2001, 57).

In fact, that U.S. official proved to be remarkably accurate in his assessment. The Awami League scored a stunning victory, garnering 166 of the 313 seats in the National Assembly. The divisions within the country were highlighted by the fact that the league captured all but two seats in East Pakistan while failing to win a single seat in West Pakistan. Meanwhile, Bhutto's PPP captured 85 seats, all in the western wing of the country, and most of those in the provinces of Punjab and Sind (Jackson 1974, 24).

According to the rules that had governed Pakistan since the last constitution was overturned in 1958, Yayha had the power to call the new assembly together at his discretion. He initially proposed March 3, 1971, as the date for the convening of the National Assembly, but Bhutto, who feared allowing the Assembly to meet before a constitution was in place (after all, would not that sequence permit a Bengali-dominated Assembly to draw up the new constitution?), rejected that date immediately. Meanwhile, in the weeks following the elections both Mujib and Bhutto made provocative statements that only served to stoke the fires of discontent in the country. In late December, Bhutto flatly stated his refusal to let the PPP sit as an opposition party in parliament, and declared that neither a new constitution nor a new government could be successfully formed without PPP participation and approval. In early January, Mujib retracted his commitment to the LFO, issuing a public demand that any constitution be based on his six-point program (Ganguly 2001, 57).

A full-blown ethnic security dilemma now existed in Pakistan. The "ethnic security dilemma, imported from international relations, stresses the competition for control of the government if its impartiality is in doubt" (Saideman and

Ayers 2000, 1130). The more the government supports, and is supported by, a single ethnic "insider" group at the expense of other, "outsider" ethnic groups in a multinational setting, the greater the likelihood that one or more of those ethnic outsider groups will feel that its security is threatened by the existing system, and thus the greater its incentive to change that system, using violence if necessary. Any attempt by the outsider group to address its inferior, insecure status will be seen as a threat to the security of the ruling ethnic group, which will then feel compelled to respond in kind.

In this case, President Yahya had to try to find a way to address the insecurity that East Pakistanis felt as a result of their region's inferior status within the Pakistani federation, without alienating his West Pakistani base. Seeking to find some compromise that would be acceptable to all the parties, Yayha arranged a conference to include himself, Mujib and Bhutto. He arrived in Dacca, East Pakistan, on March 15 in a last-ditch effort to save Pakistan from collapse. The difficult nature of Yahya's task was underscored when, on the day of his arrival, Mujib proclaimed, "The heroic struggle of the people marches forward. . . . The spirit of freedom in Bangladesh cannot be extinguished. . . . The struggle shall continue . . . until our goal of emancipation is realized." Mujib also issued thirty-one directives on how "Bangladesh shall be governed," prompting a foreign reporter to remark that the Mujib "seems to have declared the independence of East Pakistan" (Choudhury 1974, 161). Bhutto's arrival on March 21 only further complicated matters, particularly given the personal dislike that he and Mujib harbored toward each other.

Predictably, the negotiations in Dacca failed. The coup de grâce took place on March 22, 1971, when Mujib formally demanded that power be completely devolved from the central government and turned over to the two regions of the country. President Yahya was inalterably opposed to Mujib's demand, and rejected it on the spot. On March 25 a dejected Yahya returned to West Pakistan and gave the nod to a military action that was designed to destroy Bengali opposition to the central Pakistani state. That night, the military launched the now-infamous Operation Searchlight. According to many accounts, wholesale carnage ensued, including the slaughter of thousands of unarmed civilians.

In a classic example of the spillover effect (the impact of events within the borders of one state "spilling over" into another state), millions of terrified East Pakistanis fled their homes for India. Eventually, some ten million refugees from East Pakistan ended up in India, although it is important to note that the refugees came in several waves throughout 1971, and some of these waves of population movement seemed to be sparked by Indian-sponsored guerrilla activity in East Pakistan. In addition to the massacres and the refugee crisis, another result of Operation Searchlight was that Sheikh Mujib was taken into custody and held by the Pakistani government.

Even G. W. Choudhury, who served in Yahya's cabinet, admitted, "The Pakistan Army's brutal actions, which began at midnight on March 25, 1971, can never be justified. The Army's murderous campaign in which many thousands of innocent people including women, the old and sick, and even children were brutally murdered . . . constituted a measureless tragedy." Choudhury suggests that the brutality of the assault indicated a deep, ethnic-based hatred of Bengalis on the part of Punjabis, and goes on to speculate, based on his conversations with Yahya after the scale of Operation Searchlight became obvious, that by March 23 Yahya had lost control over the decision-making process to militant elements within the army (Choudhury 1974, 181–83).

Outside of Dacca, the Pakistani army faced a far tougher job in subduing the challenge to its rule in East Pakistan. Bengali regiments, many of whom had been quietly ordered away from Dacca by central commanders just prior to March 25 in order to make the army's job easier there, rallied against the national army. On March 26, a Bengali officer stationed in the East Bengal seaport of Chittagong declared the formation of a provisional government for the new state of Bangladesh. Several weeks later, after a government in exile was formed in India, Bengali independence was proclaimed once again. Finally, by the end of May 1971, the army declared that the revolt was crushed (Choudhury 1974, 188). This assumption, like so many others by Pakistani governmental institutions during this period, proved to be far removed from reality.

In New Delhi, the Indian government faced potentially grave economic, social, and political challenges as a result of the crisis. A report written by India's Institute for Defense Studies and Analysis claimed that the refugees would cost India $900 million per year, an economic burden that, if accurate, was obviously too much for India to bear (Stoessinger 2001, 127). In addition, the population influx threatened the existing tribal balance in the Indian states of Tripura and Meghala and increased economic pressure in particular in Tripura and West Bengal, all areas which had experienced a growth in antigovernment sentiment in the second half of the 1960s (Sisson and Rose 1990, 180–81).

The longer the refugee crisis lingered, the greater the likelihood that a full-blown domestic crisis might erupt in India. The secessionist movement in East Bengal might stimulate the emergence of a separatist movement among the disaffected population of West Bengal—what political scientists call the demonstration effect. The demonstration effect refers to the phenomenon whereby people in one territory draw inspiration from, and emulate, the protests and movements they observe in another territory. Here it is also useful to recall the previously mentioned study by Saideman and Ayers, which showed that irredentist demands are most likely to emerge in a situation in which a disaffected group's kin dominate a neighboring state (Saideman and Ayers 2000, 1136). In this case, the most likely goal of West Bengali activists would be the creation of a single state encompassing the entire Bengali diaspora.

The Indian government was clearly concerned in 1971 about the uncertain impact that the secessionist drive in East Bengal might have on Indian West Bengal (Sisson and Rose 1990, 180). Would an independent Bangladesh make an irredentist claim on West Bengal? Would Indian Bengalis push for union with their kin to the east? Certainly, the U.S. government was aware of what was at stake for India in the crisis. During a June 3 meeting at the White House, National Security Advisor Henry Kissinger and U.S. Ambassador Harold Keating identified three issues which, in their view, made India particularly sensitive to the situation in East Pakistan: the possibility that the Awami League, which was perceived to be sympathetic to India, might not take its "rightful" place at the head of the central government in Pakistan; the deep ties between West Bengalis and

East Bengalis; and the fear that over time the resistance movement in East Pakistan would become so radical that it would cause serious problems for India's security interests (Gandhi 2002).

With this uncertain (and potentially dangerous) situation looming on the horizon, and yet equally aware that a successful war against Pakistan would gravely weaken India's longtime foe and pay big domestic dividends to the ruling Congress Party in India on the eve of state elections scheduled for early 1972, the Indian government decided in the summer of 1971 that gradual escalation of the conflict in East Pakistan, to the point of direct intervention by India, would be the best policy (Sisson and Rose 1990, 206–8). Prime Minister Gandhi's immediate goals were to reduce the building internal pressure on the Indian state, to ensure that any postsecessionist regime in Bangladesh would be pro-Indian in its policy orientation, and specifically to reduce the possibility that an independent Bangladesh carved out of Pakistan would make irredentist claims on Indian West Bengal (Sisson and Rose 1990, 206–7). Thus Pakistan's domestic crisis created intolerable conditions in India, which in turn engendered pressure from India on Pakistan to resolve the crisis, which eventually resulted in another Indo-Pakistani war.

Conflict Spiral and the Indo-Pakistani War of 1971

On March 31 both houses of the Indian Parliament passed a resolution that equated the actions of Pakistani troops with genocide, demanded that power in East Pakistan be transferred to Mujibur, and proclaimed that "the people of East Bengal . . . will receive the wholehearted sympathy and support of the people of India" (Jackson 1974, 36). Interestingly, while Indian decision makers, including Gandhi, defined the developing crisis as a threat to India's interests, a few observers argued early in the crisis that the situation might be a blessing, because it could create the conditions that would result in the division of Pakistan. For example, K. Subrahmanyam, director of the highly respected, government-funded Indian Institute of Defense Studies and Analyses, commented in an April 5 newspaper article that the violence in East Pakistan provided "an opportunity (to dismember Pakistan) the likes of which will never come again" (Choudhury 1974, 211; Ganguly 2001, 63–64; Sisson and Rose 1990, 149).

Far from an emotional plea to spill Pakistani blood, Subrahmanyam offered a reasoned argument for why, in his view, the benefits of Indian intervention would outweigh the costs. First, he argued that the costs of attempting to absorb ten million or more refugees would far exceed the costs of another war with Pakistan. Second, he feared that failing to respond to the current refugee crisis would encourage Pakistan to push other ethnic minority groups into India. Third, he believed that, because China had no direct stake in the conflict, it would not intervene to defend Pakistan. Although it would take several months, Subrahmanyam's view came to be widely accepted in decision-making circles in India (Ganguly 2001, 64).

Initially, however, the Indian government envisioned a political solution that would include the release of Sheikh Mujib, the repatriation of all refugees—Muslim and Hindu alike—and a negotiated resolution to the crisis in Pakistan. At first, Mrs. Gandhi chose the path of caution, expressing outrage over the military operation in East Pakistan, announcing India's support for the Awami League, and allowing its political leadership and their guerrilla allies to take refuge in India. She stopped short, however, of ordering direct Indian military intervention in the crisis, providing overt material support for the blossoming rebel movement in the east, or formally recognizing the Bangladeshi government in exile as a sovereign body (Sisson and Rose 1990, 143). At this point, Gandhi seemed willing to give Pakistan some breathing room to arrive at a political compromise that would be acceptable to all the parties involved on the ground—the Pakistani government, the Awami League, the refugees, and the Indian government.

Very quickly, however, the Indians discovered that the Pakistanis, having defined the situation in East Pakistan as a military challenge rather than a political problem, came to believe by May that the military threat had subsided, and thus that the crisis had subsided. The generals in charge in Pakistan simply did not believe that the Bangladeshi rebels could defeat the Pakistani army. Nor did Pakistan believe that India would use its own ground forces to support its erstwhile East Bengali allies. Finally, the Pakistanis continued to cling to the belief that the international community defined the unity of Pakistan as a core interest worth guaranteeing in the face of any Indian threat (Sisson and Rose 1990, 162–63).

The decision by an aggrieved ethnic group to seek secession is driven by domestic events and conditions; the success of a secessionist movement, however, is by and large determined by "international politics, by the balance of interests and forces that extend beyond the state" (Horowitz 1981, 167). The militarization of the conflict by Pakistan, and the growing support for Subrahmanyam's view regarding the benefits of taking a more activist policy, drove India to support the creation of a guerrilla force to carry the fight to Pakistani forces stationed in East Pakistan. In fact, given the comparative military weakness of the Bangladeshi rebel forces, Indian support for the guerrillas was crucial. India provided arms, training and sanctuary to the newly formed Mukti Bahini (MB), or "Liberation Army." Originally known as the Mukti Fauj, or "People's Army," the guerrilla army included irregulars who had been fighting for independence from Pakistan as well as East Pakistanis who had been members of the central army of Pakistan prior to Operation Searchlight. By mid-April, the Indian government already had a rudimentary military structure in place for the guerrillas and had named a commander, Col. A. G. Osmani, a former officer in the Pakistani army. By early May, Osmani was already plotting military strategy for his forces. The creation of the MB was supported by the centrist Awami League, which, absent its jailed leader Sheikh Mujib, sought to consolidate its control over the independence movement by excluding radical leftists from the ranks of the MB (Jackson 1974, 55–57).

Both the guerrillas and their Indian sponsors recognized that time was of the essence, given the fact that the monsoon season began in the region in June and lasted until September. The rains would severely hamper the mobility of Pakistani forces, meaning that they would be easy targets. In addition, the waterlogged roads would make it extremely difficult for the Pakistani army to respond quickly to guerrilla strikes on economic and infrastructure targets. As they prepared for their military campaign, the belief that weather conditions would give the MB an advantage in the field drove the Awami League to reject President Yahya's overtures to explore a compromise solution to the conflict (Jackson 1974, 58–59).

At the same time that India quietly increased its ability to utilize military pressure against Pakistan through the MB, in public the Indians clamored for UN intervention in support of a political solution that would "stop any further influx of refugees and ensure their early return under credible guarantees for their future safety and well-being." However, the Gandhi government further warned that "if the world does not take heed, we shall be constrained to take all measures as may be necessary to ensure our own security and the preservation and development of the structure of our social and economic life" (quoted in Jackson 1974, 60). Gandhi's position was that India supported a diplomatic solution to the crisis, but only if the details of a diplomatic solution met India's demands. Otherwise, in the absence of a political settlement that matched India's interests, the Indians would press forward with the military option. In fact, by mid-July Gandhi and her top advisors had privately come to the conclusion that direct armed intervention by Indian forces would be required to resolve the crisis in East Pakistan satisfactorily (Sisson and Rose 1990, 206).

For reasons that have already been discussed in some detail, it is clear that the long-term balance of power clearly favored India in 1971. However, for a brief period of time from late June through early August, the balance of threats seemed to be shifting against India. First, after a brief drop in the number of refugees moving from East Pakistan into India, the refugee flow increased once more, with the U.S. government estimating in August that about fifty thousand refugees per day were flooding across the border (Gandhi 2002). The fact that the increase in refugees came after a brief period of reduced refugee flows further reinforced the sense in New Delhi that the situation on the ground was getting worse, not better.

Several events in the international system also reinforced India's growing sense of strategic insecurity. On June 22 the *New York Times* reported that a ship had sailed from New York City loaded with U.S. military equipment bound for Pakistan. Later, two more ships bearing military equipment left for Pakistan. Although technically the story was correct, the importance of the event was overstated; the shipment comprised the paltry $5 million in aid that managed to survive the previously mentioned State Department–directed arms cutoff to Pakistan. At the time, however, the news of the arms shipment triggered outrage in the U.S. Congress (Kissinger 1979, 859). The news of the shipment also caused great consternation in India, where the government worried that these shipments might represent the tip of the iceberg in terms of a renewal of U.S. arms transfers to Pakistan.

Around this time, several other events in the foreign policy arena also caused concern in New Delhi. Recall that on July 15 the U.S. and China announced their diplomatic breakthrough. After this announcement, an attempt by India in late July to improve relations with China was rebuffed by the Chinese. Meanwhile, the Americans were sending mixed signals to India on what U.S. policy would be in the event of a Chinese attack on India. Also in late July, eager to put pressure on the Indians in order to finally seal the Treaty of Friendship and Cooperation, the Soviets stated that their South Asian policy was still driven by the "spirit of Tashkent," which was grounded in an even-handed approach to Indo-Pakistani relations. Finally, there was the emerging reality that the international community would not force Pakistan to recognize the independence of Bangladesh (Ganguly 2001, 65; Jackson 1974, 61, 72).

In response to this sudden increase in threats to India's interests, the Treaty of Friendship and Cooperation with the USSR looked much more attractive to India than ever before. This was particularly true given Article 9 of the treaty, which required that in the event either party was attacked by a third party, consultation would occur with an eye toward removing the threat (Ganguly 2001, 65). The fact that it took just twenty-four hours for the details of the treaty to be worked out and for the agreement to be signed and ratified highlights the eagerness on the part of India to bolster its international security at that juncture (Jackson 1974, 71–72).

In addition to signing the alliance pact with the Soviet Union, India also looked to the MB to help India regain the initiative in East Pakistan. In response to President Yahya's announcement in late June that he planned to transfer political power to civilian rulers in four months, in July the Awami League swore an oath to fight the war until victory was achieved. On August 9, in a move apparently designed to placate his own domestic hardliners, President Yahya announced that Mujib would be put on trial for treason. "Yahya did not grasp his peril," Henry Kissinger later recalled; he "was certain to mobilize even greater world pressures and fuel Indian intransigence" (Kissinger 1979, 868).

Throughout August the MB experienced increasing success in its military operations. Part of this growing success stemmed from the increasing control which India, fearful that ideological divisions among Bangladeshi independence forces might weaken the movement, exercised over the MB (Jackson 1974, 78). By increasing their influence over the MB, the Indians enforced solidarity, while also enhancing the organization's military efficiency and effectiveness. By the end of the month the MB began to undertake naval strikes, sinking several coastal vessels and river boats. The immediate objective of these naval attacks was as much economic as it was military. The MB wanted to choke off jute and tea exports from East Pakistan to the global markets, thereby robbing the central Pakistani government of desperately needed capital (Jackson 1974, 77–78).

Up to this point, a fairly symmetrical conflict spiral had been occurring, with both India and Pakistan contributing equally to increased tension through each state's provocative moves and statements. However, beginning in September the Indo-Pakistani conflict spiral became increasingly asymmetrical, with Pakistan attempting to cool the situation and to internationalize the issue, while India sought to increase the military pressure on Pakistan and to freeze the international community out of any discussions on how to resolve the crisis. The negative effect which the crisis in East Pakistan had on India's domestic system was the primary catalyst for India's increasingly provocative and bellicose policy stance throughout the fall of 1971 (Sisson and Rose 1990, 206).

In September, Yahya, aware of the growing success of Indian-backed MB forces in the field and sensing that he had overplayed his hand with the announcement that Mujib would be tried, reversed course. On September 1 he named a civilian governor to head East Pakistan. A day later, press restrictions were lifted in Pakistan. On September 5 a general amnesty was proclaimed for all civilians and military personnel who had engaged in antigovernment activities in East Pakistan, with the notable exception being those individuals who had already been charged with crimes. Although Mujib was still slated to be tried, Yayha quietly told the Americans that he would not be subject to the death penalty if convicted. On September 8 an East Bengali was named to head Pakistan's UN delegation. On the eighteenth Yahya announced that the new constitution that was to be drawn up by a panel of experts would be subject to review and change by the legislature. Two days later, the government announced that a new round of elections would be held to fill East Pakistan's empty legislative seats (earlier, the government had decided that only 88 of the 167 Awami League members who had won slots in 1970 would be allowed to sit in the legislature) (Jackson 1974, 81; Kissinger 1979, 871).

The new spirit of goodwill which Yayha sought to convey at this time was designed to reach out to India and to the broader international community as well. First, he hoped to meet some of India's demands, thus denying them a legitimate rationale to intervene in the conflict (Sisson and Rose 1990, 222). Second, with the UN's annual session opening in New York, the Pakistani leader hoped to highlight his willingness to seek a compromise solution to the crisis with the help of the international community. In addition, Yahya's announcement that Mujib would not face the death penalty earned Pakistan some brownie points with the American government. In response, on October 1 Richard Nixon requested an additional $250 million for relief efforts in Pakistan.

Yahya's political offensive did little, however, to reverse the spiral toward general war. Even while Pakistan seemed to seek a diplomatic settlement in early September, India put its troops on general alert at the beginning of September, with Pakistan responding by reinforcing its position along the Indo-Pakistani border. On September 9, India moved its sole armored division and an additional armored brigade toward the border. On the sixteenth the Americans received reports that India planned in early October to slip another nine thousand MB guerrillas into East Pakistan from India. When pressed by the Americans to rein in the guerrillas, India claimed to have no control over their activities. In addition, India, with diplomatic support from the Soviet Union at the UN, rejected the idea of placing UN personnel on the ground in India to assist them in dealing with the refugee crisis, going so far as to refuse to allow UN representatives to come to the refugee camps to explain Yahya's offer of amnesty.

The escalation toward war continued in October. On October 8 an Indian official told Henry Kissinger that if the crisis was not resolved to its liking by the end of the year, India would be forced to take matters into its own hands. India's increasingly bellicose stance on the situation was no doubt reinforced by a promise from the Soviet Union that the Soviets would support India with a military airlift in the event of war (Kissinger 1979, 874). On October 17, President Yahya repeated a suggestion he had made previously that both countries withdraw their troops from the border regions. Both Gandhi and her minister of defense rejected the proposal, with the defense minister warning that "if war is thrust upon us by the Pakistani military junta, we will not withdraw from occupied Pakistani territory, come what may." A final diplomatic foray into the burgeoning crisis by the UN bore no fruit in late October, when UN Secretary General U Thant's call for international peacekeepers to be stationed on both sides of the Indo-Pakistani border was accepted by Pakistan but rejected by India.

Meanwhile, on October 22 Indian reservists were called up, and by the end of October, the Indian government had fully committed itself to send troops across the border into East Pakistan (Jackson 1974, 90–91, 101). The military plan that was being drawn up called for a short operation, lasting a maximum of three weeks and beginning sometime in late November or early December. The Indians preferred that time frame for several reasons. It allowed for the rivers in East Pakistan to subside after the monsoon season, thus making them easier to cross; it increased the likelihood that the Himalayan passes would be closed by the first winter snows, thus greatly decreasing the likelihood of Chinese intervention; it allowed Mrs. Gandhi time to tour the Western capitals, including Washington, thus underscoring the appearance that India was willing to exhaust all diplomatic options before "reluctantly" choosing war; and it gave India ample time to prepare its own military forces and build the strength of MB forces in preparation for the operation (Sisson and Rose 1990, 208–9).

Throughout November the Indians continued to prepare for the probability that another war with Pakistan would erupt in the near future. In early November, President Yahya surprised the Americans when he accepted a U.S. proposal for a unilateral Pakistani withdrawal from the border. In return, Yahya asked that Indian troops pull back as well shortly after a Pakistani withdrawal. In addition, Yayha told the U.S. that he supported the idea of America making a public announcement that the aid pipeline to Pakistan had been completely shut down. Yahya was even willing to take the humiliation of having the announcement made by the U.S. during an official state visit by Indira Gandhi to Washington that was planned for early November. Finally, the embattled Pakistani leader told the U.S. that he was ready to meet with Awami League members, possibly including representatives designated by Sheikh Mujib (Kissinger 1979, 878).

Indira Gandhi embarked on her "peace tour" of western capitals at the end of October. Prior to her meeting in Washington with Richard Nixon, Gandhi pressed India's case in Brussels, Vienna, and London. At each stop, she hammered home the Indian government's core arguments regarding the East Pakistan crisis: She blamed the Pakistani government for the "genocide" that was taking place in East Pakistan, complained that the refugees were placing an extreme burden on India, refuted the claim that what was happening was an "Indo-Pakistani" dispute (since such an acknowledgment would have legitimized diplomatic intervention by the United Nations), called for a quick resolution that recognized the legitimate aspirations of the people of East Pakistan, and claimed that while India did not seek war, it might be forced to take such a course if the refugee crisis was not resolved (Sisson and Rose 1990, 194).

Of course, the most important stop was in Washington, DC. Just prior to the trip, she received reassurance from the Kremlin that Soviet and Indian interests were in perfect harmony on the issue of East Pakistan. To underscore their point, the Soviets began airlifting military equipment to India on November 1, which was just prior to Gandhi's arrival in Washington (Ganguly 2001, 66; Kissinger 1979, 877).

From the U.S. perspective, the results of Gandhi's meetings with Richard Nixon were decidedly mixed. Reflecting the agreement that had been struck with Yahya, the U.S. president promised to suspend the transfer of any further military assistance to Pakistan. Nixon's assurances on this issue undoubtedly increased the Indian leader's belief that the U.S. was not prepared to use military leverage in order to deter Indian aggression. Her confidence was further bolstered by reports that the Soviets had indicated that they were willing to bring military pressure to bear on China if that country attacked India (Choudhury 1974, 220; Ganguly 2001, 66).

At the same time, Nixon asked Gandhi to delay any direct Indian military intervention in the conflict, since he believed that he was close to brokering a breakthrough in talks between the Pakistani government and the Bangladeshi government in exile (Jackson 1974, 98). In any event, the Americans asked, what was the harm in waiting to see how Yahya's plan for civilian rule in Pakistan played out? According to Yahya's own timetable, the power transfer was slated to occur at the beginning of January. In the opinion of top American policymakers, it was inevitable that, at the very least, East Pakistan would gain autonomy, if not absolute independence.

Ironically, according to Kissinger's interpretation of Gandhi's frame of mind at the meetings in Washington, it was precisely the Indian president's fear that Yahya was serious about reform that drove her to accelerate the path toward war (Kissinger 1979, 880). The Americans correctly suspected that Gandhi's "peace tour" was by and large an elaborate hoax designed to signal India's "peaceful intentions," even as preparations of a war with Pakistan were well under way (Sisson and Rose 1990, 209). Both the Pakistani government (as evidenced in Yahya's promises earlier in the month), and moderates within the Awami League, seemed open to Nixon's diplomatic effort. However, the Indian government, fearful that a U.S.-sponsored diplomatic settlement might allow Pakistan to remain unified, balked. In fact, in her meetings with Nixon, Gandhi may have tipped her hand regarding India's ultimate goal when she argued that in addition to East Bengal, other regions of Pakistan, including Baluchistan and the Northwest Frontier, deserved greater autonomy (Kissinger 1979, 881).

India's military involvement in East Pakistan accelerated substantially around the time of the Nixon-Gandhi meeting. Indian units began quietly slipping across at the end of October. For months, in the face of loud protests from Pakistan, India had sponsored, directed, trained and supplied the MB. Now, Indian units had begun to move back and forth across the border into East Pakistan (Choudhury 1975, 209).

On November 21 the *New York Times* reported that Yahya Khan had offered Pakistan's "hand of friendship" to India. The same day and the day after, tensions escalated as India sent tanks into East Pakistan, purportedly in response to Pakistani shelling. In retrospect, this for all practical purposes marked the beginning of the 1971 Indo-Pakistani War, although it would not turn into a full-blown war until December 3. As had been planned by the Indians, on November 23 the MB launched an offensive against the Chaugacha junction, and on November 29 that location fell to MB forces. Meanwhile, reports continued to emerge out of the region that Indian involvement in the fighting was intensifying; on November 29 the Indians became involved in a battle with Pakistani forces near Hilli, East Pakistan.

Although some Indian forces entered and remained on Pakistani territory in late November, the actual number of Indian forces involved was fairly small. MB units were given responsibility for a good deal of the ground fighting, thus at least partially masking India's increasing direct participation in the fighting. Moreover, many of the "battles" that were fought during this period were actually little more than skirmishes, with the Pakistanis exaggerating both the ferocity of the fighting and the number of Indian troops involved in an effort to force the international community to put pressure on India to halt the operation. For example, on November 28 reporter James P. Sterba of the *New York Times* described the fighting as "a series of border skirmishes short of all-out war." On December 2, just a day before full war erupted, Sterba wrote in the *Times* that "the actual level of combat between Pakistani and Indian troops appears to be fairly light, with both sides placing more emphasis on the propaganda war than on combat."

Meanwhile, Indian commanders continued to describe their actions as defensive in nature (Jackson 1974, 102). Suspicious of India's true intentions, the Nixon administration finally rammed a freeze on arms exports to India down the throat of the State Department. In addition, Nixon demanded complete cut off of U.S. economic assistance to India, to which the State Department replied that a better approach would be to suspend economic aid to both states. At the same time, a debate began within the U.S. government regarding the nature and extent of America's treaty obligations to Pakistan. Again, the battle lines were drawn between the State Department, which argued that the U.S. had no legal obligation to assist Pakistan, and Kissinger, who feared that the U.S. was "conducting itself like a shyster looking for legalistic loopholes" (Kissinger 1979, 894–95).

Although the U.S. seemed to be moving ever so slowly in the direction of taking a more active role in protecting Pakistan in order to deter further Indian aggression, a decision by Yahya rendered the issue a moot point. As Indian forces continued their advance into East Pakistan, and mindful that traditional Pakistani military doctrine rested on the assumption that "defense of the east lay in the west," Yahya took the fateful decision to expand the war by launching an offensive along the western border. As was often the case as the crisis unfolded, Pakistan's calculations regarding the choice to widen the war seem, in retrospect, irrational.

Pakistani Decision Making and the 1971 War

International relations and foreign policy scholars have long been interested in analyzing the possible causal relationship between the quality of the foreign policy decision-making process and the quality of the policy that is produced by that process. In his seminal book *Essence of Decision* (1971), Graham Allison identifies three models of decision making—rational actor, organizational process, and bureaucratic politics—and applies each model to American policymaking during the Cuban missile crisis. The rational actor model, which is assumed to be the ideal approach, argues that elites identify an objective or objectives, gather information, engage in an objective, well-informed cost-benefit analysis of their policy options, choose the policy that is most likely to maximize their objectives at the lowest possible cost, implement the policy, and then carefully monitor the success or failure of the policy (Cashman 1993, 77–78).

Contrary to the rational actor model, the **organizational process model** assumes that both policy choice and policy implementation are significantly determined and constrained by preexisting organizational processes and plans. These organizational biases have an important implication for foreign policy decision making: Organizational standard operating procedures (SOPs) create routines for managing the flow of information and implementing decisions; the routines seriously constrain the ability of policy elites to develop and implement innovative responses to new crises as they emerge. Obviously, then, the organizational process is an impediment to rational decision making (Cashman 1993, 86–87).

Finally, the bureaucratic politics model depicts foreign policy as the outcome of pulling and hauling between various policy elites, each of whom wants to protect his or her own "turf" (i.e., the interest of the government agency they represent). The individuals who head agencies take an extremely parochial view on policy issues; their stance on an issue is likely to be shaped by their calculations on how the issue affects their agency, and they often equate the interests of their agency with the interests of the state. As the famous phrase goes, the bureaucratic politics model assumes that "where you stand (on an issue) depends on where you sit" (Cashman 1993, 89–91).

In 1971 a rational Pakistani regime would have understood that its power disadvantage vis-à-vis India rendered the chances for victory in any war with India exceedingly small. In fact, two years after the war, retired major general Fazal Muqeen Khan claimed that Pakistani leaders realized after 1965 "it had become economically impossible for Pakistan to keep pace with (India). . . . Under these circumstances all that Pakistan could do was to avoid war with India and to strive to resolve disputes through political and diplomatic means." If, in fact, this is an accurate depiction of the mindset of Pakistani decision makers, it would seem to indicate that top elites understood the balance of power and tailored their policies accordingly (and rationally).

However, the *Report of the Commission of Inquiry—1971 War*, the Pakistani government's official inquiry into the war, tells quite a different story. Not only did policymakers fail to incorporate a nuanced understanding of the balance of power in South Asia into their calculations, but in addition the claim was made in the summer of 1971 that, owing to Pakistan's increased military presence in the eastern wing and to the country's strengthened alliance with China, a two-front offensive war with India was now possible. Although those changes were never formally adopted into Pakistan's strategic planning (in particular, war planners ultimately decided that the best strategy was to continue to emphasize the utility of offensive operations on the western front while hoping to fight a holding action in the east), the fact that they were introduced into the discussion indicates just how far off base the Pakistanis were in terms of grasping the perilous military balance facing Pakistan vis-à-vis India in 1971. In response to what he believes to be Fazal Muqeem's inaccurate and self-serving depiction of "rational" Pakistani decision making prior to and during the 1971 crisis, Amin remarks that "no one at the helm of affairs was ready to think so realistically and rationally" (Amin 2001).

On the other hand, the available evidence indicates that policymaking by the Pakistani military regime toward East Pakistan exhibited some of the characteristics of bureaucratic politics. Typically, where the bureaucratic politics model is relevant, "policy options are linked to institutional interests. Options are not likely to be put forward nor supported unless they reflect some institutional preference" (Cashman 1993, 92). In this case, a special subtype of bureaucratic politics existed in Pakistan: Because the military so thoroughly dominated the halls of political power in 1971, the preferences and interests of the military were given precedence in government policy. Most important, the Pakistani government doggedly clung to the view throughout much of 1971 that the crisis in East Pakistan was a military problem which required a military solution. Crushing the revolt would remove the threat that had placed "the military's corporate interests and West Pakistani economic interests at unacceptable risk" (Sisson and Rose 1990, 160).

Of particular importance in the case of Pakistan is the military's dominant role in the government. It has long been argued that so-called garrison states, i.e., those states which undertake substantial and prolonged mobilizations of their economies and societies in preparation for war, become more and more militarized over time. Of critical importance is the fact that "militarized states tend to monopolize the flow of information vital to decision-making" in the hands of military elites. "Military rule," observes Julian Schofield, "contributes to war by introducing a systematic bias in decision-making" (Schofield 2000, 132, 134).

For example, decision-making structures in military regimes tend to be overly streamlined, so that just a few military officers have a monopoly over the state's military and defense policies. Furthermore—and this is not surprising—the leaders of military regimes tend to blur the line between defense policy and foreign policy, with foreign policy being seen primarily as a tool to protect the military interests of the state. Thus the slot of foreign minister almost invariably is handed to a military officer, whose institutional bias leads him to favor a military solution to external crises (Schofield 2000, 134).

In addition, military rulers tend to pattern the structure of their governmental decision making after the hierarchical structure of decision making that they are most familiar with from their experiences in the armed forces. Thus rigid SOPs are followed which allow for little deviation. Because of these SOPs, it is difficult to assimilate unexpected information, which retards the government's ability to respond in a rational fashion to a crisis (Schofield 2000, 134).

In a conceptual discussion at the beginning of his examination of Pakistani decision making, Schofield identifies four biases which make the militarized state more war-prone. First, because the militarized state lacks the competence to engage in a sophisticated political analysis of foreign policy issues, there is a tendency to focus on foreign threats and the possibility of war. Second, due to the obsession with the balance of power, military regimes will exaggerate the benefits to be gained from a perceived window of opportunity to strike a blow at an external adversary. Third, such regimes often ignore the domestic implications of foreign policy choices, and because of their lack of expertise in the arena of foreign policy, they find it difficult to predict the behavior of allies—both their own and those of their enemies. Fourth, once a crisis erupts, military regimes have a strong preference to escalate toward war as quickly as possible, the idea being to destroy the enemy's military capabilities rather than to convince it to make a political choice to change its behavior (Schofield 2000, 135).

In analyzing Pakistani decision making within the context of the 1971 crisis, it is important to begin by noting that Yahya Khan came to power in 1969 with the support of his fellow military officers. He then constructed a decision-making structure in which military officers occupied every top post within the government. Moreover, access to Yahya was carefully controlled by Lt. Gen. S. M. G. Peerzada, who served as principal staff officer. Generally speaking, only those military officers with a long history of friendship and association with Yahya were given access to the president, although top-level civil service secretaries were able as well at times to circumvent their agency chiefs and gain access directly to the president's office (Sisson and Rose 1990, 24–25). Meanwhile, the formal civilian cabinet was relegated to dealing with the mundane administrative tasks. Eventually the civilian cabinet was disbanded altogether in February 1971, a month *before* the army carried out its operation in East Pakistan. In addition, the civil service bureaucracy was decimated, with a number of civilian administrators who had served under the Ayub Khan regime being purged by Yahya and his cronies (Burki 1986, 62).

Yahya served as president, army supreme commander, and chief martial law administrator. In dealing with the East Pakistan crisis, and in the planning and conduct of the war he relied on a small group of advisors, all of whom were officers in the army. The fact that Pakistan's war policy was being decided by a tiny coterie of army officers, all of whom were stationed in West Pakistan, meant that relations between headquarters and field commanders (especially in East Pakistan), and between the army and the other branches of the armed forces, were "difficult and uneasy—fraught with personal and inter-service rivalries, with misunderstandings, and with simple incomprehension" (Jackson 1974, 108). Jackson's language in describing the difficult task of policy formulation and implementation underscores the relevance of the bureaucratic politics model in this case.

Organizational process also played a role in undermining the rationality of Pakistani decision making during the crisis. In *The Report of the Commission of Inquiry*, the Pakistani government found that the strategy of attacking India on the western front in an effort to seize as much Indian territory as possible while fighting what amounted to a defensive war on the eastern front was expressed formally in War Directive No. 4, issued by Ayub Khan on August 9, 1967. In fact, this was simply a restatement of the failed strategy of the 1965 war. Although several factors were reassessed by Pakistan's General Headquarters in the summer of 1971, including the impact of both Pakistan's "alliance" with China and India's Treaty of Friendship and Cooperation with the Soviet Union, no substantial revisions were made to the strategy that had been expressed in the 1967 document. As the Commission of Inquiry noted in its report, a number of events since 1967, and in particular developments since March 1971 such as the revolt in East Pakistan and India's massive military buildup (supplemented by its treaty with the USSR), should have triggered a serious reappraisal of the assumptions and strategies contained within Directive No. 4. In essence, the belief that "defense of the east began in the west" had become an unquestioned assumption at the core of Pakistan's military planning; it was the standard plan for fighting a war with India, and Pakistani policymakers were unable to move off of that plan in light of new information and developments.

A final piece of the puzzle of irrational Pakistani decision making may be provided by applying the concept of groupthink, first developed by social psychologist Irving Janis (1982). This syndrome strikes "when group members' striving for unanimity overrides their motivation to realistically appraise alternative courses of action" (Cashman 1993, 112). The evidence suggests that groupthink may have plagued Pakistani decision making during the crisis. Yahya's advisors "circled the wagons," pushing him to take a hard line against Mujib and the Awami League, and insulating him from those who might advocate other policy options. In the words of one former Pakistani government official, Yahya's sources of information and advice were limited to close confidants "who provided only those reports and assessments that were pleasing to the ears of their boss." For example, twice during the crisis Yahya sent delegations to China to feel out the Chinese on the level of support Pakistan could expect to receive from Beijing in the event that war broke out with India. In both cases, the delegations simply lied to Yahya upon their return to Pakistan; he was led to believe that China would provide active, steadfast support for Pakistan if a war with India erupted, when in fact the Chinese had offered Pakistan only vague statements that China would support the territorial unity of Pakistan (Choudhury 1975, 212–13). More generally, the unwillingness to elicit information and advice from civilian foreign policy experts, the failure to reexamine long-held assumptions and preferences, and the tendency to explain away past policy failures (such as the 1965 war) all suggest that the top circle of decision making in Pakistan was infected by groupthink.

In addition, as predicted by Schofield's model of nonconstitutional military regimes, the Pakistani government proved utterly incapable of accurately predicting the response of the international community to the war. Because of their crude understanding of foreign policy in general and great power politics in particular, the Pakistanis failed to discern the fact that the Soviet Union, which felt threatened by the Sino-American breakthrough, saw a potential Indian victory as a useful tool for humiliating China and the U.S. Furthermore, by counting on intervention by China and/or the United States, Pakistan took into account neither the desire on the part of the Chinese to avoid a militarized confrontation with their more powerful Soviet neighbors, nor Nixon's desire to improve relations with both China and the USSR at a time when the U.S. was trying to extricate itself from Vietnam.

As the conflict spiral accelerated in the late fall, a general consensus emerged in Pakistan to take the initiative in launching a full-scale war. However, although it is true that a consensus emerged among Pakistani decision-making elites in late November that war with India was required—and moreover that Pakistan should strike first on the western front—it is also true that multiple, contradictory currents of opinion existed in Pakistan in 1971 regarding the underlying logic for the proposed war. One stream of thought argued that Pakistan's main aim in the war should be to capture as much territory as quickly as possible, in an effort to set up a "land for peace" tradeoff with the Indians—the scenario that was envisioned in War Directive No. 4. A second school, obsessed with Pakistan's standing claim to Kashmir, believed that any war with India should focus on seizing and holding that particular region. Finally, a third school of thought sought to balance against India by internationalizing the conflict, in hopes that the UN, the U.S., China, and others would intervene once a war started and force India to back away from its confrontational policy toward Pakistan. According to the logic of that particular argument, Pakistan should fight a limited conflict which could be sustained until the international community in-tervened. Given the muddled nature of Pakistani decision making during this time, it is not surprising that no solid choice seems to have been made among these three irreconcilable objectives. To some extent, all three goals were pur-sued in the war; none were even remotely achieved (Jackson 1974, 113).

In order to complete our analysis of Pakistani decision making, a brief note on Yahya Khan's individual psychological and cognitive make-up is in order. The evidence suggests that Yahya was guilty of relying too much on cognitive short-cuts—specifically, **stereotyping** and wishful thinking—in dealing with the crisis, which may have made it difficult for him to engage in a rational analysis of Pak-istan's policy options. In particular, Yahya relied on broad stereotypes to analyze and predict the actions of his enemies.

For example, he assumed, as did most West Pakistanis, that neither the Ben-galis of East Pakistan nor the Hindus of India possessed the fighting qualities nec-essary to defeat Pakistan's army. In the words of a retired Pakistani officer, the "Martial Races Theory" created a "superiority complex" that "played a major role in the wishful thinking" that led Pakistani decision makers to believe that India could not rationally choose to launch a war on Pakistan, and that in the event that India did make the irrational choice to attack, the superiority of the Muslim warriors would overcome India's numerical advantage in men and equip-ment (Amin 2000). In addition, he personalized the conflict between Pakistan and India, using the derisive term "that woman" in public settings to refer to In-dira Gandhi (Stoessinger 2001, 126, 130).

The stereotyped images Yahya held regarding his foes are extremely signifi-cant, given the emphasis that military regimes place on balance of power in mak-ing foreign policy. Yahya's perception that both Bengalis and Hindus, by their na-tures, were not good fighters, along with his dismissive comments regarding Gandhi (based at least partially on her gender), undermined his ability to engage in a rational calculation regarding the costs and benefits of going to war with India in 1971. "The Pakistani nation had been fed on propaganda about (the) mar-tial superiority of their army," laments Amin (2001), and this propaganda nur-tured a widely held view that Pakistan's supposed qualitative advantage in the fighting capability of its soldier-warriors would more than make up for its quan-titative disadvantage in troop strength and equipment. Anchored in these stereo-types, Yahya "wished" himself into believing that Pakistan was destined to win a war with India. Unfortunately for Yahya, the Pakistani president did not have a rational decision-making structure in place to act as a useful check against his irrational images and policies.

Before closing this discussion on decision making, it is important to note that India's decision-making structure was not completely dissimilar from the struc-ture in Pakistan. As Sisson and Rose (1990) chronicle, similar to the system in Pak-istan, decision making in India tended to be dominated by a small circle of indi-viduals, in this case a few of Indira Gandhi's most trusted friends and cabinet ministers. The most influential advisors to the prime minister during the 1971 cri-sis included the heads of her personal secretariat (P. N. Haskar prior to July 1971 and P. N. Dhar thereafter), G. Parthasarthy (a close confidant who held no formal post), D. P. Dhar (former envoy to the Soviet Union), K. C. Pant and R. N. Mirdha (the two ministers of state responsible for home affairs), and an interministerial committee comprised of several cabinet secretaries. One critical difference, however, was that in India the military was kept at arm's length in terms of its control over policy decisions as the crisis evolved. Unlike in Pakistan, where military officers controlled both military and foreign policy (an arrangement which resulted in a tendency to conflate the two spheres into a single issue area dominated by military interests), in India any input into government decision making from the military had to be channeled through the defense minister, Jagivan Ram. Despite the fact that the core group of decision makers was "quite small and homogenous," and thus perhaps vulnerable to many of the same irrational tendencies that plagued Pakistani decision making, civilian control over the decision-making process enhanced the ability of Indian decision makers to engage in rational decision making in 1971 (Sisson and Rose 1990, 138–41).

SUMMARY

As is the case with all wars, a number of factors contributed to the outbreak of the 1971 war between India and Pakistan. At the international level, Britain's colonial management of India heightened the intercommunal tension between Hindus and Muslims. The British employed a classic divide-and-rule strategy in colonial India, encouraging Hindus and Muslims to mobilize themselves according to their unique religious identities. This policy was so successful that, as Britain prepared to withdraw from India, the Muslim minority demanded a separate independent state. Anxious to pull out of its colonial commitments as quickly as possible, the plan which Britain devised for dividing the territory pleased neither Hindus nor Muslims. The status of hundreds of "princely territories" remained unresolved, and the viability of Pakistan, with its two territorial wings separated by more than one thousand miles of Indian territory, was open to serious question.

After the British withdrawal and the founding of the independent states of India and Pakistan, both of the new states proclaimed a policy of nonalignment within the context of the Cold War. In fairly short order, however, first Pakistan and then India found themselves drawn into the Cold War vortex, as each state sought assistance from one or both of the superpowers. In particular, Pakistan's decision to join the Baghdad Pact and SEATO placed it firmly in America's corner, and drove the Soviets to seek better relations with India. Although for a period of time during the 1960s U.S. and Soviet interests converged in South Asia—both superpowers supported India in order to thwart Chinese expansion in the region—by the late 1960s the U.S. under Nixon moved back toward a discernable pro-Pakistan tilt in its foreign policy, and the Soviet Union pressed India to sign the Treaty of Friendship and Cooperation, something India eventually did in 1971. Meanwhile, China, which had border disputes with India and was involved in a struggle with the USSR for influence in the communist world, strengthened its existing alliance with Pakistan and forged a new relationship with the United States.

In short, the activities of the great powers in South Asia fueled the conflict environment in the region by bolstering the confidence of the two regional combatants that they could count on great power protection in the event of another war. In the end, of course, Pakistan would discover much to its chagrin that it had grossly overestimated the amount of support which China and the U.S. would offer to Pakistan as the crisis grew, and severely underestimated the degree to which the Soviets would back India.

At the dyadic level, given the history of tension and warfare between the two states it is not surprising that the decisions which each state made in an effort to increase its own security were perceived as threats by the other state. As 1971 unfolded, a new conflict spiral emerged between India and Pakistan. Moves taken in the name of national security by one state motivated the other state to respond in the name of its own national security.

In the Indo-Pakistani case, there seems to be some gap between the broad perception in the international community at the time of which party was the main driving force behind the 1971 conflict spiral and the objective reality of primary responsibility for the spiral. Specifically, although most of the world perceived Pakistan as being the aggressor in initiating and maintaining the conflict spiral, the evidence discussed in this chapter indicates that although Pakistan's ill-conceived and morally reprehensible crackdown on the Awami League provided the first spark for renewed Indo-Pakistani tensions, thereafter it was India's determination to manipulate the crisis to its strategic advantage, which kept the conflict spiral going. It is true that Pakistan's leadership misperceived that a window of opportunity existed to fight and win a general war by launching a preemptive strike on December 3 along the western border with India. Such a war was deemed necessary by the Pakistanis because they feared the dismemberment of the country, an outcome which represented an unacceptable loss to the Pakistani national leadership. However, it is also critical to note that, by the eve of the war, the fires of conflict had been stoked first by India's support for the MB, and then by direct Indian involvement in the fighting in East Pakistan. Thus while the Pakistanis incorrectly calculated that a window of opportunity existed to strike at India, thereby arresting their growing sense of vulnerability vis-à-vis India and its MB allies, the Indians correctly perceived that the conditions were ripe for India to use the crisis to weaken, if not destroy, Pakistan and therefore to shift the balance of power in the region even more clearly in its own favor.

At the state level, irredentism played some role in explaining India's decision to intervene in what was in theory a domestic crisis in Pakistan. India had never accepted the partition of Bengal by the British into Indian West Bengal and Pakistani East Bengal. From the Indian perspective, the people of Bengal were of a single national stock, and deserved to be united again in a single territorial unit. On a larger scale, many in the Indian government were still rankled by the partition of colonial India, the result of which was the creation of Pakistan. It is undoubtedly the case that some in India still dreamed of the reintegration into India of the Muslim provinces which formed independent Pakistan.

At the substate level, the military Pakistani government in particular was plagued by irrational decision making. The military regime in Pakistan displayed many of the characteristics that are commonly found in military regimes where constitutional constraints are lacking: an overly centralized decision-making structure; too much reliance on SOPs; an inability to gather, assimilate, and interpret unexpected information; lack of access to top decision makers for those who disagree with existing policy; an overreliance on military capability analysis as the main determinant of policy; an inability to predict with accuracy the behavior of interested third party actors as the crisis unfolds; and, in the case of Pakistan, a refusal to depart from traditional Pakistani military doctrine, which argued that the defense of East Pakistan depended first and foremost upon the defense of West Pakistan.

At the individual level, Pakistan's President Yahya Khan carried many of the stereotypes that were commonly found among West Pakistanis. Specifically, he believed that, by their nature, West Pakistanis were better suited to fight and win wars than were either Bengalis or Hindus. In addition, given the language he used when discussing the growing conflict, it appears that Yahya assumed that the fact that his adversary, Indira Gandhi, was a woman gave him a distinct advantage when it came to fighting and winning a war. These stereotypes allowed Yahya and his colleagues at the top of the Pakistani government to believe that Pakistan might actually be able to fight and win a two-front war against India.

THE WAR AND ITS AFTERMATH

In an effort to emulate Israel's opening gambit in the Six-Day War of 1967, Pakistan launched a "surprise" air assault on Indian air bases in northwestern India on December 3. The Pakistani offensive was an utter failure. Having anticipated the attacks, India had moved its military aircraft into reinforced concrete bunkers. The following day, the Indian air and naval forces launched a coordinated counterattack, striking hard at the key port city of Karachi. As a result of the assault, a number of oil installations were destroyed, and Karachi's harbor was effectively blocked (Ganguly 2001, 67–68).

On the ground, fierce fighting ensued, as the Pakistanis sought desperately to protect their state from total collapse. The tenacity with which Pakistani forces fought in the west "to save Pakistan" may have been well founded. In Washington, reliable intelligence was received that Gandhi's war plan was as grandiose as some in the Nixon administration had suspected: to begin with the "liberation" of Bangladesh, followed by a military thrust designed to "liberate" all of Kashmir, and finally to turn to the absolute destruction of Pakistan's military. If successful, the plan would almost surely result in the complete disintegration of Pakistan (Kissinger 1979, 901).

On the other hand, Sumit Ganguly, a well-respected expert on the Indo-Pakistani conflict, claims that no reliable independent evidence exists to support Kissinger's contention that India sought the complete destruction of Pakistan in 1971 (Ganguly 2001, 69). However, it is important to note that the Americans apparently believed that the Indians had the intention to carry the war to the absolute limit, as evidenced by the fact that Nixon ordered a U.S. naval task force to sail for the Bay of Bengal on December 12. The naval maneuver was meant to highlight U.S. support for the territorial integrity of what remained of Pakistan (i.e., for West Pakistan, now that East Pakistan's independence was a foregone conclusion) and to give the Soviets cause to move with caution in the event that

China decided that it had to enter the war in order to save Pakistan from total destruction (Kissinger 1979, 912). In addition to these stated reasons for the U.S. ship movements, it is also likely that the maneuver was a belated and rather half-hearted gesture meant to show that, at a time when the U.S. was seeking a way out of Vietnam, it could be counted on to come to the aid of its friends.

Meanwhile, in East Pakistan, the Indian air force had even more success. In short order, nearly half of Pakistan's air force was destroyed, and bombing runs by MiG-21s damaged Pakistan air strips so severely that the few planes that survived the Indian onslaught were unable to take off or land. On the ground, utilizing a blitzkrieg strategy of swift thrusts designed to capture large amounts of territory as quickly as possible, by December 8 Indian forces, augmented by MB fighters, surrounded the city of Dacca. In the midst of the fighting, Indira Gandhi recognized Bangladesh on December 6. On December 16 the remaining Pakistani forces in Dacca fled, and the Indian army took full control of the city. On the seventeenth Indira Gandhi declared a cease-fire. President Yahya quickly reciprocated, and the war came to a close.

As a result of the war, Bangladesh gained its long-sought-after independence. A desperately poor but very proud country, Bangladesh jealously guarded its sovereignty and independence in the face of Indian pressure to accept the role of a quasi-client state of India. In terms of its relations with the superpowers, although the Soviet Union plied Bangladesh with military assistance, the United States poured three times more money than the USSR into the UN's relief fund for Bangladesh.

India's star ascended in South Asia, reaching its apex in 1974 when the Indians successfully exploded a nuclear device. From 1971 until 1998, when Pakistan successfully tested its own nuclear bomb, India enjoyed unquestioned military hegemony over South Asia. However, its economy struggled mightily, at least partially due to the costs of the 1971 war. Strikes and acts of civil disobedience increased markedly in the early to mid-1970s. The opposition to Gandhi was further fueled when the Allahabad High Court invalidated her 1971 election. In a stunning development, on June 25, 1975, Gandhi declared a state of emergency and suspended civil rights for Indian citizens. During the era that followed, a period of time her opponents branded the "Reign of Terror," thousands were jailed, the government practiced forced sterilization as a method for reducing urban overcrowding, and slum dwellers were evicted in the name of "beautification projects." After being out of office for three years beginning in 1977, Gandhi returned to power in 1980, but she was assassinated by her Sikh bodyguards on October 31, 1984 (Heitzman and Worden 1996).

In Pakistan, retribution for the country's failures on the battlefield came swiftly. After having been reassured by their leaders for years of Pakistan's military superiority, the rapid defeat at the hands of India caught most Pakistanis completely off guard. Pakistanis were humiliated to discover that not only was their country now split in two, Pakistan also had lost its status as the largest Muslim country in the world. Violent demonstrations rocked the country as soon as news of the war's outcome reached the Pakistani people; on December 20, Yahya Khan stepped down and Zulfiqur Ali Bhutto assumed power as the president. Although he failed to democratize Pakistan's political system and Pakistan's economy failed

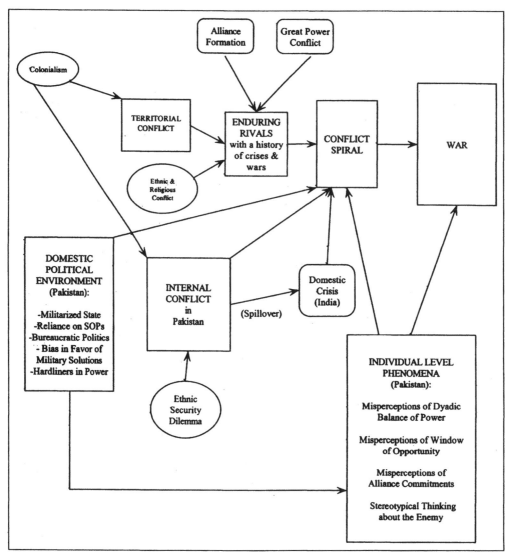

Chart 5.1. The Indo-Pakistani War of 1971: Causal Factors

to respond to Bhutto's policy of Islamic socialism, he strengthened Pakistan's ties with the wealthy Islamic oil states and convinced the U.S. to partially lift the embargo on the transfer of U.S. arms to Pakistan. In 1977, Bhutto was overthrown by Gen. Muhammad Zia. Under Zia's leadership, Pakistan entered an era of growing isolation from the rest of the world, a trend that was reversed finally in the early 1980s, when Pakistan cooperated with the U.S. and Saudi Arabia in opposing the Soviet invasion of Afghanistan (Blood 1995).

For the great powers, the 1971 Indo-Pakistani War reinforced one trend that had existed since 1965: growing Soviet influence in South Asia. On the other hand, China saw a key regional ally significantly weakened, and thus by extension its own influence reduced. Sino-Pakistani relations entered a state of gradual decline in the years following the war. For the U.S., Pakistan's loss represented the first in a series of defeats for American allies in the third world during the 1970s. In South Vietnam, Nicaragua, and Iran the U.S. suffered the loss of key third world allies during the decade of the 1970s. Little did U.S. officials realize that, just ten years after the fall of the shah of Iran and the Soviet invasion of Afghanistan took place in 1979, the Berlin Wall would come tumbling down, marking the demise of the Soviet Union and the end of the Cold War.

6

The Iran-Iraq War

For the better part of the 1980s, the two most powerful states in the Persian Gulf were locked in mortal combat with each other. The world community looked on with great anxiety as two of the world's largest producers of petroleum seemed intent on destroying each other. Lasting eight years, the Iran-Iraq War was one of the longest conventional wars in the twentieth century—longer than either World War I or World War II. The magnitude of this war led one observer (al-Khalil 1990, 261) to classify it as the first (and thus far only) "great war" among the countries of the third world, a war in which the masses of people on both sides were mobilized for war on a tremendous scale. The conflict resulted in casualties numbering between one and one and a half million. But the full intensity of the war can perhaps only be appreciated by understanding that Iraq, with a total population of approximately sixteen million, put fully 10 percent of its population under arms: At the height of the war its army reached one million, and another six hundred thousand citizens belonged to its militia. By 1986 every male under the age of fifty-one was put on military call in Iraq. The country spent $95 billion on the war effort, much of it borrowed. It allocated 57 percent of its GDP on the war (Iran spent 12%). In fact, the combined cost of the war to both sides, in terms of both direct and indirect war damage, has been estimated at about $1.19 trillion (Hiro 1991, 1–4, 251).

As with many wars, the Iran-Iraq War has ancient roots as well as more immediate causes. We shall examine both sets of factors.

ROOTS OF WAR: LONG-TERM CAUSES

Enduring Rivals

You will remember from previous chapters that certain pairs of states called enduring rivals interact differently than do other pairs of states; they are much more prone to conflict and violence. Indeed, such long-term rivals have been responsible for roughly half of all the wars, militarized disputes, and violent changes of territory in the last two centuries (Geller and Singer 1998, 23). While modern Iran and Iraq may be classified as enduring rivals, the rivalry of the two

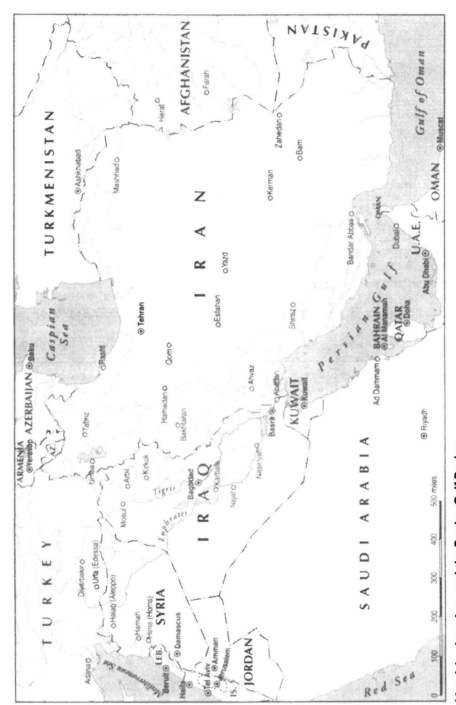

Map 6.1.   Iran, Iraq, and the Persian Gulf Region

peoples located on these territories precedes the present century. Arabs in present-day Iraq won their independence from the Persian Sassanian empire in AD 637 at the battle of Qadisiya. Conflicts later arose between the Ottoman Turks, who occupied present-day Iraq, and the Persian empire, now Iran, in the sixteenth century and became endemic in the mid-seventeenth century (Hiro 1991, xxii; Grummon 1982, 3).

Detached from the Ottoman Empire as a consequence of the Turkish defeat in WWI, Iraq first became a British mandate and then eventually gained its independence in 1932 under the rule of the British-installed Hashemite dynasty. To its east, the rule of Persia's Qajar dynasty was overthrown in 1921 in a coup d'état led by Reza Khan, the commander of the elite Cossack Brigade. Five years later Reza Khan crowned himself Shah (Emperor) Reza Pahlavi, instituting the Pahlavi dynasty. Eight years later the shah changed the name of his country from Persia to Iran—"Land of Aryans." In 1941, with Europe imperiled by the Axis powers, the Allies, worried about the shah's pro-fascist leanings and his country's oil wealth and strategic location, sent Reza Pahlavi into exile. They replaced him on the throne with a more pliant ruler, his son, Mohammed Reza Pahlavi. The British and the Russians then occupied Iran for the duration of the war.

The Cold War followed hard on the heels of World War II, and the Gulf region was soon embroiled in the global conflict between East and West. Along with Iran, British-dominated Iraq was a charter member of the 1951 Central Treaty Organization (CENTO), the U.S.-led, anti-Soviet alliance in the Middle East. Indeed, the organization was referred to as the Baghdad Pact, indicating the central position of Iraq in CENTO. However, after the 1958 revolution in Iraq which overthrew the Hashemite monarchy, Iraq denounced its pro-Western allegiances and courted Soviet support. Iran and Iraq thus emerged on different sides of the Cold War divide and as rivals for geopolitical leadership in the Persian Gulf. Their competition for regional dominance was aided and abetted by the two superpowers.

Iraq became one of the Soviet Union's primary clients in the Middle East, and the USSR sought to build up Iraqi military might in the region. The governing elites in Baghdad perceived themselves as the leaders of the forces of secular republicanism, Arab socialism, and militant Arab nationalism. One of the tenets of Iraq's ruling Ba'athist (Renaissance) Party was that the Arab nation must be rejuvenated by replacing the archaic system of rule by monarchy, which it saw as a creation of Western imperialism, with secular republics (Grummon 1982, 8). This placed Iraq at odds with not only Iran but also its Arab neighbors, such as Saudi Arabia and the Persian Gulf emirates.

On the other hand, under Shah Mohammed Reza Pahlavi, Iran remained a member of CENTO and a major ally of the United States. Indeed, Iran was one of the two "pillars" of U.S. policy in the region—the other being Saudi Arabia. Thus in the 1960s and 1970s, the conflict between Iran and Iraq took on the appearance of an ideological contest between the conservative, pro–status quo, pro-Western and promonarchical Iran and the radical, revolutionary, pro-Soviet, and anti-monarchical Iraq (Hiro 1991, 15). While all-out war between Iran and Iraq was avoided until 1980, between 1934 and 1980 the two rivals were involved in seventeen militarized disputes, most of these (fourteen) occurring between 1960 and 1980 (Geller and Singer 1998, 152).

With Britain preparing to withdraw from the area east of Suez in the late 1960s, Iran—prodded by the United States—became more assertive in the region. Teheran's leaders came to see Iran as the policeman of the region, with a mission to counter the forces of radical revolution. Iran opposed radical movements in the Middle East, developed ties to Israel, and was hostile to pan-Arabism and Arab socialism as practiced by Nasser's Egypt and by the Ba'ath Party governments in Iraq and Syria. The shah had already embarked on a long-term military modernization program, and this program accelerated considerably in the 1970s. Though Iran's initial edge in national power might have been offset by Iraqi economic growth in the early 1970s, this edge was short-lived (Tammen et al. 2000, 75–77). After the 1973 oil crisis, the Iranian economy took off and its military power was enhanced accordingly. Military spending, which accounted for about 5.6 percent of Iran's GNP in 1969, reached 15 percent of GNP in 1978 (Geller and Singer 1998, 147). Much of the spending went toward purchases of sophisticated weaponry that the U.S. sold to the shah to buttress Iran's position as a bulwark against Soviet influence in the region.

In addition to Iran's three-to-one population advantage over Iraq, by the mid-1970s it was clear that Iran's military buildup, based on American technology, had given it clear military superiority over Iraq. Indeed, until the early 1970s Iraq's army was perhaps best characterized as no more than a "robust police force" (Pelletiere 1992, 13). However, Iranian foreign policy and the Iranian military buildup fueled an arms race and Iraq doubled the size of its army after 1973.

The Iranian military buildup created a classic security dilemma by increasing the level of threat perceived by Iraqi leaders and setting off a conflict spiral that lasted from 1969 to 1975. While the Iranian buildup frightened Iraq, it emboldened Iran. In 1969 the shah repudiated the longstanding agreement with Iraq on the crucial Shatt-al-Arab waterway. Iraq responded by reviving the issue of Arabistan (called Khuzistan by Iran), an area of Arab population in eastern Iran periodically claimed by Iraq. The government in Baghdad announced the creation of a rebel organization to fight for the independence of Khuzistan Arabs from Iran—the Popular Front for the Liberation of Arabistan. In retaliation, in January 1970 Iranian government officials provided weapons and tactical advice to a group of disgruntled retired Iraqi military officers who were plotting a coup. The attempt failed and Iraq responded by breaking off diplomatic relations with Iran in May 1970 and expelling expatriate Iranians from Iraqi soil. Iran countered by launching military maneuvers near Iraq's central border region and by assisting the rebellion of Iraqi Kurds in the north of Iraq. Fighting escalated dramatically in Iraq's Kurdish region, and full-scale war appeared to be a very distinct possibility.

Interactions between Iran and Iraq in the period between 1969 and 1975 were intensely conflictual and extremely threatening. This pattern is typical of relations between enduring rivals, whose interactions exhibit high levels of hostility as they lurch from crisis to crisis. However, this six-year conflict spiral was temporarily short-circuited before it ended in all-out war by the signing of the Algiers Accords in early 1975. Peaceful relations lasted only four years however, and a second, more deadly, spiral of hostility broke out after the Iranian Revolution in 1979. We will return to this story a little later in the chapter.

Territory

International relations scholars know that of all the issues that can draw states into violent conflicts, those involving territory are the most dangerous. The rivalry between Iraq and Iraq was greatly intensified by unresolved territorial disputes, many of which combined geographic and economic interests. Slightly over half of the world's oil reserves are in the Persian Gulf and much of these reserves are located in Iran and Iraq (Hiro 1991, 2). Resource-related disputes broke out over the exploration for oil in the Persian Gulf and over how to properly divide the continental shelf areas belonging to Iran and Iraq in the gulf. Additionally, Iran and Iraq share common oil fields along their land-based borders. To the extent that one side vigorously pumped resources from this common pool of petroleum, the other claimed to have been victimized by deliberate economic warfare by its rival. Water rights were also disputed. Many of Iraq's rivers originate in the mountains of Iran and flow into the Tigris. Iranian diversion of these waters adversely affected Iraqis downstream (Swearingen 1988, 413–14).

The long, contiguous land border shared by Iraq and Iran presented numerous opportunities for disputes and many areas were claimed by both states. Contributing to the six-year conflict spiral, border clashes broke out in 1970 and in 1972 along Iraq's oil-rich central border region with Iran, an area where the territorial boundaries had been continuously disputed. More serious fighting occurred in early 1974, and a UN-mediated cease-fire, negotiated in May, broke down by the summer of the same year.

In November 1971 Iran added fuel to the fire by seizing three islands in the Strait of Hormuz that belonged to two of the Arab Gulf emirates—Abu Musa, Greater Tunb, and Lesser Tunb. Combined with the islands already possessed by Iran, these additional territories greatly enhanced Iranian ability to control the Strait of Hormuz, and thus entry to or exit from the Persian Gulf. Iraq responded by condemning Iranian imperialism and by once again cutting off diplomatic relations with Iran. The Iraqi regime also deepened its relations with its superpower protector, signing a fifteen-year Treaty of Friendship and Cooperation with the USSR in April 1972. Even though this was not a military alliance, it symbolized the potential for the expansion of Soviet influence in the region. The Nixon administration paid close attention and responded a month later with a decision to increase its military assistance to Iran. Nixon pledged that Iran would be permitted to buy any American-made nonnuclear military weaponry in its inventory, a favor that the U.S. granted to none of its other allies. The U.S. also increased its efforts at instigating a full-scale Kurdish rebellion inside Iraq. Iranian military intervention in Iraq's Kurdish north (prodded by the U.S.) increased substantially from 1972 to 1975. Predictably, Iraq retaliated by increasing its aid to the Popular Front for the Liberation of Arabistan inside Iran.

The most important territorial dispute centered on the Shatt-al-Arab (literally, the Arab River), a 120-mile waterway created by the confluence of the Tigris and Euphrates Rivers, which then flows into the Persian Gulf. The final third of this river forms the southernmost section of the border of Iran and Iraq. The waterway is critical for both economic and military/strategic reasons. It is perhaps most important to Iraq because it is crucial to Iraq's ability to transport its petroleum down the Tigris, through the Shatt, and into the Persian Gulf and thence to the rest of the world. Except for its access to the Persian Gulf through the Shatt, Iraq is a land-locked country. Its single, large commercial port, Basra, is situated forty-seven miles up the Shatt, and its other harbor facility, Fao, is located at the mouth of the Shatt. Although Iran has a major oil facility at Abadan on the Shatt and a port at Khorramshahr, it has a large coast on the Persian Gulf and is not nearly as dependent on the Shatt for the transhipment of goods.

Because of the importance of the Shatt, the Ottoman Empire, which controlled the area that became Iraq after the end of WWI, entered into treaty agreements with Persia, the precursor to the modern state of Iran, setting the boundaries between themselves. The 1847 Treaty of Erzurum provisionally fixed the boundary at the east bank of the waterway, giving Persian vessels freedom of navigation in the Shatt, but granting sovereignty and control of the Shatt to Turkey. In other words, the Shatt was Ottoman territory. This arrangement was continued into the modern age by the British/Russian–brokered 1913 Constantinople Accords and by a revised, British-mediated Iran-Iraq Frontier Treaty in 1937. The later two agreements adjusted the boundary in Persia/Iran's favor somewhat around the two major Iranian cities on the Shatt—Khorramshahr and Abadan. At Abadan the boundary was set at the *thalweg*, the middle of the main navigable channel of the river. In all other places the boundary remained at the east bank, favoring Iraq. These arrangements were somewhat unusual because, at least in the twentieth century, in most situations where a river forms the border between two countries, the exact boundary for the entire length of the river is the *thalweg*.

Iran's concerns were both symbolic and economic. The treaty did not reflect the true power realities of Iran-Iraq relations; it gave unequal legal status to the two states, with Iran in a decidedly inferior position. Just as important, the treaty placed Iraq in charge of commerce on the Shatt. Iraq controlled piloting and the maintenance of river channels through dredging, and it benefited from the payment of tolls on the river. As a result, the Iranians first demanded the *thalweg* as the boundary for the entire Shatt in 1932. After repeatedly being rebuffed on this issue, in 1969 the shah unilaterally abrogated the 1937 agreement and claimed the *thalweg* as the boundary. Iran sent its gunboats into the channel and placed naval and air forces on full alert. The Iraqis complained fruitlessly to the United Nations and retaliated by expelling thousands of Iranian pilgrims visiting Shi'a shrines in Iraq. The propaganda war increased on both sides. Military units were concentrated along both sides of the border, leading to occasional military clashes beginning in 1970. As we have already mentioned, Iranian bullishness on the Shatt and on other issues propelled a conflict spiral and an arms race that did not end until the two countries settled the boundary issue six years later.

In the June 1975 Algiers Accords, Iraq gave in to Iranian demands and accepted the *thalweg* as the boundary of the Shatt. For its part, Iran promised to set up a joint commission to demarcate the exact land boundary and to return to Iraq several disputed pieces of territory in the central border region, including the strategic heights of Zain al Qaws and Saif Saad, which Iran had forcibly annexed. This last promise remained unfulfilled. The territories in question, which contain plentiful reserves of petroleum and a high concentration of ethnic Persians, remained in Iran's possession throughout the 1970s, but when the Khomeini government came to power in Teheran in 1979, Iraq placed increased pressure on Iran to make good on the earlier promises.

The treaty was such a bitter pill to swallow and was so controversial that the Iraqi president refused to sign the agreement; instead, it was left to Vice President Saddam Hussein, the chief negotiator of the agreement, to sign the document. Hussein apparently considered the agreement to be a personal humiliation—a document negotiated under duress occasioned by the distinct possibility of all-out war with the more powerful Iranian military (Grummon 1982, 10; Chubin and Tripp 1988, 23). As president, Hussein vowed to restore Iraq's sovereignty over the Shatt. From the perspective of prospect theory, we could reasonably conclude that Hussein never really fully accommodated to this loss; he did not accept the Algiers Accords as representing a new, legitimate status quo. Later, in 1980, when he framed the conflict with Iran, he would be able to justify Iraq's use of violence as preventing the loss of the pre-Algiers status quo.

However important these territorial grievances were, and even though Iraq used territorial justifications for its attack on Iran in 1980, it should be remembered that once the Iraqis were on the defensive militarily, all these territorial issues became negotiable and were ultimately abandoned after the war's end. Territorial issues added to the general rivalry between Iran and Iraq and helped to initiate the conflict spiral in 1969, but they were probably not the decisive factor in the war's outbreak in 1980.

Religion

In addition to longstanding territorial disputes, the two rivals were split by religious differences. Although both countries belong to the vast Islamic world that stretches from the westernmost edge of North Africa and proceeds through the Middle East and South Asia to the Indonesian archipelago, this Islamic world is certainly not united. While the majority of Muslims worldwide are members of the Sunni sect, a significant minority of Muslims are members of the Shi'a branch of Islam. Iran is the center of the Shi'ite world and the vast majority of its people (90–97 percent) are Shi'a.

On the other hand, Iraq was ruled by a Sunni political elite from the central part of the country. This was not a recent development; Sunnis have been politically dominant since the sixteenth century, whether under Ottoman rule, the post-WWI British Mandate, the subsequent Hashemite Monarchy or the post-1958 Ba'athist republic. The numerical majority of the population (between 55 and 65%) were, however, Shi'a adherents, as were the vast majority (perhaps as many as 85%) of army personnel (Hiro 1991, 2, 22; Pelletiere 1992, 29; Turner 1985, 148–49). Southern Iraq, including the area around the Shatt, is dominated by Shi'a Arabs. Some of the holiest Shi'a shrines, such as Karbala and Najaf, are on Iraqi territory and are under the control of the secular government in Baghdad. Pilgrimages by Iranians to holy places in Iraq were therefore subject to regulation by the government in Baghdad. As a general principle, Shi'ism finds itself opposed to secular authority, and many Shi'a clerics, therefore, opposed the secular political system constructed by the Ba'athist regime. As a result, Iraqi Shi'a were frequently subjected to repression by the Sunni government in Baghdad.

Within weeks of the shah's renunciation of the Shatt treaty in 1969, Iraq responded with a campaign of repression against Shi'a clerics. Shi'a antigovernment riots took place in southern Iraq in 1975 and 1977. All were brutally suppressed by the government.

Both the shah's government in Teheran and the Sunni government in Baghdad were initially strongly secular in orientation. That is, they supported what Americans would refer to as a separation of church and state. Indeed, this was one of the major tenets of the ruling Ba'athist Party in Iraq. However, the Iranian Revolution of 1979 brought to power in Teheran a government based on theocratic principles and institutions—one in which the highest religious authorities were also the dominant political authorities. The existence in Teheran of a theocracy dominated by conservative Shi'a clerics introduced an ideological element in the conflict between Iran and Iraq. The Iranian Revolution promoted a struggle between the universalistic religious ideology of the new Islamic regime in Iran and secular Arab nationalism in places like Iraq.

After the Khomeini government took power in Teheran, Iran began to meddle in religious affairs in Iraq—a violation of the Algiers Accords. Although fundamentalists in Iran focused primarily on the toppling of secular regimes rather than protecting Shi'a brethren in other states, the two goals could not be totally separated. Khomeini attempted to rally the repressed Shi'a in Iraq to revolt against Saddam Hussein's secular Sunni government. Indeed, there were Shi'a riots in Iraq once again in 1979 and 1980. The Iraqi response was predictable. In March 1980 Saddam Hussein outlawed the leading Shi'a movement—al Daawa al Islamiya (Islamic Call)—on pain of death. There is little doubt that Khomeini's Iranian Revolution created the fear that Islamic fundamentalism, with its emphasis on theocratic forms of government, would spread among Shi'a in southern Iraq as well as to neighboring countries in the region. Countries with significant Shi'a minorities were at risk, especially if they were ruled by hereditary monarchies—branded as "un-Islamic" by Khomeini (Hiro 1991, 3). As a result, not only was Iraq threatened by the Islamic Revolution in Iran, but the Saudis, the Kuwaitis, and the other Persian Gulf monarchies were imperiled as well.

From the vantage point of history one might argue that the Shi'a threat to Saddam Hussein's regime was not so significant in September 1980 that Iraq needed to wage all-out war against Iran to destroy it. Not only were Shi'a groups like al Daawa relatively small, but they had been largely crushed before the war broke out in 1980 (al-Khalil 1990, 265). Ultimately, the war against Iran was launched from predominately Shi'a territory in Iraq, and Iraqi Shi'a remained loyal to the state throughout the war. Nevertheless, the perception that Shi'a unrest threatened the Ba'athist regime was probably a powerful consideration by Saddam Hussein and his advisers. And it was certainly true that, in spite of Baghdad's successful short-term repression of Shi'a activity, Shi'a opposition constituted a "menacing long term problem" in the context of the Islamic Revolution next door in Iran (Dawisha 1980, 142).

Ethnic/Cultural Conflict

The territorial and religious conflicts between Iran and Iraq were compounded by ethnic and nationalistic factors. While most Iraqis are Arabs by ethnicity and speak Arabic, the majority of Iranians are Persian and speak Farsi. However, both countries are truly multiethnic in composition. Iraq has a significant Kurdish minority: Approximately 20 percent of Iraqis are ethnic Kurds, and Kurds make up the majority of those who live in northeastern Iraq. The Kurds are primarily Sunni Muslims by religion, but they are not Arabs. They are a multistate nation, living within the borders of Iraq, Iran, Turkey, and Syria, but they have no state of their own—a situation that has caused considerable trouble for their host governments. Iran, with a total population of about thirty-eight million, is home to about four million Kurds. Iran's other ethnic communities include ten million Azerbaijani Turks in the northwest, one and a half million Baluchis in the southeast, and approximately one million Arabs along its western frontiers in Khuzistan. Persians probably make up no more than half of Iran's total population, though their political dominance is not the least in doubt (Turner 1985, 150).

Mutual antipathy of Iranians and Iraqis toward each other based on ethnicity (Persians versus Arabs) or race (Aryans versus Semites) is perhaps best thought of as part of the cultural baggage available to be mobilized by political leaders at the outbreak of war as both sides begin to demonize each other. It is not a direct cause of the war, but it is a condition which adds to the generally negative content of mutual relations and which makes the decision for war easier.

More important, both governments had for many years been involved in the politics of ethnic subversion. As we have already seen, in response to Iran's 1969 repudiation of the 1937 treaty regarding the Shatt, Iraq renewed its own claim to the Arab-populated province of Khuzistan in western Iran. It organized a rebel group on Iranian soil (the PFLA) and began propaganda broadcasts to Arabs in Khuzistan, encouraging them to revolt against the shah's rule.

Prior to the 1975 Algiers Accords, both governments were involved in funneling support to the ethnic Kurdish rebel organizations on the other side of the border to fight against their governments, though Iran's support for Iraqi Kurdish rebels far outweighed Iraq's support for Iranian Kurds and it did more damage. The northern Kurdish region is of vital economic importance to the Iraqi regime, as 60 percent of Iraq's oil revenues came from these areas. Fighting in northern Iraq had broken out in 1969 over Baghdad's broken promises to the Kurdish leader Mullah Mustafa Barzani to grant the Kurds autonomy within Iraq. As we have seen, by 1972, the shah, encouraged by the U.S., made a major commitment to Barzani's Kurdish rebels. Not only did Iran provide U.S. and Israeli weaponry to Kurdish rebels, but Iranian units assisted with artillery and air support near the border, and by January 1975 the shah had infiltrated two regiments of his own uniformed army into "liberated" Kurdish areas of Iraq (Hiro 1991, 16). Border skirmishes also broke out between Iranian and Iraqi military units away from Kurdish areas. Before the dust settled, Iraq had suffered about sixty thousand military and civilian casualties in the fighting (Helms 1984, 118).

Recognizing the imminent danger of a devastating all-out war and the need to devote government attention to economic development, the two governments decided to sign a truce in 1975. In return for agreeing to Iran's demands concerning the Shatt-al-Arab in the Algiers Accords, the Iranians closed the border to Kurds and agreed to stop supporting the rebellious efforts of Kurds in Iraq. In fact, both sides agreed in Article 3 of the accord to end "any infiltration of a subversive nature from any source." The end of Iranian support for Iraqi Kurds, and the simultaneous end of support from the American CIA, permitted Iraq's military to suppress the rebellion in the north. Indeed, the Kurdish revolt collapsed in roughly two weeks.

The Iranian Revolution initiated a significant change in the Kurdish situation. Once Khomeini assumed power in Iran in 1979, the ethnic and religious cards were played again. Iran began once more to assist Iraqi Kurds, and it meddled in the southern Iraqi province of Basra, inciting Shi'ites against Saddam Hussein's government. It became clear fairly quickly that the new regime in Iran was unwilling to preserve the cooperation initiated by the Algiers Accords. Iraq responded in kind. Fighting between Iranian Kurds and Revolutionary Guards started up within two months of Khomeini's victory. This renewed fighting in Iranian Kurdistan, coupled with agitation by Iranian Arabs in Khuzistan and repeated pipeline explosions, all pointed to renewed Iraqi interference in Iran (Grummon 1982, 12). These actions convinced Iranian leaders that Iraq was once again engaged in subversion.

IMMEDIATE/SHORT-TERM FACTORS

The Algiers Accords ended the six-year conflict spiral and allowed Iran and Iraq to concentrate on their internal political problems and also to bring to fruition their plans for economic modernization. While some have characterized the 1975–1980 interlude as a period of "watchful tension" based on a fragile truce (Chubin and Tripp 1988, 23), the post–Algiers Accords era was a period of at least *relative* quiet, normalcy, and even cooperation in the relations between Iran and Iraq. As Martin Malin (1997, 385–86) describes it:

> Between 1975 and the departure of the Shah from Iran amidst the Revolutionary turmoil of early 1979, relations between Iran and Iraq were completely normalized. Trade relations expanded. The numbers of Iranian Shi'ite pilgrims visiting holy sites in Iraq mushroomed. . . . The Shah was accorded full respect in the Iraqi press. Iran and Iraq formed a united front within OPEC. . . . Cooperation over internal security matters was extensive. When rioting against the Iraqi government by Shi'ite opposition groups erupted in 1977, the Shah dispatched the Empress Farah Diba to the Iraqi holy sites to address the crowds and help the government restore order. Likewise, Iraq made no effort to exploit the Shah's domestic difficulties when his country descended into revolutionary chaos. In fact, at the Shah's request, Khomeini was expelled from Iraq for his anti-Shah rhetoric in 1978. Finally, even after the Shah had fallen, Iraq cautiously welcomed the new regime in Teheran [and] expressed hope that the friendly relations that had grown in recent years would continue.

Iraq's numerous attempts at cooperation with postrevolutionary Iran were unsuccessful. It was only after Iraqi efforts to maintain normal relations had failed that Iraq started down the path to a military confrontation. It is therefore necessary to address those immediate circumstances that made continued cooperation difficult and which pushed the two rivals toward a renewed conflict spiral.

The Iranian Revolution and the Changing Perception of Threat

Iraq initially responded warmly to the success of the Iranian Revolution. Certainly the Ba'athist leadership was heartened by the creation of an anti-Western government in Iran and by Iran's near 180-degree turn in foreign policy, including its withdrawal from the pro-Western CENTO alliance. Iraq's attempts at normal relations, however, were not reciprocated.

From the perspective of the Iraqi leadership, the perception of a threat from revolutionary Iran grew more and more compelling. One of the central tenets of Iran's Islamic fundamentalist movement, that an "Islamic government" was the only legitimate form of government in the Islamic world, represented a basic challenge to the existing secular state system in the Middle East in general and to the stability of Iraq in particular. To Khomeini and the Iranian leadership on the other hand, Iraq's secular Ba'athist ideology represented a repudiation of Islamic principles. Throughout the region, concern grew that the government in Teheran would seek to export the revolutionary principles of Islamic fundamentalism, sowing the seeds of revolution throughout the region. Indeed, some highly placed followers of Khomeini considered the geographic expansion of the Revolution to be the regime's primary mission (Pelletiere 1992, 29). Khomeini did nothing to dispel these notions; quite the contrary. In a speech on February 11, 1979, proclaiming the success of his Revolution, he declared, "We will export our revolution to the four corners of the world because our revolution is Islamic" (Hiro 1991, 32). Like Lenin and the Bolshevik revolutionaries in 1917, Khomeini and his followers believed that the success of the Revolution at home required its expansion abroad; if Iran did not spark other fundamentalist Islamic revolutions, it would be vulnerable to its external opponents, who would band together to bring down the Iranian Revolution (Walt 1996, 215; Moin 1999, 251, 265). Iraq made a particularly good target for the spread of revolution because it had a secular government, it oppressed its own Shi'a citizens, and there were six major Shi'a shrines inside Iraq. Iran's revolutionaries saw it as their duty to support oppressed Muslims in the gulf region—like Iraq's Al Daawa organization—who might attempt to depose their corrupt and/or secular rulers (Hiro 1991, 28).

Despite the rather significant internal chaos that accompanied the construction of the new Islamic government in 1979 and 1980, the Revolution in Iran was going through a "euphoric" phase. Cooperation between the two governments became more and more difficult as the struggle for power within Iran had a direct impact on relations with Iraq (Malin 1997, 393). Emboldened by the success of the Revolution, Iranian political elites came to believe that it was a historic force capable of overcoming all obstacles. With a glorious lack of restraint, Iran's leaders launched verbal assaults on external opponents, indulging in rhetorical attacks on Baghdad with virtually no regard for their effect across the border and without thought that they might bring any adverse reaction. Indeed, they seemed to be possessed of a sense of invulnerability, denying that their words might produce any negative consequences in the real world. In reality, behaviors in Teheran and Baghdad were tightly coupled; actions taken by one side became the justification for actions by the other. Statements and actions in the foreign policy realm in Iran became part and parcel of the internal struggle for political power, as politicians of all stripes found that verbal pummeling of Iraq's secular political leadership was useful in proving their revolutionary and Islamic credentials. Even President Bani Sadr, a political moderate, proclaimed the Iraqi people would overthrow the Ba'athist government, and he rejected the Iraqi demand that Iran turn over the lands promised to Iraq in the Algiers Accords (Walt 1996, 216; Chubin and Tripp 1988, 34; Pelletiere 1992, 32). By the spring of 1980 the export of Islamic fundamentalist revolution had become an officially proclaimed government policy.

As part of this internal political process, Iranian support for Iraqi Shi'a opposition groups intensified. And this automatically increased the level of threat perceived by Iraq. Iranian actions and threats produced Iraqi counter threats and counter actions. The situation gave incentive as well as protective political cover for Saddam Hussein's repression of Iraqi Shi'a. And conversely, Iraqi rhetoric and domestic repression of its Shi'a population provided protective political cover for attacks by Iran's radical clergy on political moderates who wished to resolve issues through diplomacy.

By 1980 Iraqi leaders were coming to the conclusion that what was at stake was nothing less than the potential breakup—inspired by Iranian officials—of the Iraqi state into thirds: a northern Kurdish state, a southern Shi'a Arab state, and a rump state in the center of primarily Sunni Arabs. And this perception created the belief that actions must be taken to protect the Iraqi state from destruction. Furthermore, Saddam Hussein's own political insecurity precluded a patient and conciliatory approach to the new regime in Teheran. He could not wait until the new Iran put on a more moderate face, and he could not afford to appear weak or irresolute in the face of Iranian taunts and threats (Pelletiere 1992, 33). Iran's refusal to respond positively to Iraq's attempts at continued good relations provided evidence that the Islamic Republic was not interested in cooperation.

The Iranian Revolution and the Changing Distribution of Power

Meanwhile, the internal situation in Iran itself was chaotic. The old regime of the Pahlavi Dynasty was quickly replaced in 1979 by the government of Ayatollah Khomeini; nevertheless, there was great political unrest and instability inside Iran. The initial broad coalition of antishah forces began to disintegrate. A vicious power struggle took place as the assorted revolutionaries of the Left and the Right who had toppled the shah engaged in a power struggle among themselves. The moderate head of the provisional government, Mehdi Bazargan, was forced to share power with a Revolutionary Council dominated by radical clerics who belonged to the Islamic Republican Party (IRP). Radical clerics also dominated the Iranian Parliament (majlis). After Bazargan was forced to resign in November 1979 over the hostage crisis involving American diplomats, the power struggle played itself out primarily between the moderate president of the Islamic Republic, Abdolhassan Bani Sadr (elected in January 1980), and the radical clerical forces of the IRP. Bani Sadr, who supported the Islamic transformation but was opposed to direct clerical rule, allied himself with liberal politicians, moderate clerics, and the militant left-wing Islamic Mujahedin e Khalq.

While Iraqi leaders increasingly felt threatened by the Iranian Revolution, they also saw in this period of domestic unrest a short-term window of opportunity in which old scores could be settled. Iraqi leaders perceived a situation in which—for a limited period of time—the costs of war might be minimal and the chances of success substantial. The military balance, roughly two to one in Iran's favor (due primarily to its three-to-one manpower advantage and its American arsenal), had now shifted dramatically. Compared to Iraq's army of 242,000 men, by late 1980 Iran's army was about half of its former size—roughly 240,000 men (or less) instead of the 415,000 (or more) it had in 1979. Many units were only at half strength, as desertions were estimated to be at 60 percent. The term of enlistment was halved and training was neglected. Iran canceled orders for military goods and cut the defense budget severely. Military spending fell from about 15 percent of GNP to about 7.3 percent. Meanwhile, U.S. military support ended, creating a scarcity of spare parts for the Iranian military machine. Iran's helicopter force was mostly grounded, and only 30 percent of its tanks were operational (Chubin and Tripp 1988, 33; Pelletiere 1992, 35; Malin 1997, 399).

Khomeini and his followers were naturally suspicious of the loyalty of the military, which they tended to see as an instrument of the shah's repression; accordingly, they had unleashed a reign of terror against the military leadership. Hundreds of officers were shot or imprisoned. By some estimates, between 30 and 50 percent of officers between the ranks of major and colonel had been purged. Virtually all senior generals were dismissed or executed (Hickman 1982, 17–18; Turner 1985, 156; IISS 1981; Roberts 1996, 42–46). In the wake of the old regime, Iran created a new politically bifurcated military, with President Bani Sadr in charge of the regular army and the clerics in charge of the new Revolutionary Guards. The authority of the remaining officers was undercut by the presence of political "commissars" attached to each unit by a committee of clerics. The military appeared restive and unreliable; it fought back halfheartedly. In July 1980, Revolutionary Guards foiled a coup attempt by Iranian army units. In August, Revolutionary Guards fought once again with the army. By November 1979, the U.S. Department of Defense declared that the Iranian army was "no longer an effective military force" (Roberts 1996, 41). While threatening Iraq, Iran had simultaneously set about the destruction of its own means of defense.

Iran's economic situation had similarly deteriorated during and immediately after the Revolution. Due to strikes and political turmoil in the oil regions and the subsequent mass departure of foreign technicians, oil production plummeted to a tenth of the normal output. This caused a shortage on the world market with subsequent price increases for producing states (like Iraq), but Teheran suffered a drastic drop in government oil revenues. With its economy in a shambles, the government had been forced to finance over one half of its $40 billion national budget though deficit (Sick 1985, 92, 165–66; Levy and Froelich 1985, 137).

Meanwhile, Iraq, aided by the Soviet Union, had continued its military buildup unabated throughout the 1970s. Its military spending went from 14 percent of GNP in 1972 to 21 percent in 1980. Its military had virtually doubled in size since 1973; by 1980 it had approximately 242,000 men in its armed services—about the same as in Iran (Turner 1985, 156; Chubin and Tripp 1988, 294). Exact estimates of the military balance and of the broader balance in national capabilities vary, but it seems clear that a power transition had taken place; Iran's pre-Revolution military advantage over Iraq had disappeared and Iraq had either drawn even or had even overtaken its rival militarily. With regard to the purely military balance, one estimate is that Iraq went to war with a five-to-one advantage in military forces (Pelletiere 1992, 40). Most estimates of the military balance, however, put it at rough parity, with quantitative Iraqi superiority in tanks and Iranian superiority in combat aircraft (Brown and Snyder 1985, 120; IISS 1981; Chubin and Tripp 1988, 294–305). Examination of various broader measures of national power indicates that by 1980 the new balance was more on the order of 60 to 40 in Iran's favor. Iraq had rapidly approached parity with Iran but had not quite overtaken its rival (Geller and Singer 1998, 150; Tammen et al. 2000, 76; Parasiliti 1997, 19).

In sum, a stunning shift had taken place in the dyadic military balance and in the more general distribution of national capabilities. The Iranian Revolution had allowed Iraq to achieve a rough equality with Iran. Since enduring rivalries are quite sensitive to unstable military balances, the presence of such a dramatic shift in power was sure to have an impact on the relations between long-term rivals such as Iran and Iraq and might substantially increase the probability of war.

Historically, perceptions of an easy military victory by one side have been a major ingredient in the decision for war. By 1980 Iraqi leaders came to believe that an invasion into Iran would be short and easy. Saddam Hussein predicted that a mere two-week campaign would produce victory. This misperception can be attributed to a variety of factors: an overestimation of Iraqi abilities, faulty military intelligence, a lack of understanding of the Iranian Revolution and the nature of the enemy, and perhaps a strong dose of wishful thinking. The overly positive assessment of the chances for Iraqi military success was probably abetted by Iranian emigrés, including former Iranian president Sharpur Bakhtiar and Gen. G. A. Oveissi, who exaggerated for Saddam Hussein the reports of Iranian weakness and economic decline. Hussein was encouraged to believe that the middle class was widely opposed to the new Islamic Republic, that pro Shah supporters would aid Iraqi liberation efforts and that Kurdish and Arab minorities in Iran would welcome an invasion: Either a coup would occur or the government would collapse (Pelletiere 1992, 35).

Iraq, of course, correctly perceived a change in the nature of Iranian intentions, and it was not alone in this assessment. Other Arab states in the region felt equally threatened by Islamic fundamentalism in Iran. Shi'a Muslims made up 30 percent of Kuwait's population and 70 percent of Bahrain's population. Saudi Arabia had about 500,000 Shi'a concentrated in its eastern oil regions (Pelletiere 1992, 29). Saudi leaders believed the threat from Islamic fundamentalism to be so great that they organized a cooperative security arrangement in the Gulf area to counter the threat. In the summer and fall of 1979 Iraq began to cooperate with Saudi Arabia against the mutual threat. And in the spring of 1980 Iraq negotiated security arrangements with other Arab states as well. Finally, in August 1980, a month before the invasion, Iraq secured the backing of Saudi Arabia and Kuwait for a military operation against Iran, backing that would result in many billions of dollars in grants and loans to Iraq during the war. This expectation of foreign assistance was an important factor, perhaps even a necessary factor, in Iraq's decision to go to war (Levy and Froelich 1985, 137).

Meanwhile, not only were Iranian leaders preoccupied with the dynamics of their Revolution, but the seizure of the American embassy in Teheran in November 1979 and the ensuing hostage crisis focused what limited international attention the Iranian leaders could muster on its relations with the "Great Satan." While Iraq increased its anti-Iranian rhetoric and its punitive measures toward Shi'a inside Iraq, and while it conspicuously built up its military might (purchasing arms, recalling its draftees, strengthening its border posts), Iran took few military steps to counter the threat; indeed, it continued to decimate its own army. This lack of Iranian response to Iraqi toughness may have further encouraged Saddam Hussein and his advisers to reach for adventuristic solutions (Chubin and Tripp 1988, 34). Additionally, the seizure of the U.S. embassy and the subsequent triumph of radicals over moderates in Iran probably convinced Iraqi leaders that the threat from the Iranian Revolution would continue rather than decline (Grummon 1982, 9).

Thus the Iranian Revolution produced two important effects in Iraq: perceptions of political insecurity and perceptions of military opportunity. Iraqi leaders perceived a long-term threat that the spread of Islamic fundamentalist ideas, aided by Iranian political authorities, would ignite Shi'a revolts in Iraq, but they also perceived that the present chaos in Iran presented a unique, immediate strategic opportunity to Iraq. There was a window of opportunity that would not be open indefinitely.

The International Environment

The regional and international political balance had also shifted considerably in the wake of the Iranian Revolution—to the detriment of Iran. After American diplomats had been taken hostage in Teheran in November 1979, Iran was diplomatically isolated. In spite of their weakened global position, the Iranians turned down an offer of Soviet assistance. Having freed itself from American hegemony, Iran's leaders were understandably unwilling to subordinate themselves to a new political master, especially a country led by "godless Communists." Moreover, the Soviet invasion of Afghanistan in December 1979—undertaken to support the Communist government in Kabul in its struggle against Islamic "freedom fighters"—dramatically worsened Soviet relations with the Islamic world.

On the other hand, in 1980 Iraq was near the height of its power. Due largely to a surge in oil prices on the world market, its economy, the second largest producer of oil within OPEC, was in good shape. Personal incomes were rising and economic development programs had succeeded in modernizing agriculture, creating new industries, and building public housing for the masses.

On the international front, the door was open for Iraq to play a leading role in regional politics. Egypt, Iraq's major rival, was shunned by the Arab world for signing a separate peace with Israel at Camp David. Saddam Hussein had himself achieved some success in rallying the Arab world against the Camp David Accords by convening two Pan-Arab Conferences. Furthermore, the threat of Islamic fundamentalism to Saudi Arabia and the Persian Gulf emirates made Arab states in the gulf suddenly dependent on Iraqi military power for the protection of their vital national interests.

What Saddam Hussein lacked was a single, dynamic achievement that might serve as a symbol of his leadership. However, if Iraq could defang the threat of

Iranian fundamentalism, reverse the humiliating concessions made to Iran in the Algiers Accords, and detach Arab land (Iranian Khuzistan) from the Persians, this would surely improve his claim to Arab leadership. And since Baghdad had already been selected as the site of the 1982 Non-Aligned Conference, Saddam Hussein would, assuming a victory over Iran, be in a position not only to assume the role of the undisputed leader of the Persian Gulf region and the Arab world, but perhaps also to grasp Fidel Castro's mantle as leader of the nonaligned movement (al-Khalil 1990, 270–76). The "politics of international prestige" was almost certainly a major consideration in the mind of the Iraqi leader.

Individual Psychological Factors and Perceptions

The ideological premises and worldviews of the leaders in Teheran and Baghdad and their perceptions of the immediate situations they faced in 1979 and 1980 also made it difficult for the two states to cooperate (Malin 1997, 395–96). Because Iraq initiated the war and because the primary decisions for war were made by its leader, and because the literature on Iranian leaders is fairly sparse, our discussion of the impact of psychological factors in this case will focus mainly on the perceptions, personality, and worldview of Iraqi President Saddam Hussein.

The conflict escalated significantly after the Revolution in Iran brought Khomeini to power in February 1979 and after Vice President Saddam Hussein ousted his colleague and mentor, President Ahmad Hassan al Bakr, in July of the same year. Though Saddam Hussein was slated to become president later in the year, there was apparently considerable backroom maneuvering by his opponents to prevent his elevation. Hussein preempted their moves by inducing Bakr to step down early. Announcing the discovery of a plot against himself, he then initiated a purge of political opponents, ending in the execution of many of his rivals in the senior ranks of the party and government (Pelletiere 1992, 28). From this point onward, political power in Iraq was even more greatly concentrated in the hands of Saddam Hussein and a very narrow circle of insiders (Chubin and Tripp 1988, 17). At the top of the political establishment in Baghdad sat one of the most ruthless leaders of modern times.

The decision by Saddam Hussein and his advisers to attack Iran was based on a number of crucial misunderstandings or miscalculations derived from faulty perceptions. The Iraqi leadership overestimated its own capabilities and it underestimated both the military capabilities and the resolve of its opponent. Specifically, Iraqi leaders believed:

1. Islamic fundamentalism would spread to the Shi'a in Iraq and this would undermine the regime's authority. (In fact, the Shi'a stayed loyal to Iraq during the war.)
2. Sunni Arabs in Khuzistan would rise up against the Islamic Republic if Iraqi forces entered Iran. (They did not.)
3. The general discord in Iran and the ayatollah's presumed lack of popularity would deprive the Iranian government of the unity needed to prosecute a war against Iraq. An Iraqi invasion might even precipitate an overthrow of the Khomeini regime. (It did not.)

4. Iraqi military superiority would lead to a relatively easy victory. (It did not.)

It is easier to outline these misperceptions than to explain why they might have occurred. A closer look at Saddam Hussein's psychological makeup and his worldview might shed some light on this question, however.

Saddam's character derives from a particular blend of cultural and psychological attributes. Saddam Hussein, whose name means "the fighter who stands steadfast," was born in 1937 to a peasant family near Tikrit in central Iraq. His father died before he was born, and in accordance with the custom of the region, his mother married his paternal uncle, a man who was reportedly abusive to Saddam. At the age of ten, when his wishes for further education were denied by his family, Saddam left home and subsequently took up residence with his maternal uncle, Kairallah Talfa, in Tikrit. Kairallah became not only his father figure but also his political mentor as well. Kairallah, who was a cousin of the future president, Ahmad Hassan al Bakr, had been jailed by the authorities for his nationalist, anti-British activities. He impressed young Saddam with his nationalism, his hatred of foreign powers, and his tales of glory (Post 1990, 386–87).

Saddam grew up in a culture of violence and established himself early as a political leader who would not hesitate to do "whatever it took." Having joined the Ba'athist Party at age twenty, at age twenty-two he was selected to lead a team to assassinate Iraq's leader, Gen. Abdul Karim Qassem, in October 1959. The mission failed, and Saddam fled to Syria and then Egypt.

While Western psychologists have never had the opportunity to subject the Iraqi leader to personal interviews, nevertheless his background and his personality have been scrutinized from afar. Saddam has been described by psychologists in the United States as possessing a narcissistic personality; in fact, one psychologist terms him a "malignant narcissist" (Post 1990, 384–401). Hussein's malignant narcissism is made up of a group of closely related personality traits.

Saddam was an extremely ambitious man with an exalted self-image. He had "messianic" dreams of glory and identified himself with the Babylonian king Nebuchadnezzar, who conquered Jerusalem in 586 BC, and with Saladin, who defeated the Crusaders in 1187. He saw himself as a great world leader like Gamal Abdul Nasser (his personal hero), Mao Tse-tung, Ho Chi Minh, Tito, and Fidel Castro (Post 1990, 387, 395). He believed that his role was to unite the Arab world—a role consistent with the Ba'athist Party's emphasis on the concept of pan-Arabism—but his grandiosity led him to overestimate his own strength. His enormous vanity and pride also led him to construct a cult of the personality. His personal glorification was government policy: Pictures and statues of President Hussein dotted the landscape of Iraq.

As one would suspect of a narcissist, Hussein was sensitive to personal slights, equated criticism with disloyalty, and possessed a strong paranoid orientation. A basic axiom of Saddam's was "he who is not totally with me is my enemy" (Post 1990, 390). He tended to perceive conspiracies against himself and Iraq, and behind these conspiracies he was likely to see the hands of foreign enemies, such as the U.S., Israel, or Iran. He used these perceived threats to justify his aggression toward others. He saw himself surrounded by enemies but was generally unable to understand his own role in creating these enemies.

Saddam's personality suggests a strong trait of dominance, associated with the belief that "he could cow and repress his foes into submission" (Chubin and Tripp 1988, 7). His psychological compulsion to dominate others in personal relations was transferred to the international arena. He tended to treat countries in much the same way he treated individuals: He tried to dominate them. Saddam was a power seeker who displaced his own personal, psychological need for power onto the domestic and international arena and rationalized it as being in the public good (Post 1993, 50). His drive for power was virtually unlimited; he was relatively unrestricted by pangs of conscience, by the suffering of others, or by past loyalties. Saddam sought power, but he also sought glory, reputation, and prestige.

Unconstrained aggression was an important facet of this personality constellation. Saddam was ruthless in the acquisition and maintenance of his own power. For instance, he was a key figure in mounting the successful 1968 coup that brought the Ba'athists to power in Iraq but crucial to that success was the assistance of the government's chief of military intelligence, Abdul Razzaz al Nayef. Hussein repaid Nayef's loyalty by ordering his capture, exile, and eventual assassination (Post 1990, 388). The classic story of Saddam's ruthlessness and his paranoia takes place during the early stages of the Iran-Iraq War. In 1982, after Iran had begun its counteroffensive and Iraq was looking for a way out of the war, Khomeini's terms included, as a precondition for a settlement, that Saddam first step down as leader. At a meeting of his cabinet, Saddam asked his ministers to speak freely and offer advice on Khomeini's conditions. The minister of health unwisely took the bait and suggested Saddam step down. Hussein thanked him for his candid advice. The man was quickly arrested and his body sent to his wife in a black bag, chopped to bits. With such a demonstration of the consequences of unwanted advice, it is no wonder that Saddam was unlikely to have the benefit of judicious counsel from his advisers. His purges of disloyal advisers left him surrounded by toadies and sycophants whose inability to critically assess his policies and plans contributed to the potential for miscalculation (see Renshon 1993a, 89 on this).

Some have explained Hussein's uncontrolled aggression as "narcissistic rage," which consisted of extremely violent reactions to "narcissistic injuries"— challenges or events that blocked his narcissistic striving or called into question his self-image (Renshon 1993b, 344). Such rage, often triggered by conspicuous defeats, developed alongside a compulsion to right a wrong, to undo a hurt, and to perform acts of revenge. In a fit of such rage, the narcissist shows complete disregard for any rational limitations in his attempt to obtain revenge. In sum, the sensitivity to slights, the tendencies toward dominance and aggression, and the vast psychological energy devoted to ego defense meant that the more threatened Hussein was, the more threatening he became in return.

While these traits do not describe someone with a pleasant personality, Saddam Hussein did not suffer from a psychotic disorder. He was not irrational, though he was dangerous in the extreme (Post 1993, 49). He was capable of seeing the difference between fantasy and reality, he was rational rather than impulsive, and he was capable of acting with deliberation and even patience (Post 1990, 392). However, in Post's analysis, "while he is psychologically in touch with reality, he is often politically out of touch with reality. Saddam's world is narrow and distorted, and he has scant experience out of the Arab world. . . . Moreover, he is surrounded by sycophants, who are cowed by Saddam's well founded reputation for brutality and are afraid to contradict him" (Post 1990, 392).

While Western analysts agree on Saddam's character and personality, there is some disagreement on the derivation of his "malignant narcissism." One analyst has suggested that his drive for power and his messianic dreams of glory were created by underlying self-doubts and subconscious feelings of insecurity that were derived from his difficult early childhood (Post 1990, 394). Power, therefore, acted as a compensatory device for Saddam. Others have suggested that Saddam's drive for power and his use of aggression to achieve and maintain power were merely the result of reinforcement. Rather than being deprived as a child, Saddam may have been indulged—in his dreams of glory and in his aggression. And he may simply have learned as an adult—in the milieu of Iraqi politics where there were few legal or political restraints on the use of force—that violence was an effective method of attaining and keeping power (Winter 1993, 108–13; Renshon 1993b, 343). In any case, deprivation or positive reinforcement, the result is the same: a sense that he was entitled to take what he wanted (Renshon 1993b, 343).

Finally, we must note that many of the traits cited above are common to a number of leaders in the region (e.g., Nasser, Assad, and others). What Western analysts see as unusual, Arab observers might see as commonplace. In the Middle East, as elsewhere, personality traits are almost always the result of the interplay between culture and individual psychology.

Saddam Hussein's perceptions of the situation in 1980 are crucial, and these perceptions were certainly affected by his worldview and his personality. Given his paranoia and obsession with power and security, given his perceived loss of face regarding the earlier Algiers Accords and his need to "even the score," and given his predilection for resolving problems with violence, it is quite possible that he perceived a deadly threat to his power from Iranian-backed Shi'a in Iraq that necessitated a preventive war (al-Khalil 1990, 272; Chubin and Tripp 1988, 20). It is likely that he perceived himself to be locked in a life and death struggle with Khomeini over the issue of Iraqi Shi'a and simultaneously in a position to attain certain of his messianic dreams of regional and global leadership, if he could pull off a victory over Iran. While the benefits of a victorious war were potentially great, the costs of failure in a war with Iran were equally great, especially for Hussein himself. Under such circumstances leaders frequently engage in wishful thinking as a subconscious way of avoiding potential problems. Saddam Hussein's overestimation of Iraqi capabilities and his underestimation of Iran's capabilities to respond to an attack certainly look from the outside to exhibit elements of wishful thinking.

Across the border, Saddam Hussein was faced with an adversary with an equally strong personality. Ayatollah Ruhollah Khomeini has been described by his biographer as possessing a number of somewhat contradictory traits. He was autocratic in style, intolerant, austere, introverted, self-righteous, decisive, and combative. At times he was capable of incredible invective against his perceived enemies, with a seeming loss of control. On the other hand, he could be politically quite sensitive to the needs and views of others, he was capable of monumentally pragmatic behavior, and he was a calculating populist politician whose every move was carefully planned (Moin 1999, 37, 44, 63–64, 219, 226–27, 258, 295).

Khomeini believed that the great powers were innately hostile and aggressive; he divided the world into oppressors (the two superpowers, their allies, and puppets) and the oppressed. In his eyes the Iraqi government oppressed the Shi'a faithful in Iraq. He had assimilated the traditional Shi'a version of history as an oppressed community, historically wronged; in such a situation, it was the duty of the faithful to seek revenge, since only through revenge could injustices be put right (Moin 1999, 17). (Khomeini's own father had been killed when Ruhollah was about six months old, and his family assiduously lobbied the shah for justice.) As a religious authority, Khomeini had come to the radical theological conclusion that he had attained the status of one "who acts as a vessel through which the divine outpourings reach man" (Moin 1999, 296–97; 48–51). He believed in the use of force and violence in carrying out God's commands, and he saw his own anger as the anger of God (Moin 1999, 266, 273, 295). He tended to see the world as a struggle between truth and falsehood and therefore saw the world in blacks and whites, without shades of gray. This Manichaean worldview precluded compromise and had a significant effect on Iranian foreign policy. Khomeini regarded Saddam as an infidel and frequently compared the war with Iraq to the Prophet Mohammed's war against infidels (Moin 1999, 17, 236; Walt 1996, 213–14).

Additionally, Khomeini may have harbored a personal grudge against Hussein. The ayatollah was exiled by Iran's shah to Iraq in 1965, over a decade prior to the Revolution. He proved too troublesome in nearby Iraq, and in 1978 the shah prevailed upon Saddam Hussein to adhere to the principles of the Algiers Accords. Khomeini was expelled from Iraq and forced to seek refuge in Paris. Apparently, the Ayatollah never forgave Saddam Hussein for this. Thus the conflict spiral between the rival states was influenced by the personalities, beliefs, and perceptions of the leaders in the two states.

The two leaders were alike in many ways. Both believed absolutely in themselves, as well as their political doctrines. Both tended to view virtually any action by their opponents as evidence of malign intent. Both were strong-willed, intransigent men who could not be intimidated. Although both were rational and capable of retreat, they both found it difficult to back down in the face of threats. Neither was likely to respond productively to bullying by the other, especially since they each perceived the other to be domestically unpopular and easily deposed (Hiro 1991, 37; Walt 1996, 254; Chubin and Tripp 1988, 9). Furthermore, to back down would have created negative domestic consequences for both leaders.

Ultimately, however, we must admit that the personalities of the two men had a limited impact on the outbreak of the war. Any Iraqi leader, regardless of his personality or worldview, would probably have responded to Iranian provocations (and Iranian weakness) in much the same way. The threat of a Shi'a uprising in Iraq was a real one, though by the late summer of 1980 the internal crackdown on Shi'a dissidents had made it a fairly remote one. Nevertheless, the threats were real, the grievances were real, and the conflicts of interest were real. But these were also disputes that might have been settled by different leaders through dialogue and negotiation. The psychological make-ups of Hussein and Khomeini help to some degree to explain why violence was chosen instead.

Political Culture and Domestic Political Structure

The propensity of the political elite to rely on the use of force to settle domestic as well as international disputes was well established in the political culture of the Iraqi leadership. Indeed, there appeared to be an "excessive faith" in the efficacy of such methods (Pelletiere 1992, 23–24; Chubin and Tripp 1988, 7). Further, the autocratic nature of the Iraqi regime and the relative absence of norms associated with nonviolent conflict resolution placed little inhibition on the political elite to use caution. Saddam Hussein himself is a product of the conspiratorial and persecuted Ba'athist underground of the late 1950s, a milieu in which ruthless methods were commonplace. Once in power the Ba'athists tended to see domestic opposition as counterrevolutionary threats. Moreover, domestic opposition was likely to be seen as linked to perceived subversive interventions by the U.S., Iran, and Israel in the internal affairs of Iraq that justified the use of force against the regime's opponents (Chubin and Tripp 1988, 16).

Cultural factors interacted with internal political structures in both countries. The development of democratic institutions was inhibited by cultural norms in each state. The lack of democratic institutions that might limit the power of executive branch leaders in foreign affairs and convert public pressure into government policy probably played a role in the radicalization of policies in both Teheran and Baghdad (Malin 1997, 395). In Iraq, the lack of democratic machinery meant, at a minimum, that the Iraqi decision for war was probably not fully analyzed or debated—leading to the possibility of miscalculation (Malin 1997, 397–98). In addition, the fact that Saddam Hussein insisted on surrounding himself with "yes men" meant that he did not receive the full range of information and advice required for optimal decision making. In Iran the presence of a transitional government in which control over foreign policy was both poorly institutionalized and somewhat decentralized meant that foreign policy became the object of dispute between the various factions. Correspondingly, foreign policy became politicized. In the revolutionary political atmosphere of Teheran, reversing the conflict spiral with Iraq became difficult because moderate and pragmatic politicians who wished to pursue policies of compromise, accommodation and diplomacy could be successfully attacked by their domestic opponents as being counterrevolutionary, un-Islamic, and soft on Iran's enemies (Walt 1996, 258–59).

As John Vasquez (1993, 198–224) points out in his steps-to-war theory, war between rival states is likely only if hardliners are in power in at least one of the state. If hardliners are in power in both states, the likelihood that conflicts will escalate to violence is extremely high. In both Iran and Iraq, hardliners rather than accommodationists were in power.

Dyadic Interaction: Conflict Spirals

There was no single incident, no catalyst, like the sinking of the *Maine* in 1898 or the assassination of Archduke Franz Ferdinand in 1914, that triggered the Iraqi decision to go to war against Iran. Instead, a series of interactions between the two states continually ratcheted up the degree of conflict between them, perversely affecting the domestic political situations in each country (see Pelletiere 1992, 33). We have already seen that a six-year conflict spiral was triggered in 1969 by Iran's renunciation of the 1937 Frontier Treaty. This spiral was terminated just short of war by the Algiers Accords. However, with the advent of the Iranian Revolution, another spiral soon began.

In conflict spirals, the prevailing dynamic is that conflictual actions by one side increase the perception of threat and hostility in the other, which lead to responses that are equally conflictual or even more conflictual. These reciprocal hostilities are further propelled by blowback onto domestic politics in both states; hostile acts by the rival state create domestic political support for even tougher measures and decrease the political influence of accommodationists who seek to defuse the crisis. At some point neither side may be capable, politically, of avoiding war.

Conflictual interactions between Iran and Iraq centering on the Shi'a opposition in Iraq began to spiral out of control beginning in 1979. Shi'a riots had become a major challenge to the Ba'athist government in 1977—even before the Iranian Revolution. As vice president, Saddam Hussein had countered Shi'a political activity with a two-pronged approach. On the one hand, there was a severe crackdown against members of al Daawa and other dissident Shi'a leaders; on the other hand, development assistance and other economic enticements were offered to the Shi'a masses. When Khomeini took power in Iran in 1979, a leading Iraqi Shi'a religious authority, Ayatollah Mohammed Bakr al Sadr of Najaf, warmly welcomed the event and warned that now that Iran's Shah had been toppled, other tyrants might be dealt with as well—a thinly veiled reference to Saddam Hussein. He was later to issue a religious edict that, because of state repression of Shi'a, the Iraqi regime was un-Islamic and that dealings with it were forbidden (Hiro 1991, 35). Sadr was a theorist of militant Islam, a reputed leader of al Daawa, and a man with close ties to Ayatollah Khomeini. In fact, Khomeini named Sadr to be the head of the "Supreme Council of the Islamic Revolution of Iraq"—an honor certainly not meant to endear him to Saddam Hussein. In June 1979, just as he was setting off to visit Khomeini in Iran, Ayatollah Sadr was seized and placed under house arrest, triggering another wave of Shi'a riots in Najaf and Karbala. More arrests and bloodshed followed. Saddam Hussein ordered the destruction of Khomeini's former residence in Iraq and the deportation of his representatives. At the very least, the events of the spring and summer of 1979 encouraged the perception that Shi'a unrest was largely due to subversive meddling by the new revolutionary government in Teheran (Chubin and Tripp 1988, 26).

Despite sincere efforts by Iraq and the Bazargan government in Iran to resolve their differences, by the fall of 1979 Shi'ite unrest throughout the upper Persian Gulf region led to another round of threats and demands. Iraq ended diplomatic relations with Iran following repeated attacks by Iranian Revolutionary Guards on Iraq's embassy in Teheran and on its various consulates.

The Khomeini government retaliated with an ideological offensive. It began providing material as well as rhetorical support for the Shi'a underground in Iraq in the fall of 1979. Radio broadcasts from Teheran and Ahwaz beamed propaganda into Iraq. In September, Ayatollah Rhouhani called for the annexation of Bahrain (where Shi'a constituted a majority) and the export of revolution throughout the Persian Gulf. In newspaper interviews, speeches, and official pronouncements Khomeini loudly condemned those rulers in the Islamic world who placed nationalism, Arab or state, above Islam. The unnamed target of this rhetorical attack was, of course, Saddam Hussein, one the leaders most associated with Arab nationalism.

Saddam countered by trying to manipulate his public relations image. He made appearances at shrines and within the Shi'a areas of Iraq, and he made use of Islamic history and Islamic symbols in his public appearances so that people would see him as a pious and practicing Muslim. But the repression also continued. In March 1980 nearly a hundred opposition figures were executed by the regime; half were members of al Daawa. Membership in that organization was now made retroactively punishable by death.

Al Daawa responded to this latest round of repression with subversive violence: assassinations and assaults on police and army stations and on party officials. Most prominently, it attempted to assassinate Information Minister (later Vice Premier) Tariq Aziz on April 1, 1980. Aziz survived, though several students were killed in the attempt. A roundup of Shi'a militants produced a confession from one man—described as "an Iraqi of Iranian origin"—who claimed to have been ordered to assassinate the vice premier by Ayatollah Khomeini himself at a meeting in Khomeini's home town of Qom in Iran (Chubin and Tripp 1988, 26; Pelletiere 1992, 31). Incredibly, the funeral procession for the victims of the assassination was itself attacked with another grenade just as it passed an Iranian school in Baghdad, resulting in another death. These two events heightened the regime's anger at Iran, which it believed was associated with the assassination plot. Seeking to root out the Shi'a underground, Saddam ordered bombings of Iranian border towns, expelled both Iranian residents of Iraq and Iraqi citizens of Iranian descent and ordered the execution of certain Shi'a leaders who had supported the Iranian Revolution. Thousands of Shi'a were arrested in Najaf, Karbala, and in the largest Shi'a township in Baghdad. A campaign was initiated to deport any Iraqi who had even the slimmest connection with Iran—by birth, marriage, or name (Chubin and Tripp 1988, 27). Finally, to add to his pan-Arab credentials, Saddam Hussein also demanded that Iran vacate the three islands in the gulf that had been taken a decade earlier and return them to their Arab owners.

The spiral of hostility continued upward. Hussein ordered that Ayatollah Sadr be executed along with his sister, and this was carried out secretly on April 8—a week after the attempted assassination of Tariq Aziz. When the execution became public knowledge about a week later, Khomeini responded with another verbal broadside, accusing the Iraqi regime of starting a war against Islam. He called on the Iraqi army and the Iraqi people to rise up and overthrow Saddam. More concretely, the Iranian government began training Iraqi Shi'a guerrilla fighters, while continuing its assistance to Iraqi Kurds. Iraq responded by an act of punitive reciprocity—increasing its aid to Iranian Kurds and to Arabs in Iranian Khuzistan. It also stepped up expulsion of Shi'a "fifth columnists," expelling perhaps sixteen thousand Iraqis of Iranian origin (Hiro 1991, 35). Border skirmishes became more numerous and more deadly in the summer of 1980. The level of hostile rhetoric increased as well, with Saddam Hussein threatening to "cut off the hand" of anyone trying to interfere in Iraq. He warned, "Iraq is prepared to enter into any kind of battle to defend its honor and sovereignty" (Chubin and Tripp 1988, 27). It was around this time—sometime in the spring of 1980—that Saddam Hussein may have begun to formulate plans for war against Iran (Chubin and Tripp 1988, 27; Grummon 1982, 16). The primary motivation for war was Iran's continued incitement of Iraqi Shi'a against the government in Baghdad (Dawisha 1980, 146).

Internal politics in each country worked to ratchet upward the hostility in the foreign policies of Iran and Iraq. In Iran, according to one scholar (Malin 1997, 396), "The aggressive foreign policy rhetoric, which mixed Iranian nationalism with a universalistic imperative to 'export' the Islamic revolution, served to marginalize critics on the left and kept the popular classes mobilized by directing their energies outward." Moreover, Iraqi meddling with Iran's Kurdish and Arab minorities provided an excuse for religious ideologues to take control of Iranian foreign policy by blaming Iraq for Iran's internal strife. The revolutionary government of Iran, perceiving its own internal political vulnerability, found a perfect scapegoat in the secular, Sunni government in Baghdad. A "tough" Iranian foreign policy toward Iraq became an important litmus test in the internal struggle for power. And Muslim clerics in Iran used the issue as a tool in their successful attempt to oust moderate leaders like Bazargan (Malin 1997, 396–97).

Baghdad's Sunni leaders also perceived themselves to be politically vulnerable, especially when it came to Iraqi Shi'a who sympathized with the Iranian Revolution. Just as Iraq's use of internal repression against its domestic Shi'a opponents reverberated across the border in Teheran, Baghdad found its own scapegoat in the revolutionary Shi'a regime in Iran in order to rally greater public support. Because each country could blame its internal political problems on foreign plotters, dual elite vulnerabilities led to dual scapegoating.

While Iraqi leaders probably initially hoped that the United States and pro-Shah forces within Iran would topple Khomeini, the failure of two attempted coups mounted by pro-Shah military officers in late May and early July 1980 (backed by Iraq) sent the message that if the revolutionary regime in Iran were to be toppled, Iraq would have to play a direct role (Hiro 1991, 36). No internal forces capable of that task remained. With this in mind, in August, Iraq apparently won the backing of Saudi Arabia and Kuwait for a military operation against Iran. The end game was now near.

All-out war, when it came, did not emerge out of the peaceful blue autumn skies. Low-level warfare had broken out long before the "real" war. Iran claimed to have been the target of an astounding 434 military attacks and 363 airspace violations by Iraq in the eighteen months before the war; Iraq claimed itself to be the victim of 544 Iranian violations of its land and airspace (Swearingen 1988, 406). During the month of August, Iraq had positioned approximately three hundred tanks in the long-disputed central border area opposite Qasr-e Shirin, and by the end of that month heavy shelling by the Iraqis apparently forced the evacuation of civilians around Qasr-e Shirin and Naft-e Shah. On September 2, 1980, there were clashes between Iranian and Iraqi military forces along the border. On the fourth Iran shelled two Iraqi towns and its air force bombed inside Iraqi territory. This was followed by two notes sent by Iraq to the head of the Iranian embassy in Baghdad. The notes demanded renegotiation of the 1975 Algiers agreement, an end to Iranian-sponsored border violence, and the evacuation of the two territories in Kermanshah province promised to Iraq in the Algiers Accords, along with an ultimatum that Iraq would seize these lands if they were not immediately returned. Iran responded with artillery fire. On the seventh and tenth Iraq took the long-disputed strategic heights of Zain al Qaws and Saif Saad. On the twelfth and thirteenth it took five more border posts. All of these military actions were apparently routs by the Iraqis (Grummon 1982, 13).

Hence by September 10 Saddam Hussein had successfully taken those strips of land that had up to this point been the main territorial bones of contention between the two states. Nevertheless, on the seventeenth Saddam Hussein accused Iran of violating the Algiers Accords, charging that Iran was guilty of some 187 border violations in the previous four months. Consequently, he declared the treaty to be abrogated, demanding the Iranian ships now use Iraqi pilots in the Shatt and fly the Iraqi flag. Additionally, Iraq charged that the region of Ahwaz ("Arabistan") had been wrongfully ceded to Iran in the 1847 Treaty of Erzerum, since its inhabitants were mostly Arab. Last, Iraq demanded that Iran return to their owners the three islands taken in the Gulf of Hormuz by the shah a decade earlier.

Saddam Hussein's motivation is impossible to ascertain for certain. It is quite possible that he initiated a **brinkmanship crisis**, using the techniques of coercive diplomacy against Iran, believing that Iran could be forced into backing down and acceding to Iraqi demands, and if it did not, Iraq would be able to defeat its rival in a short, limited war fought for limited goals. Indeed, Saddam said on several occasions that he did not desire war. He presumed that Khomeini would recognize the relative weakness of his position and, as Iraq had done in 1975, would make concessions to his stronger neighbor. Saddam's strategy was in some ways a mirror image of the 1975 situation, when Iraq itself had been compelled by superior force to make concessions in order to prevent a wider war. Saddam had drawn certain lessons about the consequences of being on the wrong side of a power imbalance from his previous crises with Iran and he may have presumed that the Iranians had drawn the same lessons (Chubin and Tripp 1988, 23, 29). The demands in the Iraqi ultimatum, like the Austrian ultimatum to Serbia in 1914, pushed the opponent to the limit of what was politically feasible and were perhaps even designed to be rejected. Iran, true to form, refused to consider them. Heavy fighting broke out along the Shatt, and on the twentieth Iran called up its reserves.

Finally, on September 22, Iraq launched a frontal attack on Iran spearheaded by an attempt by the Iraqi air force to destroy Iran's air capabilities through bombing of ten Iranian airfields. Ten divisions in all were sent forward, with five armored divisions crossing the border and striking against military and economic targets in Iran. Iran was only able to respond with parts of two divisions of its own (Chubin and Tripp 1988, 36). Iraq seized Iranian territories in the central region and along the Shatt. However, the all-important air attack utterly failed to destroy Iran's capabilities.

Iraq's initial goals in the war appeared to be limited (Pelletiere 1992, 34). Officially they were Iranian recognition of Iraq's sovereignty over land and waters (the Shatt), Iranian restraint from interfering in Iraq's internal affairs, Iranian adherence to principles of good neighborly relations, and Iran's return of the islands in the Persian Gulf to the United Arab Emirates. The strategy for the achievement of these goals was an Israeli-type blitzkrieg attack on Iran's Khuzistan province to be completed in less than two weeks; an all-out invasion of Iran was never contemplated (al-Khalil 1990, 259; Wright 1980, 282–87). Khuzistan held several advantages. Since the province contained nearly all of Iran's oil, the seizure of the major oil areas around Khorramshahr and Abadan would deny crucial revenues to Iran. Moreover, since it bordered the Shatt, control of the province would solidify Iraq's ability to detach the Shatt from Iran. Alternatively, possession of Khuzistan might provide a useful bargaining chip that could be offered back to Iran in return for Iraqi sovereignty over the Shatt (Swearingen 1988, 414–15). Finally, as 80 percent of the province's population was made up of ethnic Arabs, many Iraqis probably believed (inaccurately as it turned out) that the local population might support their "liberation" from Iran.

The war was perceived to be short and inexpensive (Malin 1997, 395). If Iraq was lucky, the war might provide the knockout blow to the Khomeini regime, ending the threat to Iraq. At worst, the invasion would give Iraq useful bargaining chips in negotiating its demands.

SUMMARY

The stage for war between Iran and Iraq was set by a number of important long-term background conditions. The two states were enduring rivals who tended to see each other as opponents and who had engaged in numerous conflicts in the two decades prior to 1980, narrowly averting full-scale war in 1975. The dyadic conflict was impelled by territorial disputes that were considered unresolved by Iraq, ethnic and religious differences, and foreign allegiances along the Cold War divide. The most important proximate cause of the war, however, was the Iranian Revolution. Khomeini's victory and the establishment of an Islamic Republic in Iran based on theocratic principles, and Iran's words and deeds on behalf of its Revolution, created perceptions of threat and fears on the part of others. Khomeini's commitment to spread Islamic revolution, along with the use of foreign policy as a tool of internal politics, meant that subversive Iranian support for Iraqi Shi'a and Iraqi Kurds would increase.

Iraqi leaders, perceiving their regime to be vulnerable to Kurdish and Shi'a revolts instigated by Iran, retaliated in kind. A conflict spiral of words and deeds ensued, with the two countries trading diplomatic denunciations, propaganda efforts, acts of sabotage and subversion, incitements to revolt among the other side's disaffected populations, and small-scale military attacks that escalated to full-scale warfare. In each country internal problems could be blamed on the other. The Iranian Revolution not only changed the perception of threats in the region but also changed the distribution of power. Internal unrest in Iran, along with the decimation of traditional military forces and the questionable loyalty of the remnants, created a power transition and opened a window of opportunity in which Iraq could seriously contemplate war against its larger rival. Iraq's decision to use force against Iran was made more likely by prevailing regional and international conditions that isolated Iran and induced Saudi Arabia and Kuwait to guarantee support to Iraq in its use of force against Iran. Finally, the probability that war would result from the conflict spiral was undoubtedly accelerated by the personalities of the two protagonists and the misperceptions of the attackers.

AFTERMATH

Six days after the attack began, the UN Security Council urged an end to hostilities and Iraq announced its readiness to accept a cease-fire if Iran accepted its rights over the Shatt. Teheran rejected the UN cease-fire request and Hussein offered one of his own, also rejected by Iran—setting the tone for the next eight years. Unable to stop what he had started by achieving gains with minimal costs and unable to get Teheran to accept "the logic of force," Hussein continued the assault, taking Khorramshahr on November 10 and placing other cities in the Khuzistan area—Abadan and Dezful—under siege.

By September 1981 the Iraqi initiative was over and the Iranians had regained Abadan; in March 1982 they regained the Dezful area. This prompted a statement by Saddam in April 1982 that he would be willing to withdraw if Iran assured Iraq that this would end the fighting. The Iranians once again refused to stop fighting. On April 29, 1982, Iran launched a major counteroffensive in the southern sector that culminated in the retaking of Khorramshahr. By the end of May Iraqi forces had been pushed back to the original boundary with Iran and the tide of battle had changed.

The Israeli invasion of Lebanon in June 1982 prompted an appeal to Iran and Iraq by Islamic countries to end the war so that the Muslim world could unify against Israel. Iran refused. For the next six years Iraq would be fighting defensively to prevent Iran from occupying Iraqi territory; simultaneously, Iraq would attempt to inflict enough military and economic pain on Iran to influence the government in Teheran to agree to end the fighting.

Iraq was aided in its efforts by copious loans from the Arab world—Kuwait and Saudi Arabia in particular. It was also assisted by the Soviet Union, which by the mid-1980s firmly supported Saddam Hussein's attempt to beat back the threat posed by Iranian Islamic fundamentalism. By some estimates, $7 billion in aid was transferred from Moscow to Baghdad between 1986 and 1988. For its part, the United States granted $2 billion in commodity credits and shared crucial intelligence information with the Iraqi regime (Bill and Springborg 1993, 294–95).

The war had become a defensive war of survival for Iraq, now placed in the position of trying to thwart continual Iranian thrusts up and down the front. The short-term advantages that Iraq had in 1980 were offset by Iran's long-term trump card—its tremendous numerical superiority in human beings capable of being mobilized for war. Not only were a series of land fortifications constructed to defend against the Iranians—who had begun using human wave assaults—but by 1984 Iraq also began to use chemical weapons against the Iranian onslaughts. Complementary to the army's defense of the land was the increased use of air power against Iranian infrastructure to increase the costs of war and to compel a

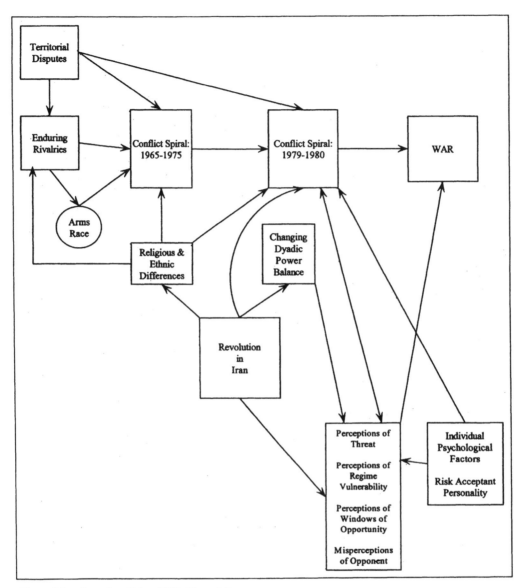

Chart 6.1.   Iran-Iraq War 1980: Causal Factors

settlement. In 1984 Iraq escalated its air attacks on Iran's cities and economic infrastructure. Iran responded by shelling Basra. The air attacks against cities were temporarily ended by a UN-mediated agreement not to attack civilian populations. This agreement failed to hold, and at times of particular military stress throughout the war, Iraq resorted to air attacks on Iranian population centers and economic targets, which led to subsequent Iranian retaliation in kind. In addition to oil installations, power generators, industrial plants, communication centers, and hydroelectric dams, some targets were chosen for their symbolic value to the clerical leadership in Iran—Qom, Isfahan, and Teheran itself. Iranian ships and ships carrying Iranian oil were also targeted, in order to further damage the Iranian economy but also to pressure the international community to use its influence to bring the war to an end.

The final years of the war saw continued Iranian offensive efforts against Iraqi territory (against Basra and the southern marshes and the Fao Peninsula, against the central sector, and in Iraqi Kurdistan, where Iranian forces were in league with dissident Iraqi Kurds), a continuation of the tanker war on both sides, and Iraqi air attacks against economic targets in Iran (such as the oil facilities at Kharg Island). Finally, in July 1987 the UN Security Council unanimously passed Resolution 598 calling for a cease-fire and the withdrawal of forces. Iraq accepted the resolution on condition that Iran also agree. Iran refused. Hussein then announced his own five-point peace plan. By now both sides were militarily and economically exhausted by the war. Finally, Khomeini reluctantly accepted the UN Resolution 598 in July 1980, a year after it was passed by the Security Council. The cease-fire went into effect on August 20, at which point Hussein turned his military's attention to the rebellious Kurds in the north, putting down the rebellion with poison gas.

Once the cease-fire was in effect, Iran and Iraq commenced talks in Geneva to negotiate a postwar settlement. The discussions were stalled almost immediately. Two years later, after Iraq's attack on Kuwait in August 1990 and the subsequent construction of an international coalition against Iraq, Hussein hastily concluded a postwar agreement with Iran to prevent Iran from joining with the international coalition in its military actions against Iraq. The price? Every issue was settled on Iranian terms: the *thalweg* as the international boundary for the Shatt, the determination of the land boundaries, and the control of territory in the central region. Thus by 1990 the scorecard had been finalized. For its invasion of Iran in 1980, Iraq had fought a bloody eight-year war and had gained absolutely nothing.

7

The Iraq War

In time, history provides fitting names for wars. The names are usually derived from certain unique features or characteristics of the conflict that provide meaning and context and even a certain amount of color—the War of Jenkins' Ear, the Soccer War, the War of the Austrian Succession, the Napoleonic Wars. Sometimes, names change with the passage of time: Who knew in 1918 that there would be another world war three decades later? The First World War was simply called the Great War. At present, the 2003 U.S. war against Iraq is usually referred to as the Iraq War. In years to come, however, it is possible that the war may acquire another, more suggestive title. Plentiful candidates exist.

What salient features of the conflict might spur future commentators to devise an appropriate name for the Iraq War? Many argue that, in retrospect, it was a war of choice, an optional rather than a necessary war. Perhaps future history books will refer to it as America's Optional War. Though President Bush was at one point forced to admit that Saddam Hussein's government had not been directly linked to the bombing of the World Trade Centers and the Pentagon on September 11, 2001, the war was certainly proclaimed to be part of the global war on terrorism. Perhaps it should be called the Second American War against Terror—the war in Afghanistan being the first. The invasion of Iraq was also justified by the Bush administration as a preemptive war against an immediate threat (though it is probably more accurately defined as a war of prevention against a potential long-term threat), and the doctrine of preemptive war has become quite controversial. Perhaps later students of war will come to know this war as the American War of Preemption, preserving the administration's inappropriate terminology. Ultimately, the invasion of Iraq was a war associated with a particular president and administration. It is difficult, though not impossible, to believe that other presidents and other administrations would have chosen the same course of action given the same circumstances. Perhaps it will eventually be known as Mr. Bush's War. Nevertheless, in keeping with contemporary attributions, we will simply refer to it as the Iraq War and let history take its course.

Given the recent nature of the war and the public's limited access to official papers and documents, much of what is said in this chapter will be somewhat speculative. Nevertheless, the broad outlines of an explanation for the war can

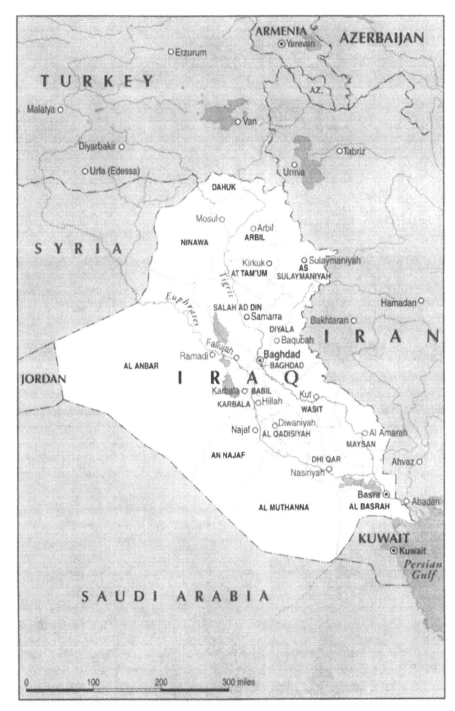

Map 7.1. Iraq

be ascertained from a host of "instant histories," memoirs, and reports of various official investigative commissions. What emerges from these accounts is a war whose causes are somewhat unique. Many of the causal factors generally identified by the theoretical literature on interstate war are absent here. No territorial disputes existed between the United States and Iraq; the two countries do not even share a border. No grand systemic power transitions were underway in which the position of the global leader, the United States, was put in peril by a "rising challenger." Indeed, the systemic transformation that ended the Cold War created a unipolar system with the U.S. as the sole and unchallenged superpower. No dyadic power transitions were brewing either; certainly no Iraqi economic or military buildup was underway that threatened to reduce the U.S.-Iraqi military balance to parity or near-parity. The severe imbalance of capabilities in favor of America meant that Iraq could never directly threaten the U.S., at least not in any conventional way. No arms races or competitive alliance constructions were under way, and no real conflict spiral seemed to be brewing. In the period prior to the outbreak of war, neither country was experiencing internal unrest or civil conflict; in neither country were the incumbent political elites seriously threatened with a loss of their political power. Quite the contrary, in the United States the president's approval ratings reached 90 percent in the aftermath of the Afghan war, and his party had just increased its representation in both houses of Congress in the 2002 elections. What then explains this war?

The most powerful explanations of the war are associated with short-term phenomena. Few long-term root causes seem relevant. The Iraq War highlights the importance of factors at the individual level: the personality of leaders, their worldviews, and their perceptions and misperceptions. The war serves as a strong reminder to us of the difference between the operational milieu (the world as it really is, and the world in which policies are actually carried out) and the psychological milieu (the world as perceived by decision makers, whether or not accurate). Political leaders act according to the latter rather than the former (Sprout and Sprout 1965).

We will start our examination of the war with a brief summary of the historical background to the conflict between the U.S. and Iraq and take a look at the decisions of the Bush administration after the attacks on the World Trade Center and the Pentagon on September 11, 2001. We will then be in a position to make some assessments of the factors that led to the outbreak of war.

BACKGROUND TO WAR: THE GULF WAR AND UN INSPECTIONS

The historical background to the war is, by now, well known. On August 2, 1990, Saddam Hussein's Iraq invaded Kuwait, and President George H. W. Bush quickly proclaimed, "This will not stand." Both the United Nations and the United States undertook immediate action to get Iraq to withdraw. The UN Security Council mandated economic sanctions and authorized a military blockade and an air embargo to enforce those sanctions. President Bush, concerned initially that Iraq would follow up its annexation of Kuwait with an attack on Saudi Arabia, prevailed on that country to permit U.S. forces to defend it. U.S. troops were sent to the Persian Gulf as part of Operation Desert Shield, and President Bush patiently built an impressive international coalition—including Arab states such as Egypt, Syria, and Saudi Arabia—that was willing to confront Iraq. By November 1990, with Saddam still refusing to leave Kuwait, Bush decided to give the coalition forces an "offensive option" and doubled the number of U.S. forces in the Persian Gulf. If Iraq would not go, it could be compelled to go. Threats were now backed with real capabilities.

On November 29 the Security Council passed Resolution 678, giving an ultimatum to Iraq: UN members were authorized to use "all means necessary" to bring about Iraq's withdrawal from Kuwait and to restore international peace and security if Iraq did not withdraw by January 15, 1991. When Iraq remained defiant, Bush ordered aerial bombardment to begin on January 16. Coalition air strikes continued for five weeks without inducing Iraq to withdraw. Finally, on February 22, the president issued another ultimatum, with noon on the next day as the deadline for Iraq's withdrawal. When that deadline passed, the ground war (Operation Desert Storm) began. Iraqi forces were quickly routed and retreated back across the border. After a mere one hundred hours of ground combat, President Bush announced a cease-fire on February 27. U.S. and coalition forces chose not to destroy the Iraqi military forces or to occupy Baghdad or to overthrow the government. Neither did they choose to support rebellious internal Iraqi factions attempting to bring down Saddam's government in the wake of the war.

By the end of the first week in March a Shi'a revolt had broken out in the southern part of the country, followed by a Kurdish revolt in the north. Both were probably encouraged by the president's words to the Iraqi people to overthrow their government. Both were brutally put down by Saddam Hussein's remaining military units, including crack Republican Guard units that had escaped from Kuwait.

Why didn't the U.S. take advantage of the situation to intervene in the civil conflict and topple Saddam Hussein's government? The record points to numerous reasons. First, coalition forces clearly lacked a Security Council mandate to do so; their mission was merely to expel Iraq from Kuwait. Second, an American attempt to overthrow Iraq's government would have been opposed by Arab states, thus splitting the politically fragile anti-Iraq coalition. Third, if U.S. forces intervened in the rebellion, it would be impossible to prevent Iranian forces from intervening in the Shi'a area in southern Iraq—a scenario to be avoided at all cost. Fourth, Turkey, an important NATO ally, was adamantly opposed to assisting the rebels. If the Kurdish insurgency in northern Iraq was successful, it might embolden Turkish Kurds to press their own political demands and reignite a long-standing conflict in southeastern Turkey. Fifth, no American leader wanted an Iraq that would be split by civil war into three parts—an independent Kurdish north, a Shi'a south with ties to Iran, and a Sunni "rump state" in the center. Such a situation would make it impossible for Iraq to play its traditional role as a counterbalance to Iranian power. Sixth, most administration officials believed that Saddam Hussein was likely to be overthrown in an internal coup, making U.S. intervention unnecessary. Finally, continuing the war would have led to increased casualties for U.S. forces who might be locked into a lengthy occupation with no "exit strategy" in sight—a scenario that would lessen public support for the war and for President Bush in his bid for reelection in 1992.

Instead, U.S. and British forces confined their response to the construction of no-fly zones, first in the north and later in the south. This mission, called Operation Provide Comfort, prohibited Iraq from using fixed-wing aircraft in the zones and made it possible for international aid agencies to lend assistance to the Shi'a and the Kurds without the threat of Iraqi air strikes.

In the Gulf War's aftermath, the UN Security Council passed, and Iraq accepted, Resolution 687, imposing certain obligations on the defeated state. Iraq was to destroy its nuclear, biological, and chemical weapons under UN supervision. (Nuclear, biological, and chemical weapons are all referred to as weapons of mass destruction, or WMD.) Iraq was prohibited from making any attempt to acquire such weapons or their components in the future, it was not permitted to possess ballistic missiles beyond a range of 150 kilometers, and it had to allow UN inspectors to search for prohibited weapons and destroy them. The United Nations Special Commission (UNSCOM) was created to inspect Iraq's chemical, biological, and missile programs, while the International Atomic Energy Agency (IAEA) inspected Iraq's nuclear weapons program. Both organizations were headed by Swedish diplomats: UNSCOM by Rolf Ekeus and the IAEA by Hans Blix. If the UN inspectors could at some point confirm that Iraq no longer possessed the banned weapons programs, then the economic sanctions on Iraq could be lifted.

Once allowed into the country, inspectors began their search and destroy mission. Almost all of Iraq's remaining Scud missiles were discovered and dismantled. Significant stocks of chemical weapons (CW) were promptly located and destroyed. Biological weapons (BW) were more problematic: Iraq claimed not to have any, but UNSCOM suspected otherwise.

As we now know, and as the Commission on the Intelligence Capabilities of the United States Regarding Weapons of Mass Destruction (CIC 2005, 511) has succinctly summarized,

> Saddam Hussein initially judged that the sanctions would be short-lived, that Iraq could weather them by making a few limited concessions, and that Iraq could successfully hide much of its preexisting weaponry and documentation. Accordingly, Iraq declared to the United Nations part of its ballistic missile and chemical warfare programs, but not its biological or nuclear weapons programs. But after initial inspections proved much more intrusive than Baghdad expected, Saddam became concerned. In order to prevent discovery of his still-hidden pre-1991 WMD programs, Saddam ordered Hussein Kamil to destroy large numbers of undeclared weapons and related materials in July 1991.

Saddam's battle with the inspectors suffered a grievous blow in 1995. Hussein Kamel al-Majid, one of Saddam Hussein's sons-in-law and, as director of Iraq's Military Industrial Commission, chief of all of Iraq's WMD programs, defected to Jordan. Kamel told UN inspectors that not only did Iraq have biological agents, but it also had succeeded in weaponizing some of them—anthrax, botulinim toxin, and aflatoxin. He also reported new details of CW production and use. He claimed, however, that he had ordered all BW and CW destroyed in 1991. As a result of Hussein Kamel's defection, Saddam Hussein—apparently believing that his WMD programs were now "blown"—surrendered a massive pile of documents on

Iraqi BW and CW programs that he maintained Kamel had hidden on his chicken farm. Iraq also revealed its remaining research facilities, which UNSCOM promptly demolished (Blix 2004, 29–30; Lopez and Cortright 2004, 93).

Iraq's nuclear weapons program deserves special attention. In 1991 UN inspectors discovered an Iraqi nuclear industry more advanced than was previously believed. Prior to the Gulf War, Iraq had been able to secretly enrich uranium without detection by the IAEA. This was somewhat shocking at the time, but it was also learned that Iraq had not used modern centrifuge type enrichment (though they later began to develop this process). Instead, they had used the older electromagnetic isotope separation (EMIS) process used by the Manhattan Project in World War II—a very slow, labor- and energy-intensive process. Inspectors found that the Iraqi nuclear program produced only minuscule amounts of plutonium and under a half kiloton of uranium. The latter was enriched to only about 4 percent of U-235, far less than the 80 to 90 percent needed for a bomb (Blix 2004, 18, 23–24; Risen 2006, 96–97).

Kamel confided that in 1990, just prior to the Gulf War, he had ordered a crash program to make nuclear weapons using fissionable material from a research reactor. But that effort too had failed. Much of Iraq's nuclear industry was destroyed by coalition bombing during the Gulf War—mostly by accident since the EMIS facilities were unknown at the time (Risen 2006, 100). And what was not destroyed in the war was rather quickly discovered and dismantled by inspectors. By 1994 the IAEA had removed all fissionable material from Iraq, and all nuclear facilities in the country had been destroyed.

While much of Iraq's WMD capacity lay in ruins at the end of the Gulf War or was destroyed shortly thereafter by inspectors, a great deal of uncertainty remained. Kamel revealed that Iraq had not completely abandoned its WMD programs. It retained basic materials, designs, personnel, and some dual-use equipment, and it maintained intact its major BW facility at Al-Hakam, all of which would enable it to restart production after UN inspectors left (Siffrey and Cerf 2003, 315n). Iraq also tried to hide documents associated with its CW/BW programs. Most important, the destruction of the stockpiles was kept secret and Iraq "chose to obfuscate whether it actually possessed WMD" (CIC 2005, 506). Saddam's 1991 instructions to subordinates to destroy the weapons (and the acts of destruction themselves) were rarely documented, leaving a significant gap between what Iraq was known to have possessed, and what inspectors actually found. Even Iraqis themselves were in the dark. Saddam most likely consulted only a handful of officials about the decision to dismantle WMD and apparently revealed the secret to his generals only in late 2002 (CIC 2005, 513).

According to one analyst (Pollack 2004, 83–85) Kamel's defection led Saddam Hussein to the conclusion that Iraq would be unable to preserve a "just in time" WMD program that would give Iraq the capability to produce banned weapons on a moment's notice. Instead, he appears to have decided that Iraq should cut its program back to an absolute bare minimum. Fatefully, however, as we have seen, Saddam Hussein also decided to create the impression that his weapons potential was still intact. The impression worked: Most foreign observers bought the deception, thereby laying the basis for the later U.S. justification for military action. Why would Hussein foster this dangerous illusion? Postwar interviews with

Saddam Hussein and others suggest that the deception primarily was seen as a way to maintain a deterrent against Iraq's traditional foe, Iran, not the United States (Graham 2004, 33; CIC 2005, 511–13).

Generally speaking, between 1991 and 1998 Iraqi compliance with its obligations under Resolution 687 was spotty, dilatory, and grudging. Attempts to deceive inspectors were often blatant. In some cases Iraqi agents moved files and burned documents while inspectors waited for facilities to be opened for them (Blix 2004, 33). Inspectors made significant discoveries and destroyed numerous weapons, but not because the Iraqis made it easy for them. UNSCOM and the IAEA destroyed chemical agents, biological agents, missiles, and huge portions of Iraq's infrastructure related to prohibited weapons production, including its entire nuclear infrastructure.

By 1998, the two UN agencies had still not given Iraq a clean bill of health, and they pushed Iraq to permit inspections of presidential palaces and other areas that had previously been off limits. Iraq's refusal to permit these searches led to the decision in December to withdraw inspectors from Iraq. The United States and Britain retaliated with four days of punitive air strikes on Iraqi WMD sites and other military targets (Operation Desert Fox). Between 1998 and 2002, with UNSCOM and the IAEA gone, there were no weapons inspections carried out inside Iraq. The United States and its partners had lost their crucial eyes "on the ground"; consequently, their confidence in assessing the status of Iraq's banned military programs deteriorated considerably.

At this point Congress, in an attempt to prod the Clinton administration into taking more decisive action against Iraq, passed the Iraq Liberation Act, which declared that "it should be the policy of the United States to support efforts to remove the regime headed by Saddam Hussein from power." Congress authorized a small sum, up to $97 million, for regime change. The money went primarily to aid and train exiled opposition forces, such as Ahmed Chalabi's Iraqi National Congress, but the law specifically barred the direct use of U.S. military force.

Added to the list of irritants associated with Iraq was the strong possibility that Saddam Hussein's government was behind a bungled assassination attempt against former president George H. W. Bush in April 1993 in Kuwait. Seventeen suspects were apprehended before they could carry out the plan, and the leader of the rather feckless group, Wali al-Ghazali, fingered Iraq. He confessed, probably after being tortured, that the Iraqi Intelligence Service had given the order to assassinate the former president (Bamford 2004, 256–59). Some analysts doubt the whole episode, suggesting that Kuwati officials fabricated the story in order to curry favor with the United States (see Kaufman 2004, 15–16). Two months after the attempt, the Clinton administration retaliated with a Tomahawk cruise missile attack on Iraqi intelligence headquarters in downtown Baghdad.

By the dawn of the twenty-first century the United States–Iraq relationship had taken on some of the aspects of a rivalry. The conflict relationship is of rather recent origins—dating only to Iraq's attack on Kuwait in 1990—and therefore does not qualify as an enduring rivalry, which normally requires at least six militarized international disputes (MIDs) over a period of twenty to twenty-five years. Instead, the U.S.-Iraq relationship might be characterized as a "proto-rivalry," a category of short-term, potential rivalries that tend to terminate early

(Goertz and Diehl 2000, 228–37). William Thompson (2001, 560) puts forward three criteria for **strategic rivalries** that are based on the mutual perception of rivalry rather than on participation in militarized disputes. The actors must regard each other as competitors capable of "playing in the same league," as the source of actual or latent threats that have the potential to become militarized, and as enemies. The U.S.-Iraq relationship certainly fits Thompson's second and third criteria, but the first is problematic. It is doubtful that the U.S. leaders saw Iraq as capable of playing in the same league. While most rivalries are between two major powers or two minor powers, a major-minor rivalry, such as this, takes place "when minor powers become something more than nuisances in the eyes of the major power decision-makers" (Thompson 2001, 565). By 2003 the United States and Iraq had fought one major war, U.S. fighter planes controlled the air space over northern and southern Iraq and were engaged in weekly combat in those zones, and the U.S. appeared as the chief protagonist in maintaining UN sanctions and the inspection regime in Iraq. Moreover, after 9/11 the U.S. began to see Iraq not only as a regional threat but also as a more wide-ranging strategic threat to the United States. As one of the three countries in the president's "axis of evil," it was certainly more than a "nuisance."

Whether the U.S.-Iraq relationship can be called an enduring rivalry, a proto-rivalry, or a strategic rivalry (or none of the above) is probably less important than the fact that U.S. leaders clearly perceived Iraq in the way that rivals perceive each other. They saw Iraq as a threat to U.S. national interests, expected further conflict with Iraq, believed that the conflicts could not be resolved peacefully, and believed that coercive bargaining strategies were necessary to deal with Iraq.

THE BUSH ADMINISTRATION, 9/11, AND IRAQ: THE DECISION FOR WAR

The Iraq Agenda Pre-9/11

The George W. Bush administration came to office in January 2000. Many of its members had served in the previous Bush administration and saw Iraq as "unfinished business" and were committed to regime change in Iraq. Many thought the decisions to end the Gulf War early and to refrain from assisting the Shi'a and Kurdish revolts were ill advised. Chief among the Iraq hawks were Vice President Dick Cheney, who had been the secretary of defense in the earlier Bush administration, and Deputy Secretary of Defense Paul Wolfowitz, who had been Cheney's undersecretary of defense for policy and one of the few who had actually argued at the time for a continuation of the war. Defense Secretary Donald Rumsfeld, who had not held a position in the previous Bush administration but had served as the first President Bush's unofficial emissary to Saddam Hussein, shared their views. The hawks' nemesis was Secretary of State Colin Powell, who as chairman of the Joint Chiefs of Staff (JCS) in 1991 had been one of the chief proponents of an early end to the war.

The new Bush team was so concerned about Iraq that when the outgoing Clinton administration was setting up preinaugural national security briefings for the incoming foreign policy team, Cheney insisted that Iraq should be "Topic

A" in the foreign policy briefings, in spite of warnings by Clinton and others that the number one threat to the U.S. would be al Qaeda (Woodward 2004, 9).

Within days of the presidential inauguration, the new administration was working on strategy for Iraq. On January 30, 2001, at the first meeting of the National Security Council (NSC), Condoleezza Rice, the president's national security adviser, introduced the topic of Iraq's destabilizing effect on the gulf region. Rice turned the meeting over to Director of Central Intelligence (DCI) George Tenet, who then showed photos purporting to indicate Iraqi chemical or biological weapons factories (Suskind 2004a, 70–75). President Bush assigned tasks. The State Department was directed to come up with a new, more focused economic sanctions policy for Iraq. The CIA was to intensify intelligence gathering on Iraq's WMD and its ties to terrorist groups. Treasury was to develop more options for financially squeezing Iraq. And Defense Secretary Rumsfeld and the JCS were to look at military options, including putting U.S. ground forces in the Kurdish north and the Shi'a south, as well as supporting opposition groups within Iraq (Suskind 2004a, 75). Clearly, Iraq was near the top of the foreign policy agenda at the earliest stages.

The NSC met on Iraq again on February 1st. Rumsfeld provided a background memo for the meeting laying out the argument that in the post Cold War world the U.S. faced an emerging peril: the proliferation of WMD in the hands of countries opposed to the United States. It was not just traditional great power opponents like China and Russia that posed the threat but also "rogue states" like Iraq, Iran, and North Korea. When Powell presented the State Department's "targeted sanctions" approach to Iraq, Rumsfeld belittled the role of economic sanctions and emphasized "going after Saddam" and bringing about regime change in Iraq. "Imagine," he argued, "what the region would look like without Saddam and with a regime that's aligned with U.S. interests. . . . It would change everything in the region and beyond it. It would demonstrate what U.S. policy is all about" (Suskind 2004a, 85). The discussion then focused on how to achieve regime change.

Treasury Secretary Paul O'Neill, who was present at the early NSC meetings on Iraq, believes that "from the start, we were building the case against Hussein and looking at how we could take him out and change Iraq into a new country. And, if we did that, it would solve everything. It was all about finding *a way to do it*" (Suskind 2004a, 86).

Discussion of a tougher policy toward Iraq permeated down through the various layers of the national security bureaucracy: from the National Security Council, to the meeting of the principals (the NSC members meeting without the president), to the meetings of the deputies (the number two–level officials in each department), to lower-level interagency committees (see box 7.1). In the first six months of the new administration, the Department of Defense and the State Department wrote several policy briefs on the possibility of intervention in Iraq (Suskind 2006, 22).

The deputies committee—made up of officials from the Department of State, Department of Defense, CIA, NSC, and other agencies and chaired by Stephen Hadley, the deputy national security adviser—met several times on Iraq in the late spring and summer of 2001 (Woodward 2004, 21) At a deputies meeting on

Box 7.1. Bush Administration Policy Units.

President of the United States

National Security Council / War Cabinet
President George W. Bush
Vice President Dick Cheney
Secretary of State Colin Powell
Secretary of Defense Donald Rumsfeld
Director of Central Intelligence George Tenet
President's Assistant for National Security Affairs Condoleezza Rice
Chairman, Joint Chiefs of Staff, Gen. Hugh Shelton/Richard Myers
Treasury Secretary Paul O'Neill
Attorney General John Ashcroft
And others, as the president directs, such as:
FBI Director Robert Mueller
White House Chief of Staff Andrew Card
VP Chief of Staff I. Lewis Libby
Deputy Assistant for National Security Affairs, Stephen Hadley

Principals committee
Heads of departments and agencies meeting without the president,
chaired by Dr. Rice

Deputies committee
Deputy Assistant for National Security Affairs Stephen Hadley (chair)
Deputy Secretary of State Richard Armitage
Deputy Secretary of Defense Paul Wolfowitz
Deputy Director of Central Intelligence John McLaughlin
VP Chief of Staff I. Lewis Libby
Vice Chair of the Joint Chiefs of Staff Gen. Richard Myers (followed by
Gen. Peter Pace)
And others, such as Deputy White House Chief of Staff Joshua Bolton

terrorism in April, Wolfowitz took the position that al Qaeda, the terrorist group responsible for the attacks on two U.S. embassies in Africa in August 1998 and on the USS *Cole* in October 2000 while at port in Yemen, had to be state sponsored, and that the United States had to go after Iraq (Clarke 2004, 30).

The deputy-level process led to discussions by the principals about the possible direct use of U.S. military force against Iraq. Wolfowitz apparently backed a "draft plan" to send U.S. military forces from Kuwait in a quick strike to occupy the oil fields in southern Iraq—an area that accounted for roughly two-thirds of Iraq's oil production. The idea was to establish a foothold in this "enclave" from which the U.S. could support Iraqi opposition forces in an effort to precipitate an internal revolt. Secretary Powell thought the idea absurd and, as Woodward (2004, 22) describes, he advised the president not to get stampeded into the decision, that it was not as easy as he might believe. Bush assured him that he was "in no hurry to look for trouble." No policy recommendations were sent to the president at this time, and summer vacation plans put Iraq on hold. Powell's approach had temporarily carried the day. The U.S. would try to keep Saddam Hussein "in his box" without direct military force.

One week before the 9/11 attack, at a meeting of the principals on the subject of terrorism, Rumsfeld argued that Iraq should be a priority of the war on terrorism: "Whatever we did on this al Qaeda business, we had to deal with the other sources of terrorism" (Clarke 2004, 237–38). At this point, however, direct U.S. military intervention was not yet in the cards. The Bush administration's strategy for bringing about regime change attached itself to the thin reed of supplying military, economic, and political support to Iraqi opposition groups (Woodward 2004, 21). This relatively timid approach was about to change.

A New World: The Bush Administration and Iraq after 9/11

At 8:46 am on Thursday, September 11, 2001, American Airlines Flight 11 crashed into the north tower of the World Trade Center in New York. Approximately seventeen minutes later United Airlines Flight 175 hit the south tower. At 9:37 American Airlines Flight 77 smashed into the Pentagon. Another flight, United Airlines 93, whose target was the Capitol Building in Washington, crashed short of its target in a field outside Shanksville, Pennsylvania, when its hijackers were overcome by valiant passengers. Al Qaeda's simultaneous attacks on the World Trade Center and the Pentagon were in many ways a "hinge event"—an action that changed the political orientation of President Bush and the course of U.S. foreign policy. It ignited a white-hot appreciation of the nature of the new, post–Cold War threats to the United States and of the nation's vulnerabilities to new enemies. Specifically, 9/11 shifted attention within the administration away from great powers politics and on to the links between international terrorism, rogue regimes, state sponsors of terrorism, and access to weapons of mass destruction. In Washington, mindsets were transformed and world events, including U.S.-Iraqi relations, began to be seen through a different set of conceptual lenses.

The president immediately laid down a marker. The United States would retaliate not only against those who had carried out the attack (al Qaeda) but also against those states who supported and assisted the attackers. He declared, "We will make no distinction between terrorists who committed these acts and those who harbor them." This surely meant the Taliban regime in Afghanistan, where Osama Bin Laden and the al Qaeda leadership had been given refuge, but it might be extended to many other states, including Iraq. The statement gave the neoconservative (or neocon) faction in the Bush administration and their hawkish allies a wedge to begin advocating for regime change in Iraq under the heading of antiterrorism. While links between al Qaeda and Saddam Hussein were not readily apparent, many in the Bush administration felt they must exist. Moreover, with inspectors absent from Iraq for almost three years and the increased chance that Iraq might acquire viable WMD programs, the Bush administration now confronted the possibility that Iraq, as a state that sponsored terrorism, might make these weapons available to al Qaeda or other terrorist groups. Intelligence on potential dangers posed by Iraq was now seen in a new light, as was the problem of deterring Saddam Hussein and "keeping him in his box" (Fallows 2004a, 54; Woodward 2004, 27).

While it was instantly clear that al Qaeda was responsible for the 9/11 attacks—it took less than a day for the CIA to identify the hijackers as al Qaeda members—many in the administration were drawn to Iraq. Within hours of the attack on the Pentagon, Rumsfeld discussed with his staff the possibility of U.S. military strikes against Iraq and sent a note to Gen. Richard Myers about potential retaliation against Iraq. In the meetings with the president that night he argued that the focus should be on states that supported terrorism, like Iraq (Woodward 2004, 24; Daalder and Lindsay 2003, 99; Bamford 2004, 285; 9/11 Report 2004, 330, 335; Lemann 2004, 157). Rumsfeld's position was strongly seconded by his deputy, Paul Wolfowitz, a leader of the neocons, who argued that the attacks were too sophisticated and complicated to be the work of some ragtag group of terrorists. They had to be state sponsored, and that meant Iraq (Clarke 2004, 30). Wolfowitz began to push the Iraqi connection to 9/11 in conference calls to Cheney and others (Bamford 2004, 285).

The president created a "War Cabinet" of relevant senior officials to deal with the crisis. At morning and afternoon meetings of the War Cabinet on Friday, September 12, Rumsfeld raised the issue of whether the 9/11 terrorist attacks might give the U.S. an opportunity to attack Iraq immediately. He argued that if the United States was serious about combating international terrorism, Iraq would have to be addressed. The Pentagon, of course, had been working for several months already on a plan for regime change in Iraq. On the other hand, it had no plan for Afghanistan. Moreover, the lack of targets in Afghanistan—where the Taliban government sheltered Osama Bin Laden and his al Qaeda network—suggested to Rumsfeld that the U.S. should consider bombing Iraq. Wolfowitz supported making Iraq the primary target in the war on terrorism. The president's reaction was that the U.S. needed to change the government in Iraq, not merely hit it with cruise missiles, as the Clinton administration had done. The initial conclusion of the War Cabinet on the twelfth was that the first stage in the war on terrorism should focus on al Qaeda and Afghanistan; however, there would be a second stage in that war and Iraq could be addressed later (Woodward 2002, 48–49; Woodward 2004, 25; Clarke 2004, 31; Suskind 2004a, 184).

Iraq was clearly on the president's mind, however. In the evening, Bush took aside the NSC's terrorism coordinator, Richard Clarke, and a few others, and pushed them to find a link between the 9/11 attacks and Saddam Hussein. When Clarke responded that the intelligence analysis on al Qaeda's responsibility was solid, the president pressed further to "see if Saddam was involved. Just look. I want to know any shred. . . . Look into Iraq" (Clarke 2004, 32). Clarke's follow-up memo, sent to Rice on the eighteenth, stated that "no compelling case" could be found for Iraqi participation in the planning or the execution of the strikes. Rice's chief aide on Afghanistan, Zalmay Khalilzad, concurred in the assessment (National Commission 2004, 334). Nevertheless, in the first months after the

9/11 attack, the CIA found itself under pressure from the White House, the vice president's office and the secretary of defense to find some connection between Saddam Hussein and al Qaeda (Suskind 2006, 190–91).

Discussion of U.S. responses to the 9/11 attack continued at a weekend meeting of the War Cabinet at Camp David, commencing on Saturday, September 15. In addition to the president, the attendees were Cheney, Rice, Hadley, Powell, Armitage, Rumsfeld, Ashcroft, Mueller, Tenet, Wolfowitz, and Cofer Black, chief of the DCI's Counterterrorist Center (National Commission 2004, 332). Military planners had been asked to draw up scenarios for an attack on Iraq as well as Afghanistan, and JCS chair Hugh Shelton was prepared to talk about military options in Iraq if the issue was raised. The Defense Department briefing paper identified three priority targets for the war on terrorism: al Qaeda, the Taliban, and Iraq (National Commission 2004, 335; Fallows 2004a, 56; Woodward 2002, 79). When the discussion shifted to Iraq in the Saturday morning session, Wolfowitz took the lead in making the case for striking Iraq in the first round of the war on terrorism. He estimated that there was between a 10 and 50 percent chance that Saddam Hussein was involved in the 9/11 attacks. Even if Iraq was not involved, if the United States was serious about the war on terrorism, it would have to go after Saddam sometime. Moreover, while an attack on mountainous Afghanistan might prove problematic, Iraq was "doable." Hussein's oppressive and corrupt regime might just crack under outside military pressure (National Commission 2004, 335; Woodward 2002, 83; Suskind 2004a, 187–88; Daalder and Lindsay 2003, 104). Wolfowitz appeared to be supported by his boss, Secretary Rumsfeld.

Wolfowitz has since suggested that he was speaking for his boss, and that in a coffee break with the president, he agreed that the military options that had been put on the table were less than satisfactory. He brought up the "enclave strategy":

> It would be very simple to enable the Iraqi opposition to take over the southern part of the country and protect it with American air power. That would have included a large chunk of Saddam's oil reserves. And the President said, 'That's an imaginative idea; how come you didn't say so?' And I said . . . 'It is not my place to contradict the chairman of the joint chiefs unless the secretary of defense asks me to do so.' In fact . . . in the directive . . . the president signed to Rumsfeld to put together a plan for Afghanistan, it specifically mentions the option of taking control of the southern part of Iraq in some form. (Bowden 2005, 120)

The opposition at the Camp David meetings to targeting Iraq was heavy. Secretary of State Powell argued that the U.S. needed allies in the war against terrorism, but focusing on Iraq would undercut the United States' ability to build a strong international coalition against al Qaeda and the Taliban. The president himself appeared to have strong reservations about the Iraq scenario, and the military was not asked at this point to present a plan of action. In the end, Cheney joined Powell, Tenet, and Card in opposing military action against Iraq; Rumsfeld abstained (National Commission 2004, 335; Woodward 2002, 84–91). Iraq was temporarily off the table, and the Saturday afternoon session focused entirely on Afghanistan.

Back in Washington at an NSC meeting on Monday the seventeenth, the president summed up his feelings about Saddam and Iraq: "I believe Iraq was involved, but I'm not going to strike them now. I don't have the evidence at this point" (Woodward 2002, 99). However, the president wanted to keep his options open. At the Monday meeting, Bush signed a top secret order directing the Defense Department to begin planning for military options in Iraq, including the possibility of occupying Iraqi oil fields (National Commission 2004, 335; Bamford 2004, 287). At a meeting on September 19 between Bush, Cheney, and Tenet, the president pushed Tenet once again to investigate links between Saddam Hussein and al Qaeda. He specifically asked him to investigate a reputed meeting, later deemed not to have occurred, between the leader of the 9/11 hijackers, Mohammed Atta, and an Iraqi intelligence official in Prague (Suskind 2006, 23).

Meanwhile, Powell was to draft an ultimatum to the Taliban, the president would sign an "intelligence finding" authorizing CIA operations in Afghanistan, and General Shelton was to draw up detailed military plans for Afghanistan. The man in charge of military options was Gen. Tommy Franks, commander of Central Command (CENTCOM), which had responsibility for the Middle East and Persian Gulf area. Franks had actually pushed for more robust planning for a possible war in Iraq during the summer before 9/11, but his recommendations had been turned down by the president. CENTCOM now began "dusting off" these plans (National Commission 2004, 336). But Afghanistan was still first on the agenda.

In his speech to Congress on September 20, Bush issued an ultimatum to Afghanistan's Taliban government. It must close all terrorist camps and hand over every terrorist, Osama Bin Laden included. There would be no negotiation and no discussion; the Taliban must act and act immediately. "They will hand over the terrorists, or they will share their fate," Bush stated. On the day of his speech, President Bush intimated to Prime Minister Blair of Great Britain that the Taliban was not the only concern; he declared that he was determined to oust Saddam Hussein at some point as well (Burrough et al. 2004, 236). In the end, the Taliban refused to cooperate. Phase one of the war on terrorism officially began on October 7, 2001, as the U.S.-led coalition began the bombing of Taliban positions in Afghanistan. In his televised address to the nation, President Bush said, "Today we focus on Afghanistan, but the battle is broader. Every nation has a choice to make. In this conflict, there is no neutral ground. If any government sponsors the outlaws and killers of innocents, they have become outlaws and murderers themselves. And they will take that lonely path at their own peril."

By mid-November, Kabul had fallen to the U.S.-supported Northern Alliance, and throughout the country Taliban and al Qaeda forces were defeated or forced to withdraw—though Osama Bin Laden and Taliban leader Mullah Omar eluded capture. Serious consideration of a U.S. military operation against Iraq appears to have begun very soon thereafter. The relative ease with which the U.S. and its allies had toppled the Taliban was certainly a spur for those who wished to initiate regime change in Iraq. Without an official presidential policy decision, quite a few U.S. agencies began to act as if a war with Iraq was next. In late October, the State Department even began to make plans for a postwar transition in Iraq (Fallows 2004a, 56).

Also in late October 2001, the CIA began seeing intelligence traffic indicating a potential terrorist attack with a radiological device or "dirty bomb"—though the evidence was far from firm. Tenet briefed the president on this threat and indicated that Iraq was one of the countries most likely to supply terrorists with the radiological material to construct such a weapon. The president apparently "went through the roof." He ordered the War Cabinet to make nuclear terrorism their highest priority (Daalder and Lindsay 2003, 118–19). In short order, the president was to receive more alarming news about the potential distribution of WMD to terrorists. A nuclear black market centered around Pakistan's most revered scientist, A. Q. Khan, had been discovered and Pakistan had detained two nuclear scientists who had met with Osama Bin Laden in Afghanistan (Lantis and Moskovitz 2005, 98–99). A potential link between al Qaeda and a nuclear armed state had been discovered.

On November 21, well before control over Afghanistan had been consolidated, the president asked Secretary of Defense Rumsfeld about the status of the U.S. war plan on Iraq. The president spurred his chief civilian military adviser to action: "Let's get started on this" (Woodward 2004, 1–2). Arguably, this was the first concrete step toward war taken by the president. His request led to a high level, top secret military planning process in the hands of CENTCOM commander Tommy Franks and his operations director, Gen. Gene Renuart. Rumsfeld directed them to think about an attack as early as April or May 2002 (Woodward 2004, 43; Lantis and Moskovitz 2005, 99). Phase two was now getting serious. From this point on, military planning would develop a powerful momentum toward war that would be difficult to reverse.

On December 12, with the president at his home in Crawford, Texas, the War Cabinet met via secure video hookup. General Franks presented a briefing on the Iraq war plan and discussed the preparations that would be necessary in order to carry out a military operation. In order to assure U.S. ability to use the military option in the future, Bush agreed—as a noncommital first step—to triple U.S. forces in Kuwait and to fund an upgrade of facilities in Qatar. He told Rumsfeld, "We need to get started doing some of these things" (Woodward 2004, 63). The president had secretly set in motion the military wherewithal to pursue a war against Iraq at some point in the near future.

A public hint at the direction U.S. policy was going to take was delivered in the president's state of the union message on January 29, 2002. President Bush declared that Iran, Iraq, and North Korea constituted an "axis of evil." The three states were singled out as posing "a grave and growing danger" because of their programs to develop WMD and the possibility that they could provide these weapons to terrorists, "giving them means to match their hatred." Moreover, the president warned that "time is not on our side. I will not wait on events, while dangers gather. I will not stand by, as peril draws closer and closer. The United States of America will not permit the world's most dangerous regimes to threaten us with the world's most destructive weapons." The speech was essentially a justification for a war with Iraq and a preview of the policy of the use of preemptive military force. A further hint of the preemption policy came in the president's West Point graduation speech on June 1, 2002, in which he suggested that deterrence and containment might not work in the post 9/11 world: "If we wait for threats to fully materialize, we will have waited too long . . . the war on terror will not be won on the defensive. We must take the battle to the enemy, disrupt his plans, and confront the worst threats before they emerge. . . . Our security will require all Americans . . . to be ready for preemptive action when necessary to defend our liberty and to defend our lives."

The president and his team began to introduce a new issue into its foreign policy rhetoric. The issue was not whether Iraq could be contained and deterred from menacing the other states in its region; the issue now was a potential attack on the U.S. by Iraq or terrorist groups aided by Iraq (see Kaufman 2004 on this point).

Early in 2002 CIA head George Tenet and his chief of Iraq operations briefed President Bush, Vice President Cheney, and Cheney's chief of staff, I. Lewis "Scooter" Libby. The CIA had done a "lessons learned" study of previous covert operations in Iraq. First, the agency concluded that the U.S. had a credibility problem in Iraq; we had deserted our allies too many times in the past. To restore our credibility we would have to show "seriousness," and the most important sign of this would be preparation for a massive military invasion. Second, Tenet emphasized that covert action could *not* overthrow Saddam; the dictator was a master at sniffing out coups and then snuffing them out. Regime change on the cheap was unlikely. Tenet put a mere 10–20 percent chance of success on any covert operation against Saddam. Only a full-scale military invasion could bring about regime change. The CIA was now an advocate for military action in Iraq (Woodward 2004, 71–73; Woodward 2002, 330). As a result of these discussions, the president, on February 16, signed a new intelligence order calling for the CIA to begin covert action to support a U.S. military effort to bring about regime change. The order authorized increased support for the Iraqi opposition, increased intelligence gathering efforts in Iraq, preparations for the deployment of CIA paramilitary teams and U.S. Special Forces in Iraq, and the use of sabotage and disinformation operations in Iraq.

By February 20, 2002, the first covert CIA team had entered northern Iraq (Woodward 2002, 329–30; Woodward 2004, 108). In March, operations in Afghanistan were scaled back and CIA commandos began filtering into Iraq. In mid-2002 a new CIA task force on Iraq had been created (Gellman and Linzer 2004). By the end of July, the president had ordered about $700 million to be spent, and he approved roughly thirty projects related to a military attack on Iraq, reprogramming money already appropriated by Congress. Rice's NSC staff was put in charge of the Executive Steering Group, which was to oversee the coordination of all these actions (Woodward 2004, 137; Ricks 2006, 48–49). By late fall, sixty thousand U.S. troops were in the gulf region (Mann 2004, 348). To many, it appeared that the decision for war was becoming locked in. When Richard Haass, the head of the policy planning staff at the State Department, talked with Rice in June to express his doubts about the military option, he received the distinct impression that the decision had been made (Lemann 2004, 158).

In the summer of 2002, official discussion in Washington centered on three potential options for dealing with Iraq: logistical and intelligence support for Iraqi opposition forces that might result in inciting an internal, military coup against Saddam Hussein, the provision of air and limited ground support for an assault carried out by opposition groups, and a full-scale U.S. military intervention in Iraq (Lantis and Moskovitz 2005, 99). Option three increasingly held the edge over the competition.

The now-famous Downing Street Memo, revealed during the 2005 British election campaign, suggests that the psychological Rubicon had already been crossed in Washington by July 2002. The memo, by David Rycroft, is a summarization of a high-level meeting of Prime Minister Blair with his national security team on July 23, 2002, on the topic of Iraq. The head of Britain's foreign intelligence service, MI6, Sir Richard Dearlove, known as C, briefed the group on his recent meeting in Washington with DCI Tenet and other Bush administration officials three days earlier. In the memo's retelling (Danner 2005, 71): "C reported on his recent talks in Washington. There was a perceptible shift in attitude. Military action was now seen as inevitable. Bush wanted to remove Saddam Hussein, through military action, justified by the conjunction of terrorism and WMD. But the intelligence was being fixed around the policy. The NSC had no patience with the UN route, and no enthusiasm for publishing material on the Iraq regime's record. There was little discussion in Washington of the aftermath after military action."

Foreign Secretary Jack Straw said, "It seemed clear that Bush had made up his mind to take military action, even if the timing was not yet decided," and Defense Secretary Geoffrey Hoon reported that "the most likely timing in U.S. minds for military action to begin was January (2003)." Thus the British perception of the decision process in the U.S. was that the decision for war had essentially been made by late July and that the only questions left had to do with how to justify the use of force and actually set the military option in motion politically.

At the highest levels of government, as Washington prepared for the military option in Iraq, Secretary of State Powell and his deputy, Richard Armitage, appeared most concerned at the gathering momentum toward war. Both were veterans of the war in Vietnam and were acutely aware of the potential pitfalls of U.S. intervention on foreign soil. Their concern, however, appeared to be more about the tactical questions of *how* to proceed toward war rather than the fundamental question of *if* the administration should take that course. By this time, Powell had apparently come to the conclusion that the war could not be stopped and that his only chance was to have some influence on the way it took place (Lemann 2004, 158). Powell managed to arrange a meeting on August 5 with Bush and Rice to make the case for greater caution. He discussed the potential "downsides" of a war—militarily, diplomatically, and politically. He warned the president of potential unintended consequences of war, uttering the famous "pottery barn rule": If you break it, you'll own it. The thrust of his message was that the U.S. could not and should not do this alone; the task required a coalition like the one put together by the president's father in the Gulf War. And if we wanted allies, we would have to go through the UN Security Council. But, Powell warned, the international "cover" provided by the UN might lead to an outcome quite different than what the president had in mind: UN action might actually be able to solve the crisis with Iraq and eliminate the need for war. Both Powell and Rice thought the meeting went well; the president had heard an alternative point of view that needed to be expressed (Woodward 2004, 148–51).

The principals met on August 14 to discuss a draft of a national security presidential directive (NSPD) to be issued by the president. (NSPDs were the president's "marching orders" to his national security bureaucracy; they constituted official government policy, signed by the president.) The document's title was "Iraq: Goals, Objectives and Strategy." Among the goals listed: "Free Iraq in order to eliminate Iraqi weapons of mass destruction . . . to prevent Iraq from breaking out of containment and becoming a more dangerous threat to the region and beyond. . . . End Iraqi threats to its neighbors, to stop the Iraqi government's tyrannizing of its own population, to cut Iraqi links to and sponsorship of international terrorism, to maintain Iraq's unity and territorial integrity. And liberate the Iraqi people from tyranny, and assist them in creating a society based on moderation, pluralism and democracy" (Woodward 2004, 154–55). The goals and the rationale were agreed on; there was something in this list for everyone. The strategy for achieving the goals was a matter of some contention, however.

As it happened, the president was scheduled to address the UN General Assembly in September. Powell told the president it would be unimaginable for the president to make the speech without mentioning Iraq; the question was what exactly the president should say. The principals agreed that the president's speech should be about Iraq. They also agreed that he should not ask for a formal declaration of war. Other than that, there was little agreement on what the president should say (Woodward 2002, 335–36). A bureaucratic fight would now ensue to determine the content of that speech and U.S. policy.

At the NSC meeting with the president two days later the debate focused on whether the president should accept Powell's recommendation to specifically ask the UN for a resolution on Iraq. In spite of the skepticism of Cheney and Rumsfeld, a tentative decision to pursue a "two-track strategy" (both military and diplomatic approaches) was made. Powell was able to convince Bush that asking the UN for a resolution on Iraq was a necessary first step for war; without this the U.S. would be bereft of allies. Moreover, if the U.S. was to have allies, Britain was crucial. And what was crucial for Britain was that the use of military force had to be preceded by a permissive Security Council resolution—just as in the 1991 Gulf War. For reasons of domestic politics in London, the road to Baghdad had to run through New York. This was the bottom-line message conveyed to Bush, Powell, and Rice by British prime minister Tony Blair, his Foreign Minister Jack Straw, and by David Manning, Blair's national security adviser. (Daalder and Lindsay 2003, 139; Woodward 2002, 347; Woodward 2004, 155–57, 177–78). The Aussies and the Spanish were equally adamant on this point.

Later meetings of the principals and NSC in early September continued the discussion. Cheney led the hawks in opposing a Security Council resolution. In his view, the UN was a tar pit, and the search for a resolution would be a neverending process that would tie American hands, waste time, and eventually fail to accomplish U.S. goals. According to Woodward (2002, 346; Woodward 2004, 176), Powell believed that "Cheney was beyond hell-bent for action against Saddam. It was as if nothing else existed." He believed Cheney was "terrified" by the prospect that the UN/diplomatic track might actually work, thereby eliminating the option for war (Woodward 2004, 157). Cheney, supported by Rumsfeld and others, fought an intense rear-guard struggle against asking for a UN resolution up until the final minutes before the speech. In the end, Powell (and Tony Blair, who made a critical visit to Bush on September 7 to plead for the Security Council option) won on the question of tactics. It was decided that Bush's speech to the UN should include a request for a Security Council resolution on Iraq (Woodward 2002, 345–48; Woodward 2004, 174–76).

The UN Diplomatic Gambit and Weapons of Mass Destruction

President Bush's speech to the General Assembly on September 12, 2002, made homage to both the Cheney and Powell factions. It singled out Iraq as a "grave and gathering danger" and a country that had failed to comply with numerous UN resolutions. It challenged the UN to prove its relevance by enforcing Iraqi compliance with its disarmament obligations, but it also promised that the U.S. "would work with the UN Security Council for the necessary resolutions." It promised both multilateral action and unilateral action, warning that if the UN failed to act, the U.S. would: "We cannot stand by and do nothing while dangers gather." In a week's time, the president would ask the support of another body—Congress. The diplomatic track running through the United Nations was coupled with a request that Congress support a resolution authorizing the president to use force against Iraq, thereby putting teeth into the administration's exercise of coercive diplomacy.

The administration began a public relations push to "sell" the idea of an increased threat from Iraq and to generate public support for a preventive war. Bush, Cheney, Rumsfeld, and others made speeches declaring that Saddam Hussein was bent on harming the United States, that he could be neither deterred nor contained, that he supported international terrorists and had cooperated with Osama bin Laden and al Qaeda, that he had chemical and biological weapons and was close to getting nuclear weapons, and that he could give these weapons to terrorists to use against the United States. Secretary Rumsfeld declared that U.S. intelligence had "bullet-proof" evidence of links between Iraq and al Qaeda, and President Bush said in September, "The first time we may be completely certain he [Saddam Hussein] has nuclear weapons is when, God forbid, he uses one." Similar lines were delivered by other administration officials in what was clearly a concerted attempt to manage public opinion.

On September 17 the administration's *National Security Strategy* document was published (see box 7.2). It further outlined the neoconservative view that the policies of containment and deterrence might not be effective in the post 9/11 global environment and that use of preemptive military force might be necessary to fight terrorists and their state sponsors. For the first time in history, the United States had formally adopted a preventive war policy as the center of its military strategy.

With national and international organizations debating the necessity of war, the administration had to make its case about the threat from Iraq. An important part of this process was an assessment by the U.S. intelligence community about the degree of Iraq's noncompliance with its disarmament obligations, the extent of its WMD programs, and the threat it posed to the region and to the United States. The primary means by which the various U.S. intelligence agencies come

Box 7.2. The National Security Strategy of the United States of America (Excerpts).

It has taken almost a decade for us to comprehend the true nature of this new threat. Given the goals of rogue states and terrorists, the United States can no longer solely rely on a reactive posture as we have in the past. The inability to deter a potential attacker, the immediacy of today's threats, and the magnitude of potential harm that could be caused by our adversaries' choice of weapons, do not permit that option. We cannot let our enemies strike first.

In the Cold War . . . we faced a generally status quo, risk-averse adversary. Deterrence was an effective defense. But deterrence based only upon the threat of retaliation is less likely to work against leaders of rogue states more willing to take risks, gambling with the lives of their people, and the wealth of their nations. . . .

Traditional concepts of deterrence will not work against a terrorist enemy whose avowed tactics are wanton destruction and the targeting of innocents; whose so-called soldiers seek martyrdom in death and whose most potent protection is statelessness. The overlap between states that sponsor terror and those that pursue WMD compels us to action.

For centuries, international law recognized that nations need not suffer an attack before they can lawfully take action to defend themselves against forces that present an imminent danger of attack. Legal scholars and international jurists often conditioned the legitimacy of preemption on the existence of an imminent threat—most often a visible mobilization of armies, navies, and air forces preparing to attack.

We must adapt the concept of imminent threat to the capabilities and objectives of today's adversaries. Rogue states and terrorists do not seek to attack us using conventional means. They know such attacks would fail. Instead, they rely on acts of terror and, potentially, the use of weapons of mass destruction—weapons that can be easily concealed, delivered covertly, and used without warning. . . .

The United States has long maintained the option of preemptive action to counter a sufficient threat to our national security. The greater the threat, the greater is the risk of inaction—and the more compelling the case for taking anticipatory action to defend ourselves, even if uncertainty remains as to the time and place of the enemy's attack. To forestall or prevent such hostile acts by our adversaries, the United States will, if necessary, act preemptively.

The United States will not use force in all cases to preempt emerging threats, nor should nations use preemption as a pretext for aggression. Yet in an age where the enemies of civilization openly and actively seek the world's most destructive technologies, the United States cannot remain idle while dangers gather.

to agreement on the analysis of a particular issue is through a National Intelligence Estimate (NIE)—a document hammered out by the heads of the intelligence agencies summarizing the community's collective "best guess" about a particular topic. The previous NIE on Iraq, dating to 2000, had refrained from making a categorical declaration that Iraq had weapons of mass destruction. It focused primarily on the presence of WMD *programs* and the *development* of chemical and biological weapons; its assessment of Iraq's nuclear program was merely that the program had not been abandoned.

NIEs are usually requested by Presidents contemplating important policy decisions. This was not the case with regard to Iraq; instead, the request was made by Congress. Senate Democrats had pressed for an up-to-date NIE after hair-raising speeches about the Iraqi threat by the president and the vice president. Senators wanted to hear what the intelligence community said before they voted on the war resolution requested by the president. The 2002 NIE, now seen as a monumentally flawed document, was the product of a several-week rush job. The document was completed on October 1, and an unclassified version was made available to the public. (The following is based on United States 2002a; see also Woodward 2004, 197–99; Pollack 2004, 80; Priest and Pincus 2004, 34; Kaufman 2004, 11, 38; Kinsella 2004, 14). The new NIE declared, "Baghdad has chemical and biological weapons as well as missiles with ranges in excess of UN restrictions; if left unchecked it will probably have nuclear weapons during this decade. . . . Since inspections ended in 1998, Iraq has maintained its chemical weapons effort, energized its missile program, and invested more heavily in biological weapons; in the view of most agencies, Baghdad is reconstituting its nuclear weapons program."

The consensus of the intelligence community was that Iraq had renewed production of chemical agents (a blistering agent, mustard gas, and several nerve agents: sarin, cyclosarin, and VX). And although it confessed that there was no specific information on Iraq's CW stockpile, it nevertheless stated that Iraq probably had at least one hundred metric tons of CW agents, and possibly as much as five hundred metric tons, much of which was probably produced within the last year with rebuilt capabilities. The NIE also declared that Iraq possessed biological weapons and had active development, production and weaponization programs that were now more advanced than before the Gulf War and that Iraq could quickly produce a variety of BW agents, including anthrax. It put the chances that Iraq possessed smallpox at fifty-fifty. These judgments were expressed with "high confidence."

The NIE also expressed "high confidence" that Iraq was continuing or even expanding its nuclear weapons program. It stated that "Iraq probably would not be able to make a weapon until 2007 to 2009, owing to inexperience in building and operating centrifuge facilities to produce highly enriched uranium." But if Iraq were to obtain fissile material from outside sources, the NIE predicted that it could actually make a nuclear weapon "within several months to a year."

The report declared that Iraq possessed a covert force of up to a dozen prohibited Scud missiles and was developing and deploying new missiles with prohibited ranges. The report also maintained that Iraq could launch unmanned aerial vehicles (UAVs or drones) that could deliver BW or perhaps CW against U.S.

troops and U.S. allies in the region, and perhaps even against the U.S. homeland, if brought into range. On the other hand, the report declared that Saddam Hussein was unlikely to initiate an unprovoked attack against the U.S. with WMD. And no hard proof was put forward for the claimed stockpiles of existing weapons. The intelligence agencies hedged their bets considerably, and the State Department's Intelligence and Research division (INR) filed eleven pages of disagreements. Most of the dissenting views were not declassified until July 2003. Neither the president nor his NSC adviser read the entire ninety-two-page classified report, and only a few members of congress read more than the five-page executive summary (Ricks 2006, 61). Casual readers were likely to get a false sense of consensus from the intelligence community.

Much of the "evidence" behind these assessments is now seen as having been inaccurate, contrived, or overstated. Moreover, the errors in the NIE were not random; they were all in the direction of overstating Iraqi capabilities. A report in 2004 by the Senate Select Committee on Intelligence and a presidential commission (the Commission on the Intelligence Capabilities of the United States Regarding Weapons of Mass Destruction, also known as the Silberman-Robb commission) concluded that the NIE's findings were uniformly incorrect, constituted a major intelligence failure, and in many cases simply did not reflect the evidence known at the time. Indeed, strong contrary evidence was available to government analysts, and many intelligence officers had serious doubts about Iraq's alleged WMD programs.

For instance, it turned out that the unmanned aerial vehicles (UAVs or drones) were made purely for observation and surveillance. They were not designed for chemical or biological agents and did not carry warheads. By January 2003 the director of U.S. Air Force Intelligence had come to this conclusion, but the U.S. Air Force lost the intelligence debate. The UAV scare was based on two ambiguous pieces of intelligence: a report that an Iraqi general had expressed interest in purchasing autopilots and gyroscopes for the UAV program and information that a U.S. manufacturer had included topographic mapping software in its shipment to Iraq. (This had been done as a matter of standard procedure by the manufacturer and not at the request of Iraq.) The Silberman-Robb commission (CIC 2005, 505) determined that the U.S. "Intelligence Community was too quick to characterize evidence that contradicted the theory that UAVs were intended for BW delivery as an Iraqi 'deception' or 'cover story.'"

Second, the administration's claims concerning Iraqi stockpiling and production of biological weapons were almost entirely based on the judgment that Iraq possessed mobile labs for the production of biological weapons. This judgment, in turn, rested precariously on evidence derived almost entirely from a single unreliable source, code-named Curveball. Curveball was an Iraqi chemical engineer who provided information to German intelligence, which in turn shared his debriefing information with the U.S., but U.S. agents had no direct contact with Curveball. Curveball intelligence was managed by the Defense Intelligence Agency's Defense HUMINT Service, which took no responsibility for checking his reliability or veracity. Curveball turned out to be a fabricator and the brother of an aide to Ahmed Chalabi, head of the Iraqi National Congress and a favorite of Pentagon neocons (CIC 2005, 439–42; Ricks 2006, 91). He had been fired from the Iraqi facility in question years before the activities he described were alleged to have taken place. While some CIA agents had doubts about Curveball's reliability, these doubts did not make their way up to the highest levels of the political food chain. Inspections after the war have proved that the trucks in question produced hydrogen for weather balloons and that Iraq had, in fact, unilaterally destroyed its remaining BW agents in 1991 and 1992. A second source for Iraq's BW program also existed, but had been declared to be a fabricator by the Defense Intelligence Agency (DIA), though this detail failed to make its way to Powell and other principals (Ricks 2006, 91).

Third, the claim that Iraq possessed CW stockpiles and was expanding its CW production was similarly flawed. It was based on overreliance on ambiguous overhead satellite imagery that showed heavy activity of "Samarra-type" Iraqi trucks transshipping unknown materials into and out of various military depots, including suspected CW sites from March 2002 to early 2003 (CIC 2005, 475). The conclusions based on this ambiguous imagery constituted an enormous inferential leap. In fact, the Silberman-Robb commission suggests that the perceived massive "increase" in transshipments was simply an artifact of the increased volume of satellite images taken. The Iraqis weren't using more trucks, we were just taking more pictures of them (CIC 2005, 484–85). Postwar inspections showed that no CW stockpiles existed and that there was no evidence that Iraq had restarted CW production. The "Samarra trucks" were not involved in transshipments of chemical weapons.

The fourth error was that Iraq had reconstituted its nuclear program. The NIE claimed that Iraq had purchased specialized aluminum alloy tubes that were a crucial component (rotors) in rebuilding its gas centrifuges to enrich uranium. This proved to be inaccurate. The tubes were designed for conventional (and unprohibited) military purposes. As the IAEA and U.S. Department of Energy (DOE) experts had maintained all along, they were components for rocket shell casings that Iraq had been using for roughly fifteen years—the Nasser 81-mm mobile rocket launcher. The tubes themselves never entered Iraq; they were intercepted in Jordan in June 2001. Iraq had no uranium enrichment capability of any type nor any means of reconstituting it in the near future.

The chief culprit in this story seems to have been the U.S. Army's National Ground Intelligence Center (NGIC), the presumed experts on conventional warfare technology, who declared that the tubes in question were a poor choice for rockets and that no known rocket used this alloy, even though the U.S. Mark 66 Hydra and the Italian Medusa (on which the Nasser 81-mm was based) both used it. Apparently unaware of the specifications for the Nasser 81 rockets, the NGIC clearly failed to search for readily available basic facts and information.

The NGIC shared responsibility in this matter with others. The CIA and its Weapons Intelligence, Nonproliferation and Arms Control Center (WINPAC) concurred that the tubes must be intended for use in centrifuges. When a test of the tubes by a contractor at the government's Oak Ridge laboratories suggested that the tubes were not strong enough for use in centrifuges, the CIA took issue with the contractor's methodology. The CIA also withheld information about the American Hydra and Italian Medusa rockets from the NGIC. Finally, the CIA refused to convene the authoritative panel charged with resolving technical disputes of this nature—the Joint Atomic Energy Intelligence Committee (CIC 2005, 426–29; Linzer and Gellman 2004).

The Senate Select Committee concluded that the CIA knowingly "skewed" its reports and "stacked" the evidence. It "withheld some evidence that did not accord with its conclusions, circulated other data in ways the Senate said was 'at a minimum, misleading' and tried to tilt ostensibly independent consulting reports toward the conclusion that the tubes were evidence of a nascent Iraqi nuclear program" (Linzer and Gellman 2004).

A fifth error also related to Iraq's nuclear program. There was an unsubstantiated claim that Iraq had attempted to obtain uranium yellowcake from Niger, a claim the CIA itself eventually assessed as "highly dubious" in a footnote to the NIE. The claim was based on a purported contract between Iraq and the government of Niger, now widely viewed as a crude forgery—the Niger official whose signature is on the document was not even in the government at the time of the purported contract. Even if Iraq had purchased yellowcake, it would have been useless since Iraq had no ability to enrich the uranium into weapons-grade U-235. (Bamford 2004, 331; Blix 2004, 108, 154, 211, 227–34; Halper and Clarke 2004, 216; Barstow, Broad, and Garth 2004; Priest and Pincus 2004, 34; Kaufman 2004, 24–27).

As part of this comedy of errors, the Energy Department supported the NIE conclusion that Iraq was "reconstituting its nuclear program" on the basis of the yellowcake claim considered suspect by the CIA and the State Department's INR. The CIA supported the conclusion based on their analysis, from WINPAC, of the validity of the centrifuge claim, seen as entirely wrong-headed by the Energy Department, INR, and the IAEA (Barstow, Broad, and Garth 2004).

At any rate, with the official judgment of the intelligence community now in hand, in the second week of October Congress passed the president's war resolution: 296 to 133 in the House and 77 to 23 in the Senate. Without declaring a formal state of war, Congress authorized the president to use U.S. armed forces "as he determines to be necessary and appropriate in order to—(1) defend the national security of the United States against the continuing threat posed by Iraq; and (2) enforce all relevant United Nations Security Council resolutions regarding Iraq." The uranium and centrifuge claims and the potential nuclear threat posed by Iraq appeared crucial in garnering congressional support for the resolution (Halper and Clarke 2004, 214; Kaufman 2004, 31). Moreover, the congressional vote reflected public opinion. By late 2002, polls indicated that strong majorities in the U.S. believed that Saddam Hussein had WMD, had nuclear weapons, would strike the U.S. eventually with WMD, and had assisted the 9/11 terrorists. A majority also supported a preemptive invasion of Iraq (Kaufman 2004, 30–31).

On November 8 the UN Security Council voted unanimously for Resolution 1441. The resolution—the product of a long and difficult negotiation—declared that Iraq was, and continued to be, "in material breach" of UNSC Resolution 687. It gave Iraq a "final opportunity" to comply with the UN resolutions. It required that Iraq submit a fully accurate and complete declaration of all WMD programs and stated that any false statements or omissions in this document would constitute a "material breach" of its obligations. It reminded Iraq that "serious consequences" would result from a further material breach. It declared that

Iraq's continued development of WMD, its support for terrorism, and its repression of its own population presented an ongoing threat to international peace and security. It recalled, in two places, the authority (given in 1990) to UN members in Resolution 687 to use "all means necessary" to gain Iraqi compliance with UN resolutions. It demanded that Iraq permit weapons inspectors to return to Iraq and grant them unrestricted access to all sites. (The United Nations Monitoring, Verification and Inspection Committee, or UNMOVIC, created by the Security Council in December 1999 to replace the defunct UNSCOM, was set to work with the IAEA to carry out these inspections. UNMOVIC was headed by Hans Blix, and the IAEA by Mohamed ElBaradei.) And finally, the resolution determined that the Security Council would reconvene upon receipt of any report of Iraqi noncompliance. A "material breach" would lead the council "to consider the situation and the need for compliance."

The resolution was purposely vague. The United States interpreted Resolution 1441 as giving members a blank check to take action against Iraq if it was guilty of any further material breaches. Other states were adamant that such action could only be taken by a future vote of the Security Council.

In light of the apparent solidarity in the Security Council and the buildup of U.S. forces in Kuwait, Iraq immediately (November 13) agreed to unrestricted inspections and UNMOVIC started work in late November. On December 7, Iraq submitted a 12,200-page declaration of its WMD programs. The document contained little new information and declared that Iraq had no remaining stocks of banned weapons. The CIA performed an instant analysis of the declaration and declared it to be false because it contained significant omissions—about mobile labs, attempted purchases of yellowcake, aluminum tubes, and drones. This line of argument was strongly pursued by Vice President Cheney, who claimed the declaration was patently false and not in compliance with Resolution 1441 and therefore constituted grounds for war. But President Bush and his other advisers were more cautious (Woodward 2004, 234–35). The diplomatic track would have to be pursued, at least for a little longer. The inspections would continue.

The central issue for UN inspectors concerned the presence of chemical and biological weapons. While documents indicated that at one time Iraq possessed certain amounts of various types of these agents, it was unclear how much of these weapons remained. UNSCOM had found and destroyed many of these supplies between 1991 and 1998, but not the total amounts known to have previously existed. Iraqi officials maintained that Iraq itself had disposed of the remaining amounts in 1991 by pouring chemical and biological agents into the ground. Unfortunately, the destruction of these weapons was not witnessed by UN inspectors, and the records of the process had been destroyed (Blix 2004, 162).

UNMOVIC and IAEA inspections in early December 2002 uncovered a few artillery shells with mustard gas in a site previously inspected by UNSCOM and a crate of warheads designed for chemical weapons, though without the chemical agents themselves, and a few documents suggesting Iraq had once investigated uranium enrichment by the use of lasers (Blix 2004, 96, 117, 167). No activities were found with regard to a nuclear program. That was it.

By the end of December 2002, as roughly one hundred thousand U.S. forces were being deployed to the Persian Gulf region and as the U.S. began calling up

National Guard and Reserve forces, things began to come to a head. In a crucial meeting on December 21, Tenet and his deputy at the CIA, John McLaughlin, made the intelligence community's latest case for the presence of WMD in Iraq. The administration's rationale for war—the presence of WMD in Iraq, not Iraqi connections to al Qaeda and 9/11, not human rights violations—lay in the balance. Bush, Cheney, Rice, and Card were present. The president was clearly unimpressed. Woodward (2004, 249) describes the scene:

> Bush turned to Tenet; "I've been told all this intelligence about having WMD and this is the best we've got?"
> From the end of one of the couches in the Oval Office, Tenet rose up, threw his arms in the air. "It's a slam dunk case!" the DCI said.
> Bush pressed. "George, how confident are you?"
> . . . "Don't worry, it's a slam dunk!"

This assurance by the CIA chief was enough to seal the deal; the president appeared satisfied. Presidential boots had begun to slide down the slippery slope of foreign intervention and war.

National Security Adviser Condoleezza Rice normally did not see it as her job to offer personal advice to the president unless she was asked; her job was to see to it that the president got the facts and heard the arguments of all his advisers. She asked questions, she coordinated between the various foreign policy departments and agencies, and she ran "the process." In late December Bush finally asked Rice whether she thought the country should go to war. Her response was a firm yes. She argued that U.S. credibility was at stake; the country was engaged in a strategy of coercive diplomacy with Iraq, and as part of that strategy the president had made a threat. If Saddam Hussein refused to reveal his WMD, we couldn't let him off the hook; we had to make good on our threat to use force. The inspections could not be allowed to continue indefinitely (Woodward 2004, 251–54). Bush never directly asked Rumsfeld, or Powell or any of the other principals, whether they thought the U.S. should go to war with Iraq. He thought he had a good idea of where they stood (Woodward 2004, 251–52). Rice's advice confirmed the direction the president was already leaning toward. At the end of December 2002 the president gave the order to send more than two hundred thousand forces to the Persian Gulf. General Franks had already moved his CENTCOM headquarters from Tampa to Qatar.

An interesting "black hole" in our knowledge of the war is that we do not know for sure when the fundamental decision for war was made or how it was made. There appears not to have been an NSC "now or never/up or down" debate on the issue, and different observers have different views on when the president made up his mind. Paul O'Neil believes the decision was made in the earliest days of the administration; Cheney thinks it was in January 2002 at the time of the "axis of evil" speech (Lemann 2004, 157). The Downing Street Memo suggests the summer of 2002 at the latest. Risen (2006, 79–80) reports that the CIA's Middle East station chiefs were called to a "come-to-Jesus meeting" in London in November 2002 by their superiors, who told them the debate was over and war was imminent. Woodward points to early January 2003; by then Rumsfeld was telling the president that he would quickly lose the option of *not* going to war

(Woodward 2004, 261–62). Early that month the president told Rice that "we're going to have to go to war" (Woodward 2004, 254).

Preparations for war had been put into place and were beginning to develop a momentum of their own. By January 13 the decision for war had become firm: The president told Saudi ambassador Prince Bandar and Secretary of State Powell that "it" was going to happen. But at this point there was no public announcement; the military buildup required a certain amount of secrecy and political camouflage to be successful. The diplomatic track had to be allowed to run its course—though not for long. By the twenty-fourth General Franks had delivered the final war plan to Secretary Rumsfeld and the new JCS chief, Gen. Richard Myers. U.S. forces already in the region had ballooned to one hundred thousand.

The UN process could not be allowed to vegetate interminably. Bush was impatient; as Rice explained to the 9/11 Commission, the president was tired of "swatting flies." The time for action was nearing. It was decided that Powell would have to make the case to the Security Council that inspections were not working and that Iraq was continuing to violate its obligations to disarm. Then perhaps the Security Council could be persuaded to vote for a resolution permitting the use of force; if not, the United States would have exhausted all peaceful options and would take the bit in its own teeth with a "coalition of the willing." The administration had constructed a neat policy trap. If UN inspectors found WMD in Iraq, Saddam Hussein would be unmasked as having committed a material breach of the UN resolutions, justifying the use of force. If no weapons were found, we could conclude that he was cheating because he had hidden them from inspectors—also a material breach. It was a win-win situation.

In the meantime (January 27), the initial report to the Security Council by UNMOVIC head Hans Blix contained a mixed bag. While Blix declared that Iraq had not yet genuinely accepted disarmament, and while there were discrepancies between the number of chemical weapons Iraq had originally possessed and those presumably destroyed, as yet there had been no major discoveries of stockpiles of chemical or biological weapons. He neither asserted nor excluded the existence of WMD in Iraq. And IAEA head Mohamed ElBaradei reported no evidence that Iraq had revived its nuclear program or had any physical capability to produce nuclear weapons. (He also avowed that the infamous aluminum tubes were for short range missiles rather than a uranium centrifuge.) The following evening, in the annual state of the union address, President Bush mentioned that the British government learned that Saddam Hussein had sought uranium yellowcake from an African nation, reviving the disputed claim that IAEA head ElBaradei would publicly shoot down a week later.

Bush could not simply write off the UN process. The major sticking point was that the "coalition of the willing" would not be willing to use force without a first attempt at a Security Council resolution authorizing force. Bush had to try, even if the effort failed. Prime Minister Blair drove this point home to Bush on January 31. He made it clear that for domestic political purposes in Britain, there must at least be an attempt to get a resolution. Secretary Powell's multimedia presentation to the United Nations on February 5 kicked off this attempt.

As eyes around the world were glued to television sets, Powell briefed the Security Council on U.S. intelligence concerning Iraq's continued violations. He presented a collage of information whose goal was to convince UN members and global opinion that U.S. intelligence services had found a "smoking gun"—concrete evidence of Iraqi violations of its obligations to disarm. With the CIA's Tenet sitting behind him, Powell showed satellite photos of "cleaned up" WMD sites in Iraq and played intercepted recordings of Iraqi commanders giving suspicious orders. He cited "human sources" who told of warheads being dispersed with biological weapons and of mobile biological weapons labs. (At this point both Tenet and Powell were unaware that the reliability of Curveball and other informants had been challenged by subordinates.) He accused the Iraqis of making UAVs with the ability to deliver BW and CW at long ranges. Powell reiterated the administration's position toward Saddam Hussein: "Should we take the risk that he will someday use [WMD] at a time and a place and in a manner of his choosing? . . . The United States will not and cannot run that risk for the American people. Leaving Saddam Hussein in possession of weapons of mass destruction for a few more months or years is not an option, not in a post September 11 world" (Whitney 2005, 106).

Behind closed doors American, British, and Spanish diplomats attempted to craft a resolution to permit force against Iraq that would be agreeable to the required nine state majority in the Security Council, including the other permanent members. But the negotiations were a tough sell. The French, the Germans, and the Russians were strongly opposed to the use of force in the immediate future. The French threatened a veto, and President Chirac and his foreign minister, Dominique de Villepin, argued that nothing in the current situation justified going to war.

For the Bush administration, very little justified continued restraint. On February 7, President Mubarak of Egypt sent his son, Gamal, to Bush with a message. Saddam Hussein might be looking for asylum. What would the American response be? Bush's answer was that any country that took him in would be harboring a terrorist. The U.S. would give no assurances (Woodward 2004, 314). If Saddam Hussein were to slink off in the middle of the night, the security problems would still remain. The U.S. would still have to act.

Blix made his dreaded second report to the Security Council on Friday, February 14. The message did not bode well for those who wished to obtain Security Council permission for the use of force. No prohibited biological or chemical weapons had been found and Iraq was deemed to be cooperating with the inspectors. Millions of protesters marched in major cities around the world that weekend, demonstrating against a war in Iraq. Global attention was focused on New York, Washington, and Baghdad.

In the last week of February, the United States, Britain, and Spain began circulating a draft Security Council resolution that would declare that Iraq had failed to make use of its "final opportunity," thereby permitting UN members to take military action to ensure Iraq's disarmament. Meanwhile, U.S. troop strength in the Persian Gulf had reached 200,000 by the end of February, and by the first week of March, a combined force of 250,000 troops was in the region. On March 7, UNMOVIC reported that Iraqi cooperation with inspections had improved. And while inspectors discovered about one hundred Al Samoud II missiles with ranges just beyond the allowable 150 kilometers, Iraq agreed to cooperate in their destruction. About seventy were destroyed prior to the war (Blix 2004, 190).

By March 12 the attempt to devise a Security Council resolution acceptable to a nine-member majority collapsed. On the sixteenth Bush met with Blair and Spanish prime minister Aznar in the Azores, where they agreed at long last to pull the plug on negotiations. On March 17 the administration asked UNMOVIC head Hans Blix to remove the inspectors from harm's way.

At 8:00 that night, the president, in a televised speech to the nation, announced an ultimatum: Saddam Hussein and his sons were given forty-eight hours to leave the country "so that disarmament can proceed peacefully." The president explained:

> Intelligence . . . leaves no doubt that the Iraqi regime continues to possess and conceal some of the most lethal weapons ever devised. . . .
>
> We are acting now because the risks of inaction would be far greater. In one year, or five years, the power of Iraq to inflict harm on all free nations would be multiplied many times over. With these capabilities, Saddam Hussein could choose the moment of deadly conflict when they are strongest. We choose to meet the threat now, where it arises, before it can appear suddenly in our skies and cities. (Whitney 2005, 169–70)

Two days later, on the morning of March 19, President Bush gave the order to execute Operation Iraqi Freedom. The war had begun.

Let us now look at some of the factors that were crucial to the outbreak of this war, beginning with the international system level of analysis.

INTERNATIONAL SYSTEM LEVEL CHANGE: THE END OF THE COLD WAR

The structure of the international system changed dramatically in the course of a few years between 1989 and 1991. Starting with elections in Poland in 1989, one by one, the Soviet bloc countries in Eastern Europe voted out their Communist Party governments and elected opposition parties to power. By the end of 1991 the Soviet Union itself had disintegrated into fifteen separate, independent states, some of which embarked on a truly noncommunist path. The Warsaw Pact alliance was dissolved, as was the Council of Mutual Economic Assistance (also known as COMECON), the Soviet-led economic bloc. And with these changes, the Cold War bipolar system ceased to exist.

In its place was a new post–Cold War system that seemed something of a historic oddity. Military power was oddly distributed; while several major powers and some middle powers had nuclear weapons, there was only one military power with true global reach—the United States. The system could be perceived differently by different observers. Academic specialists created a whole new cottage industry to analyze the post–Cold War arrangement. The global structure was variously described as: a unipolar system dominated by the U.S. as a global hegemon, a unipolar system without hegemony, a multipolar system with multiple actors sharing economic, political, and military power, and a hybrid "uni-multipolar" system having a single superpower but with several significant major powers. Others felt that while the system might be experiencing a "unipolar moment," it would quickly return to multipolarity. (See, for instance, Brooks and Wohlforth 2002; Fettweis 2004; Huntington 1999; Krauthammer 1990–1991, 2002–2003; Mastanduno 1997; Wilkinson 1999; and Wohlforth 1999.)

A decade after the collapse of the Soviet Union, the evidence for unipolarity was becoming clearer. The gap between the system's topmost power and the others was unprecedented. On all measurable indices of power—military capabilities, economic strength, technological advancement, strategic location, resource base, political stability, and cultural allure—the U.S. had clear preeminence, with no serious challenger in sight on any dimension, let alone on a combination of them. The U.S. spent more on its military than the next ten to twenty states combined, depending on the measurements used for comparison. And it did this with capacity to spare, spending only about 3.5 percent of its gross domestic product on the military. With the world's dominant air force and the only truly global navy, only the U.S. had the capacity to project its power to any spot on the globe. It also had a qualitative technological military advantage, based on the fact that it spent more on military research and development than most of the rest of the world combined. Moreover, military effort by potential rivals—as measured by military spending as a percent of GDP—had not been substantially increased. Indeed, defense spending in most major powers had been declining relative to GDP. Nor had any rival states formed military alliances to counterbalance U.S. dominance (Wohlforth 1999, 9–22; Brooks and Wohlforth 2002, 21–31; Fettweis 2004, 90–93).

At the turn of the new century, the U.S. economy was the largest in the world. Its GDP in 2002 was over $10 trillion, roughly thirty times that of Russia, ten times that of China, and over two and a half times that of Japan. Moreover, no rival was "catching up." The U.S. economy grew by 27 percent in the 1990s, almost twice the growth rate of the European Union and triple the Japanese rate. Its economic edge was buttressed by a level of investment in technological development unmatched by its economic rivals; for instance, in the 1990s the U.S. spent twenty times what the Chinese spent on technological development (Brooks and Wohlforth 2002, 21–31; Fettweis 2004, 90–93).

In sum, far from being a temporary phenomenon, the degree of unipolarity from 1990 to 2002 actually increased as the United States' potential rivals lost ground relative to the U.S. (Krauthammer 2002–2003, 552). As the United States contemplated war against Iraq, it was more powerful in both absolute and relative terms than ever before. Indeed, the margin of superiority held by the global leader may have been greater than at any time in history (Brooks and Wohlforth 2002, 21; Fettweis 2004, 92).

A strong case could be made that objective structural conditions within the international system at the start of the new century made U.S. intervention in Iraq more likely. The system was, at a minimum, conducive to preventive war by the global superpower. Unipolarity is, by definition, a global structure in which one state's capabilities are too great to be counterbalanced but not so concentrated as to result in a true global empire (Wohlforth 1999, 9). Under these conditions, "hegemonic war" or world wars over global leadership will be unlikely.

Because of the vast disparity of power between the global leader and its rivals, there can be no misperception over the true military balance. There may be dissatisfied states in the system, but there will be no dissatisfied states with the capability to challenge the system's superpower. This is the logic of "hegemonic stability theory" as found in Modelski and Thompson's (1989) long cycle theory and Gilpin's (1981) hegemonic war theory.

However, the small probability of a great power war does not mean that all wars will be less likely. If it is true that power is most effectively checked by counterbalancing power, unipolarity meant that after 1991 the United States was released from many of the normal constraints imposed on it by the countervailing power of rivals. Its military might endowed it with a wide assortment of policy choices—at a time when its increased relative power would lead to increased interests and goals. It could use its predominant military capabilities to neutralize threats to its security, to maintain access to resources, or to promote human rights and democracy. Importantly, it could use its military force against small states without fear that the system's major powers would intervene. The U.S. could attack Iraq without fear of military consequences, a situation that was manifestly not true during the bipolar Cold War. Thus twenty-first-century unipolarity would provide an opportunity for the U.S. that it lacked prior to the collapse of the Soviet bloc.

Leaders rarely believe their state is secure enough, and this applies even to leaders of strongest states (Mearsheimer 2001, 2, 34). Indeed, preventive wars appeal to leaders intent on maintaining their positions in the global hierarchy. (This axiom is inherent in the September 2002 National Security Strategy of the United States of America.) The problem with being the system's "top dog" is that the future will always tend to look worse than the present. Hegemonic powers keep a wary eye on all long term threats. And, as prospect theory tells us, "actors are prone to accept great risks when they believe they will suffer losses unless they act boldly" (Jervis 2005, 587).

As we have noted, the structure of the international system, and what this means for any particular country's foreign policies, is a matter of perception, subject to various interpretations. Therefore, we will need to turn to the individual level of analysis and look at the belief system or worldview of Bush administration officials and how these beliefs affected their perceptions of the international system and the threats the United States faced from transnational terrorist groups and from Iraq.

THE INDIVIDUAL LEVEL

Contending Worldviews in the War Cabinet

Belief systems help leaders to "construct" their own visions of the world—visions that may or may not help them understand reality. It is difficult to make sense of the decision for war by the Bush administration without an examination of the underlying belief systems of the president and his top-level advisers. Their distinct worldview colored their understanding of the nature of the international system in the post–Cold War world, guided their assessment of the threats that faced the United States, and informed their analysis of the immediate situation in Iraq. It was the prism through which they interpreted the past and the present, and it was the lens through which they dreamed about the future.

The Vulcans: Realists, Neoconservatives, and Assertive Nationalists

Members of President Bush's top-level foreign policy team have often been referred to as the "Vulcans" (Mann 2004). This was a term applied by Condoleezza Rice to the group of foreign policy specialists who advised George W. Bush in his presidential campaign in 2000. The name stuck when the Bush administration took office. While the Vulcans shared many common views, they were not a monolithic group; significant divisions existed. However, the similarities in worldview outweigh the differences. Vulcans of all stripes shared a set of interrelated ideas. (This section draws on Mann 2004, xvi–xvii, 329, 362–63; Halper and Clarke 2004, 9–22; Boot 2004, 20–28; and Daalder and Lindsay 2003, 13–16, 36–49, 85.)

Vulcan Similarities

First, the Vulcans argued that the United States was not in decline. Quite the contrary; the end of the Cold War had made clear that the U.S. was a global superpower without parallel. Far from declining in power, the U.S. was increasing its power relative to both its allies and its rivals. The world had been transformed from a bipolar system into a unipolar system. This meant that the U.S. no longer needed to make concessions or compromises with other countries, especially with morally disreputable regimes. Nor were alliances or multilateral agreements required for U.S. action abroad. Allies might prove to be more of a hindrance than a benefit; they would only constrain U.S. freedom of action.

Second, the Vulcans believed that because of its position of global predominance the U.S. should assert its role as global leader, actively promoting international peace and security, but also creating and shaping a global environment friendly to U.S. interests and principles. Moreover, the U.S. should work to ensure that no other power was ever in a position to challenge it—a goal that required a sustained high level of budgetary support for the U.S. military.

Third, the group focused on traditional security issues and emphasized the importance and utility of military power. The Vulcans were dedicated to increasing U.S. military power, and they believed it was important to demonstrate U.S. strength and the willingness to use force. Weakness encouraged others to strike against the U.S. Moreover, there was a conviction that, as the president said, "the best defense is a good offense" (Daalder and Lindsay 2003, 83–85).

Fourth, they believed states were still the key actors in the international system, not transnational interest groups or other nonstate actors. One implication of this was that to be successful, international terrorist groups must be backed by states. U.S. counterterrorist activities could therefore focus on states who supported terrorist groups.

Fifth, the Vulcans argued that although the end of the Cold War had changed the nature of threats that the U.S. had to face, the United States still lived in a dangerous, Hobbesian world. Their view of the world was, at least for the short term, pessimistic: Military conflict is the norm; trust and cooperation are elusive.

Sixth, in the post–Cold War world, the nature of threats had changed so that the old tools of deterrence and containment were no longer appropriate or workable. Deterrence and containment might be ineffective against terrorist groups without territory or assets to protect, and one could not count on deterrent threats having an effect on irrational dictators in "rogue states." With the declining utility of deterrence and containment, the new security environment might require that the U.S. take preemptive military action to deal with threats.

Seventh, the Vulcans all believed (though with varying degrees of intensity) in **American exceptionalism**, that the United States was special and different, a country whose values are universally admired, a country that used its military power for good, and a country that was indispensable to global progress. The U.S. should use its power to promote American values abroad, especially the values of political democracy and freedom (including economic freedom). In this belief, the Vulcans were guided by the concept of a democratic peace: A world of substantially more democratic states would be substantially more peaceful because democratic states do not go to war with each other. Thus the spread of liberal democratic values increases U.S. security.

Within this general worldview, differences appeared. Three recognizable subgroups can be identified: traditional realists, assertive nationalists, and neoconservatives.

Realists and Assertive Nationalists

Early in the Bush administration it appeared that traditional realists were the dominant faction. Realists like Condoleezza Rice, Colin Powell, and Powell's deputy at the State Department, Richard Armitage, tended to be more pragmatic and cautious than the neocons. Their views were more akin to the foreign policy movers and shakers in the first Bush administration—National Security Adviser Brent Scowcroft (Rice's mentor), Secretary of State James Baker, and President G. H. W. Bush himself—and ultimately, former secretary of state Henry Kissinger. Applying the "lessons of Vietnam," they tended to be more hesitant to use U.S. military power abroad. And they were therefore skeptical of using the military to engage in peacekeeping missions and nation building. They were extremely reluctant to use U.S. force abroad to build democracy and support human rights. They saw this as an "idealistic" exercise unrelated to U.S. vital national interests. Finally, they tended to be fairly "internationalist" in outlook, placing more value on the usefulness of international institutions, great power diplomacy, and the need to cooperate with traditional allies than would others within the Vulcan camp. They focused their attention primarily on foreign relations with major powers like Russia and China.

A second group, located at the top levels of the administration, held considerable power. Called assertive nationalists (Daalder and Lindsay 2003, 15), they were conservative realists like Vice President Dick Cheney and Secretary of Defense Donald Rumsfeld, who were skeptical of the neocons' crusading zeal and their emphasis on nation building and human rights—though they agreed with their emphasis on U.S. exceptionalism and unilateralism. They merely wished to use U.S. power to defeat the nation's enemies and counter threats to national interests. Like the neocons, however, they were deeply skeptical of diplomacy, international institutions, and international law (Halper and Clarke 2004, 14; Daalder and Lindsay 2003, 15–16, 47). This faction of the Vulcans was the most unilateralist and most conscious of the need to preserve U.S. freedom of action (Boot 2004, 24–26). They also believed that traditional realists like Powell were too cautious in the use of force and too constrained by the lessons of Vietnam. They argued that timidity in the use of force projected an image of American weakness (Daalder and Lindsay 2003, 134).

Neoconservatives

The third group, neoconservatives, occupied posts at the secondary level in the Bush administration, though not at the highest levels. The list of neocons includes Paul Wolfowitz, deputy secretary of defense; Douglas Feith, undersecretary of defense for policy; I. Lewis Libby, chief of staff to Vice President Cheney; Steven Hadley, deputy national security Adviser; Elliot Abrams, NSC staff assistant for the Near East, Southwest Asian, and North African Affairs; Richard Perle, member and one-time chair of the Defense Policy Board until he resigned in February 2004; John Bolton, undersecretary of state for arms control and international security affairs and later U.S. ambassador to the UN; Peter Rodman, assistant secretary of defense for international security affairs; and Zalmay Khalilzad, NSC staffer for Afghanistan and Iraq policy, then U.S. ambassador to Afghanistan, and then ambassador to Iraq.

Neoconservatives tended toward a more Manichaean and puritanical approach to international politics than the realists; they saw issues in terms of absolute moral categories: good versus evil. And they saw other countries as easily divisible into two camps—"with us or against us." They often spoke about the need for "moral clarity" in U.S. foreign policy. The words of President Bush's spring 2002 West Point address gave voice to this moralistic approach: "Moral truth is the same in every culture, in every time, and in every place . . . there can be no neutrality between justice and cruelty, between the innocent and the guilty. We are in a conflict between good and evil, and America will call evil by its name."

The neocons were uncomfortable with the realists' pragmatism, their emphasis on maintaining international stability, their emphasis on diplomacy, their willingness to work with authoritarian regimes (and with multilateral institutions), and with the relative lack of moral content in the foreign policies they espoused. Instead, they championed the use of American power to upset the current international status quo by promoting democracy, human rights and free markets abroad through forceful regime change. They proposed to stimulate radical change in the Middle East in order to "drain the swamp" and eliminate the conditions that fostered terrorism. They believed that the collapse of communist governments from 1989 to 1991 signaled the victory of economic capitalism and political democracy and their acceptance as universal values. They accepted the validity of "the democratic peace"—the idea that democratic countries do not fight each other and that a world of democratic states would therefore be a more peaceful world. They believed that a state's behavior is shaped by its political systems. Authoritarian states were conflict prone, aggressive, and untrustworthy (Jervis 2005, 577–79).

As a result, neocons espoused a kind of muscular Wilsonian idealism, or "Wilson on steroids." While the goal of traditional realists had been to maintain international stability, neoconservatives were true radicals. Their goals were "transformational"; they sought to shape the global environment to make it consistent with American values. Consequently, they supported the use of U.S. military forces for purposes of "nation building." (What they actually mean by this term is "state building," the construction of new, democratic political institutions.) For the neoconservatives, the promotion of democracy was a central aspect of the identity of the United States (Monten 2005, 113).

Neocons had long focused on Iraq as a major threat to U.S. interests. Two of their number, Perle and Wolfowitz, had pressed the elder President Bush to oust Saddam Hussein at the end of the 1991 Gulf War (Halper and Clarke 2004, 147). In 1992, in the aftermath of the Gulf War, Wolfowitz, Libby, and Khalilzad were responsible for a draft of the Defense Planning Guidance document written for Defense Secretary Cheney that proposed that the U.S. block the emergence of any potential competitor, championed unilateral use of U.S. power, advocated preemptive use of U.S. force, and identified Iraq and North Korea as primary trouble spots for the U.S. (The draft was leaked to the press, creating such a furor that Cheney had to revise it.)

Neocons also were very supportive of Israel. In 1996, while Clinton occupied the White House, several neocons who would later be part of George W. Bush's foreign policy team—Richard Perle, Douglas Feith, and David Wurmser (first a State Department official and then Cheney's Middle East expert)—had hired themselves out as consultants to the incoming Israeli prime minister, Benjamin Netanyahu. Their report not only advised Netanyahu to make a "clean break" with the Oslo peace process and ditch the "land for peace" approach in negotiations but also advised him to accept a preemptive military doctrine. The consultants suggested that Israel could resolve its problem with the Palestinians by launching a preemptive strike against Lebanon, and then escalate the conflict to encompass a regional war against Syria and Iraq, with the goal of removing Saddam Hussein from power. The result would be to remake the Middle East and "roll back" the threat to Israel from its neighbors. For neocons, Iraq—with its educated, urban population and its potential for an active civil society—seemed an especially good candidate for a democratic transition in the Arab world (Bamford 2004, 261–65; Halper and Clarke 2004, 106–7, 148). Wisely, Netanyahu rejected the plan.

In January 1998 Wolfowitz, Perle, Rumsfeld, Khalilzad, Bolton, and other neocons associated with the Project for the New American Century (PNAC), signed an open letter to President Clinton supporting the use of U.S. military force to oust Saddam Hussein. And Wolfowitz testified a month later before the House International Relations Committee that the only way to eliminate the threat posed by Hussein's attempt to acquire WMD would be regime change in

Iraq. Thus when Wolfowitz presented the arguments for an attack on Iraq at the crucial Camp David meeting four days after 9/11, he was rolling out a well-oiled neocon template for action in the Middle East.

The neocons' scenario for the future in the Middle East started with the ouster of Saddam Hussein in Iraq (brought about through preemptive use of U.S. military force if necessary), which would then lead to a rebuilt Iraq with democratic institutions, that would in turn lead to a seismic upheaval in the Arab world. Democracy in Iraq would lead to a "demonstration effect": The wave of democratization would spill over into Jordan, Morocco, Lebanon, Egypt, Kuwait and Saudi Arabia. Dominoes would fall, but this time the good guys would win. The triumph of democracy would have many positive effects. It would "dry up the swamp" of poverty, repression, corruption, and poor governance that planted the roots of terrorism in the Middle East. The overthrow of Iraq would deliver a strong message of U.S. power to countries like Iran and Syria. Moreover, the new Iraq would become the United States' key ally in the area (replacing Saudi Arabia), providing secure access to petroleum, and pursuing a more tolerant policy toward Israel in the bargain. Finally, there was a belief that "the road to Jerusalem ran through Baghdad," that regime change in Iraq was a necessary first step in creating the conditions for an acceptable peace in the Middle East.

The neocons were much more likely than the realists to claim that the U.S. ability to rely on the tools of deterrence and containment was declining. They believed that rogue states were generally risk acceptant and accident prone (Jervis 2005, 579) and tended to be led by "madmen"; likewise, terrorists were seen as fanatic "true believers" who had little to lose and had no fixed base of operations or territory of their own. Thus the new security environment required that the U.S. take preemptive military action to deal with threats. Reacting in a purely defensive manner might be too late and too costly. In reality, what the neocons called preemption included both military preemption against imminent threats and preventive war against speculative, long-term threats.

In contrast to realists, and like assertive nationalists, neocons tended to be unilateralists rather than multilateralists. They were "hostile toward nonmilitary multilateral institutions and instinctively antagonistic toward international treaties and agreements" (Halper and Clarke 2004, 11). However, they were not hostile to alliances per se, just to permitting multilateral institutions a veto over U.S. action (Boot 2004, 24). They did, however, tend to see the United States' traditional European allies as being less useful or necessary than previously. Their approach to international affairs tended to be more confrontational than that of the realists.

Neocons were also more supportive than the realists of U.S. unipolar primacy. They accepted what academics have referred to as the hegemonic stability theory—that the world is more stable during periods in which a single state holds undisputed military, economic, and political primacy, and they sought to extend the era of American primacy by maintaining a military capability "beyond challenge" by any state or coalition of states. Essentially, they assumed that as a response to U.S. leadership, other states would bandwagon with the U.S. rather than balance against it (Monten 2005, 148). They believed that as the dominant state in the global system, the U.S. had a special role and the normal rules of the system did not apply to it. Some neocons talked about a new Pax Americana and saw the United States as a benign imperial power providing a "moral framework" for a new world order.

Finally, neocons also led the way in identifying the development of WMD by rogue states as the most important strategic threat to the United States. They emphasized that new U.S. military technologies making weapons more accurate permitted the U.S. to fight a more "surgical" war—and one with fewer casualties. This development would make military intervention more feasible—politically as well as militarily—than in the past. The revolution in military technology was also instrumental in making feasible the strategy of military preemption. Moreover, preemptive military force could be used in service of the strategy of "counterproliferation" to prevent rival states from attaining weapons of mass destruction or the capability to deliver them.

The three worldviews or belief systems we have discussed above encompass elements of what has been called an "operational code," which, according to Alexander George (1980), contains both the underlying philosophical assumptions about (international) politics and the tactical elements of how one can best achieve one's political goals. Box 7.3 is adapted from George's classification of the content of operational codes—posed as questions—and contains the authors' estimation of the operational code of neoconservatives.

INDIVIDUAL LEVEL OF ANALYSIS

The Personality and Worldview of President Bush

Before we address the belief system of President Bush, let us first look at some aspects of his personality and leadership style that have a bearing on the decision for war. Recent assessments give us a fairly consistent picture. President Bush is depicted as decisive, impatient, short-tempered, competitive, action-oriented, and results-oriented. He has a strong sense of the certainty of his own beliefs and dislikes ambiguity and self-doubt. He is reluctant to recognize and admit errors. He places a high value on persistence and "resolve." He appears to have strong drives for power and dominance, and he requires loyalty from his advisers. He has a sense of superiority, but not a deep sense of self-confidence. As the underachieving "black sheep" of a powerful political family, from whom little was expected, he is somewhat prickly about his rise to power and has become increasingly protective of the correctness of his decisions. Though smart, he is not a complex thinker. He enjoys being president (Lemann 2004, 150–57; Daalder and Lindsay 2003, 89; Suskind 2004b).

President Bush also sees himself as someone who will act boldly and "seize the opportunity to achieve big goals" and make dramatic changes; he declines to "play it safe." Unlike his father, who admitted to being weak on "the vision thing," George W. Bush is described as being "drawn to big, landscape-changing ideas" (Woodward 2004, 88; Daalder and Lindsay 2003, 32; Lemann 2004, 150, 164). These traits suggest that Bush is a risk-acceptant decision maker rather than risk averse. The combination of risk acceptance and the pursuit of "big goals" creates the possibility that when mistakes are made, they will be made on

Box 7.3. The Neoconservative Operational Code.

A. Philosophical Questions

1. Q: *What is the essential nature of politics? Harmony or conflict? What is the fundamental character of one's opponents?*
    A: It's a Hobbesian world in which conflict is endemic. The nature of at least some enemies—such as rogue states and global terrorist organizations—is that they are evil and they hate America and its democratic institutions. On the other hand, a world of democratic states would be much more harmonious.

2. Q: *What are the prospects for the eventual realization of one's fundamental values and goals? (Optimistic or pessimistic?)*
    A: Optimistic. The United States has an opportunity to restructure the world so as to increase democracy and freedom. American values will become universally accepted; the American model of democratic capitalism has no serious rival in the post–Cold War world. U.S. leadership will produce bandwagoning by others.

3. Q: *Is the future predictable? In what sense and to what extent?*
    A: Yes, at least in the long-term. Democracy and freedom will spread throughout the world, though there may be short-term setbacks.

4. Q: *How much control can political leaders have over historical developments? What is the role of the individual in shaping history? What is the role of chance in human affairs?*
    A: Leaders with the courage to pursue large goals can make a difference.

B. Instrumental Questions

1. Q: *What is the best approach for selecting goals or objectives? (For instance, on the basis of purely unilateral national interest or on the basis of multilateral considerations involving self-restraint?)*
    A: American national interest should have clear priority over other goals.

2. Q: *How are goals pursued most effectively? (For instance, through force or diplomacy? Unilaterally or multilaterally? Through threats or promises of rewards?)*
    A: Unilateralism is preferred to multilateralism. Threats of force, especially those made by states with unrivaled military power, are effective. However, deterrence, defense, and containment may not work against rogue states and terrorists; preemptive force may be necessary. Countries are more likely to be taken advantage of if they rely on rewards. Appeasement doesn't work.

3. Q: *How are risks calculated, controlled, and accepted? (For instance, through slow escalation of one's actions or through a fait accompli?)*
    A: The lesson of Vietnam is that escalation is unlikely to be effective. The lesson of 9/11 is that the risk of inaction is greater than the risk of taking military action.

4. Q: *What is the best timing of action to advance one's interests? (What, for instance, is the utility of preemption or surprise? Should force be used simultaneously with negotiation? Should one only negotiate from strength?)*
    A: In the current era timing is extremely crucial. Time is not on our side. The United States cannot afford to wait until threats are manifest. Preemption may be preferable to defense.

5. Q: *What are the utility and role of different means for advancing one's interests?*
    A: Military means are more effective than liberal critics believe them to be—especially in the hands of a dominant hegemonic power.

a grand scale. Jervis (2005, 581) suggests that the shock of 9/11, and the concomitant increase in danger and uncertainty, made Bush more willing to take risks to prevent further acts of terrorism.

What do we know about the George W. Bush's general outlook? President Bush has a complex set of interrelated views that are tied to his personal convictions. First, Bush is probably the most religious president since Jimmy Carter. Bible study is part of his daily regimen. Prompted by his own family's outrage at his drinking, and aided by the intervention of the reverend Billy Graham, George W. Bush became a "born again" Christian in 1985, when he was thirty-nine years old. Many have reported that he believes his calling as president is to carry out God's will and that he views his role as part of a divine mission to lead his nation at a critical moment in history (Daalder and Lindsay 2003, 87–89; Didion 2003, 84; PBS 2004; Wallis 2003, 2–4). Suskind (2004b) reports that in a meeting with Amish farmers in Pennsylvania in 2004 Bush said, "I trust God speaks through me."

The president sees the war on terrorism and the war against Iraq in the context of his perception of a divine mission (Wallis 2003, 3–5). In the words of President Bush in his speech at the National Cathedral after 9/11, "Our responsibility to history is already clear: to answer these attacks and rid the world of evil." He sees fighting the war on terrorism as the "calling" of his generation (Woodward 2004, 91). In his January 2002 state of the union address he said, "History has called America and our allies to action and it is both our responsibility and our privilege to fight freedom's fight." In a speech on the first anniversary of the 9/11 tragedy, the president said, "I believe there is a reason that history has matched this nation with this time. . . . We know that God has placed us together in this moment." Bush sees the U.S. as having a responsibility to promote freedom, but even this is placed in a religious context. In the president's words, "Freedom is not America's gift to the world. Freedom is God's gift to everybody in the world" (Woodward 2004, 88–89).

Those close to the president say that after the attacks of 9/11, he found his "mission in life" (Wallis 2003, 3). Jervis (2005, 585) suggests that "Bush's response to September 11 may parallel his earlier religious conversion and owe something to his religious beliefs, especially in his propensity to see the struggle as one between good and evil. There is reason to believe that just as his coming to Christ gave meaning to his previously aimless and dissolute personal life, so the war on terrorism has become, not only the defining characteristic of his foreign policy, but also his sacred mission."

Second, based in part on his religious convictions, Bush has a tendency to see the world in Manichaean terms, as a moral struggle between the forces of good and evil, with the United States representing good (Wallis 2003, 4). After 9/11 he declared to other countries that in the war on global terrorism, "Either you are with us, or you are with the terrorists." No middle ground was to be allowed. The president made countless references to evil, an indication that for him foreign policy had a moral dimension. In his speech to congress September 20, 2001, the president declared: "Freedom and fear, justice and cruelty, have always been at war, and we know that God is not neutral between them." Moreover, Bush's certainty and his inability to reflect critically on his own decisions are probably byproducts of his faith, his belief in a divine plan, and his simplistic good versus evil approach to issues (Wallis 2003, 4).

Third, Bush appears to be an "ideological thinker." As we have seen, he works more or less deductively from moral, religious, and political principles rather than inductively from empirical facts. He is a fundamentalist rather than a rationalist; his approach to information and ascertaining "the truth" does not lend itself to nuanced, complex thinking. In Isaiah Berlin's famous comparison of the hedgehog and the fox—"the fox knows many things, but the hedgehog knows one big thing"—President Bush is clearly a hedgehog. He is not a seeker of facts or opinions. His decision style is to make decisions quickly "without detailed study and investigation" (Suskind 2006, 72). The president seems to have a remarkable lack of curiosity about issues. He is predisposed to believe things on faith and principle without examining evidence and to hold these beliefs with absolute certainty. He is a "true believer" rather than a pragmatist. Suskind (2004b) reports that a Republican who had worked for President Reagan and the first President Bush told him, regarding George W. Bush, that "he dispenses with people who confront him with inconvenient facts. . . . He truly believes he's on a mission from God. Absolute faith like that overwhelms a need for analysis. The whole thing about faith is to believe things for which there is no empirical evidence." The president trusts intuition over facts; he tells his advisers that he relies on his "gut" to make decisions or he "prays over it." When Senator Joe Biden presented his concerns in the Oval Office to the president about the situation in Iraq in the months after the end of combat, he asked the president, "How can you be so sure when you know you don't know the facts?" The president's reply was, "My instincts" (Suskind 2004b).

What Is George W. Bush's Foreign Policy Orientation?

It is an open question where George W. Bush fits into the three foreign policy orientations outlined above. Unschooled in foreign affairs until his campaign tutorials by the Vulcans, one might be tempted to say that George W. Bush was at least initially an "empty vessel" into which various strands of Vulcan thought were poured. His campaign rhetoric and his early pronouncements as president seemed to place him in the traditional realist camp. Candidate Bush made quite a few statements unbecoming a neocon. He said the U.S. would refrain from intervention abroad in areas where vital U.S. interests were not at stake, he opposed the temptation to engage in nation building (Somalia, Kosovo, Haiti) and to commit troops overseas, and he declared that "military power is not the final measure of might." To the extent that he talked about Iraq, his solution was to "isolate" it rather than invade it. Moreover, he argued that the United States should be "humble abroad." His main adviser in the preelection "tutorial" process, Rice, was primarily a realist whose analytical focus was on traditional threats posed by major powers such as China (rather than Iraq). Her January/February 2002 article in *Foreign Affairs*, "Campaign 2000: Promoting the National Interest," which laid out the Bush foreign policy message, made no mention of the use of force for regime change or the promotion of democracy abroad or a doctrine of preemptive war.

Ultimately, however, Bush appears to have been "converted" by the neocons (and by the like-minded assertive nationalists) after September 11. There is no question that September 11 transformed George W. Bush (Halper and Clarke 2004, 135–38; Jervis 2005, 580–81). This is to be expected. What we know about how and when individuals undergo changes in images and worldviews suggests that such transformations are most likely to occur if the individual's views are not yet very rigid and if there are dramatic events that challenge one's current view and compel the individual to reassess his or her thinking to deal with the events (Deutsch and Merritt 1965). Moreover, change is more likely if it does not involve a change in the individual's core beliefs.

What were the changes to President Bush's worldviews after 9/11? He came to believe that in the current global environment, deterrence and containment (and even traditional measures of defense) might not be effective strategies against rogue states or terrorists who were developing WMD and that one might have to adopt preemptive strategies. He came to see terrorism as a greater threat to the United States than previously. He accepted that democratic transformations in the Middle East might be an important solution to the spread of terrorism. He believed that "if people were given freedom and democracy, that would begin a transformation process in Iraq that in years ahead would change the Middle East" (Woodward 2004, 412, 428). And he adopted a more proactive and assertive set of tactics to achieve the goal of spreading democracy and promoting American values. These changes were primarily instrumental rather than philosophic. The president did not have to change his fundamental view of the world. Indeed, the attacks on 9/11 probably reaffirmed his view that the world was a dangerous place, that international law and organizations could not protect the United States, and that terrorists were not really "stateless" but were aided and abetted by rogue states like Afghanistan (Daalder and Lindsay 2003, 79–80).

Once the 9/11 attacks had taken place, the president (and perhaps Rice as well) gravitated toward the neocon position held by Wolfowitz, Libby, Hadley, and Perle. And it is that subset of worldviews which guided the president's view of the global situation and his view of the proper U.S. response to the post–Cold War environment. For a man whose intellectual underpinnings in foreign affairs were of rather short standing, and therefore somewhat tenuous, the leap was not so breathtaking. After all, realists, assertive nationalists, and neoconservatives share quite a few beliefs. The transition from one to another is significant, but not earthshattering. The neocon approach clearly fit with certain aspects of his broader ideology, his temperament, and his personality.

Individual Level: Perceptions and Misperception

Although it is difficult to lump all of the top-level decision makers in the Bush administration together, nevertheless most U.S. leaders held similar perceptions about the global situation and the conflict with Iraq. Many of these perceptions and misperceptions were important in moving U.S. policy toward war. Among these perceptions were: (1) the perception of a unipolar international system in which the U.S. played the role of global leadership, (2) perception of a grave and growing threat from Iraq, (3) perception of an easy victory, and (4) perception of an advantage from an offensive, preventive strike.

Perceptions of the International System

Let us return to our discussion of the international system. Between 1989 and the end of 1991, the Berlin Wall had been torn down, communist governments in eastern Europe had collapsed, the Warsaw Pact had been abolished, and the Soviet Union itself had been rendered into fifteen independent states. The Cold War was over. The structure of the international system was changing at warp speed. What would be the essential characteristic of the new global structure? What should the United States' strategy be in response to changes in the global system? As proponents of the constructivist approach to international politics argue, system structure itself never directly determines the behavior of states. The structure of the international system affects state behavior indirectly; it is mediated through ideational and cultural factors such as images and perceptions, established norms, ideology, learning processes, socialization, social interaction and the practices of statecraft, and other cultural phenomena (Desch 1998, 167; Hopf 1998, 173).

Given a high degree of structural uncertainty about the changing system, the nature of the post–Cold War system was, as we have seen, open to interpretation. President George H. W. Bush, on whose watch these monumental events took place, talked vaguely about a "new world order." For the first President Bush, that generally meant a world in which major powers, having no fundamental conflicts among them, would be able to cooperate together for the common good. The United Nations and its Security Council could, at last, be effective instruments of world peace and security. Because of great power cooperation, the world would be a safer and more peaceful place. The bipolar world would give way to a multipolar world in which the U.S. would be the leading state, but political, economic and military power would be dispersed among China, Japan, the European Union, the new Russia, and other states. President George H. W. Bush and President Clinton both emphasized multilateralism and the use of international organizations as a way of accommodating and reassuring other major powers that the U.S. would not attempt to use its power to impose its will on others (Mastanduno 1997, 61–62).

As we have seen, the neoconservatives and their allies had another view of the newly born international system. With the bipolar Cold War over, the world had become unipolar, with the United States as the world's only true superpower (or hegemonic power), and the only state capable of global leadership. In this world, cooperation with others through international institutions would be useful, but not necessary. Because of its position as a hegemonic power, the U.S. would be in a position not just to lead the world, but if necessary to impose its will on the world. The U.S. should take advantage of what neoconservative columnist Charles Krauthammer called the "unipolar moment." Unfortunately, the new international system would not be more peaceful or less threatening. The nature of the threats would simply be different, with the primary threat coming from rogue states, like Iraq, that develop weapons of mass destruction.

The best hope for safety would come from "American strength and will—the strength and will to lead a unipolar world, unashamedly laying down the rules of world order and being prepared to enforce them" (Krauthammer 1990–1991, 33). To the extent that there was international stability, it would be the product of U.S. hegemonic leadership.

Both views, that of George H. W. Bush and the neocons, were compatible with the changing international situation. It was a matter of seeing the glass as half empty or half full. Neither was foreordained to become the dominant position of the U.S. government; we make of the world what we will. Which view became dominant would depend on the mix of individuals in office. That mix changed considerably in January 2001. Gone were Clinton's Democratic multilateralists. The traditional realists of the first Bush administration, represented by Colin Powell, were marginalized. The dominant faction now consisted of a coalition of neocons and assertive nationalists, and the events of 9/11 shifted the balance even further in their direction.

The neocons and their allies saw the world as unipolar. The logical implication of this was that the United States found itself in a world in which it could pursue its own national interests, as it defined them, create new rules of the game, and dispense with the strictures imposed by international institutions, international law, and alliance considerations. The U.S. had the unrivaled power to shape the world in its own image—to promote free market capitalism, free trade, political democracy, and human rights—without constraint. We could promote regime change in Iraq because it was in our interest to do it and because we *could* do it.

The perception of a unipolar global structure, plus the perceived threat from rogue states with WMD, plus the perceived opportunity presented by the nation's capabilities, led the Bush administration to attempt to reshape the international system (Jervis 2005, 588).

Perceptions of Threat

The constructivist approach to international relations reminds us that threats are socially constructed: "Since what constitutes a threat can never be stated as an *a priori*, primordial constant, it should be approached as a social construction of an Other" (Hopf 1998, 199). Power in the hands of some states is seen as more threatening than it is in the hands of others. This is the insight conveyed in Stephen Walt's famous "balance of threats" thesis—that states are more likely to balance against perceived threats than against sheer power (Walt 1987). Leaders of states act towards others on the basis of meanings or identities they have attributed to them (Wendt 1992, 396). Identities are, by their nature, relational and based on mutual interaction.

We can safely say that in the minds of most Bush administration officials, Iraq was identified as a rogue state, a sponsor of terrorists, a revisionist state, a human rights violator, a dictatorship, and a serial aggressor—the embodiment of evil. These negative perceptions of Iraq were created and confirmed in a decade of U.S.-Iraqi dyadic interaction since the end of the Gulf War. The relationship was one of rivalry and confrontation (by both), resistance (by Iraq) and punitive action (by the U.S.). Iraq constantly attempted to evade arms inspectors and economic sanctions, and it played military cat-and-mouse games with the American and British pilots in the two no-fly zones. It was one of the few states that refused to denounce the terrorist attacks of 9/11. All these considerations led to an American perception of Iraq as a threat and to the belief that U.S. security required regime change in Iraq.

These negative perceptions of Iraq were dramatically worsened by the events of 9/11. Cheney in particular appeared "preoccupied" with links between Iraq and al Qaeda (Lantis and Moskowitz 2005, 97). He sought out experts and began to read all that he could about Islam and the Middle East (Daalder and Lindsay 2003, 130).

Given that almost everyone saw Iraq as a threat, and given that many in the government had pursued regime change in Iraq virtually since Inauguration Day, once the CIA had determined that regime change could not be attained on the cheap by subversion or coup, the policy menu shrunk to the single option of a military invasion. The intellectual judgment for the necessity of this action focused on the presumed presence of WMD in Iraq, its continued violation of the UN inspection regime, and the consequent security threat Iraq posed to the region. After 9/11, the link between WMD technology, rogue states, and terrorists became solidified in the minds of many administration officials. The problem was not just that Iraq might pose a threat to its Arab neighbors and to Israel. The presumed threat expanded to include the possibility that Saddam Hussein would make his WMD available to terrorists who would use them against U.S. citizens, bases, property and perhaps even on U.S. soil. Many believed that Iraq posed the most dangerous threat of all: It might have, or quickly come to possess, nuclear weapons. The president, echoing his intelligence agencies, feared that Iraq could have a nuclear bomb in a year if it had fissile material. On the eve of the war, Vice President Cheney said flatly, "We believe he [Saddam Hussein] has, in fact, reconstituted nuclear weapons." The threat was not necessarily seen as immediate or imminent, but as a speculative, conditional, future threat.

Since no weapons of mass destruction have been found in Iraq, it is necessary to examine how the U.S. government got it so wrong.

Evaluation of the Perceived Threat: Did Iraq Possess Weapons of Mass Destruction?

It is undisputable that Iraq had several types of chemical and biological weapons prior to the Gulf War. Hussein had used poison gas against the Kurds and the Iranians. He possessed them but did not use them during the Gulf War. Between 1991 and 1998 UN inspectors discovered and destroyed chemical weapons in abundance: 40,000 chemical munitions, 480,000 liters of live chemical agents, and 3,000 tons of precursor chemical, along with equipment for the production of chemical agents (Lopez and Cortright 2004, 93). Biological weapons, including anthrax warheads, were also found. Missiles were located and destroyed. And the Iraqi nuclear weapons complex was also demolished.

But did Iraq possess WMD in the months and years prior to the 2003 war? No one knew for sure. The crux of the issue was that Iraqi documents indicated that a certain number of biological and chemical weapons had once existed, and UN inspectors could document that a large number of these had been found and destroyed, but there were still some weapons unaccounted for—the most worrisome being anthrax, VX, and botulinum toxin (Daalder and Lindsay 2003, 165). The Iraqis claimed these had been destroyed, but no evidence of this existed.

Most U.S. officials and intelligence agents, as well as UN weapons inspectors and foreign intelligence services, believed biological and chemical weapons existed somewhere. President Bush agreed. In July 2003 he declared, "There's no doubt in my mind" about the existence of these weapons (Daalder and Lindsay 2003, 166).

We know now that no such weapons existed. It is quite probable that after 1991 none of Iraq's WMD programs existed except at a vague planning level (Kaufman 2004, 29). In October 2004, Charles Duelfer, head of the Iraq Survey Group, issued his report on the seventeen-month U.S. effort to locate WMD after the defeat of Hussein's government. Duelfer reported the following conclusions to Congress in 2004 (Priest and Pincus 2004; Priest 2004; Whitney 2005, 247–327):

1. Iraq's CW stockpile had been destroyed in 1991, and there were no indications of an effort to resume research in or production of chemical weapons. There was no active CW program at the time of the U.S. invasion.
2. Iraq destroyed its undeclared stocks of BW in 1991 and 1992. It apparently abandoned its ambition to obtain advanced biological weapons by 1996, and there was no evidence of an attempt to reconstitute the BW program. There was no active BW program at the time the war started. (And there was no evidence at all of any smallpox virus program—past or present.)
3. Iraq's nuclear weapons program ended in 1991, and there was no effort to restart it. In fact, Iraq's ability to reconstitute its nuclear program progressively decayed after 1991.
4. With respect to illegal long-range missiles, there was no evidence of any of Iraq's older Scud missiles. Iraq did attempt to extend the range of its missiles beyond the range allowed by the UN. It had designs for long-range missiles and had procured components for this effort. These illegal missiles and production facilities were discovered by UNMOVIC when inspectors returned to Iraq in 2003, and they were dismantled with Iraqi compliance.
5. Saddam Hussein "aspired" to develop a nuclear capacity and intended to rebuild CW and BW programs at some point in the future, once UN sanctions had ended, but he had no formal plan to do this and no administrative structure existed to carry out the reconstruction of any WMD program. With regard to nuclear programs, he certainly had no existing capability to restart a program.

In sum, at the time of the U.S. invasion, Iraq had no WMD, but it did possess the necessary industrial equipment and the scientists who might be used to restart certain WMD programs in the future. The most likely program to restart would be mustard gas and nerve agents, which could be reconstituted within a year.

The Senate Select Committee on Intelligence reported that evidence of Iraq's illegal programs had been ignored, exaggerated, misrepresented, and selectively used. All the errors, moreover, were in the same direction: They all served to buttress the argument that Iraq was more threatening than it was in reality (Powers 2004, 87). How did this happen?

INDIVIDUAL AND SUBSTATE ANALYSIS: WHY THE MAJOR FAILURE OF INTELLIGENCE ANALYSIS?

Ten interrelated factors, at the individual and substate level, combined to push the Bush administration to overrate the threat posed by WMD in Iraq.

First, many individuals in the Bush administration had by this time come to adopt image structures reflecting what Henry Kissinger (1962, 201) once called the "inherent bad faith model." In this mindset, the level of trust in other states is so completely lacking because of past experiences that no good deed is recognized. Individuals who hold this type of image structure are capable of explaining away virtually any apparently positive behavior by an opponent (such as the destruction of weapons). There is nothing the opponent can do to change its original image in the mind of the beholder. Hostile negative images are preserved in spite of real world changes. Inherent bad faith models are typically held by leaders of countries who see themselves as enduring rivals. Certainly, most U.S. officials were predisposed to view words and deeds by Iraqis as being purposefully misleading and deceitful. Unfortunately, this was probably also the administration's view with regard to UN inspectors (Blix 2004, 261).

Second, it is a basic maxim of political institutions that public officials will see the world in light of their institutional interests and attempt to maximize these interests. For instance, all government agencies can be counted on to attempt to increase their budgets, their personnel, their missions, and their political influence. These are principles associated with the bureaucratic politics model (Allison 1971). If an institution, such as the infamous NKVD during the time of Stalin's purges, is charged with finding threats to the state and rooting out spies and enemies, it will damn well find threats, spies, and enemies. It is in its institutional interests to do so. In so doing, it proves its own necessity, increases its political influence, and gives itself leverage in attaining even more resources, personnel, and influence. In short, if the president and vice president believe that Iraq is a threat, then U.S. intelligence agencies can be expected to find evidence that Iraq is a threat. The result is that the intelligence community tells political leaders what they think they wish to hear.

Third, to some extent, all agencies charged with protecting national security tend to rely on a process of worst-case analysis. If they do not identify threats to the national security, they are negligent. They tend therefore to find opponents where none exist, and having found those opponents, they ask themselves what is the worst they could do to us if they wish us harm. From there it is a short step to assume that they do in fact intend to harm us and that the potential danger is in fact real. Thus, threats are perceived to exist when they do not, or small threats are interpreted as large threats. Indeed, the CIA was created in 1947 largely to prevent the kind of intelligence disaster that led the U.S. to discount the Japanese threat to Pearl Harbor. The primary purpose of the institution, as understood by its members, is to warn of impending threats (Powers 2004, 91).

Secretary of Defense Rumsfeld believed that intelligence tended to "understate problems, that bad things too often went undetected for years" (Woodward 2004, 174). Rice agreed with this assessment and memorably argued, "We don't want the smoking gun to be a mushroom cloud" (Woodward 2004, 179). Assuming the worst about Iraq appeared logical. After all, Iraq had at one time possessed chemical weapons, had used them on Iran and the Kurds, had fired missiles at Iran, Saudi Arabia, Bahrain, and Israel, and had started two wars in eleven years. Once inspections had ended, it was "natural" to assume that Saddam Hussein would resume his quest for nuclear weapons (Powers 2004, 89).

The failure to predict the terrorist attacks of 9/11 was, of course, also on everyone's mind. CIA director Tenet believed that no one, after 9/11, "wanted to be caught understating a potential threat"—his organization least of all (Woodward 2004, 438–39). The tendency toward worst case analysis was strengthened by the time of the October 2002 NIE because it was clear that U.S. forces might soon be engaged against an enemy with WMD (CIC 2005, 534). Clearly, it would be a smaller error to report a threat that would later prove to be nonexistent than to fail to report a threat that later proved to be real. Intelligence agents were never punished for the former, but things would go badly if they failed to report a threat that turned out to be real only in the aftermath of some disaster. Worst case analysis seemed to be a prudent approach to threats; it appeared to be in the national interests as well as the interest of U.S. intelligence organizations.

Tenet's assurance on December 21, 2002, that the evidence in favor of the existence of illegal WMD programs in Iraq was a "slam dunk" convinced the president and his skeptical secretary of state. Most doubts were swept aside, and doubts held by lower-level analysts did not always make it to the top of the political food chain. (Powell was unaware of the questionable reliability of source Curveball when he addressed the Security Council about Iraq's WMD.) At the top, the lack of dissenting opinions gave the appearance that the evidence was much more solid than it in fact was.

Fourth, Rumsfeld, Tenet, Rice and the others were well aware of past failures of the U.S. intelligence community to identify threats in timely fashion. These failures had led to lessons of history that served as guides to future policies. Intelligence analysts were mindful of the history of Iraq's past production and use of WMD and its successful attempts at concealment of those weapons technologies (CIC 2005, 411). For the Bush administration, one relevant lesson of history was that U.S. intelligence organizations often miss or underestimate important threats to national security. After the Gulf War, inspectors found that prewar assessments of Iraq's chemical and biological weapons programs had been underestimated. More critically, prior to the Gulf War, the U.S. intelligence community had predicted that Iraq was five to seven years away from developing nuclear weapons. Inspections after the Gulf War seemed to indicate that Iraq was substantially closer to the construction of a nuclear weapon than previously thought possible. At least, this was the interpretation of the situation perceived by Bush administration officials. Iraq was deemed, in 1991, to be perhaps no less than a year away from its goal, two at most—closer than even the previous worst-case estimates. Secretary Rumsfeld called the old predictions "flat wrong," and in September 2002, the president claimed that Iraq had been a mere six months away from developing a nuclear weapon.

These statements were wildly inaccurate. In fact, Iraq's crash program in 1990–1991 was a failure. The enrichment program was considerably behind schedule, with only a small fraction of the necessary equipment (electromagnetic separators and gas centrifuges) in place, and Iraq produced only micrograms of enriched uranium. In addition, Iraqi scientists had not yet produced a weapons design by 1991. In retrospect, the pre–Gulf War U.S. estimate was fairly realistic. If Iraq had been allowed to continue its programs, it might have been able to produce a weapon by 1996 (Kaufman 2004, 20–28; Priest and Pincus 2004, 34). Thus the "lesson of the Gulf War" was based on myths. Nevertheless, by 2002 U.S. intelligence analysts feared the possibility of a surprise about Iraqi nuclear programs (CIC 2005, 414). To prevent being burned again by underestimating the threat, analysts "systematically discounted" less malignant interpretations of Iraq's WMD potential (CIC 2005, 431–32).

For Vice President Cheney there were two other crucial lessons learned from the earlier Gulf War and from the terrorist attacks on 9/11: Time is not on our side and the risk of inaction in the face of threats is worse than the risk of taking action (Blix 2004, 71). Both lessons served to push the administration toward the use of preventive force as a way of dealing with the perceived threat from Iraq.

Fifth, normal human psychological processes predispose individuals to rely on their already existing and strongly held beliefs. Beliefs are remarkably resistant to change. The concept of cognitive consistency helps to explain why human decision makers, beset by conflicting and ambiguous information, tend to ignore information that does not fit with their preexisting images of the world. Cognitive processes work to prevent individuals from holding inconsistent beliefs and images. Individuals find ways to ignore or explain away information that conflicts with their current images and beliefs. Thus when we look at the world, we tend to see those things that we expect to see, based on our present images of the world. And if we come across information that we do not expect, the human mind is capable of distorting those disconcerting pieces of information into something more consistent with our other images and beliefs.

A major conclusion of the Silberman-Robb commission (CIC 2005, 430) was that the U.S. Intelligence Community took as its starting point the premise that Iraq possessed CW/BW stockpiles, that they had been successfully concealed, and that Iraq was reconstructing all of its WMD programs, including its nuclear weapons programs. Incoming evidence was filtered through this intellectual prism. Moreover, there was no effort made to question this basic premise or put forward alternative explanations for the lack of evidence of WMD in Iraq. The commission concluded: "The analytical flaw was not that this premise was unreasonable (for it was not); rather, it was that this premise hardened into a presumption, and analysts began to fit the facts to the theory rather than the other way around." The result was that "analysts effectively shifted the burden of proof, requiring proof that Iraq did *not* have active WMD programs rather than requiring affirmative proof of their existence" (CIC 2005, 527).

Since much of the evidence of Iraq's WMD programs was ambiguous or missing or presumed to be the product of deliberate disinformation, it was relatively easy to dismiss any contrary assessments. They could simply be chalked up to Iraq's proven "denial and deception" program. When inspectors failed to find weapons, this was not necessarily taken as proof that weapons didn't exist; rather, it simply confirmed the assumption that Iraq was effectively hiding its WMD programs. For instance, when source Curveball pointed out the location of a mobile BW lab and U.S. satellites were unable to find it, CIA's WINPAC simply assumed it had been effectively concealed (CIC 2005, 452). Similarly, the Army's NGIC interpreted the Iraqi claim that the high-strength aluminum tubes were really for use in short-range rockets as "a poorly disguised cover story" with the result that "the thesis that the tubes were destined for centrifuges took on the quality of a hypothesis that literally could not be disproved: both confirming and contradictory facts were construed as supportive evidence" (CIC 2005, 432). In fact, as the Silberman-Robb commission (CIC 2005, 527) concluded, "In some instances analysts' presumptions were so firm that they simply *disregarded* evidence that did not support their hypotheses. . . . Rather than weighing the evidence independently, analysts accepted information that fit the prevailing theory and rejected information that contradicted it."

During the spring of 2002, the CIA's assistant director for collection devised a program in which the agency recruited U.S.-based family members of Iraqi scientists to return to Iraq to visit their relatives and interview them to determine the status of Iraq's WMD programs. Some thirty Iraqi scientists were thus interviewed by their American relatives. Risen (2006, 85–107) reports that all thirty reported (accurately) that Iraq's nuclear, chemical and biological weapons had been destroyed and abandoned. The CIA ignored this crucial intelligence. The report was not included in any of the CIA's assessments; it was not disseminated to other intelligence agencies, or shared with senior policymakers in the departments of State or Defense, the NSC, or the White House.

When a defector who had been a source on Iraq's reputed CW program was evaluated as wildly unreliable (he absurdly reported on a new Iraqi weapon that combined chemical, biological, and nuclear weapons properties), the information he supplied was nevertheless retained within the system "because analysts simply rejected those parts of his reporting that seem implausible and accepted the rest" because it fit their assumptions (CIC 2005, 487). Discordant information was ignored or reinterpreted so as to maintain conformity with the dominant interpretation. The weapons *did* exist; they were not found because Saddam Hussein had successfully hidden them from inspectors!

Sixth, the belief that Saddam Hussein was hiding WMD and had restarted WMD production after inspectors left in 1998 was so pervasive throughout the administration that it would be difficult for single individuals to challenge that assumption (Daalder and Lindsay 2003, 166; CIC 2005, 515). The "conventional wisdom" that Iraq was effectively hiding its WMD programs was shared so widely by most Bush officials that it had become part of the institutional culture of the administration; indeed it could be said to be a core belief of the president's team. (It was also inextricably connected to another core belief: Saddam had to be overthrown.) The institutional culture produced an "echo chamber effect" in which all the "right" or preferred interpretations rebounded off each other, and agencies and officials confirmed each other's biases. This conventional wisdom led to several results, including the failure to apply rigorous tests of evidence to the collection of intelligence and the sloppy validation and vetting of dubious intelligence sources who nevertheless produced the "right" answers (CIC 2005, 404–5).

Seventh, the foreign intelligence services with whom U.S. agencies worked tended to share the same raw intelligence and analysis about the presence of WMD in Iraq. Analysts in the British intelligence community and in Egypt had come to that conclusion, but so had some within the French and German intelligence communities (Blix 2004, 71, 127, 194). Even UNMOVIC head Blix had a gut feeling that Iraqi WMD did exist (Blix 2004, 112). The "cross-fertilization" of similar viewpoints among intelligence organizations was fairly strong. To some degree, the consensus was the result of "circular reporting" in which multiple agencies may have unknowingly relied on the same unreliable sources, providing them with "false corroboration" of their reports (CIC 2005, 538). In some cases, the effect of cross-state information sharing was more insidious. Bamford (2004, 307–12) notes a study done by retired general Shlomo Brom for the Tel Aviv University's Jaffe Center for Strategic Studies that concludes that Israel's intelligence community was unable to discover any evidence of WMD in Iraq and in fact knew that Iraq had no WMD stockpiles but nevertheless "hyped" the Iraqi threat to the U.S. in the months before the war because it didn't want to interfere with the president's plan for war.

Eighth, one member of President Bush's team, Vice President Cheney, assumed an unofficial role in the administration to look out for the really big threats and to examine the potential for major disasters, a role similar to what Alexander George (1972) has called a "Cassandra's Advocate." Early on, his focus was on the possession of WMD in the hands of "rogue states" and terrorists. He discounted the threat from al Qaeda, apparently under the impression that such a terrorist organization must have the backing of a state sponsor like Iraq in order to pull off such well-planned, coordinated attacks against U.S. targets all over the world. Al Qaeda was just a little guy; Iraq had to be the "big kahuna." With such a powerful member of the administration ringing the alarm bells, there was very little chance that Iraq would be ignored.

Suskind (2006, 62, 163–68) takes the argument farther. He maintains that after the discovery of a potential link between Pakistani nuclear scientists and Al Qaeda in October 2001, the Vice President began to take the approach that "even if there is a one percent chance" of terrorists getting WMD, the U.S. had to "treat it as a certainty in terms of our response" and act immediately. With regard to such "low-profile, high-impact" events, the U.S. would have to respond. And not having clear evidence of such an impending event should not restrain us; we might never have absolute proof. For safety's sake, the standard of proof would have to be low; mere suspicion would become the "threshold for action." Suskind calls this the "one percent doctrine" or the "Cheney Doctrine" and sees it as the framework taken by the administration in its approach to the issue of Iraq. An obvious corollary to the doctrine was preventive war.

Ninth, the compartmentalization of the intelligence process meant that different parts of the intelligence community had different information and no parts of it had all the relevant intelligence about Iraq. In these circumstances, when the vice president made speeches saying that the administration was certain that Iraq had active BW, CW, and nuclear programs, the apparent certainty of conclusions served to dampen the skepticism of intelligence analysts, who might simply conclude that the principals at the top of the political pyramid might have access to certain classified "crown jewels" that underlings had not seen (Ricks 2006, 51). They must know more than we do.

Tenth, while it was difficult to know Iraq's military capabilities, it was equally hard to fathom Saddam's motives and intentions. Saddam had WMD in the past; he had used them. If he had destroyed them as he claimed, why couldn't he just demonstrate this to the inspectors and thereby induce the UN to end sanctions? Why subject the country to over a decade of economic sanctions and a loss of oil revenue estimated at $100 billion (Woodward 2004, 298)? Why dismantle the weapons and then pretend to have them, giving inspectors a hard time? Why, especially, given the negative consequences of the bluff? Americans wouldn't have done this; it wouldn't be rational. It made no sense for Iraq to subject inspectors to such harassment if Iraq had no weapons to protect.

Some answers to this dilemma are provided by the report of the administration's own Iraq Survey Group. The report, based on postwar interrogation of Saddam Hussein and his captured associates as well as documents found in Iraq, concluded that Iraq's weapons programs were primarily a response to Iranian programs, and that Iraqi resistance to inspection might have been designed to fool the Iranians into thinking that Iraq still possessed WMD. Saddam himself believed that WMD had saved Iraq twice, once when Iraq faced defeat at the hands of Iran in the long Iran-Iraq War and again in 1991 to prevent an invasion of Baghdad by coalition forces in the Gulf War (Whitney 2005, 249). In the 1991 war Saddam had given directions to use chemical and biological weapons if the United States invaded Baghdad. Thus WMD were deemed vital for deterrence against Iran and the U.S. Moreover, Saddam Hussein believed that whatever Iraq did, the U.S. would not permit the UN to end sanctions (Graham 2004, 33). Cooperation would not lead to positive results.

Finally, there is the possibility that the intelligence process was "politicized," that political leaders pressured the intelligence community to produce an analysis of the situation in Iraq that would conform to the desires of the president and his advisers. We will discuss this shortly in the section on substate level decision processes.

INDIVIDUAL LEVEL OF ANALYSIS: OPTIMISM AND RATIONAL CHOICE

Historically, optimistic perceptions have been associated with decisions for war (Blainey 1973). After the U.S. victory in Afghanistan, those who had supported regime change in Iraq emphasized the likelihood that Saddam Hussein's government would crumble as the Taliban had done in Afghanistan. Moreover, as that war wound down, U.S. military assets could be easily transferred to Iraq. A set of interrelated perceptions were involved. First, just as in 1991, the perception was that success would be sure and swift and the number of casualties low (Daalder and Lindsay 2003, 131–32). While the U.S. military had become more technologically proficient in the years after the first Gulf War, the Iraqi military had been substantially degraded by war and sanctions. Because of the inherent illegitimacy of Saddam Hussein's regime, Iraqi forces, prompted by a U.S. propaganda effort, could be persuaded to lay down their arms. Indeed, Secretary Rumsfeld's plan to use a minimal number of troops in a rapid drive toward Baghdad was based on this assumption—which proved to be correct. Moreover, the U.S. had numerous reports of Iraqi brigade-division commanders who promised U.S. contacts that they would join against Saddam once the invasion began (Bowden 2005, 113). When the time came, none did.

A second perception, held by Cheney, Rumsfeld and others, was that Americans would be greeted as liberators rather than occupiers, greeted with flowers rather than bombs. Saddam Hussein was a brutal tyrant, and anyone, Muslim or non-Muslim, who rescued the Iraqi people from his evil clutches would surely be welcomed as a savior. Consequently, the postwar period was deemed to be fairly rosy, something on the order of the U.S. occupation of Germany after WWII. State building would lead to a stable democracy in Iraq. Moreover, the postwar nation-building costs for the U.S. were presumed to be low. In retrospect it is apparent that these perceptions of the immediate postwar situation were substantially divorced from reality. While the analysis of the threat from Iraq had been subjected to worst-case analysis, the analysis of the postwar situation was the product of best-case analysis.

Other perceptions fit into the same complex of ideas. For instance, it was perceived that "time was not on our side" and that "the risk of inaction was greater than the risk of action." Moreover, the lesson of Israel's attack on the Iraqi nuclear reactor in 1981 was that preemption could be extremely useful against rogue states pursuing WMD programs. This lesson—combined with the lesson from inspections after the Gulf War that major WMD programs could be successfully hidden from inspection—was a powerful incentive to take immediate action before the threat emerged full blown.

As the Bush administration viewed the problem, a military solution appeared to be a logical, reasonable solution to a difficult problem. Explanations of war based on rational choice theory tell us that national leaders decide for war when the expected utility (or gains) from war exceed the expected losses. According to the preeminent scholar in this field: "The size of the expected gains or losses depend on (a) the relative strengths of the attacker and the defender; (b) the value the attacker places on changing the defender's policies, relative to the possible changes in policies that the attacker may be forced to accept if it loses; and (c) the relative strengths and interests of all other states that might intervene in the war" (Bueno de Mesquita 1981, 46).

The perceived calculus within the Bush administration probably amounted to the following:

1. The perceived costs—economic, military, political—were believed to be low, especially given a rapid military assault using minimal forces and "smart" weapons. And the costs of postwar nation building would be small and borne primarily by Iraq itself and by our allies.
2. The relative military power of the U.S. and Iraq was seen as being highly imbalanced in favor of the U.S.

3. The probability of success in achieving regime change was believed to be high.
4. The outcomes (or utility) of a military invasion—the ouster of Saddam Hussein, the destruction of Iraq's WMD capabilities, the demonstration effect on U.S. enemies, the establishment of democracy, the ability to remove U.S. forces from Saudi Arabia and to secure U.S. access to Iraqi oil, and so on—were seen as highly desirable and beneficial. This was especially so when compared to the outcomes associated with refraining from the use of force—continuation of Saddam's rule, continued loss of U.S. credibility, continued threat from Iraq's WMD program and from the proliferation of WMD to terrorists, and continued regional instability.
5. The likelihood of any military counter intervention by any state to assist Iraq was seen as nil. No state had a real interest in perpetuating the regime of Saddam Hussein, let alone the capability to achieve this in the face of U.S. power.
6. In terms of timing, there was a perceived advantage accruing to a preventive use of force.

A rational calculation, therefore, made the option of military force a "slam dunk" to the president and his advisers. One simple explanation of the war therefore is simply that the expected utility of using force far outweighed the expected utility of restraint.

The rational choice argument fits quite nicely with Vasquez's (1993, 64–65) argument that wars between pairs of states that are unequal in power (**wars of inequality**) have different causes than wars between states that have equal capabilities (wars of rivals). He argues that wars of inequality are more likely to be associated with the "logic of preponderance and of opportunity" in which the strong seek dominance and the weak are unable to prevent it. War initiation in these situations is "more likely to be governed by rationalistic cost-benefit considerations" and is consistent with expected utility theory. In wars of inequality the strong initiate wars because they can and because they have an opportunity.

A final word about the rational calculation of policy choices should be mentioned. It deals with the issue of risk. Prospect theory is usually seen as an amendment to the expected utility theory. While expected utility theory emphasizes the maximizing of gains as the decision makers' primary motivation, prospect theory emphasizes the minimization of losses. It argues that individuals are likely to take greater risks to prevent losses than they are to make gains. In this case, U.S. policymakers were clearly motivated by both potential gains and by preventing potential losses. And they saw the risk of inaction to be high, while the risks of war were believed to be relatively low. Proponents of prospect theory, such as Robert Jervis (Glenn 2002, 15), would argue that in the post-9/11 world, U.S. leaders might see the U.S. as perpetually in the realm of potential losses from international terrorists—a realm in which it is "almost certain the status quo will deteriorate quickly unless we act." While this may be too much of a stretch, the Bush administration was certainly willing to take substantial risks to prevent future losses, especially if those losses were of the same order of magnitude as the 9/11 attacks. When you add in the president's generally risk-acceptant orientation toward problem solving and the vice president's one percent doctrine, whatever real risks existed from an invasion of Iraq would have seemed infinitesimally small in comparison to the potential losses that might accrue from inaction. In the Iraq war calculation, the push of gains maximization and the pull of loss prevention both edged the administration in the same direction.

SUBSTATE LEVEL OF ANALYSIS: GROUPTHINK OR BUREAUCRATIC POLITICS?

Process counts. *How* policies are made helps to determine *what* the policies are. Scholarly analysts of foreign policy typically attempt to examine how certain inappropriate or flawed decision-making processes lead to policy disasters by reducing critical thought and rational policy analysis. Two problematic decision processes are identified by academic specialists: groupthink (Janis 1982) and bureaucratic politics (Allison 1971). The two models are theoretically distinct, have entirely different characteristics, and produce poor decisions through entirely different mechanisms.

Groupthink leads to poor decisions because the individuals making the decision are so committed to maintaining the group's internal cohesion that they are unwilling to critically assess the assumptions and policy proposals of other group members, especially those of the group's leader. Few alternatives are discussed, few outsiders are consulted, debate is limited, and dissent is stifled. Group harmony and consensus are valued more than finding the best policy. On the other hand, bureaucratic politics produces poor decisions because each member of the group seeks to enhance the interests of his or her own institution at the expense of the national interest. The process is conflictual and political rather than consensual, as individuals fight over contending goals and policies. Two potential results of the process are possible. Either a "lowest common denominator" policy is chosen that can be supported by all of the relevant actors. Or a policy is determined by the members of a "winning" coalition and imposed over the objections of a smaller group of losers. Groupthink and the bureaucratic politics model are presumed to be mutually exclusive. In reality, however, we can often find some evidence of both processes in any particular government.

The decision-making process in the Bush administration might best be characterized as a mildly dysfunctional cross between groupthink and the bureaucratic politics model. While the Bush administration's foreign policy decision group was not cohesive and it contained people with different worldviews, nevertheless, their views did not diverge that much on the ideological spectrum. The dominant coalition used the levers of bureaucratic politics to reduce the effective pool of decision makers and to reduce the options, creating in effect a kind of groupthink environment.

Aspects of Groupthink in the Bush Administration

As in groupthink environments, there was a tendency not to challenge the positions of the group leader. The president's advisers might challenge one another, but there is little evidence that anyone felt comfortable challenging the president and forcing him to reexamine his views and assumptions. Once it became known that the president preferred a particular course of action—military intervention to bring about regime change—dissent was muted if not ended. Loyalty to the president was a common characteristic of his advisers; the president wanted loyal team players and his advisers understood this. Suskind (2004b) believes the president's intolerance of doubters and critics increased after 9/11. Bush's "with us or against us" mentality applied to his own government as well as to foreign countries.

The Vulcans took their lead from the president. As Bruce Buchanan has noticed in another context (the abuse of prisoners held in Baghdad), there was a "tendency for everybody to take signals from the president, that this is what we need to do and we're not going to let irritants of a lesser nature divert us from our course" (Allen 2004, 6). In the words of another analyst (Suskind 2004b): "If a president fishes, people buy poles; if he expresses displeasure, aides get busy finding evidence to support the judgment." *New York Times* reporter James Risen has a similar take on the situation. He concludes that the president and his closest advisers created a "fevered" prowar climate in the government that spread through the ranks because "Bush sent signals of what he wanted done; without explicit presidential orders, the most ambitious got the message" (Risen 2006, 61). Rumsfeld put a more positive spin on this dynamic in his interview with Woodward (2004, 181): "We don't vote. . . . What happens is discussion takes place, pros and cons are considered and we participate in those. The president begins leaning in a certain direction. [Then] people say, well, if that's the direction, you need to understand that the alternative direction has these advantages and disadvantages and the one you're leaning toward has this advantage and disadvantage and begin anticipating the problems that can accrue."

Also consistent with groupthink, there was a tendency to close the process to outsiders and not to solicit their advice, particularly if it might rock the boat. Unlike John Kennedy and Bill Clinton, who developed extensive direct lines of communication from the president to lower-level government officials and staffers and who often sought out advice and expertise from specialists inside and outside the government, President Bush preferred to consult only with his immediate circle of advisers—people with whom he felt comfortable. This was a small, closed circle and they rarely consulted with outsiders (Lemann 2004, 152). Christopher DeMuth, the head of the conservative American Enterprise Institute, observed that the close circle of advisers around the president was "both exclusive and exclusionary. . . . It's a too tightly managed decision-making process. When they make decisions, a very small number of people are in the room, and it has a certain effect of constricting the range of alternatives offered" (Suskind 2004b). Moreover, Bush, unlike "policy wonk" presidents like Clinton, was not an avid reader. He received information primarily in oral form, and primarily from his top advisers. Bob Woodward asked Bush if he ever sought advice on the Iraq problem from his father, from outsiders like Brent Scowcroft and others. His response was, "I have no outside advice. . . . The only true advice I receive is from our war council. . . . I didn't call around asking 'What the heck do you think we ought to do?'" (Lemann 2004, 159).

Since participation in the process was limited, the scope of internal debate was also limited. For instance, Halper and Clarke (2004, 218) make the following judgment:

> The environment in which the administration proceeded to war obstructed the systemic checks and balances that would have produced necessary questions requiring answers before military boots hit Iraqi soil. Important questions were not asked because the administration's policymaking culture had become highly politicized in support of the neo-conservative agenda. Either policymakers were "with the program" or they were consigned to outer darkness. . . . This was a major institutional failure. . . . The NSC, in particular, failed to fulfill its responsibility to . . . rationalize the differing perspectives of the State and Defense Departments, and to constrain special interest agendas such as those of the neo-conservatives.

In a similar vein, Paul Light makes the following observation of the Bush policy team: "The way this group of people operates is to have this kind of echo chamber in which they hear what they want to hear, see what they want to see. . . . They have no formal or informal method for challenging themselves, and that is a perfect recipe for [disastrous decisions]" (Allen 2004, 6).

The options available for top-level decision makers to discuss were limited because the president's inner circle tended to filter out views incompatible with already established lines of policy. The State Department's Richard Haass told Nicholas Lemann (2004, 159), "Those who didn't buy in [to the military option] were excluded"—a classic characteristic of groupthink processes.

The lack of internal debate over a variety of options also stemmed from the tendency toward self-censorship, very much as predicted by groupthink. As we have seen, the one man most opposed to the group consensus for preemption was Powell. Unlike his colleagues, Powell was nervous about the policy of preemption and thought that an immediate threat had to be present to justify use of military (Woodward 2004, 129). However, Powell was a career soldier with a strong sense of loyalty to the commander in chief. He might run contrary proposals up the flagpole, but when they were hauled down, he always saluted.

One of the main features of the process, and one that reflects groupthink as well as the personal style of the president, was the excessively haphazard and unstructured decision-making process. As Risen (2006, 665) notes, "After 9/11, the moderating influences of the slow-moving bureaucracy were stripped away. The president and his principals . . . held almost constant, crisis-atmosphere meetings, making decisions on the fly. Instead of proposals gradually rising up through the normal layers of government, they were introduced and imposed from above. Debate was short-circuited. Interagency reviews of new initiatives were conducted on the run." After interviewing several high-level Bush administration officials, journalist James Fallows (2004b, 73) came to a similar conclusion: "There is no evidence that the president and those closest to him even talked systematically about the 'opportunity costs' and trade-offs in their decision to invade Iraq. No one has pointed to a meeting, a memo, a full set of discussions about what America would gain and lose."

Associated with this defective process were the absence of critical analysis and the lack of willingness to reexamine original assumptions, potential risks and hazards, and to generally think about how the policy might fail. Powell himself believed that no one in the president's leadership group could "break through to insist on a realistic assessment" of events and policies. There was no one who could go to Bush and say, "Pay attention, you're in trouble" (Woodward 2004, 415).

Suskind (2004b) argues that after the initial months of the administration, a particularly closed decision style, centered on the president's lead, developed: "a disdain for contemplation or deliberation, an embrace of decisiveness, a retreat from empiricism, a sometimes bullying impatience with doubters and even friendly questioners. . . . He didn't second-guess himself; why should they?" It was a style that reflected the president's own personality and style: "This is one key feature of the faith-based presidency: open dialogue, based on facts, is not seen as something of inherent value. It may, in fact, create doubt, which undercuts faith. It could result in a loss of confidence in the decision-maker and, just as important, by the decision-maker" (Suskind 2004b).

The president himself, as Fred Greenstein observes, is not one who is disturbed by second thoughts, self-doubts or regrets; he does not like to reconsider policy decisions. He doesn't ask a lot of question. He wants action and solutions, and once he gets them he does not look back (Woodward 2002, 256). He "'doesn't turn over the rock' to see what might be waiting to bite him" (Allen 2004, 6). While the president himself rarely showed any doubts once policies had been made, it was likewise clear to his advisers that they should also dispense with their doubts and get fully on board. Bush's advisers knew that "little was more appealing to President Bush than showing resolve" (Woodward 2004, 81). Doubts, uncertainty, and hand-wringing were considered to be signs of weakness. His advisers understood this. The administration was certainly "protective" of its decisions and spent little time revisiting basic assumptions or policies.

Lemann (2004, 158) summarizes a process that is consistent with groupthink. He argues that, unlike John Kennedy during the Cuban Missile Crisis, George W. Bush did not conduct a policy process "in which a President, at the brink of war, elaborately seeks all possible information, tries to expose himself to every argument, and debates with his top officials the consequences of every possible course of action." The apparent lack of a formal, rigorous policy process fit the president's personal style of decision making perfectly (Suskind 2006, 225).

Aspects of Bureaucratic Politics in the Bush Administration

Several aspects of the Bush administration's foreign policy process indicate a typical bureaucratic politics environment. One could certainly not define the War Cabinet as a cohesive group—the one factor seen by Janis as the essential ingredient for the presence of groupthink. Indeed, as Woodward (2004, 415) reports, two of the president's principal advisers, Powell and Cheney, were barely on speaking terms. The main line of internal conflict ran between the relatively moderate State Department on one side and on the other, a more hawkish coalition based in the Defense Department, the vice president's office, and the top levels of the CIA. Rice and her NSC staff were to some degree caught in the middle of this policy struggle.

As Allison's bureaucratic politics model would predict, individuals representing a variety of government organizations—State, DOD, CIA, NSC, the vice president's staff—held somewhat differing positions that were generally related to their institutional bases. Arguments were frequently heated within deputies meetings, principals meetings and in full-scale NSC/War Cabinet meetings. Although Bush was the dominant presence in the War Cabinet, "he does not either guide or take part in the exchanges that would lead to a decision" (Lemann 2004, 159). Ideally, Bush and Rice wanted the advisers to disagree and argue over policy issues as a way of raising and clarifying options and determining their strengths and weaknesses (Daalder and Lindsay 2003, 61). However, O'Neill reports that NSC meetings tended to be highly "formal and scripted, both procedurally and intellectually" (Suskind 2004a, 288). Most real debate occurred in meetings without the president.

Wolfowitz, in his infamous interview with *Vanity Fair*, acknowledged that senior level officials had many reasons for going to war, but the "truth is that for reasons that have a lot to do with the U.S. government bureaucracy, we settled on the one issue that everyone could agree on which was weapons of mass destruction as the core reason" (2003). The strong implication is that the administration wanted regime change in Iraq, but had a difficult time agreeing on a rationale that might be presented to the world, to Congress and to the American public. It also implies that for some in the administration WMD was not the primary reason for the war.

The military invasion of Iraq addressed several goals and was thereby supported by different factions for different reasons. It would eliminate a threat of the use of WMD by Iraq and the possibility that Iraq would offer WMDs to terrorists for use against the U.S., result in a democratic transition in Iraq that could trigger a wider transition in the Arab world, allow the U.S. to withdraw its troops from Saudi Arabia, reduce the threat to Israel, retaliate for the attempted assassination of the president's father, demonstrate U.S. resolve to use force against those who opposed it and strengthen deterrence, serve as a successful test case of the administration's preemptive war strategy, strengthen deterrence, secure control over Iraq's oil reserves and make possible business deals between U.S. oil interests and the state of Iraq, and solidify the president's domestic political position as a "war president."

One possible outcome in bureaucratic politics model decision processes is that factional infighting leads to the victory of one faction over another, rather than to a compromise policy that reflects a lowest common denominator. In the American system, when institutional representatives favor differing solutions, it is the role of the national security adviser and her staff to integrate the views of the contenders and forge compromise solutions. When the adviser is unable to forge these compromises, the president must then choose among the options.

In the decision to attack Iraq, the neocons, in coalition with the assertive nationalists, won the argument and gained the support of the president. The neocon coalition won the "war for Bush's mind," while the realists lost and the State Department had to "stand down." The only concessions made to the realists in the State Department were that Iraq was put off for the second round of the war on terrorism and that the road to war was allowed temporarily to run through the UN Security Council, but only because doing so would not disturb the military's time line for Iraq.

While most of the main actors were neocons or (like Cheney and Rumsfeld) were comfortable with the neocon agenda, State Department officials were not. Powell; his deputy, Richard Armitage; Richard Haass, the director of policy planning; and Gen. Anthony Zinni, the department's Middle East adviser, were dissenters. They pushed the administration to use the tools of diplomacy—the things the State Department does best—and tried to put off the use of force, the domain of the Pentagon. However, in many ways, Powell had become co-opted. He was seen as someone who was not fully on the team, and his dissent was expected. Once Powell had said his piece, he could be ignored and he would fall in line once the president had made a decision. In some ways then, the major dissenter was "domesticated"—a situation consistent with groupthink and with the bureaucratic politics model (see Thomson 1973, 102). Powell's victories were of the tactical variety. His dissent affected the way the administration went to war, but not whether it would go to war.

The net effect of the bureaucratic struggle was something that looked like groupthink. The moderates in the State Department had been allowed to play in the game, but they were driven into self-censorship and into confining their criticism to tactical issues in order to stay on the playing field. Thus a small group of decision makers were able to control the agenda and the options and ensure that nothing stood in the way of the president's predisposition for a preventive war against Iraq.

Another piece of the bureaucratic puzzle is the presence of a separate power center close to the Oval Office. Given the president's relative lack of knowledge and experience in foreign affairs and given the splits between the realists and the neocons, President Bush relied heavily on Cheney to help sort out the differences and determine the path that policy was to take. To maximize his power, Cheney set up his own staff of about a dozen foreign policy advisers independent of Rice and the president's NSC staff, creating what was essentially another independent foreign policy agency. Cheney appeared to be in charge of much of the administration's foreign policy portfolio, especially matters related to WMD (Mann 2004, 275–76; Daalder and Lindsay 2003, 59; Halper and Clarke 2004, 120–21; Suskind 2006, 61, 69). Indeed, Powell noted that "things didn't really get decided until the president had met with Cheney alone" (Woodward 2004, 392). Halper and Clarke (2004, 120) cite presidential historian Douglas Brinkley who believes Cheney "is the vortex in the White House on foreign policymaking. Everything comes through him." Since Cheney had been a chief proponent of forceful regime change in Iraq, this arrangement created a powerful bureaucratic ally for the neocons in the Pentagon (Mann 2004, 369). Risen (2006, 64) suggests that "the dominant power relationship" in the foreign policy bureaucracy was between Rumsfeld and Cheney and that the two "had a back channel where the real decision making was taking place, and that larger meetings were often irrelevant." The political deck was stacked in favor of the hardliners.

The **constructivist** approach to international politics tells us that ideas play an important role in determining foreign policy. What foreign policymakers believe plays an important role in determining the policies pursued by governments. But how do ideas, like preemption and regime change, get translated into policy? One answer is that ideas become enshrined in policies through the work of **policy entrepreneurs**. Drawing on the work of John Kingdon (1984) political scientists have defined policy entrepreneurs as individuals who attempt to initiate fundamental policy changes—policies that may not be consistent with the institution's previous view of its mission (Checkel 1993, 278; Mintrom 1997, 739). Policy entrepreneurs are "idea men," intellectual "peddlers" (Checkel 1993, 276). They attempt to promote and gain support for their preferred policies through a variety of methods: identifying (and defining) problems, shaping and framing the policy debate, crafting arguments that appeal to target groups, networking, and building political coalitions (Mintrom 1997, 739–40).

It should be obvious by now that neocons centered around Paul Wolfowitz played the role of policy entrepreneurs on Iraq. A solid neocon network was securely in place—in second-tier positions in the Defense Department, the NSC, and the vice president's office. They successfully built a political coalition with other hardliners, such as Rumsfeld and Cheney, who supported preemptive military force against Iraq. And through their allies in the media, they gathered public support for the connection between Iraq, WMD, and terrorism.

But neocon policy entrepreneurs needed something else—an opening provided by a change in international situation. As Checkel illustrates in his work on Gorbachev's adoption of radically non-Marxist foreign policy ideas, the interaction of domestic level factors and international system level factors helps to explain radical policy changes. In the Soviet case the presence of receptive leader (Gorbachev) plus a changing international environment (the resurgence of capitalist economies, the new Cold War and Reagan's Strategic Defense Initiative, the Soviet disaster in Afghanistan, etc.) created *"policy windows* through which policy entrepreneurs could jump" (Checkel 1993, 273). As we have seen, the international system changed significantly with the collapse of the Soviet Union. It changed even more significantly, at least as far as the Bush administration was concerned, on September 11, 2001.

At this point it was possible to conceptually redefine the post–Cold War world in ways that would have been impossible earlier. New dangers and new priorities could be identified; new strategies and tactics could be designed. It was, so to speak, a "new ball game." The policy window had just opened. Those, like the neocons, who had ready interpretations for this new situation (a unipolar system in which the major threat was from rogue states with WMD programs who supported terrorists) and ready strategies to deal with it (preemptive or preventive wars to promote regime change) were now in a position to make an impact on the policy process. There now appeared to be problems for which they had appropriate answers, and this gave them an edge in the bureaucratic competition with moderates in the State Department. A receptive leader awaited their advice, but without the shock of 9/11, it is not at all clear that George W. Bush would have become a war president.

The decision for war had a certain feeling of inevitability about it. After the 9/11 attacks there was an informal understanding that although al Qaeda and the Taliban took priority, Iraq would have to be dealt with and dealing with Iraq meant the use of military force. Once it became clear that regime change in Iraq could not be done through reliance on coups or internal revolts or Iraqi dissidents, discussions about Iraq tended to focus not on whether a military invasion was a good idea, but on the military considerations of how it might take place, how many troops would be necessary, when it could start, how long it would take, and what was the best way to justify it to Congress, the public, and the UN (Mann 2004, 336; Woodward 2004). There does not seem to have been a particular moment at which the decision was made. And at no point did any of the principals argue to the president that a military intervention should not be made. Top-level advisers were hesitant to tell the president that a U.S. occupation would worsen the United States' position in the world, dramatically increase the chances of anti-American terrorism, or add to instability in the Middle East. We find scant evidence in any of the accounts of White House decision making that any of the president's advisers argued that a preemptive attack on Iraq was immoral, illegal, or likely to be ineffective (let alone counterproductive) in attaining the nation's goals.

Because War Cabinet meetings and NSC meetings tended to be military briefings rather than general discussions on policy, Secretary Powell decided to seek some time alone with the president to discuss the general idea of war. During his meeting with Bush (with Rice also attending), he warned the president that war could not be done unilaterally. It could destabilize Arab governments friendly to the U.S.; it could suck the life out of every other foreign policy initiative and harm the war on terrorism; it could adversely affect the oil market; and building democracy in Iraq might be extremely difficult. But he did not counsel the president not to do it. His message was, "If you're going to do it, here are some things you ought to consider." He was careful not to directly challenge the goal of regime change set by the president (Woodward 2004, 148–51). And the president was careful never to directly ask Powell whether he recommended going to war.

In the meantime, virtually every U.S. government institution with foreign policy responsibility was carrying on as if war was coming. The bureaucratic momentum—in the form of military planning, intelligence planning, and the prepositioning of forces and material abroad—made it difficult to reverse course; if, indeed, anyone was interested in doing this.

Effects of Bureaucratic Politics on Threat Assessment

The assessment of Iraq's WMD capabilities was affected by a combination of individual level factors and institutional factors, primarily those associated with bureaucratic politics. When disagreements exist within the U.S. intelligence community (as they did) about the nature of the threat, the summing up of the community's views in an NIE may be shaded in the way that intelligence analysts believe will be well received by those at the top. More insidiously, political officials may put pressure on analysts to produce a particular result. In other words, the intelligence process may become politicized, at least in the broad sense of that term. Here we return to a topic we touched on earlier.

One of the most compelling statements of the politicization of the process comes from the Downing Street Memo. It reports the distinct impression of Sir Richard Dearlove, the head of Britain's MI6, after meeting with Tenet and others in Washington on July 20, 2002, that "the intelligence and facts were being fixed around the policy" of the military overthrow of Saddam Hussein (Danner 2005, 71).

The Senate Select Committee on Intelligence found no evidence of direct attempts at manipulation of intelligence nor did it find any evidence that any U.S. intelligence officers had been pressured or coerced to change their judgments in order to produce a desired result. Likewise, the Silberman-Robb commission found that "no analytical judgments were changed in response to political pressure to reach a particular conclusion" (CIC 2005, 545). Neither did the commission find any manipulation of information or analysis to please what was perceived to be the desired conclusion of top-level decision makers (CIC 2005, 546). However, in the commission's own words (CIC 2005, 547–48), it was clear that "analysis was shaped—and distorted—by the widely shared (and not unreasonable) assumption . . . that Saddam retained WMD stockpiles and programs. This strongly held assumption contributed to a climate in which the Intelligence Community was too willing to accept dubious information as providing confirmation of that assumption. . . . Some analysts were affected by this 'conventional wisdom' and the sense that challenges to it—or even refusals to find its confirmation—would not be welcome."

Stories, many unconfirmed, abound about the pressure felt by various intelligence officers working for the CIA, State Department, FBI, and DIA to produce evidence of Iraq's WMDs and Iraqi links with al Qaeda. Pressure came from senior officials in the White House (Rice, Cheney and Libby) and the Defense Department (Rumsfeld, Wolfowitz and Feith). Kaufman (2004, 39–40) reports that Wolfowitz exerted pressure on CIA and DIA analysts in 2001 and 2002 to support the contention that Saddam Hussein had been responsible for the 1993 bombing of the World Trade Center. Vice President Cheney and his chief of staff, Lewis Libby, made several visits to CIA headquarters in Langley, Virginia to look at raw intelligence on Iraq and perhaps to pressure analysts to produce evidence that would justify a war (Bamford 2004, 333–37; Kaufman 2004, 39–40).

Bamford recounts a source who worked for the CIA's Weapons, Intelligence Nonproliferation and Arms Control Center (WINPAC) who told him the group never uncovered any proof of WMD in Iraq. He said, "Where I was working, I never saw anything—no one else there did either." But there appeared to be pressure from political officials above. The pressure worked. Bamford's source relates that one division head in WINPAC told his staff that "if Bush wants to go to war, ladies and gentlemen, your job's to give him a reason to do so" (Bamford 2004, 333–34). The Silberman-Robb commission found that "WINPAC analysts described an environment in which managers rewarded judgments that fit the consensus view . . . and discouraged those that did not" (CIC 2005, 549).

James Risen's interviews of many members of the U.S. intelligence community led him to conclude that CIA officials from top to bottom in the agency were generally uninterested in Iraq, focusing instead on al Qaeda and a potential long term threat from Iran, and had doubts about Iraq's possession of WMD (and its links to al Qaeda). However, their doubts "were stifled because of the enormous pressure that officials at the CIA and other agencies felt to support the administration. George Tenet and his senior lieutenants became so focused on providing intelligence reports that supported the Bush administration's agenda, and so fearful of creating a rift with the White House, that they created a climate within the CIA in which warnings that the available evidence on Iraqi WMD was weak were either ignored or censored" (Risen 2006, 109).

Skeptics at the CIA were pushed aside or "smacked down" (Risen 2006, 111). The CIA's Iraq Operations Group had turned into an advocacy group leading the charge for war within the agency (Risen 2006, 77). Suskind (2006, 308) reports that many of the agency's analysts had become disenchanted with the process because they believed that there was "little point in even sending reports up the chain" because it was clear the top-level policymakers would simply reject reports that did not support their views. A further clue to the politicization of the intelligence process is the unusual feature that as intelligence about Iraq moved up the institutional chain, the conclusions tended to take on greater certainty and fewer qualifications, the exact opposite of what normally happens in the intelligence process (Ricks 2006, 55).

The report by the Senate Select Committee on Intelligence included an email sent by a senior CIA official to a subordinate concerning the latter's doubts about the reliability of Curve Ball's information on Iraq's BW program. The memo was sent the day before Secretary Powell's speech to the UN. "Keep in mind the fact that this war's going to happen regardless of what Curve Ball said or didn't say and that the Powers That Be aren't terribly interested in whether Curve Ball knows what he's talking about" (Isikoff 2005, 59).

Paul Pillar, the CIA officer in charge of Near East and South Asian intelligence from 2002 to 2005, and the man responsible for coordinating intelligence on Iraq, has also concluded that the intelligence community's work was politicized. He argues that the Bush administration turned the relationship between intelligence and policymaking upside down. They "used intelligence not to inform decision making, but to justify a decision already made" (Pillar 2006, 17–18). Ultimately, Pillar argues that although the intelligence community's assessments of Iraq were flawed, they got many things right. For him, the fundamental problem was that "official intelligence analysis was not relied on in making even the most significant national security decisions because the administration had already made up its mind on what policy to follow" (Pillar 2006, 15). He confirms that CIA officers understood that the U.S. would invade Iraq and that it would "frown on or ignore" any analysis that was contradictory to this policy and would welcome any analysis supportive of such an outcome. Thus there was a natural bias in favor of the administration's policy preferences. But the main route through which politicization was achieved was the constant and persistent queries put to the intelligence community to turn over certain rocks (Iraqi WMD, an Al Qaeda link to Saddam Hussein) rather than others. This may have led to self-deception among policymakers who "can easily forget that he is hearing so much about a particular angle in briefings because he and his fellow policymakers have urged the intelligence community to focus on it" (Pillar 2006, 24).

Professional objectivity can also be compromised by a desire to be "part of the team" (CIC 2005, 549). In the Bush administration George Tenet had become more than just the president's chief adviser on intelligence matters, he had become an integral part of the administration's policymaking team. All directors of the CIA know that their careers, and their influence, will rise or fall depending on their relationship with the president. Tenet also understood that he "owed" Bush for keeping him in the job after the 2000 election and for protecting him from the political fallout from the 9/11 disaster. He was predisposed, therefore, to provide the president with what he wanted (Powers 2004, 93; Risen 2006, 20; Pillar 2006, 27).

A central question is whether the president himself understood that the "official" intelligence picture offered to him was skewed, but used the intelligence anyway to gain public and congressional support. The report of the Democratic members of the Senate Armed Services Committee, released by Senator Carl Levin, states that many of the president's closest aides—Rumsfeld, Wolfowitz, Libby, and Hadley—knew that some parts of the intelligence were skewed (NYT 2004). And top officials, according to Kaufman (2004, 9), "knew what policy they intended to pursue and selected intelligence assessments to promote that policy based on their political usefulness, not their credibility." While it was apparent to many inside the administration that the intelligence about Iraq's WMD was not as conclusive as its spokesmen had said, there is scant evidence that these reservations reached the president (Woodward 2004, 354–56). For instance, it is almost certain that the president did not read the entire 2002 NIE on Iraq and might therefore have been unaware of the substantial lack of consensus on the issue of Iraqi WMD. "What the president knew and when he knew it" is still an open question. Perhaps we will never truly know the answer.

SUMMARY

The Iraq War is a war in which an almost nonexistent threat to the United States from Iraq was magnified into an impending security threat of the first order that appeared to require the drastic step of preventive war. The overperception of threat was enhanced by the existence of several factors: a faction in power who perceived the situation in Iraq to be unfinished business and thus deserving of a top position on the administration's agenda, an ambiguous (and perhaps unknowable) level of real threat from the presence of illegal WMD in Iraq, institutional/bureaucratic forces that pushed the administration toward a worst-case assessment of the threat, a politicized process of intelligence collection and analysis that led to the disregard of evidence contrary to the administration's preconfirmed views of the threat, lessons of history that led the administration to conclude that time was against it and that the danger of inaction was high, the belief that even the suspicion of low-probability high-impact events required that the U.S. respond to them as if they were certain, and the presence of a major hinge event (the attacks of 9/11) that increased feelings of threat and vulnerability as well as the necessity for action.

The preference for the use of military force as the primary tool to deal with the perceived threat was enhanced by multiple forces: the existence of a hardline majority coalition within the administration (made up of neocons and assertive nationalists), many of whom acted as policy entrepreneurs who pushed the idea of a threat from Iraq along with a solution of preventive war to create regime change; an active president prone to take risks and reluctant to reevaluate assumptions in order to achieve big goals; a policy team that deferred to its leader and engaged in self-censorship when confronted with policy disagreement; a haphazard and unstructured decision-making process that failed to nurture critical thinking; a decision-making process that was relatively closed to outsiders and tended to limit available options and the scope of internal debate; a strategy of coercive diplomacy from which the administration could not back down; increasing bureaucratic momentum created by massive deployments of troops and material to the Persian Gulf; a changing and somewhat ambiguous unipolar international system perceived to reduce constraints on U.S. action; and a rational calculation in which the probability of success was deemed to be high, the potential costs deemed to be low, and the probable outcomes were deemed to be entirely beneficial. The result was a war that was, in retrospect, largely unnecessary.

AFTERMATH

By early 2007 U.S. military fatalities in Iraq had risen to more than three thousand, with other coalition forces accounting for well over two hundred more fatalities. The vast majority of these deaths came after the initial fighting with Iraqi forces had ended. The number of Iraqi military and civilian casualties is essentially unknowable, but independent organizations put the number at over 50,000, though it is possibly much higher. The United Nations reported that Iraqi civilian deaths had risen to more than one hundred per day by June 2006, and Baghdad had become the most dangerous city in the world. Iraq is beset by massive internal violence, whether one chooses to characterize it as an insurgency or an all-out civil war. The necessity of a continued U.S. presence in Iraq to maintain order has stretched the human resources of the military thin. Tours of duty have been extended and the "ready reserve" has had to be called up. The monetary cost of the war has soared well beyond original official estimates. In 2004 and 2005, the cost to U.S. taxpayers of the occupation in Iraq was running at about five billion dollars a month, for a total cost in mid-2006 of well over two hundred billion dollars (Ricks 2006, 431).

The Iraq War has initiated significant changes in the Middle East and Persian Gulf as well as in the global arena, some of which were foreseeable and desired, others unintended, unforeseen and undesired. The war has led to the overthrow of Saddam Hussein and to a process of democratization in Iraq—a state-building and nation-building project whose future is uncertain and fraught with troubles. It had led to pressure on neighboring Arab regimes, like Egypt, Syria, Saudi Arabia, and Lebanon, to adopt democratic institutions and practices. Arguably, it has played a minor role in Libya's decision to put an end to its nuclear ambitions. The presence of U.S. forces has also led to the influx of foreign jihadists into Iraq, which is now

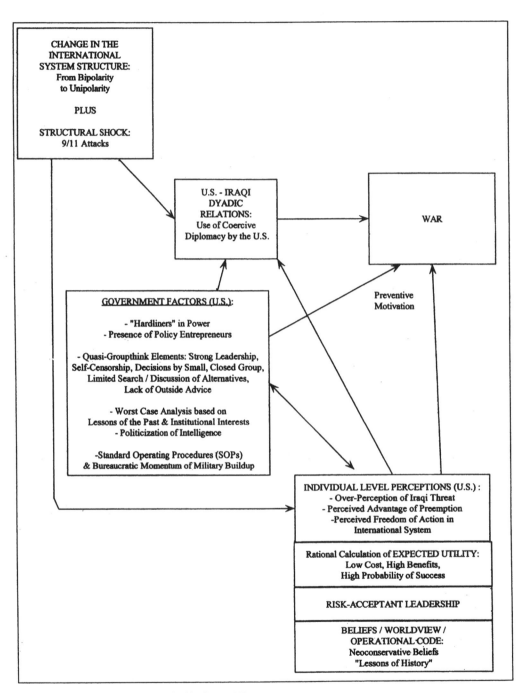

Chart 7.1. The Iraq War of 2003: Causal Factors

a central battlefield in the war on terror, as Iraq has become the training ground for the next generation of Islamist terrorists. It has touched off an internal civil struggle in Iraq carried out by Iraq insurgents and foreign jihadists using both guerrilla tactics and terrorist methods. The war has tarnished the credibility of the U.S. intelligence community; it has raised concerns that the global hegemon has chosen to disregard international law in its willingness to use torture and cruel and degrading punishment of detainees and its use of "extraordinary rendition" to send detainees to other countries known for their use of torture; it has dramatically increased anti-American feelings around the world, including countries within the American alliance system; it has established a claim to the legality of preventive war that may serve as a dangerous rationale for other countries to settle scores with their rivals; and it has increased the incentive for rogue states like Iran and North Korea to actually attain nuclear weapons as a fait accompli that might deter U.S. intervention.

8

Conclusion

We set off on this examination of the causes of war with several assumptions:

1. There is no single causal factor that is responsible for war.
2. Most wars are due to multiple factors that interact with one another.
3. These factors are found at different levels of analysis.
4. These factors will vary from case to case, and no two cases of war are likely to result from exactly the same combination of forces.
5. It may be possible, nevertheless, to identify certain repeated dangerous patterns of interaction between causal factors; these patterns may take the shape of causal chains that sequentially link causal factors together.

We have used process tracing to develop case studies of seven wars from the last one hundred years as a kind of "first cut" to determine the feasibility of identifying such patterns.[1] The cases were selected on the basis of several nonrigorous criteria. First, we attempted to select cases that would be inherently interesting to students of international relations. Second, we attempted to select a set of wars that were fairly diverse with regard to time period, geographical area, and whether the participants were major powers or minor powers. We did not rigorously attempt to select a representative sample of wars; we cannot therefore claim that our results are in any way representative of the larger class of interstate wars in recent history. With that caveat, we will now attempt to see where our first cut has led us.

All five assumptions appear to be abundantly justified. No war appears to be caused by a single factor or adequately explained by a single theory. In every case multiple causal factors at several levels of analysis combined to contribute to the initiation of war. These factors have simultaneous, mutually reinforcing effects that interact with each other to increase the probability of war. While the factors most responsible for war vary somewhat from case to case, there are significant uniformities as well. Our findings in these seven cases appear to substantiate the most recent wave of scholarship in research on the "causes of war" (see Geller and Singer, 1998; Thompson 2003; Vasquez 2004; Bennett and Stam 2004).[2] Table 8.1

represents a summary of our subjective judgments of which factors best explain the occurrence of each of the seven wars.

While there was considerable variation from case to case in the identity of those factors that contributed most to the presence of war, we nevertheless found that certain strong patterns or tendencies emerged. These patterns consist of clusters of factors that were repeatedly found to coexist in the period prior to the outbreak of war. As such, we may consider them to be "dangerous patterns" of interaction between states.

TWO TYPES OF WAR

What we see rather clearly fits John Vasquez's (1987, 1993) classification of wars as either wars of rivalry or wars of inequality. We did not set out necessarily to find this dichotomy; nevertheless, its existence is fairly clear. Despite the fact that we have only one example of major power–minor power war in our set of cases (the Iraq War), the distinction is compelling. It is worth quoting Vasquez (1993, 64–65) at some length here:

> Wars between equals, I call *wars of rivalry*, and wars between unequals, I call *wars of inequality*. It is assumed that wars between equals are more oriented to the logic of balance of power and prey to its deficiencies—such as mutual fear, suspicion and insecurity; arms races; and the temptation of preventive war. Wars between unequals lack all of these characteristics. These wars are more oriented to either the logic of preponderance of power and of opportunity or to the logic of revolution, depending on who is the initiator. Unlike wars between equals, where both sides tend to employ the same logic because they perceive the situation from a similar foundation of capability, wars between unequals involve two parties who employ different logics and initiate wars for different reasons—the strong seeking dominance and the weak liberation.

Since our findings fit Vasquez's categories exceedingly well, we will use his terminology.

WARS OF RIVALRY (PATTERN A)

It is reasonably clear that the dominant pattern that has emerged and the one that applies to most of our cases is a pattern of interaction between rivals or relative equals. It is a pattern that involves the linkage of several causal factors, and it is a pattern that, with certain important additions, fits the one described in John Vasquez's (1987, 1993) steps-to-war model. This pattern, allowing for some individual case distinctions, applies to World War I, the Pacific theater in World War II, the Six-Day War, the 1971 Indo-Pakistan War, and the Iran-Iraq War. In addition, it loosely fits the Ethiopia-Eritrea War, a case addressed in detail in the companion website for this book.[3] We will refer to this pattern as Pattern A.

What, then, does this dominant pattern look like?

Factor One: Conflict Spirals

First, it is abundantly clear that wars do not occur "out of the blue." They are preceded by dyadic (or multilateral) interactions that have the appearance of relatively symmetrical conflict spirals in which each opponent responds to the other's prior moves—or at least to the perceived moves of the other state. Typically, these actions and reactions tend to produce higher and higher levels of intensity, hostility and threat over time. Wars of rivalry tend to be wars of escalation: *All* of our cases involving relative equals produced conflict spirals. This is clearly the pattern one sees in the two global wars—WWI and WWII in the Pacific—as well as in the four minor-minor wars: the Six-Day War, the Iran-Iraq War, the Ethiopia-Eritrea War, and the 1971 Indo-Pakistani War, though in the latter, the conflict was at times asymmetric, as the Pakistanis attempted (unsuccessfully) to reverse the spiral and reduce the level of hostility. Some of the conflict spirals resulted in preemptive wars, the Six-Day War being the prime example. Other conflict spirals ended in preventive wars; this was the logic of the Pacific theater in World War II and to some extent the Ethiopia-Eritrea War. In 1914 the German decision for war had *both* preventive and preemptive motivations.

In these conflict spirals, as Vasquez (1987, 1993) notes, realpolitik policies and actions propel the spiral to higher and higher levels of hostility. The use of coercive diplomacy, threats and ultimatums, the construction of alliances, arms buildups, mobilizations and military alerts, attempted faits accomplis, and demonstrations of commitment all act as provocations rather than inducements to cooperation and restraint. They all create conditions that make it extremely difficult for the states involved to avoid war. As the spiral continues, leaders on both sides begin to conclude that their options are being exhausted, that their opponents are unwilling to resolve the issue in a way that is acceptable, and that their opponents cannot be allowed to continue doing what they are doing. This was certainly true of Germany, Austria, and Russia in 1914; and it was true of both the U.S. and Japan in 1941, Israel and the Arab states in 1967, India and Pakistan in 1971, and Iran and Iraq in 1980.

Just as wars do not occur out of the blue, neither do the conflict spirals themselves. The European spiral associated with the July Crisis of 1914 was in many ways a continuation of the repetitive crisis interactions between an increasingly polarized set of rival European powers. The two Moroccan crises and the Balkan crises between 1905 and 1913 set the stage for the July Crisis of 1914 that centered around unresolved issues in the Balkans. The conflict spiral between Japan and her western rivals that preceded the Pacific phase of World War II was linked to a regional war in Asia initiated by Japan in 1931. It was given momentum by the outbreak of World War II in Europe, and European rivalries and conflicts tended to intersect with those in the Asian theater. The 1967 spiral in the Middle East constituted merely the latest phase of conflict interactions between Israel and her neighbors that dated to 1948. The participants were rivals who had been involved in earlier wars with each other and between whom there were still fundamental unresolved issues. The spiral in South Asia in 1971 also represented a continuation of crisis interactions between a pair of rivals who had already fought two wars and who had been involved in escalating and deescalating patterns of conflictual interaction dating to their independence in 1947. The conflict spiral between Iran and Iraq in 1980 had similar origins. It arose from the still smoldering embers of the previous 1965–1975 conflict spiral between the two rivals, a spiral that had just barely avoided the step of all-out war.

In the last three conflicts—between Israel and her Arab neighbors, between India and Pakistan, and between Iran and Iraq—an ethno-religious dimension interlocked with territorial and political dimensions.

Conflict spirals can be relatively short and intense or relatively lengthy. The July Crisis that led up to World War I lasted approximately five weeks; the spiral that preceded the Six-Day War was roughly two months in duration. On the other hand, the Ethiopian-Eritrean conflict spiral began in the summer of 1997, picked up considerable speed in late 1997, and ended in war in early May 1998. The Bangladesh crisis lasted a full eight months, and the period between Khomeini's coming to power in January 1979 in Iran and the outbreak of war in September 1980 was well over eighteen months. The protracted Japanese-American spiral was considerably longer. A slow-burning fuse was lit between the two by the Manchurian Incident in 1931, but the spiral became intense in January 1940, when the U.S. terminated the U.S.-Japan Treaty of Commerce. War came almost two years later.

While conflict spirals are typically thought to develop out of security dilemmas in which the attempts by one state to increase its perceived need for greater security have the effect of decreasing the security of others, we find that conflict spirals may be generated in ways that do not resemble classic security dilemmas. Only the conflict spiral associated with World War I appears to arise out of classic security dilemma situations in which unilateral acts motivated by the desire for greater security by one side lead to escalatory reactions by a rival. Similarly, although the logic of the security dilemma assumes that the primary motivation of national leaders is fear and insecurity, we find that in some cases this defensive motivation based on fear is frequently coupled with desire for gains and benefits in ways that are hard to disentangle. Leaders have multiple motivations.

For instance, the spiral preceding the Iran-Iraq War appears at best to be a partial fit with the classic security dilemma model. The Iranian actions which set off the conflict spiral with Iraq were not at all related to a security buildup. In fact, the Iranian military was in the process of self-destruction. Iranian actions toward Iraq were the product of revolutionary élan rather than insecurity or fear. While Saddam Hussein was concerned about the Shi'a threat to the integrity of the Iraqi regime emanating from Iran, and while one of his motivations was fear, there were other motivations behind his actions as well, including political and territorial gain.

In the Middle East in 1967, security calculations for one "side" to the conflict (i.e., the Arab states) were greatly complicated by the array of multilateral security challenges which each individual Arab state faced. While it is true that each of the major Arab players viewed Israel as a common enemy, it is also true that Egypt, Syria and Jordan faced threats from fellow Arab states within the context of the Arab Cold War, as well as from domestic opponents within their borders. Here it is instructive to recall that when King Hussein signed a defense pact with Egypt in late May 1967 he did so because he feared retribution from the radical Arab states, from his own hostile Palestinian population, or both. Thus a security agreement which was viewed in Israel as representing the last link in the ever-tightening Arab noose around the Jewish state actually came about as a result of Jordan's calculations that the pact would reduce the threats to its security emanating from other Arab actors.

The conflict spiral in the Pacific theater of WWII fits the classic security dilemma model even less well, since Japanese leaders' concerns had as much to do with preserving territorial gains and achieving regional superiority as protecting security, though clearly they did perceive Japanese security to be threatened. Likewise, the 1971 conflict spiral in South Asia fits the classic pattern poorly. Pakistan was threatened not by any security-driven buildup of Indian military might, but by the bloody disintegration of the bifurcated union of its own Eastern and Western parts.

What factors contribute to these Pattern A conflict spirals? In most cases, the answers are the same: rivalry, territorial disputes, domestic politics, and perceptions.

Factor Two: Rivalry

The second aspect of this dominant pattern is that the pairs of states involved in these conflict spirals are normally dyads that can be classified as rivals. They are states who see each other as rivals, who experience repeated militarized conflicts with each other, who have mutual perceptions of threat and hostility, and who expect that conflicts between themselves are not likely to be resolved peacefully. In World War I, the Six-Day War, the India-Pakistan War of 1971, and the Iran-Iraq War, all the major protagonists can be classified as enduring rivals (Goertz and Diehl 1998; Wayman 2000). If we use Thompson's (2003) criteria for strategic rivalry based on mutual perceptions, all six of the cases of wars between equals involved rivals.[4] In some of our cases, we found that multiple rivalries existed that compounded the problems found in the central rivalry.

The relationship between Iran and Iraq, the two major contenders for power in the Persian Gulf region, is a classic example of an enduring rivalry. The enduring rivalry between India and Pakistan, the two contenders for regional dominance in South Asia, produced three major wars between 1948 and 1971. And it has intersected with another regional rivalry, between India and China, in ways that sometimes exacerbated existing conflicts. The relations between Israel-Syria, Israel-Egypt, and Israel-Jordan indicate the danger of multiple rivalries that intersect around a single, central issue. The two global wars in the twentieth century both involved multiple dyadic rivalries that intersected and were mutually reinforcing. The central rivalries in 1914 would include Austria-Russia, Austria-Serbia, Britain-Germany, France-Germany, and Germany-Russia. This short list excludes multiple rivalries involving two minor players in the July crisis—Italy and the Ottoman Empire. The major rivalry in the Pacific theater of World War II was between the U.S. and Japan, but this dyadic relationship intersected with other rivalries not only in Asia—Britain-Japan, China-Japan, Russia-Japan—but also in Europe. Finally, if one relaxes the normal definitional time requirement for the existence of rivalries (that is, a twenty-year history involving several militarized crises), Eritrea and Ethiopia can be properly seen as strategic rivals.

Like India and Pakistan, which were "born" as rivals upon their independence in 1947, the secession of Eritrea from Ethiopia created a situation that was ripe for rivalry from the start.

Rivalries may be built on different foundations: ethno-religious differences were at the root of rivalries between Israel and the Arab states, between Iran and Iraq, and between India and Pakistan. All of these rivalries also had territorial dimensions to them. Other rivalries are more clearly about regional or global power and influence. This is certainly true of the various rivalries associated with the two great power wars of the twentieth century, but it is also true of the rivalries between Iran and Iraq and between India and Pakistan.

Rivalries may interact synergistically with other dyadic level phenomena to increase the likelihood of war. Among rivals, power shifts or transitions are known to be especially dangerous factors in initiating and accelerating conflict spirals. But only two wars in our set of cases were clearly preceded by dyadic power shifts between rivals—World War I and the Iran-Iraq War. In a third, the Pacific theater of WWII, the overall distribution of power between the U.S. and Japan was not actually changing, but the U.S. buildup simply threatened to make the gap between the two unbridgeable. Broader, system-wide power shifts were important only in the two global wars—as we might suspect. In the Six-Day War and the Indo-Pakistani War no significant power shifts preceded the war.[5]

Arms races and alliance building may also be connected to rivalries and conflict spirals, but they were important factors in only three of our cases—World War I, World War II, and the Six-Day War. Alliances were a peripheral factor in the 1971 Indo-Pakistani War, and arms races and alliance building did not appear important in the other wars.

Factor Three: Territorial Disputes

The third dimension of Pattern A is the presence of a dyadic conflict over territory. However, territorial disputes are not always present and may contribute only indirectly to the conflict. Territorial disputes are related to the existence of rivalries, and disputes between rivals with unresolved territorial issues tend to escalate. Direct dyadic territorial disputes were at the root of rivalries in the Middle East between Israel and her Arab neighbors, and were central to the India-Pakistan rivalry and the Iran-Iraq rivalry. They also existed in the Ethiopia-Eritrean relationship. Indeed, the existence of unresolved territorial disputes was part and parcel of what made some of these states rivals in the first place. In the pre-1914 situation in Europe, territorial disputes were central to the German-French and Austria-Hungary-Serbia rivalry, but not to other rivalries such as those between Britain and Germany or between Russia and the two Dual Alliance partners. Territorial disputes did not play a role in all of our cases, however. They were not directly involved in the U.S.-Japanese rivalry or the U.S.-Iraq rivalry, both of which were between noncontiguous states.

Although several of the wars in our set of cases were rooted in territorial disputes, ultimately the wars may not be "about" territory. Of our seven cases, only in the Ethiopia-Eritrea and Iran-Iraq cases does it appear that territorial disputes played a significant role in fueling the conflict or that a major goal in the war was the disposition of territory. However, even in these wars one must be careful not to overemphasize the role of territorial conflict. With regard to the war in the Horn of Africa, although the existence of an unsettled boundary in the Badme region and border incursions in this area provided the basic casus belli, it is difficult to argue that territorial issues were the dominant factor propelling the two countries to war. Territorial conflict was a major feature of the Iran-Iraq relationship, where the disputed Shatt al-Arab waterway was a central issue, but ultimately, as in the Ethiopia-Eritrea case, the war was only partly about territory. In the Iran-Iraq War and the Ethiopia-Eritrea War, all protagonists had other, non-territorial grievances that were equally compelling.

In the Middle East since 1948 the issue of Israel's sovereignty over the territory of Palestine has been a root cause, in one way or another, of all the conflicts between Israel and its Arab neighbors. While the Arab-Israeli conflict is rooted in a territorial dispute, the 1967 Six-Day War itself was not about territory, even though the result of the war was the Israeli occupation of five areas taken from its three neighbors. It was a war about security. While the territorial dispute over Kashmir between Pakistan and India remained unresolved in 1971, the issues at stake were different. In the 1971 war the territorial issue was one of the autonomy or independence of the Bengali portions of the original state of Pakistan—a cause which India eventually came to champion as Pakistan broke apart in civil war. But while the retention of a unified Pakistani territory was a primary motive for Pakistan, the attainment of territory was not a consideration for India. In the Pacific theater of WWII, while the central issue was Japanese occupation of its neighbors' territories, the territories in dispute belonged to China—and to the British, French, and Dutch colonial empires in Southeast Asia—not the United States. There was no direct territorial dispute between the two protagonists.

Thus far we have described a pattern somewhat, but not entirely, similar to Vasquez's steps-to-war model. The pattern starts with territorial conflicts (sometimes) as a root cause of war, leading to conflict spirals between rival states of roughly equal power that escalate to war through the use of coercive realpolitik bargaining tactics. Dyadic level phenomena—rivalries, territorial disputes, and conflict spirals—are central to the increased potential for war. However, while dyadic phenomena are of primary importance, they are not wholly responsible for the outbreak of war.

Factor Four: The Domestic Political Environment

A fourth factor leaps out of our case studies. In all the wars between equals, the domestic political situation in one (or more) of the states played a crucial role in the process that led to war. Domestic political factors increased the potential for war in several different ways in our cases.

In two cases, the Indo-Pakistani War of 1971 and the Iran-Iraq War, civil war or revolution in one state enticed a rival to initiate coercive strategies in hopes of a relatively easy victory. In these cases, the conflict spiral began in large part because of the internal domestic changes underway in one of the states. Indeed, in many ways the existence of the civil conflicts in Bangladesh and Iran was the triggering factor that set in motion the conflict interactions that led to war. The

Islamic fundamentalist revolution in Iran simultaneously increased the threat to the unity of the Iraqi state and temporarily altered the dyadic distribution of power, producing a perceived window of opportunity for Iraq. The civil conflict in Pakistan created a threat to the unity of the Pakistani state and it further increased India's dyadic power edge while creating adverse domestic conditions in India (caused by refugees) that pushed that state toward a military solution. In the absence of these domestic conflicts war was much less likely to break out between these pairs of states in this particular period of time. In a third case, the Ethiopia-Eritrea War, continued political instability and domestic armed conflict in Ethiopia led the Eritrean leadership to calculate that the TPLF government in Ethiopia was so internally weak that a war would cause it to collapse. In all three of the above cases, political leaders perceived a short-term opportunity to address a long-term threat.

In several cases—WWI, the Pacific theater of WWII, and India-Pakistan—the nature of the political system in the initiators helps greatly to explain why conflicts developed and then escalated in violence. The Japanese political system of the 1930s and 1940s had made a failed attempt at democratization and was characterized by the presence of contested institutions and by significant militarization of political decision making. Austria-Hungary was a multiethnic empire (with limited democratic institutions) inhabited by restive minorities who were enticed towards rebellion by their Slavic brothers in next-door Serbia. Rocked by the assassination of the heir apparent, it was bound to respond vigorously to any perceived challenge to its internal unity. Pakistan was a multiethnic state founded on the principle of religious identity. Like Japan, its transition to democracy was incomplete and instead the political process had become increasingly militarized.

The existence of ruling elites who were, or perceived themselves to be, politically vulnerable appears to be an important factor. In several cases—in Japan in the 1930s and 1940s, in Ethiopia in 1998, and to some extent in Germany and in Austria-Hungary in 1914—ruling elites perceived the domestic political situation to be unraveling and their own hold on power to be tenuous. None of these countries had mature democratic systems; instead, all were largely autocratic in nature or were at best semidemocratic. Two, Japan and Ethiopia, had perhaps begun democratic transitions, though in both there was considerable backsliding in this process. The potential vulnerability of elites in these cases added to the pressure to engage in risky, nationalistic, and confrontational foreign policies as a way of shoring up domestic political support for the regime. In these instances, diversionary motives lay just under the surface.

In two countries—Hirohito's Japan and Yahya Khan's Pakistan—the militarization of the political system was an important structural factor that increased the likelihood that the government would choose a violent solution to its problems. Military leaders dominated the government; military codes and worldviews prevailed; the institutional interests of the military were an important consideration; and a systematic bias existed in the decision-making process which favored military solutions for political problems. The Eritrean government also exhibited many aspects of a militarized government. The EPLF leadership in Asmara tended to rely on military solutions, with its use of force to resolve economic and territorial issues with Ethiopia being only the latest in a series of armed conflicts.

In several situations the ascendancy of hardliners to power, and/or the conversion of moderates to a more hardline position, propelled the conflict spiral forward. The assassination of Archduke Franz Ferdinand changed the internal political balance of power in the Austro-Hungarian Empire and increased the power of hardliners. By 1941 hardliners had been added to FDR's cabinet and General Tojo had become the prime minister in Japan. Sixteen months before the outbreak of the Six-Day War, a coup in Syria brought the Ba'athist regime to power, creating a radical hardline government in Damascus that put pressure on the Egyptian leader, Nasser, to take a tougher position. Moreover, the balance of power in the Israeli cabinet shifted decidedly toward the hardliners when Moshe Dayan was added as defense minister just days before the war broke out. In Pakistan, the civilian cabinet was disbanded and military control became even more centralized in February 1971 as war approached. By 1980, with the accession to power of Saddam Hussein and Ayatollah Ruhollah Khomeini, both Iran and Iraq were led by strong-willed, intransigent, and combative autocrats. In Ethiopia, intense pressure from hardline Tigrayans on President Meles Zenawi to deal with the Eritrean issue was a crucial determinant of Ethiopia's decision to respond with force to Eritrean provocations.

In several of our cases, the actions taken by one state in the conflict spiral created a blowback effect on the domestic political situation in the rival state. Japanese-American interaction in the long conflict spiral leading up to Pearl Harbor had the effect of hardening domestic opinion in both countries. Negative reactions by the opponent seemed to vindicate the approach of hardliners in each country, and elites in both countries came to the conclusion that war was inevitable and needed to be planned for. In the weeks preceding the Six-Day War, Israeli actions against Syria had an important blowback effect not only in Egypt and Syria, hardening the attitude of leaders in both governments, but also in Jordan, where Palestinians pushed King Hussein toward war. Likewise, Arab responses to the perceived Israeli threat hardened attitudes in Israel and led to the conclusion that war was inevitable. The civil war in Bangladesh, the brutality of West Pakistani repression, and the refugee crisis had a direct spillover effect on the domestic situation in India. And in the run-up to the Iran-Iraq War, the Iranian policy of supporting antigovernment Shi'a forces directly impacted the domestic political situation in Iraq, forcing Baghdad to respond aggressively to Iranian subversion.

The presence of certain dysfunctional decision-making procedures also contributed to the use of military solutions to interstate conflicts. In Germany prior to WWI and in Japan prior to WWII, logrolling among political and military interest groups led to bellicose and expansionistic policies. In Japan in 1941 and in Pakistan in 1971 (and the U.S. in 2003) we find decision-making procedures that appear to combine the institutional conflict found in bureaucratic politics with the excessive consensus-seeking nature of groupthink. The result in each case was a policy (war) that was not subjected to rigorous analysis. Political and military elites "circled the wagons" around a flawed strategy and refused to consider seriously the possibility of error. In our cases, to the extent that we can judge, neither groupthink nor bureaucratic politics appear in their pristine, textbook form. Tendencies that pushed toward consensus coexisted with conflictual elements in the decision-making process. This reinforces the findings of second-generation groupthink theorists such as Paul 't Hart that suggest that the bureaucratic politics model and groupthink are not as distinct as originally believed. Hart (1990, 121, 139–59) concludes that cohesiveness is not a necessary condition for groupthink, and that in fact there is a rather complex relationship between conflict and consensus in decision-making groups. We conclude that political factors at the state or substate level are generally underappreciated factors in the march toward war.

Factor Five: Perceptions and Misperceptions

Finally, it is starkly apparent that a fifth factor is also extremely important—the presence of certain perceptions or misperceptions by decision makers. In the crucial days and hours before the outbreak of war, the perceptions of leaders were critical. To the extent that leaders' perceptions of the world departed from reality, nonrational explanations play an important role in helping us to understand the origins of war. The leaders in our seven cases often misperceived the intentions of other countries, the degree of threat that existed, and the true distribution of military power. They sometimes perceived the existence of windows of opportunity and windows of vulnerability and the advantages of taking preemptive or preventive action. Consistent with prospect theory, leaders often perceived that their states had suffered losses or were likely to suffer losses relative to a reference point.

International system level and dyadic level phenomena may have some importance in and of themselves and independent of perceptions, but this is hard to sort out. Such factors as dyadic and systemic power shifts were largely important to the extent that they were perceived and interpreted by national leaders. System level phenomena (such as alliance formation and global power shifts) and dyadic level phenomena (such as power transitions and arms races) trigger important individual perceptions: perceptions of threat, of windows of opportunity and vulnerability, and perceptions of the advantage of preemptive or preventive use of force. (As would seem appropriate, international system factors seem to be of primary importance with regard to global wars such as WWI and WWII. They are decidedly less important for regional wars between minor powers.)

In 1914—as a result of dyadic and systemic power shifts, arms races, and alliance building—German and Austria leaders (wrongly) perceived an offense-dominated military environment and a quickly closing window of opportunity to win a two-front war against Russia and France, coupled with a rapidly approaching window of vulnerability with respect to those two powers. They initially misperceived the willingness of Russia and France to get involved in a war between Austria and Serbia as well as the willingness of Britain to aid France in a larger war on the continent. Once the crisis began, German leaders continued to misperceive the intentions of the Triple Entente and the level of threat directed at them.

In 1967 leaders in Israel, Egypt, and Syria all misperceived the intentions of the other states to some degree and imputed to them more malevolent intentions than was probably the case. Moreover, Egyptian leaders appear to have badly miscalculated the true distribution of power between Arab states and Israel, enticing them toward a more bellicose strategy. In 1971 Pakistani leaders misperceived the true dyadic distribution of power with India, inaccurately perceived a window of opportunity that might be created by a preemptive attack on India, and misperceived the willingness of China to come to their assistance if help were required.

In reaction to the revolution in Iran, Iraq's leaders also misperceived the true distribution of power between the two countries, largely because the revolutionary crisis in Iran was seen as preventing Iran from effectively mobilizing its inherently larger resource base for war. Thus Saddam Hussein and the Iraqi leadership perceived an attractive window of opportunity to settle old scores and expected a relatively easy victory in a limited war. Likewise, in 1998 Eritrean leaders miscalculated the distribution of military and political forces—in large part because they overestimated the degree of President Meles' vulnerability and the degree of political cohesion in Ethiopia. They made the same mistake that Hussein had made; they underestimated the ability of an opponent with inherently larger capabilities to mobilize these capabilities when faced with a foreign threat under conditions of domestic political crisis.

To the extent that individual level idiosyncratic factors such as misperception are important factors in the decision for war, a logical conclusion might be that it is not inevitable that conflicts between rivals should lead to war. There do appear to be choices, though the realm of available choices appeared to those who made them to be tightly constrained. War is a choice made by individual leaders. When war does break out in the final stages of a conflict spiral, the outbreak is frequently due to misperceptions and the fog of prewar. Fear is clearly the primary motivating force, though not the only one. Therefore, the initiators are frequently compelled by the logic of preemption or preventive wars (or both).

In sum, the dominant pattern that emerges from our cases of war is as follows. At the dyadic level, rivalries are formed between states out of ethnic and religious differences, out of territorial disputes, out of incompatible interests, and out of regional or global competition for relative power and influence—or out of some combination of these factors. Many of the rivalries were linked—some directly, some indirectly—to unresolved conflicts over territory. At some point a catalyst or trigger event is likely to initiate a conflict spiral. Once that spiral begins, contributing factors at the international, dyadic, state, substate, and individual levels combine to escalate the dyadic interaction toward war.

At the systemic and dyadic levels, conflict spirals are fueled by power shifts, arms races, alliance formation, and dysfunctional learning that result from repeated crises. At the state and substate levels, spirals are accelerated by the existence of militarized regimes, the ascendancy of hardliners to power, and by the use of dysfunctional decision-making processes. In some cases violent internal conflicts in one state entice opportunistic intervention by a rival. In other cases the vulnerability of elites or the political instability of transitional political systems provides incentive for aggressive foreign policies. Finally, at the individual level of analysis, the escalation of conflict spirals is almost always propelled by misperceptions of the distribution of power between protagonists, misperceptions of the intent of rival states or the level of threat they present, or by perception of windows of opportunity or vulnerability that lead to preemptive or preventive strategies. There is a degree to which almost all of our cases may be called wars of illusion; in almost no case did the leaders in the initiating country, operating in what we have called the **fog of prewar**, accurately perceive the situation in which they found themselves.[6]

Pattern A Variations

Even though wars of rivalry arise out of patterns that share many fundamental similarities, clearly no two patterns are exactly alike and it is possible to classify several variations in the dominant pattern.

The Classic Rivalry Spiral

The first variation can be called the **classic rivalry spiral**, a pattern epitomized by the Six-Day War. This is a pattern that is rooted in a territorial rivalry between Israel and her neighbors, a rivalry that also has religious and ethnic dimensions to it. The antagonists have been involved in previous crises and wars. A classic security dilemma exists in which the security measures of each side are negatively linked: efforts by one side to enhance its security are likely to be seen as threatening to the other. At some point "normal" levels of conflict-laden interaction begin to increase in intensity and a conflict spiral ensues as both sides engage in coercive countermeasures. As in 1967, such spirals are likely to involve the logic of preemptive war. As the level of threat intensifies, a point is reached at which at least one side fears that it is about to be the victim of a first strike by the other, and thus perceives that the only way to adequately defend itself is through a preemptive strike.

Domestic Instability Spiral

A second variation might be called the **domestic instability spiral**. This is essentially a classic rivalry spiral in which the conflict spiral is triggered by domestic political instability of some sort in one of the rivals, the pattern we see in the Iran-Iraq War and in the 1971 Indo-Pakistani War. Once again we have a set of classic rivalries, both of which have territorial and ethno-religious aspects. In both cases the rivals had been involved in previous wars or militarized disputes. What is different in this variation is that what triggers the latest conflict spiral is an internal political conflict in one of the rivals—a revolution in Iran and a secessionist war in Pakistan. Without these internal conflicts, the chances of external war between the rivals at that particular point in time would have been considerably less.

Complex Rivalry Spirals

A third variation is the **complex rivalry spiral** that we see in the case of the two world wars. Here we have not just dyadic rivalries but also multiple rivalries, as was also the case in the Six-Day War. Unlike the previous cases, international system level factors are much more important. A combination of the deconcentration of systemic power, a general changing of the global distribution of relative power, and dyadic power transitions all lead to increased global insecurity and perception of windows of opportunity and windows of vulnerability. Territorial disputes *per se* are less important in this pattern; prestige, status and dominance (and survival) are more compelling. Mutual fear and suspicion abound, and the logic of preventive war is in the air.

In both cases of global war, the conflict spiral that takes place has lengthy roots. The spiral that preceded World War I in the summer of 1914 was itself preceded by several previous crises that stopped short of war—at least between the major power protagonists. Essentially, we see a two-step spiral: one between 1905 and 1913 that involves the two Moroccan crises and the two Balkan wars and the July Crisis of 1914. The U.S.-Japan spiral is a decade-long process that gains momentum throughout the 1930s and reaches a fever-peak only in 1941. And it is a spiral that takes place in the context of ongoing regional wars in Europe and in Asia. In both cases the full panoply of dyadic interaction factors that tend to accelerate crises are present: arms races, alliance formation, threats, ultimatums, and other tools of coercive diplomacy.

WARS OF INEQUALITY (PATTERN B)

The Iraq War indicates the presence of a dramatically different pattern. This is in large part due to the fact that it is the only war in our set of case studies that is a major power–minor power war and a war between two states that are clearly asymmetrical in physical capabilities.

Unlike Pattern A, in which dyadic level factors centered on conflict spirals were of primary importance, in Pattern B we find that the most important explanatory factors in wars of inequality are found at the substate and individual levels of analysis. In wars of rivalry, the identity of the initiator is not a foregone conclusion. Since the primary rivals are involved in a conflict spiral that is largely symmetrical, either state might have the motivation and opportunity to initiate war, depending on the circumstances and on individual perceptions or misperceptions. The war is often unintentional, at least in the sense that neither of the rivals actually *wanted* war. In Pattern B, however, at a fairly early point in the conflict process one state desires to have war, rationally calculates the cost-benefit analysis, and sets in place a strategy to achieve its gains by the use of force. Wars of Inequality are not unwanted or inadvertent wars; they are wars of intent—though this is not to say that no miscalculations occur.

In our sole Pattern B case, the Iraq War, the primary causal factors had to do with the individual decision makers, their personalities, their worldviews and perceptions, and the dysfunctional governmental procedures through which the actual decision for war was made. There was no territorial dispute at the root of the conflict. There was no enduring dyadic rivalry, at least not in the classic sense, but the logic of conflict between rivals existed nevertheless. Though security issues may have been of importance, there was no real security dilemma, and no arms race, no competitive building of alliances, and no conflict spiral. (At the point that the Iraq War began, the government of Saddam Hussein, in its own ineffectual way, was trying to reduce the level of international tension and hostility and was cooperating with UN inspectors, but this had no effect on the United States.) To the extent that a conflict spiral was present, it was decidedly asymmetrical.

While fear may still be the primary motivation in wars of inequality, this is less clear than in wars of rivalry. In the United States, the assessment of threat emanating from Iraq was almost certainly overperceived. The structural shock of the 9/11 attacks served to raise the importance of rogue states with WMD potential and the necessity of dealing effectively with this new type of threat. There was, however, a coexisting (and probably equally weighted) motive of gain. Gains maximization appears to be just as compelling an explanation for the war as loss minimization (and prospect theory). Wars of inequality tend to be opportunistic wars based on rational cost-benefit analysis of the type described by expected utility theory. They occur because one side, the more powerful, has a strong motive, an expectation of substantial gain, an assessment of relatively low costs, and a relative certainty of success. Wars of inequality follow Thucydides' dictum from the Melian Dialogues that "the strong do what they can, and the weak do what they must."

This is not the same as saying that all governments that find themselves in the same circumstances would do the same thing. Since there are no long-term structural forces pushing the two states into conflict with each other, whether war breaks out is highly dependent on individual beliefs, on operational codes, on perceptions and on decision-making procedures. American leaders, many of whom were hardliners who held a neoconservative worldview, reacting to the shock of 9/11 and believing that time was not on their side, perceived a condition of vulnerability from the confluence of rogue states, WMD, and global terrorism. In this context, they vastly misperceived the strength of Iraqi weapons programs, Iraqi intentions, the overall threat to the U.S. from Iraq, and the ease by which a democratic regime might be brought to Iraq. A closed and unstructured decision making process and a tendency to defer to the wishes of the president added to the problem.

FINAL CONSIDERATIONS: CATALYSTS, THE INADVERTENCE OF WAR, AND FUTILITY

Several of the wars in our case studies were triggered by specific catalysts from different levels of analysis. State level phenomena acted as catalysts in three wars. World War I was ignited by the assassination of Archduke Franz Ferdinand, which exacerbated fears in the Dual Empire about Slavic nationalism and the Serb problem but also changed the internal balance of power in the country; the 1971 Indo-Pakistani War was set in motion by the Awami League's victory in the 1970 Pakistani elections and the subsequent civil war; and the Iran-Iraq War was triggered by the Islamic Revolution in Iran. In one case the conflict process was set in motion by what can only be described as a catastrophic global hinge event: The Iraq War can be traced to the 9/11 attacks on the Pentagon and World Trade Center by al Qaeda, a nonstate actor.

Other wars seem not to be initiated by any particular event. Rather, they seem to be propelled by a series of events at the dyadic level in which it is impossible to determine that one event is more critical than any other and each event is preceded by one just as important. Such is the history of the U.S.-Japanese conflict, for which it might be argued there was a gradual spiral that went back to the Manchurian Incident of 1931—ten years before the attack on Pearl Harbor. The origin of the deadly conflict spiral preceding the Six-Day War is a matter of interpretation: it can be variously traced to a general increase of militarized disputes on Israel's northeast border, the aerial skirmish between Israel and Syria in April 1967, the report of threats made by Israeli defense minister Rabin in the second week of May, or to the Egyptian request to withdraw UNEF a week later. The trigger for the Ethiopia-Eritrea War is equally murky. It developed out of a series of actions and counteractions involving economic and territorial issues over a period of many months.

In all cases except the Iraq War, there was significant potential for events or situations that might trigger a fatal conflict spiral. War was not inevitable, but enough causal factors existed in the period prior to the outbreak of these wars that a wide variety of potential events or occurrences at several levels of analysis might have served to initiate a death spiral. This is frequently referred to as the "streetcar" analogy: Catalysts are just like streetcars; if you miss the first one, another one—just as good—will come along in a few minutes (see Thompson 2003). A European-wide war in the second decade of the twentieth century could have occurred in the absence of the assassination at Sarajevo, a third India-Pakistan War could have occurred without a civil war in Bangladesh, and a third Middle East War could have happened in the mid-1960s without an aerial clash between Israeli and Syrian jets. Or they might *not* have happened.

Many of the wars in our case studies appear to be inadvertent in the sense that they were not consciously sought by the initiators—at least not as part of a long-term strategic vision. Only two, the Iran-Iraq War and the Iraq War of 2003, were consciously sought by their initiators. In both of these wars, the leadership in the attacking countries was motivated by potential gains coupled with the belief that victory was attainable at relatively small cost. In both initiating countries, leaders believed that only military solutions could truly resolve existing problems. However, even in these two cases, sorting out intentions resists easy categorization. In the Iran-Iraq War Saddam Hussein was not solely motivated by potential gains. Considerations of threat to the unity of the Iraqi state and potential loss of such unity due to Iranian meddling in Shi'a politics in Iraq were also present. And in the 2003 war, although American leaders saw great potential gains stemming from regime change in Iraq, they were also worried about potential losses that might be associated with an Iraq armed with weapons of mass destruction.

In all of the other cases, it was relatively clear that the participants did not enter the conflict spiral with the intention of war. Most leaders saw themselves as threatened by the actions of others and the primary motive was fear. This was clearly the case in Berlin, Vienna, and St. Petersburg in 1914, in Tokyo in 1941, and in Tel Aviv in 1967. In some cases, especially in 1914, the initial forceful actions were taken with the hope that they would deter war. In 1998 the invasion

Table 8.1. Causal Factors in Seven Case Studies of War.

	World War I	Pacific War	Six-Day War	Indo-Pakistani War	Iran-Iraq War	Ethiopia-Eritrea War	Iraq War
Individual personality	x			x	x		x
Beliefs / operational codes	XXX						XXX
Misperceptions	XXX	x	XXX	XXX	x	x	XXX
Perceived windows	XXX	XXX		x	XXX	x	XXX
Perceived first-strike advantage	XXX	XXX	XXX	x			x
Expected utility							XXX
Prospect theory		XXX	x	x		XXX	
Domestic conflict or elite vulnerability	x	x	x	XXX	XXX	XXX	
Political transition / democratization		XXX					
Hardliners in power	XXX	XXX	XXX	XXX	x		XXX
Militarized system		XXX		XXX		x	XXX
Dysfunctional decision making		x		x			XXX
Diversionary or scapegoat motive		x	x			XXX	

Territorial conflict	XXX	x	XXX		XXX	x	
Conflict spiral	XXX	XXX	XXX	XXX	XXX	XXX	
Security dilemma	XXX	XXX	XXX	x			
Preemptive or preventive motivation	Preempt and prevent	Prevent	Preempt	Preempt		Prevent	Prevent
Arms race	XXX	x	x	x			
Alliance formation	XXX	x	x	x			
Dyadic power shifts	XXX	x	XXX		XXX		
Dyadic rivals: single/multiple	XXX Multiple	XXX Multiple	XXX Multiple	XXX Single	XXX Single		x Single
Coercive diplomacy	XXX	XXX	XXX	x	x		x
Ethnic/religious conflict			x	x	x		
Systemic power shifts	XXX	XXX					
Global power deconcentration	XXX	XXX					
Unipolar system						x	XXX

Note: x = factor is present; XXX = factor is present and seems important; blank = factor not present or is insignificant.

of Badme was seen by the Eritrean leaders not as the initial strike in an all-out war but as creating a military fait accompli (though Eritrean leaders believed that if Ethiopia did respond with force, Eritrea was capable of winning the war). The 1971 Indo-Pakistani War occupies the middle ground on this issue. In 1971 a reluctant Indian leadership gradually came to the conclusion that war was feasible and would solve many existing problems, and a reluctant Pakistani government came to pretty much the same conclusion.

Finally, we would be remiss if we did not note that in very few cases did the initiator achieve anything near the desired best-case outcome. Germany and Austria in 1914, Japan in 1941, Pakistan in 1971, Iraq in 1980, and Eritrea in 1998 all failed in their objectives. All were defeated or effectively stalemated in a war of exhaustion. Israel in 1967 achieved its short-term goal of defending the security of the state from its external enemies. But its victory in 1967 did not prevent the subsequent Yom Kippur War of 1973 or the wars in Lebanon in 1982 or 2006—nor did it prevent the uprisings by Palestinians in the West Bank and Gaza (the *intifadas*) and the incessant terrorist attacks that have prevented any semblance of peace and security inside Israel in recent years. The United States certainly achieved its primary objectives in 2003—defeating the Iraqi army and ousting Saddam Hussein—but its long-term objectives of bringing a stable, pro-Western government to Iraq, a democratic peace to the Middle East, and a victory in the "global war on terrorism" have yet to be attained.

In the final analysis, the resort to war has often represented the triumph of wishful thinking over good sense. Even worse, it has been an exercise in futility.

NOTES

1. Six case studies are reported here: World War I, World War II in the Pacific, the Six-Day War, the India-Pakistan War of 1971, the Iran-Iraq War, and the Iraq War of 2003. The seventh case study, the Ethiopian-Eritrean War, is available on this book's website, and findings from that war are also presented in this conclusion.

2. Our conclusion is also remarkably similar to a recent overview (Goldstone 2001, 165) of decades of research by social scientists to discover the causes of internal domestic revolutions. It states that "there is no single set of factors whose absence or presence leads to revolution or nonrevolution. Rather, different factors combine in a variety of ways to produce different types and outcomes of revolutionary conflict."

3. We must admit at this point that the Ethiopia-Eritrea War resists neat characterization. We have chosen to include it in Pattern A even though in certain ways it appears to be a war of unequals. The two states were clearly not rivals, and their dyadic relationship had not been characterized by a history of disputes—militarized or otherwise. Nevertheless, the relationship between the Ethiopian TPLF and the Eritrean EPLF had been a testy one over the years of their revolt against the Dergue regime in Ethiopia, and there was considerable tension as well as cooperation between the two movements. In terms of raw power, especially as expressed as potential power based on economic and demographic resources, the two states were unequal—though not grossly so. Eritrea, though smaller and weaker demographically and economically, was a mobilized society which in some years spent as much or more on military goods than its larger neighbor. Ethiopia certainly did not treat its smaller neighbor as a weak, inferior vassal. Quite the contrary; to many Ethiopians it appeared as if its leadership was being pushed around by the Eritrean EPLF

leadership. Clearly in Thompson's (2001, 560) terminology, Ethiopia saw Eritrea as "capable of playing in the same league."

4. Although the U.S.-Iraq relationship might fit Thompson's criteria for a strategic rivalry, it is perhaps better seen as a *proto-rivalry*.

5. The Iraq War was preceded by a major reordering of power in the international system—the end of the Cold War bipolar system and the creation of a more unipolar system—but the causal effect of this on the war was rather indirect. It certainly had no effect on the dyadic balance between the U.S. and Iraq, which was already extremely lopsided.

6. This is also true in the Iraq War, the one case that we have of wars of inequality.

Glossary

accomodationists. Individuals predisposed to advocate against the use of force and support cooperative strategies based on negotiation, compromise, and the reliance on international law and organizations.

alliance formation. The forging of mutual ties of diplomatic and/or military cooperation between two or more states. Alliance formations *may* be formalized as security pacts, which typically take one of two forms: collective defense, which is designed to promote cooperation among members states in order to guarantee the security of the members of the pact from aggression by nonmember states, or collective security, which is designed to promote cooperative relations among member states in order to deter and punish aggression between members of the pact. See also *balancing* and *bandwagoning*.

American exceptionalism. The worldview, popular among some conservatives and liberals in the United States, that the U.S. is a uniquely good and benevolent country that uses its power to promote the common good in the international system. Those who subscribe to this view believe that America's values are universally admired, and that U.S. leadership is indispensable for the promotion of peace and development within the international system.

anarchy. The absence of a sovereign, overarching governing institution (such as a world government) in the international system. See also *realism*.

arms race. Competitive buildups of military armaments at higher than normal rates, usually involving two states. Arms races may be bilateral or multilateral. See also *conflict spiral* and *security dilemma*.

asymmetric conflict. A conflict interaction pattern in which the escalation of levels of hostility is not mutual.

autarky. A state strategy that aims to achieve complete economic self-reliance.

balancing. A policy of seeking to offset or "balance against" a powerful state or alliance, either by increasing one's power through internal means or through external means by becoming involved in a counter-alliance. Realists argue that balancing occurs as a response to the concentration of power in the international system. See also *alliance formation* and *bandwagoning*.

bandwagoning. A policy in which a smaller state responds to the concentration of power in the international system by forging an alliance with, rather than balancing against, the largest power.

beliefs. Opinions or convictions held by an individual regarding objects, events, people, and politics. Beliefs may be organized into a more or less integrated whole, thus forming a belief system by which an individual organizes and makes sense of the political world. See also *operational code*.

bipolar system. A condition under which there are two great powers within the international system.

blowback effect. The unanticipated impact of foreign policy decisions and events, including the choice for and conduct of war, on domestic political systems in both the initiating state and the target state.

brinksmanship crisis. A crisis tactic in which the initiator intentionally forces a conflict to the brink of war in the belief that the other side will break down and abandon its commitment when faced with the threat of force.

bureaucratic politics model. Describes a conflictual process by which governmental decisions are made by individuals representing different organizations and agencies that compete with each other to determine national policies. Since most "players" in the process tend to see foreign policy issues from the parochial perspectives of their home organizations, decisions tend to be made through political processes such as bargaining, logrolling, coalition building, and compromise, as well as through outright power struggles among competing organizations and coalitions. BPM may be seen as an alternative to the *rational choice model*.

cartelized political system. A political system in which the government is dominated by a coalition of powerful groups with narrow interests, all of whom derive parochial benefits from foreign expansion and military activities. The coalitions are maintained by logrolling tactics in which the parochial interests of each group are supported by all of the others.

civil war. A domestic conflict between the armed forces of the state and rebel forces in which the goal is to control the institutions of government. Civil wars become internationalized when the parties to the conflict forge ties with external actors to assist them in fighting the war.

classic rivalry spiral. Typically, a pattern that is rooted in a territorial rivalry between states and often has ethnic or religious components. The antagonists have been involved in previous crises and wars, and a generalized security dilemma exists that negatively links the security measures of each side: Efforts by one side to enhance its security are likely to be seen as threatening to the other. At some point "normal" levels of conflict-laden interaction begin to increase in intensity and a conflict spiral ensues as both sides engage in coercive countermeasures. Such spirals are likely to involve the logic of preemptive war as the level of threat intensifies to a point at which at least one side fears that it is about to be the victim of a first strike by the other, and thus the only way to adequately defend itself is through a preemptive strike. See also *conflict spiral theory* and *domestic instability spiral*.

coercive diplomacy. The use of threats, punitive sanctions, and demonstrations of force and commitment as part of a bargaining process designed to change the behavior of another state.

cognitive consistency. A cognitive process that occurs when an individual is faced with new (and presumably accurate) information that conflicts with that individual's current beliefs and images. Under such conditions, an individual is inclined to discount, reject, or modify the new information in order to prevent the creation of an image with incompatible components. The result is that image change is difficult and old images tend to last in the face of countervailing information.

compellence. A threat intended to make an adversary change its behavior and do something it is not currently doing.

complex interdependence. Refers to the multiple channels of interaction that connect countries together, making them sensitive and vulnerable to events in the international system and to policy decisions that are made by those with whom they are linked.

complex rivalry spiral. A pattern that is characterized by multiple rivalries. International system level factors are crucial, as a combination of the deconcentration of systemic power, a general changing of the global distribution of relative power, and dyadic power transitions all lead to increased global insecurity and perception of windows of opportunity and windows of vulnerability. Territorial disputes per se are less important in this pattern; prestige, status, and dominance (and survival) are more compelling. Mutual fear and suspicion abound, and preventive war is an attractive option.

conflict spiral theory. Assumes that states and their leaders generally respond to others on the basis of reciprocity. Leaders who face hostile, uncooperative, and threatening actions from other states will respond with hostile, uncooperative, and threatening actions of their own, which will trigger more hostile actions. Thus the level of hostility and threat will increase in subsequent interactions. The spiral may be symmetric, with both sides escalating the level of hostility, or asymmetric, with only one side doing the escalating. Once a spiral of hostile and conflictual interactions begins, it is difficult to break the cycle. See also *arms race* and *security dilemma*.

constructivism. A model of international politics which assumes that "reality" as understood by individuals does not reflect objective truth; instead, reality is the product of subjective, socially constructed and culturally determined images, expectations, beliefs, and norms.

contested institutions. In this situation, powerful domestic groups disagree about the most fundamental rules of politics, such as who should rule and what type of political and economic institutions are best for the state. Within the context of contested institutions, the military has two viable courses of action for preserving its domestic influence: the use of internal repression against its enemies or the use of external force. See also *diversionary wars*.

contiguous states. Countries that share a common border. International relations research shows that wars are much more likely to occur between contiguous states than between states that do not border each other, and that wars between contiguous states are most frequently driven by disputes over territory.

critical points. According to Doran's power cycle theory, the four points at which a state's power relative to other great powers in the international system undergoes a shift in direction or a change in the rate of its relative increase or decrease. These points are not predictable. When they come, they create the necessity for states to reevaluate their relative position in the global hierarchy.

cult of the offensive. A bias that develops within the military as an institution, favoring offensive strategies over defensive strategies, and that reflects the organizational self-interest of the military.

democratic peace. The longstanding theoretical claim that states with democratic political systems do not go to war with each other. Recent research suggests that, while this theory is correct when applied to stable, established democracies, newly democratized or democratizing systems may be particularly war-prone. See also *democratization*.

democratization. The process through which a state evolves from authoritarianism or totalitarianism toward democracy. The uncertainty and institutional weakness that exists in a democratizing state can create opportunities for powerful traditional institutions (such as predemocratic elites and their allies in the military) to push for a foreign war as a way to slow or stop the development of democracy. In addition, external foes may attempt to take advantage of the uncertainty caused by democratization by launching a military attack against the democratizing state. See also *democratic peace*.

deterrence theory. Maintains that states may successfully prevent attacks or other unwanted behavior on themselves or their allies by making threats to retaliate. Threatening behaviors are deemed to induce caution in others rather than counter-threats.

diaspora. A nation whose individual members have been dispersed across multiple territories as a result of historical conditions, which may include events such as war, persecution, or attempted genocide. A diaspora may have a home state or its people may be stateless.

diversionary wars. Wars in which political elites who face a domestic crisis attempt to unify their country and to shore up their own political positions by engaging in armed conflict with foreign opponents. The primary goal of these types of wars is to divert the attention of the public from the domestic problems that threaten the regime. See also *in-group/out-group theory* and *scapegoat war*.

domestic instability spiral. Characterized by the same patterns as the classic rivalry spiral, with the exception that the latest conflict spiral—the one that ends in war—is triggered by an internal political conflict in one of the rival states. See also *classic rivalry spiral*.

dyadic relations. The relationship between two states.

dysfunctional crisis learning. The misinterpretation or misapplication of lessons gleaned from previous interactions with a foe. One manifestation of dysfunctional crisis learning is that both winners and losers in previous conflicts within the dyad learn to be "tougher" in the next dyadic confrontation. See also *enduring rivals*.

enduring rivals. States that see each other as rivals, experience repeated militarized conflicts with each other, have mutual perceptions of threat and hostility, and expect that conflicts between themselves are not likely to be resolved peacefully. See also *dysfunctional crisis learning*.

ethnic entrepreneur. A leader who seeks to bolster his or her domestic political standing by manipulating the images and feelings held by the members of his or her ethnic group toward another ethnic group.

ethnic subversion. A policy in which a state supports the military activities and political aspirations of an ethnic group in another state in order to destabilize the domestic system of the other state.

expected utility theory. A theory of decision making which posits that a rational individual will choose the policy option that is expected to provide the biggest pay-off in terms of gains. In addition, expected utility theorizes that individuals are most likely to take risks when they calculate that doing so will lead to significant gains. See also *prospect theory* and *rational choice*.

fait accompli. A conflict strategy that is designed to establish a new situation or condition in such a way that it appears both inevitable and irreversible to one's enemy.

fog of prewar. The idea that decision making during the crisis period that precedes a war is hindered by such factors as the stress experienced by leaders, the search for cognitive consistency, the existence of motivational biases, and the dearth of timely, reliable, and accurate information. These factors lead to widespread misperceptions and uncertainty, a situation in which substantial errors of judgment are likely.

genocide. The attempt to destroy, in whole or in part, a national, ethnic, racial, or religious group.

global political culture. The norms, beliefs, values, and attitudes regarding what constitutes legitimate or illegitimate behavior within the international system during a particular era.

groupthink. A decision-making process in which a cohesive, homogeneous and insulated decision-making group strives for group unanimity and cohesion to the detriment of the task of realistically assessing the problem in front of them. Under conditions of groupthink, the decision-making unit is isolated from outside input, debate over the wisdom of current policy is absent, and there is strong pressure on members within the decision-making circle to support the group's preferred option for the future.

hardliners. Political leaders who, on the basis of their beliefs, advocate a confrontational approach towards a rival state. Typically, hardliners maximize the state's demands vis-à-vis the rival state, refuse to compromise with their enemies, and advocate the use of force as a legitimate and effective first option in the event the rival state refuses to accede to their demands.

hegemonic stability theory. A theory that asserts that the concentration of power in a single dominant state promotes greater cooperation and decreases the occurrence of war in the international system. See also *power transition theory*, *regimes*, and *unipolar system*.

hegemonistic nationalism. A particularly virulent form of nationalism in which the state believes that its nation deserves a state, while other nations do not. Because this belief is based on feelings of national superiority, hegemonistic nationalism may lead to a policy of aggression toward other, supposedly inferior nations.

hegemony. A condition in which a single great power (the hegemon) has the preponderance of both military and economic capabilities within an international system. Hegemons are able to make and enforce international rules and regimes regarding monetary and trade relations, the rules of international law and international conflict, and conflict resolution.

historical analogies. A psychological technique that involves attempting to use the lessons derived from past events to guide current decisions and policies.

immediate causes of war. Proximate events and decisions that contribute directly to the outbreak of war between two or more states.

in-group/out-group theory. The theoretical claim that a conflict with an external foe often increases internal cohesion within a group.

internationalization. The externalization of an intrastate war through direct military intervention or the provision of military, economic, and diplomatic support by outside actors.

interstate war. Sustained armed combat between two or more sovereign states that results in a minimum of one thousand battle deaths.

intrastate war. Sustained armed combat between two or more combatant organizations (one of which is usually the state) within the boundaries of a state. Examples of types of conflict that fall within the category of intrastate war are civil wars, revolutions, and wars of secession. See also *civil war, revolution,* and *wars of secession.*

irredentism. A state's claim to an adjoining territory (which it may have previously occupied), based on shared ethno-national ties with a portion of the population of the adjoining territory, or the demand by a minority national group in one state to link themselves to an adjoining state based on ethno-national ties with the majority in the adjoining state.

kick 'em while they're down wars. Wars in which one state calculates that it can take advantage of a temporary shift in the dyadic balance of power and go to war with a normally more powerful rival because of domestic instability within their rival state.

levels of analysis. An approach to studying international relations in which causal factors are aggregated into several levels. Although various theorists disagree on the appropriate number and classification of levels, this work uses five levels of analysis: the individual level, the substate level, the nation-state level, the level of dyadic (bilateral) interaction between states, and the international system level.

logrolling. A tactic of compromise and consensus building between organizations within the state in which each organization gets what it wants most in return for tolerating the adverse effects of the policies enacted by its intrastate, organizational partners.

long cycle theory. Argues that the international system goes through recurring periods, roughly one hundred years in length, each of which is marked by the ascension of a dominant power (*hegemon*), followed by a period of power maintenance by the hegemon, and finally the decline of the old hegemon and the ascension of a new, dominant power. The theory assumes that war is the most likely agent for major change in the system as the new hegemon uses war to defeat and replace the declining hegemon.

long-term (or root) causes of war. Underlying conditions, cycles, structures, and patterns of relations that create the context under which war between two states becomes more likely.

militarized political system. A system in which military leaders dominate the government, the decision-making structure of the state resembles that which is used in the military, the institutional interests of the military play a critical role in shaping the state's policies, and there is a bias toward resolving political problems via military means.

mirror image. A psychological technique that involves the tendency to invest in one's enemy the opposite of the positive characteristics seen in oneself.

misperceptions. Occur when an individual's understanding of the world does not correspond to reality, especially when information is missing or incomplete, a condition that occurs quite often in international politics, where secrecy and deception are practiced to keep rivals and opponents (and even allies) from knowing what they wish to know.

motivated bias. A bias that appears in one's rational calculations or in one's perception of others that is due to emotional and psychological processes such as ego defense rather than a bias that is purely due to cognitive limits on one's rationality.

multiple rivalries. A dangerous situation in which a number of overlapping conflict dyads exist within the context of a confined geographic space.

multipolar system. A condition under which there are three or more dominant states of relatively equal power in the international system.

nationalism. A strong sense of shared, exclusive communal identity, which typically may be based on such characteristics as language, ethnicity, religion, race, culture, or common historical experiences. See also *hegemonistic nationalism*.

offense-defense balance theory. A theory of war which focuses on two causal factors. The first is a perception of the existence of windows of opportunity and vulnerability that are brought on by shifts in global and/or dyadic distributions of power. The second is the perception that the offense/defense balance is in favor of offensive forces and strategies.

operational code. The crucial beliefs and assumptions held by an individual regarding politics and how best to achieve one's political goals.

organizational process model. Assumes that both policy choice and policy implementation are significantly determined and constrained by preexisting organizational processes and plans. These organizational biases have an important implication for foreign policy decision making: Organizational standard operating procedures create routines for managing the flow of information and implementing decisions; the routines seriously constrain the ability of policy elites to develop and implement innovative responses to new crises as they emerge.

perceptions. An individual's image of the world and events in it. Our perceptions of events and actions in the international environment are filtered through our *beliefs* and *operational codes*.

personality. A leader's basic orientations toward himself or herself and toward his or her world. The leader's personality traits, combined with the psychological makeup and *beliefs* of the leader, shape his or her general foreign policy orientation. Key traits and factors include leaders' need for power, their self-esteem, their desire to affiliate with others, their need to dominate others, their relative level of egotism, and where they fall on a scale ranging from being an extrovert to being an introvert.

policy entrepreneurs. Individuals who attempt to initiate fundamental policy changes that may not be consistent with the institution's previous view of its mission.

power cycle theory. Argues that the capabilities of major powers, relative to other members of the great power system, follow a cyclical path of growth, maturation, and decline. The theory asserts that states are most prone to war when they reach one of four critical points in the cycle. Critical points indicate a change in a country's previous trend in the cycle as either rising or declining in power relative to others. The more countries that are going through critical points, the greater the chance of war. See also *critical points, long cycle theory,* and *power transition theory.*

power transition theory. As originally formulated, the theory asserts that the potential for war is greatly increased when the power capabilities of a major power challenger who is dissatisfied with the international status quo rapidly reaches a level equal to (or almost equal to) that of the hegemonic leader who is the defender of the global status quo. It is now used more broadly to apply to all dyadic pairs of states. Power transitions lead to greater perceptions of threat and anxiety, to perceptions of windows of opportunity and windows of vulnerability, and eventually to war. See also *hegemonic stability theory, long cycle theory,* and *power cycle theory.*

preemptive war. A war that is launched based on the assumption that an attack from an opponent is imminent and thus there is an advantage to striking first.

preventive war. A war that is launched based on the assumption that, due to shifts in the dyadic balance of power, the attacking state has a better chance to prevail in the present than in the future. This generally involves a perception that a current window of opportunity is closing and a window of vulnerability is emerging.

process tracing. An analytical approach to the study of war that uses variables derived from the theoretical and empirical literature to trace the causal process by which initial conditions or root causes combine with more immediate or proximate factors to develop, over time, into war. Process tracing seeks to identify which clusters of variables are most likely to result in war.

prospect theory. A theory of decision making which assumes that individuals think in terms of gains and losses, rather than net assets (as is assumed under *expected utility theory*). As a result, according to prospect theory individuals focus on deviations from a reference point (usually the status quo) in analyzing a situation and making a decision. Contrary to *expected utility theory,* prospect theory argues that individuals are most likely to take risks when they calculate that doing so increases their possibility of minimizing losses in something which they value.

proximate causes of war. See *immediate causes of war.*

psychological makeup. See *personality*.

rational choice (or rational actor model). A model that assumes that states, as unified rational actors, undertake the following steps in making a decision: identify and place goals in the order of their importance, list the policy alternatives available for achieving those goals, calculate the costs and benefits of the expected outcomes of each alternative, and choose the policy that will produce the best outcome (in terms of the balance of costs and benefits). See also *expected utility theory*.

realism. A theoretical school that argues that, much as individuals in their daily lives are obsessed with their own welfare and survival, states are obsessed with their own security and survival in the international system. Thus realism assumes that all states seek to maximize or maintain their power in order to ensure their security in the anarchic global system. See also *anarchy* and *security dilemma*.

realpolitik. The strategies and tactics that are linked to the exercise of power by states within the international system.

regimes. Norms, rules, principles, institutions, and decision-making procedures around which actors' expectations converge in a given international issue area. Typically, regimes are created by, and reflect the interests of, the dominant state within the international system. See also *hegemonic stability theory*.

revisionist states. States that are dissatisfied with the current distribution of power, prestige, status, and economic benefits within the current international system, thus leading them to seek to overturn the existing global norms and balance of power within the international system.

revolution. The transformation through mass action of the fundamental political, economic, social, and cultural institutions of the state, usually involving the use of violence. Although revolutions are first and foremost a domestic phenomenon, they have serious implications for the possibility of interstate conflict by increasing uncertainty and anxiety in the international system, causing an abrupt shift in the distribution of power within the system, making it difficult to measure power accurately and increasing the level of threat perceived by the revolutionary state and by its rivals.

rivals. See *strategic rivals*.

scapegoat war. A subset of the diversionary war category in which political elites justify launching a foreign war by pointing to the supposed involvement of another state in fomenting problems within the elites' domestic system. See also *diversionary wars*.

security dilemma. Occurs when one state attempts to increase its own security by building up its military capabilities, involving either the acquisition of more or better weapons or the forging of new alliances. Under the security dilemma, when one state increases its own security, other states feel less secure, and they respond to the perception of a growing threat by taking measures to increase their own security, which in turn decreases the security of the first state once again. In the end, all states feel less secure in spite of—or more correctly because of—the measures they take to increase their security. See also *arms race, conflict spiral*, and *realism*.

status discrepancy. A situation in which the prestige accorded to a state within the international system does not match its actual economic and military capabilities.

stereotyping. A psychological technique that involves the creation of a set of broad assumptions regarding the culture, character and behavior of another group of people.

strategic rivals. A dyad in which each state regards the other as a competitor whose actions and policies pose an immediate and/or latent military threat to its own core interests. The states involved tend therefore to deeply distrust each other and to expect that conflicts between them will not be settled peacefully. Such dyadic rivals tend to become involved in a series of militarized crises and are highly prone to war.

two-level game model. A model of international diplomacy which depicts states as engaging in bargaining at two theoretically distinct but interactive levels as they seek to arrive at a mutually acceptable agreement: Level I, which involves the negotiations in the international system between two or more states, and Level II, which is the bargaining that occurs within each state as political leaders address the demands and desires of interested domestic parties regarding the outcome of the negotiations at Level I. Each side has a "win set" of possible outcomes (terms or conditions) that it will accept. If the win sets of the two states overlap—that is, if they both contain some identical conditions—then an agreement is possible. The larger each side's win set, the more likely the two win sets will overlap and that an agreement can be reached.

unipolar system. A condition under which the international system is dominated by a single great power. See also *hegemonic stability theory*.

wars of inequality. warfare between states of unequal strength. See also *wars of rivalry*.

wars of rivalry. warfare between states of roughly equal strength. See also *wars of inequality*.

wars of secession. A domestic war in which a segment of the population, based in a subregion of the country, seeks to break away in order to form their own state. Wars of secession often become internationalized as the parties to the war seek external assistance. In addition, wars of secession may also become externalized when a bordering state shares an ethnic tie with one of the parties involved in the war.

window of opportunity. The perception by state leaders that conditions have created a temporary opportunity to prevail against a rival in warfare.

window of vulnerability. The perception by state leaders that conditions will increase their state's vulnerability to attack by a rival in the future

wishful thinking. A psychological technique for coping with stress in which an individual ignores or downplays negative information and evaluations, thus allowing the individual to assume that his or her policy choices will result in a desired outcome. See also *motivated bias*.

world systems theory. A theory of international political economy which applies Marx's class-based analytical approach to the global capitalist economy. World systems theory divides the globe into three categories of states: the core states (the great capitalist industrialized powers, including the United States, Western Europe, and Japan); the semiperiphery states (the relatively less advanced but industrialized states of Eastern Europe, Russia, and some East Asian states such as Singapore and Taiwan); and the periphery states (the poorest states, covering much of the lesser-developed world, whose primary functions in the world capitalist economy are to provide cheap natural resources and labor, as well as markets for manufactured items that are produced in the core and the semiperiphery). The theory presumes that because the capitalist world economy has persisted for several centuries through several cycles of hegemonic rise and fall, fundamental change can only occur via an overthrow of the global capitalist system, which logically would require a large-scale war.

References

Allen, Mike. 2004. "Management Style Shows Weaknesses." *Washington Post*, June 2, A6.

Allison, Graham. 1971. *Essence of Decision: Explaining the Cuban Missile Crisis*. Boston: Little, Brown.

Amin, Agha Humayun. 2000. "The Pakistan Army from 1965–1971." *Defence Notes*. On line at www.defencejournal.com/2000/nov/pak-army.html (June 21, 2003).

———. 2001. "The 1971 War: An Examination of the Strategic Concept of War." *Defence Notes*. On line at www.defencejournal.com/2001/jan/1971-war.html (June 21, 2003).

Andersen, Roy R., Robert F. Seibert, and Jon G. Wagner. 1998. *Politics and Change in the Middle East*. 5th ed. Upper Saddle River, N.J.: Prentice-Hall.

Aruri, Naseer H. 1988. "Palestinian Nationalism Since 1967: An Overview." In *The Arab-Israeli Conflict: Two Decades of Change*, edited by Yehuda Lukacs and Abdallah M. Battah, 71–82. Boulder, Colo.: Westview Press.

Ayoob, Mohammad. 1995. *The Third World Security Predicament: State-making, Regional Conflict, and the International System*. Boulder, Colo.: Lynne Rienner.

Baghdadi, Abdul Latif. 1977. *Mudhakkirat* (Memoirs). Cairo: al-Maktab al Hadith.

Bajpai, Shankar K. 2003. "Untangling India and Pakistan." *Foreign Affairs* (May–June): 112–26.

Bamford, James. 2004. *A Pretext for War*. New York: Doubleday.

Barstow, David, William Broad, and Jeff Garth. 2004. "How the White House Embraced Disputed Arms Intelligence." *New York Times*, October 3. On line at www.nytimes.com/2004/10/03/international/middleeast/03tube.html (October 3, 2004).

Beasley, W. G. 1987. *Japanese Imperialism, 1898–1945*. Oxford: Oxford University Press.

Bennett, D. Scott, and Allan C. Stam. 2004. *The Behavioral Origins of War*. Ann Arbor: University of Michigan Press.

Bergus, Douglas C. 1996. "The View from Washington." In *The Six-Day War: A Retrospective*, edited by Richard B. Parker, 189–236. Gainesville: University Press of Florida.

Bickerton, Ian J., and Carla L. Klausner. 1998. *A Concise History of the Arab-Israeli Conflict*. 3rd ed. Upper Saddle River, N.J.: Prentice-Hall.

Bill, James A., and Robert Springborg. 1993. *Politics in the Middle East*. New York: Harper Collins.

Bix, Herbert. 2000. *Hirohito and the Making of Modern Japan*. New York: Harper Collins.

Blainey, Geoffrey. 1973. *The Causes of War*. New York: Free Press.

Blix, Hans. 2004. *Disarming Iraq*. New York: Pantheon.

Blood, Peter R., ed. 1995. *Pakistan: A Country Study*. 6th ed. Washington, D.C.: Federal Research Division, Library of Congress.

Boot, Max. 2004. "Neocons." *Foreign Policy* 140:20–28.

Bowden, Mark. 2005. "Wolfowitz: The Exit Interviews." *Atlantic Monthly*, July/August, 110–22.

Brecher, Michael. 1980. *Decisions in Crisis: Israel, 1967 and 1973.* Berkeley and Los Angeles: University of California Press.

Brooks, Stephen, and William Wohlforth. 2002. "American Primacy in Perspective." *Foreign Affairs* 81 (4): 20–33.

Brown, James, and William P. Snyder. 1985. "The Iran-Iraq War: Introduction." In *The Regionalization of Warfare*, edited by James Brown and William P. Snyder, 119–25. New Brunswick, N.J.: Transaction Books.

Brown, L. Carl. 1996. "Origins of the Crisis." In *The Six-Day War: A Retrospective*, edited by Richard B. Parker, 13–73. Gainesville: University Press of Florida.

Brown, L. Carl, and Richard B. Parker. 1996. "Introduction." In *The Six-Day War: A Retrospective*, edited by Richard B. Parker, 1–12. Gainesville: University Press of Florida.

Brown, W. Norman. 1972. *The United States and India, Pakistan, and Bangladesh.* 3rd ed. Cambridge: Harvard University Press.

Bueno de Mesquita, Bruce. 1981. *The War Trap.* New Haven: Yale University Press.

Burke, S. M. 1973. *Pakistan's Foreign Policy: An Historical Analysis.* Oxford: Oxford University Press.

Burki, Shahid Javed. 1986. *Pakistan: A Nation in the Making.* Boulder, Colo.: Westview Press.

Burrough, Bryan, Evgenia Peretz, David Rose, and David Wise. 2004. "The Path to War." *Vanity Fair*, May.

Buruma, Ian. 2003. *Inventing Japan.* New York: Modern Library.

Butow, Robert J. C. 1961. *Tojo and the Coming of the War.* Princeton: Princeton University Press.

Byman, Daniel, and Kenneth Pollack. 2001. "Let Us Now Praise Great Men." *International Security* 25 (4): 107–46.

Calleo, David. 1978. *The German Problem Reconsidered.* Cambridge University Press.

Carr, E. H. 2001. *The Twenty Years' Crisis.* New York: Palgrave.

Cashman, Greg. 1993. *What Causes War? An Introduction to Theories of International Conflict.* New York: Lexington.

Chawla, Shalini. 2001. "Pakistan's Military Spending: Socio-Economic Dimensions." *Strategic Analysis* 25 (August).

Checkel, Jeff. 1993. "Ideas, Institutions, and the Gorbachev Foreign Policy Revolution." *World Politics* 45:271–300.

Choucri, Nazli, and Robert North. 1975. *Nations in Conflict.* San Francisco: W. H. Freeman.

Choudhury, G. W. 1974. *The Last Days of United Pakistan.* Bloomington: Indiana University Press.

———. 1975. *India, Pakistan, Bangladesh, and the Major Powers: Politics of a Divided Sub-Continent.* New York: Free Press.

Chubin, Shahram, and Charles Tripp. 1988. *Iran and Iraq at War.* Boulder, Colo.: Westview Press.

Churchill, Randolph S., and Winston S. Churchill. 1967. *The Six Day War.* Boston: Houghton Mifflin.

Clarke, Richard. 2004. *Against All Enemies: Inside America's War on Terror.* New York: Free Press.

Claude, Inis, Jr. 1962. *Power and International Relations.* New York: Random House.

Cobban, Helena. 1984. *The Palestinian Liberation Organization.* Cambridge: Cambridge University Press.

Cohen, Stephen P. 2002. "The Nation and the State of Pakistan." *Washington Quarterly* 25 (3): 109–22.

Commission on the Intelligence Capabilities of the United States Regarding Weapons of Mass Destruction (CIC). Laurence Silberman and Charles Robb, co-chairs. 2005. "Case Study: Iraq." In Whitney, *WMD Mirage*, 402–554.

Crowley, James. 1974. "A New Asian Order: Some Notes on Prewar Japanese Nationalism." In *Japan in Crisis*, edited by B. Silberman and H. D. Harootunian. Princeton: Princeton University Press.

Daalder, Ivo, and James Lindsay. 2003. *America Unbound: The Bush Revolution in Foreign Policy*. Washington, D.C.: Brookings Institution.

Danner, Mark. 2005. "The Secret Way to War." *New York Review of Books*, June 9, 70–74.

Dassel, Kurt. 1998. "Civilians, Soldiers and Strife: Domestic Sources of International Aggression." *International Security* 23 (1): 107–40.

Dawisha, Adeed. 1980. "Iraq: The West's Opportunity." *Foreign Policy* 41:134–53.

———. 2000. "Arab Nationalism and Islamism: Competitive Past, Uncertain Future." *International Studies Review* 2 (Fall): 79–90.

Desch, Michael. 1998. "Culture Clash: Assessing the Importance of Ideas in Security Studies." *International Security* 23 (1): 141–70.

Deutsch, Karl, and Richard Merritt. 1965. "Effects of Events on National and International Images." In *International Behavior*, edited by Herbert Kelman, 132–87. New York: Holt, Rinehart and Winston.

Didion, Joan. 2003. "Mr. Bush and the Divine." *New York Review of Books*, November 6, 81–86.

Diehl, Paul F., ed. 1998. *The Dynamics of Enduring Rivalries*. Urbana: University of Illinois Press.

Diller, Daniel C., ed. 1991. *The Middle East*. 7th ed. Washington, D.C.: Congressional Quarterly.

Donaldson, Ronald H. 1973. "Soviet Political Aims in South Asia." Paper submitted to the Twenty-fifth Annual Meeting of the Association for Asian Studies. Chicago, March 30–April 1.

Doran, Charles F. 1989. "Power Cycle Theory of Systems Structure and Stability: Commonalities and Complementarities." In *Handbook of War Studies*, edited by Manus Midlarsky, 83–110. Ann Arbor: University of Michigan Press.

———. 1991. *Systems in Crisis*. Cambridge: Cambridge University Press.

———. 2000. "Confronting Principles of the Power Cycle: Changing Systems Structure, Expectations and War." In *Handbook of War Studies II*, edited by Manus Midlarsky, 332–68. Ann Arbor: University of Michigan Press.

Doran, Charles F., and Wes Parsons. 1980. "War and the Cycle of Relative Power." *American Political Science Review* 74:947–65.

Dower, John. 1986. *War without Mercy: Race and Power in the Pacific War*. New York: Pantheon.

Duelfer, Charles. 2004. Report of the Iraq Survey Group. Quoted in "Excerpts from the Weapons Report." *Washington Post*, October 7, 33.

Eckhardt, William. 1991. "War-Related Deaths Since 3000 BC." *Bulletin of Peace Proposals* (December).

Ekstein, Michael, and Zara Steiner. 1977. "The Sarajevo Crisis." In *British Foreign Policy under Sir Edward Grey*, edited by F. H. Hinsley. Cambridge: Cambridge University Press.

Eriksson, Mikael, and Peter Wallensteen. 2003. "Armed Conflict, 1989–2003." *Journal of Peace Research* 41 (5): 625–36.

Fallows, James. 2004a. "Blind into Baghdad." *Atlantic Monthly*, January/February, 52–74.

———. 2004b. "Bush's Lost Year." *Atlantic Monthly*, October, 68–84.

Farsoun, Samih K., and Christina E. Zacharia. 1997. *Palestine and the Palestinians*. Boulder, Colo.: Westview Press.

Fawzi, Muhammad. 1980. *Harb al-Thalath Sanawat* (The Three Years War). Heliopolis: Dar al-Mustaqbil al-Arabi.

Fearon, James. 1995. "Rationalist Explanations for War." *International Organization* 53:567–87.

Feis, Herbert. 1950. *The Road to Pearl Harbor*. Princeton: Princeton University Press.

Ferguson, Niall. 1999. *The Pity of War: Explaining World War I*. New York: Basic Books.

Fettweis, Christopher. 2004. "Evaluating IR's Crystal Balls: How Predictions of the Future Have Withstood Fourteen Years of Unipolarity." *International Studies Review* 6 (1): 79–104.

Fujiwara, Akira. 1973. "The Role of the Japanese Army." In *Pearl Harbor as History*, edited by D. Borg, S. Okamoto, and D. Finlayson. New York: Columbia University Press.

Galtung, Johann. 1964. "A Structural Theory of Aggression." *Journal of Peace Research* 1:95–119.

Gandhi, Sajit, ed. 2002. "Nixon Presidential Materials Project: National Security Project." On line at www.gwu.edu/-nsarch/NSAEBB/NSABB/79 (July 26, 2004).

Ganguly, Sumit. 1994. *The Origins of War in South Asia: The Indo-Pakistani Conflict since 1947*. 2nd ed. Boulder, Colo.: Westview Press.

———. 1995. "War without End: The Indo-Pakistani Conflict." *The Annals of the American Academy of Political and Social Sciences* 541 (September): 167–78.

———. 2001. *Conflict Unending: India-Pakistan Tensions since 1947*. Washington, D.C.: Woodrow Wilson Center Press.

Geller, Daniel S. 1998. "The Stability of the Military Balance and War among Great Power Rivals." In Diehl, *Dynamics of Enduring Rivalries*, 165–90.

———. 2000. "Material Capabilities: Power and International Conflict." In *What Do We Know About War?* edited by John A. Vasquez, 259–77. Lanham, Md.: Rowman & Littlefield.

Geller, Daniel S., and J. David Singer. 1998. *Nations at War: A Scientific Study of International Conflict*. Cambridge: Cambridge University Press.

Gellman, Barton, and Dafna Linzer. 2004. "Afghanistan, Iraq: Two Wars Collide." *Washington Post*, October 22, A1, A14–15.

George, Alexander. 1972. "The Case for Multiple Advocacy in Making Foreign Policy." *American Political Science Review* 66:751–85.

———. 1980. "The Operational Code: A Neglected Approach to the Study of Political Leaders and Decision Making." In *The Conduct of Soviet Foreign Policy*, edited by E. Hoffman and F. Fleron, 165–90. New York: Aldine.

Gilbert, Arthur N., and Curtis Holmes. 1996. "Scar Wars: Dueling, Democracy, and the Production of Truth." Paper presented to University of Denver Democracy Conference.

Gilpin, Robert. 1981. *War and Change in World Politics*. Cambridge: Cambridge University Press.

Gleditch, Nils Petter, Peter Wallensteen, Mikael Eriksson, Margareta Sollenberg, and Harvard Strand. 2002. "Armed Conflict, 1946–2001: A New Dataset." *Journal of Peace Research* 39 (5): 615–37.

Glenn, David. 2002. "Calculus of the Battlefield." *Chronicle of Higher Education*, November 8, A14–16.

Goertz, Gary, and Paul F. Diehl. 1992. "The Empirical Importance of Enduring Rivalries." *International Interactions* 18:151–63.

———. 1998. "The 'Volcano Model' and Other Patterns in the Evolution of Enduring Rivalries." In Diehl, *Dynamics of Enduring Rivalries*.

———. 2000. "(Enduring) Rivalries." In *Handbook of War Studies II*, edited by Manus Midlarsky, 222–67. Ann Arbor: University of Michigan Press.

Goldstone, Jack. 2001. "Toward a Fourth Generation of Revolutionary Theory." *Annual Review of Political Science* 4:139–87.

Gordon, Michael. 1974. "Domestic Conflict and the Origins of the First World War: The British and German Cases." *Journal of Modern History* 46:191–236.

Graham, Bradley. 2004. "A Leader with an Eye on His Legacy." *Washington Post*, October 7, A33.

Grummon, Stephen R. 1982. *The Iran-Iraq War: Islam Embattled*. New York: Praeger.

Halper, Stefan, and Jonathan Clarke. 2004. *America Alone: The Neo-Conservatives and the Global Order*. Cambridge: Cambridge University Press.

Hart, Paul 't. 1990. *Groupthink in Government*. Baltimore: Johns Hopkins University Press.

Heitzman, James, and Robert L. Worden, eds. 1989. *Bangladesh: A Country Study*. 2nd ed. Washington, D.C.: Federal Research Division, Library of Congress.

———. 1996. *India: A Country Study*. 5th ed. Washington, D.C.: Federal Research Division, Library of Congress.

Helms, Christine Moss. 1984. *Iraq: Eastern Flank of the Arab World*. Washington, D.C.: Brookings Institution.

Hensel, Paul R. 2000. "Territory: Theory and Evidence on Geography and Conflict." In *What Do We Know About War?* edited by John A. Vasquez, 57–84. Lanham, Md.: Rowman & Littlefield.

Hickman, William F. 1982. *Ravaged and Reborn: The Iranian Army, 1982*. Washington, D.C.: Brookings Institution.

Hiro, Dilip. 1991. *The Longest War: The Iran-Iraq Military Conflict*. New York: Routledge, Chapman and Hall.

Holsti, Ole, Robert North, and Richard Brody. 1968. "Perception and Action in the 1914 Crisis." In *Quantitative International Politics*, edited by J. David Singer, 132–58. New York: Free Press. Reprinted in *Classics of International Relations*. 3rd ed., edited by John Vasquez, 200–210. Upper Saddle River, N.J.: Prentice Hall, 1996.

Hopf, Ted. 1998. "The Promise of Constructivism in International Relations Theory." *International Security* 23 (1): 171–200.

Horowitz, Donald L. 1981. "Patterns of Ethnic Separatism." *Comparative Studies in Society and History* 23 (April): 165–95.

Hull, Isabel. 1982. *The Entourage of Kaiser Wilhelm II: 1888–1918*. Cambridge: Cambridge University Press.

Huntington, Samuel. 1958. "Arms Races: Prerequisites and Results." In *Public Policy* 8:41–86, edited by C. J. Friedrich and S. E. Harris.

———. 1993. "The Clash of Civilizations?" *Foreign Affairs* 72 (3): 22–49.

———. 1996. *The Clash of Civilizations and the Remaking of World Order*. New York: Simon and Schuster.

———. 1998. "The Clash of Civilizations Goes Nuclear." *New Perspectives Quarterly*, June.

———. 1999. "The Lonely Superpower." *Foreign Affairs* 78 (2): 35–50.

Huth, Paul K. 1988. *Extended Deterrence and the Prevention of War*. New Haven: Yale University Press.

———. 2000. "Territory: Why Are Territorial Disputes between States a Central Cause of International Conflict?" In *What Do We Know About War?* edited by John A. Vasquez, 85–110. Lanham, Md.: Rowman & Littlefield.

Huth, Paul, D. Scott Bennett, and Christopher Gelpi. 1992. "System Uncertainty, Risk Propensity, and International Conflict among the Great Powers." *Journal of Conflict Resolution* 36:478–517.

Ike, Nobutaka. 1967. *Japan's Decision for War: Records of the 1941 Imperial Conferences.* Stanford, Calif.: Stanford University Press.

Ikenberry, G. John. 2002. "America's Imperial Ambition." *Foreign Policy* 81 (5): 44–60.

International Institute for Strategic Studies (IISS). 1981. *The Military Balance, 1980–81.* London: IISS.

Iraq Survey Group. 2004. "Excerpts from the Comprehensive Report of Charles A. Duelfer, Special Adviser to the DCI and Leader of the Iraq Survey Group, on Iraq's WMD." In Whitney, *WMD Mirage.* 247–327.

Iriye, Akira. 1987. *The Origins of the Second World War in Asia and the Pacific.* London: Longman.

Isikoff, Michael. 2005. "A Wicked Curveball." *Newsweek*, April 11, 59.

Jackson, Robert. 1974. *South Asian Crisis: India, Pakistan and Bangladesh; a Political and Historical Analysis of the 1971 War.* New York: Praeger.

Janis, Irving L. 1982. *Groupthink: Psychological Studies of Policy Decisions and Fiascoes.* 2nd ed. Boston: Houghton-Mifflin.

Jansen, Marius. 2000. *The Making of Modern Japan.* Cambridge: Belknap/Harvard University Press.

Jepperson, Ronald, Alexander Wendt, and Peter Katzenstein. 1996. "Norms, Identity, and Culture in National Security." In *The Culture of National Security*, edited by P. Katzenstein, 33–75. New York: Columbia University Press.

Jervis, Robert. 1976. *Perception and Misperception in International Politics.* Princeton: Princeton University Press.

———. 1978. "Cooperation under the Security Dilemma." *World Politics* 30:167–214.

———. 1989. "Rational Deterrence: Theory and Evidence." *World Politics* 41:183–207.

———. 1994. "Political Implications of Loss Aversion." In *Avoiding Losses/Taking Risks: Prospect Theory and International Conflict*, edited by Barbara Farnham, 23–40. Ann Arbor: University of Michigan Press.

———. 2005. "Understanding the Bush Doctrine." In *American Foreign Policy: Theoretical Essays.* 5th ed., edited by G. John Ikenberry, 576–99. New York: Pearson/Longman.

Jervis, Robert, Richard Ned Lebow, and Janice Gross Stein. 1985. *Psychology and Deterrence.* Baltimore: Johns Hopkins University Press.

Joll, James. 1992. *The Origins of the First World War.* 2nd ed. New York: Longman.

Kagan, Donald. 1995. *On the Origins of War.* New York: Doubleday.

Kahneman, David, and Amos Tversky. 1979. "Prospect Theory: An Analysis of Decision Under Risk." *Econometrica* 47:263–91.

Kaiser, David E. 1983. "Germany and the Origins of the First World War." *Journal of Modern History* 55:442–74.

———. 1990. *Politics and War: European Conflict from Philip II to Hitler.* Cambridge: Harvard University Press.

Kak, Kapil. 1998. "Pakistan: A Geo-Political Appraisal." *Strategic Analysis* 22 (November).

Kato, Shuichi. 1974. "Taisho Democracy as the Pre-Stage for Japanese Militarism." In *Japan in Crisis*, edited by B. Silberman and H. D. Harootunian, 217–36. Princeton: Princeton University Press.

Kaufman, Chaim. 2004. "Threat Inflation and the Failure of the Marketplace of Ideas." *International Security* 29 (1): 5–48.

Kennedy, Paul. 1984. "The First World War and the International Power System." *International Security* 9 (1): 7–39.

———. 1987. *The Rise and Fall of the Great Powers.* New York: Random House.

Kerr, Malcolm. 1971. *The Arab Cold War: Gamal Abdul Nasser and His Rivals: 1958–1970.* 3rd ed. Oxford: Oxford University Press.

al-Khalil, Samir. 1990. *Republic of Fear.* New York: Pantheon.

Khouri, Fred J. 1985. *The Arab-Israeli Dilemma*. 3rd ed. Syracuse, N.Y.: Syracuse University Press.

Kingdon, John. 1984. *Agendas, Alternatives and Public Policy*. Boston: Little, Brown.

Kinsella, David. 2004. *Regime Change: Origins, Execution, and Aftermath of the Iraq War*. Belmont, Calif.: Wadsworth-Thomson.

Kissinger, Henry. 1962. *The Necessity for Choice*. New York: Doubleday.

———. 1979. *White House Years*. Boston: Little, Brown.

Krauthammer, Charles. 1990–1991. "The Unipolar Moment." *Foreign Affairs* 70 (1): 23–33.

———. 2002–2003. "The Unipolar Moment Revisited." *National Interest* 70:5–17. Reprinted in *American Foreign Policy: Theoretical Essays*, edited by G. John Ikenberry, 550–64. New York: Pearson/Longman.

Kugler, Jacek, and Douglas Lemke. 2000. "The Power Transition Research Program: Assessing Theoretical and Empirical Advances." In *Handbook of War Studies II*, edited by Manus Midlarsky, 129–63. Ann Arbor: University of Michigan Press.

Kulkarni, V. B. 1973. *India and Pakistan: A Historical Survey of Hindu-Muslim Relations*. Bombay: Jaico Publishing House.

LaFeber, Walter. 1997. *The Clash: U.S.–Japanese Relations Throughout History*. New York: W. W. Norton.

Lake, David. 2003. "International Relations Theory and Internal Conflict: Insights from the Interstices." *International Studies Review* 5:81–89.

Lantis, Jeffrey, and Eric Moskowitz. 2005. "The Return to the Imperial Presidency? The Bush Doctrine and U.S. Intervention in Iraq." In *Contemporary Cases in U.S. Foreign Policy*, edited by Ralph G. Carter. Washington, D.C.: Congressional Quarterly Press.

Lebow, Richard Ned. 1981. *Between Peace and War: The Nature of International Crises*. Baltimore: Johns Hopkins University Press.

———. 1984. "Windows of Opportunity: Do States Jump Through Them?" *International Security* 9 (1): 147–86.

———. 2000–2001. "Contingency, Catalysts, and International System Change." *Political Science Quarterly* 115 (4): 591–616.

———. 2003. "A Data Set Named Desire: A Reply to William R. Thompson." *International Studies Quarterly* 47:475–78.

Lemann, Nicholas. 2004. "Remember the Alamo: How George W. Bush Reinvented Himself." *New Yorker*, October 18, 148–61.

Lemke, Douglas. 2002. *Regions of War and Peace*. Cambridge: Cambridge University Press.

Leng, Russell. 1983. "When Will They Ever Learn? Coercive Bargaining in Recurrent Crises." *Journal of Conflict Resolution* 27:379–419.

Levi, Ariel, and Glen White. 1997. "A Cross-Cultural Exploration of the Reference Dependence of Crucial Group Decision under Risk." *Journal of Conflict Resolution* 41:792–813.

Levy, Jack. 1981. "Alliance Formation and War Behavior: An Analysis of the Great Powers, 1495–1975." *Journal of Conflict Resolution* 25:581–614.

———. 1983. *War in the Modern Great Power System, 1495–1975*. Lexington: University Press of Kentucky.

———. 1987. "Declining Power and the Preventive Motivation for War." *World Politics* 40 (1): 82–107.

———. 1988. "Domestic Politics and War." In *The Origin and Prevention of Major Wars*, edited by R. Rotberg and T. Rabb, 79–99. Cambridge: Cambridge University Press.

———. 1989. "Organizational Routines and the Causes of War." In *Choices in World Politics*, edited by Bruce Russett, Harvey Starr, and Michael Stoll, 150–80. New York: W. H. Freeman.

———. 1990–1991. "Preferences, Constraints, and Choices in July 1914." *International Security* 15 (3): 151–86.

———. 1991. "The Role of Crisis Mismanagement in the Outbreak of World War I." In *Avoiding War*, edited by Alexander George, 62–102. Boulder, Colo.: Westview Press.

———. 1993. "The Diversionary Theory of War: A Critique." In *Handbook of War Studies*, edited by Manus Midlarsky, 259–88. Ann Arbor: University of Michigan Press.

———. 1994a. "An Introduction to Prospect Theory." In *Avoiding Losses/Taking Risks: Prospect Theory and International Conflict*, edited by Barbara Farnham. Ann Arbor: University of Michigan Press.

———. 1994b. "Prospect Theory and International Relations: Theoretical Applications and Analytical Problems." In *Avoiding Losses/Taking Risks: Prospect Theory and International Conflicts*, edited by Barbara Farnham, 119–46. Ann Arbor: University of Michigan Press.

———. 1997. "Prospect Theory, Rational Choice, and International Relations." *International Studies Quarterly* 41:87–112.

Levy, Jack, and Mike Froelich. 1985. "Causes of the Iran-Iraq War." In *The Regionalization of Warfare*, edited by James Brown and William P. Snyder, 127–43. New Brunswick, N.J.: Transaction Books.

Lieven, D. C. 1983. *Russia and the Origins of the First World War*. New York: St. Martin's.

Linzer, Dafna, and Barton Gellman. 2004. "CIA Skewed Iraq Reporting, Senate Shows." *Washington Post*, July 11, A19.

Lopez, George, and David Cortright. 2004. "Containing Iraq: Sanctions Worked." *Foreign Affairs* 83 (4): 90–103.

Love, Kennett. 1969. *The Twice-Fought War: A History*. New York: McGraw-Hill

Lustick, Ian. 1996. "To Build and Be Built: Israel and the Hidden Logic Behind the Iron Wall." *Israel Studies* 1 (Spring): n.p. On line at http://iupjournals.org/israel/iss1.html (July 14, 2001).

Lynn-Jones, Sean M. 1986. "Detente and Deterrence: Anglo-German Relations, 1911–1914." *International Security* 11 (2): 121–50.

———. 1995. "Offense-Defense Theory and Its Critics." *Security Studies* 4:660–91.

Maechling, Charles, Jr. 2000. "Pearl Harbor: The First Energy War." *History Today* 50 (12): 42–48.

Maier, Charles S. 1989. "Wargames: 1914–1919." In *The Origin and Prevention of Major Wars*, edited by Robert Rotberg and Theodore Rabb, 249–80. Cambridge: Cambridge University Press.

Malin, Martin. 1997. "Is Autocracy an Obstacle to Peace? Iran and Iraq, 1975–80." In *Paths to Peace*, edited by Miriam Fendius Elman, 373–404. Cambridge, Mass.: MIT Press.

Mann, James. 2004. *The Rise of the Vulcans: The History of Bush's War Cabinet*. New York: Viking.

Mansfield, Edward, and Jack Snyder. 1995. "Democratization and the Danger of War." *International Security* 20 (1): 5–38.

———. 2005. *Electing to Fight: Why Emerging Democracies Go to War*. Cambridge, Mass.: MIT Press.

Mansfield, Peter. 1991. *A History of the Middle East*. New York: Penguin Books.

Marder, Arthur. 1981. *Old Friends, New Enemies*. Oxford: Clarendon Press.

Marshall, Monty. 1999. *Third World War*. Lanham, Md.: Rowman & Littlefield.

Massouli, François. 1999. *Middle East Conflicts*. Northampton, Mass.: Interlink Publishing.

Mastanduno, Michael. 1997. "Preserving the Unipolar Moment: Realist Theories and U.S. Grand Strategy after the Cold War." *International Security* 21 (4): 49–88.

McDermott, Joseph. 1995. "Modern Japan and War: A Problem with a Past." In *War: A Cruel Necessity?* edited by Robert Hinde and Helen Watson, 183–95. London: Tauris.

McInerney, Audrey. 1994. "Prospect Theory and Soviet Policy Towards Syria, 1966–1967." In *Avoiding Losses/Taking Risks: Prospect Theory and International Conflict*, edited by Barbara Farnham, 101–18. Ann Arbor: University of Michigan Press.

McMahon, Robert J. 1994. "Balancing the Scales." In *The Cold War on the Periphery*, by Robert J. McMahon. New York: Columbia University Press. Accessed at Columbia International Affairs Online.

Mearsheimer, John. 2001. *The Tragedy of Great Power Politics*. New York: Norton.

Metz, Helen Chapin, ed. 1989. *Iran: A Country Study*. Washington, D.C.: GPO.

Mintrom, Michael. 1997. "Policy Entrepreneurs and the Diffusion of Innovation." *American Journal of Political Science* 41 (3): 738–70.

Mitra, Subrata. 2001. "War and Peace in South Asia: A Revisionist View of India-Pakistan Relations." *Contemporary South Asia* 10 (November): 361–79.

Modelski, George, and William R. Thompson. 1989. "Long Cycles and Global War." In *Handbook of War Studies*, edited by Manus Midlarsky, 23–54. Boston: Unwin Hyman.

Moin, Baqer. 1999. *Khomeini: Life of the Ayatollah*. New York: St. Martin's Press.

Monten, Jonathan. 2005. "The Roots of the Bush Doctrine: Power, Nationalism, and Democracy Promotion in U.S. Strategy." *International Security* 29 (4): 112–56.

Mueller, John. 1989. *Retreat from Doomsday: The Obsolescence of Major War*. New York: Basic Books.

Mutawi, Samir A. 1987. *Jordan in the 1967 War*. Cambridge: Cambridge University Press.

Nanda, B. R., ed. 1976. *Indian Foreign Policy: The Nehru Years*. Honolulu: University Press of Hawaii.

National Commission on Terrorist Attacks upon the United States. 2004. *The 9/11 Commission Report*. New York: Norton.

Nayar, Kuldip. 1972. *Distant Neighbors: A Tale of a Subcontinent*. Delhi: Vikas Publishing House.

New York Times (NYT). 2004. "How to Skew Intelligence." Editorial. October 23. On line at www.nytimes.com/2004/10/23/opinion/23sat1.html (October 23, 2004).

Oren, Michael B. 1999. "Did Israel Want the Six Day War?" *Azure* 7 (Spring). On line at www.shalem.org.il/azure/7-Orem.html.

Organski, A. F. K., and Jacek Kugler. 1980. *The War Ledger*. Chicago: University of Chicago Press.

Orme, John. 1987. "Deterrence Failures: A Second Look." *International Security* 11 (4): 96–124.

Parasiliti, Andrew T. 1997. "Iraq's War Decisions, 1978–1991." Draft of chapter 1 of the author's dissertation, Johns Hopkins University.

Parker, Richard B. 1993. *The Politics of Miscalculation in the Middle East*. Bloomington: Indiana University Press.

———. 1996. "Conclusions." In *The Six-Day War: A Retrospective*, edited by Richard B. Parker, 289–320. Gainesville: University Press of Florida.

Paul, T. V. 1994. *Asymmetric Conflicts: War Initiation by Weaker Powers*. Cambridge: Cambridge University Press.

Pelletiere, Stephen C. 1992. *The Iran-Iraq War: Chaos in a Vacuum*. New York: Praeger.

Pelz, Stephen. 1974. *Race to Pearl Harbor*. Cambridge: Harvard University Press.

Peri, Yoram. 1988. "From Political Nationalism to Ethno-Nationalism." In *The Arab-Israeli Conflict: Two Decades of Change*, edited by Yehuda Lukacs and Abdallah M. Battah, 41–53. Boulder, Colo.: Westview Press.

Pfetsch, Frank R., and Christoph Rohloff. 2000. "KOSIMO: A Databank on Political Conflict." *Journal of Peace Research* 37 (3): 379–89.

Pillar, Paul. 2006. "Intelligence, Policy and the War in Iraq." *Foreign Affairs* 85 (2): 15–27.

Pollack, Kenneth M. 2004. "Spies, Lies and Weapons: What Went Wrong?" *Atlantic Monthly*, January/February, 78–92.

Post, Jerrold M. 1990. "The Persian Gulf Crisis." Statement before the U.S. House of Representatives Committee on Foreign Affairs, December 11, 381–401. Washington, D.C.: GPO.

———. 1993. "The Defining Moment of Saddam's Life: A Political Psychology Perspective on the Leadership and Decision Making of Saddam Hussein during the Gulf Crisis." In *The Political Psychology of the Gulf War: Leaders, Publics, and the Process of Conflict*, edited by Stanley Renshon, 49–66. Pittsburgh: University of Pittsburgh Press.

Powers, Thomas. 2004. "How Bush Got It Wrong." *New York Review of Books*, September 23, 87–93.

Priest, Dana. 2004. "Hussein's Aims, Capabilities Often Differed." *Washington Post*, October 8, A7.

Priest, Dana, and Walter Pincus. 2004. "U.S. Almost All Wrong on Weapons." *Washington Post*, October 7, A1, A34.

Public Broadcasting System (PBS). 2003. "The War Behind Closed Doors." Transcript. *Frontline*, February 20.

———. 2004. "Frontline: The Jesus Factor." On line at www.pbs.org/wgbh/pages/frontline/shows/jesus/president/spirituality.html (October 26, 2004).

Putnam, Robert. 1988. "Diplomacy and Domestic Politics: The Logic of Two-Level Games." *International Organization* 42:427–60.

Quandt, William B. 1992. "Lyndon Johnson and the June 1967 War: What Color Was the Light?" *Middle East Journal* 46 (Spring): 198–228.

Rajagopalen, Rajeesh. 1999. "Neorealist Theory and the India-Pakistan Conflict—2." *Strategic Analysis* 23 (January).

Rasler, Karen, and William R. Thompson. 2000. "Global War and the Political Economy of Structural Change." In *Handbook of War Studies II*, edited by Manus Midlarsky, 301–31. Ann Arbor: University of Michigan Press.

Reich, Bernard. 1996. "The Israeli Response." In *The Six-Day War: A Retrospective*, edited by Richard B. Parker, 119–52. Gainesville: University Press of Florida.

Remak, Joachim. 1995. *The Origins of World War I: 1871–1914*. 2nd ed. Fort Worth, Tex.: Harcourt, Brace.

Renner, Michael. 1999. *Ending Violent Conflict*. Worldwatch Paper 146. Washington, D.C.: Worldwatch Institute.

Renshon, Stanley A. 1993a. "Good Judgment, and the Lack Thereof, in the Gulf War: A Preliminary Psychological Model with Some Applications." In *The Political Psychology of the Gulf War: Leaders, Publics, and the Process of Conflict*, edited by Stanley A. Renshon, 67–105. Pittsburgh: Pittsburgh University Press.

———. 1993b. "The Gulf War Revisited: Consequences, Controversies, and Interpretations." In *The Political Psychology of the Gulf War: Leaders, Publics, and the Process of Conflict*, edited by Stanley A. Renshon, 329–57. Pittsburgh: Pittsburgh University Press.

Riad, Muhammad. 1986. *Amrika wa al-Arab* (America and the Arabs). Cairo: Dar Mustaqbil al-Arabi.

Ricks, Thomas. 2006. *Fiasco: The American Military Adventure in Iraq*. New York: Penguin Press.

Risen, James. 2006. *State of War: The Secret History of the CIA and the Bush Administration*. New York: Free Press.

Roberts, Mark J. 1996. *Khomeini's Incorporation of the Iranian Military*. McNair Paper 48. Washington, D.C.: National Defense University.

Rohl, John C. G. 1987. *The Kaiser and His Court.* Cambridge: Cambridge University Press.

Rosati, Jerel A. 2000. "The Power of Human Cognition in the Study of World Politics." *International Studies Review* 2 (Fall): 45–75.

Russett, Bruce. 1972. *No Clear and Present Danger: A Skeptical View of the U.S. Entry into World War II.* New York: Harper and Row.

Russett, Bruce, and Harvey Starr. 2000. "From Democratic Peace to Kantian Peace: Democracy and Conflict in the International System." In *Handbook of War Studies II,* edited by Manus Midlarsky, 93–128. Ann Arbor: University of Michigan Press.

Sabrosky, Alan Ned. 1989. "From Bosnia to Sarajevo: A Comparative Discussion of Interstate Crises." In *Choices in World Politics,* edited by Bruce Russett, Harvey Starr, and Michael Stoll, 62–75. New York: W. H. Freeman.

Safran, Nadav. 1969. *From War to War.* New York: Pegasus Publishing.

Sagan, Scott D. 1986. "1914 Revisited: Allies, Offense and Instability." *International Security* 11 (2): 151–75.

———. 1988. "The Origins of the Pacific War." In *The Origin and Prevention of Major Wars,* edited by Robert Rotberg and Theodore Rabb, 323–52. Cambridge: Cambridge University Press.

Saideman, Stephen M., and R. William Ayers. 2000. "Determining the Causes of Irredentism: Logit Analyses of Minorities at Risk Data from the 1980s and 1990s." *Journal of Politics* 62 (November): 1126–44.

Sample, Susan. 2000. "Military Buildups: Arming and War." In *What Do We Know about War?* edited by John A. Vasquez, 165–95. Lanham, Md.: Rowman & Littlefield.

Sanjian, Gregory S. 1999. "Promoting Stability or Instability? Arms Transfers and Regional Rivalries, 1950–2001." *International Studies Quarterly* 43:641–70.

Sarkees, Meredith, Frank W. Wayman, and J. David Singer. 2003. "Inter-State, Intra-State, and Extra-State Wars: A Comprehensive Look at Their Distribution over Time, 1816–1997." *International Studies Quarterly* 47:49–70.

Schofield, Julian. 2000. "Militarized Decision-Making for War in Pakistan: 1947–71." *Armed Forces and Society* 27 (Fall): 131–48.

Senate Select Committee on Intelligence. 2004. "Report on the U.S. Intelligence Community's Prewar Intelligence Assessment on Iraq." Available at http://intelligence.senate.gov/iraqreport2.pdf.

Shalev, Michael. 1992. *Labour and the Political Economy of Israel.* Oxford: Oxford University Press.

Shlaim, Avi. 2001. *The Iron Wall: Israel and the Arab World.* New York: W. W. Norton.

Sick, Gary. 1985. *All Fall Down: America's Tragic Encounter with Iran.* New York: Random House.

Siffrey, Micah, and Christopher Cerf, eds. 2003. *The Iraq War Reader.* New York: Touchstone.

Singer, J. David, and Melvin Small. 1972. *The Wages of War, 1816–1965.* New York: John Wiley & Sons.

Sisson, Richard, and Leo E. Rose. 1990. *War and Secession: Pakistan, India, and the Creation of Bangladesh.* Berkeley and Los Angeles: University of California Press.

Sivard, Ruth Leger. 1991. *World Military and Social Expenditures 1991.* Washington, D.C.: World Priorities.

———. 1994. *World Military and Social Expenditures 1994.* Washington, D.C.: World Priorities.

———. 1996. *World Military and Social Expenditures 1996.* Washington, D.C.: World Priorities.

Small, Melvin. 1980. *Was War Necessary? National Security and U.S. Entry into War.* Beverly Hills, Calif.: Sage.

Small, Melvin, and J. David Singer. 1982. *Resort to Arms: International and Civil Wars, 1816–1980.* Beverly Hills, Calif.: Sage.

Snyder, Jack. 1982. *The Ideology of the Offensive: Military Decision Making and the Disasters of 1914.* Ithaca: Cornell University Press.

———. 1984. "Civil-Military Relations and the Cult of the Offensive, 1914 and 1984." *International Security* 9 (1): 108–46.

———. 1985. "Perceptions of the Security Dilemma in 1914." In Jervis, Lebow, and Stein, *Psychology and Deterrence*, 153–79. Baltimore: Johns Hopkins University Press.

———. 1991. *Myths of Empire: Domestic Politics and International Ambition.* Ithaca: Cornell University.

Sprout, Harold, and Margaret Sprout. 1965. *The Ecological Perspective on Human Affairs.* Princeton: Princeton University Press.

Stein, Janice Gross. 1991. "The Arab-Israeli War of 1967: Inadvertent War Through Miscalculated Escalation." In *Avoiding War: Problems of Crisis Management*, edited by Alexander L. George, 126–58. Boulder, Colo.: Westview Press.

———. 1993. "The Security Dilemma in the Middle East: A Prognosis for the Decade Ahead." In *The Many Faces of National Security in the Arab World*, edited by Baghat Korany, Paul Noble, and Rex Brynen, 56–75. New York: St. Martin's Press.

Stein, Rob. 2004. "Study Cites 100,000 Civilian Deaths in Iraq." *Washington Post*, October 29.

Stevenson, David. 1991. "Militarization and Diplomacy in Europe before 1914." *International Security* 22 (1): 125–61.

Stoessinger, John G. 2001. *Why Nations Go to War.* 8th ed. New York: St. Martin's Press.

———. 2005. *Why Nations Go to War.* 9th ed. New York: St. Martin's Press.

Sullivan, Michael J., III. 1991. *Measuring Global Values: The Ranking of 162 Countries.* New York: Greenwood Press.

Suskind, Ronald. 2004a. *The Price of Loyalty.* New York: Simon and Schuster.

———. 2004b. "Without a Doubt." *New York Times Magazine*, October 17. On line at http://nytimes.com/2004/10/17/magazine/17BUSH.html (October 17, 2004).

———. 2006. *The One Percent Doctrine.* New York: Simon and Schuster.

Swearingen, Will D. 1988. "Geopolitical Origins of the Iran-Iraq War." *Geographical Review* 78 (4): 40–416.

Taliaferro, Jeffrey. 2004. *Balancing Risks: Great Power Intervention in the Periphery.* Ithaca: Cornell University Press.

Tammen, Ronald, J. Kugler, D. Lemke, A. Stam, M. Abdollahian, C. Alsharabati, B. Efird, and A. F. G. Organski. 2000. *Power Transitions: Strategies for the 21st Century.* New York: Chatham House.

Thapliyal, Sangeeta. 1998. *Strategic Analysis* 22 (October). *The Report of the Commission of Inquiry—1971 War.* Declassified by the Government of Pakistan. On line at http://pub15.ezboard/worldofspiesfrm11.shoMessageRange?topicID=10.topic&start=21 &stop=3 (July 15, 2003).

Thompson, William R. 2001. "Identifying Rivals and Rivalries in World Politics." *International Studies Quarterly* 45:557–86.

———. 2003. "A Streetcar Named Sarajevo: Catalysts, Multiple Causation Chains, and Rivalry Structures." *International Studies Quarterly* 47:453–74.

Thomson, James C. 1973. "How Could Vietnam Happen? An Autopsy." In *Readings in American Foreign Policy: A Bureaucratic Perspective*, edited by Morton Halperin and Arnold Kanter, 98–110. Boston: Little, Brown.

Tibi, Bassam. 1993. *Conflict and War in the Middle East, 1967–91.* New York: St. Martin's Press.

Trachtenberg, Marc. 1990–1991. "The Meaning of Mobilization in 1914." *International Security* 15 (3): 120–50.

Trumpener, Ulrich. 1976. "War Premeditated? German Intelligence Operations in July 1914." *Central European History* 6.

Turner, Arthur Campbell. 1985. "Nationalism and Religion: Iran and Iraq at War." In *The Regionalization of Warfare*, edited by James Brown and William P. Snyder, 144–63. New Brunswick, N.J.: Transaction Books.

United States. 2002a. "Key Judgments: National Intelligence Estimate, October 1, 2002." On line at www.ceip.org/files/projects/npp/pdf/iraq/declassifiedintellreport.pdf.

———. 2002b. "The National Security Strategy of the United States of America." On line at www.whitehouse.gov/nsc/nss.html (October 16, 2002).

Vagts, Alfred. 1959. *A History of Militarism.* London: Hollis and Carter.

Vali, Ferenc A. 1976. *Politics of the Indian Ocean Region: The Balances of Power.* New York: Free Press.

Van Evera, Stephen. 1984. "The Cult of the Offensive and the Origins of the First World War." *International Security* 9 (1): 58–107.

———. 1985. "Why Cooperation Failed in 1914." *World Politics* 38:80–117.

———. 1994. "Hypotheses on Nationalism and War." *International Security* 18 (Spring): 5–39.

———. 1998. "Offense, Defense, and the Causes of War." *International Security* 22 (4): 5–43.

———. 1999. *Causes of War: Power and the Roots of Conflict.* Ithaca: Cornell University Press.

Vasquez, John. 1987. "The Steps to War: Toward a Scientific Explanation of Correlates of War Findings." *World Politics* 40:108–45.

———. 1993. *The War Puzzle.* Cambridge: Cambridge University Press.

———. 1998. "The Evolution of Multiple Rivalries prior to World War II in the Pacific." In Diehl, *Dynamics of Enduring Rivalries.* 191–224.

———. 2004. "The Probability of War, 1816–1992." *International Studies Quarterly* 48:1–27.

Waite, Robert G. L. 1990. "Leadership Pathologies: The Kaiser and the Führer and the Decisions for War in 1914 and 1939." In *Psychological Dimensions of War*, edited by Betty Glad. Newbury Park, Calif.: Sage.

Wallace, Michael D. 1979. "Arms Races and Escalation: Some New Evidence." *Journal of Conflict Resolution* 23:3–16.

———. 1982. "Armaments and Escalation: Two Competing Hypotheses." *International Studies Quarterly* 26:37–56.

Wallerstein, Emmanuel. 1974. *The Modern World-System.* New York: Academic Press.

Wallis, Jim. 2003. "Dangerous Religion: George W. Bush's Theology of Empire." *Sojourners Magazine*, September–October. On line at www.sojo.net/index.ctm?action=magazine .article&issue=soj0309&article=030910 (October 26, 2004).

Walt, Stephen. 1987. *The Origins of Alliances.* Ithaca: Cornell University Press.

———. 1996. *Revolution and War.* Ithaca: Cornell University Press.

Waltz, Kenneth. 1979. *Theory of International Politics.* Reading, Mass.: Addison-Wesley.

Wayman, Frank W. 2000. "Rivalries: Recent Disputes and Explaining War." In *What Do We Know About War?* edited by John A. Vasquez, 219–34. Lanham, Md.: Rowman & Littlefield.

Weart, Spencer. 1998. *Never at War: Why Democracies Will Not Fight One Another.* New Haven: Yale University Press.

Wendt, Alexander. 1992. "Anarchy Is What States Make of It: The Social Construction of Power Politics." *International Organization* 46 (2): 391–425.

———. 1998. "Constructing International Politics." In *Theories of War and Peace*, edited by M. Brown, O. Cote Jr., S. Lynn-Jones, and S. Miller, 416–26. Cambridge: MIT Press.

White, Ralph K. 1968. *Nobody Wanted War*. New York: Doubleday.

Whitney, Craig, ed. 2005. *The WMD Mirage*. New York: Public Affairs.

Wieland, Carsten. 2001. "Ethnic Conflict Undressed: Patterns of Contrast, Interest of Elites, and Clientelism of Foreign Powers in Comparative Perspective—Bosnia, India, and Pakistan." *Nationalities Papers* 29:207–41.

Wilkinson, David. 1999. "Unipolarity Without Hegemony." *International Studies Review* 1 (12): 141–72.

Williamson, Samuel R., Jr. 1979. "Theories of Organizational Process and Foreign Policy Outcomes." In *Diplomacy*, edited by Paul G. Lauren, 137–61. New York: Free Press.

———. 1989. "The Origins of World War I." In *The Origin and Prevention of Major Wars*, edited by Robert Rotberg and Theodore Rabb, 225–48. Cambridge: Cambridge University Press.

———. 1991. *Austria-Hungary and the Origins of the First World War*. New York: Macmillan.

Winter, David G. 1993. "Personality and Leadership in the Gulf." In *The Political Psychology of the Gulf War: Leaders, Publics, and the Process of Conflict*, edited by Stanley A. Renshon, 107–17. Pittsburgh: Pittsburgh University Press.

Wirsing, Robert. 1994. *India, Pakistan, and the Kashmir Dispute: On Regional Conflict and Its Resolution*. New York: St. Martin's Press.

Wohlforth, William C. 1987. "The Perception of Power: Russia in the Pre-1914 Balance." *World Politics* 39: 353–81.

———. 1999. "The Stability of a Unipolar World." *International Security* 24 (1): 5–41.

Wohlstetter, Roberta. 1962. *Pearl Harbor: Warning and Decision*. Stanford, Calif.: Stanford University Press.

Wolfowitz, Paul. 2003. "Wolfowitz Interview with Vanity Fair's Tannenhous." May 9. News transcript from the United States Department of Defense. On line at http://scoop.co.nz/mason/stories/WO0305/S00308.htm.

Woodward, Bob. 2002. *Bush at War*. New York: Simon and Schuster.

———. 2004. *Plan of Attack*. New York: Simon and Schuster.

Wright, Claudia. 1980. "Implications of the Iran-Iraq War." *Foreign Affairs* 59 (Winter 1980–1981).

Zartman, I. William. 1996. "The United Nations Response." In *The Six-Day War: A Retrospective*, edited by Richard B. Parker, 74–118. Gainesville: University Press of Florida.

Index

Note: Page numbers in italics indicate illustrations.

About the Authors

Greg Cashman is professor in the Department of Political Science at Salisbury University in Salisbury, Maryland, where he is the program coordinator for International Studies. He is the author of *What Causes War? An Introduction to Theories of International Conflict*. He received his Ph.D. from the Graduate School of International Studies at Denver University.

Leonard C. Robinson is associate professor in the Department of Political Science at Salisbury University in Salisbury, Maryland. He has published articles on Middle East politics in *Arab Studies Journal* and the *Muslim World*. He received his Ph.D. from the Department of Political Science at the University of Utah.